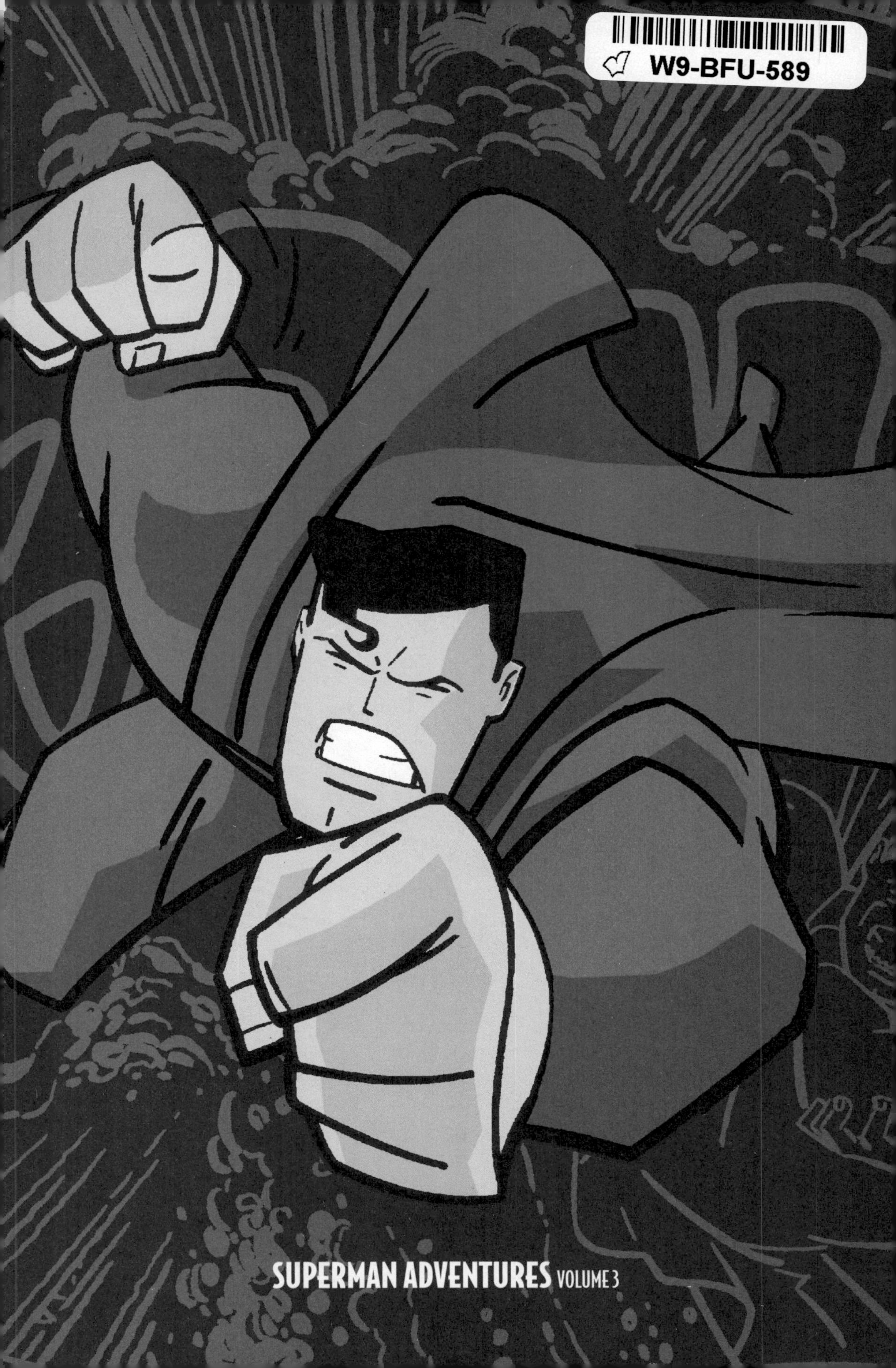
SUPERMAN ADVENTURES VOLUME 3

SUPERMAN ADVENTURES VOLUME 3

MARK MILLAR CHRIS DUFFY DEVIN K. GRAYSON JORDAN B. GORFINKEL EVAN DORKIN SARAH DYER writers
ALUIR AMANCIO NEIL VOKES BRET BLEVINS MIKE MANLEY pencillers
TERRY AUSTIN STAN WOCH inkers
RICK TAYLOR MARIE SEVERIN LEE LOUGHRIDGE colorists
LOIS BUHALIS KEVIN CUNNINGHAM letterers
RICK BURCHETT TERRY AUSTIN MARIE SEVERIN collection cover artists

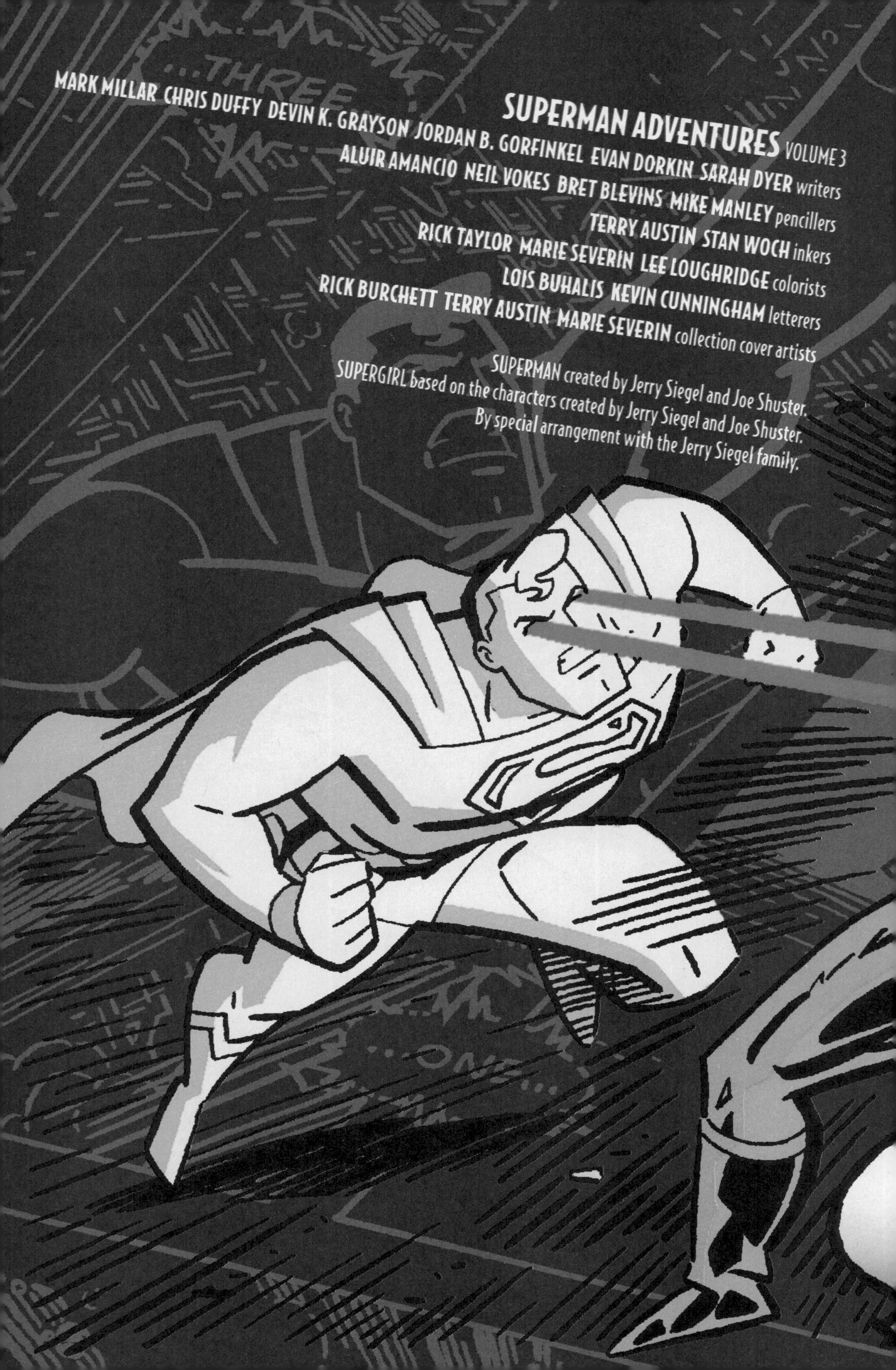

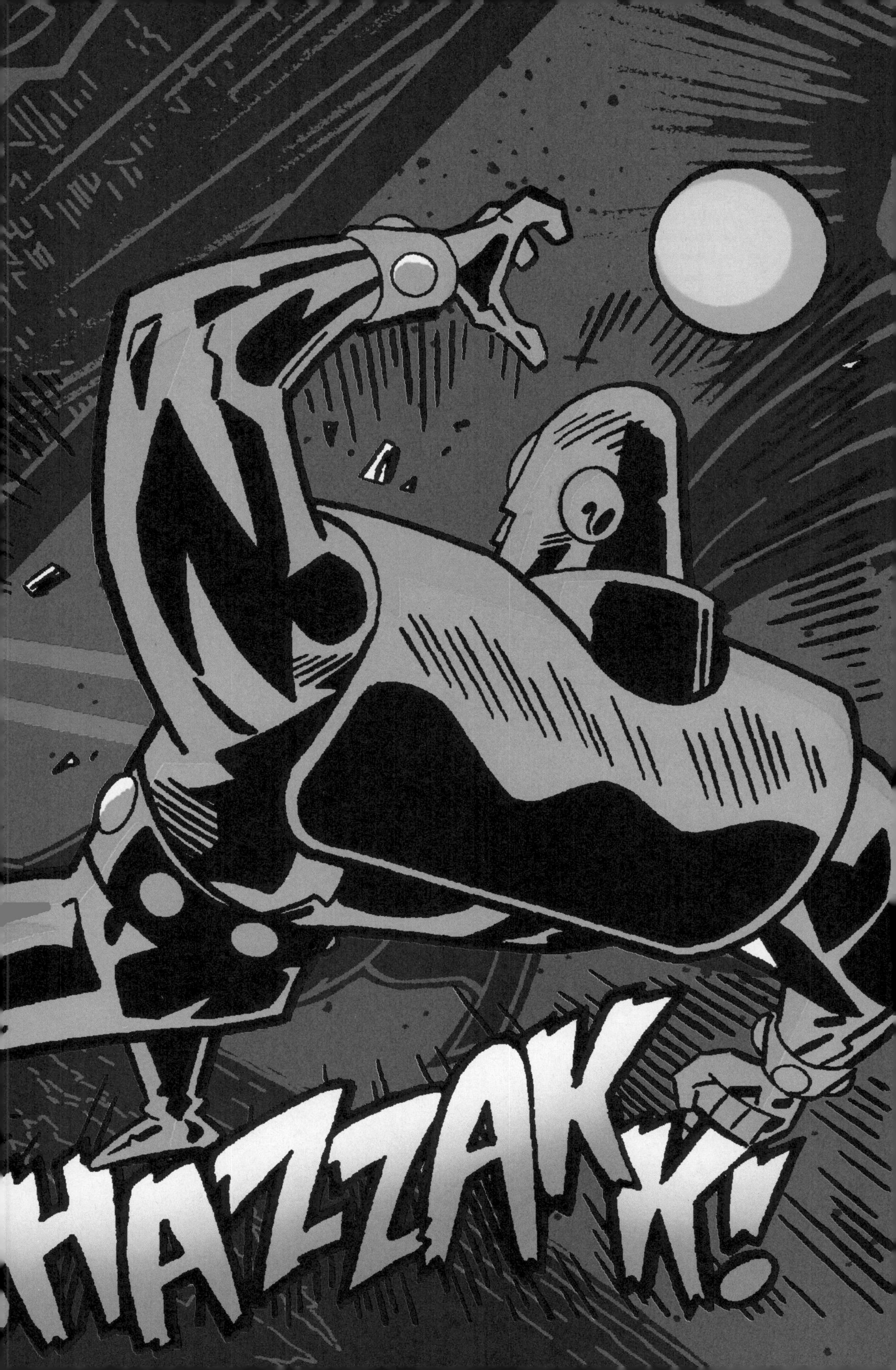
HAZZAKK!

MIKE McAVENNIE Editor – Original Series
MAUREEN McTIGUE, FRANK BERRIOS Assistant Editors – Original Series
JEB WOODARD Group Editor – Collected Editions
ERIKA ROTHBERG Editor – Collected Edition
STEVE COOK Design Director – Books
LOUIS PRANDI Publication Design

BOB HARRAS Senior VP – Editor-in-Chief, DC Comics

DIANE NELSON President
DAN DiDIO Publisher
JIM LEE Publisher
GEOFF JOHNS President & Chief Creative Officer
AMIT DESAI Executive VP – Business & Marketing Strategy,
Direct to Consumer & Global Franchise Management
SAM ADES Senior VP – Direct to Consumer
BOBBIE CHASE VP – Talent Development
MARK CHIARELLO Senior VP – Art, Design & Collected Editions
JOHN CUNNINGHAM Senior VP – Sales & Trade Marketing
ANNE DePIES Senior VP – Business Strategy, Finance & Administration
DON FALLETTI VP – Manufacturing Operations
LAWRENCE GANEM VP – Editorial Administration & Talent Relations
ALISON GILL Senior VP – Manufacturing & Operations
HANK KANALZ Senior VP – Editorial Strategy & Administration
JAY KOGAN VP – Legal Affairs
THOMAS LOFTUS VP – Business Affairs
JACK MAHAN VP – Business Affairs
NICK J. NAPOLITANO VP – Manufacturing Administration
EDDIE SCANNELL VP – Consumer Marketing
COURTNEY SIMMONS Senior VP – Publicity & Communications
JIM (SKI) SOKOLOWSKI VP – Comic Book Specialty Sales & Trade Marketing
NANCY SPEARS VP – Mass, Book, Digital Sales & Trade Marketing

SUPERMAN ADVENTURES VOLUME 3

DC Comics, 2900 West Alameda Ave., Burbank, CA 91505
Printed by LSC Communications, Owensville, MO, USA. 4/21/17. First Printing.
ISBN: 978-1-4012-7242-5

Library of Congress Cataloging-in-Publication Data is available.

PEFC Certified

Printed on paper from
sustainably managed
forests, controlled
sources

PEFC/29-31-337   www.pefc.org

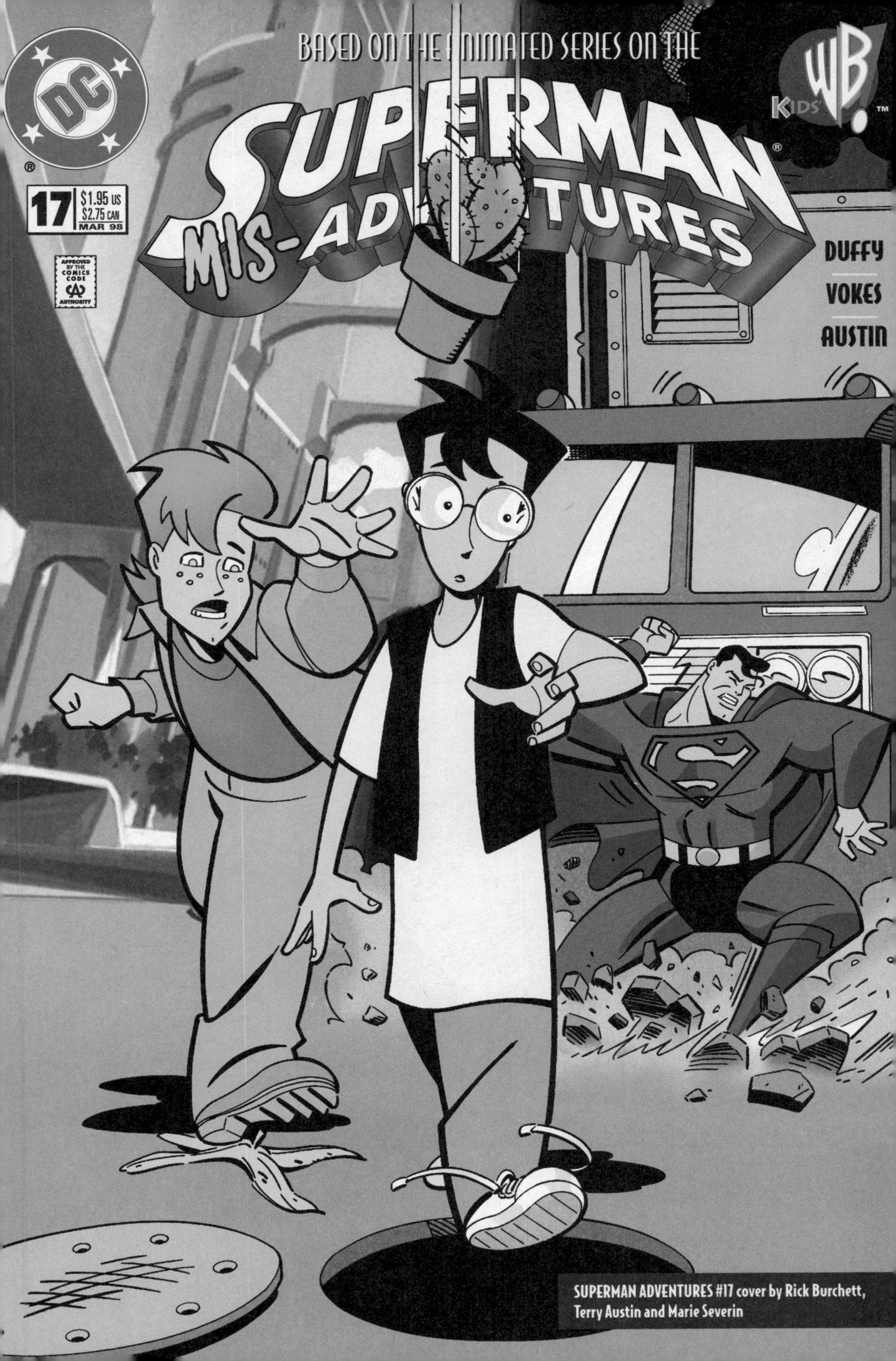
BASED ON THE ANIMATED SERIES ON THE
DC
KIDS' WB!
SUPERMAN
MIS-ADVENTURES
17
$1.95 US
$2.75 CAN
MAR 98
APPROVED BY THE COMICS CODE AUTHORITY
DUFFY
VOKES
AUSTIN

SUPERMAN ADVENTURES #17 cover by Rick Burchett, Terry Austin and Marie Severin

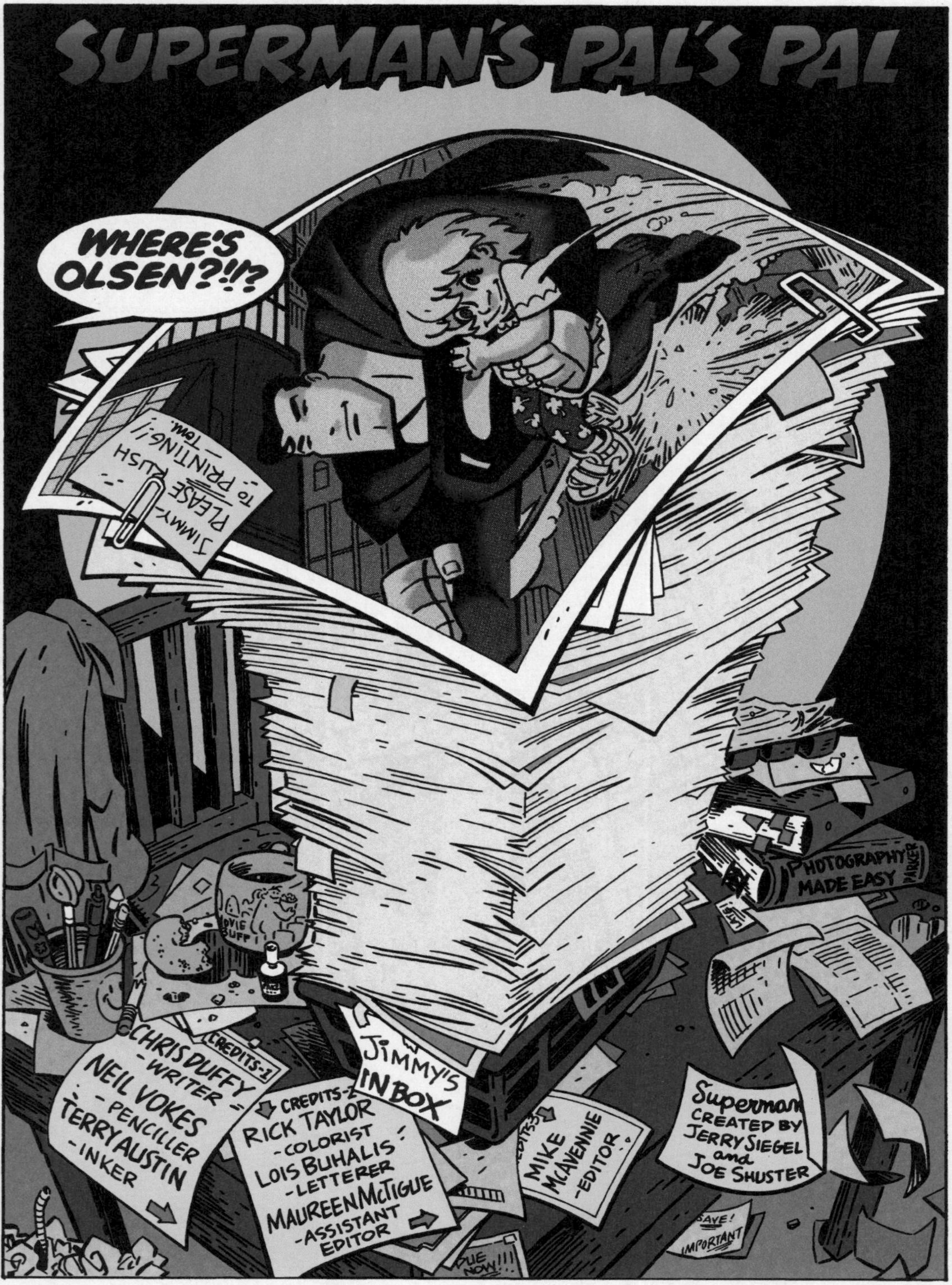
SUPERMAN'S PAL'S PAL
WHERE'S OLSEN?!!?
JIMMY- PLEASE RUSH TO PRINTING!! -Tom.
PHOTOGRAPHY MADE EASY
PARKER
CREDITS-1
CHRIS DUFFY -WRITER
NEIL VOKES -PENCILLER
TERRY AUSTIN -INKER
JIMMY'S IN BOX
CREDITS-2
RICK TAYLOR -COLORIST
LOIS BUHALIS -LETTERER
MAUREEN McTIGUE -ASSISTANT EDITOR
CREDITS-3
MIKE McAVENNIE -EDITOR
Superman CREATED BY JERRY SIEGEL and JOE SHUSTER
SAVE! IMPORTANT
DUE NOW!!!

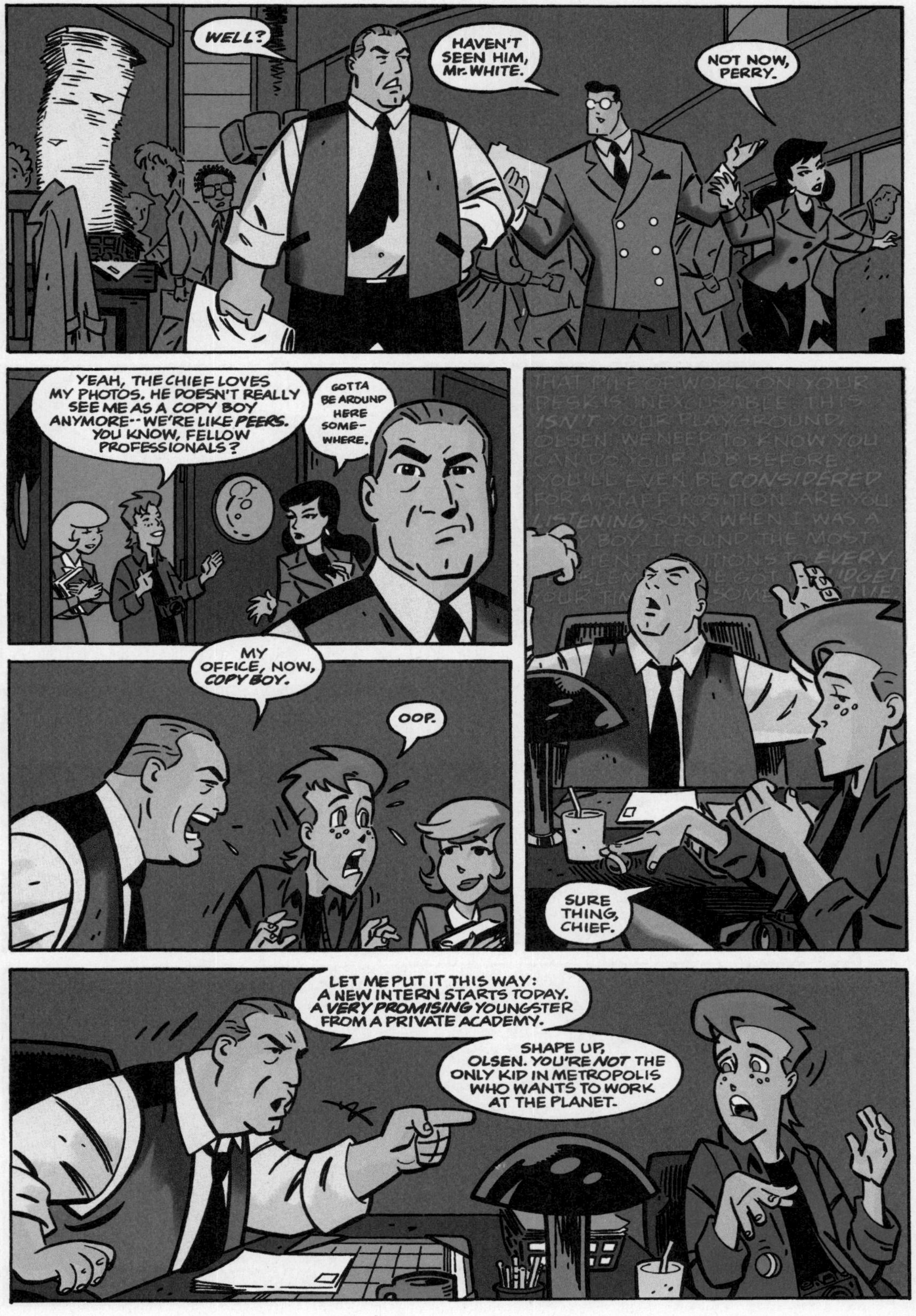
WELL?
HAVEN'T SEEN HIM, Mr. WHITE.
NOT NOW, PERRY.
YEAH, THE CHIEF LOVES MY PHOTOS. HE DOESN'T REALLY SEE ME AS A COPY BOY ANYMORE-- WE'RE LIKE PEERS. YOU KNOW, FELLOW PROFESSIONALS?
GOTTA BE AROUND HERE SOME-WHERE.
MY OFFICE, NOW, COPY BOY.
OOP.
THAT PILE OF WORK ON YOUR DESK IS INEXCUSABLE. THIS ISN'T YOUR PLAYGROUND, OLSEN. WE NEED TO KNOW YOU CAN DO YOUR JOB BEFORE YOU'LL EVEN BE CONSIDERED FOR A STAFF POSITION. ARE YOU LISTENING, SON? WHEN I WAS A
BOY I FOUND THE MOST
SURE THING, CHIEF.
LET ME PUT IT THIS WAY: A NEW INTERN STARTS TODAY. A VERY PROMISING YOUNGSTER FROM A PRIVATE ACADEMY.
SHAPE UP, OLSEN. YOU'RE NOT THE ONLY KID IN METROPOLIS WHO WANTS TO WORK AT THE PLANET.

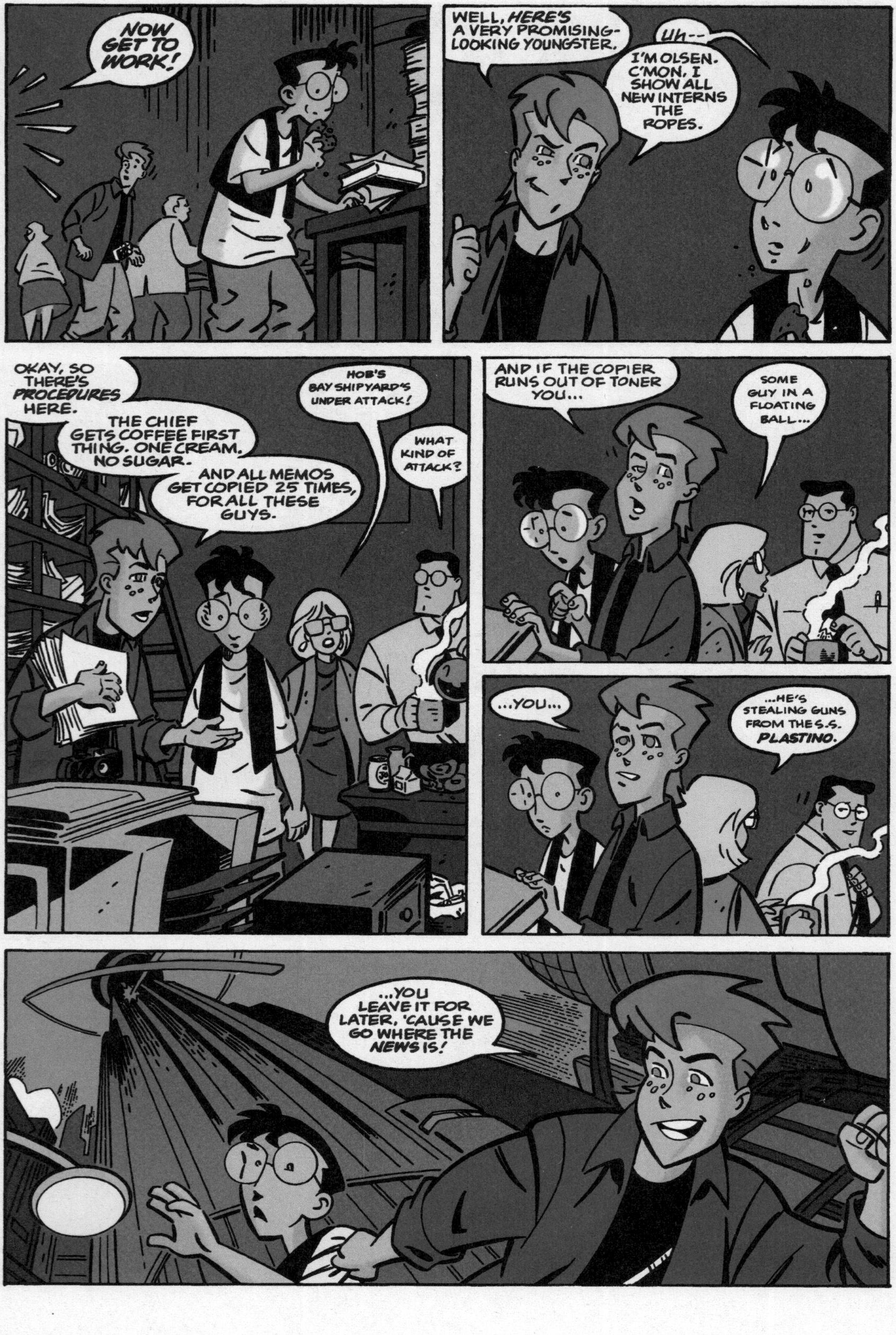
NOW GET TO WORK!
WELL, *HERE'S* A VERY PROMISING-LOOKING YOUNGSTER.
Uh--
I'M OLSEN. C'MON, I SHOW ALL NEW INTERNS THE ROPES.
OKAY, SO THERE'S *PROCEDURES* HERE.
THE CHIEF GETS COFFEE FIRST THING. ONE CREAM. NO SUGAR.
AND ALL MEMOS GET COPIED 25 TIMES, FOR ALL THESE GUYS.
HOB'S BAY SHIPYARD'S UNDER ATTACK!
WHAT KIND OF ATTACK?
AND IF THE COPIER RUNS OUT OF TONER YOU...
SOME GUY IN A FLOATING BALL...
...YOU...
...HE'S STEALING GUNS FROM THE S.S. *PLASTINO*.
...YOU LEAVE IT FOR LATER, 'CAUSE WE GO WHERE THE *NEWS* IS!

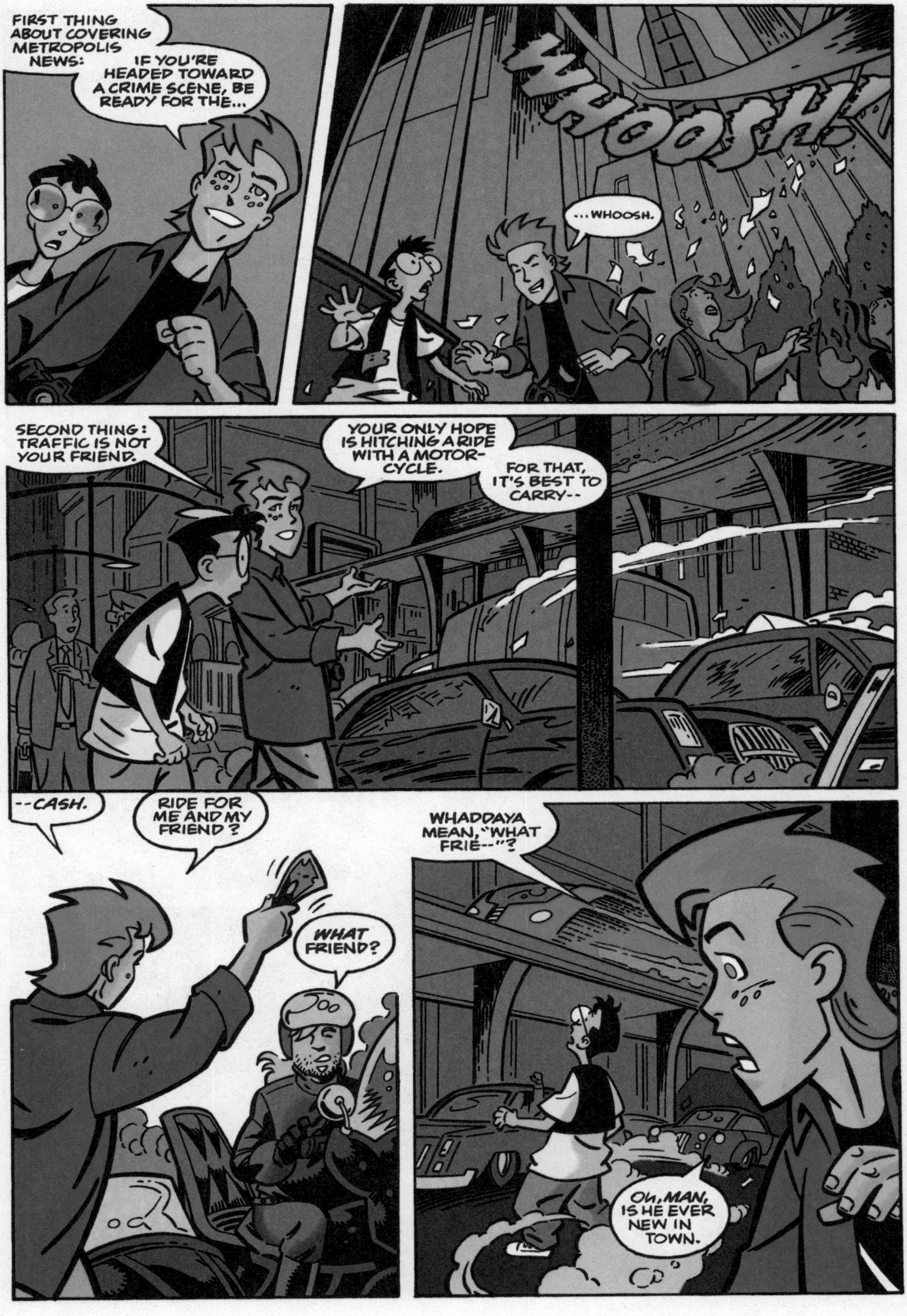

FIRST THING ABOUT COVERING METROPOLIS NEWS:
IF YOU'RE HEADED TOWARD A CRIME SCENE, BE READY FOR THE...
WHOOSH!
...WHOOSH.
SECOND THING: TRAFFIC IS NOT YOUR FRIEND.
YOUR ONLY HOPE IS HITCHING A RIDE WITH A MOTOR-CYCLE.
FOR THAT, IT'S BEST TO CARRY--
--CASH.
RIDE FOR ME AND MY FRIEND?
WHAT FRIEND?
WHADDAYA MEAN, "WHAT FRIE--"?
OH, MAN, IS HE EVER NEW IN TOWN.

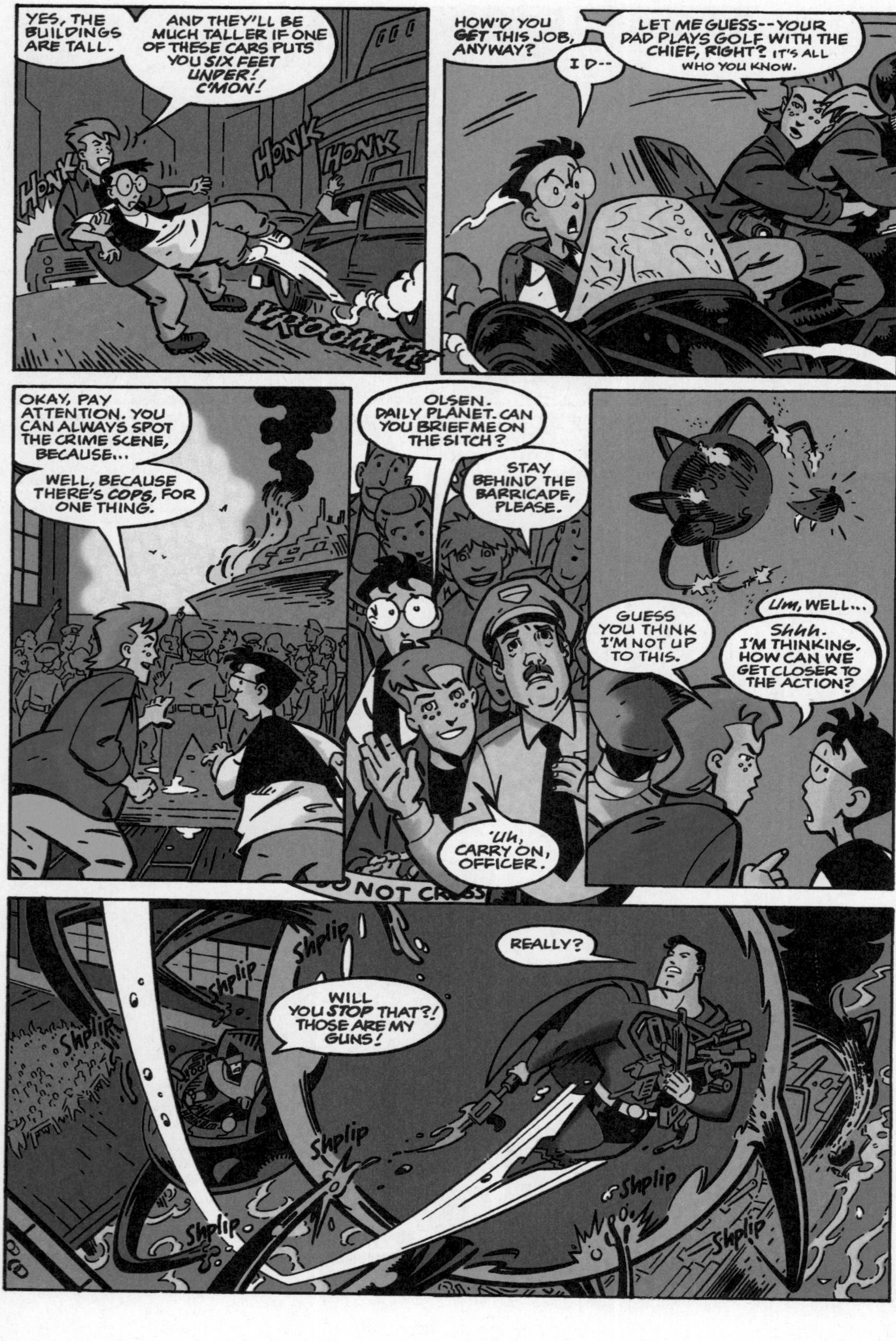
YES, THE BUILDINGS ARE TALL.
AND THEY'LL BE MUCH TALLER IF ONE OF THESE CARS PUTS YOU SIX FEET UNDER! C'MON!
HONK
HONK
HONK
VROOMM
HOW'D YOU GET THIS JOB, ANYWAY?
I D--
LET ME GUESS--YOUR DAD PLAYS GOLF WITH THE CHIEF, RIGHT? IT'S ALL WHO YOU KNOW.
OKAY, PAY ATTENTION. YOU CAN ALWAYS SPOT THE CRIME SCENE, BECAUSE...
WELL, BECAUSE THERE'S COPS, FOR ONE THING.
OLSEN. DAILY PLANET. CAN YOU BRIEF ME ON THE SITCH?
STAY BEHIND THE BARRICADE, PLEASE.
'UH, CARRY ON, OFFICER.
NOT CROSS
GUESS YOU THINK I'M NOT UP TO THIS.
UM, WELL...
SHHH. I'M THINKING. HOW CAN WE GET CLOSER TO THE ACTION?
REALLY?
WILL YOU STOP THAT?! THOSE ARE MY GUNS!
SHPLIP
SHPLIP
SHPLIP
SHPLIP
SHPLIP
SHPLIP
SHPLIP
SHPLIP

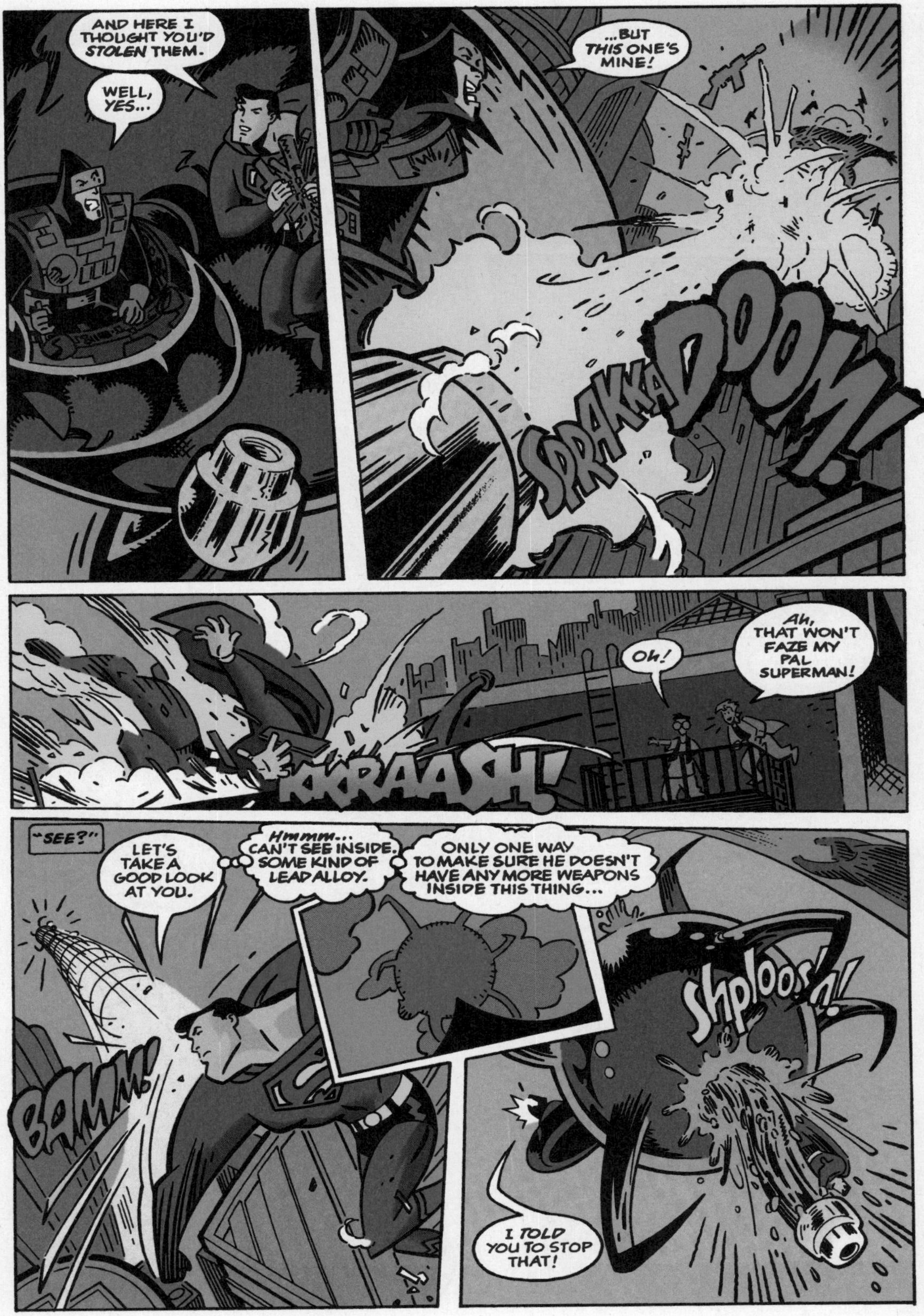
AND HERE I THOUGHT YOU'D STOLEN THEM.
WELL, YES...
...BUT THIS ONE'S MINE!
SPRAKKADOOM!!
Oh!
Ah, THAT WON'T FAZE MY PAL SUPERMAN!
KKRAASH!
"SEE?"
LET'S TAKE A GOOD LOOK AT YOU.
Hmmm... CAN'T SEE INSIDE. SOME KIND OF LEAD ALLOY.
ONLY ONE WAY TO MAKE SURE HE DOESN'T HAVE ANY MORE WEAPONS INSIDE THIS THING...
BAMM!
shploosh!
I TOLD YOU TO STOP THAT!

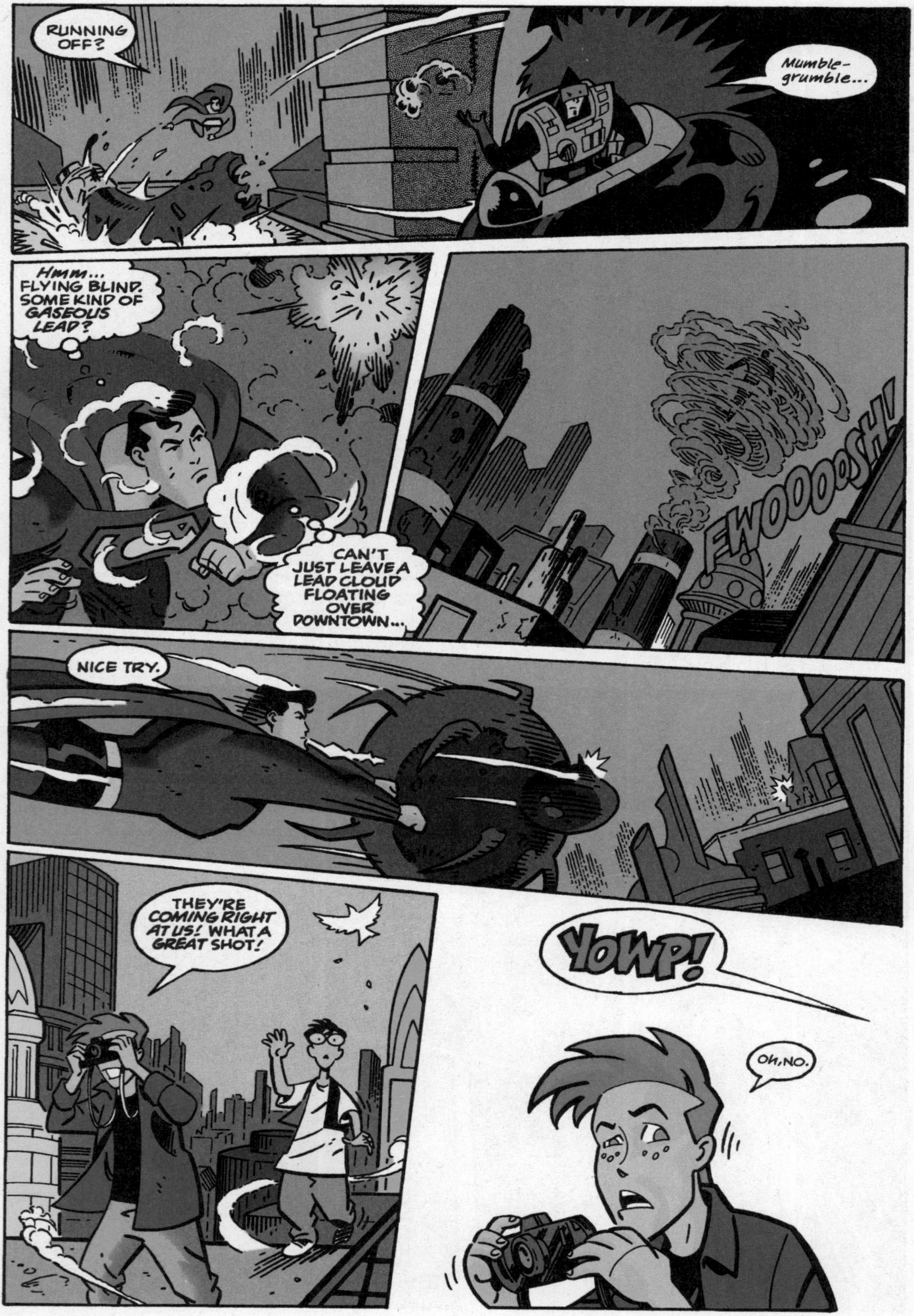
RUNNING OFF?
Mumble-grumble...
Hmm... FLYING BLIND. SOME KIND OF GASEOUS LEAD?
CAN'T JUST LEAVE A LEAD CLOUD FLOATING OVER DOWNTOWN...
FWOOOOOSH!
NICE TRY.
THEY'RE COMING RIGHT AT US! WHAT A GREAT SHOT!
YOWP!
OH, NO.

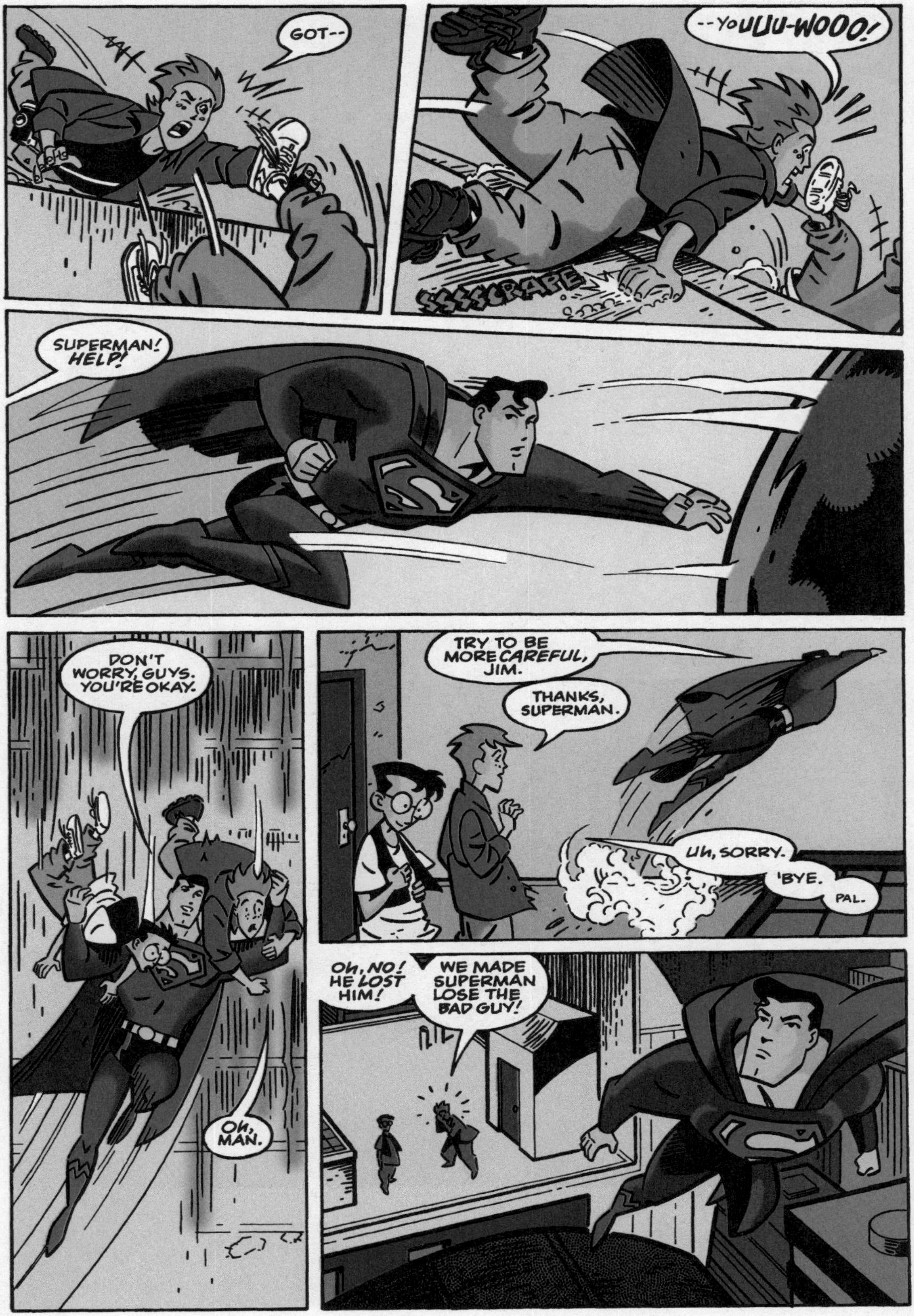
GOT--
--YoUUU-WOOO!
SSSSCRAPE
SUPERMAN! HELP!
DON'T WORRY, GUYS. YOU'RE OKAY.
Oh, MAN.
TRY TO BE MORE CAREFUL, JIM.
THANKS, SUPERMAN.
Uh, SORRY.
'BYE.
PAL.
Oh, NO! HE LOST HIM!
WE MADE SUPERMAN LOSE THE BAD GUY!

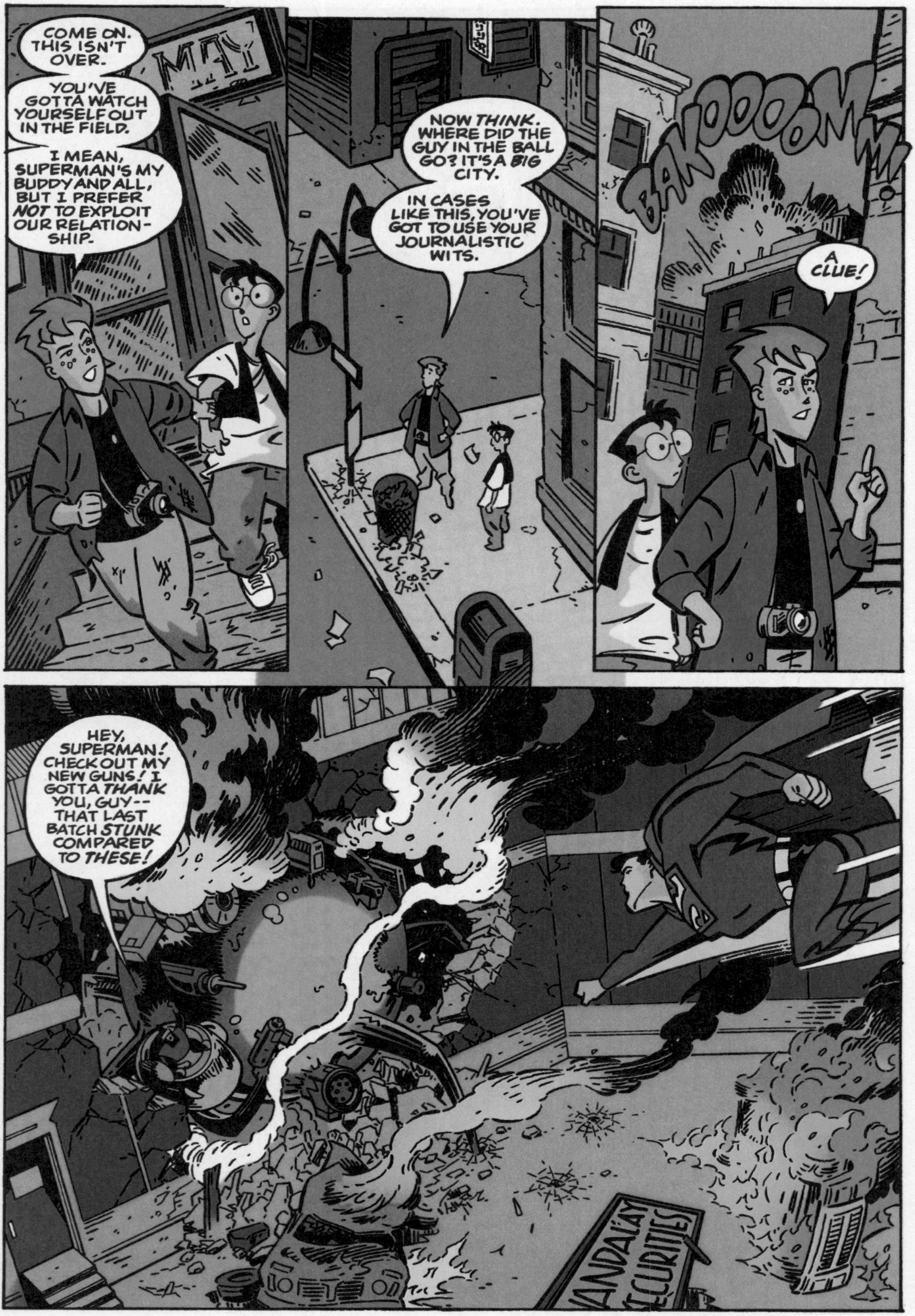
COME ON. THIS ISN'T OVER.
YOU'VE GOTTA WATCH YOURSELF OUT IN THE FIELD.
I MEAN, SUPERMAN'S MY BUDDY AND ALL, BUT I PREFER NOT TO EXPLOIT OUR RELATION-SHIP.
NOW THINK. WHERE DID THE GUY IN THE BALL GO? IT'S A BIG CITY.
IN CASES LIKE THIS, YOU'VE GOT TO USE YOUR JOURNALISTIC WITS.
BAKOOOOOMM!
A CLUE!
HEY, SUPERMAN! CHECK OUT MY NEW GUNS! I GOTTA THANK YOU, GUY-- THAT LAST BATCH STUNK COMPARED TO THESE!
VANDALAY SECURITIES

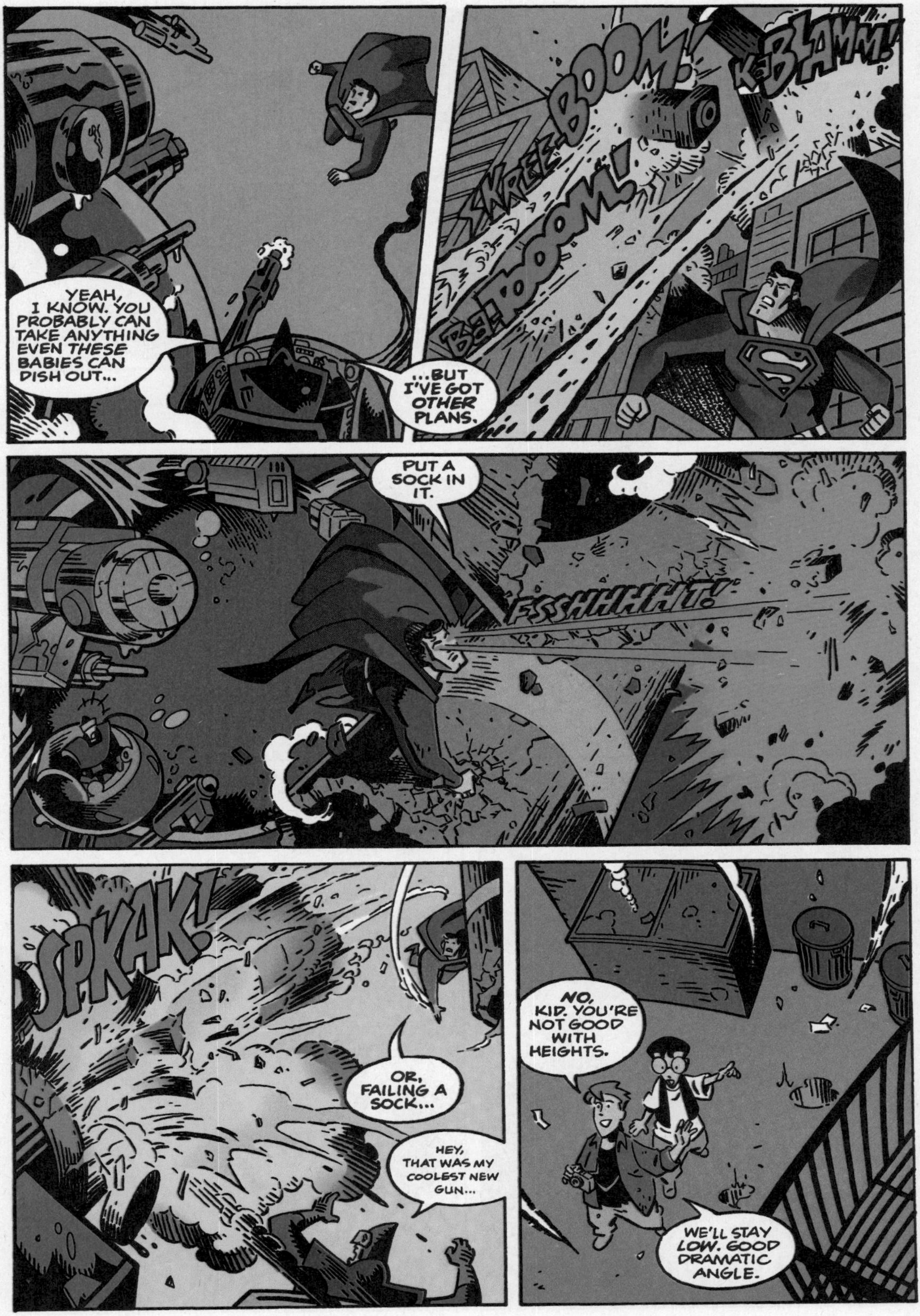
YEAH, I KNOW. YOU PROBABLY CAN TAKE ANYTHING EVEN THESE BABIES CAN DISH OUT...
...BUT I'VE GOT OTHER PLANS.
SKREE-BOOM!
KA-BLAMM!
BA-TOOOM!
PUT A SOCK IN IT.
FSSHHHHHT!
SPKAK!
OR, FAILING A SOCK...
HEY, THAT WAS MY COOLEST NEW GUN...
NO, KID. YOU'RE NOT GOOD WITH HEIGHTS.
WE'LL STAY LOW. GOOD DRAMATIC ANGLE.

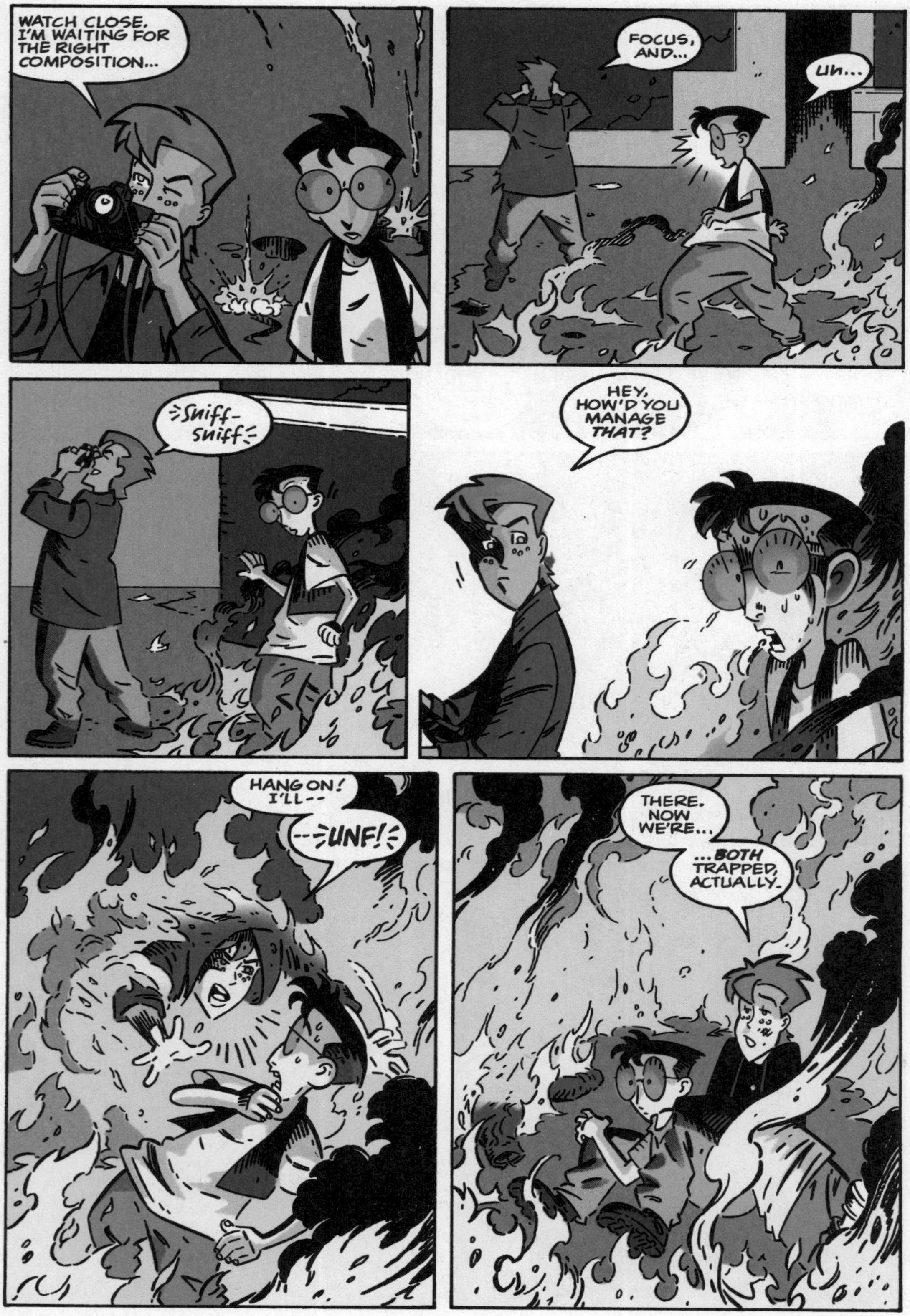
WATCH CLOSE. I'M WAITING FOR THE RIGHT COMPOSITION...
FOCUS, AND...
Uh...
Sniff-sniff
HEY, HOW'D YOU MANAGE THAT?
HANG ON! I'LL--
--UNF!
THERE. NOW WE'RE...
...BOTH TRAPPED, ACTUALLY.

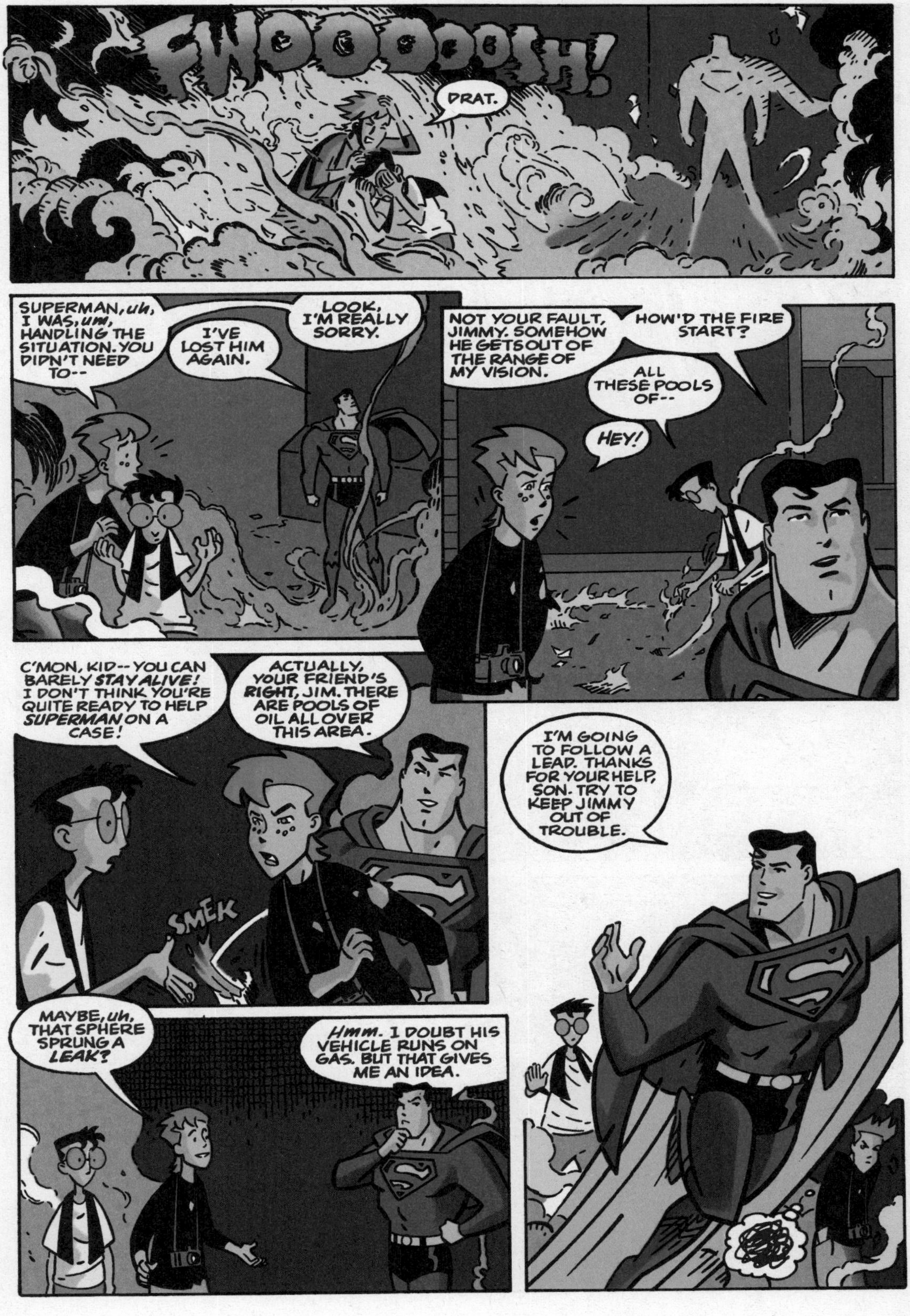
FWOOOOOSH!
DRAT.
SUPERMAN, uh, I WAS, um, HANDLING THE SITUATION. YOU DIDN'T NEED TO--
I'VE LOST HIM AGAIN.
LOOK, I'M REALLY SORRY.
NOT YOUR FAULT, JIMMY. SOMEHOW HE GETS OUT OF THE RANGE OF MY VISION.
HOW'D THE FIRE START?
ALL THESE POOLS OF--
HEY!
C'MON, KID-- YOU CAN BARELY STAY ALIVE! I DON'T THINK YOU'RE QUITE READY TO HELP SUPERMAN ON A CASE!
ACTUALLY, YOUR FRIEND'S RIGHT, JIM. THERE ARE POOLS OF OIL ALL OVER THIS AREA.
SMEK
MAYBE, uh, THAT SPHERE SPRUNG A LEAK?
Hmm. I DOUBT HIS VEHICLE RUNS ON GAS. BUT THAT GIVES ME AN IDEA.
I'M GOING TO FOLLOW A LEAD. THANKS FOR YOUR HELP, SON. TRY TO KEEP JIMMY OUT OF TROUBLE.

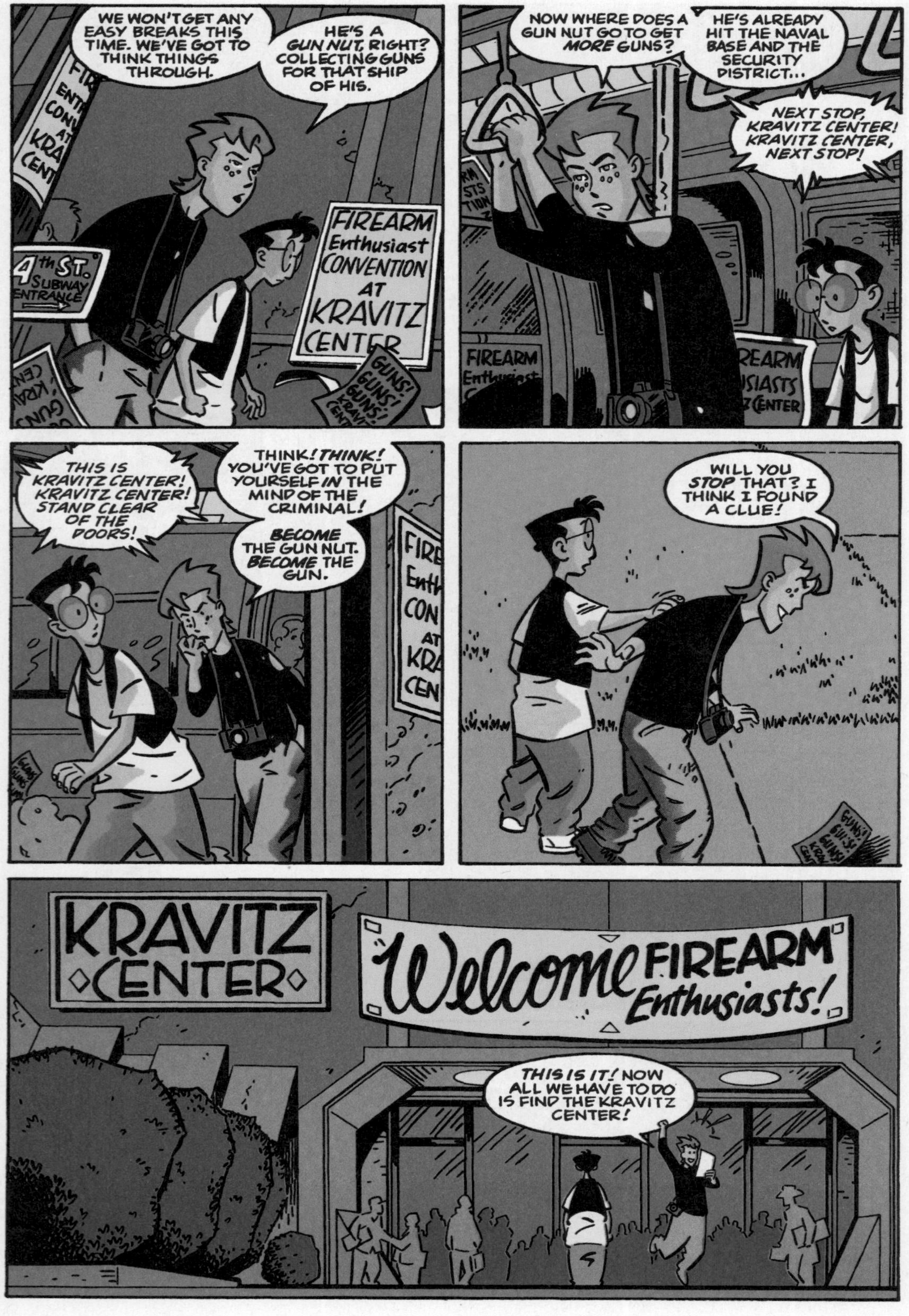
WE WON'T GET ANY EASY BREAKS THIS TIME. WE'VE GOT TO THINK THINGS THROUGH.
HE'S A *GUN NUT*, RIGHT? COLLECTING GUNS FOR THAT SHIP OF HIS.
4th ST. SUBWAY ENTRANCE
FIREARM Enthusiast CONVENTION AT KRAVITZ CENTER
GUNS! GUNS! GUNS!
NOW WHERE DOES A GUN NUT GO TO GET *MORE* GUNS?
HE'S ALREADY HIT THE NAVAL BASE AND THE SECURITY DISTRICT...
NEXT STOP, KRAVITZ CENTER! KRAVITZ CENTER, NEXT STOP!
THIS IS KRAVITZ CENTER! KRAVITZ CENTER! STAND CLEAR OF THE DOORS!
THINK! *THINK!* YOU'VE GOT TO PUT YOURSELF *IN* THE MIND OF THE CRIMINAL!
BECOME THE GUN NUT. *BECOME* THE GUN.
WILL YOU *STOP* THAT? I THINK I FOUND A CLUE!
KRAVITZ CENTER
Welcome FIREARM Enthusiasts!
THIS IS IT! NOW ALL WE HAVE TO DO IS FIND THE KRAVITZ CENTER!

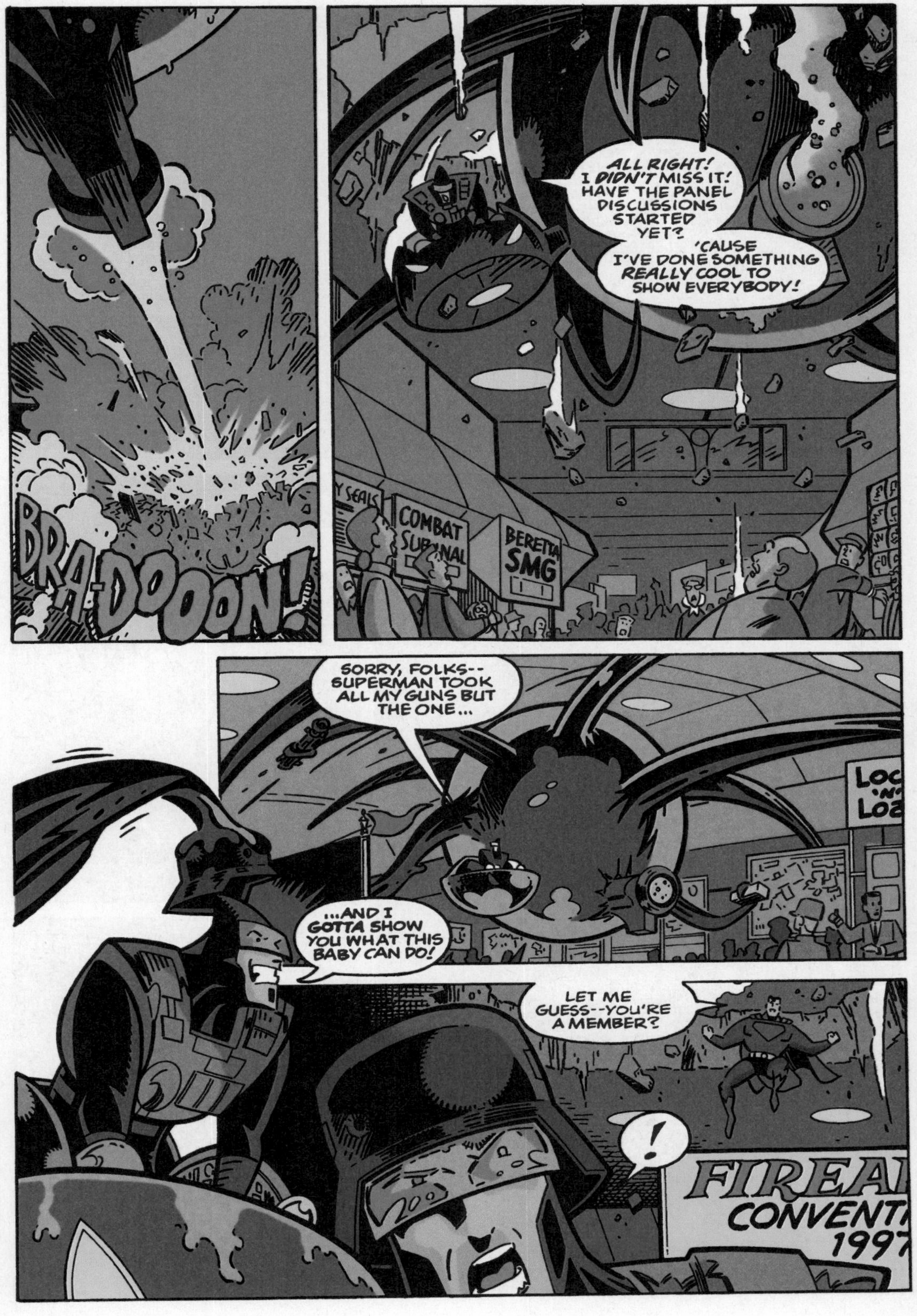
BRA-DOOOON!
ALL RIGHT! I DIDN'T MISS IT! HAVE THE PANEL DISCUSSIONS STARTED YET?
'CAUSE I'VE DONE SOMETHING REALLY COOL TO SHOW EVERYBODY!
COMBAT
BERETTA SMG
SORRY, FOLKS-- SUPERMAN TOOK ALL MY GUNS BUT THE ONE...
...AND I GOTTA SHOW YOU WHAT THIS BABY CAN DO!
LET ME GUESS--YOU'RE A MEMBER?
!
CONVENT

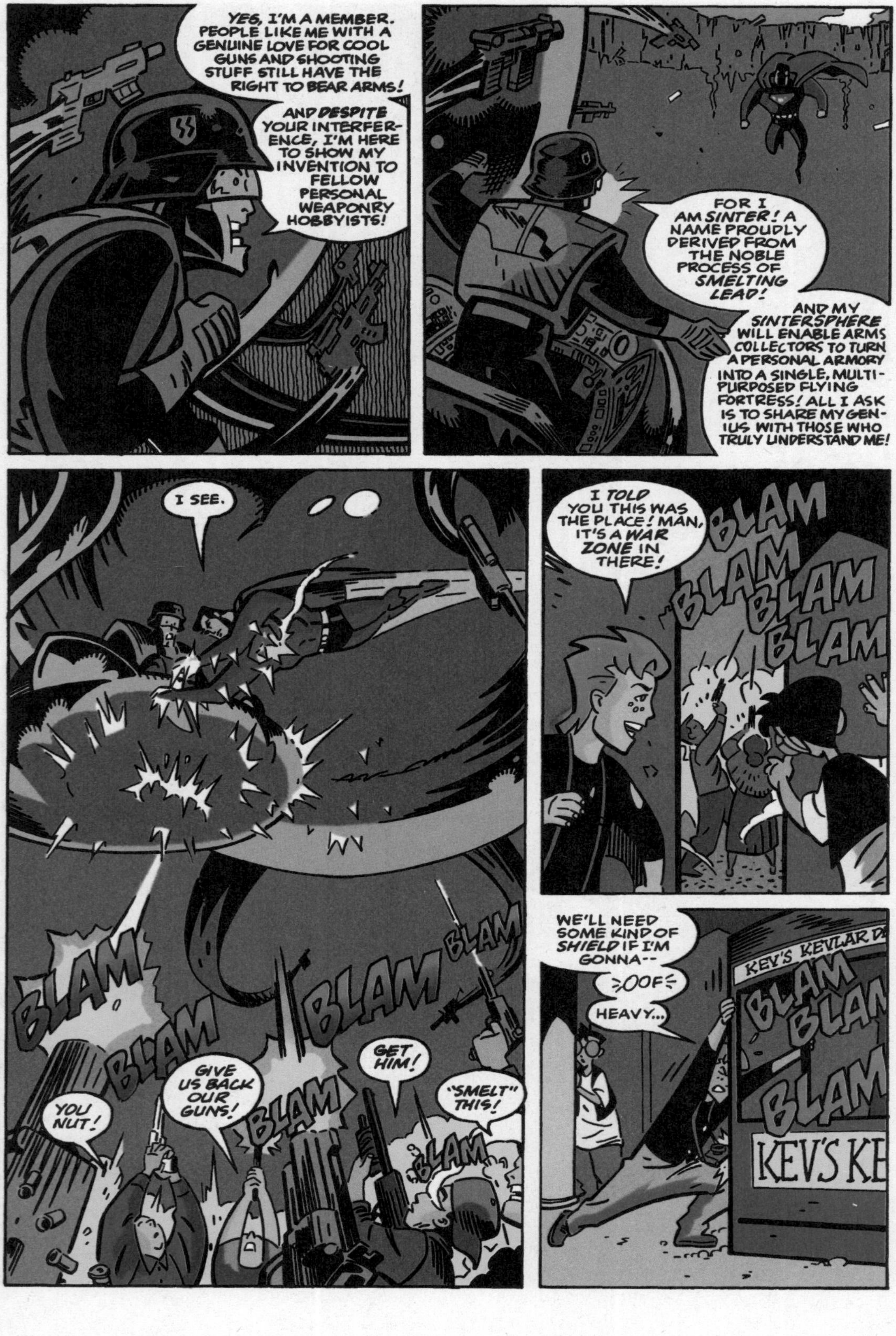
YES, I'M A MEMBER. PEOPLE LIKE ME WITH A GENUINE LOVE FOR COOL GUNS AND SHOOTING STUFF STILL HAVE THE RIGHT TO BEAR ARMS!
AND DESPITE YOUR INTERFERENCE, I'M HERE TO SHOW MY INVENTION TO FELLOW PERSONAL WEAPONRY HOBBYISTS!
FOR I AM SINTER! A NAME PROUDLY DERIVED FROM THE NOBLE PROCESS OF SMELTING LEAD!
AND MY SINTERSPHERE WILL ENABLE ARMS COLLECTORS TO TURN A PERSONAL ARMORY INTO A SINGLE, MULTI-PURPOSED FLYING FORTRESS! ALL I ASK IS TO SHARE MY GENIUS WITH THOSE WHO TRULY UNDERSTAND ME!
I SEE.
BLAM
BLAM
BLAM
BLAM
YOU NUT!
GIVE US BACK OUR GUNS!
BLAM
GET HIM!
"SMELT" THIS!
BLAM
I TOLD YOU THIS WAS THE PLACE! MAN, IT'S A WAR ZONE IN THERE!
BLAM
BLAM
BLAM
BLAM
WE'LL NEED SOME KIND OF SHIELD IF I'M GONNA--
OOF
HEAVY...
KEV'S KEVLAR
BLAM
BLAM
BLAM
KEV'S KE

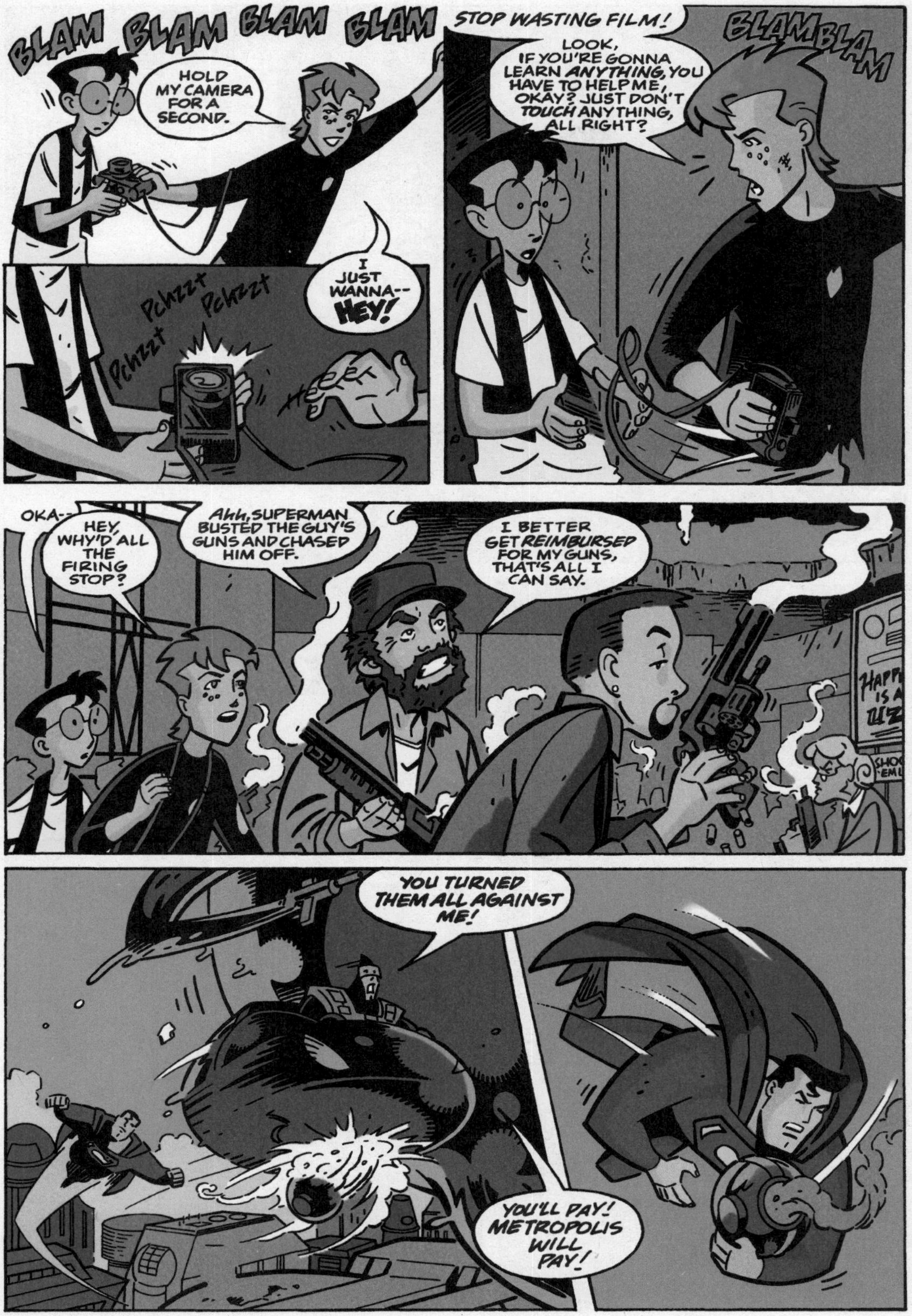
BLAM BLAM BLAM BLAM
HOLD MY CAMERA FOR A SECOND.
Pchzzt Pchzzt Pchzzt
I JUST WANNA-- HEY!
STOP WASTING FILM!
BLAMBLAM
LOOK, IF YOU'RE GONNA LEARN ANYTHING, YOU HAVE TO HELP ME, OKAY? JUST DON'T TOUCH ANYTHING, ALL RIGHT?
OKA--
HEY, WHY'D ALL THE FIRING STOP?
Ahh, SUPERMAN BUSTED THE GUY'S GUNS AND CHASED HIM OFF.
I BETTER GET REIMBURSED FOR MY GUNS, THAT'S ALL I CAN SAY.
YOU TURNED THEM ALL AGAINST ME!
YOU'LL PAY! METROPOLIS WILL PAY!

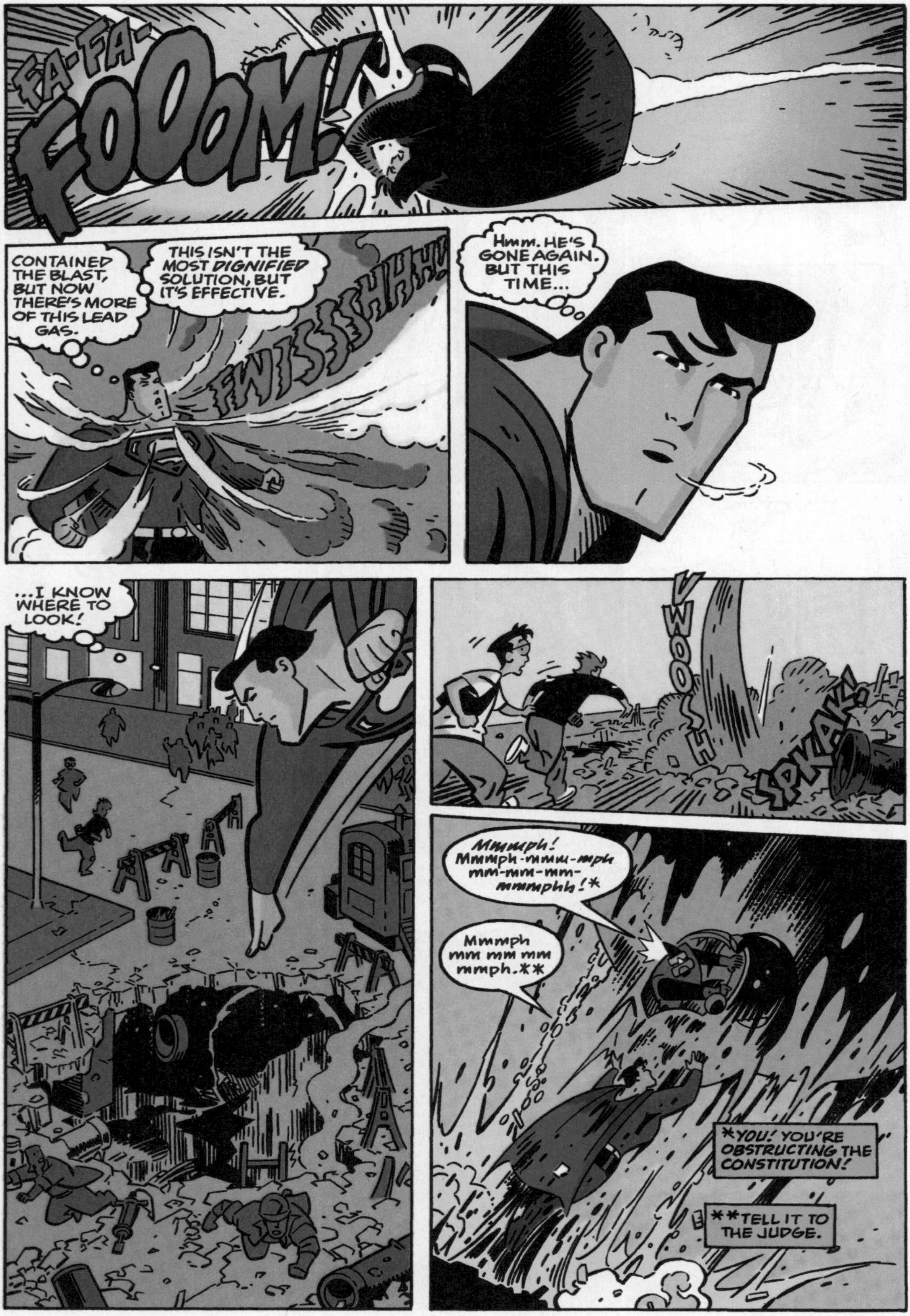
FA-FA-FOOOM!
CONTAINED THE BLAST, BUT NOW THERE'S MORE OF THIS LEAD GAS.
THIS ISN'T THE MOST DIGNIFIED SOLUTION, BUT IT'S EFFECTIVE.
FWISSSSHHH!
Hmm. HE'S GONE AGAIN. BUT THIS TIME...
...I KNOW WHERE TO LOOK!
VWOOOSH
SPKAK!
Mmmph! Mmmph-mmm-mph mm-mm-mm-mmmphh!*
Mmmph mm mm mm mmph.**
*YOU! YOU'RE OBSTRUCTING THE CONSTITUTION!
**TELL IT TO THE JUDGE.

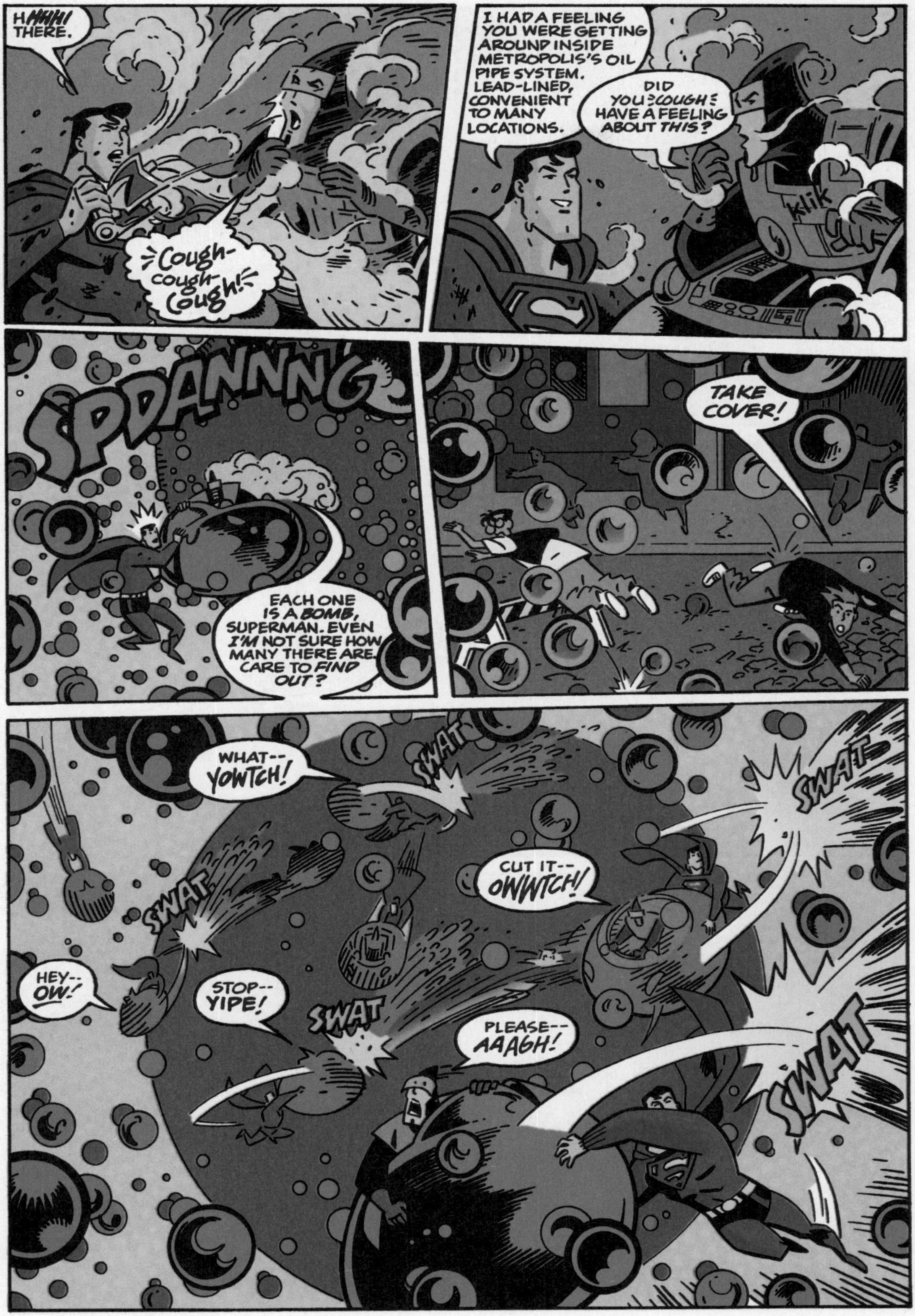
HHHHH! THERE.
Cough-cough-Cough!
I HAD A FEELING YOU WERE GETTING AROUND INSIDE METROPOLIS'S OIL PIPE SYSTEM. LEAD-LINED, CONVENIENT TO MANY LOCATIONS.
DID YOU COUGH HAVE A FEELING ABOUT THIS?
klik
SPDANNNG
EACH ONE IS A BOMB, SUPERMAN. EVEN I'M NOT SURE HOW MANY THERE ARE. CARE TO FIND OUT?
TAKE COVER!
WHAT-- YOWTCH!
SWAT
SWAT
CUT IT-- OWWTCH!
SWAT
HEY-- OW!
STOP-- YIPE!
SWAT
PLEASE-- AAAGH!
SWAT

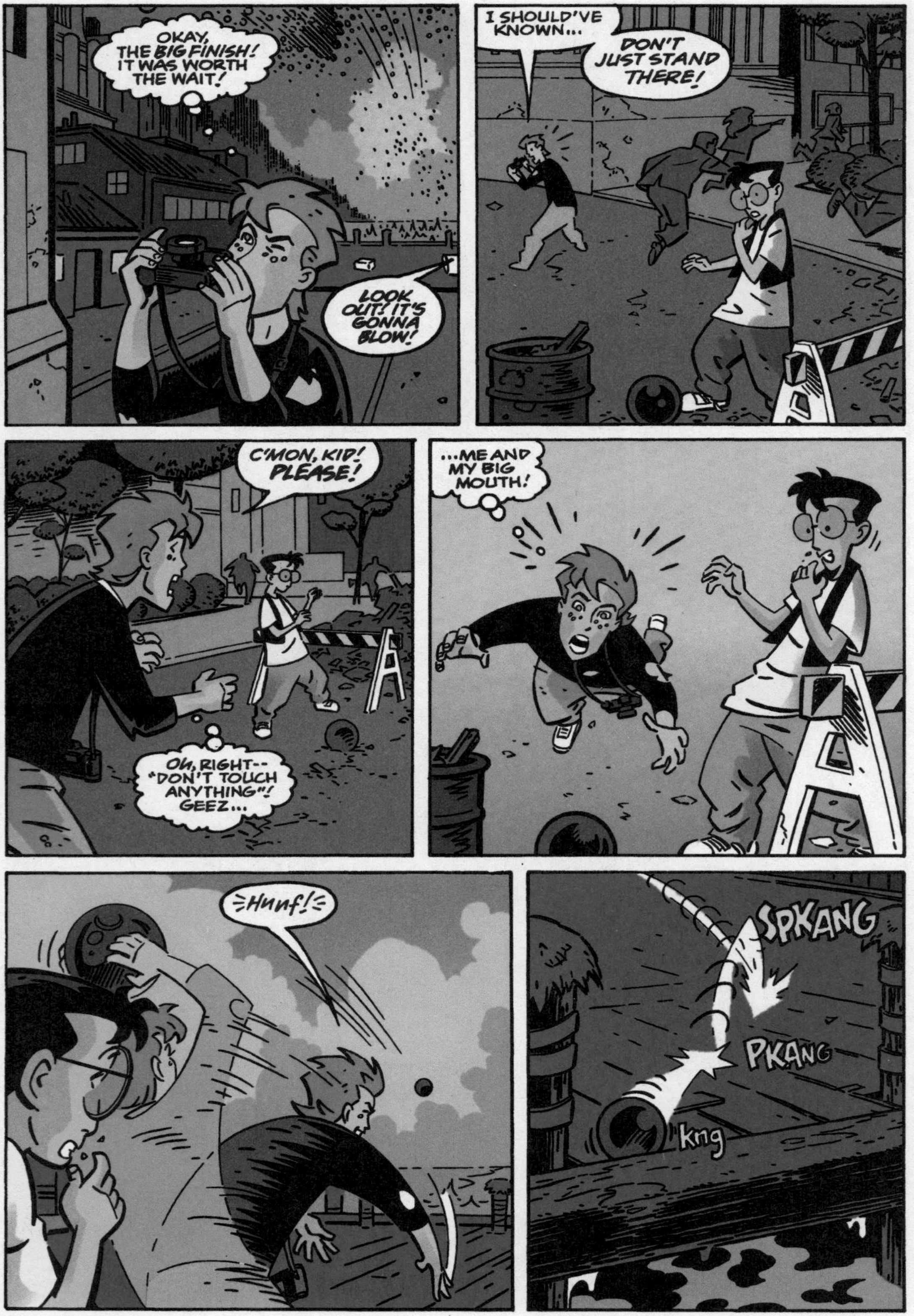
OKAY, THE BIG FINISH! IT WAS WORTH THE WAIT!
LOOK OUT! IT'S GONNA BLOW!
I SHOULD'VE KNOWN...
DON'T JUST STAND THERE!
C'MON, KID! PLEASE!
OH, RIGHT-- "DON'T TOUCH ANYTHING"! GEEZ...
...ME AND MY BIG MOUTH!
Hunf!
SPKANG
PKANG
kng

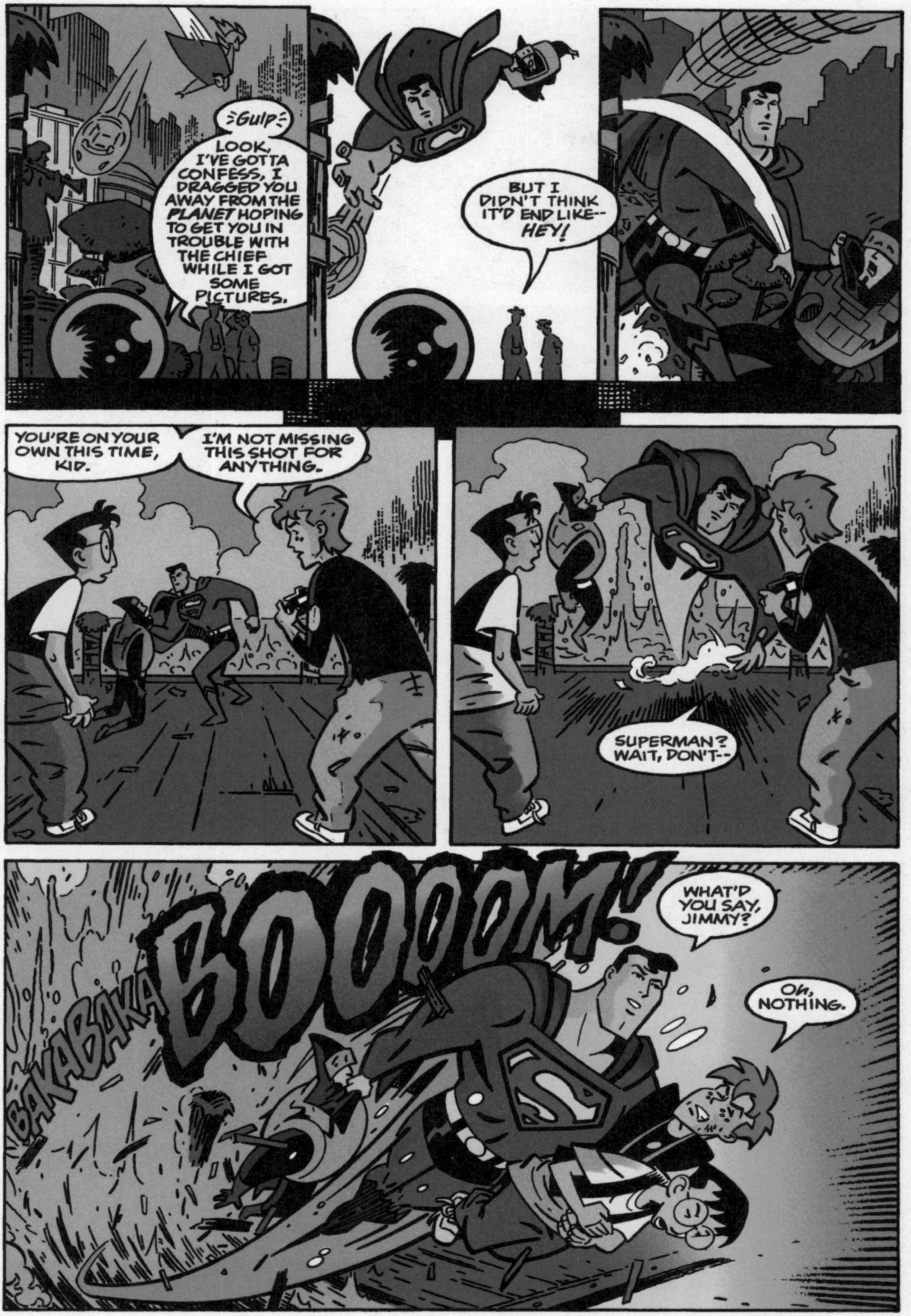
GULP
LOOK, I'VE GOTTA CONFESS, I DRAGGED YOU AWAY FROM THE PLANET HOPING TO GET YOU IN TROUBLE WITH THE CHIEF WHILE I GOT SOME PICTURES.
BUT I DIDN'T THINK IT'D END LIKE-- HEY!
YOU'RE ON YOUR OWN THIS TIME, KID.
I'M NOT MISSING THIS SHOT FOR ANYTHING.
SUPERMAN? WAIT, DON'T--
BAKABAKA BOOOOM!
WHAT'D YOU SAY, JIMMY?
OH, NOTHING.

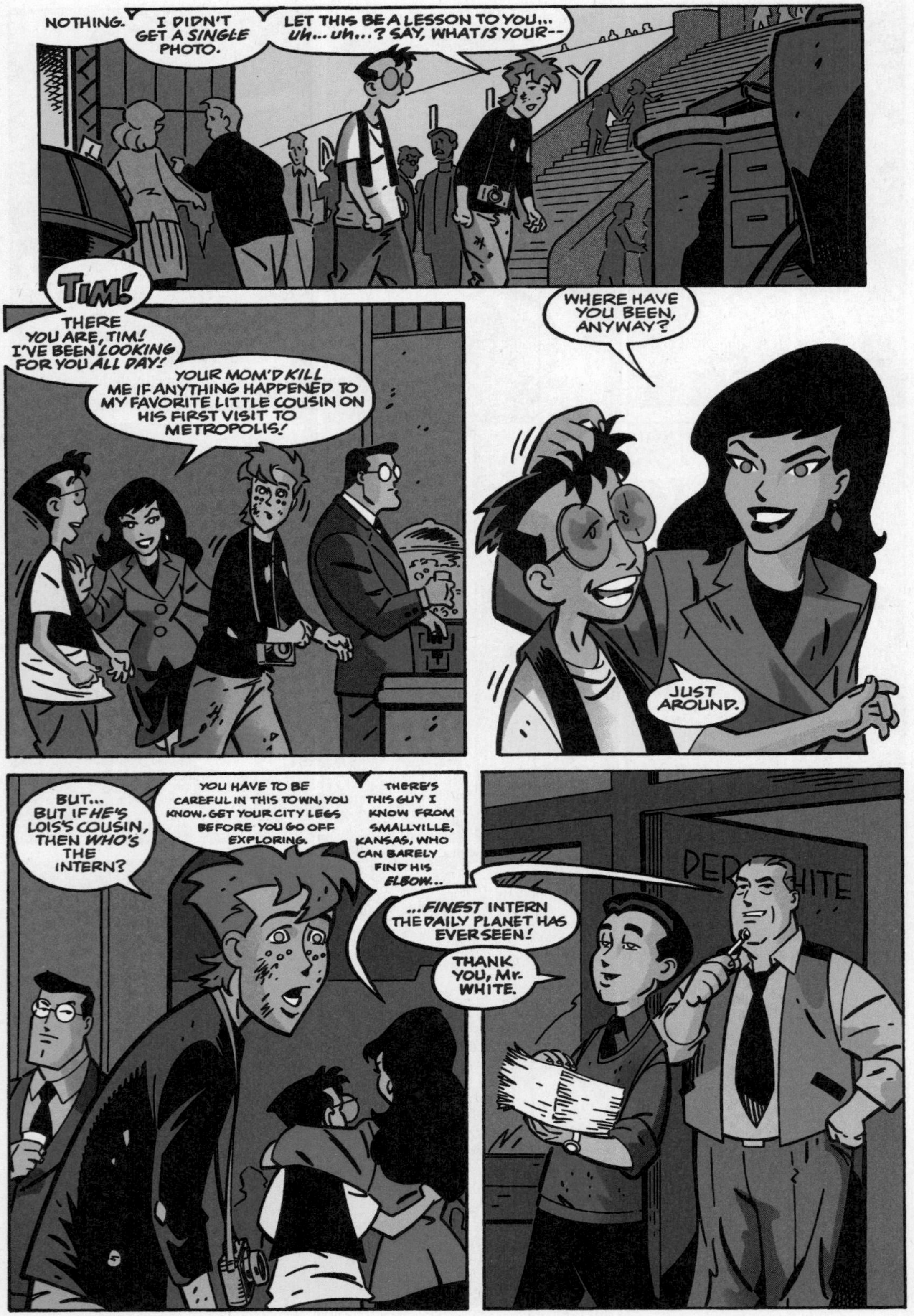
NOTHING.
I DIDN'T GET A *SINGLE* PHOTO.
LET THIS BE A LESSON TO YOU... *UH... UH...?* SAY, WHAT *IS* YOUR--
TIM!
THERE YOU ARE, TIM! I'VE BEEN *LOOKING* FOR YOU *ALL DAY!*
YOUR MOM'D *KILL* ME IF ANYTHING HAPPENED TO MY FAVORITE LITTLE COUSIN ON HIS FIRST VISIT TO METROPOLIS!
WHERE HAVE YOU BEEN, ANYWAY?
JUST AROUND.
BUT... BUT IF *HE'S* LOIS'S COUSIN, THEN *WHO'S* THE INTERN?
YOU HAVE TO BE CAREFUL IN THIS TOWN, YOU KNOW. GET YOUR CITY LEGS BEFORE YOU GO OFF EXPLORING.
THERE'S THIS GUY I KNOW FROM SMALLVILLE, KANSAS, WHO CAN BARELY FIND HIS *ELBOW*...
...*FINEST* INTERN THE DAILY PLANET HAS EVER SEEN!
THANK YOU, MR. WHITE.

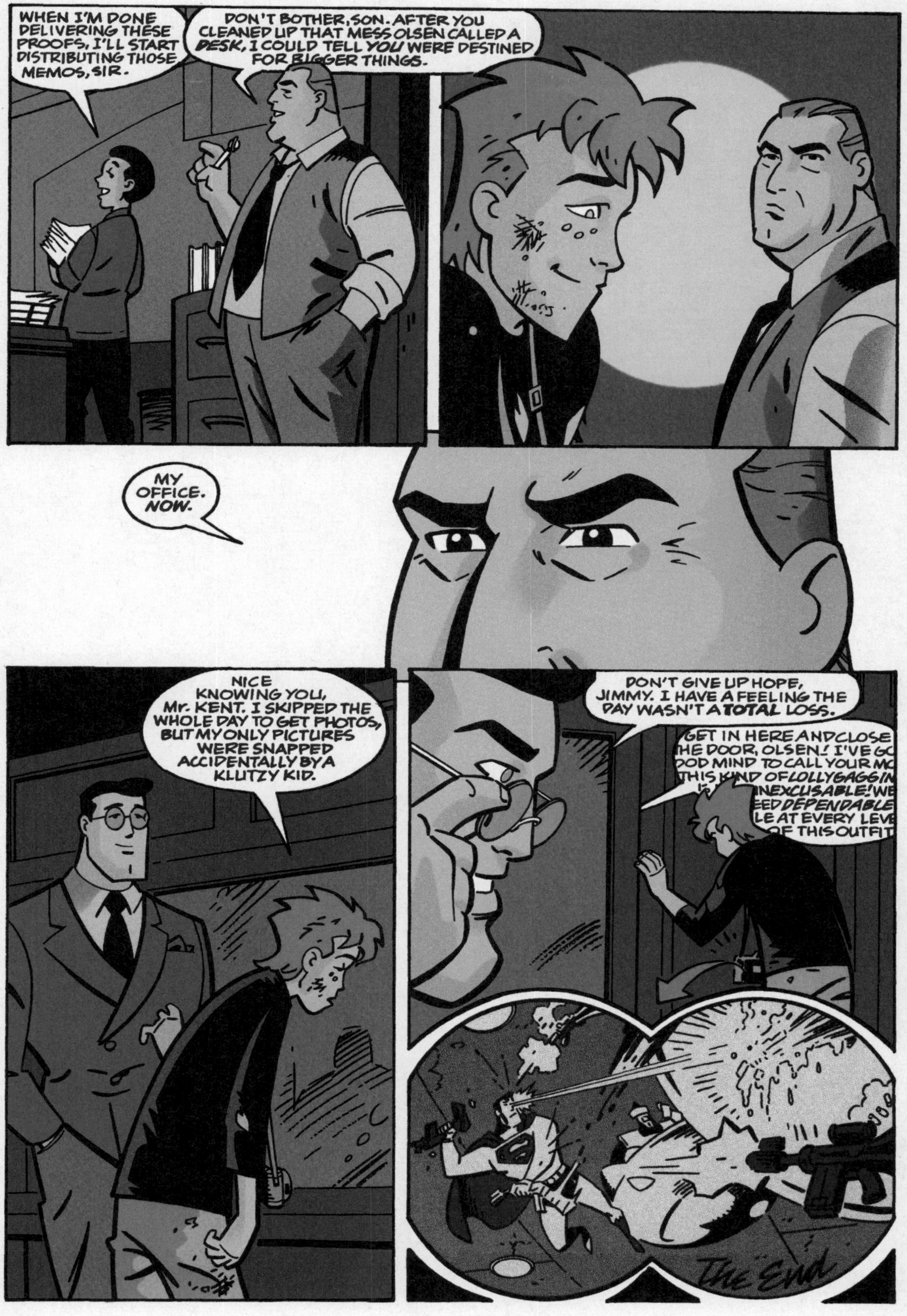
WHEN I'M DONE DELIVERING THESE PROOFS, I'LL START DISTRIBUTING THOSE MEMOS, SIR.
DON'T BOTHER, SON. AFTER YOU CLEANED UP THAT MESS OLSEN CALLED A *DESK*, I COULD TELL *YOU* WERE DESTINED FOR *BIGGER* THINGS.
MY OFFICE. *NOW.*
NICE KNOWING YOU, Mr. KENT. I SKIPPED THE WHOLE DAY TO GET PHOTOS, BUT MY ONLY PICTURES WERE SNAPPED ACCIDENTALLY BY A KLUTZY KID.
DON'T GIVE UP HOPE, JIMMY. I HAVE A FEELING THE DAY WASN'T A *TOTAL* LOSS.
GET IN HERE AND CLOSE
HE DOOR, OLSEN! I'VE GO
OOD MIND TO CALL YOUR MO
THIS KIND OF *LOLLYGAGGIN*
INEXCUSABLE! WE
EED *DEPENDABLE*
LE AT EVERY LEVE
OF THIS OUTFIT
The End

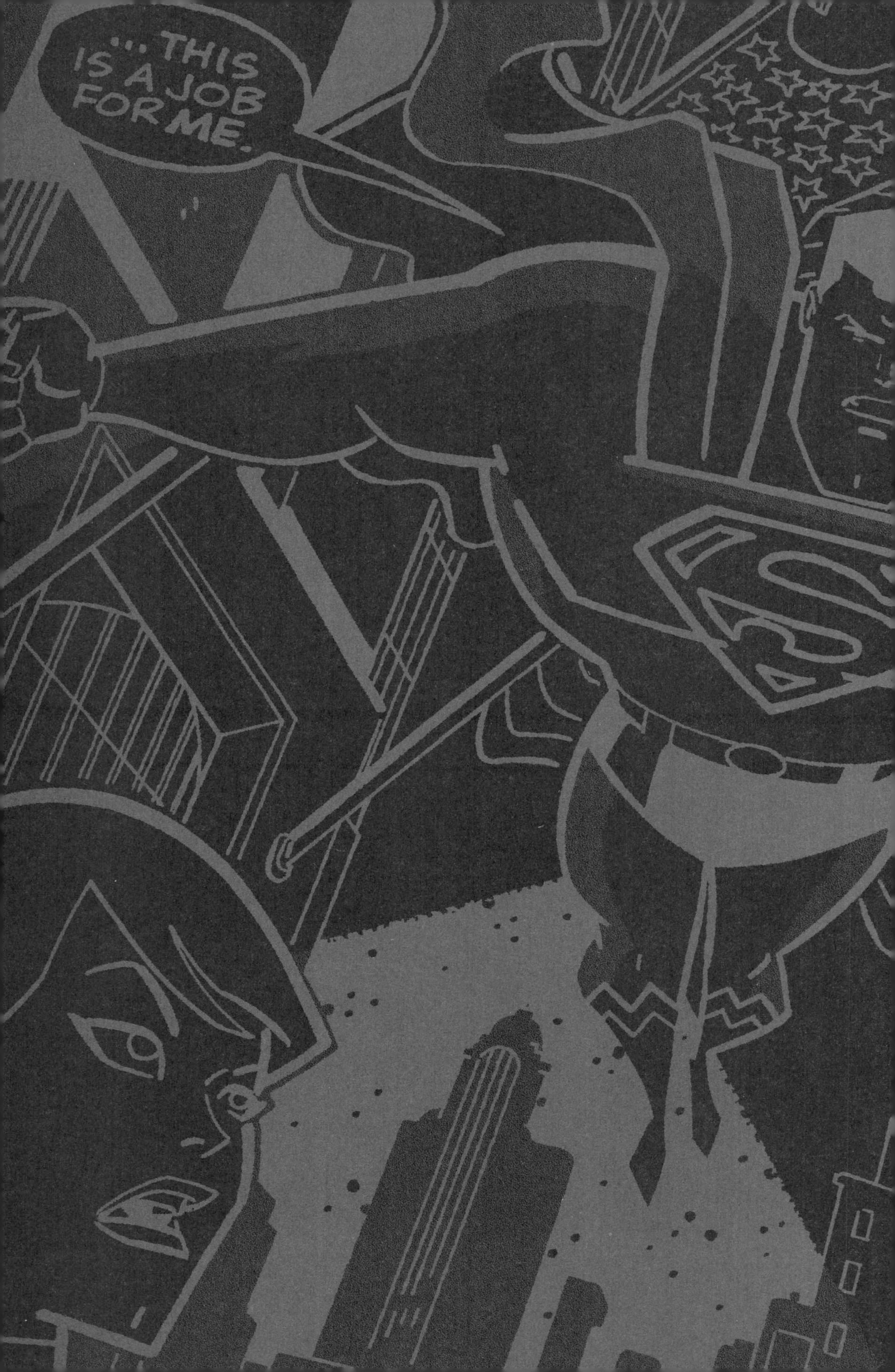
"... THIS IS A JOB FOR ME.

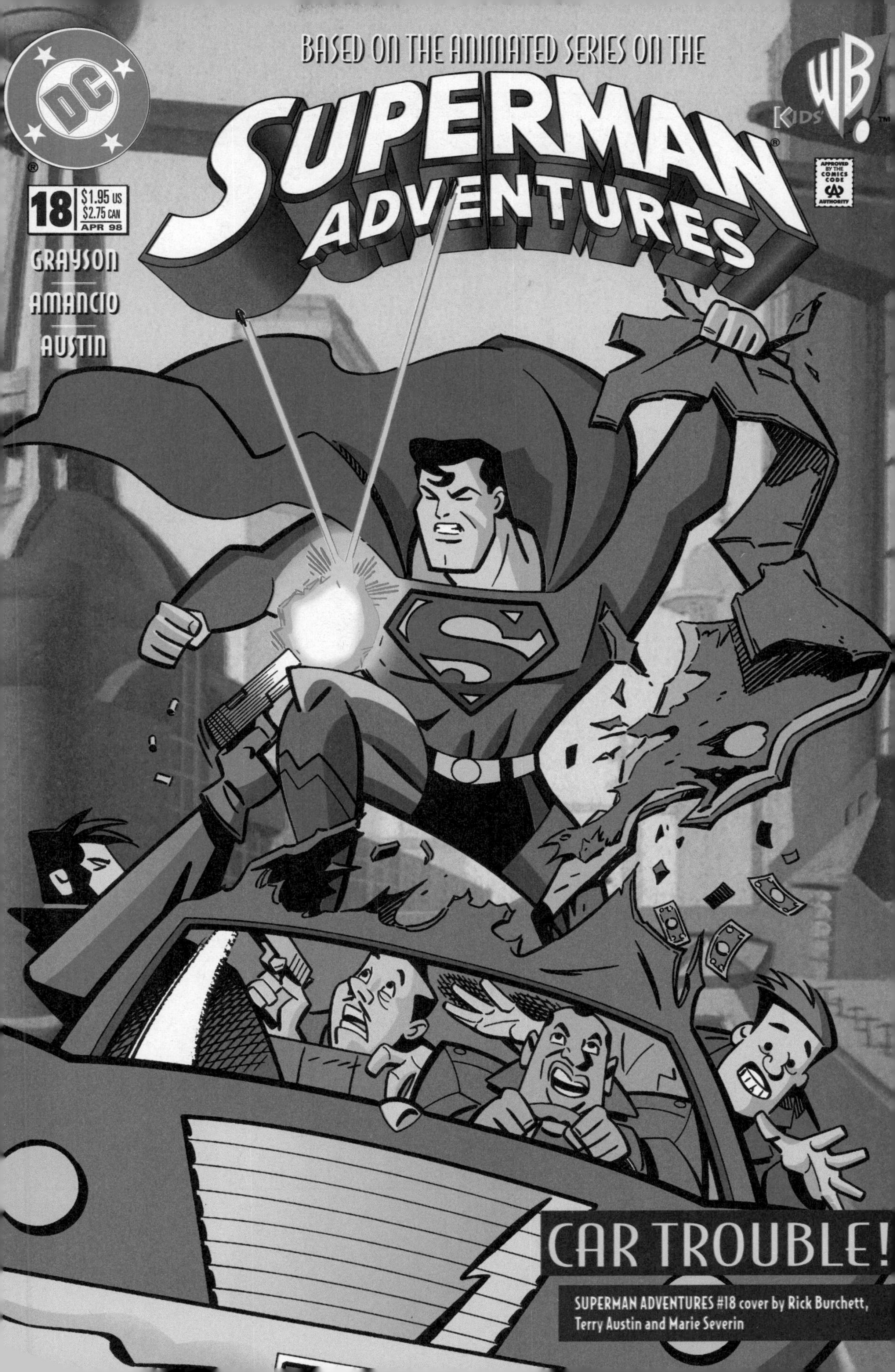
BASED ON THE ANIMATED SERIES ON THE
SUPERMAN ADVENTURES
KIDS' WB!
18 $1.95 US $2.75 CAN APR 98
APPROVED BY THE COMICS CODE AUTHORITY
GRAYSON
AMANCIO
AUSTIN
CAR TROUBLE!
SUPERMAN ADVENTURES #18 cover by Rick Burchett, Terry Austin and Marie Severin

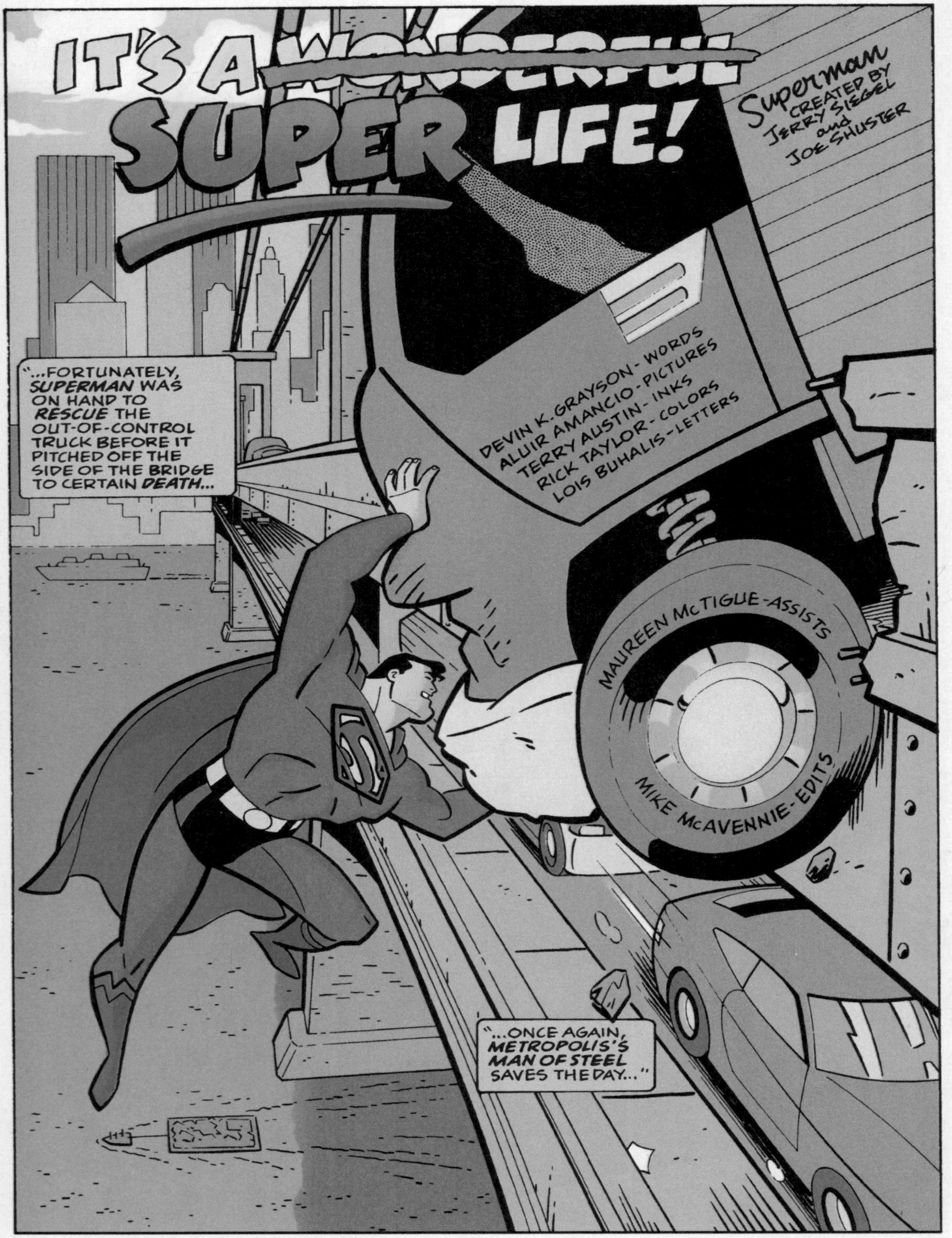

IT'S A ~~WONDERFUL~~ SUPER LIFE!
Superman CREATED BY JERRY SIEGEL and JOE SHUSTER
"...FORTUNATELY, SUPERMAN WAS ON HAND TO RESCUE THE OUT-OF-CONTROL TRUCK BEFORE IT PITCHED OFF THE SIDE OF THE BRIDGE TO CERTAIN DEATH...
DEVIN K. GRAYSON - WORDS
ALUIR AMANCIO - PICTURES
TERRY AUSTIN - INKS
RICK TAYLOR - COLORS
LOIS BUHALIS - LETTERS
MAUREEN McTIGUE - ASSISTS
MIKE McAVENNIE - EDITS
"...ONCE AGAIN, METROPOLIS'S MAN OF STEEL SAVES THE DAY..."

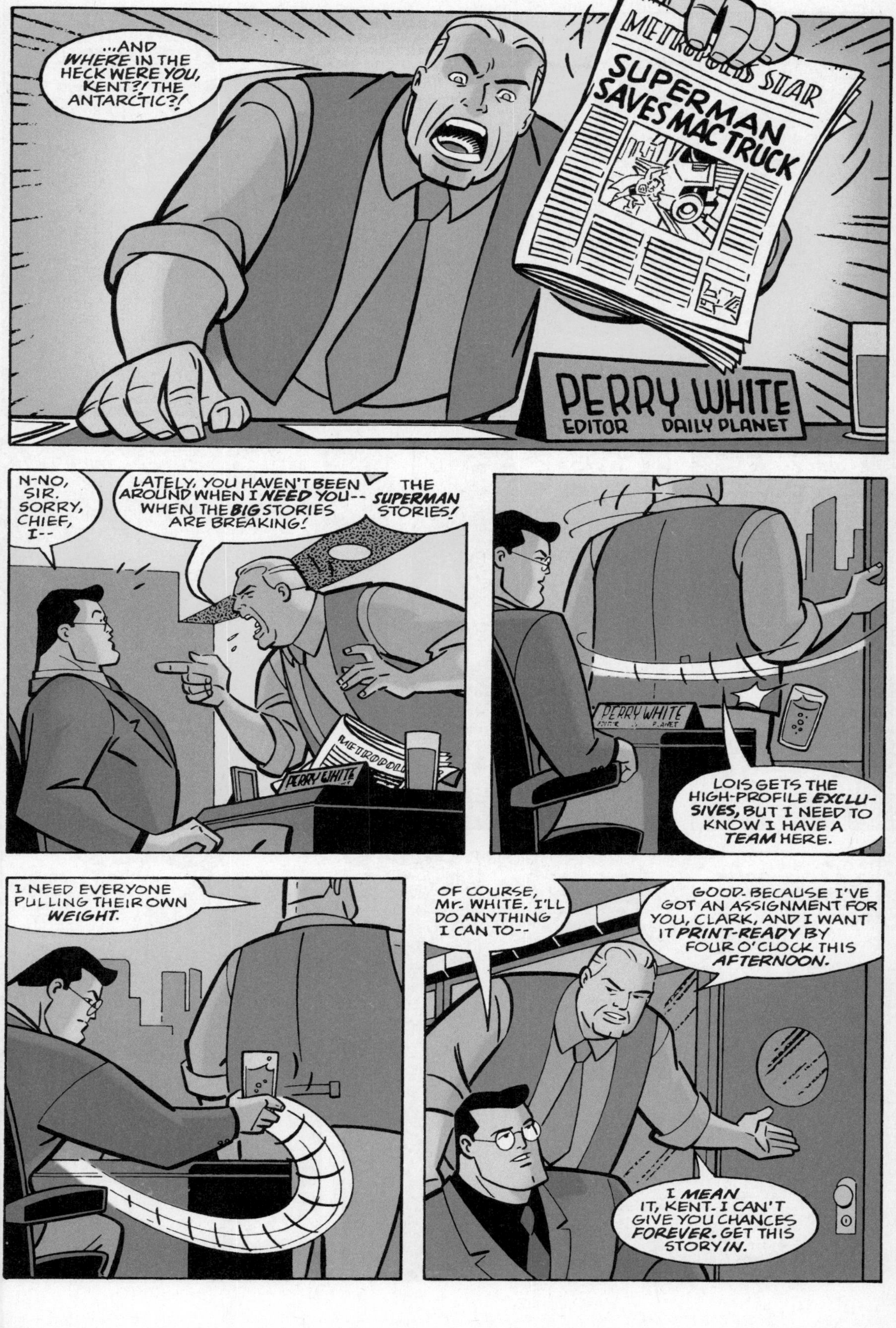
...AND WHERE IN THE HECK WERE YOU, KENT?! THE ANTARCTIC?!
METROPOLIS STAR
SUPERMAN SAVES MAC TRUCK
PERRY WHITE
EDITOR DAILY PLANET
N-NO, SIR. SORRY, CHIEF, I--
LATELY, YOU HAVEN'T BEEN AROUND WHEN I NEED YOU-- WHEN THE BIG STORIES ARE BREAKING!
THE SUPERMAN STORIES!
PERRY WHITE
LOIS GETS THE HIGH-PROFILE EXCLUSIVES, BUT I NEED TO KNOW I HAVE A TEAM HERE.
I NEED EVERYONE PULLING THEIR OWN WEIGHT.
OF COURSE, Mr. WHITE. I'LL DO ANYTHING I CAN TO--
GOOD. BECAUSE I'VE GOT AN ASSIGNMENT FOR YOU, CLARK, AND I WANT IT PRINT-READY BY FOUR O'CLOCK THIS AFTERNOON.
I MEAN IT, KENT. I CAN'T GIVE YOU CHANCES FOREVER. GET THIS STORY IN.

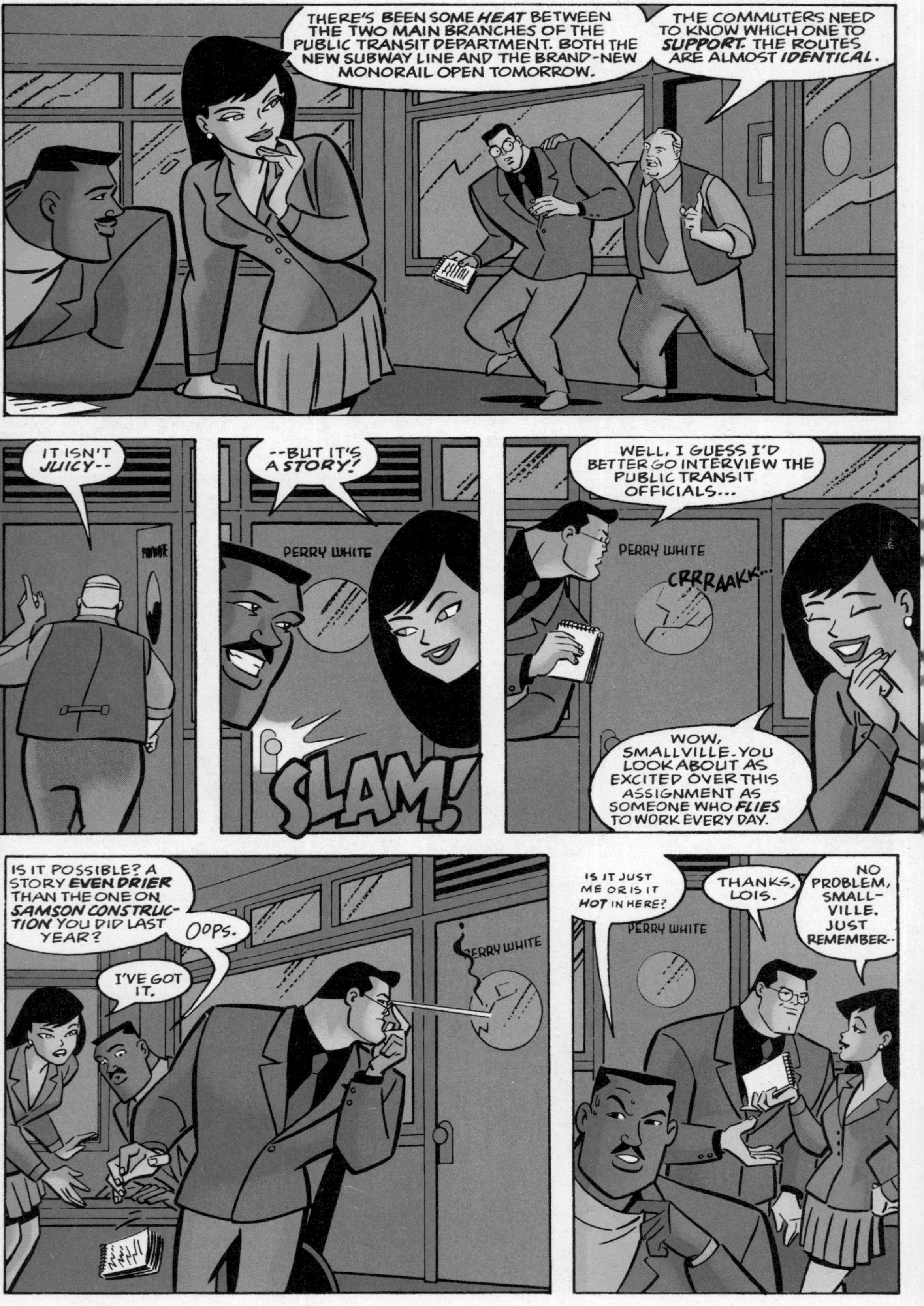
THERE'S BEEN SOME HEAT BETWEEN THE TWO MAIN BRANCHES OF THE PUBLIC TRANSIT DEPARTMENT. BOTH THE NEW SUBWAY LINE AND THE BRAND-NEW MONORAIL OPEN TOMORROW.
THE COMMUTERS NEED TO KNOW WHICH ONE TO SUPPORT. THE ROUTES ARE ALMOST IDENTICAL.
IT ISN'T JUICY--
--BUT IT'S A STORY!
PERRY WHITE
SLAM!
WELL, I GUESS I'D BETTER GO INTERVIEW THE PUBLIC TRANSIT OFFICIALS...
PERRY WHITE
CRRRAAKK...
WOW, SMALLVILLE. YOU LOOK ABOUT AS EXCITED OVER THIS ASSIGNMENT AS SOMEONE WHO FLIES TO WORK EVERY DAY.
IS IT POSSIBLE? A STORY EVEN DRIER THAN THE ONE ON SAMSON CONSTRUCTION YOU DID LAST YEAR?
OOPS.
I'VE GOT IT.
PERRY WHITE
IS IT JUST ME OR IS IT HOT IN HERE?
PERRY WHITE
THANKS, LOIS.
NO PROBLEM, SMALL-VILLE. JUST REMEMBER--

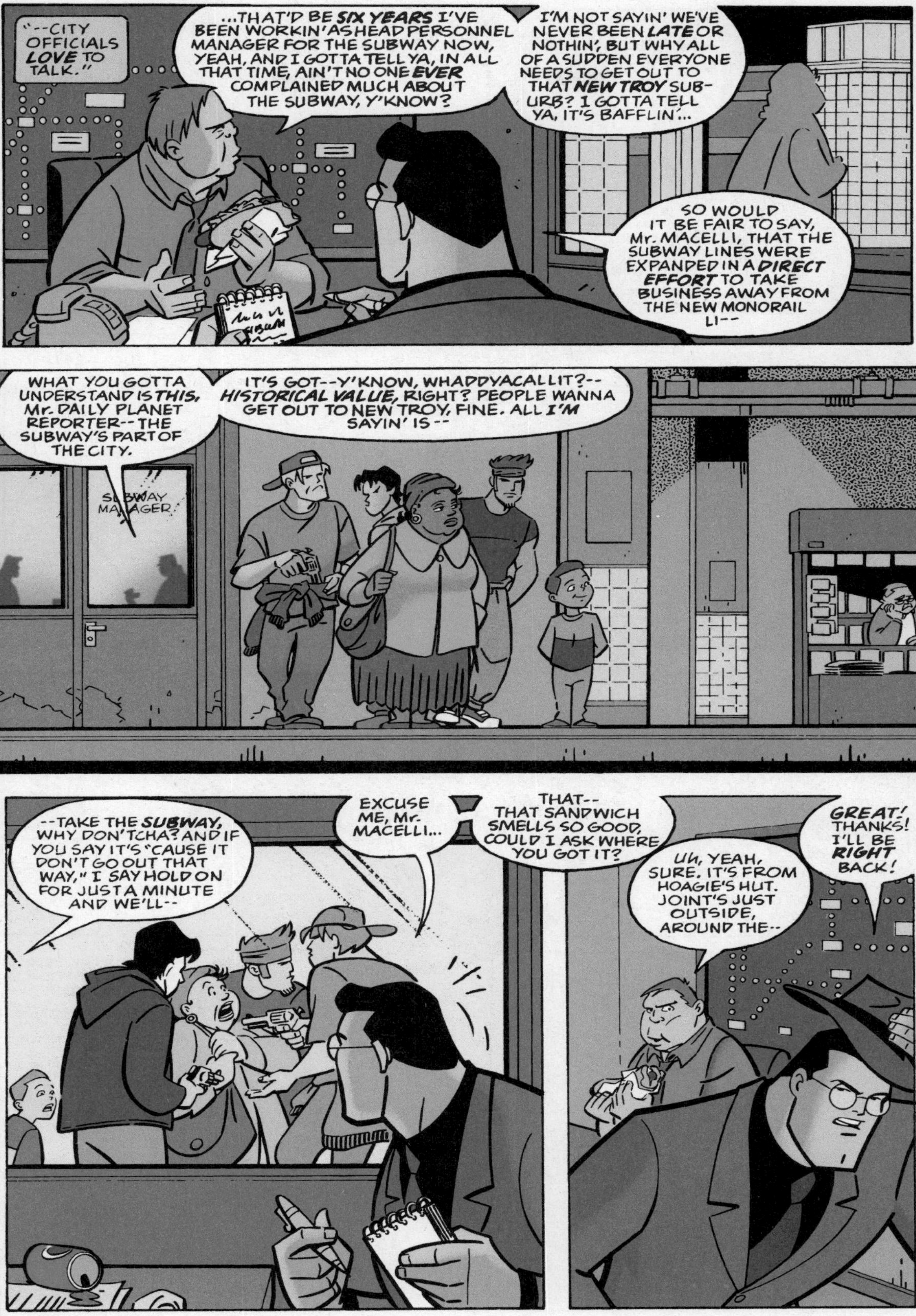
"--CITY OFFICIALS LOVE TO TALK."
...THAT'D BE SIX YEARS I'VE BEEN WORKIN' AS HEAD PERSONNEL MANAGER FOR THE SUBWAY NOW, YEAH, AND I GOTTA TELL YA, IN ALL THAT TIME, AIN'T NO ONE EVER COMPLAINED MUCH ABOUT THE SUBWAY, Y'KNOW?
I'M NOT SAYIN' WE'VE NEVER BEEN LATE OR NOTHIN', BUT WHY ALL OF A SUDDEN EVERYONE NEEDS TO GET OUT TO THAT NEW TROY SUBURB? I GOTTA TELL YA, IT'S BAFFLIN'...
SO WOULD IT BE FAIR TO SAY, Mr. MACELLI, THAT THE SUBWAY LINES WERE EXPANDED IN A DIRECT EFFORT TO TAKE BUSINESS AWAY FROM THE NEW MONORAIL LI--
WHAT YOU GOTTA UNDERSTAND IS THIS, Mr. DAILY PLANET REPORTER--THE SUBWAY'S PART OF THE CITY.
IT'S GOT--Y'KNOW, WHADDYACALLIT?--HISTORICAL VALUE, RIGHT? PEOPLE WANNA GET OUT TO NEW TROY, FINE. ALL I'M SAYIN' IS--
SUBWAY MANAGER
--TAKE THE SUBWAY, WHY DON'TCHA? AND IF YOU SAY IT'S "CAUSE IT DON'T GO OUT THAT WAY," I SAY HOLD ON FOR JUST A MINUTE AND WE'LL--
EXCUSE ME, Mr. MACELLI...
THAT--THAT SANDWICH SMELLS SO GOOD, COULD I ASK WHERE YOU GOT IT?
UH, YEAH, SURE. IT'S FROM HOAGIE'S HUT. JOINT'S JUST OUTSIDE, AROUND THE--
GREAT! THANKS! I'LL BE RIGHT BACK!

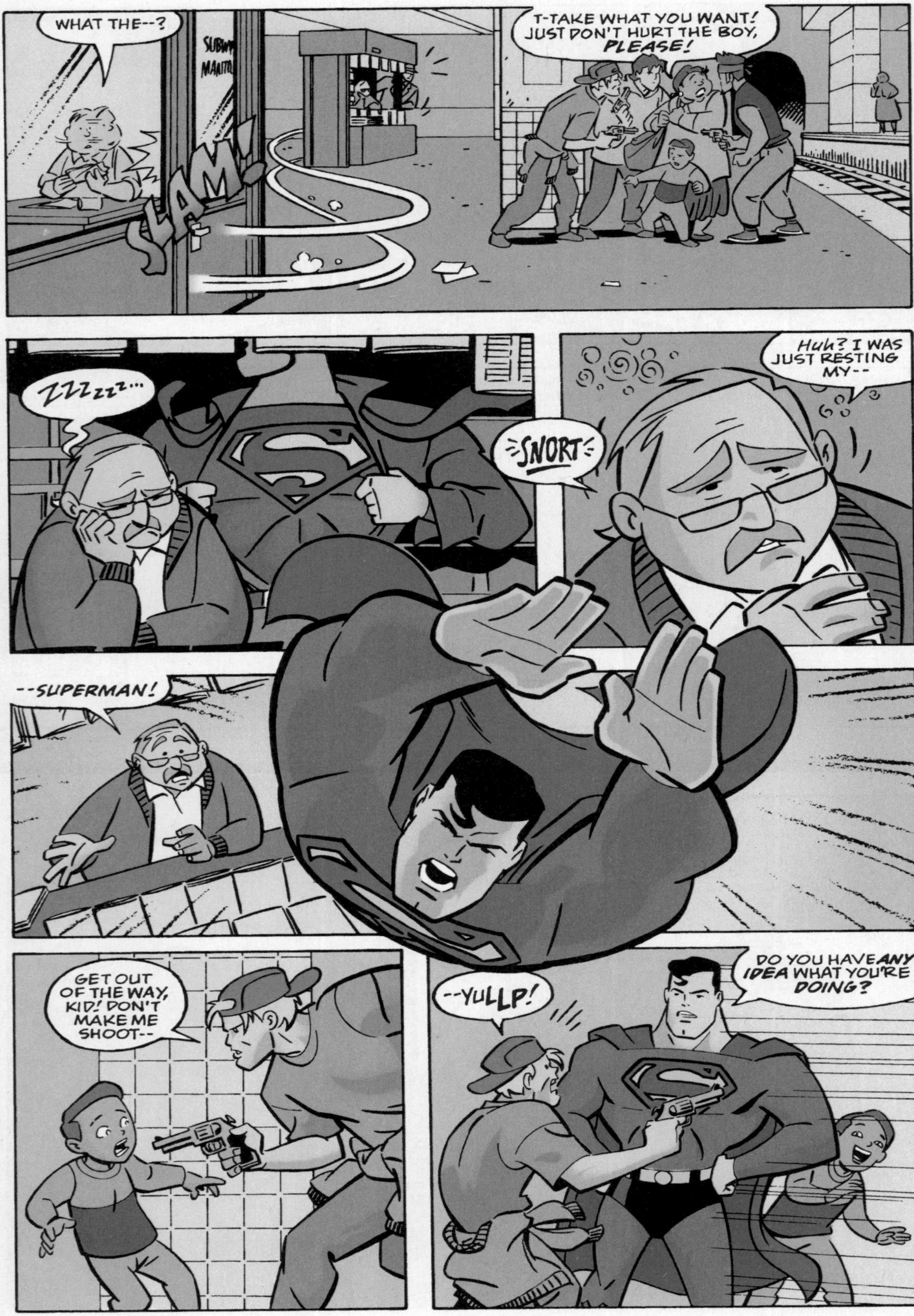
WHAT THE--?
SLAM!
T-TAKE WHAT YOU WANT! JUST DON'T HURT THE BOY, PLEASE!
ZZZzzz...
SNORT
Huh? I WAS JUST RESTING MY--
--SUPERMAN!
GET OUT OF THE WAY, KID! DON'T MAKE ME SHOOT--
--YULLP!
DO YOU HAVE ANY IDEA WHAT YOU'RE DOING?

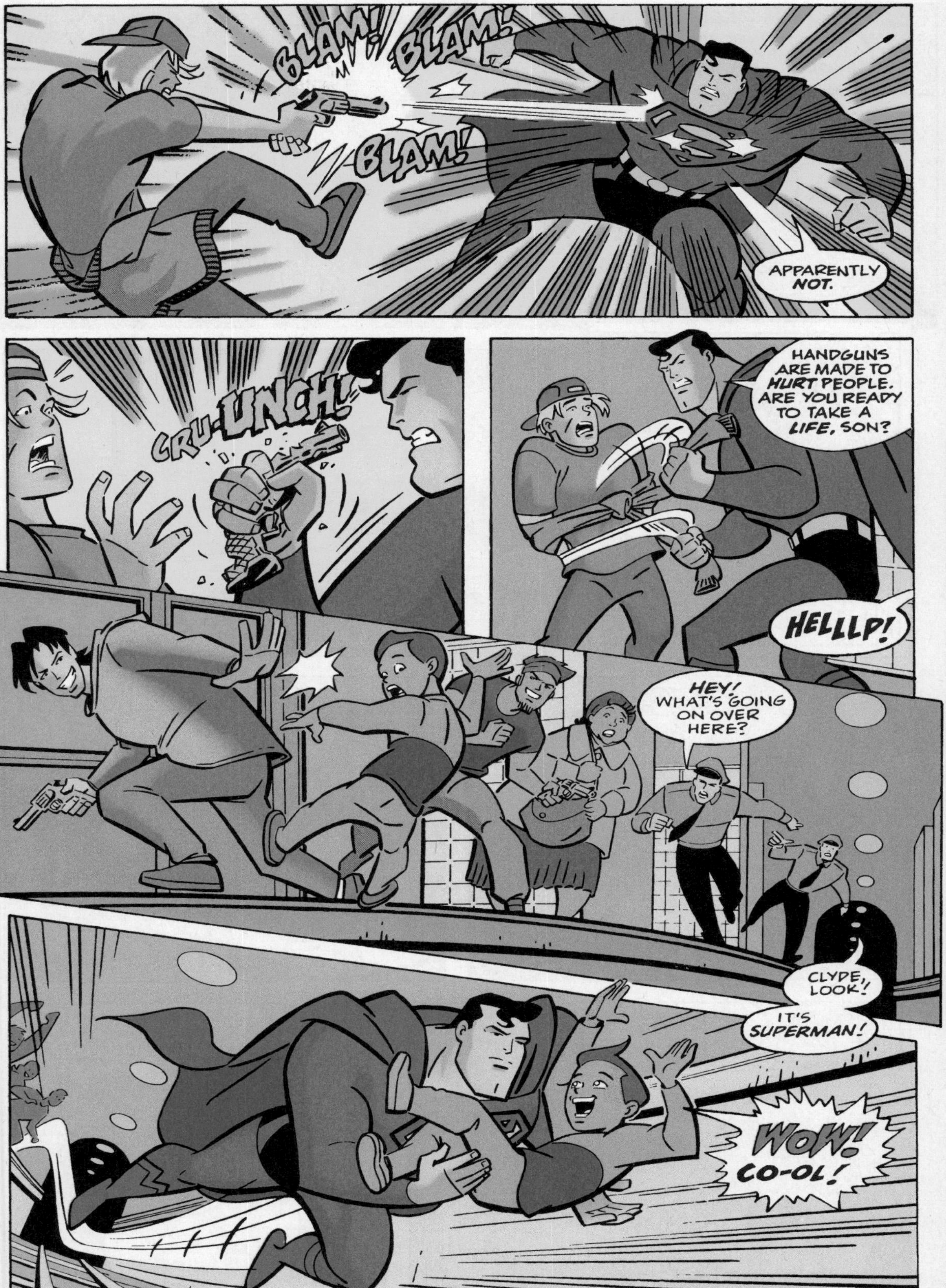
BLAM!
BLAM!
BLAM!
APPARENTLY NOT.
CRU-UNCH!
HANDGUNS ARE MADE TO HURT PEOPLE. ARE YOU READY TO TAKE A LIFE, SON?
HELLLP!
HEY! WHAT'S GOING ON OVER HERE?
CLYDE, LOOK!
IT'S SUPERMAN!
WOW! CO-OL!

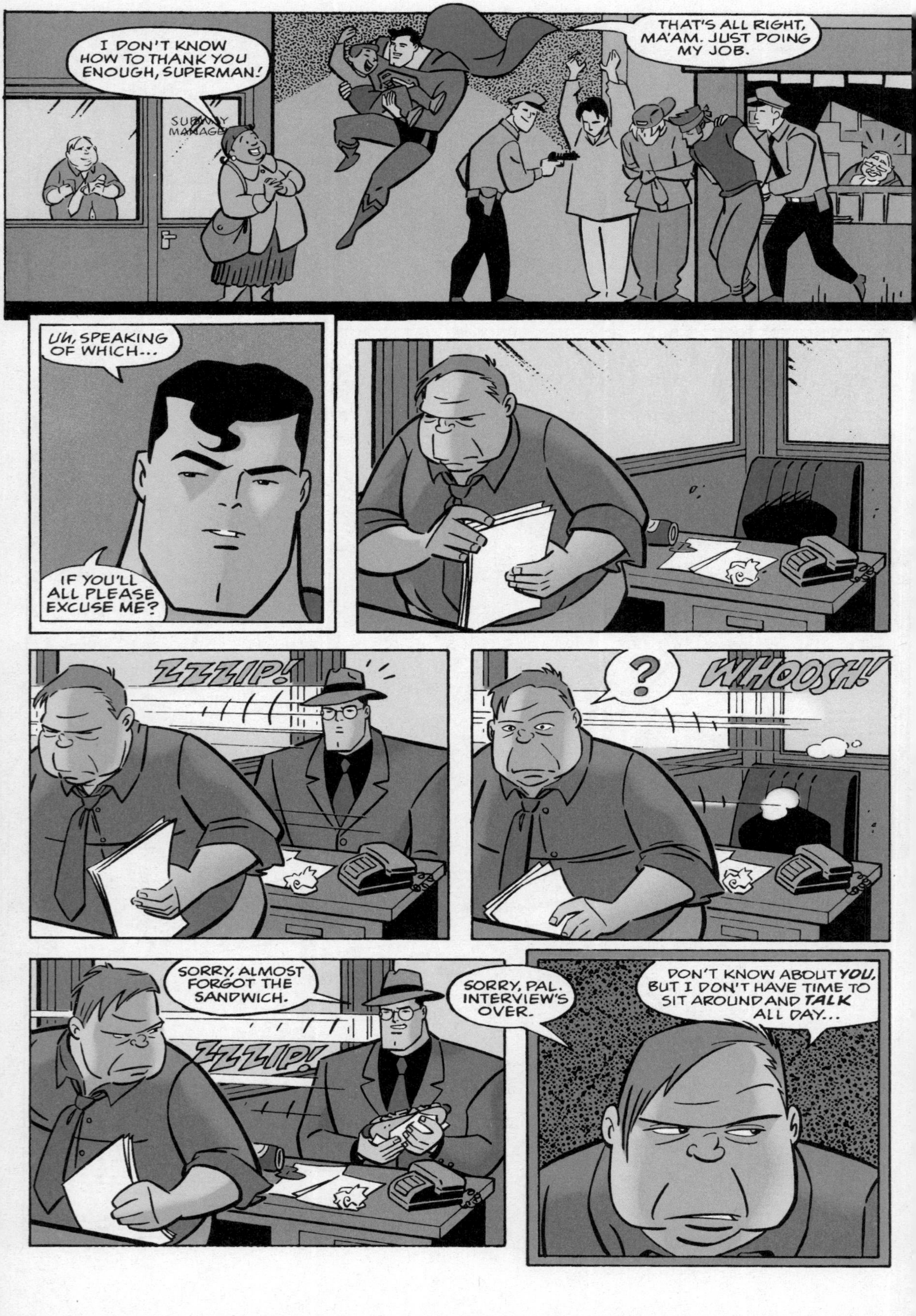
I DON'T KNOW HOW TO THANK YOU ENOUGH, SUPERMAN!
THAT'S ALL RIGHT, MA'AM. JUST DOING MY JOB.
UH, SPEAKING OF WHICH...
IF YOU'LL ALL PLEASE EXCUSE ME?
ZZZIP!
?
WHOOSH!
SORRY, ALMOST FORGOT THE SANDWICH.
ZZZIP!
SORRY, PAL. INTERVIEW'S OVER.
DON'T KNOW ABOUT YOU, BUT I DON'T HAVE TIME TO SIT AROUND AND TALK ALL DAY...

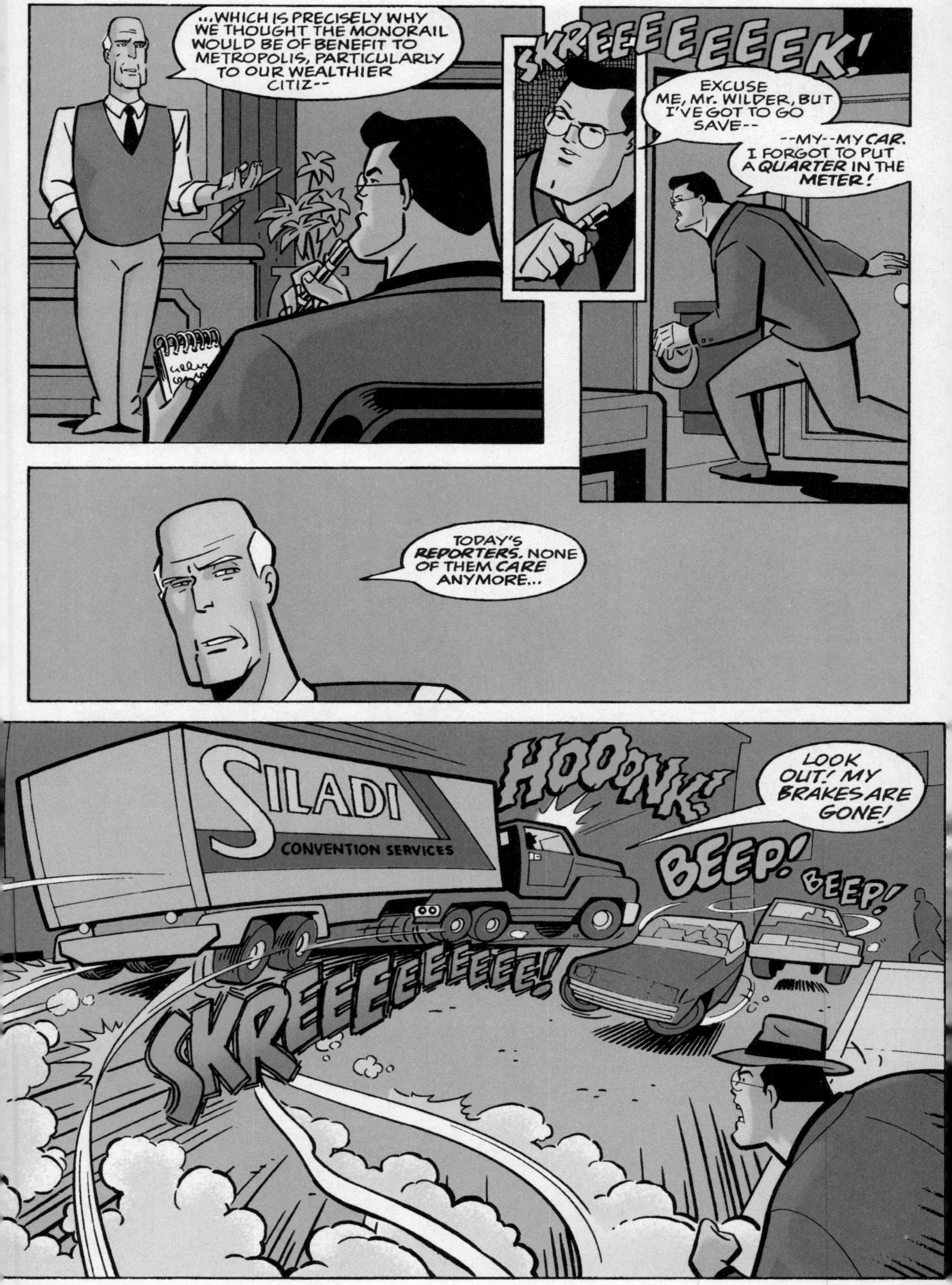
...WHICH IS PRECISELY WHY WE THOUGHT THE MONORAIL WOULD BE OF BENEFIT TO METROPOLIS, PARTICULARLY TO OUR WEALTHIER CITIZ--
SKREEEEEEEEK!
EXCUSE ME, Mr. WILDER, BUT I'VE GOT TO GO SAVE--
--MY--MY CAR. I FORGOT TO PUT A QUARTER IN THE METER!
TODAY'S REPORTERS. NONE OF THEM CARE ANYMORE...
SILADI
CONVENTION SERVICES
HOOONK!
LOOK OUT! MY BRAKES ARE GONE!
BEEP!
BEEP!
SKREEEEEEEEEE!

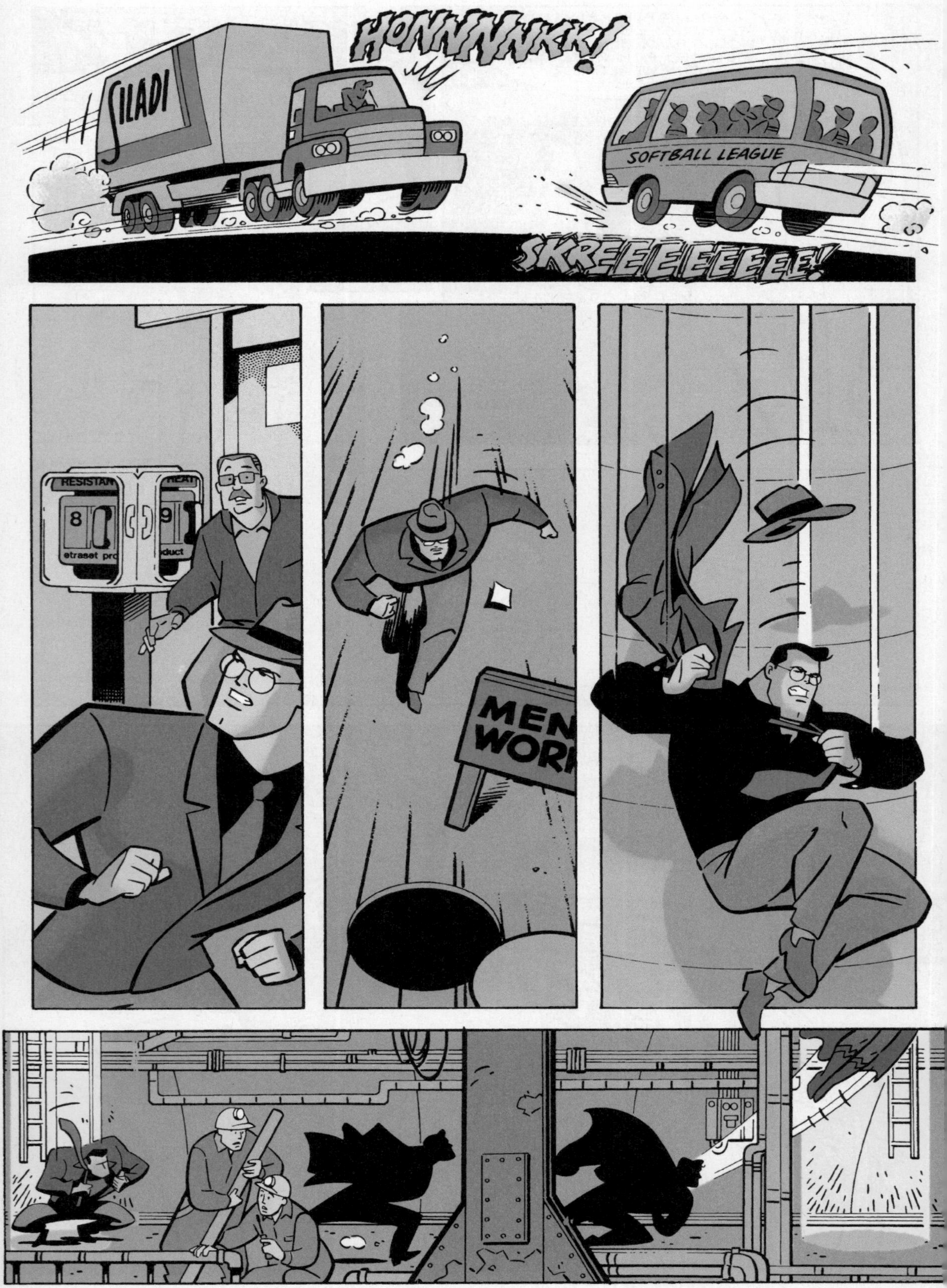
HONNNNKK!
SILADI
SOFTBALL LEAGUE
SKREEEEEEEEE!
RESISTAN
HEAT
8
9
etraset pro
oduct
MEN
WORK

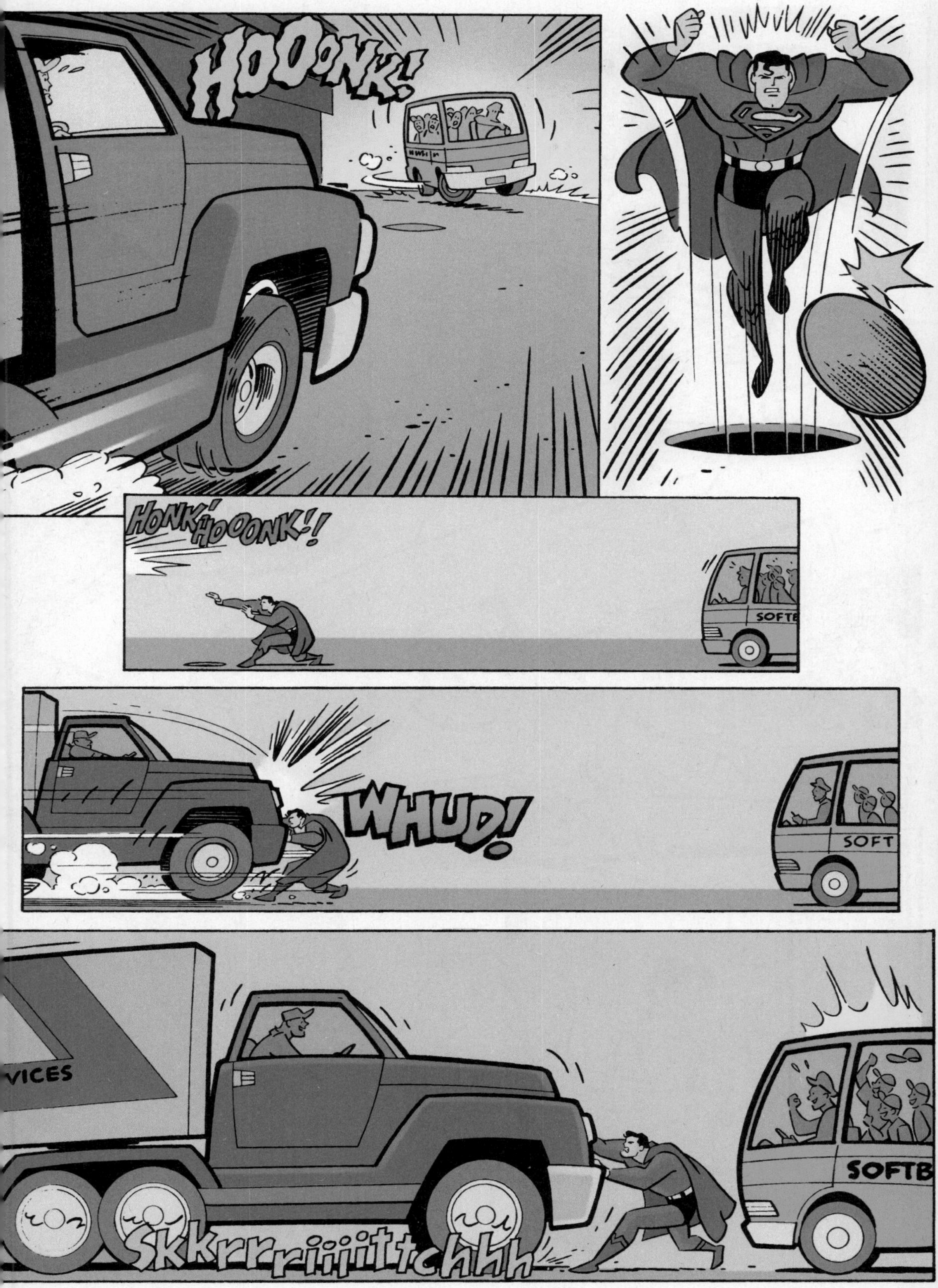
HOOONK!
HONK HOOONK!!
SOFTB
WHUD!
SOFT
VICES
SOFTB
Skkrrrriiiiittchhh

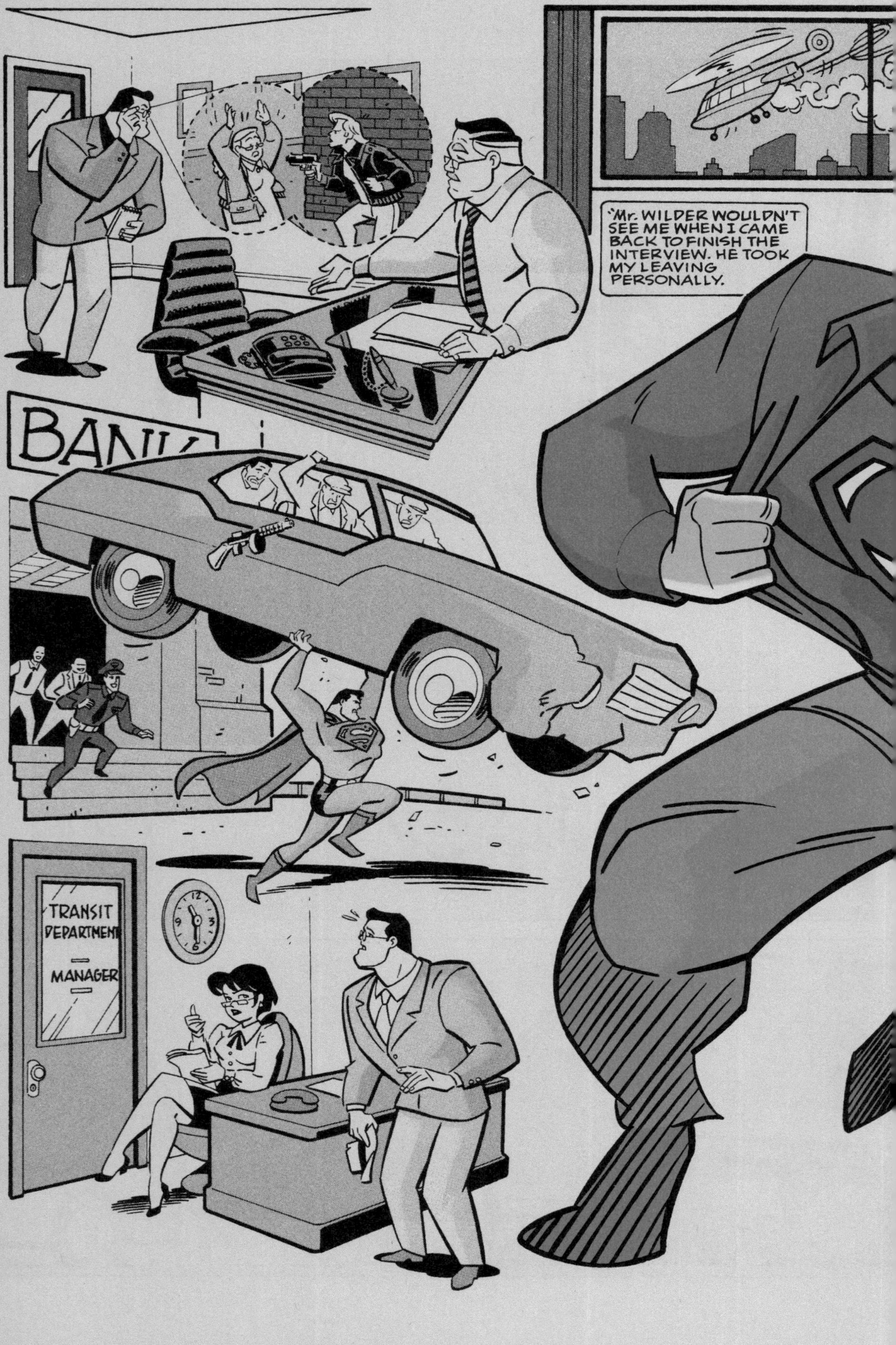
BANK
"MR. WILDER WOULDN'T SEE ME WHEN I CAME BACK TO FINISH THE INTERVIEW. HE TOOK MY LEAVING PERSONALLY.
TRANSIT DEPARTMENT
MANAGER

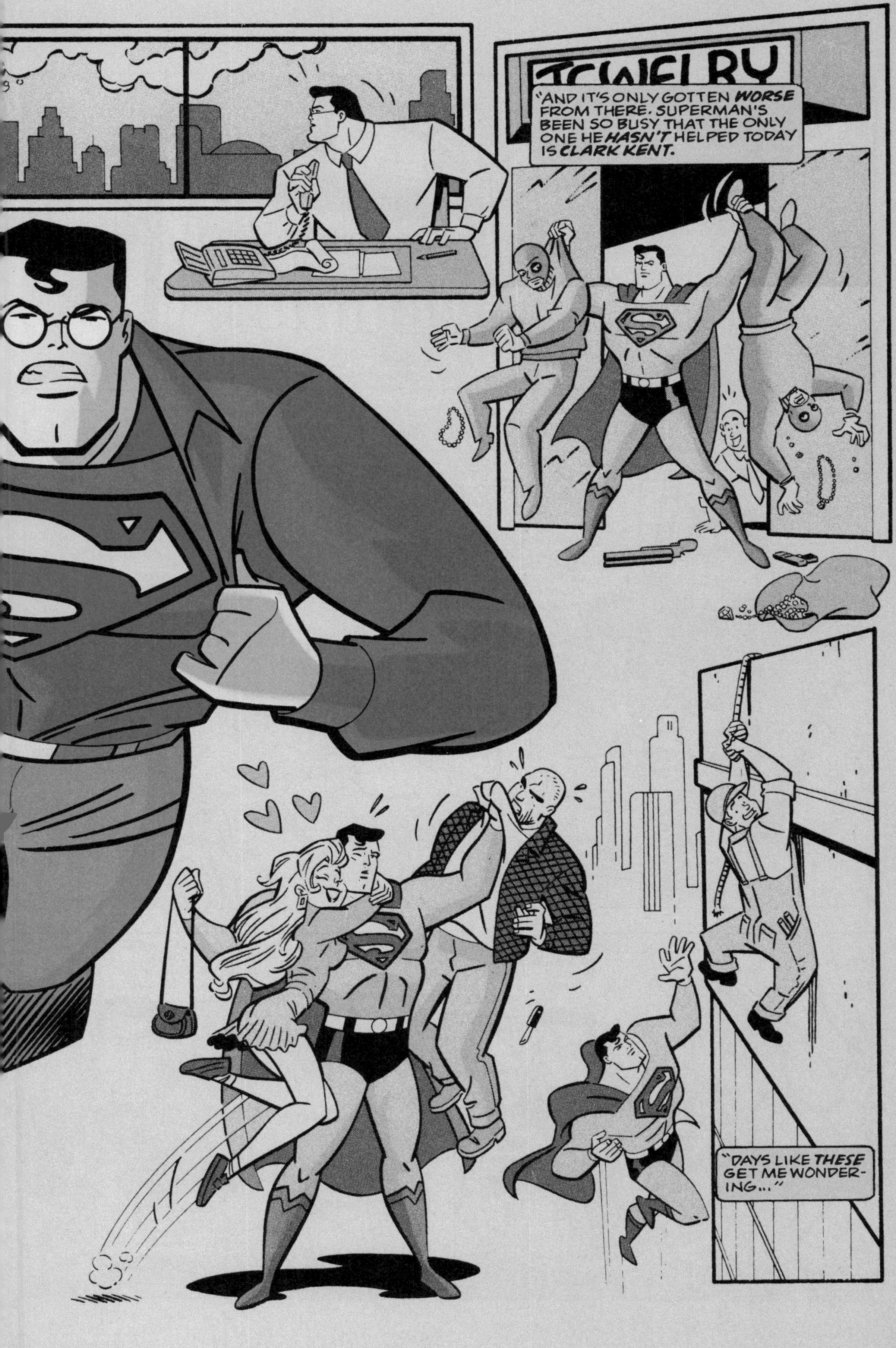
JEWELRY
"AND IT'S ONLY GOTTEN WORSE FROM THERE. SUPERMAN'S BEEN SO BUSY THAT THE ONLY ONE HE HASN'T HELPED TODAY IS CLARK KENT.
"DAYS LIKE THESE GET ME WONDERING..."

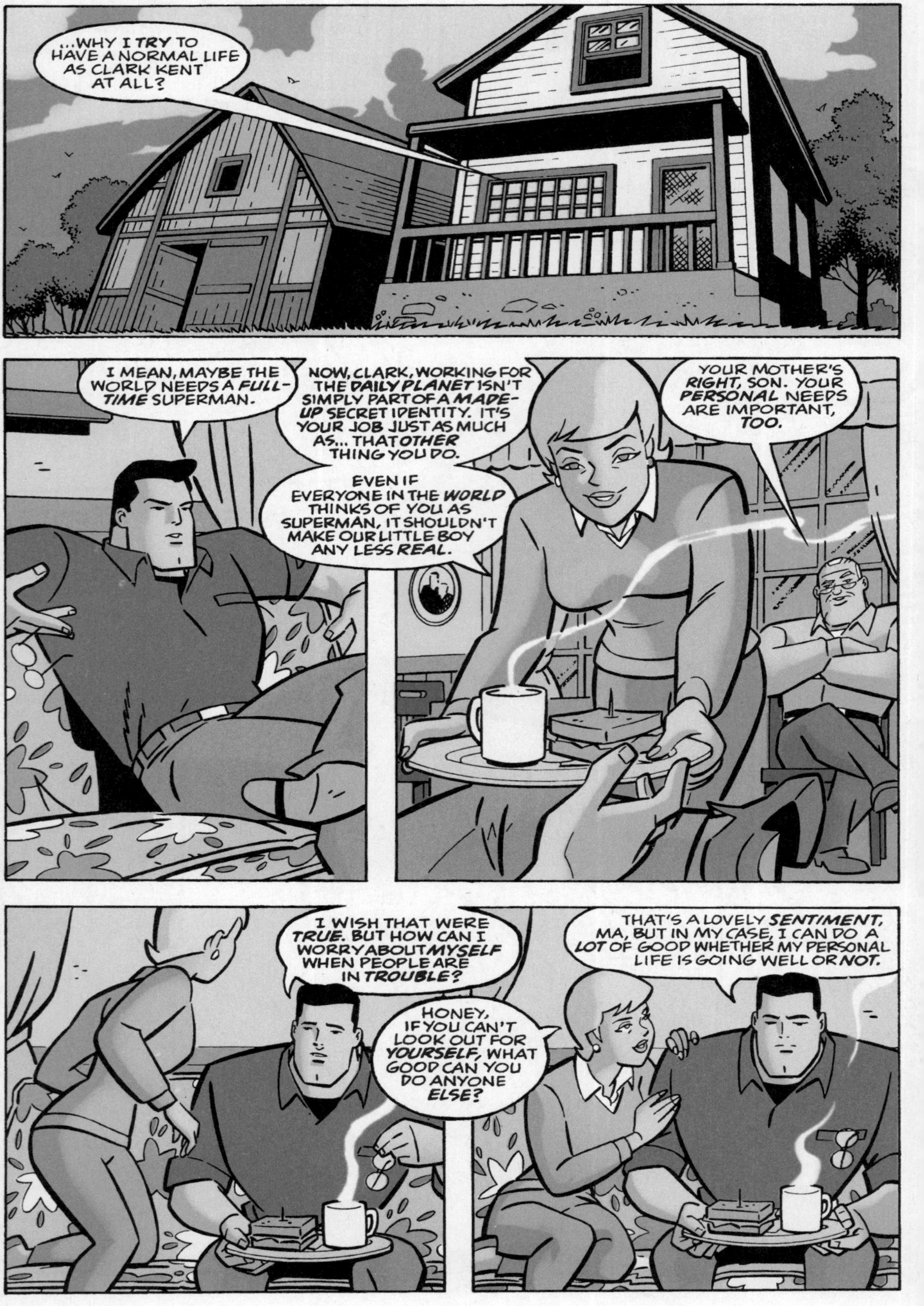
...WHY I TRY TO HAVE A NORMAL LIFE AS CLARK KENT AT ALL?
I MEAN, MAYBE THE WORLD NEEDS A FULL-TIME SUPERMAN.
NOW, CLARK, WORKING FOR THE DAILY PLANET ISN'T SIMPLY PART OF A MADE-UP SECRET IDENTITY. IT'S YOUR JOB JUST AS MUCH AS... THAT OTHER THING YOU DO.
EVEN IF EVERYONE IN THE WORLD THINKS OF YOU AS SUPERMAN, IT SHOULDN'T MAKE OUR LITTLE BOY ANY LESS REAL.
YOUR MOTHER'S RIGHT, SON. YOUR PERSONAL NEEDS ARE IMPORTANT, TOO.
I WISH THAT WERE TRUE. BUT HOW CAN I WORRY ABOUT MYSELF WHEN PEOPLE ARE IN TROUBLE?
HONEY, IF YOU CAN'T LOOK OUT FOR YOURSELF, WHAT GOOD CAN YOU DO ANYONE ELSE?
THAT'S A LOVELY SENTIMENT, MA, BUT IN MY CASE, I CAN DO A LOT OF GOOD WHETHER MY PERSONAL LIFE IS GOING WELL OR NOT.

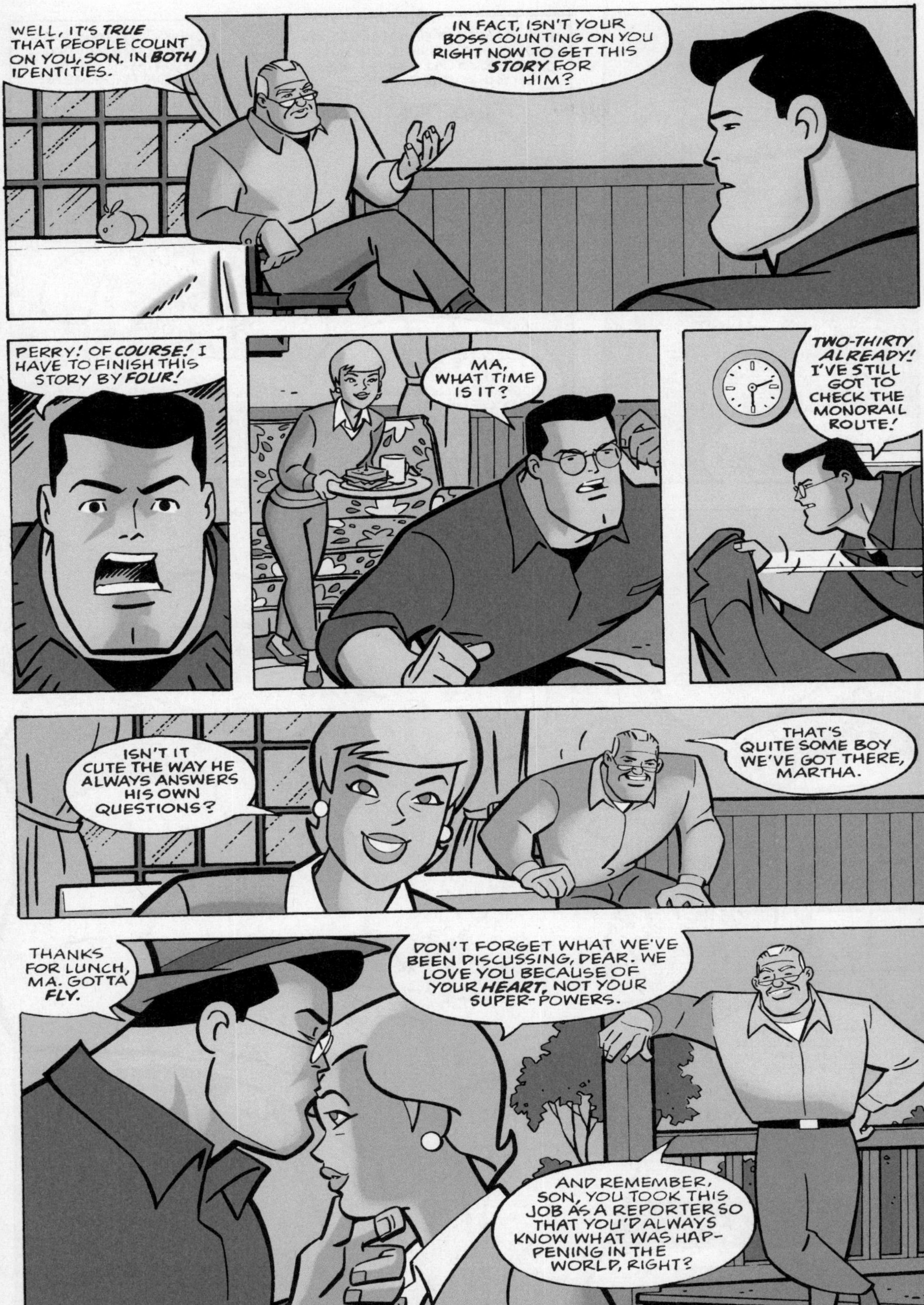
WELL, IT'S TRUE THAT PEOPLE COUNT ON YOU, SON. IN BOTH IDENTITIES.
IN FACT, ISN'T YOUR BOSS COUNTING ON YOU RIGHT NOW TO GET THIS STORY FOR HIM?
PERRY! OF COURSE! I HAVE TO FINISH THIS STORY BY FOUR!
MA, WHAT TIME IS IT?
TWO-THIRTY ALREADY! I'VE STILL GOT TO CHECK THE MONORAIL ROUTE!
ISN'T IT CUTE THE WAY HE ALWAYS ANSWERS HIS OWN QUESTIONS?
THAT'S QUITE SOME BOY WE'VE GOT THERE, MARTHA.
THANKS FOR LUNCH, MA. GOTTA FLY.
DON'T FORGET WHAT WE'VE BEEN DISCUSSING, DEAR. WE LOVE YOU BECAUSE OF YOUR HEART, NOT YOUR SUPER-POWERS.
AND REMEMBER, SON, YOU TOOK THIS JOB AS A REPORTER SO THAT YOU'D ALWAYS KNOW WHAT WAS HAPPENING IN THE WORLD, RIGHT?

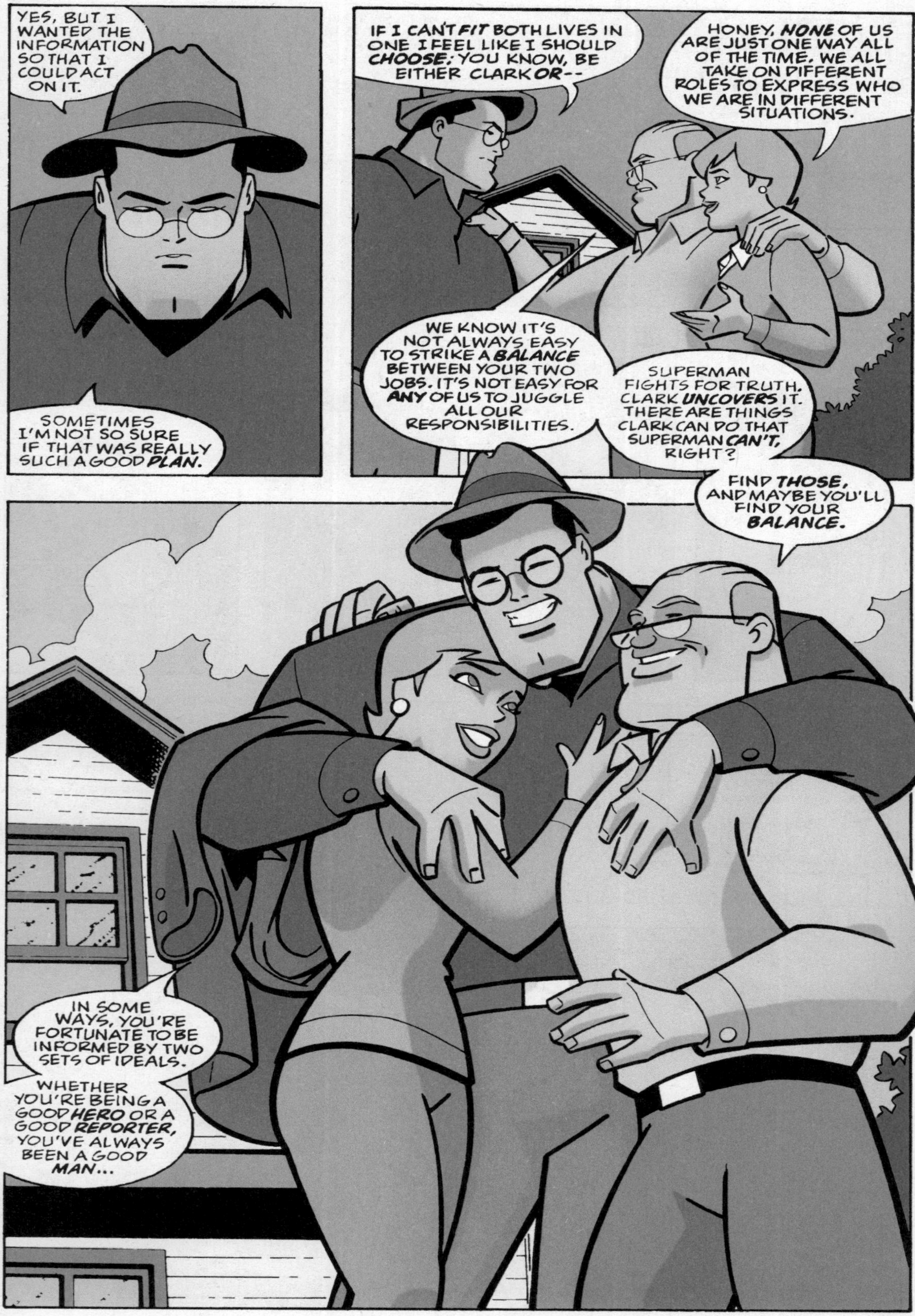
YES, BUT I WANTED THE INFORMATION SO THAT I COULD ACT ON IT.
SOMETIMES I'M NOT SO SURE IF THAT WAS REALLY SUCH A GOOD PLAN.
IF I CAN'T FIT BOTH LIVES IN ONE I FEEL LIKE I SHOULD CHOOSE; YOU KNOW, BE EITHER CLARK OR--
HONEY, NONE OF US ARE JUST ONE WAY ALL OF THE TIME. WE ALL TAKE ON DIFFERENT ROLES TO EXPRESS WHO WE ARE IN DIFFERENT SITUATIONS.
WE KNOW IT'S NOT ALWAYS EASY TO STRIKE A BALANCE BETWEEN YOUR TWO JOBS. IT'S NOT EASY FOR ANY OF US TO JUGGLE ALL OUR RESPONSIBILITIES.
SUPERMAN FIGHTS FOR TRUTH. CLARK UNCOVERS IT. THERE ARE THINGS CLARK CAN DO THAT SUPERMAN CAN'T, RIGHT?
FIND THOSE, AND MAYBE YOU'LL FIND YOUR BALANCE.
IN SOME WAYS, YOU'RE FORTUNATE TO BE INFORMED BY TWO SETS OF IDEALS.
WHETHER YOU'RE BEING A GOOD HERO OR A GOOD REPORTER, YOU'VE ALWAYS BEEN A GOOD MAN...

"...IT'S IN YOUR *NATURE*, SON."

Ooh, YOU LOOK LIKE YOU'RE IN A *RUSH*, KENT. GUESS THIS TRANSPORTATION FEATURE IS MORE EXCITING THAN WE THOUGHT...IF THAT'S POSSIBLE.

OR MAYBE IT'S JUST *DEADLINE PRESSURE* GETTING TO OUR *MILD-MANNERED* REPORTER.

HI, CLARK! NEED ANY HELP?

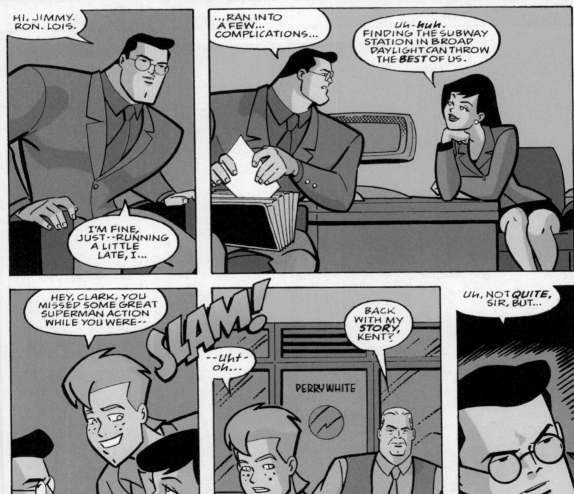

HI, JIMMY. RON. LOIS.

I'M FINE, JUST--RUNNING A LITTLE LATE, I...

...RAN INTO A FEW... COMPLICATIONS...

Uh-huh. FINDING THE SUBWAY STATION IN BROAD DAYLIGHT CAN THROW THE *BEST* OF US.

HEY, CLARK, YOU MISSED SOME GREAT SUPERMAN ACTION WHILE YOU WERE--

SLAM!

--UHT- OH...

BACK WITH MY *STORY*, KENT?

PERRY WHITE

Uh, NOT *QUITE,* SIR, BUT...

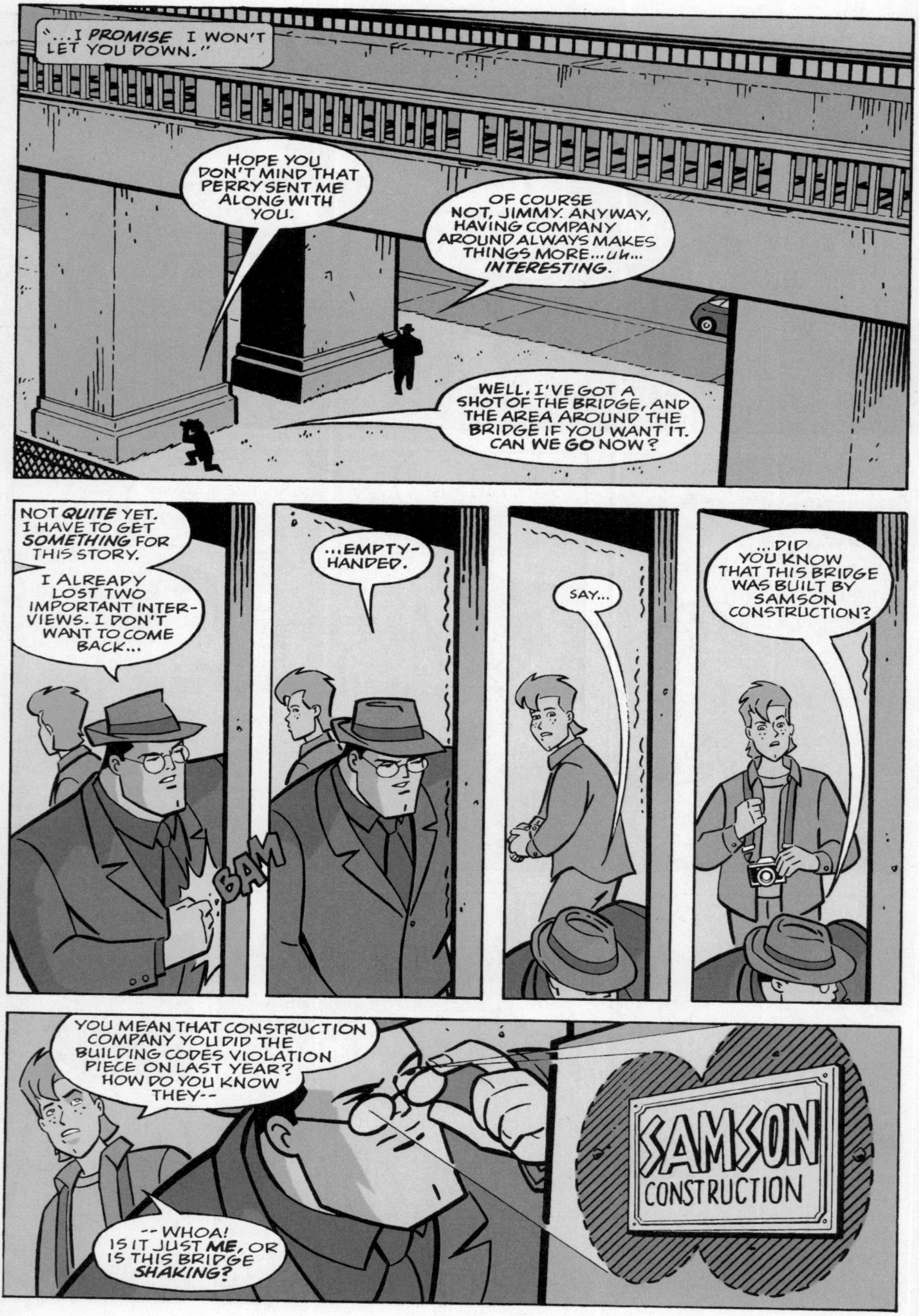
"...I PROMISE I WON'T LET YOU DOWN."
HOPE YOU DON'T MIND THAT PERRY SENT ME ALONG WITH YOU.
OF COURSE NOT, JIMMY. ANYWAY, HAVING COMPANY AROUND ALWAYS MAKES THINGS MORE...uh... INTERESTING.
WELL, I'VE GOT A SHOT OF THE BRIDGE, AND THE AREA AROUND THE BRIDGE IF YOU WANT IT. CAN WE GO NOW?
NOT QUITE YET. I HAVE TO GET SOMETHING FOR THIS STORY.
I ALREADY LOST TWO IMPORTANT INTER-VIEWS. I DON'T WANT TO COME BACK...
BAM
...EMPTY-HANDED.
SAY...
...DID YOU KNOW THAT THIS BRIDGE WAS BUILT BY SAMSON CONSTRUCTION?
YOU MEAN THAT CONSTRUCTION COMPANY YOU DID THE BUILDING CODES VIOLATION PIECE ON LAST YEAR? HOW DO YOU KNOW THEY--
SAMSON CONSTRUCTION
--WHOA! IS IT JUST ME, OR IS THIS BRIDGE SHAKING?

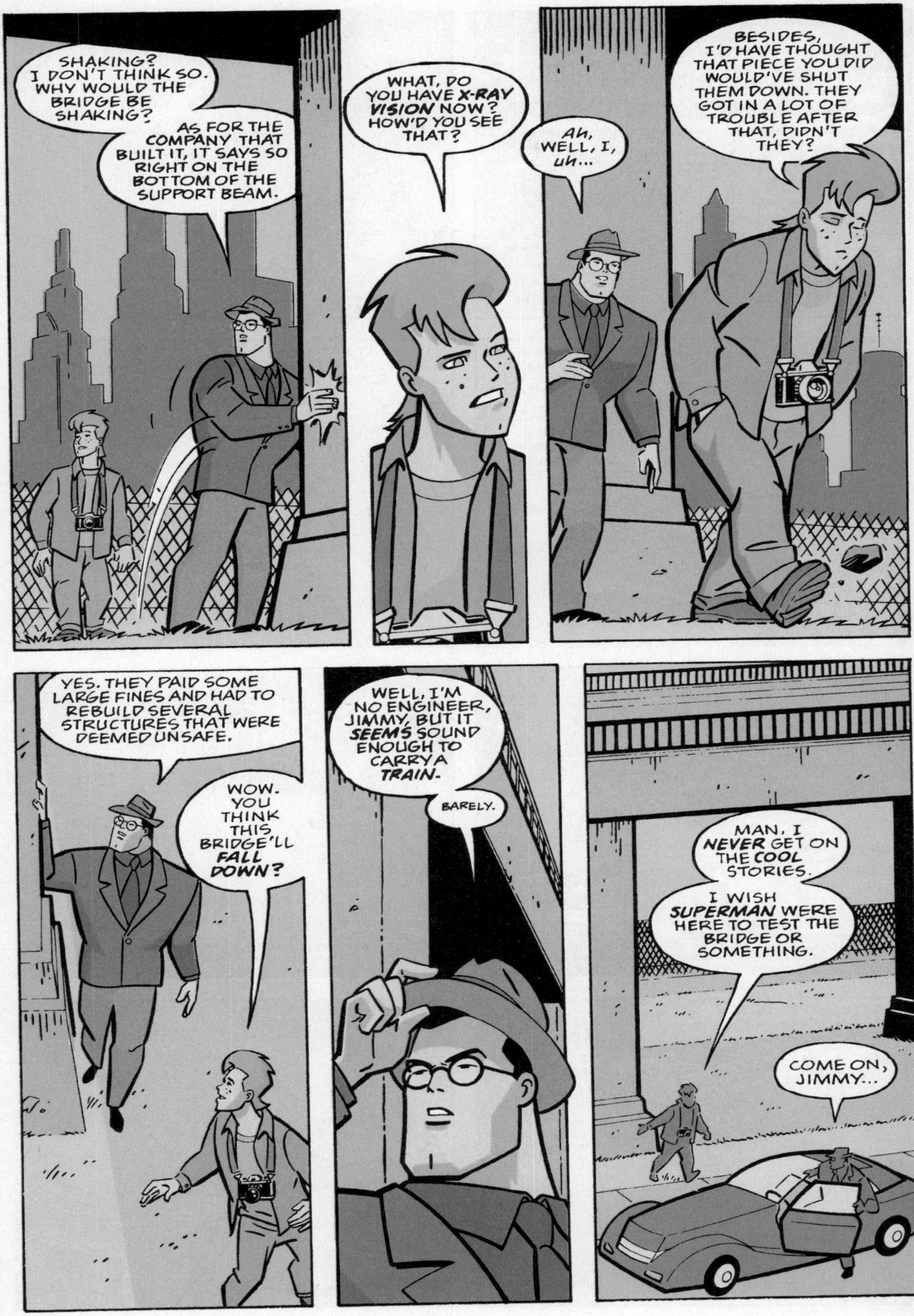
SHAKING? I DON'T THINK SO. WHY WOULD THE BRIDGE BE SHAKING?
AS FOR THE COMPANY THAT BUILT IT, IT SAYS SO RIGHT ON THE BOTTOM OF THE SUPPORT BEAM.
WHAT, DO YOU HAVE X-RAY VISION NOW? HOW'D YOU SEE THAT?
Ah, WELL, I, uh...
BESIDES, I'D HAVE THOUGHT THAT PIECE YOU DID WOULD'VE SHUT THEM DOWN. THEY GOT IN A LOT OF TROUBLE AFTER THAT, DIDN'T THEY?
YES. THEY PAID SOME LARGE FINES AND HAD TO REBUILD SEVERAL STRUCTURES THAT WERE DEEMED UNSAFE.
WOW. YOU THINK THIS BRIDGE'LL FALL DOWN?
WELL, I'M NO ENGINEER, JIMMY, BUT IT SEEMS SOUND ENOUGH TO CARRY A TRAIN.
BARELY.
MAN, I NEVER GET ON THE COOL STORIES.
I WISH SUPERMAN WERE HERE TO TEST THE BRIDGE OR SOMETHING.
COME ON, JIMMY...

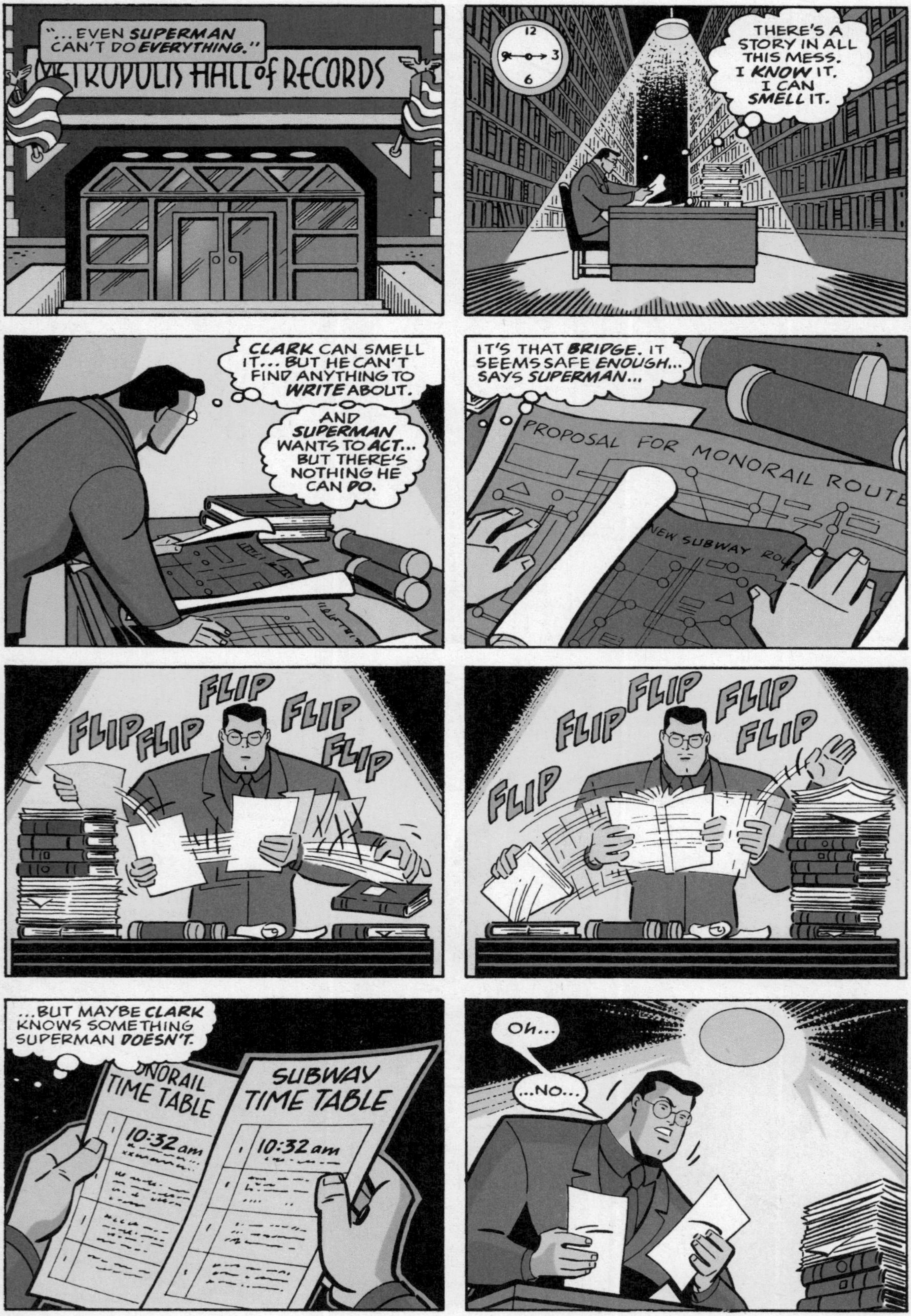
"...EVEN SUPERMAN CAN'T DO EVERYTHING."
METROPOLIS HALL of RECORDS
12 3 6
THERE'S A STORY IN ALL THIS MESS. I KNOW IT. I CAN SMELL IT.
CLARK CAN SMELL IT... BUT HE CAN'T FIND ANYTHING TO WRITE ABOUT.
AND SUPERMAN WANTS TO ACT... BUT THERE'S NOTHING HE CAN DO.
IT'S THAT BRIDGE. IT SEEMS SAFE ENOUGH... SAYS SUPERMAN...
PROPOSAL FOR MONORAIL ROUTE
NEW SUBWAY ROU
FLIP FLIP FLIP FLIP FLIP
FLIP FLIP FLIP FLIP FLIP
...BUT MAYBE CLARK KNOWS SOMETHING SUPERMAN DOESN'T.
ONORAIL TIME TABLE
10:32 am
SUBWAY TIME TABLE
10:32 am
Oh...
...NO...

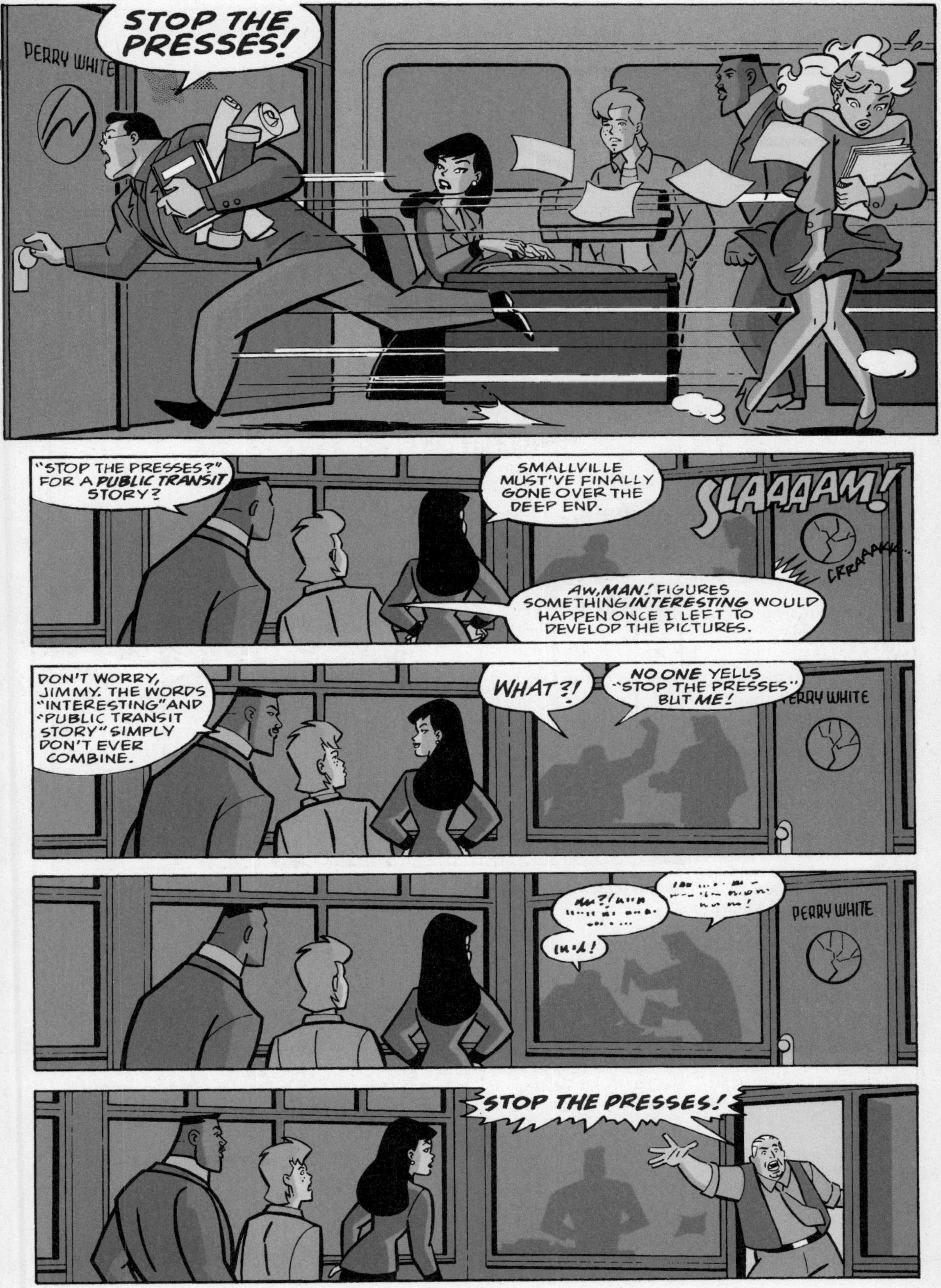
PERRY WHITE
STOP THE PRESSES!
"STOP THE PRESSES?" FOR A PUBLIC TRANSIT STORY?
SMALLVILLE MUST'VE FINALLY GONE OVER THE DEEP END.
SLAAAAM!
CRRAAAKK...
AW, MAN! FIGURES SOMETHING INTERESTING WOULD HAPPEN ONCE I LEFT TO DEVELOP THE PICTURES.
DON'T WORRY, JIMMY. THE WORDS "INTERESTING" AND "PUBLIC TRANSIT STORY" SIMPLY DON'T EVER COMBINE.
WHAT?!
NO ONE YELLS "STOP THE PRESSES" BUT ME!
PERRY WHITE
PERRY WHITE
STOP THE PRESSES!

DAILY PLANET

Early Edition   "A GREAT METROPOLITAN NEWSPAPER"   50 Cents

POTENTIAL TRAIN TRAGEDY AVOIDED

By Clark Kent

After months of competitive feuding, city officials are now cooperating to avert what could have become a potentially fatal disaster for Metropolis mass transit commuters today.

The DAILY PLANET learned yesterday that had Metropolis's new monorail and subway lines proceeded on schedule today, the two would have run through the New Troy Bridge at precisely 10:32 a.m.

Although the trains would not have collided, last-minute research proved the bridge to be incapable of supporting the weight of both trains at the same time, due to defective erection by a construction company previously cited for building code violations.

"The bridge literally would have broken apart under the weight of both trains," said engineering expert Dr. Richard Kasden. "Hundreds, if not thousands, could have been injured, or worse, killed."

The construction company that built the bridge, Samson Construction, was cited for seven separate infractions of building code regulations last year. According to Samson representative Charles Rihga, the New Troy Bridge passed all tests, but they are never the less glad that the city officials have decided to "make certain" the trains can run on the bridge.

"We aren't responsible for their poor scheduling," Rihga added. "Our

The New Troy Bridge, which could have been the site for tragedy had Metropolis's new monorail and subway lines met at 10:32 today as scheduled.

work on that bridge passed all of the minimum construction requirements. These trains weren't even in concept stages when we built the bridge, so if it can't handle the combined weight, it's not because of 'faulty construction.'"

Regardless of Mr. Rihga's comments, city officials fully intend to investigate Samson's records, and are considering what action, legal or otherwise, to take against the company.
Continued on pg.3

SUPERMAN FOILS BANK ROBBERS-p.4

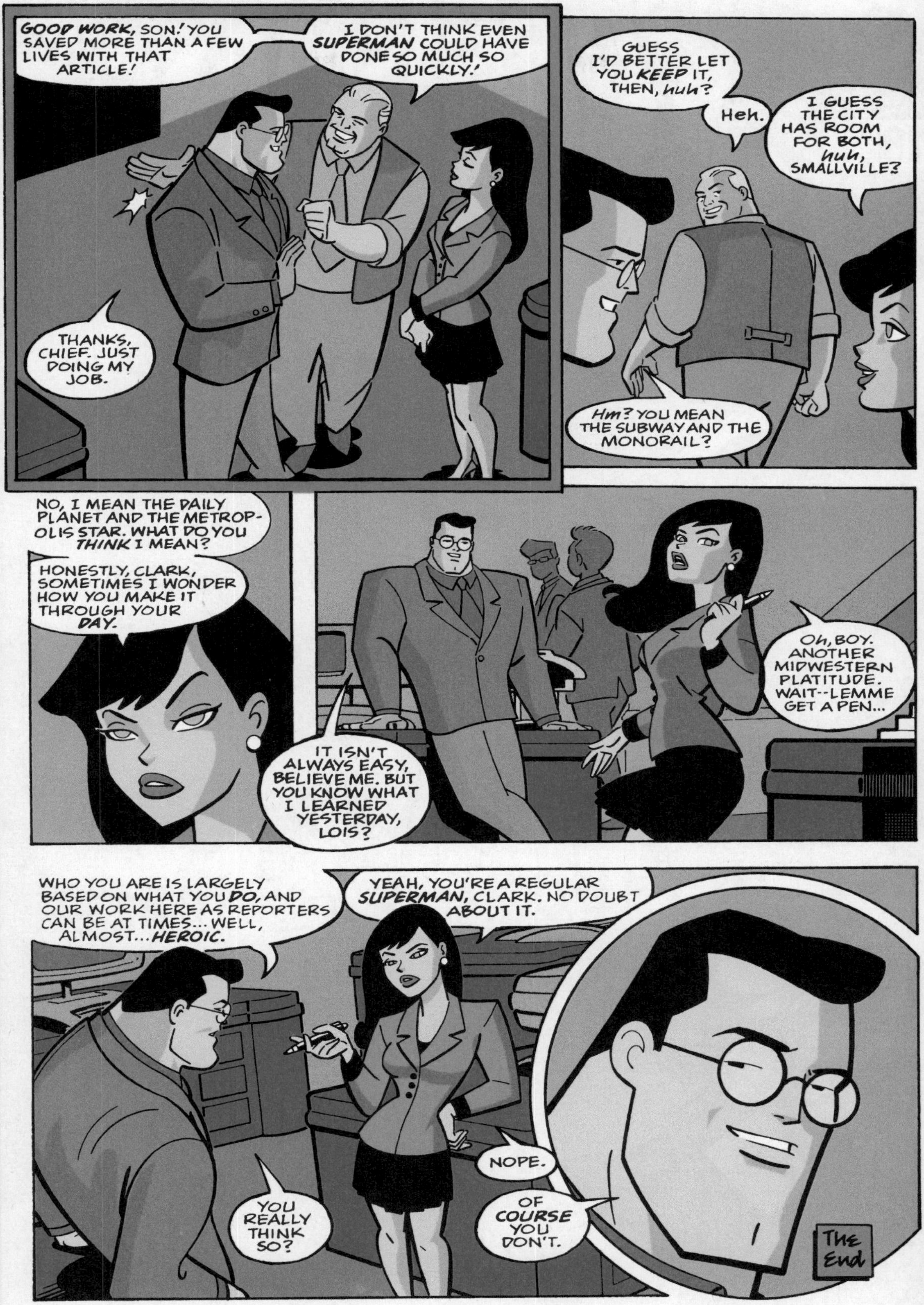
GOOD WORK, SON! YOU SAVED MORE THAN A FEW LIVES WITH THAT ARTICLE!
I DON'T THINK EVEN SUPERMAN COULD HAVE DONE SO MUCH SO QUICKLY!
THANKS, CHIEF. JUST DOING MY JOB.
GUESS I'D BETTER LET YOU KEEP IT, THEN, huh?
Heh.
I GUESS THE CITY HAS ROOM FOR BOTH, huh, SMALLVILLE?
Hm? YOU MEAN THE SUBWAY AND THE MONORAIL?
NO, I MEAN THE DAILY PLANET AND THE METROPOLIS STAR. WHAT DO YOU THINK I MEAN?
HONESTLY, CLARK, SOMETIMES I WONDER HOW YOU MAKE IT THROUGH YOUR DAY.
IT ISN'T ALWAYS EASY, BELIEVE ME. BUT YOU KNOW WHAT I LEARNED YESTERDAY, LOIS?
Oh, BOY. ANOTHER MIDWESTERN PLATITUDE. WAIT--LEMME GET A PEN...
WHO YOU ARE IS LARGELY BASED ON WHAT YOU DO, AND OUR WORK HERE AS REPORTERS CAN BE AT TIMES... WELL, ALMOST... HEROIC.
YEAH, YOU'RE A REGULAR SUPERMAN, CLARK. NO DOUBT ABOUT IT.
YOU REALLY THINK SO?
NOPE.
OF COURSE YOU DON'T.
THE End

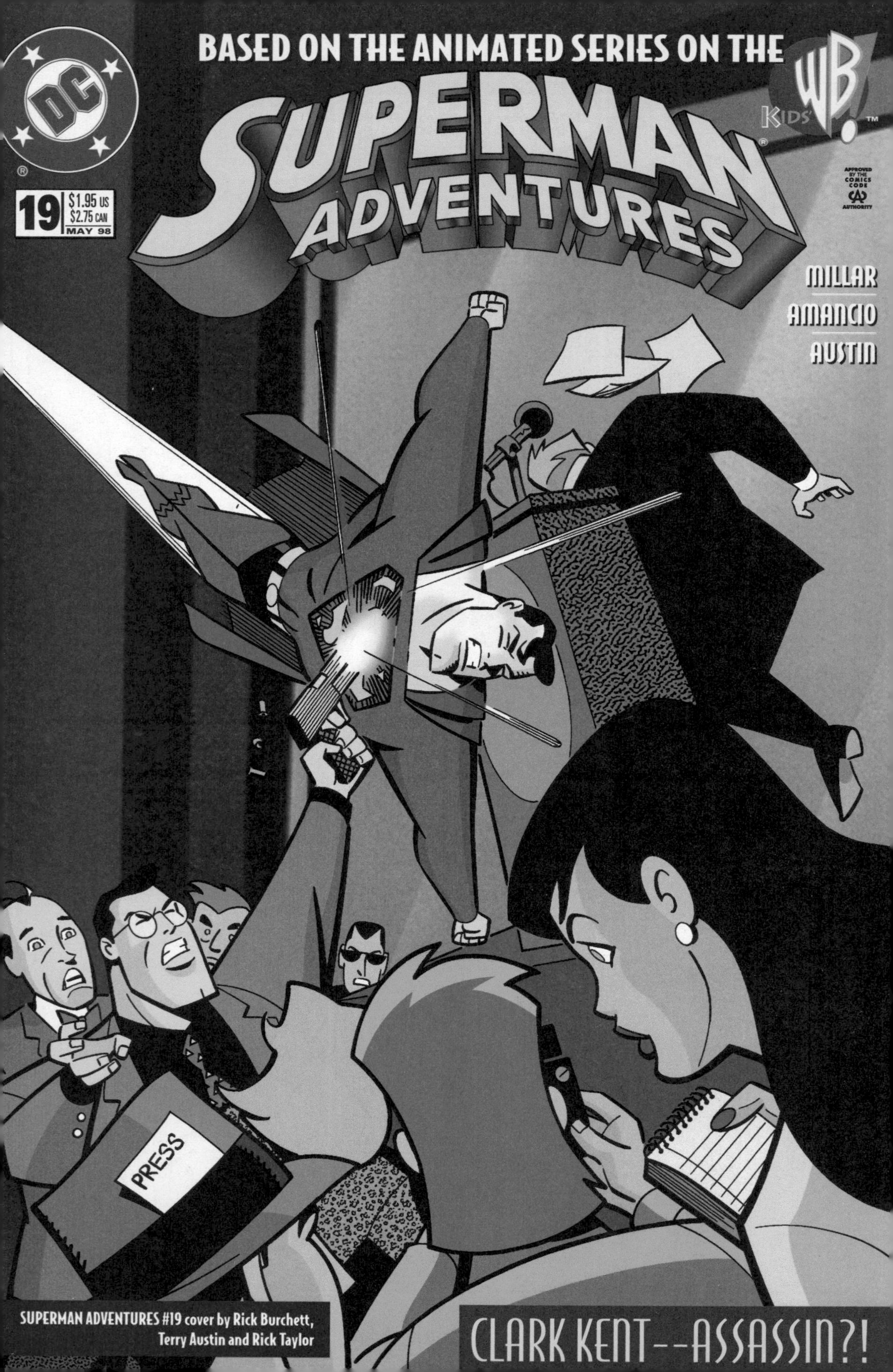
BASED ON THE ANIMATED SERIES ON THE
KIDS' WB!
SUPERMAN ADVENTURES
19
$1.95 US
$2.75 CAN
MAY 98
APPROVED BY THE COMICS CODE AUTHORITY
MILLAR
AMANCIO
AUSTIN
PRESS
CLARK KENT--ASSASSIN?!

SUPERMAN ADVENTURES #19 cover by Rick Burchett, Terry Austin and Rick Taylor

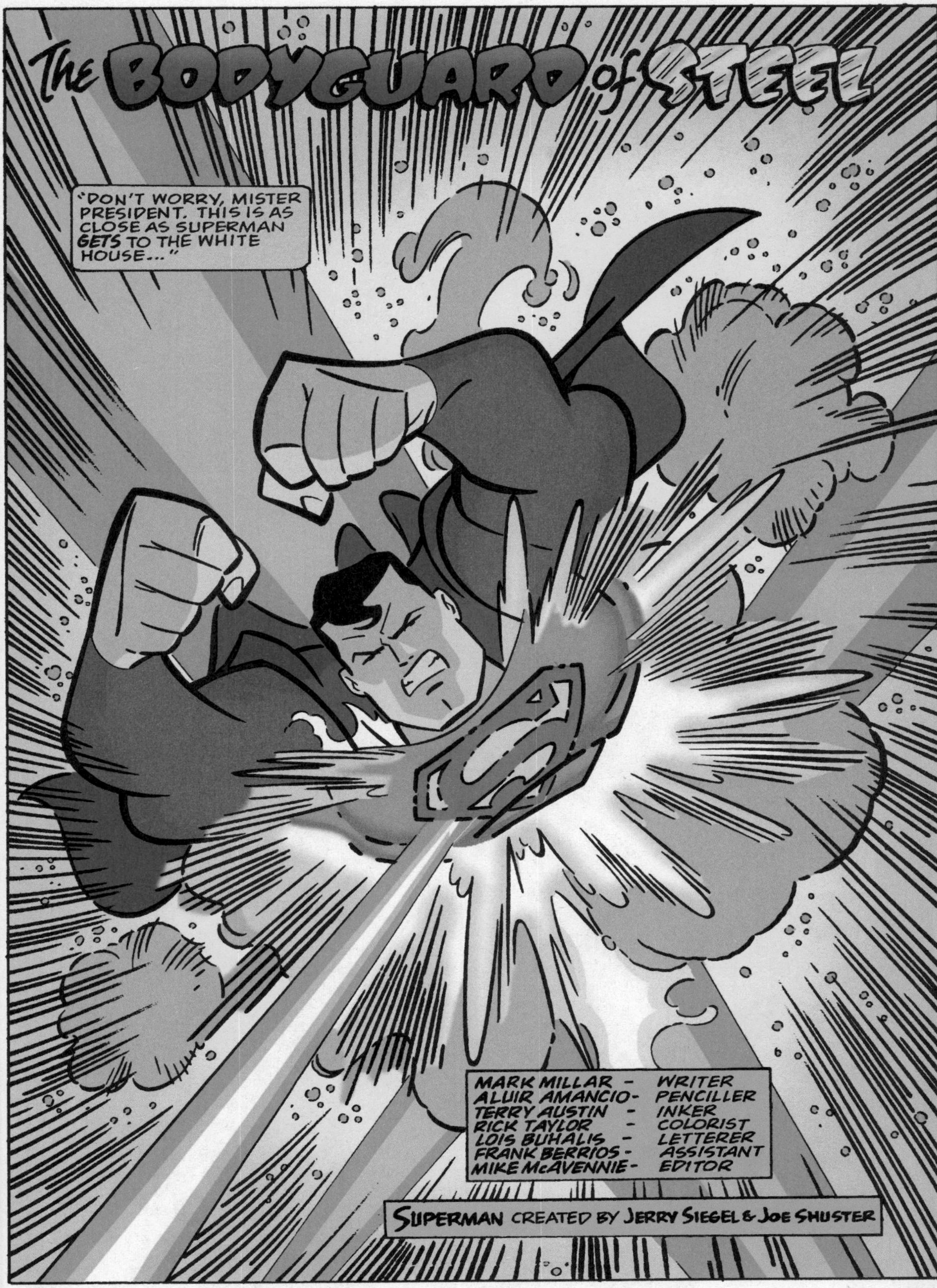
THE BODYGUARD OF STEEL
"DON'T WORRY, MISTER PRESIDENT. THIS IS AS CLOSE AS SUPERMAN GETS TO THE WHITE HOUSE..."
MARK MILLAR - WRITER
ALUIR AMANCIO - PENCILLER
TERRY AUSTIN - INKER
RICK TAYLOR - COLORIST
LOIS BUHALIS - LETTERER
FRANK BERRIOS - ASSISTANT
MIKE McAVENNIE - EDITOR
SUPERMAN CREATED BY JERRY SIEGEL & JOE SHUSTER

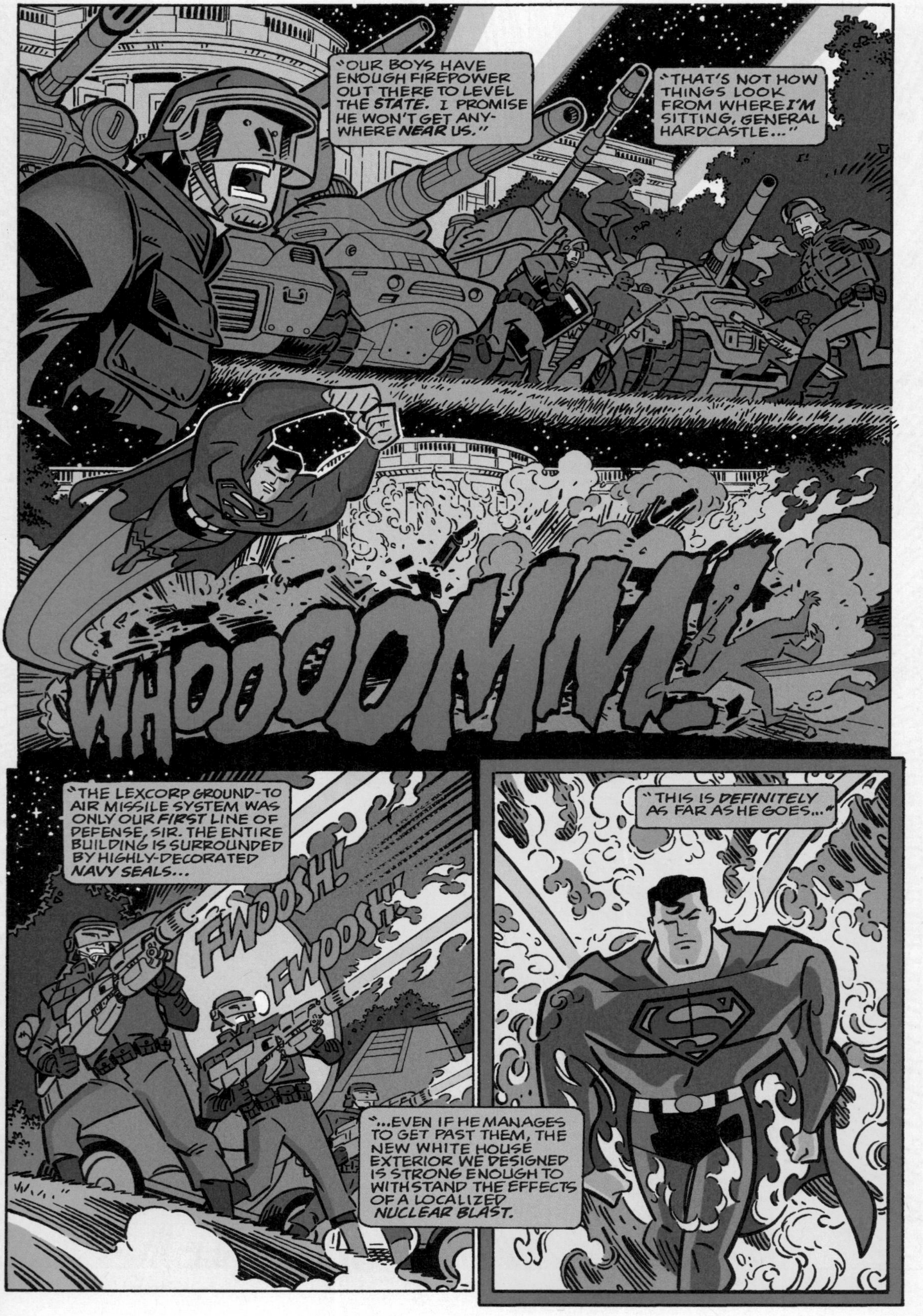
"OUR BOYS HAVE ENOUGH FIREPOWER OUT THERE TO LEVEL THE STATE. I PROMISE HE WON'T GET ANYWHERE NEAR US."
"THAT'S NOT HOW THINGS LOOK FROM WHERE I'M SITTING, GENERAL HARDCASTLE..."
WHOOOOMM!
"THE LEXCORP GROUND-TO AIR MISSILE SYSTEM WAS ONLY OUR FIRST LINE OF DEFENSE, SIR. THE ENTIRE BUILDING IS SURROUNDED BY HIGHLY-DECORATED NAVY SEALS...
FWOOSH!
FWOOSH!
"...EVEN IF HE MANAGES TO GET PAST THEM, THE NEW WHITE HOUSE EXTERIOR WE DESIGNED IS STRONG ENOUGH TO WITHSTAND THE EFFECTS OF A LOCALIZED NUCLEAR BLAST.
"THIS IS DEFINITELY AS FAR AS HE GOES..."

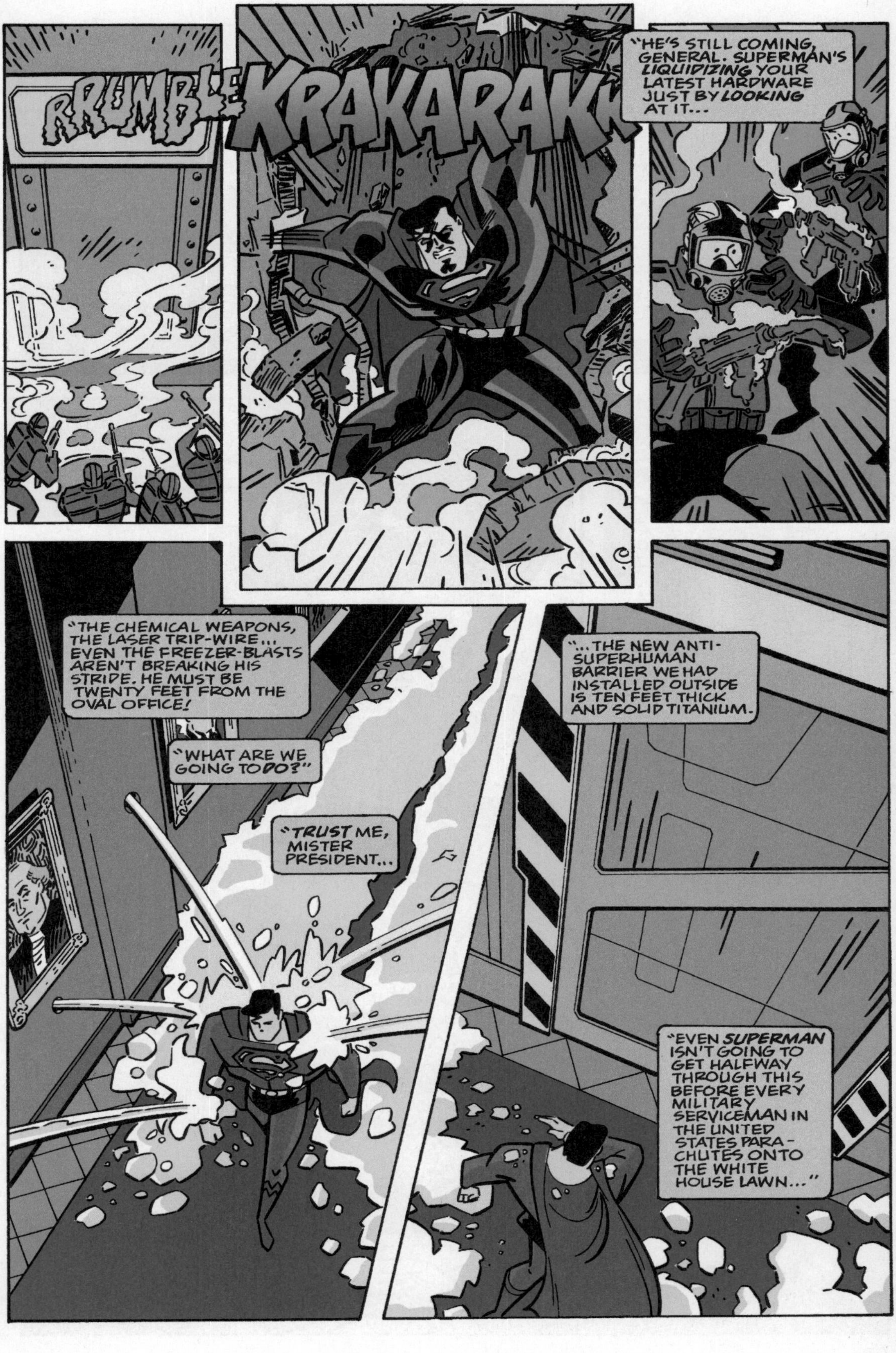
RRUMBLE
KRAKARAKK
"HE'S STILL COMING, GENERAL. SUPERMAN'S LIQUIDIZING YOUR LATEST HARDWARE JUST BY LOOKING AT IT...
"THE CHEMICAL WEAPONS, THE LASER TRIP-WIRE... EVEN THE FREEZER-BLASTS AREN'T BREAKING HIS STRIDE. HE MUST BE TWENTY FEET FROM THE OVAL OFFICE!
"WHAT ARE WE GOING TO DO?"
"TRUST ME, MISTER PRESIDENT...
"...THE NEW ANTI-SUPERHUMAN BARRIER WE HAD INSTALLED OUTSIDE IS TEN FEET THICK AND SOLID TITANIUM.
"EVEN SUPERMAN ISN'T GOING TO GET HALFWAY THROUGH THIS BEFORE EVERY MILITARY SERVICEMAN IN THE UNITED STATES PARA-CHUTES ONTO THE WHITE HOUSE LAWN..."

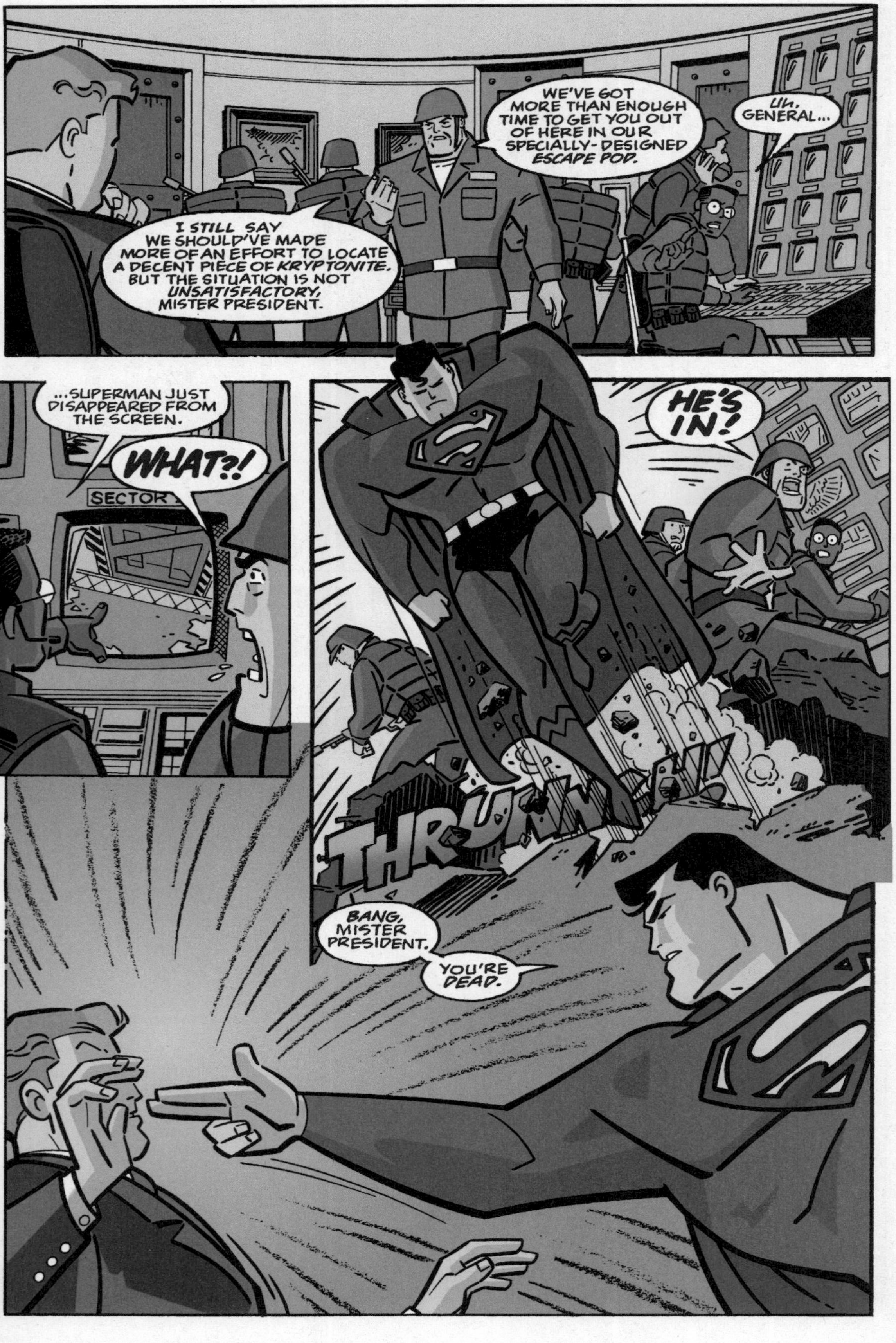
I STILL SAY WE SHOULD'VE MADE MORE OF AN EFFORT TO LOCATE A DECENT PIECE OF KRYPTONITE. BUT THE SITUATION IS NOT UNSATISFACTORY, MISTER PRESIDENT.
WE'VE GOT MORE THAN ENOUGH TIME TO GET YOU OUT OF HERE IN OUR SPECIALLY-DESIGNED ESCAPE POD.
Uh, GENERAL...
...SUPERMAN JUST DISAPPEARED FROM THE SCREEN.
WHAT?!
SECTOR
HE'S IN!
THRUNN
BANG, MISTER PRESIDENT.
YOU'RE DEAD.

SIXTY SECONDS!

GENTLEMEN, SUPERMAN HAS PROVEN BEYOND *ALL* REASONABLE DOUBT THAT THE WHITE HOUSE IS WIDE OPEN TO SUPER-HUMAN ATTACK, AND OUR DEFENSES ARE FATALLY *DEFICIENT.*

Klik!

WOULD ANYONE CARE TO OFFER AN EXPLANATION?

MISTER PRESIDENT, AS YOUR HEAD OF SECURITY, FINAL RESPONSIBILITY LIES WITH *ME*, BUT THE CONCRETE FLOOR IS AN OVERSIGHT WHICH CAN BE *EASILY* RECTIFIED.

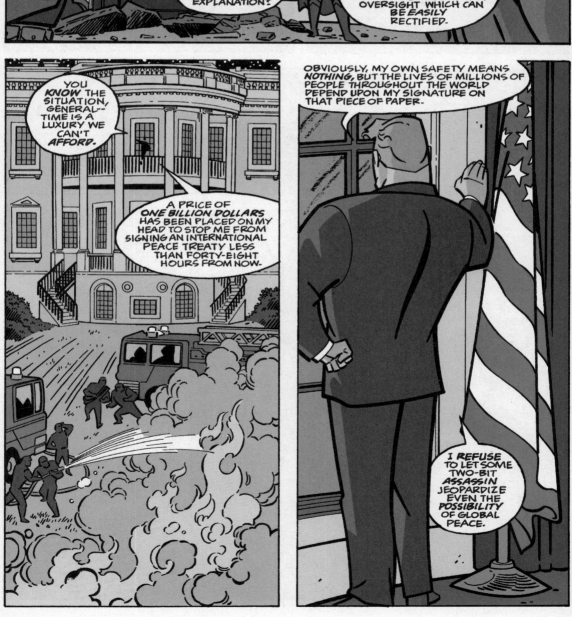

YOU *KNOW* THE SITUATION, GENERAL-- TIME IS A LUXURY WE CAN'T *AFFORD.*

A PRICE OF *ONE BILLION DOLLARS* HAS BEEN PLACED ON MY HEAD TO STOP ME FROM SIGNING AN INTERNATIONAL PEACE TREATY LESS THAN FORTY-EIGHT HOURS FROM NOW.

OBVIOUSLY, MY OWN SAFETY MEANS *NOTHING*, BUT THE LIVES OF MILLIONS OF PEOPLE THROUGHOUT THE WORLD DEPEND UPON MY SIGNATURE ON THAT PIECE OF PAPER.

I *REFUSE* TO LET SOME TWO-BIT *ASSASSIN* JEOPARDIZE EVEN THE *POSSIBILITY* OF GLOBAL PEACE.

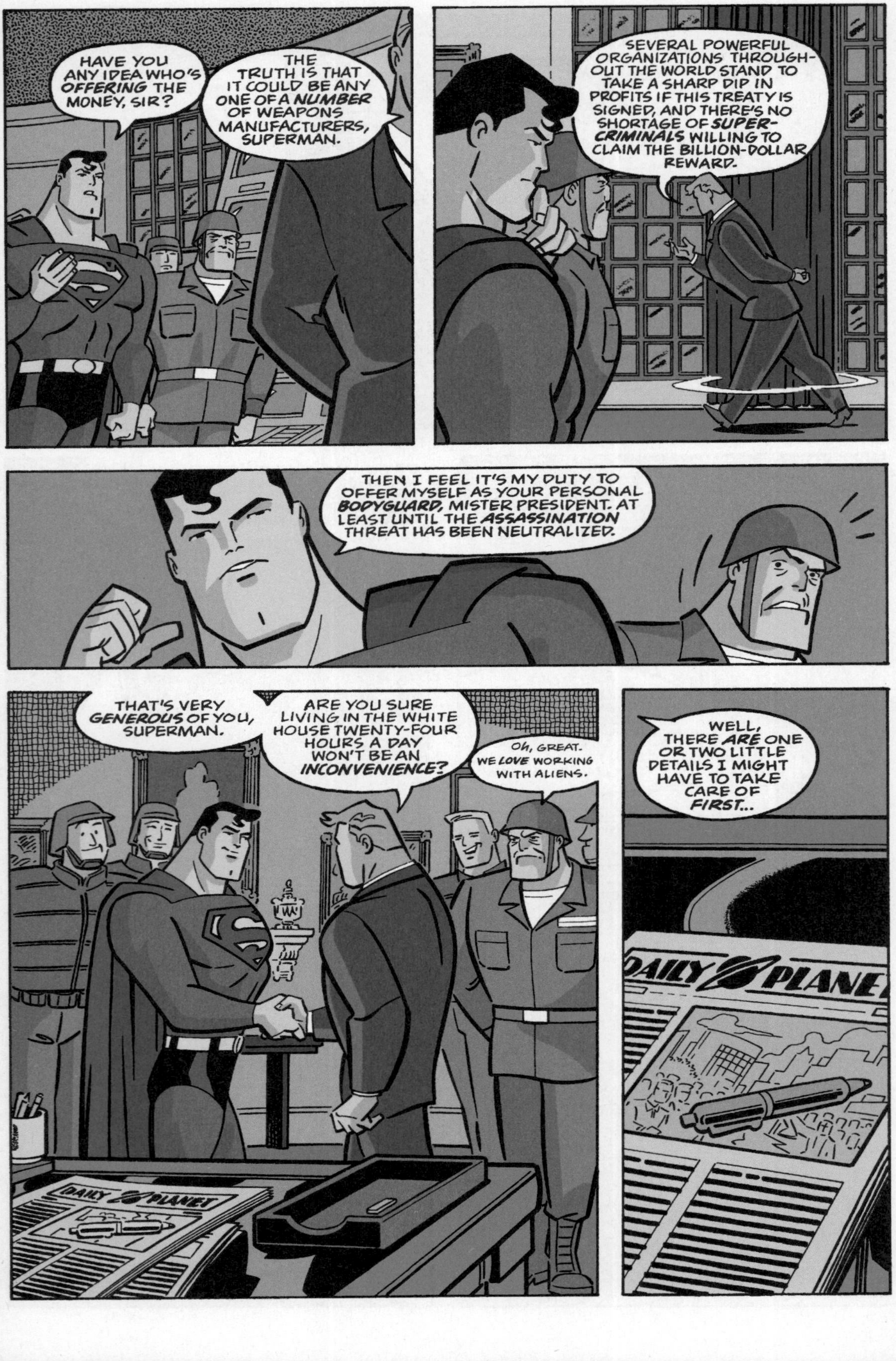
HAVE YOU ANY IDEA WHO'S OFFERING THE MONEY, SIR?
THE TRUTH IS THAT IT COULD BE ANY ONE OF A NUMBER OF WEAPONS MANUFACTURERS, SUPERMAN.
SEVERAL POWERFUL ORGANIZATIONS THROUGH-OUT THE WORLD STAND TO TAKE A SHARP DIP IN PROFITS IF THIS TREATY IS SIGNED, AND THERE'S NO SHORTAGE OF SUPER-CRIMINALS WILLING TO CLAIM THE BILLION-DOLLAR REWARD.
THEN I FEEL IT'S MY DUTY TO OFFER MYSELF AS YOUR PERSONAL BODYGUARD, MISTER PRESIDENT. AT LEAST UNTIL THE ASSASSINATION THREAT HAS BEEN NEUTRALIZED.
THAT'S VERY GENEROUS OF YOU, SUPERMAN.
ARE YOU SURE LIVING IN THE WHITE HOUSE TWENTY-FOUR HOURS A DAY WON'T BE AN INCONVENIENCE?
Oh, GREAT. WE LOVE WORKING WITH ALIENS.
DAILY PLANET
WELL, THERE ARE ONE OR TWO LITTLE DETAILS I MIGHT HAVE TO TAKE CARE OF FIRST...

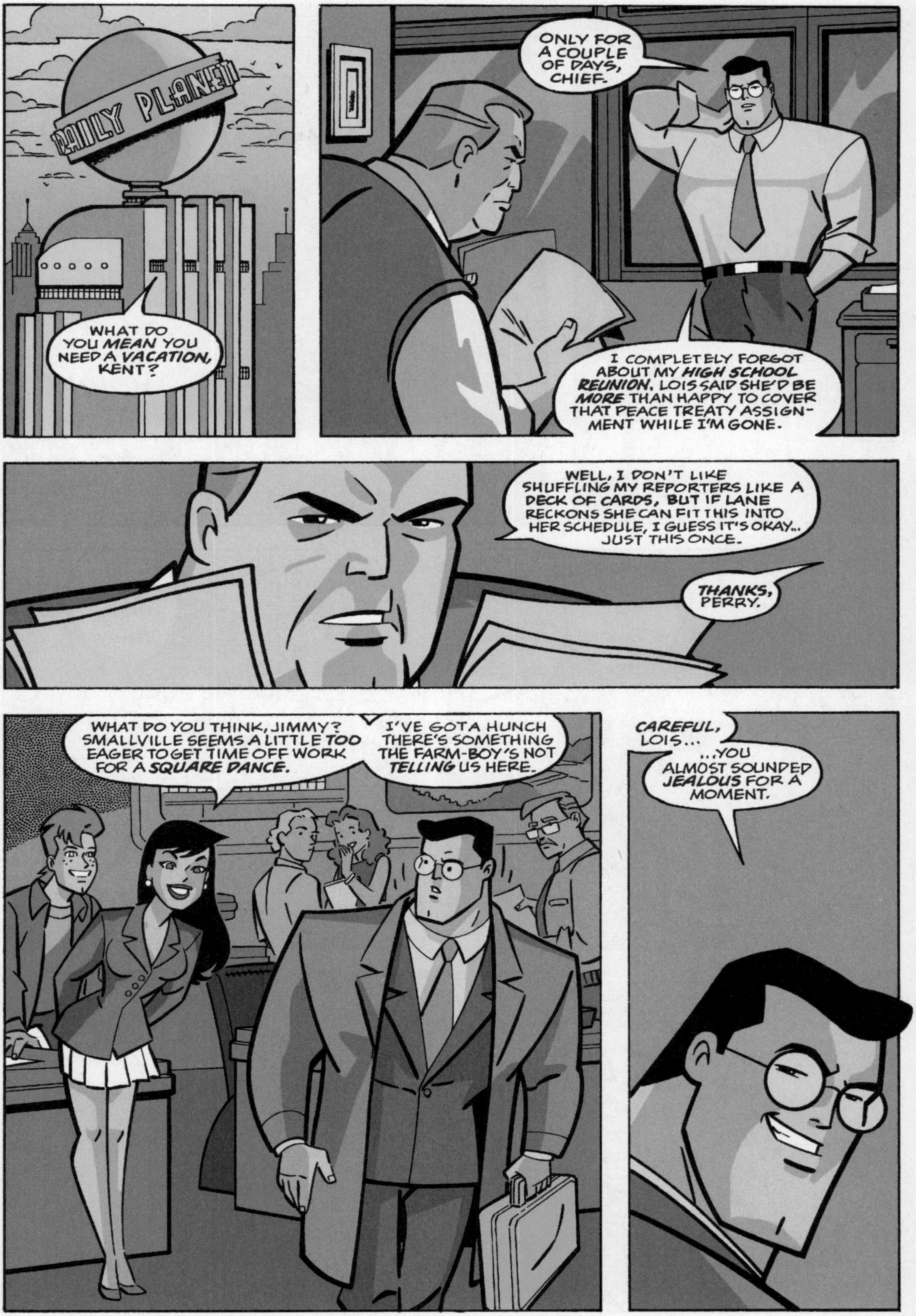
DAILY PLANET
WHAT DO YOU MEAN YOU NEED A VACATION, KENT?
ONLY FOR A COUPLE OF DAYS, CHIEF.
I COMPLETELY FORGOT ABOUT MY HIGH SCHOOL REUNION. LOIS SAID SHE'D BE MORE THAN HAPPY TO COVER THAT PEACE TREATY ASSIGNMENT WHILE I'M GONE.
WELL, I DON'T LIKE SHUFFLING MY REPORTERS LIKE A DECK OF CARDS, BUT IF LANE RECKONS SHE CAN FIT THIS INTO HER SCHEDULE, I GUESS IT'S OKAY... JUST THIS ONCE.
THANKS, PERRY.
WHAT DO YOU THINK, JIMMY? SMALLVILLE SEEMS A LITTLE TOO EAGER TO GET TIME OFF WORK FOR A SQUARE DANCE.
I'VE GOT A HUNCH THERE'S SOMETHING THE FARM-BOY'S NOT TELLING US HERE.
CAREFUL, LOIS...
...YOU ALMOST SOUNDED JEALOUS FOR A MOMENT.

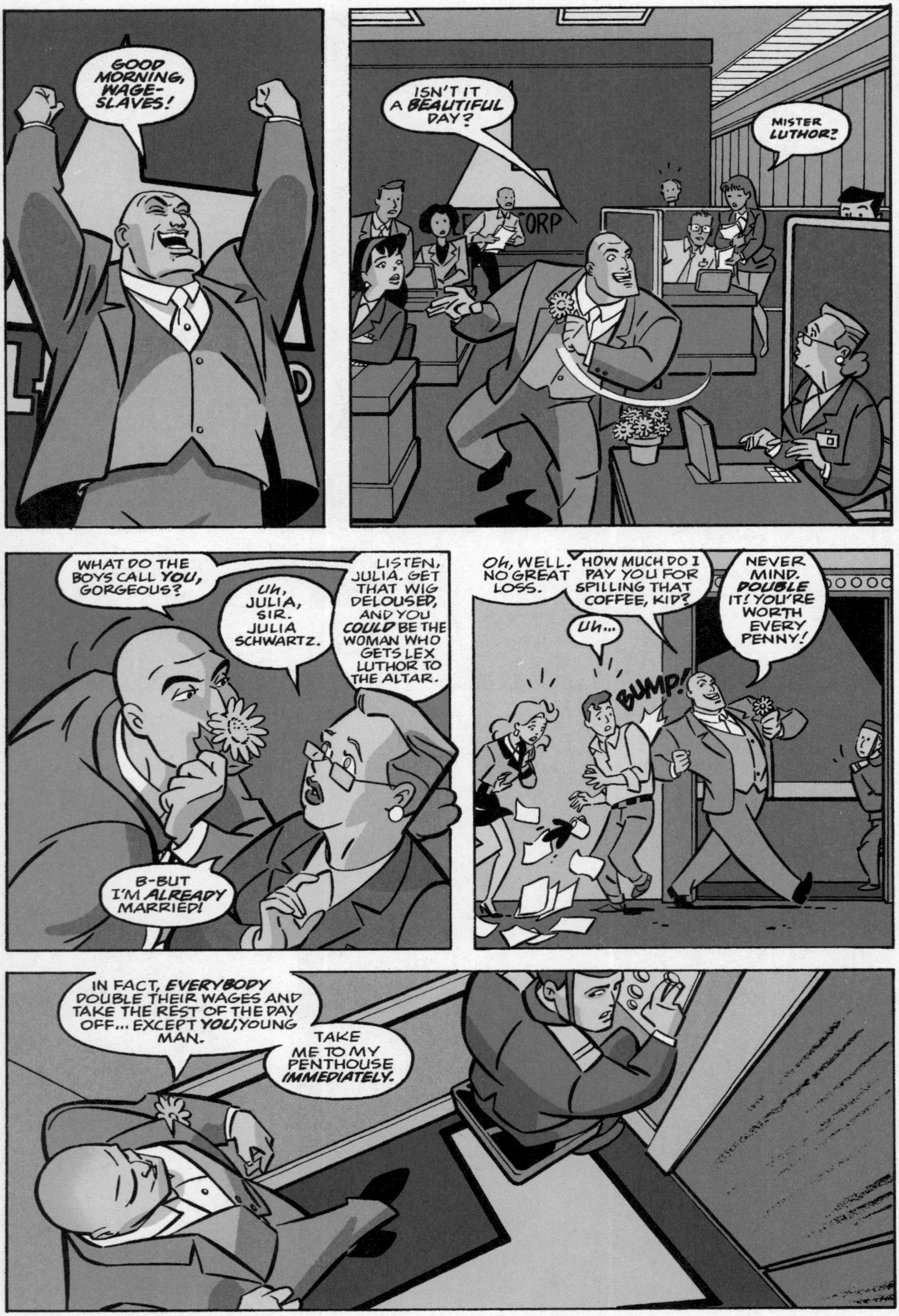
GOOD MORNING, WAGE-SLAVES!
ISN'T IT A BEAUTIFUL DAY?
MISTER LUTHOR?
ORP
WHAT DO THE BOYS CALL YOU, GORGEOUS?
UH, JULIA, SIR. JULIA SCHWARTZ.
LISTEN, JULIA. GET THAT WIG DELOUSED, AND YOU COULD BE THE WOMAN WHO GETS LEX LUTHOR TO THE ALTAR.
B-BUT I'M ALREADY MARRIED!
OH, WELL. NO GREAT LOSS.
HOW MUCH DO I PAY YOU FOR SPILLING THAT COFFEE, KID?
UH...
NEVER MIND. DOUBLE IT! YOU'RE WORTH EVERY PENNY!
BUMP!
IN FACT, EVERYBODY DOUBLE THEIR WAGES AND TAKE THE REST OF THE DAY OFF... EXCEPT YOU, YOUNG MAN.
TAKE ME TO MY PENTHOUSE IMMEDIATELY.

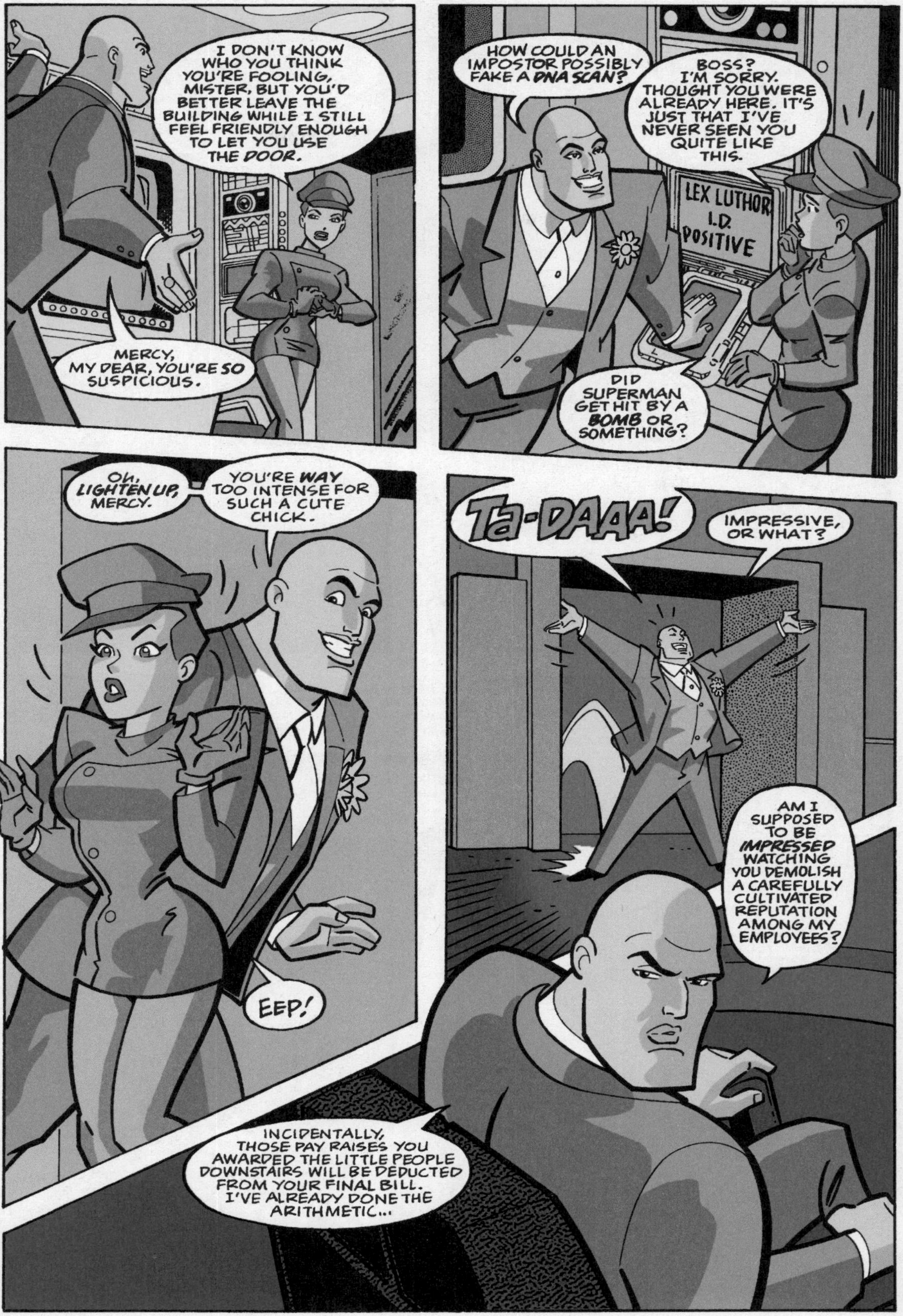
I DON'T KNOW WHO YOU THINK YOU'RE FOOLING, MISTER, BUT YOU'D BETTER LEAVE THE BUILDING WHILE I STILL FEEL FRIENDLY ENOUGH TO LET YOU USE THE DOOR.
MERCY, MY DEAR, YOU'RE SO SUSPICIOUS.
HOW COULD AN IMPOSTOR POSSIBLY FAKE A DNA SCAN?
BOSS? I'M SORRY. THOUGHT YOU WERE ALREADY HERE. IT'S JUST THAT I'VE NEVER SEEN YOU QUITE LIKE THIS.
LEX LUTHOR I.D. POSITIVE
DID SUPERMAN GET HIT BY A BOMB OR SOMETHING?
Oh, LIGHTEN UP, MERCY.
YOU'RE WAY TOO INTENSE FOR SUCH A CUTE CHICK.
EEP!
Ta-DAAA!
IMPRESSIVE, OR WHAT?
AM I SUPPOSED TO BE IMPRESSED WATCHING YOU DEMOLISH A CAREFULLY CULTIVATED REPUTATION AMONG MY EMPLOYEES?
INCIDENTALLY, THOSE PAY RAISES YOU AWARDED THE LITTLE PEOPLE DOWNSTAIRS WILL BE DEDUCTED FROM YOUR FINAL BILL. I'VE ALREADY DONE THE ARITHMETIC...

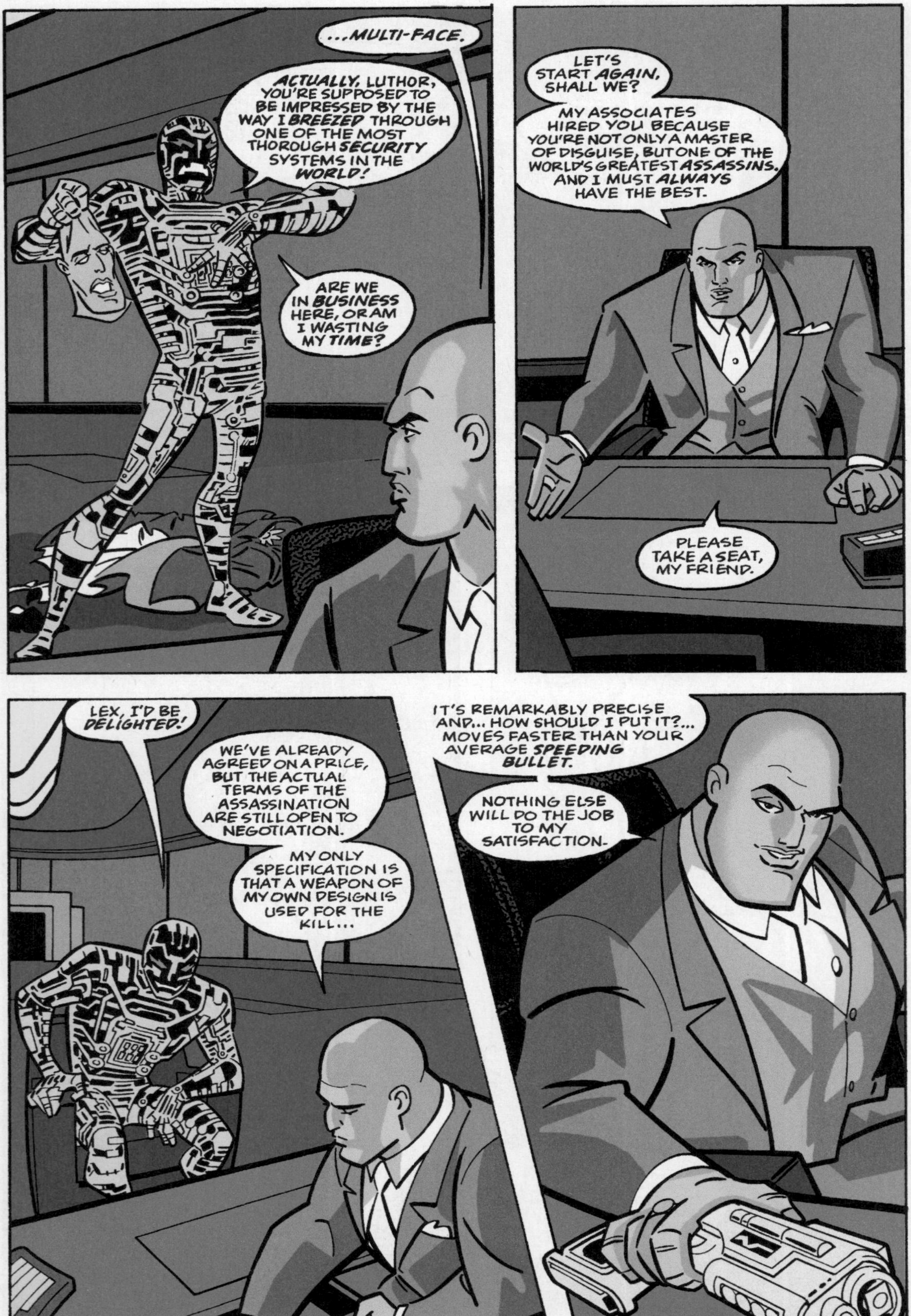
...MULTI-FACE.
ACTUALLY, LUTHOR, YOU'RE SUPPOSED TO BE IMPRESSED BY THE WAY I BREEZED THROUGH ONE OF THE MOST THOROUGH SECURITY SYSTEMS IN THE WORLD!
ARE WE IN BUSINESS HERE, OR AM I WASTING MY TIME?
LET'S START AGAIN, SHALL WE?
MY ASSOCIATES HIRED YOU BECAUSE YOU'RE NOT ONLY A MASTER OF DISGUISE, BUT ONE OF THE WORLD'S GREATEST ASSASSINS. AND I MUST ALWAYS HAVE THE BEST.
PLEASE TAKE A SEAT, MY FRIEND.
LEX, I'D BE DELIGHTED!
WE'VE ALREADY AGREED ON A PRICE, BUT THE ACTUAL TERMS OF THE ASSASSINATION ARE STILL OPEN TO NEGOTIATION.
MY ONLY SPECIFICATION IS THAT A WEAPON OF MY OWN DESIGN IS USED FOR THE KILL...
IT'S REMARKABLY PRECISE AND... HOW SHOULD I PUT IT?... MOVES FASTER THAN YOUR AVERAGE SPEEDING BULLET.
NOTHING ELSE WILL DO THE JOB TO MY SATISFACTION.

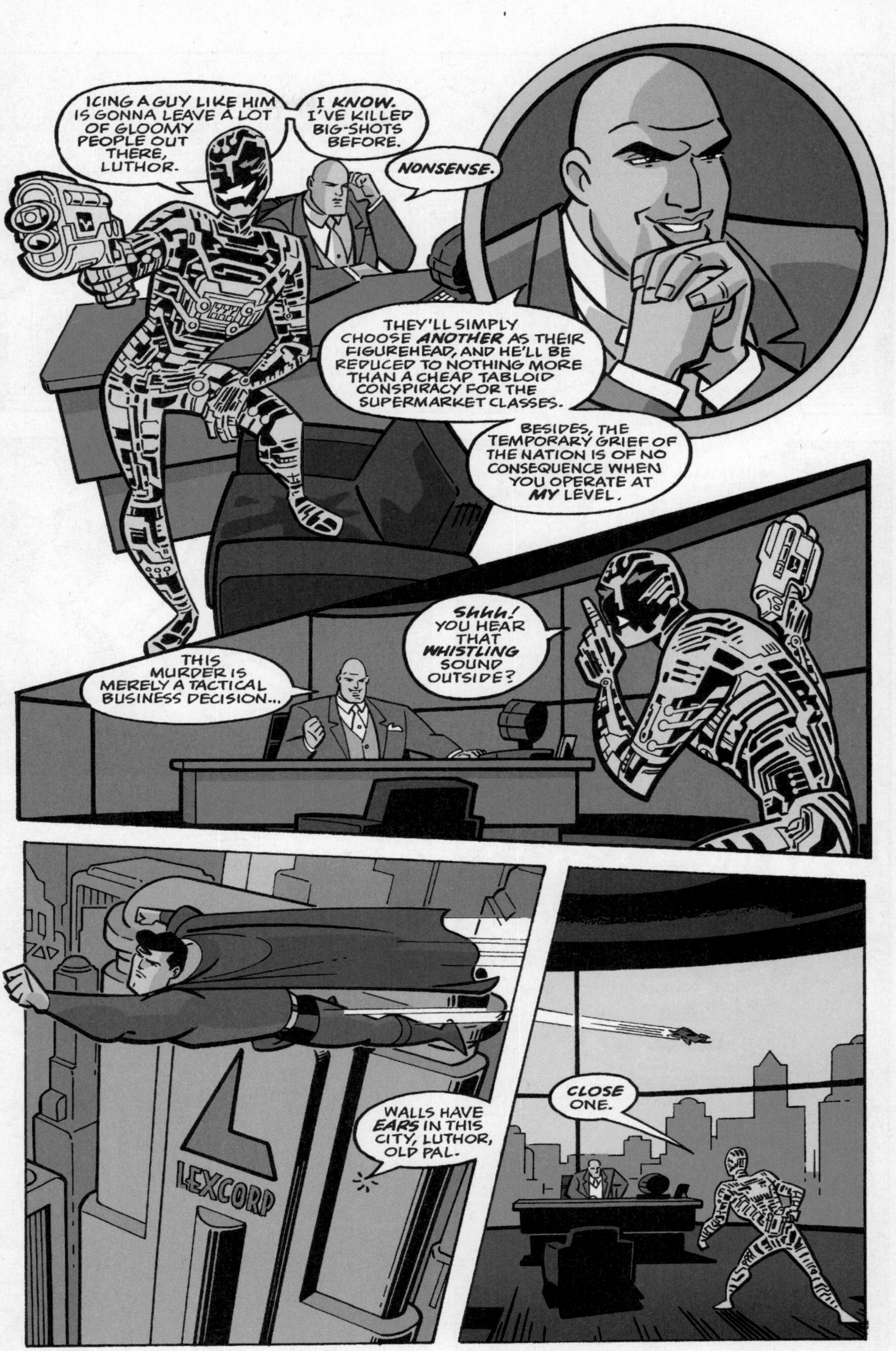
ICING A GUY LIKE HIM IS GONNA LEAVE A LOT OF GLOOMY PEOPLE OUT THERE, LUTHOR.
I KNOW. I'VE KILLED BIG-SHOTS BEFORE.
NONSENSE.
THEY'LL SIMPLY CHOOSE ANOTHER AS THEIR FIGUREHEAD, AND HE'LL BE REDUCED TO NOTHING MORE THAN A CHEAP TABLOID CONSPIRACY FOR THE SUPERMARKET CLASSES.
BESIDES, THE TEMPORARY GRIEF OF THE NATION IS OF NO CONSEQUENCE WHEN YOU OPERATE AT MY LEVEL.
THIS MURDER IS MERELY A TACTICAL BUSINESS DECISION...
Shhh! YOU HEAR THAT WHISTLING SOUND OUTSIDE?
WALLS HAVE EARS IN THIS CITY, LUTHOR, OLD PAL.
LEXCORP
CLOSE ONE.

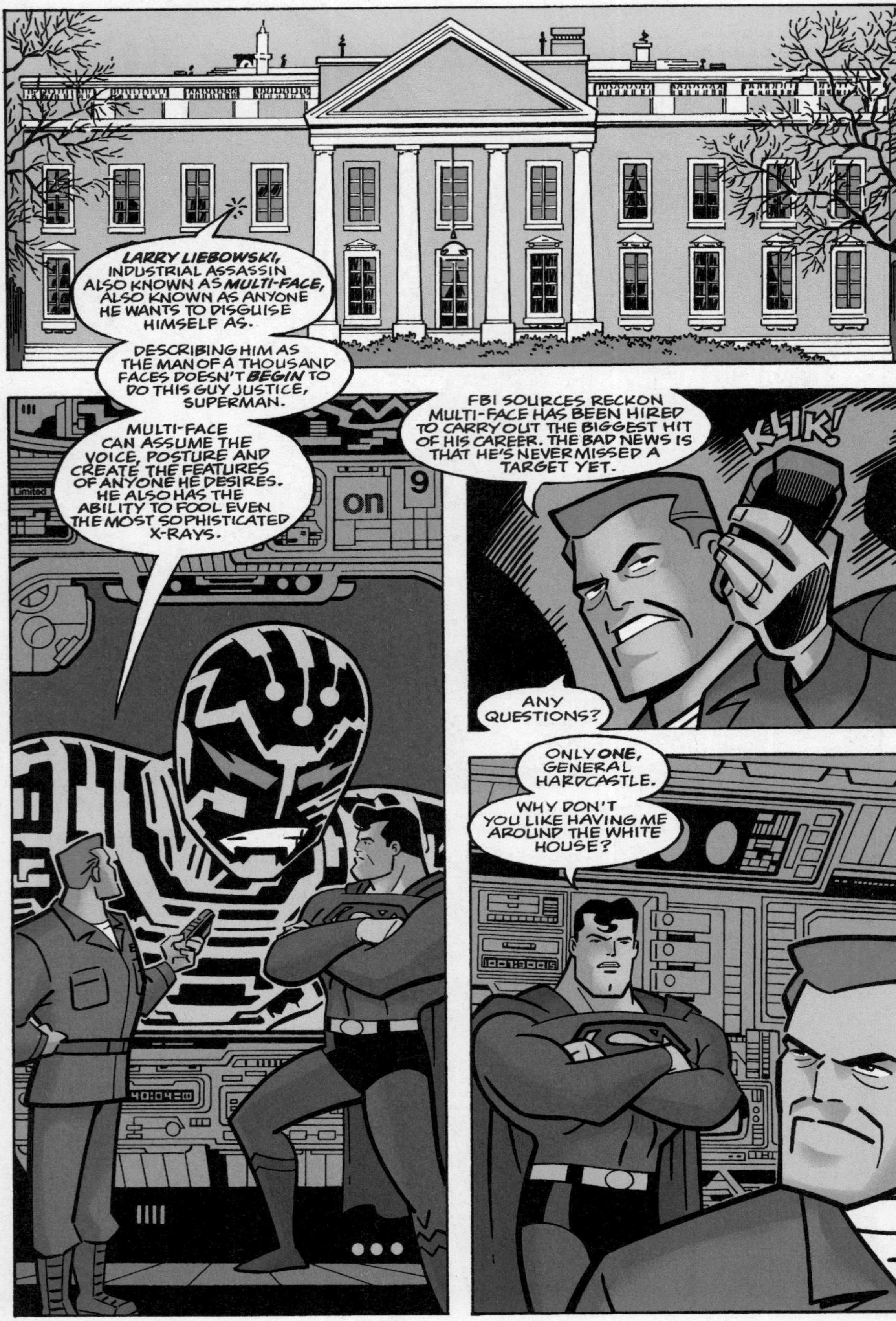

LARRY LIEBOWSKI, INDUSTRIAL ASSASSIN ALSO KNOWN AS MULTI-FACE, ALSO KNOWN AS ANYONE HE WANTS TO DISGUISE HIMSELF AS.
DESCRIBING HIM AS THE MAN OF A THOUSAND FACES DOESN'T BEGIN TO DO THIS GUY JUSTICE, SUPERMAN.
MULTI-FACE CAN ASSUME THE VOICE, POSTURE AND CREATE THE FEATURES OF ANYONE HE DESIRES. HE ALSO HAS THE ABILITY TO FOOL EVEN THE MOST SOPHISTICATED X-RAYS.
Limited
on
9
FBI SOURCES RECKON MULTI-FACE HAS BEEN HIRED TO CARRY OUT THE BIGGEST HIT OF HIS CAREER. THE BAD NEWS IS THAT HE'S NEVER MISSED A TARGET YET.
KLIK!
ANY QUESTIONS?
ONLY ONE, GENERAL HARDCASTLE.
WHY DON'T YOU LIKE HAVING ME AROUND THE WHITE HOUSE?

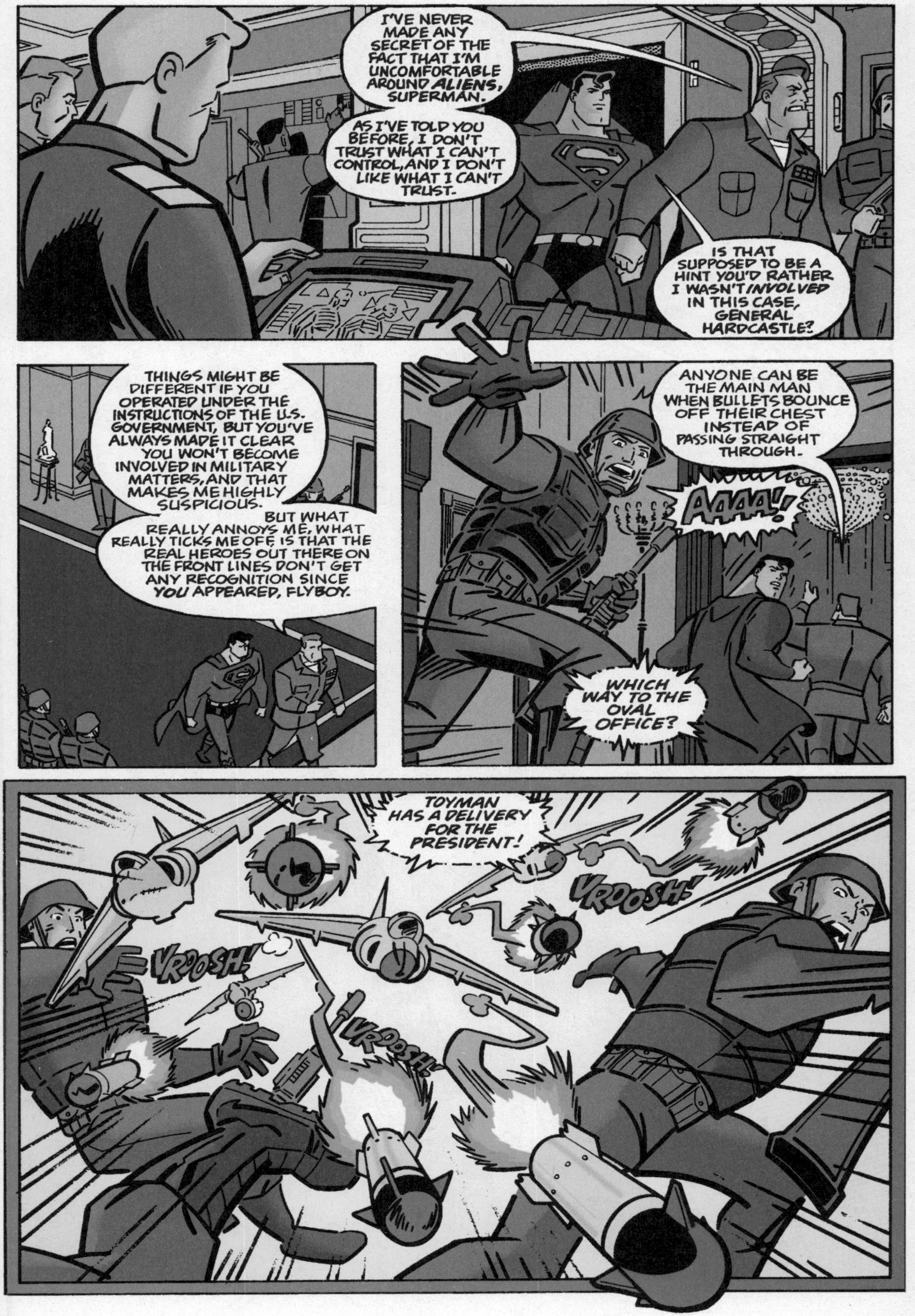
I'VE NEVER MADE ANY SECRET OF THE FACT THAT I'M UNCOMFORTABLE AROUND ALIENS, SUPERMAN.
AS I'VE TOLD YOU BEFORE, I DON'T TRUST WHAT I CAN'T CONTROL, AND I DON'T LIKE WHAT I CAN'T TRUST.
IS THAT SUPPOSED TO BE A HINT YOU'D RATHER I WASN'T INVOLVED IN THIS CASE, GENERAL HARDCASTLE?
THINGS MIGHT BE DIFFERENT IF YOU OPERATED UNDER THE INSTRUCTIONS OF THE U.S. GOVERNMENT, BUT YOU'VE ALWAYS MADE IT CLEAR YOU WON'T BECOME INVOLVED IN MILITARY MATTERS, AND THAT MAKES ME HIGHLY SUSPICIOUS.
BUT WHAT REALLY ANNOYS ME, WHAT REALLY TICKS ME OFF, IS THAT THE REAL HEROES OUT THERE ON THE FRONT LINES DON'T GET ANY RECOGNITION SINCE YOU APPEARED, FLYBOY.
ANYONE CAN BE THE MAIN MAN WHEN BULLETS BOUNCE OFF THEIR CHEST INSTEAD OF PASSING STRAIGHT THROUGH.
AAAA!
WHICH WAY TO THE OVAL OFFICE?
TOYMAN HAS A DELIVERY FOR THE PRESIDENT!
VROOSH!
VROOSH!
VROOSH!

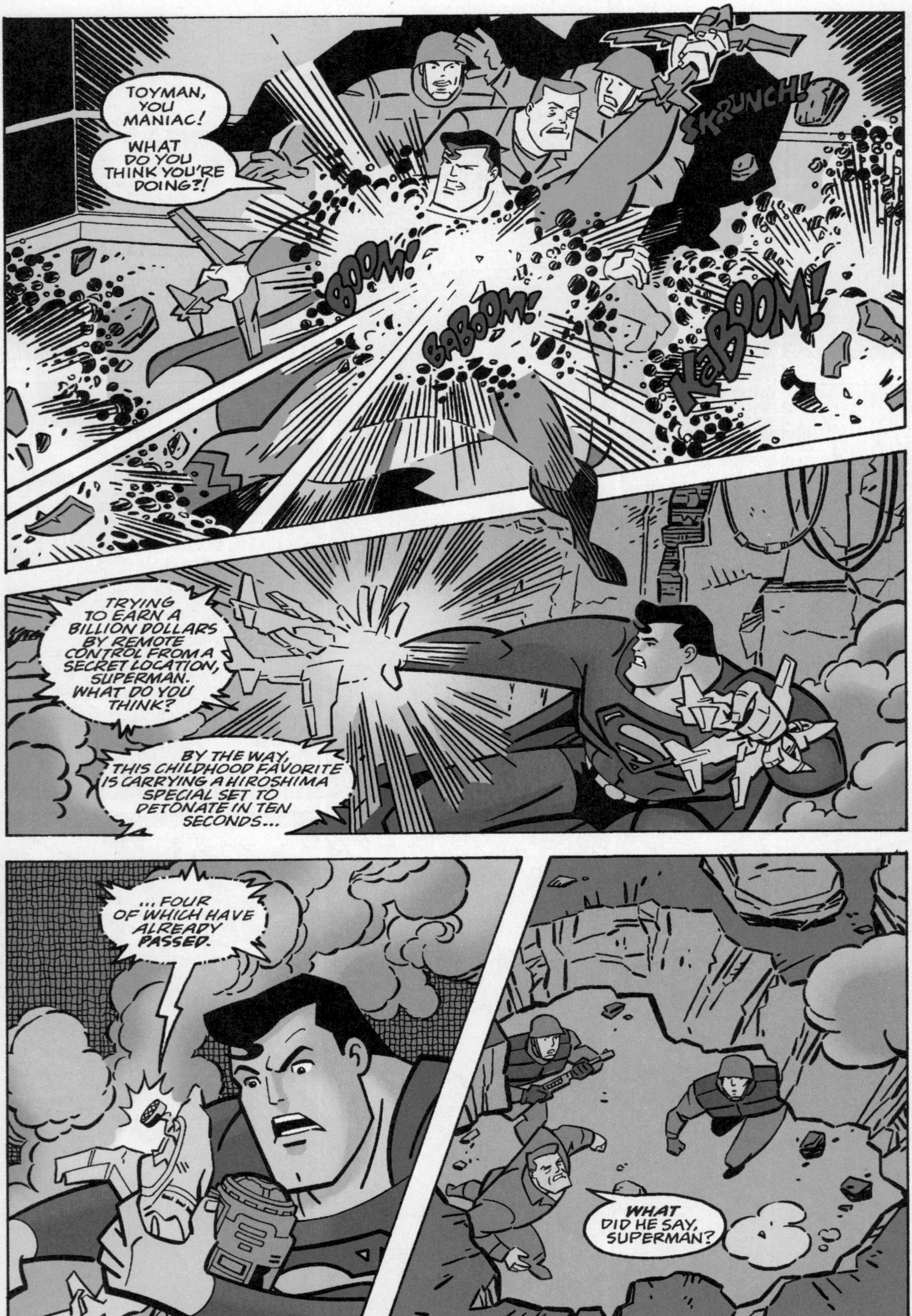
TOYMAN, YOU MANIAC!
WHAT DO YOU THINK YOU'RE DOING?!
SKRUNCH!
BOOM!
BABOOM!
KABOOM!
TRYING TO EARN A BILLION DOLLARS BY REMOTE CONTROL FROM A SECRET LOCATION, SUPERMAN. WHAT DO YOU THINK?
BY THE WAY, THIS CHILDHOOD FAVORITE IS CARRYING A HIROSHIMA SPECIAL SET TO DETONATE IN TEN SECONDS...
...FOUR OF WHICH HAVE ALREADY PASSED.
WHAT DID HE SAY, SUPERMAN?

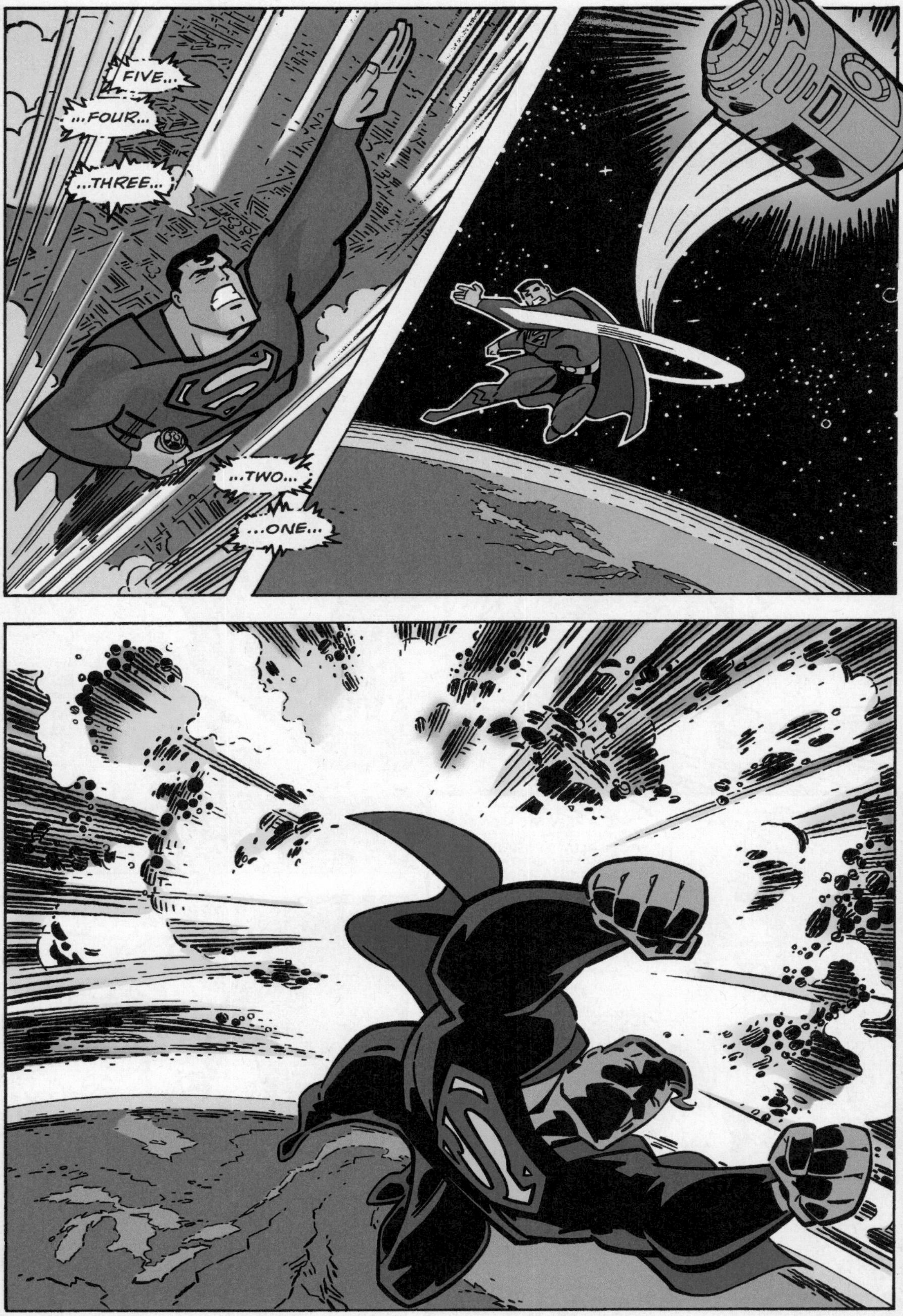
FIVE...
...FOUR...
...THREE...
...TWO...
...ONE...

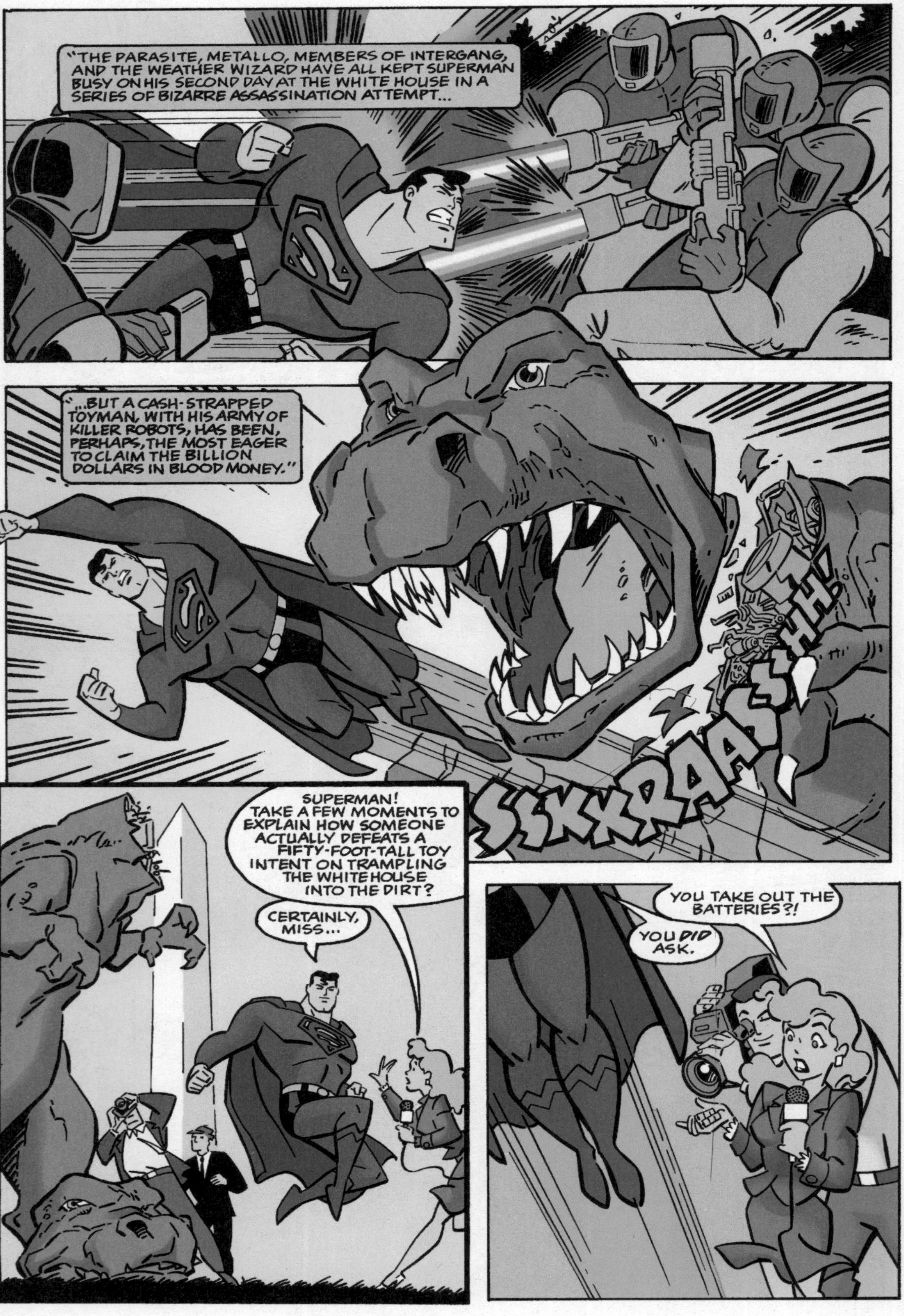
"THE PARASITE, METALLO, MEMBERS OF INTERGANG, AND THE WEATHER WIZARD HAVE ALL KEPT SUPERMAN BUSY ON HIS SECOND DAY AT THE WHITE HOUSE IN A SERIES OF BIZARRE ASSASSINATION ATTEMPT...
"...BUT A CASH-STRAPPED TOYMAN, WITH HIS ARMY OF KILLER ROBOTS, HAS BEEN, PERHAPS, THE MOST EAGER TO CLAIM THE BILLION DOLLARS IN BLOOD MONEY."
SSKKRAASSHH!
SUPERMAN! TAKE A FEW MOMENTS TO EXPLAIN HOW SOMEONE ACTUALLY DEFEATS A FIFTY-FOOT-TALL TOY INTENT ON TRAMPLING THE WHITE HOUSE INTO THE DIRT?
CERTAINLY, MISS...
YOU TAKE OUT THE BATTERIES?!
YOU DID ASK.

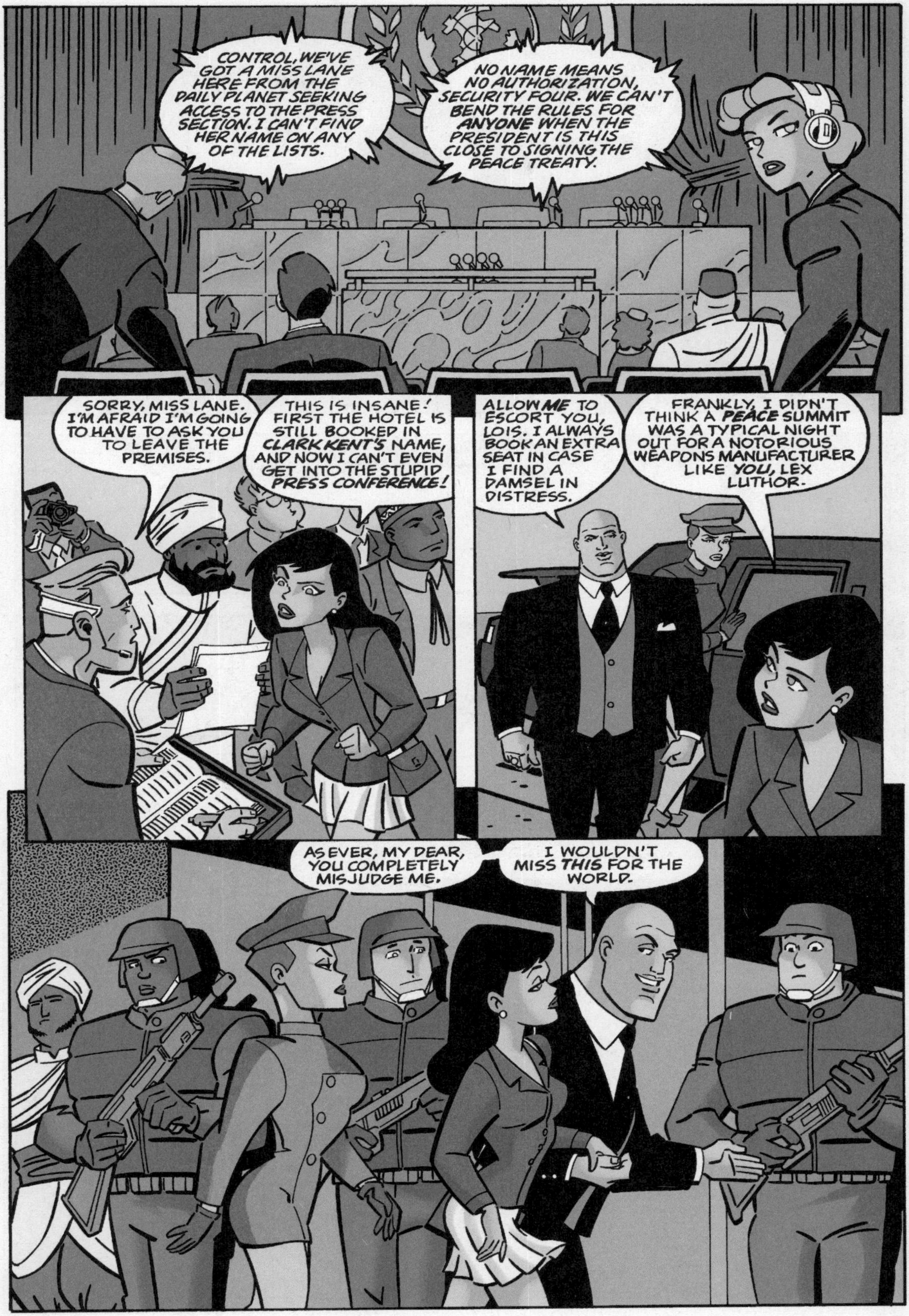

CONTROL, WE'VE GOT A MISS LANE HERE FROM THE DAILY PLANET SEEKING ACCESS TO THE PRESS SECTION. I CAN'T FIND HER NAME ON ANY OF THE LISTS.
NO NAME MEANS NO AUTHORIZATION, SECURITY FOUR. WE CAN'T BEND THE RULES FOR ANYONE WHEN THE PRESIDENT IS THIS CLOSE TO SIGNING THE PEACE TREATY.
SORRY, MISS LANE. I'M AFRAID I'M GOING TO HAVE TO ASK YOU TO LEAVE THE PREMISES.
THIS IS INSANE! FIRST THE HOTEL IS STILL BOOKED IN CLARK KENT'S NAME, AND NOW I CAN'T EVEN GET INTO THE STUPID PRESS CONFERENCE!
ALLOW ME TO ESCORT YOU, LOIS. I ALWAYS BOOK AN EXTRA SEAT IN CASE I FIND A DAMSEL IN DISTRESS.
FRANKLY, I DIDN'T THINK A PEACE SUMMIT WAS A TYPICAL NIGHT OUT FOR A NOTORIOUS WEAPONS MANUFACTURER LIKE YOU, LEX LUTHOR.
AS EVER, MY DEAR, YOU COMPLETELY MISJUDGE ME.
I WOULDN'T MISS THIS FOR THE WORLD.

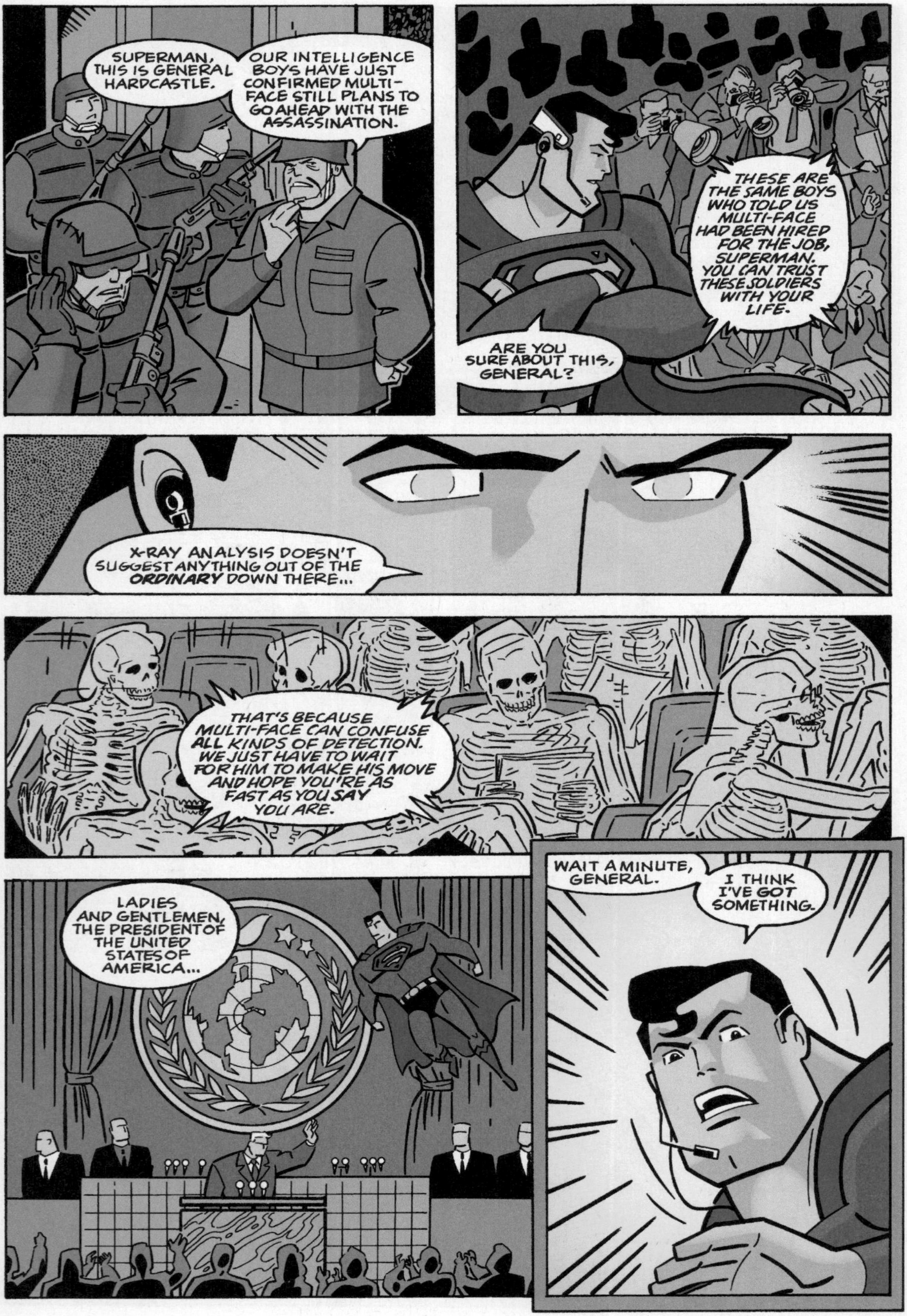
SUPERMAN, THIS IS GENERAL HARDCASTLE.
OUR INTELLIGENCE BOYS HAVE JUST CONFIRMED MULTI-FACE STILL PLANS TO GO AHEAD WITH THE ASSASSINATION.
ARE YOU SURE ABOUT THIS, GENERAL?
THESE ARE THE SAME BOYS WHO TOLD US MULTI-FACE HAD BEEN HIRED FOR THE JOB, SUPERMAN. YOU CAN TRUST THESE SOLDIERS WITH YOUR LIFE.
X-RAY ANALYSIS DOESN'T SUGGEST ANYTHING OUT OF THE ORDINARY DOWN THERE...
THAT'S BECAUSE MULTI-FACE CAN CONFUSE ALL KINDS OF DETECTION. WE JUST HAVE TO WAIT FOR HIM TO MAKE HIS MOVE AND HOPE YOU'RE AS FAST AS YOU SAY YOU ARE.
LADIES AND GENTLEMEN, THE PRESIDENT OF THE UNITED STATES OF AMERICA...
WAIT A MINUTE, GENERAL.
I THINK I'VE GOT SOMETHING.

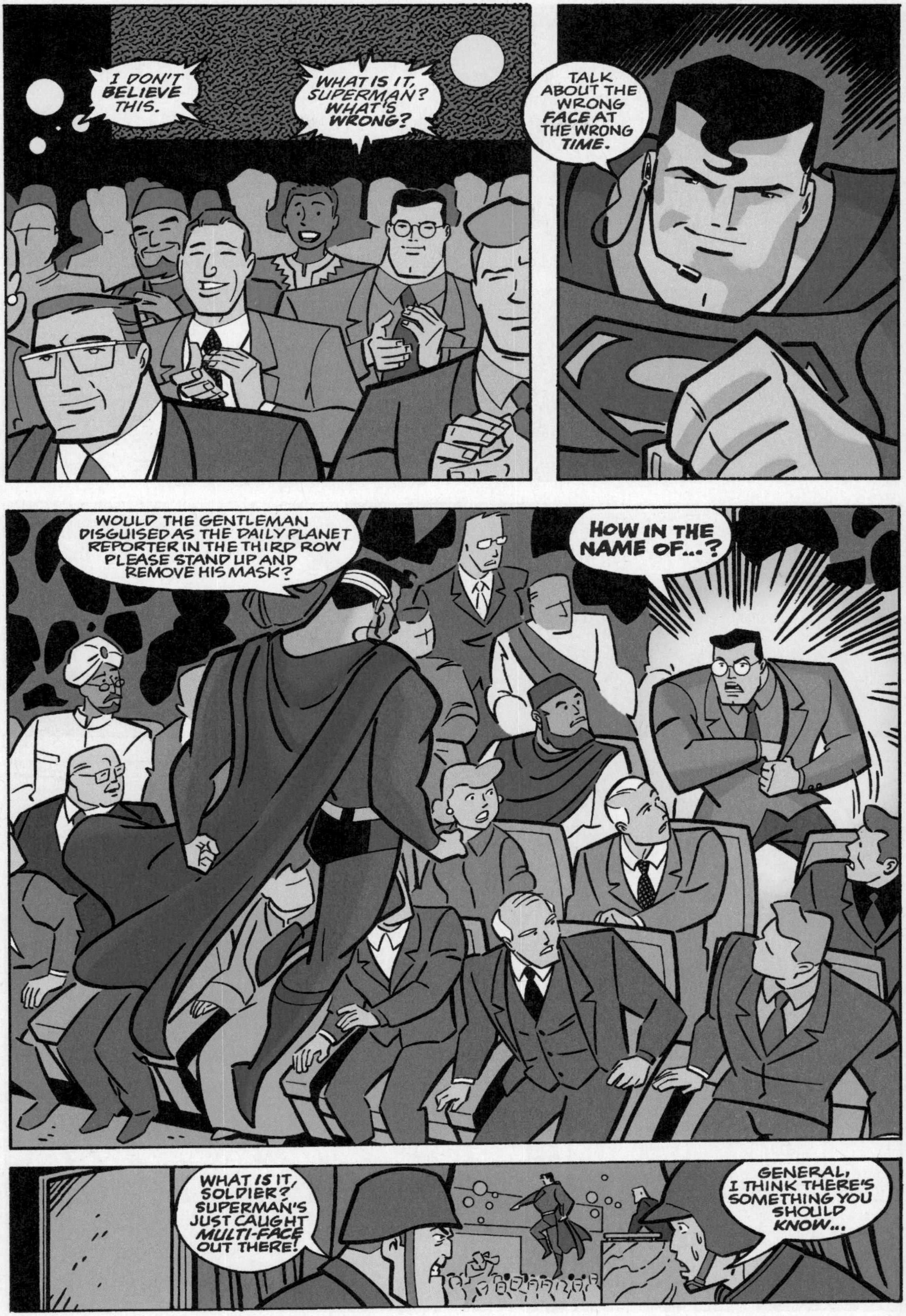

I DON'T BELIEVE THIS.
WHAT IS IT, SUPERMAN? WHAT'S WRONG?
TALK ABOUT THE WRONG FACE AT THE WRONG TIME.
WOULD THE GENTLEMAN DISGUISED AS THE DAILY PLANET REPORTER IN THE THIRD ROW PLEASE STAND UP AND REMOVE HIS MASK?
HOW IN THE NAME OF...?
WHAT IS IT, SOLDIER? SUPERMAN'S JUST CAUGHT MULTI-FACE OUT THERE!
GENERAL, I THINK THERE'S SOMETHING YOU SHOULD KNOW...

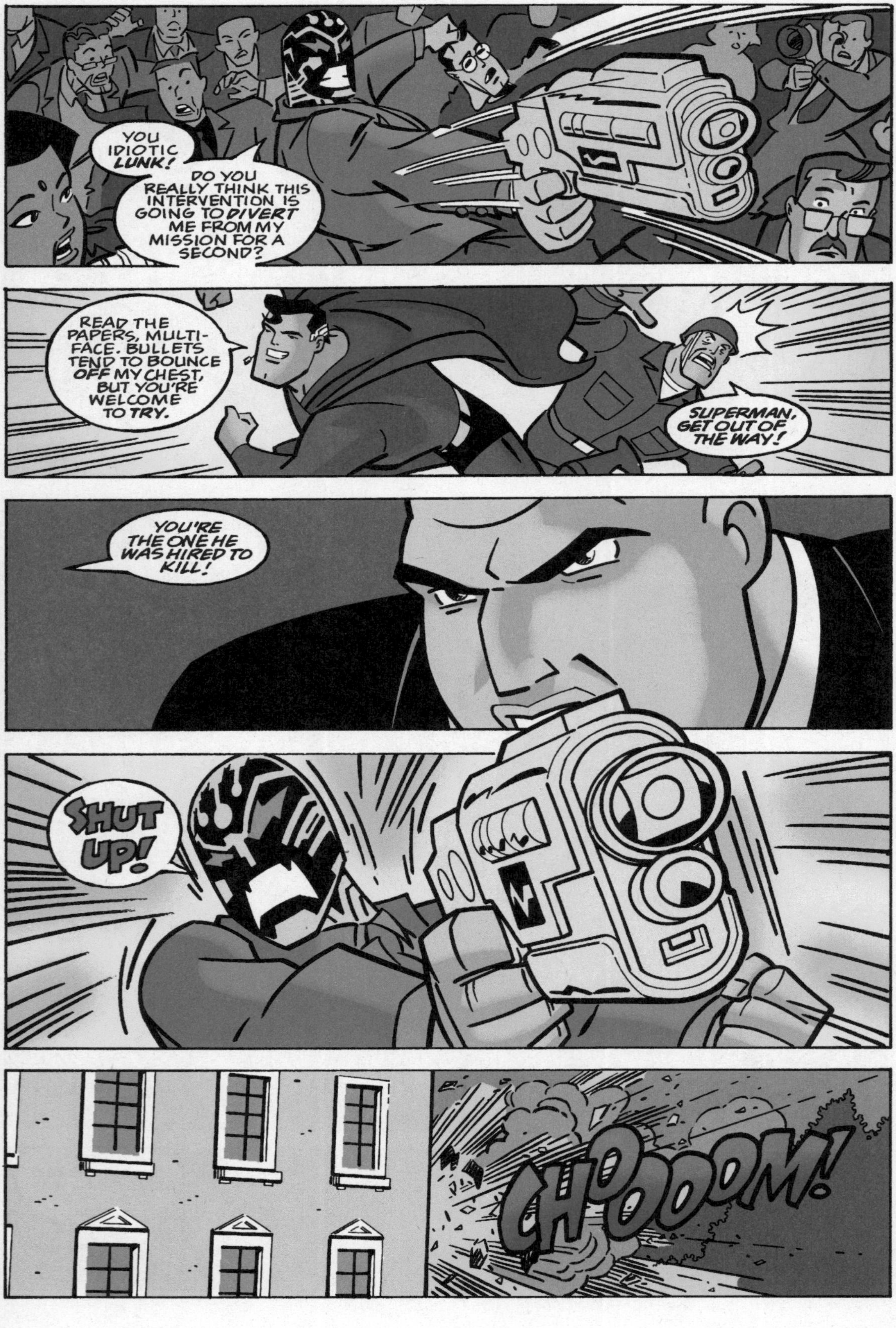
YOU IDIOTIC LUNK!
DO YOU REALLY THINK THIS INTERVENTION IS GOING TO DIVERT ME FROM MY MISSION FOR A SECOND?
READ THE PAPERS, MULTI-FACE. BULLETS TEND TO BOUNCE OFF MY CHEST, BUT YOU'RE WELCOME TO TRY.
SUPERMAN, GET OUT OF THE WAY!
YOU'RE THE ONE HE WAS HIRED TO KILL!
SHUT UP!
CHOOOOOM!

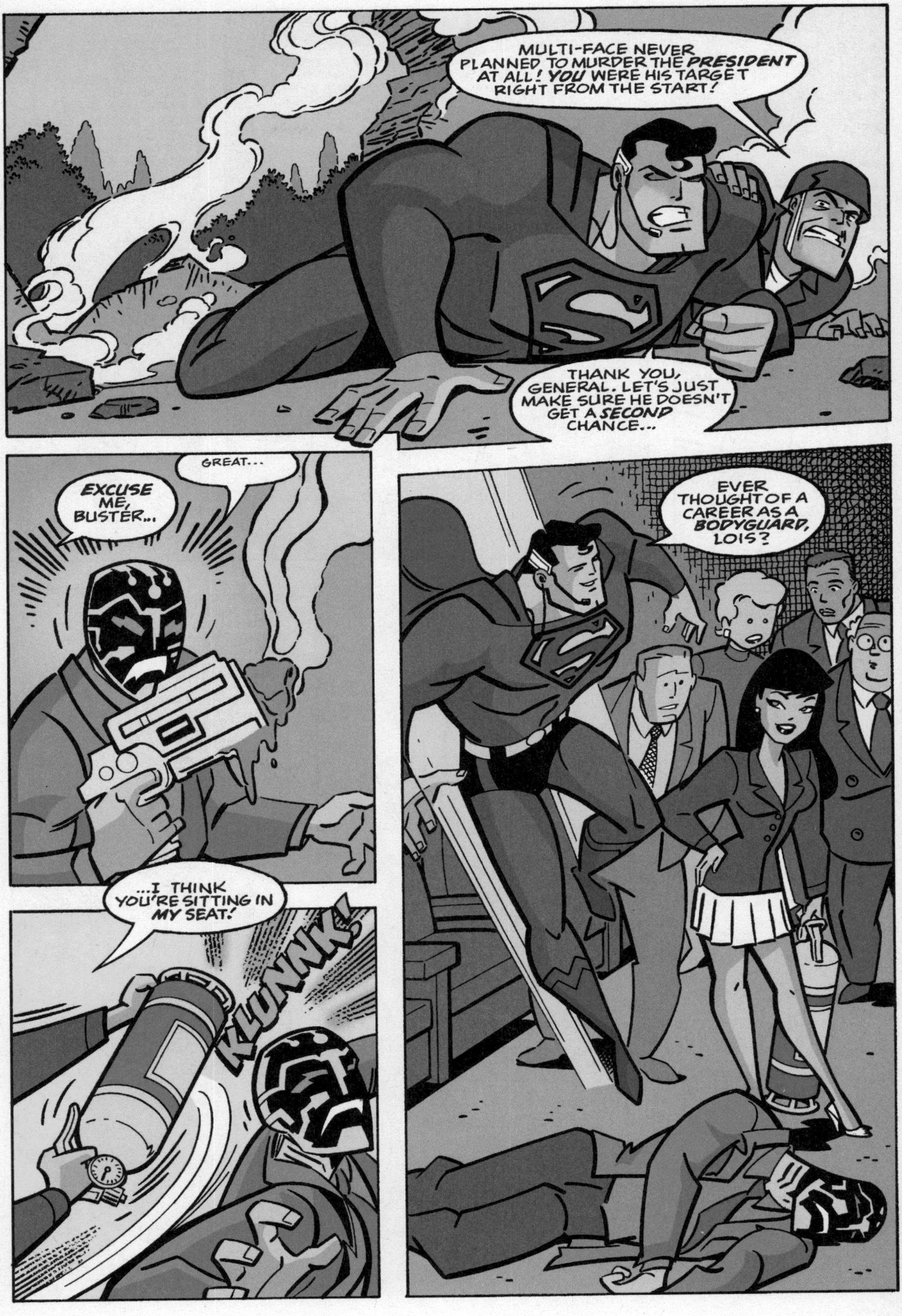
MULTI-FACE NEVER PLANNED TO MURDER THE PRESIDENT AT ALL! YOU WERE HIS TARGET RIGHT FROM THE START!
THANK YOU, GENERAL. LET'S JUST MAKE SURE HE DOESN'T GET A SECOND CHANCE...
EXCUSE ME, BUSTER...
GREAT...
...I THINK YOU'RE SITTING IN MY SEAT!
KLUNNK!
EVER THOUGHT OF A CAREER AS A BODYGUARD, LOIS?

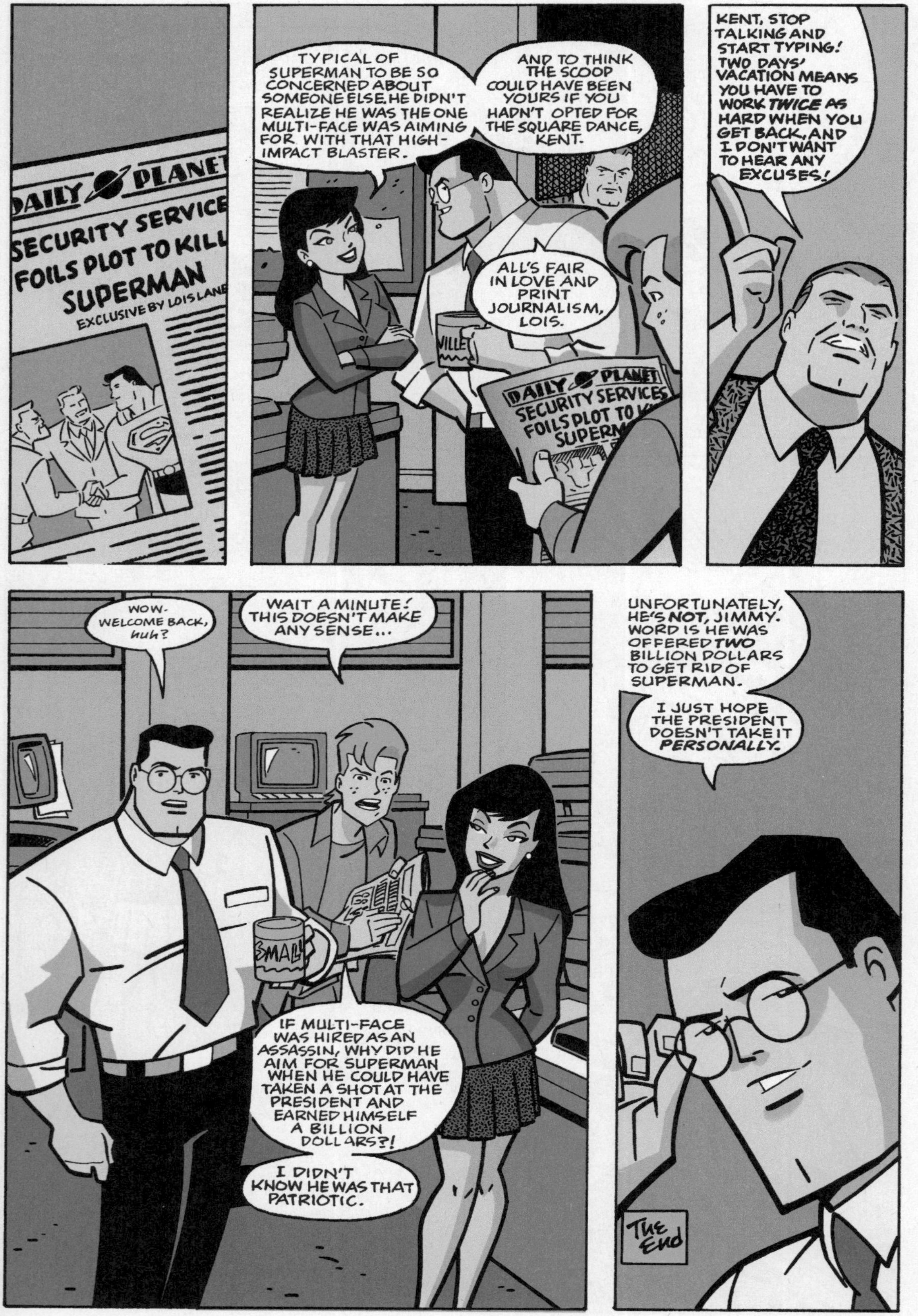
DAILY PLANET
SECURITY SERVICE FOILS PLOT TO KILL SUPERMAN
EXCLUSIVE BY LOIS LANE
TYPICAL OF SUPERMAN TO BE SO CONCERNED ABOUT SOMEONE ELSE. HE DIDN'T REALIZE HE WAS THE ONE MULTI-FACE WAS AIMING FOR WITH THAT HIGH-IMPACT BLASTER.
AND TO THINK THE SCOOP COULD HAVE BEEN YOURS IF YOU HADN'T OPTED FOR THE SQUARE DANCE, KENT.
ALL'S FAIR IN LOVE AND PRINT JOURNALISM, LOIS.
DAILY PLANET
SECURITY SERVICES FOILS PLOT TO KI
SUPERM
KENT, STOP TALKING AND START TYPING! TWO DAYS' VACATION MEANS YOU HAVE TO WORK TWICE AS HARD WHEN YOU GET BACK, AND I DON'T WANT TO HEAR ANY EXCUSES!
WOW- WELCOME BACK, huh?
WAIT A MINUTE! THIS DOESN'T MAKE ANY SENSE...
IF MULTI-FACE WAS HIRED AS AN ASSASSIN, WHY DID HE AIM FOR SUPERMAN WHEN HE COULD HAVE TAKEN A SHOT AT THE PRESIDENT AND EARNED HIMSELF A BILLION DOLLARS?!
I DIDN'T KNOW HE WAS THAT PATRIOTIC.
UNFORTUNATELY, HE'S NOT, JIMMY. WORD IS HE WAS OFFERED TWO BILLION DOLLARS TO GET RID OF SUPERMAN.
I JUST HOPE THE PRESIDENT DOESN'T TAKE IT PERSONALLY.
THE END

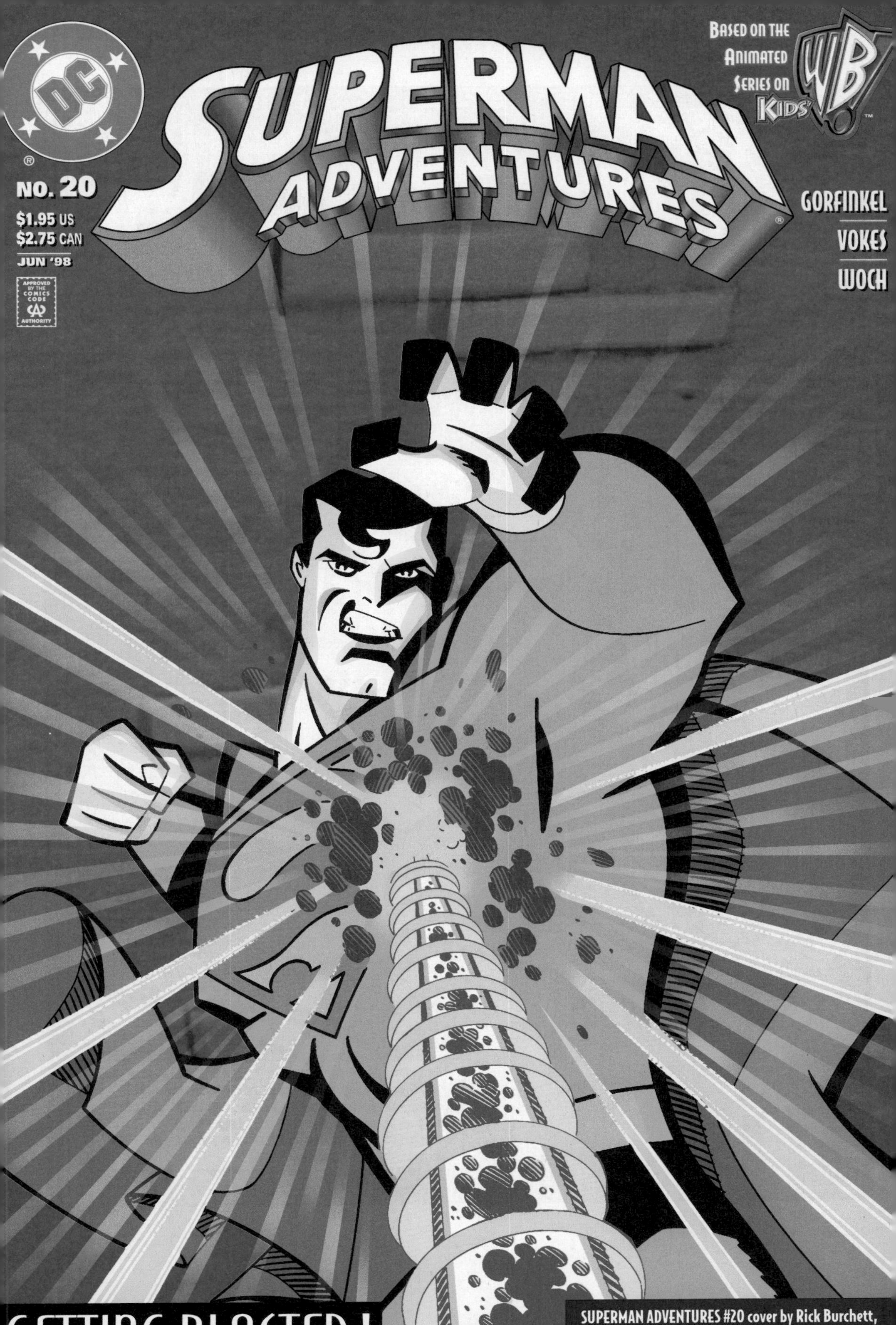
DC
SUPERMAN ADVENTURES
BASED ON THE ANIMATED SERIES ON KIDS' WB!
NO. 20
$1.95 US
$2.75 CAN
JUN '98
APPROVED BY THE COMICS CODE AUTHORITY
GORFINKEL
VOKES
WOCH

GETTING BLASTED !

SUPERMAN ADVENTURES #20 cover by Rick Burchett, Terry Austin and Rick Taylor

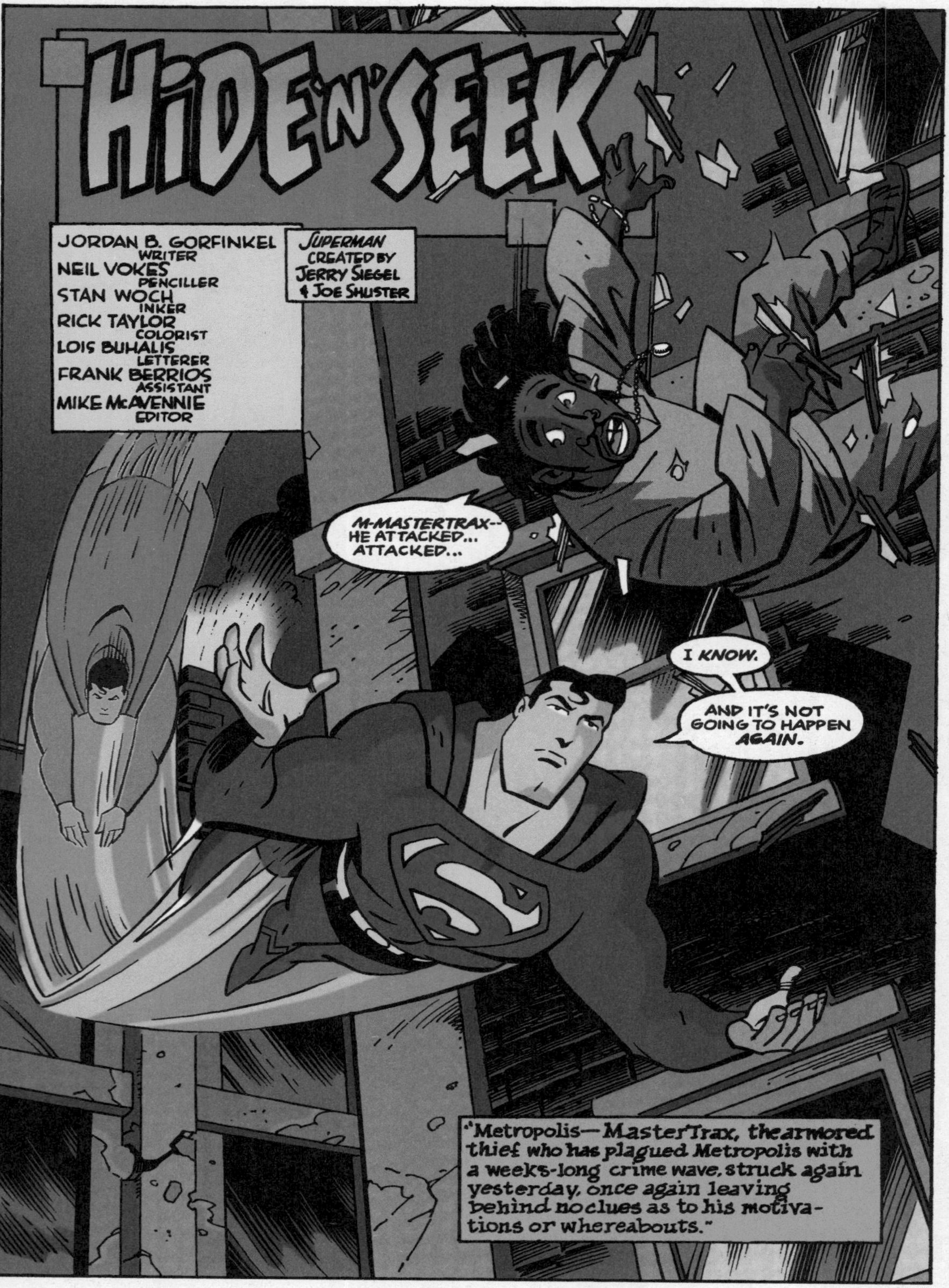
HIDE 'N' SEEK
JORDAN B. GORFINKEL WRITER
NEIL VOKES PENCILLER
STAN WOCH INKER
RICK TAYLOR COLORIST
LOIS BUHALIS LETTERER
FRANK BERRIOS ASSISTANT
MIKE McAVENNIE EDITOR
SUPERMAN CREATED BY JERRY SIEGEL & JOE SHUSTER
M-MASTERTRAX-- HE ATTACKED... ATTACKED...
I KNOW.
AND IT'S NOT GOING TO HAPPEN AGAIN.
"Metropolis—MasterTrax, the armored thief who has plagued Metropolis with a weeks-long crime wave, struck again yesterday, once again leaving behind no clues as to his motivations or whereabouts."

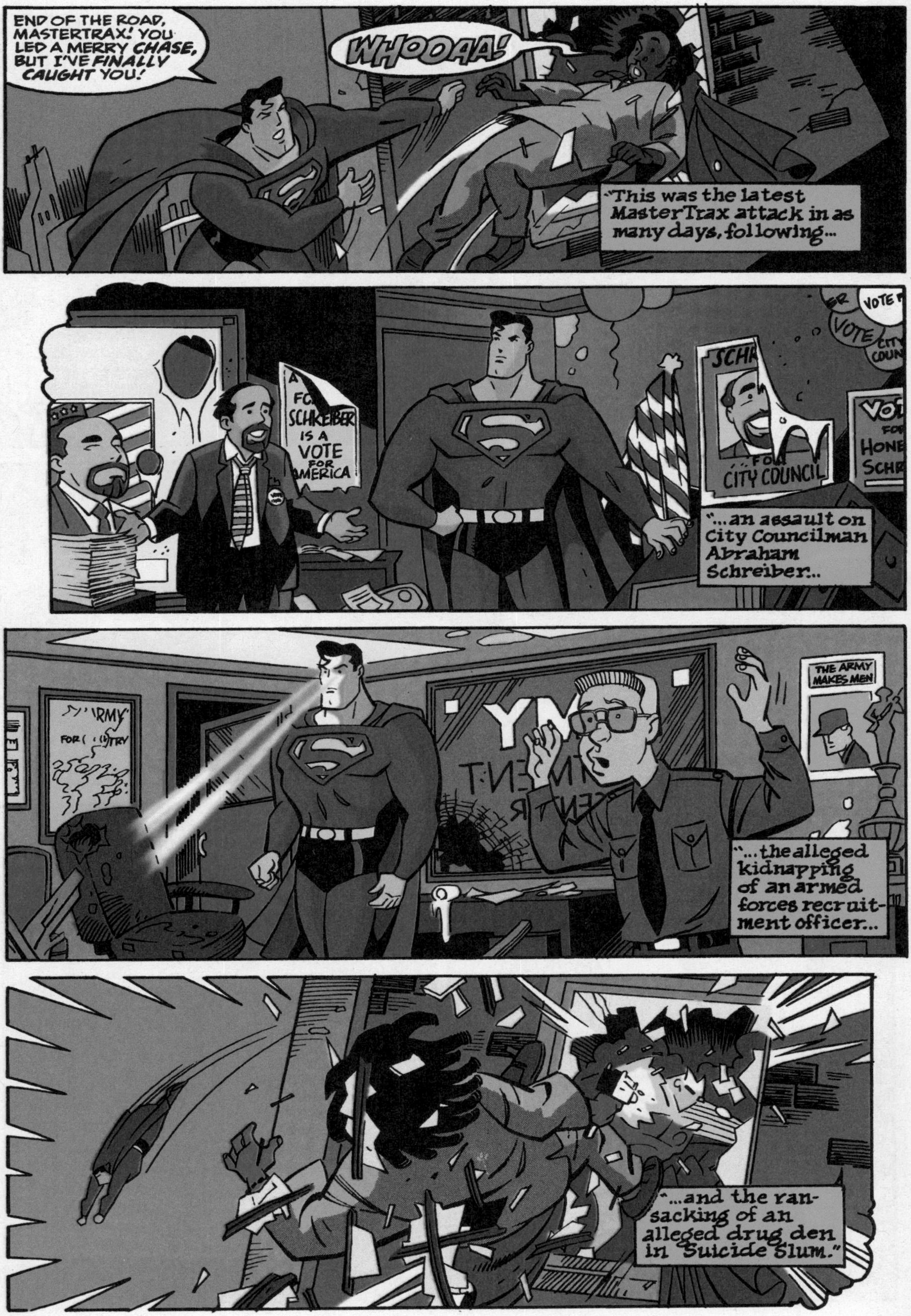
END OF THE ROAD, MASTERTRAX! YOU LED A MERRY CHASE, BUT I'VE FINALLY CAUGHT YOU!
WHOOAA!
"This was the latest MasterTrax attack in as many days, following...
VOTE
CITY COUNCIL
"...an assault on City Councilman Abraham Schreiber...
THE ARMY MAKES MEN
"...the alleged kidnapping of an armed forces recruitment officer...
"...and the ransacking of an alleged drug den in Suicide Slum."

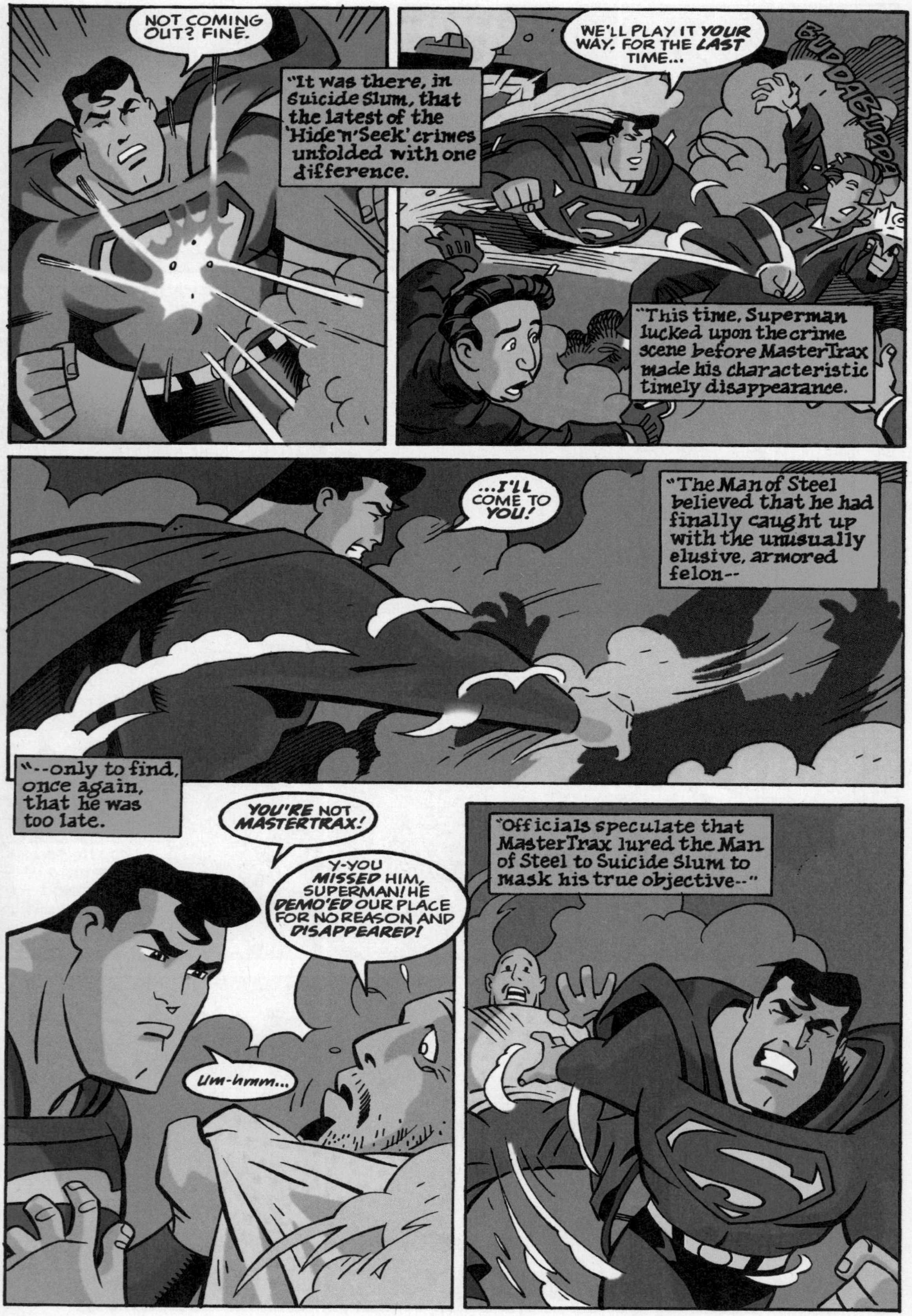
NOT COMING OUT? FINE.
"It was there, in Suicide Slum, that the latest of the 'Hide 'n' Seek' crimes unfolded with one difference.
WE'LL PLAY IT YOUR WAY. FOR THE LAST TIME...
BUDDABUDDA
"This time, Superman lucked upon the crime scene before MasterTrax made his characteristic timely disappearance.
...I'LL COME TO YOU!
"The Man of Steel believed that he had finally caught up with the unusually elusive, armored felon--
"--only to find, once again, that he was too late.
YOU'RE NOT MASTERTRAX!
Y-YOU MISSED HIM, SUPERMAN! HE DEMO'ED OUR PLACE FOR NO REASON AND DISAPPEARED!
Um-hmm...
"Officials speculate that MasterTrax lured the Man of Steel to Suicide Slum to mask his true objective--"

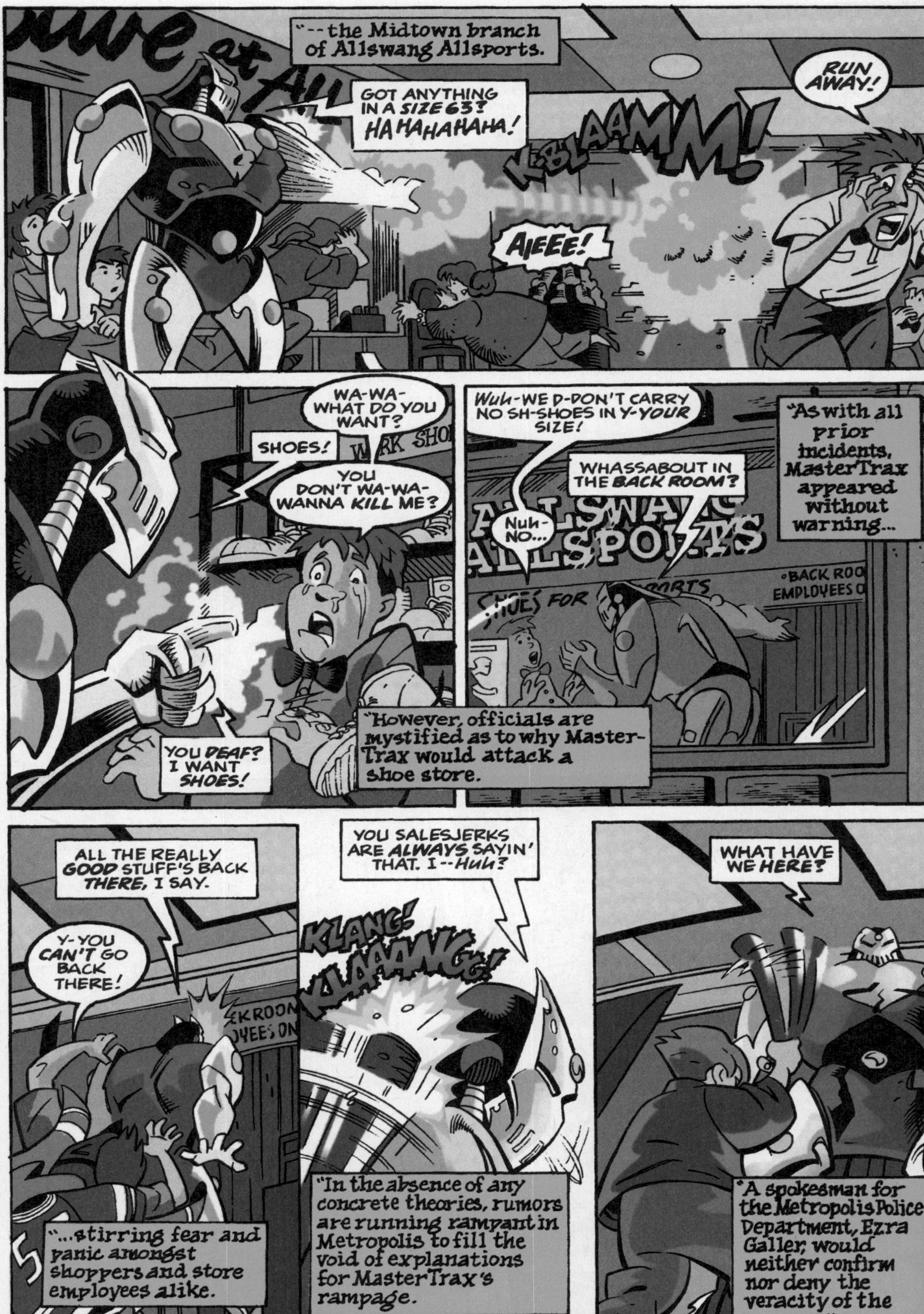
"--the Midtown branch of Allswang Allsports.
GOT ANYTHING IN A SIZE 63? HAHAHAHAHA!
RUN AWAY!
K-BLAAMM!
AIEEE!
SHOES!
WA-WA-WHAT DO YOU WANT?
YOU DON'T WA-WA-WANNA KILL ME?
YOU DEAF? I WANT SHOES!
"However, officials are mystified as to why Master-Trax would attack a shoe store.
Wuh-WE D-DON'T CARRY NO SH-SHOES IN Y-YOUR SIZE!
WHASSABOUT IN THE BACK ROOM?
Nuh-NO...
"As with all prior incidents, MasterTrax appeared without warning...
ALL THE REALLY GOOD STUFF'S BACK THERE, I SAY.
Y-YOU CAN'T GO BACK THERE!
"...stirring fear and panic amongst shoppers and store employees alike.
YOU SALESJERKS ARE ALWAYS SAYIN' THAT. I--Huh?
KLANG! KLAAAANG!
"In the absence of any concrete theories, rumors are running rampant in Metropolis to fill the void of explanations for MasterTrax's rampage.
WHAT HAVE WE HERE?
"A spokesman for the Metropolis Police Department, Ezra Galler, would neither confirm nor deny the veracity of the rumors."

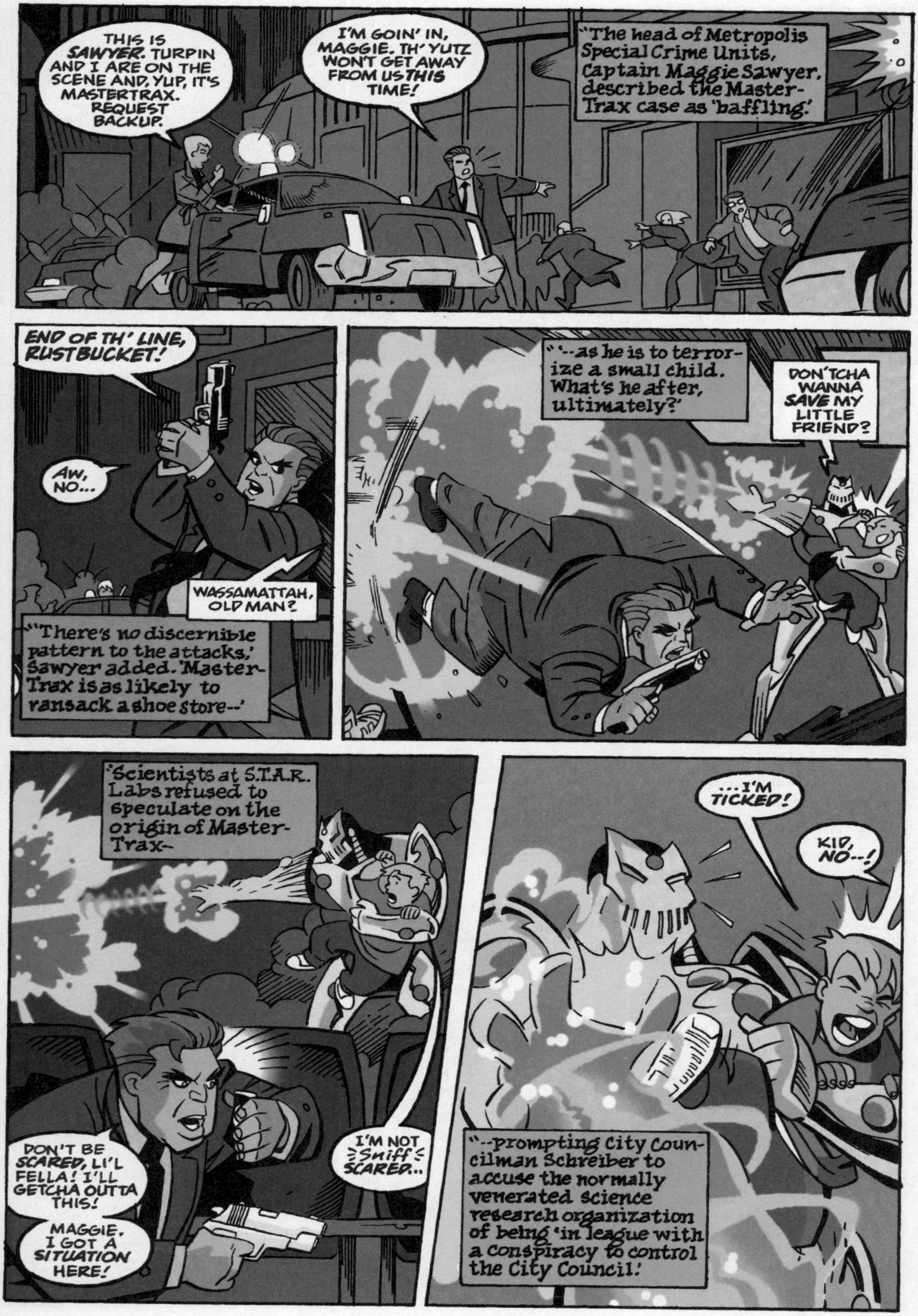
THIS IS SAWYER. TURPIN AND I ARE ON THE SCENE AND, YUP, IT'S MASTERTRAX. REQUEST BACKUP.
I'M GOIN' IN, MAGGIE. TH' YUTZ WON'T GET AWAY FROM US THIS TIME!
"The head of Metropolis Special Crime Units, Captain Maggie Sawyer, described the Master-Trax case as 'baffling.'
END OF TH' LINE, RUSTBUCKET!
AW, NO...
WASSAMATTAH, OLD MAN?
"'There's no discernible pattern to the attacks,' Sawyer added. 'Master-Trax is as likely to ransack a shoe store--'
"'--as he is to terrorize a small child. What's he after, ultimately?'
DON'TCHA WANNA SAVE MY LITTLE FRIEND?
"Scientists at S.T.A.R. Labs refused to speculate on the origin of Master-Trax--
DON'T BE SCARED, LI'L FELLA! I'LL GETCHA OUTTA THIS!
MAGGIE. I GOT A SITUATION HERE!
I'M NOT Sniff SCARED...
...I'M TICKED!
KID, NO--!
"--prompting City Councilman Schreiber to accuse the normally venerated science research organization of being 'in league with a conspiracy to control the City Council.'

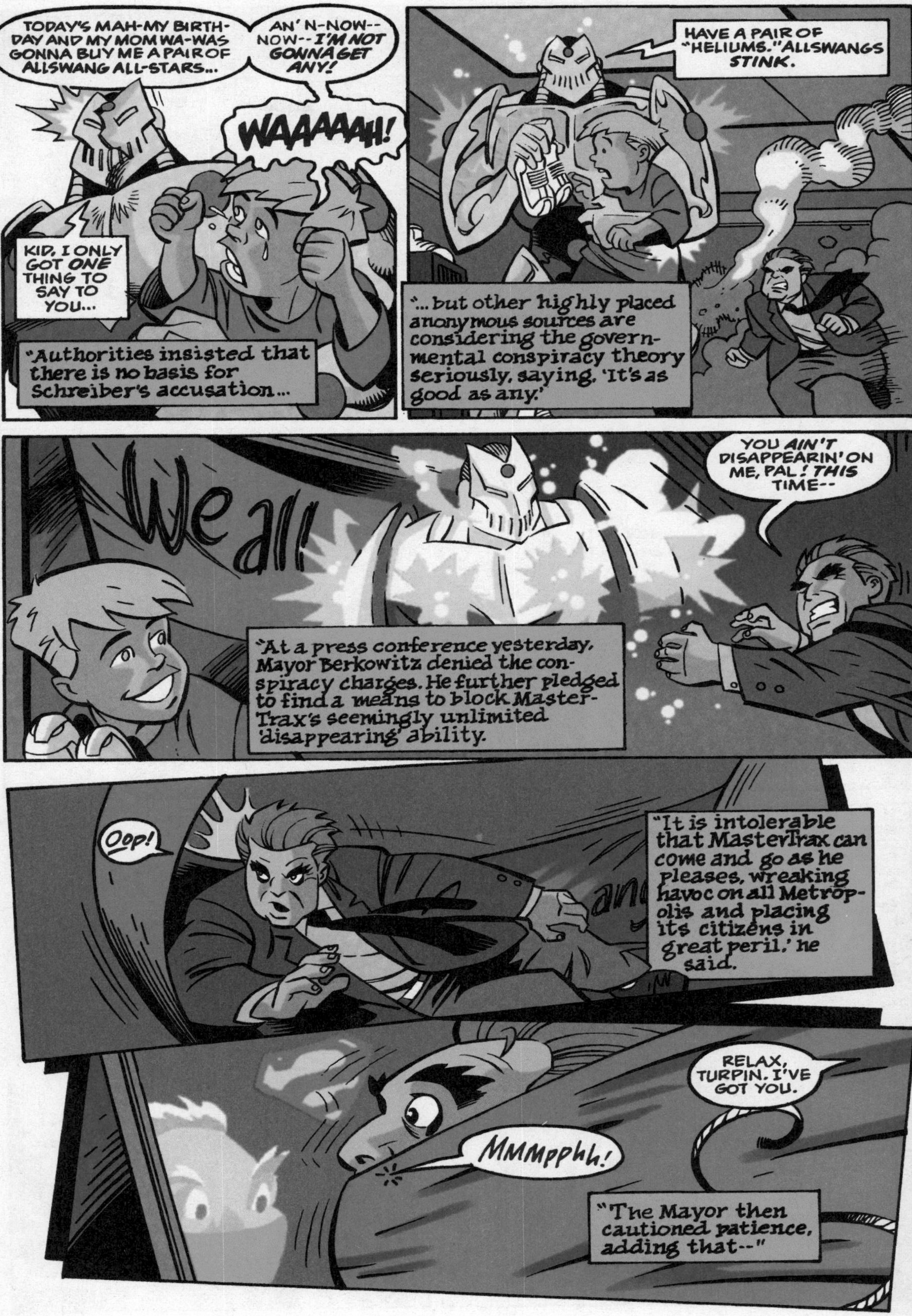
TODAY'S MAH-MY BIRTH-DAY AND MY MOM WA-WAS GONNA BUY ME A PAIR OF ALLSWANG ALL-STARS...
AN' N-NOW-- NOW-- I'M NOT GONNA GET ANY!
WAAAAAH!
KID, I ONLY GOT ONE THING TO SAY TO YOU...
"Authorities insisted that there is no basis for Schreiber's accusation...
HAVE A PAIR OF "HELIUMS." ALLSWANGS STINK.
"...but other highly placed anonymous sources are considering the governmental conspiracy theory seriously, saying, 'It's as good as any.'
We all!
YOU AIN'T DISAPPEARIN' ON ME, PAL! THIS TIME--
"At a press conference yesterday, Mayor Berkowitz denied the conspiracy charges. He further pledged to find a means to block MasterTrax's seemingly unlimited 'disappearing' ability.
Oop!
"It is intolerable that MasterTrax can come and go as he pleases, wreaking havoc on all Metropolis and placing its citizens in great peril,' he said.
RELAX, TURPIN. I'VE GOT YOU.
MMMpphh!
"The Mayor then cautioned patience, adding that--"

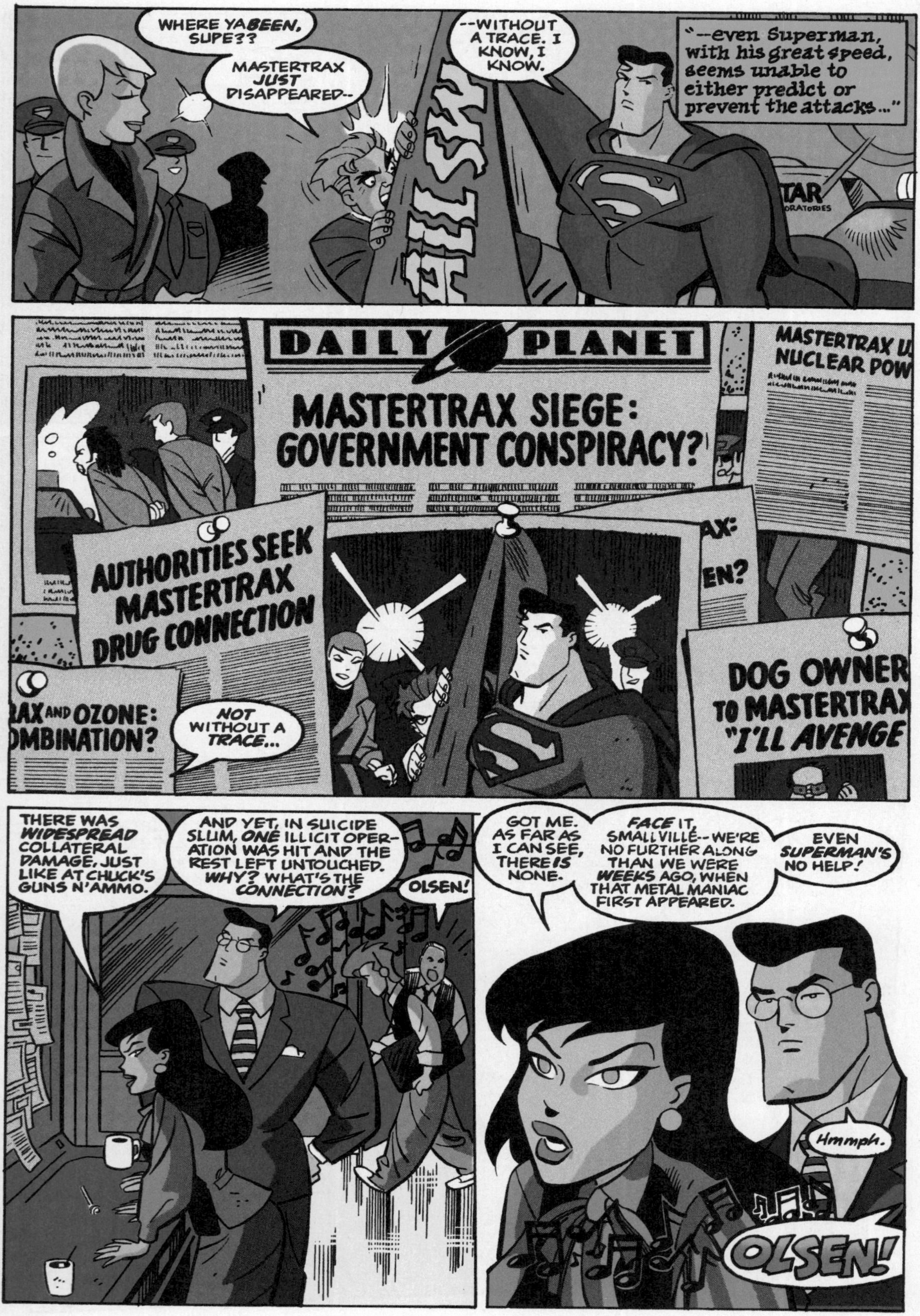

WHERE YA BEEN, SUPE??
MASTERTRAX JUST DISAPPEARED--
--WITHOUT A TRACE. I KNOW, I KNOW.
"--even Superman, with his great speed, seems unable to either predict or prevent the attacks..."
DAILY PLANET
MASTERTRAX SIEGE: GOVERNMENT CONSPIRACY?
MASTERTRAX U NUCLEAR POW
AUTHORITIES SEEK MASTERTRAX DRUG CONNECTION
RAX AND OZONE: OMBINATION?
NOT WITHOUT A TRACE...
DOG OWNER TO MASTERTRAX "I'LL AVENGE
THERE WAS WIDESPREAD COLLATERAL DAMAGE, JUST LIKE AT CHUCK'S GUNS N'AMMO.
AND YET, IN SUICIDE SLUM, ONE ILLICIT OPERATION WAS HIT AND THE REST LEFT UNTOUCHED. WHY? WHAT'S THE CONNECTION?
OLSEN!
GOT ME. AS FAR AS I CAN SEE, THERE IS NONE.
FACE IT, SMALLVILLE--WE'RE NO FURTHER ALONG THAN WE WERE WEEKS AGO, WHEN THAT METAL MANIAC FIRST APPEARED.
EVEN SUPERMAN'S NO HELP!
Hmmph.
OLSEN!

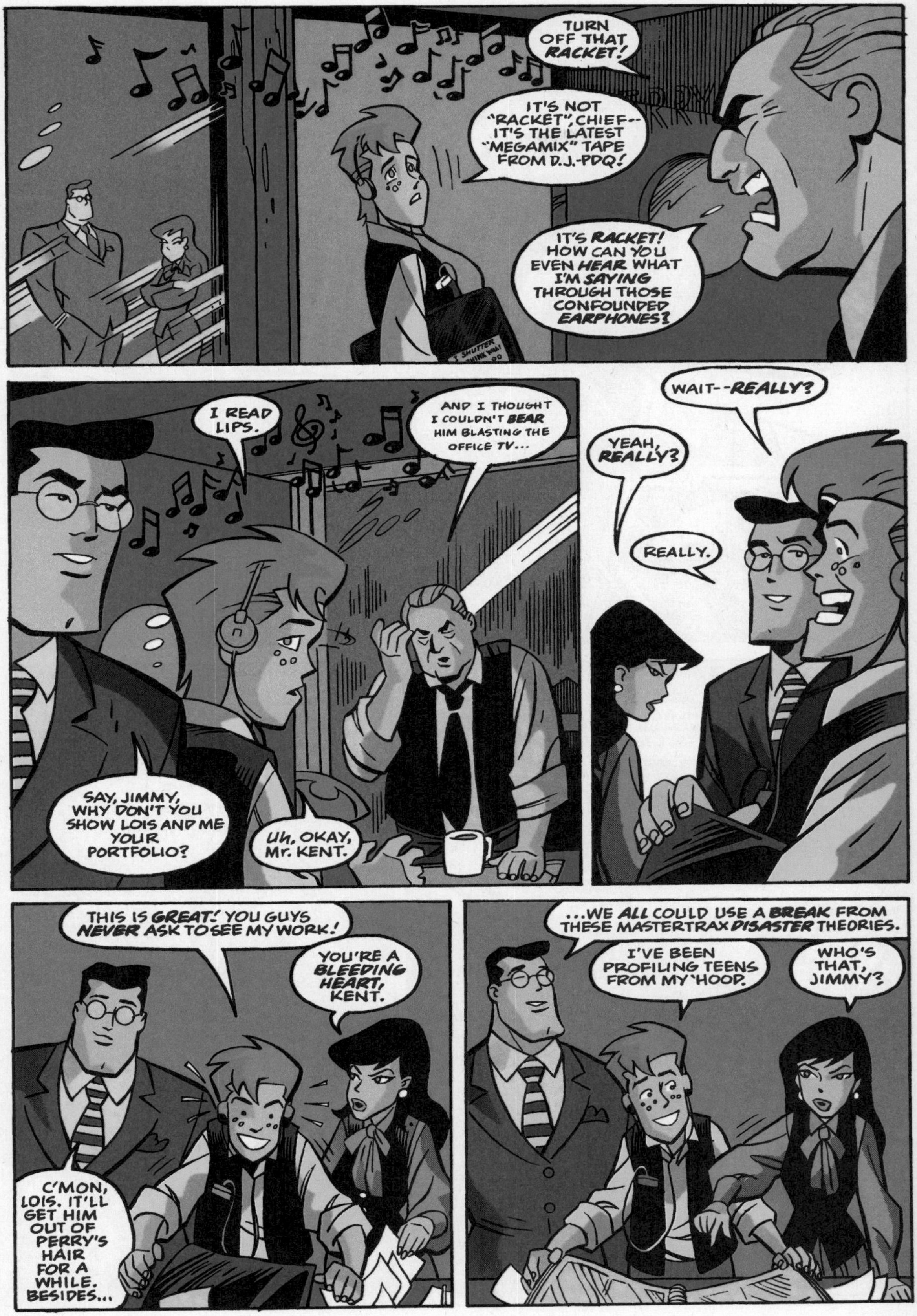
TURN OFF THAT RACKET!
IT'S NOT "RACKET", CHIEF-- IT'S THE LATEST "MEGAMIX" TAPE FROM D.J.-PDQ!
IT'S RACKET! HOW CAN YOU EVEN HEAR WHAT I'M SAYING THROUGH THOSE CONFOUNDED EARPHONES?
I READ LIPS.
AND I THOUGHT I COULDN'T BEAR HIM BLASTING THE OFFICE TV...
SAY, JIMMY, WHY DON'T YOU SHOW LOIS AND ME YOUR PORTFOLIO?
Uh, OKAY, Mr. KENT.
WAIT--REALLY?
YEAH, REALLY?
REALLY.
THIS IS GREAT! YOU GUYS NEVER ASK TO SEE MY WORK!
YOU'RE A BLEEDING HEART, KENT.
C'MON, LOIS. IT'LL GET HIM OUT OF PERRY'S HAIR FOR A WHILE. BESIDES...
...WE ALL COULD USE A BREAK FROM THESE MASTERTRAX DISASTER THEORIES.
I'VE BEEN PROFILING TEENS FROM MY 'HOOD.
WHO'S THAT, JIMMY?

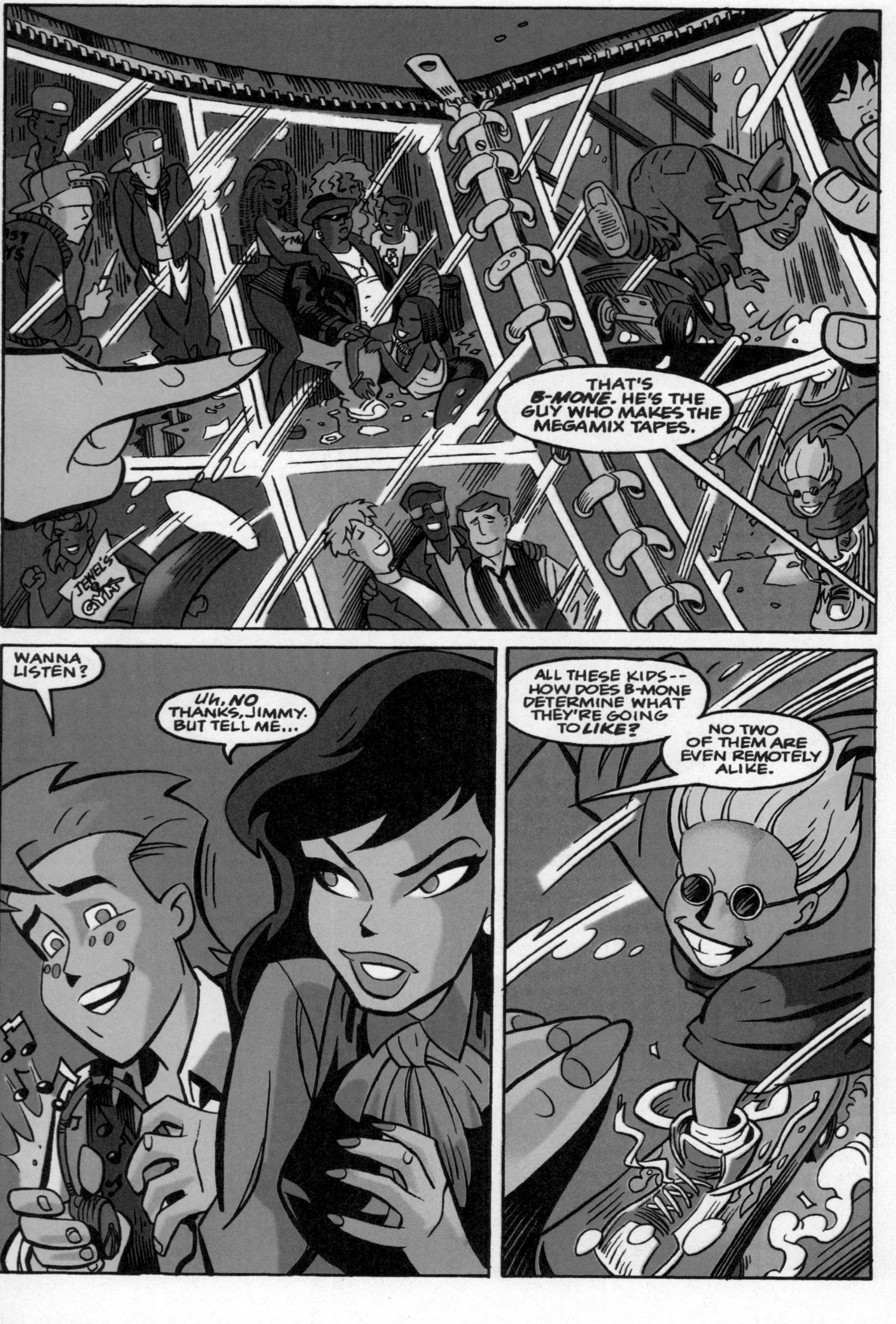
THAT'S B-MONE. HE'S THE GUY WHO MAKES THE MEGAMIX TAPES.
WANNA LISTEN?
Uh, NO THANKS, JIMMY. BUT TELL ME...
ALL THESE KIDS-- HOW DOES B-MONE DETERMINE WHAT THEY'RE GOING TO LIKE?
NO TWO OF THEM ARE EVEN REMOTELY ALIKE.

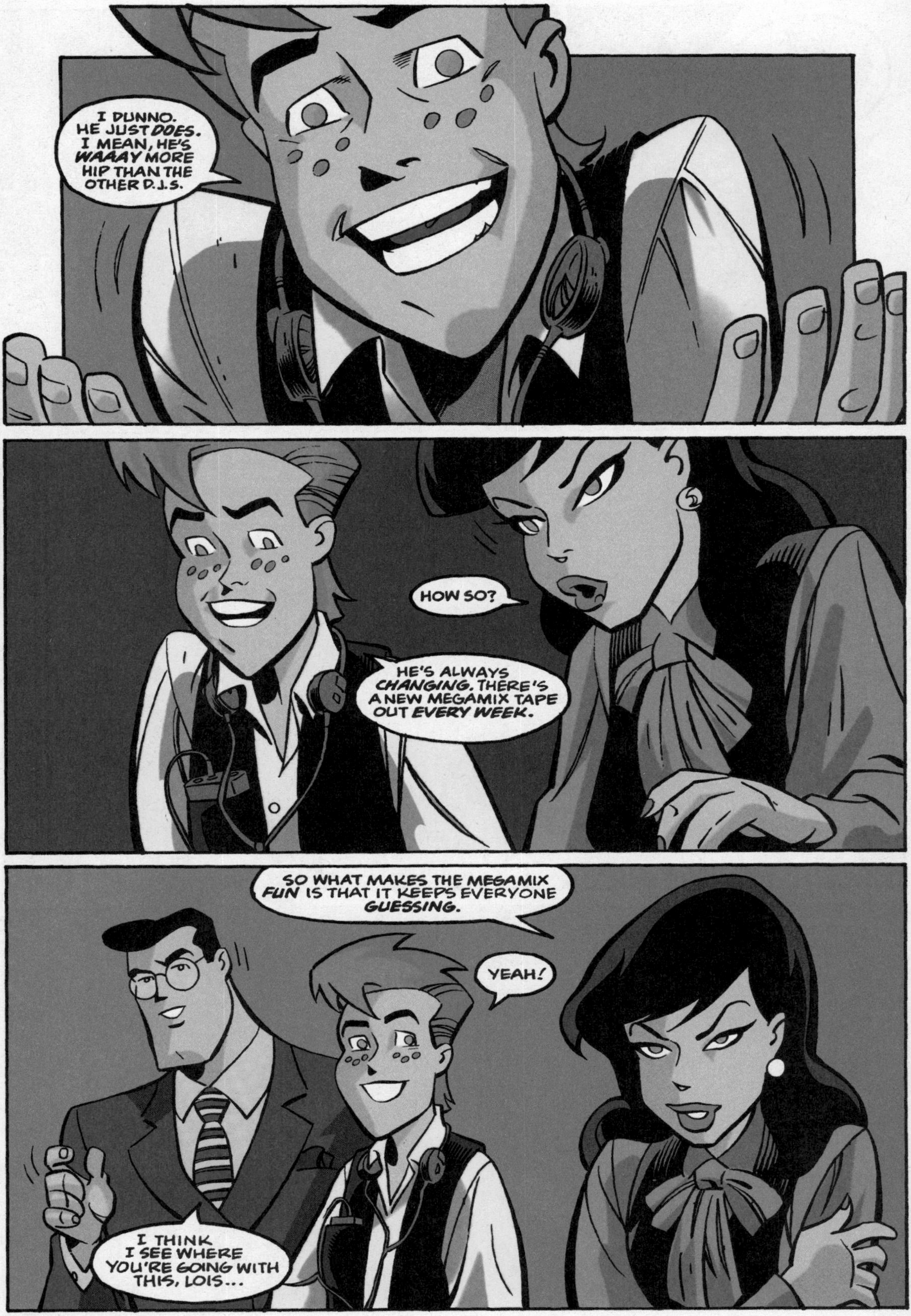
I DUNNO. HE JUST DOES. I MEAN, HE'S WAAAY MORE HIP THAN THE OTHER D.J.S.
HOW SO?
HE'S ALWAYS CHANGING. THERE'S A NEW MEGAMIX TAPE OUT EVERY WEEK.
SO WHAT MAKES THE MEGAMIX FUN IS THAT IT KEEPS EVERYONE GUESSING.
YEAH!
I THINK I SEE WHERE YOU'RE GOING WITH THIS, LOIS...

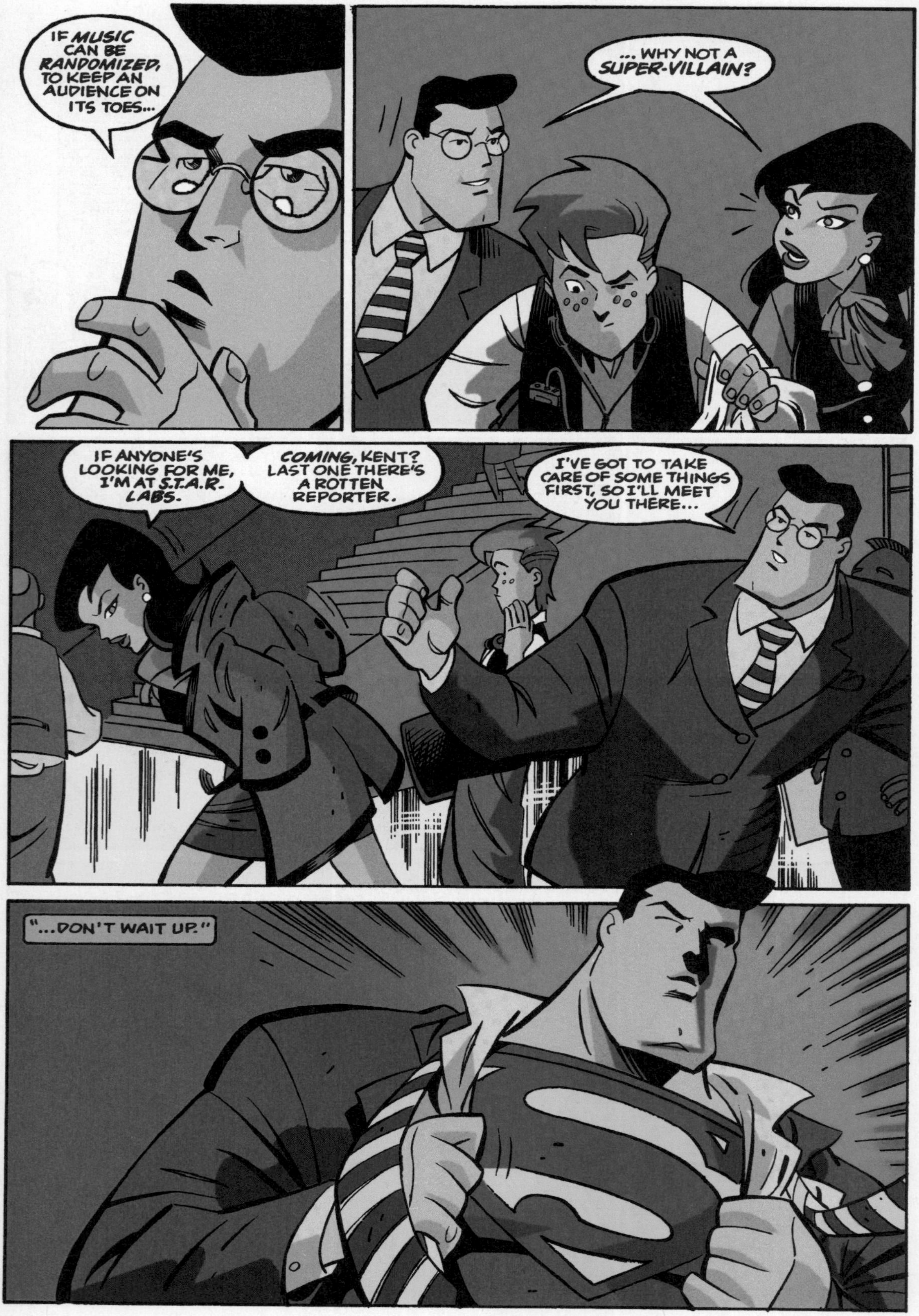

IF MUSIC CAN BE RANDOMIZED, TO KEEP AN AUDIENCE ON ITS TOES...
... WHY NOT A SUPER-VILLAIN?
IF ANYONE'S LOOKING FOR ME, I'M AT S.T.A.R. LABS.
COMING, KENT? LAST ONE THERE'S A ROTTEN REPORTER.
I'VE GOT TO TAKE CARE OF SOME THINGS FIRST, SO I'LL MEET YOU THERE...
"...DON'T WAIT UP."

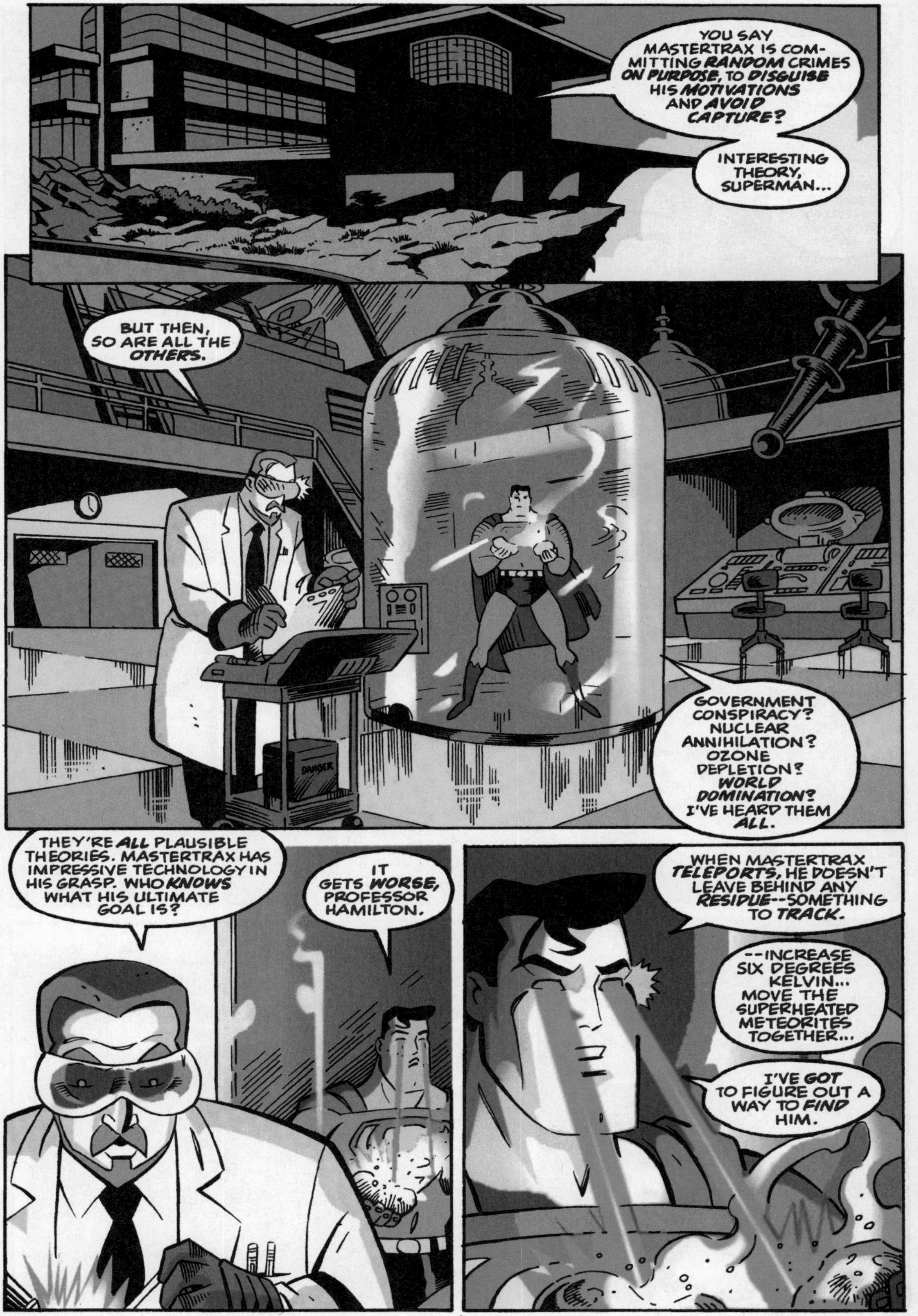
YOU SAY MASTERTRAX IS COM-MITTING RANDOM CRIMES ON PURPOSE, TO DISGUISE HIS MOTIVATIONS AND AVOID CAPTURE?
INTERESTING THEORY, SUPERMAN...
BUT THEN, SO ARE ALL THE OTHERS.
DANGER
GOVERNMENT CONSPIRACY? NUCLEAR ANNIHILATION? OZONE DEPLETION? WORLD DOMINATION? I'VE HEARD THEM ALL.
THEY'RE ALL PLAUSIBLE THEORIES. MASTERTRAX HAS IMPRESSIVE TECHNOLOGY IN HIS GRASP. WHO KNOWS WHAT HIS ULTIMATE GOAL IS?
IT GETS WORSE, PROFESSOR HAMILTON.
WHEN MASTERTRAX TELEPORTS, HE DOESN'T LEAVE BEHIND ANY RESIDUE--SOMETHING TO TRACK.
--INCREASE SIX DEGREES KELVIN... MOVE THE SUPERHEATED METEORITES TOGETHER...
I'VE GOT TO FIGURE OUT A WAY TO FIND HIM.

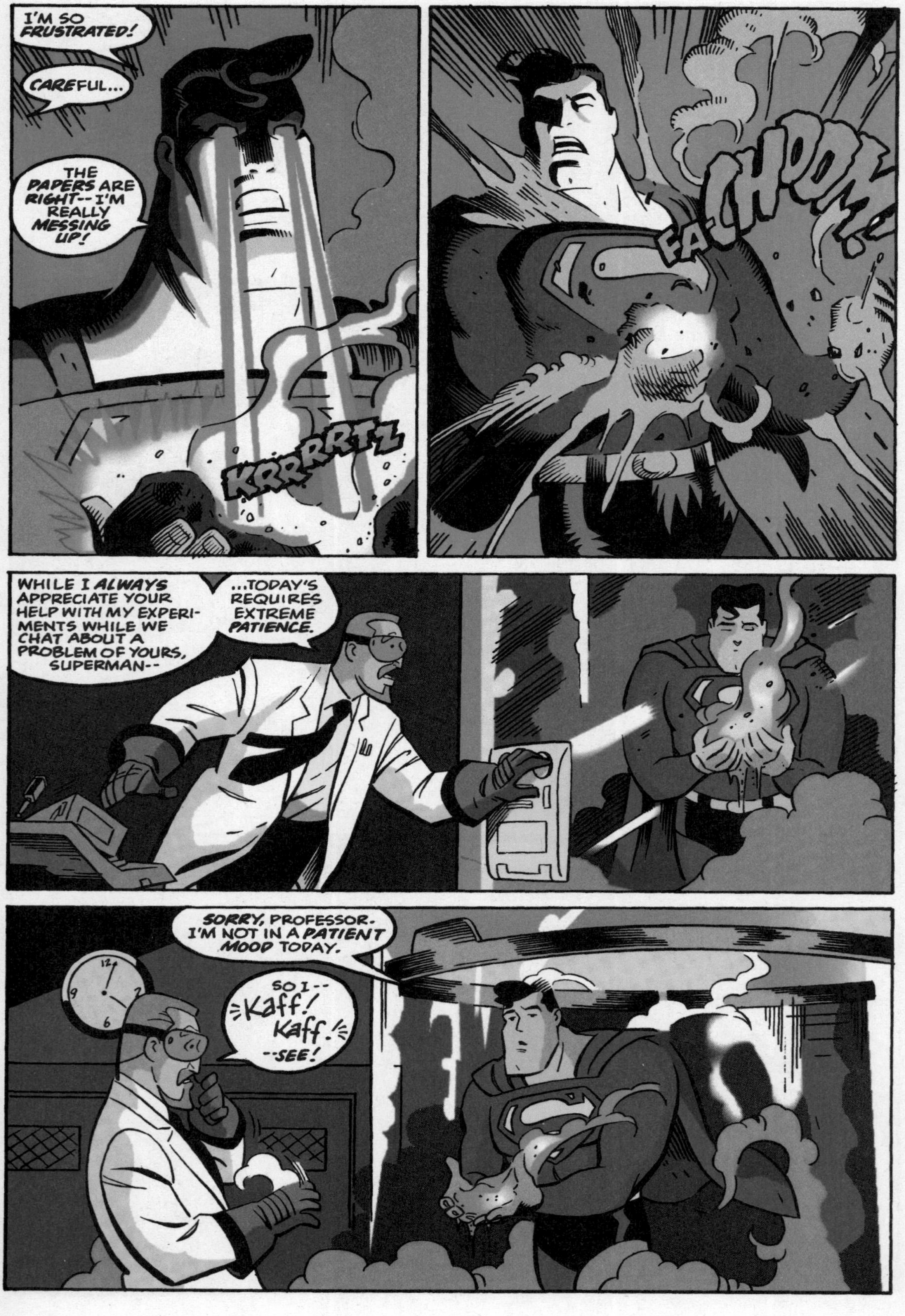
I'M SO FRUSTRATED!
CAREFUL...
THE PAPERS ARE RIGHT-- I'M REALLY MESSING UP!
KRRRRTZ
FA-CHOOM!
WHILE I ALWAYS APPRECIATE YOUR HELP WITH MY EXPERIMENTS WHILE WE CHAT ABOUT A PROBLEM OF YOURS, SUPERMAN--
...TODAY'S REQUIRES EXTREME PATIENCE.
SORRY, PROFESSOR. I'M NOT IN A PATIENT MOOD TODAY.
SO I-- Kaff! Kaff! --SEE!

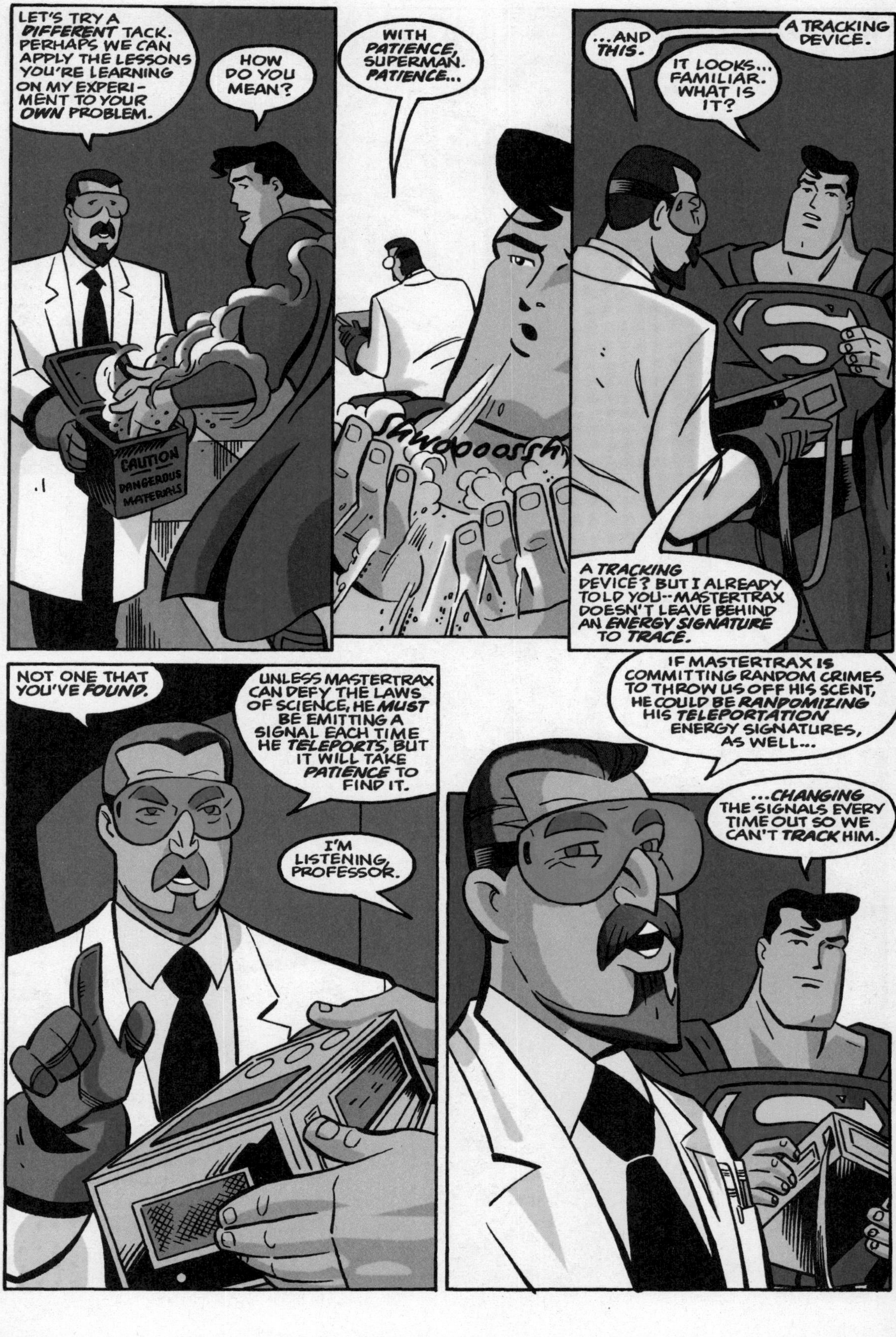
LET'S TRY A DIFFERENT TACK. PERHAPS WE CAN APPLY THE LESSONS YOU'RE LEARNING ON MY EXPERIMENT TO YOUR OWN PROBLEM.
HOW DO YOU MEAN?
CAUTION DANGEROUS MATERIALS
WITH PATIENCE, SUPERMAN. PATIENCE...
SHWOOOOOSSH
...AND THIS.
A TRACKING DEVICE.
IT LOOKS... FAMILIAR. WHAT IS IT?
A TRACKING DEVICE? BUT I ALREADY TOLD YOU--MASTERTRAX DOESN'T LEAVE BEHIND AN ENERGY SIGNATURE TO TRACE.
NOT ONE THAT YOU'VE FOUND.
UNLESS MASTERTRAX CAN DEFY THE LAWS OF SCIENCE, HE MUST BE EMITTING A SIGNAL EACH TIME HE TELEPORTS, BUT IT WILL TAKE PATIENCE TO FIND IT.
I'M LISTENING, PROFESSOR.
IF MASTERTRAX IS COMMITTING RANDOM CRIMES TO THROW US OFF HIS SCENT, HE COULD BE RANDOMIZING HIS TELEPORTATION ENERGY SIGNATURES, AS WELL...
...CHANGING THE SIGNALS EVERY TIME OUT SO WE CAN'T TRACK HIM.

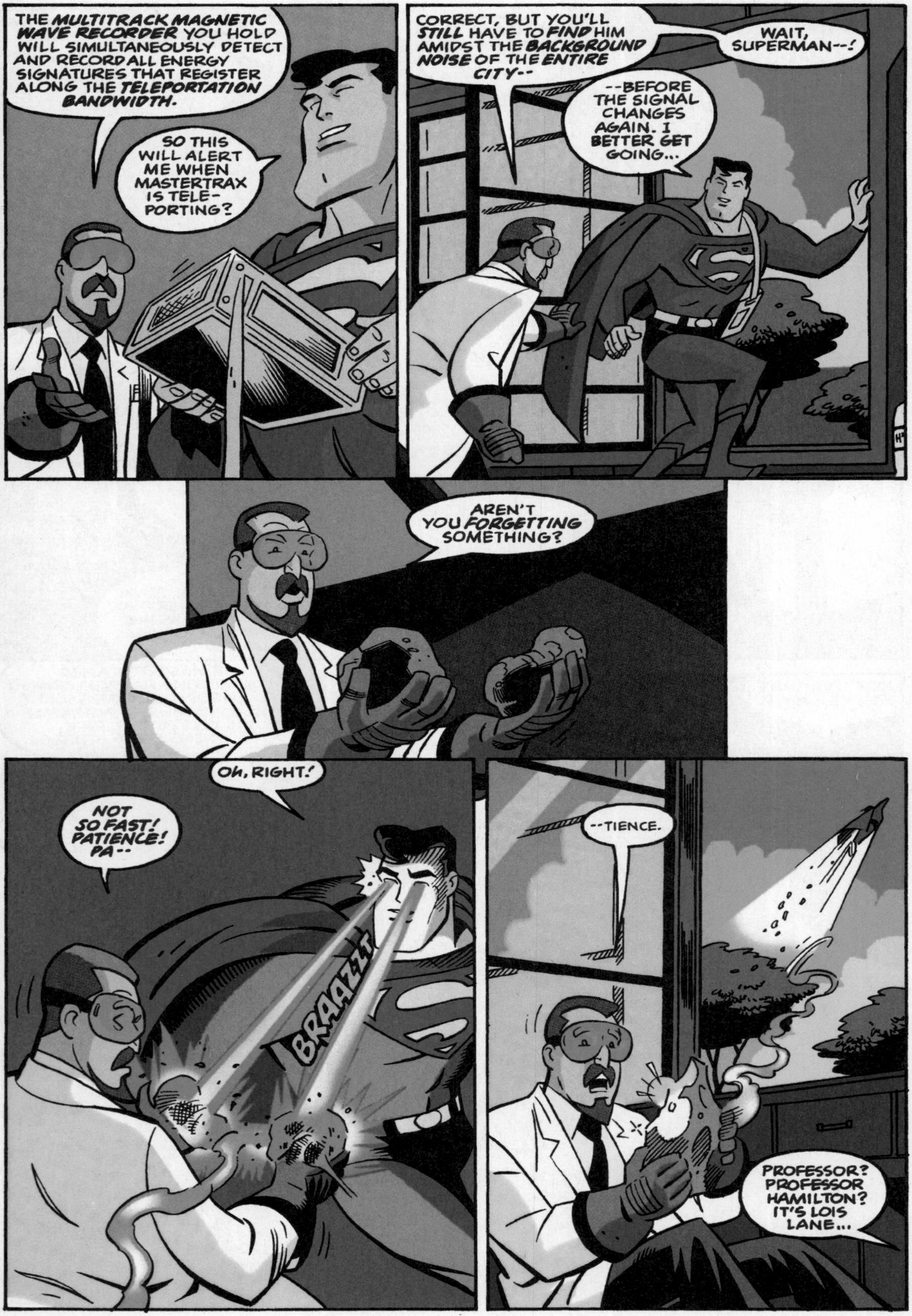
THE MULTITRACK MAGNETIC WAVE RECORDER YOU HOLD WILL SIMULTANEOUSLY DETECT AND RECORD ALL ENERGY SIGNATURES THAT REGISTER ALONG THE TELEPORTATION BANDWIDTH.
SO THIS WILL ALERT ME WHEN MASTERTRAX IS TELE-PORTING?
CORRECT, BUT YOU'LL STILL HAVE TO FIND HIM AMIDST THE BACKGROUND NOISE OF THE ENTIRE CITY--
--BEFORE THE SIGNAL CHANGES AGAIN. I BETTER GET GOING...
WAIT, SUPERMAN--!
AREN'T YOU FORGETTING SOMETHING?
OH, RIGHT!
NOT SO FAST! PATIENCE! PA--
BRAAZZZT
--TIENCE.
PROFESSOR? PROFESSOR HAMILTON? IT'S LOIS LANE...

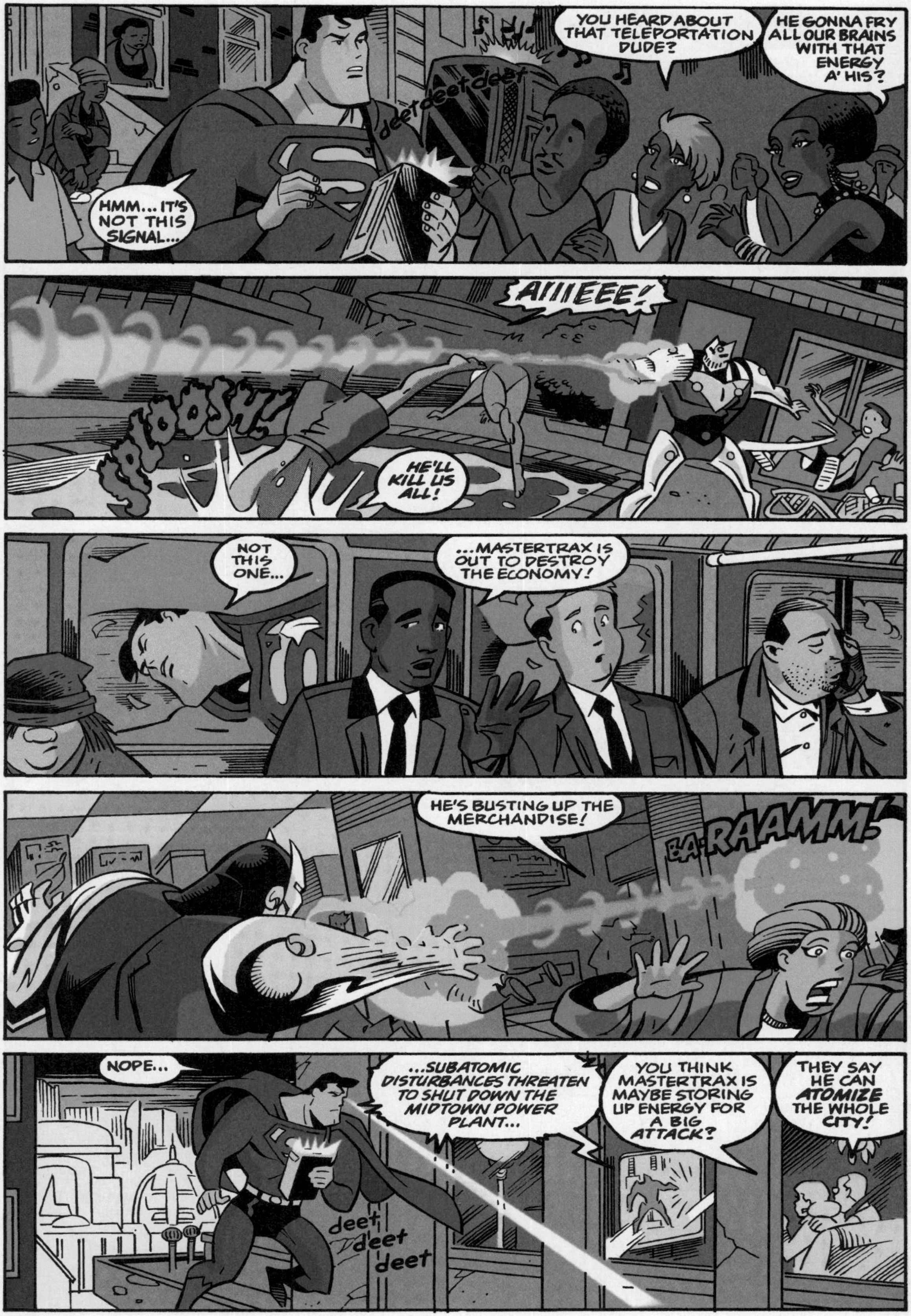
YOU HEARD ABOUT THAT TELEPORTATION DUDE?
HE GONNA FRY ALL OUR BRAINS WITH THAT ENERGY A' HIS?
deetdeetdeet
HMM... IT'S NOT THIS SIGNAL...
AIIIEEE!
SPLOOSH!
HE'LL KILL US ALL!
NOT THIS ONE...
...MASTERTRAX IS OUT TO DESTROY THE ECONOMY!
HE'S BUSTING UP THE MERCHANDISE!
BA-RAAMM!
NOPE...
...SUBATOMIC DISTURBANCES THREATEN TO SHUT DOWN THE MIDTOWN POWER PLANT...
YOU THINK MASTERTRAX IS MAYBE STORING UP ENERGY FOR A BIG ATTACK?
THEY SAY HE CAN ATOMIZE THE WHOLE CITY!
deet deet deet

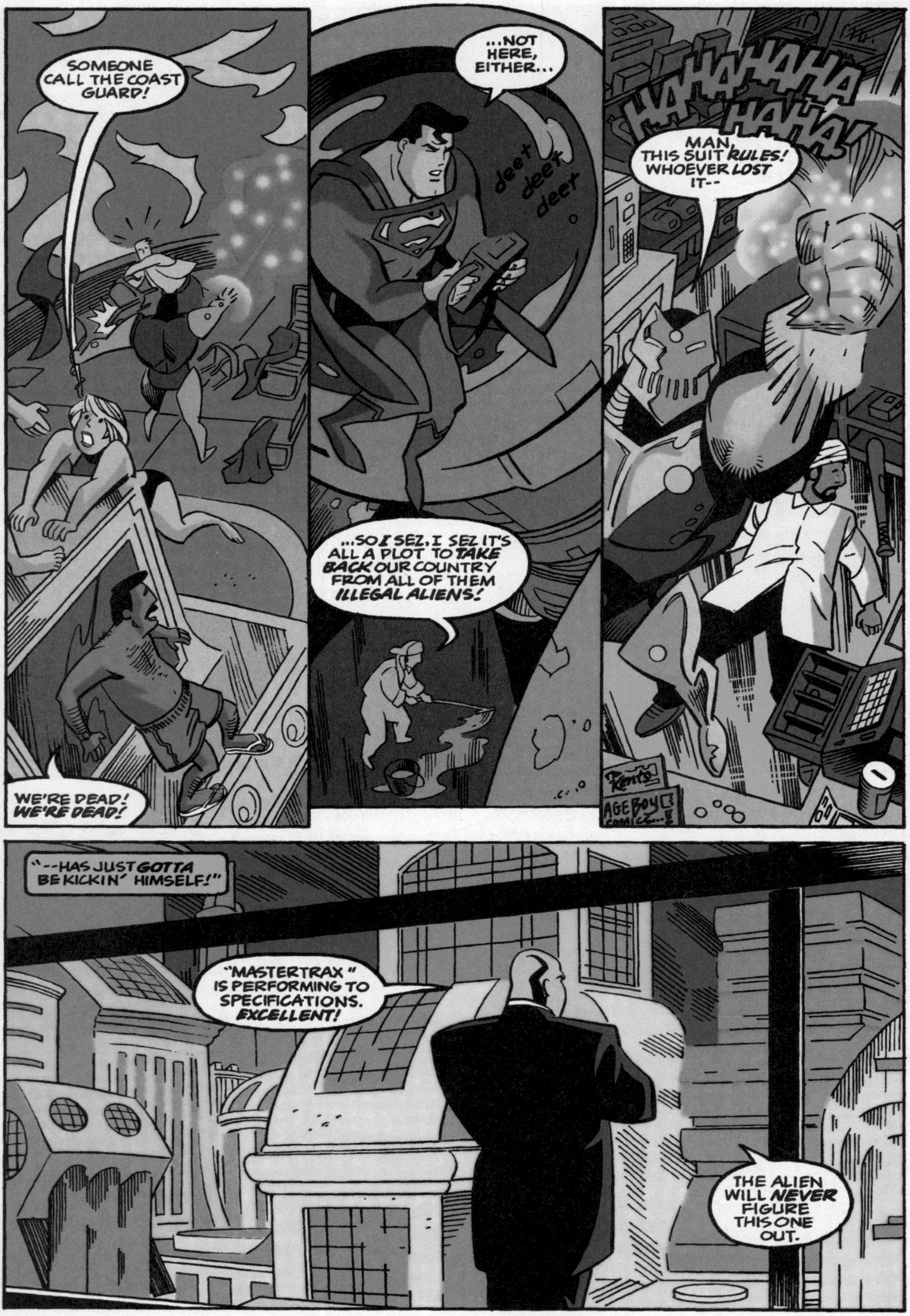
SOMEONE CALL THE COAST GUARD!
WE'RE DEAD! WE'RE DEAD!
...NOT HERE, EITHER...
deet deet deet
...SO I SEZ, I SEZ IT'S ALL A PLOT TO TAKE BACK OUR COUNTRY FROM ALL OF THEM ILLEGAL ALIENS!
HAHAHAHA HAHAHA!
MAN, THIS SUIT RULES! WHOEVER LOST IT--
Kent's
AGE BOY COMICS
"--HAS JUST GOTTA BE KICKIN' HIMSELF!"
"MASTERTRAX" IS PERFORMING TO SPECIFICATIONS. EXCELLENT!
THE ALIEN WILL NEVER FIGURE THIS ONE OUT.

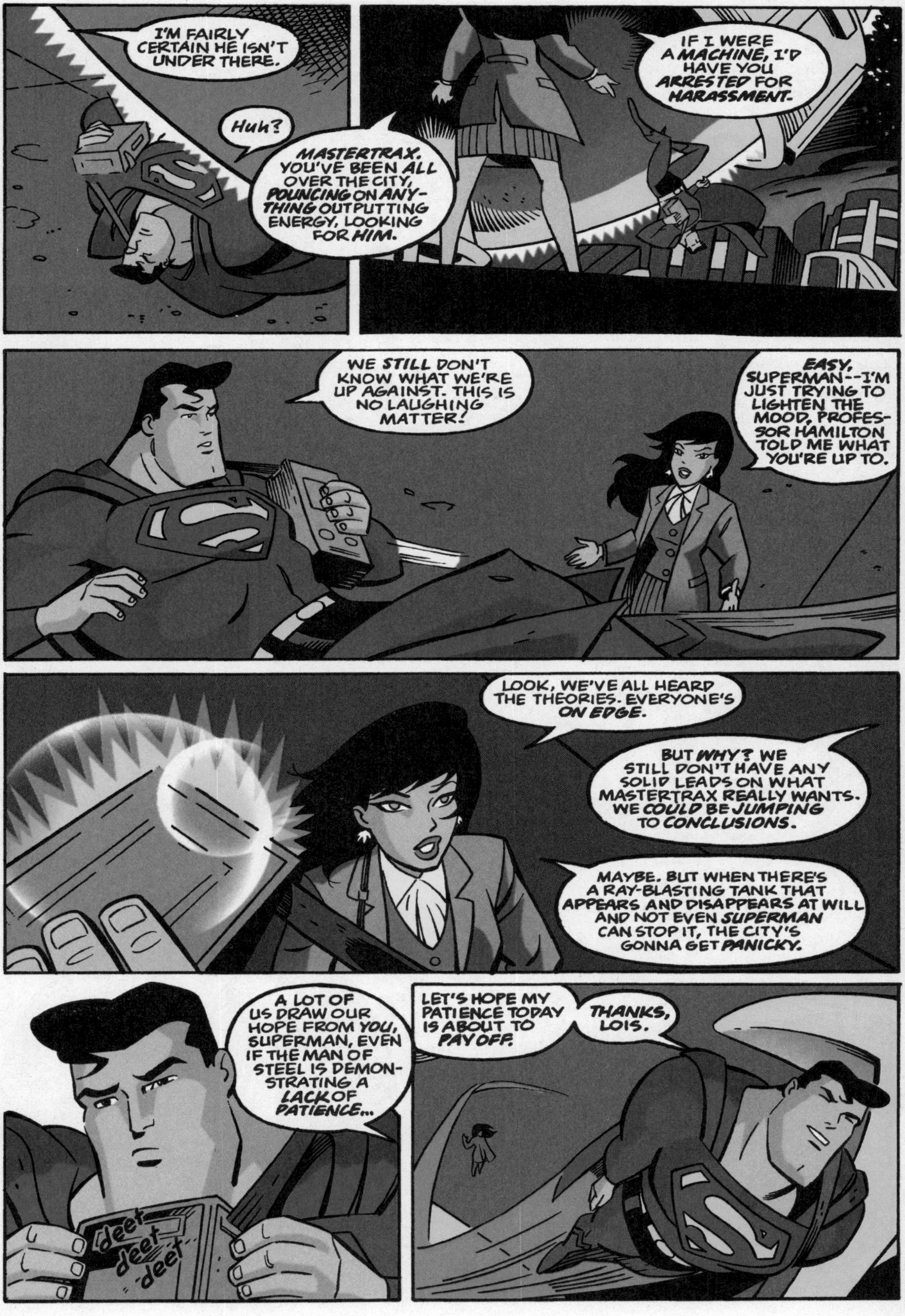
I'M FAIRLY CERTAIN HE ISN'T UNDER THERE.
Huh?
MASTERTRAX. YOU'VE BEEN ALL OVER THE CITY, POUNCING ON ANYTHING OUTPUTTING ENERGY, LOOKING FOR HIM.
IF I WERE A MACHINE, I'D HAVE YOU ARRESTED FOR HARASSMENT.
WE STILL DON'T KNOW WHAT WE'RE UP AGAINST. THIS IS NO LAUGHING MATTER!
EASY, SUPERMAN--I'M JUST TRYING TO LIGHTEN THE MOOD. PROFESSOR HAMILTON TOLD ME WHAT YOU'RE UP TO.
LOOK, WE'VE ALL HEARD THE THEORIES. EVERYONE'S ON EDGE.
BUT WHY? WE STILL DON'T HAVE ANY SOLID LEADS ON WHAT MASTERTRAX REALLY WANTS. WE COULD BE JUMPING TO CONCLUSIONS.
MAYBE. BUT WHEN THERE'S A RAY-BLASTING TANK THAT APPEARS AND DISAPPEARS AT WILL AND NOT EVEN SUPERMAN CAN STOP IT, THE CITY'S GONNA GET PANICKY.
A LOT OF US DRAW OUR HOPE FROM YOU, SUPERMAN, EVEN IF THE MAN OF STEEL IS DEMONSTRATING A LACK OF PATIENCE...
deet deet deet
LET'S HOPE MY PATIENCE TODAY IS ABOUT TO PAY OFF.
THANKS, LOIS.

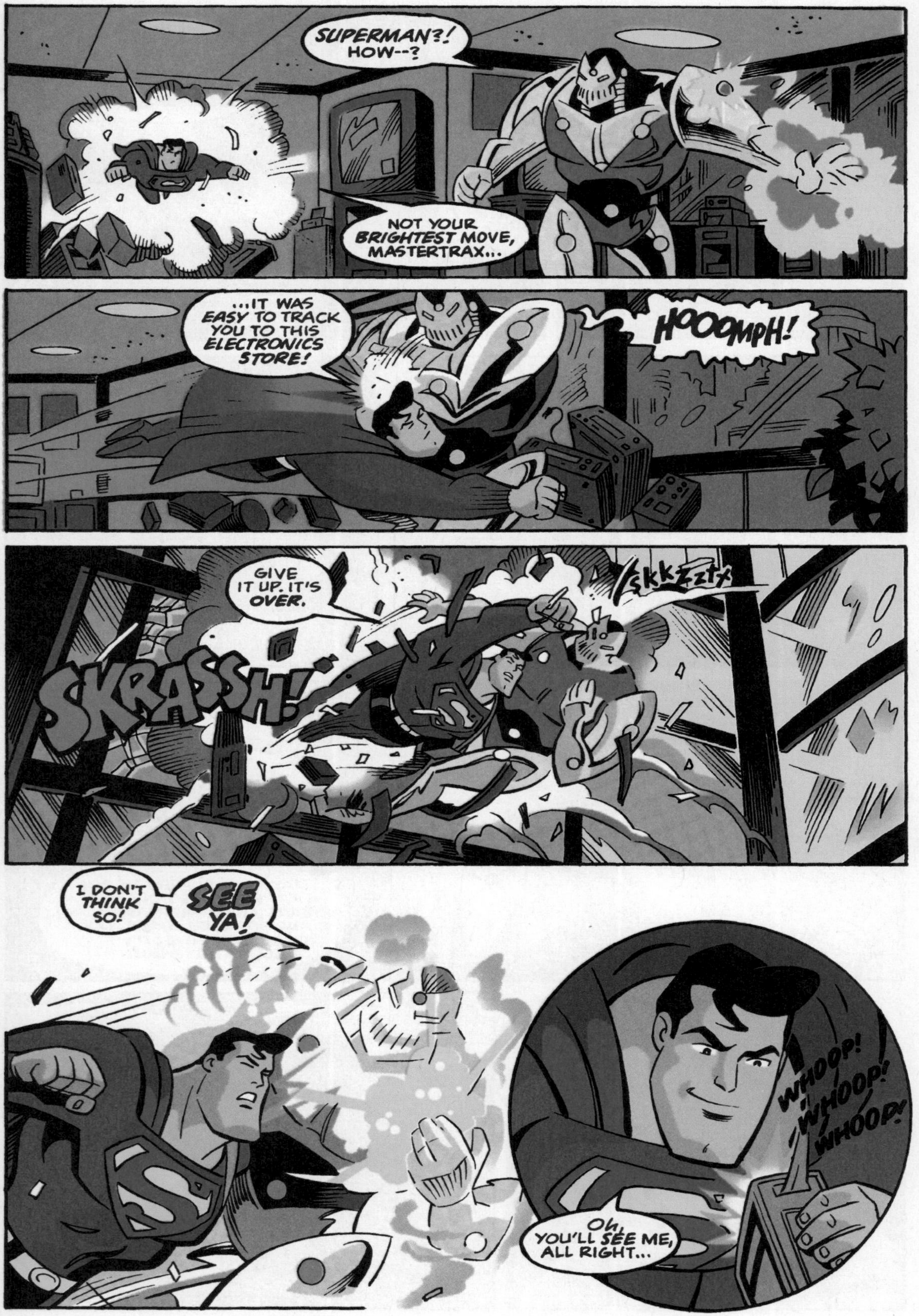
SUPERMAN?! HOW--?
NOT YOUR BRIGHTEST MOVE, MASTERTRAX...
...IT WAS EASY TO TRACK YOU TO THIS ELECTRONICS STORE!
HOOOMPH!
GIVE IT UP. IT'S OVER.
SKKZZZT
SKRASSH!
I DON'T THINK SO!
SEE YA!
WHOOP! WHOOP! WHOOP!
OH, YOU'LL SEE ME, ALL RIGHT...

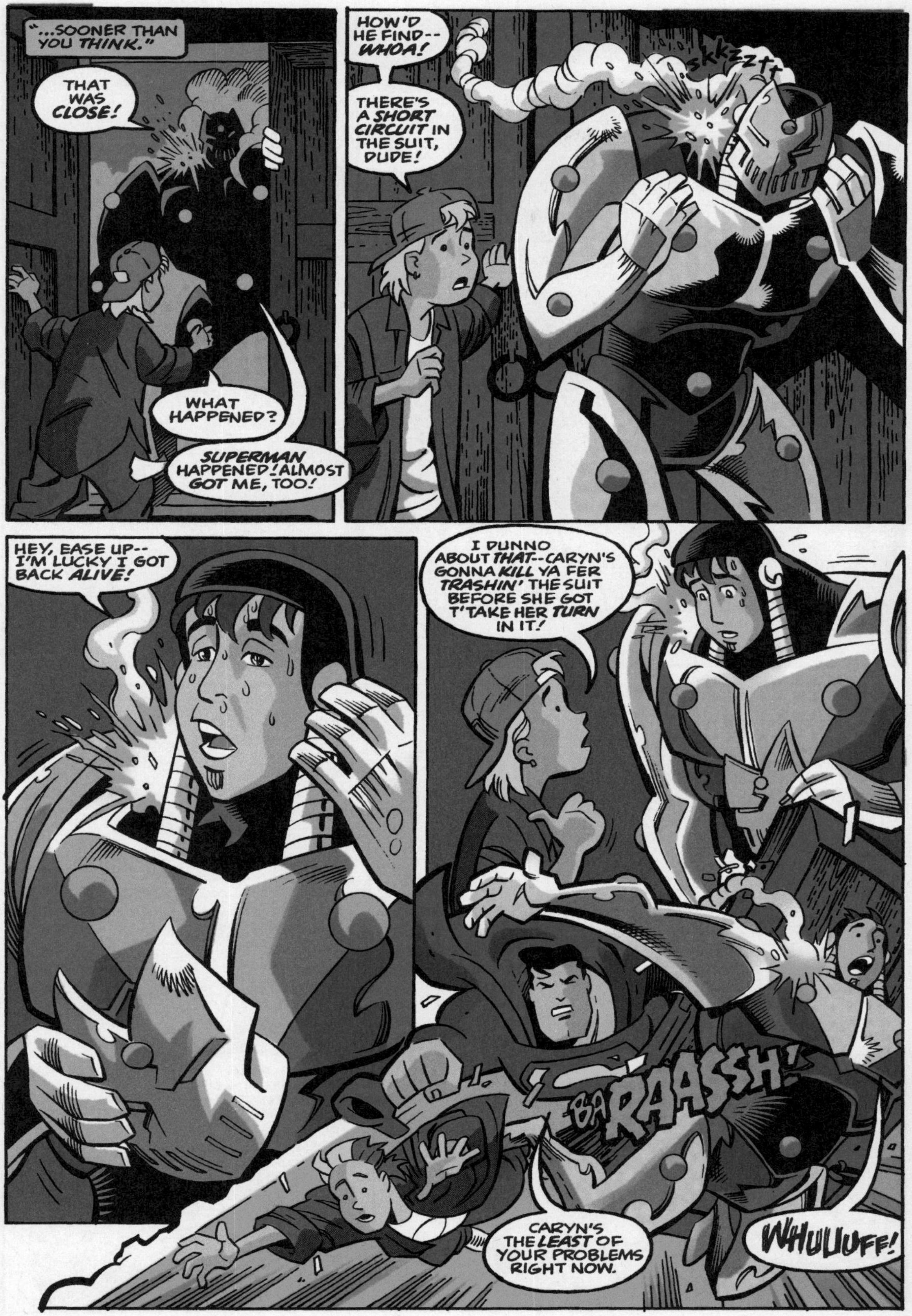

"...SOONER THAN YOU THINK."
THAT WAS CLOSE!
WHAT HAPPENED?
SUPERMAN HAPPENED! ALMOST GOT ME, TOO!
HOW'D HE FIND-- WHOA!
THERE'S A SHORT CIRCUIT IN THE SUIT, DUDE!
SKKZZTT
HEY, EASE UP-- I'M LUCKY I GOT BACK ALIVE!
I DUNNO ABOUT THAT--CARYN'S GONNA KILL YA FER TRASHIN' THE SUIT BEFORE SHE GOT T'TAKE HER TURN IN IT!
BA RAASSH!
CARYN'S THE LEAST OF YOUR PROBLEMS RIGHT NOW.
WHUUUFF!

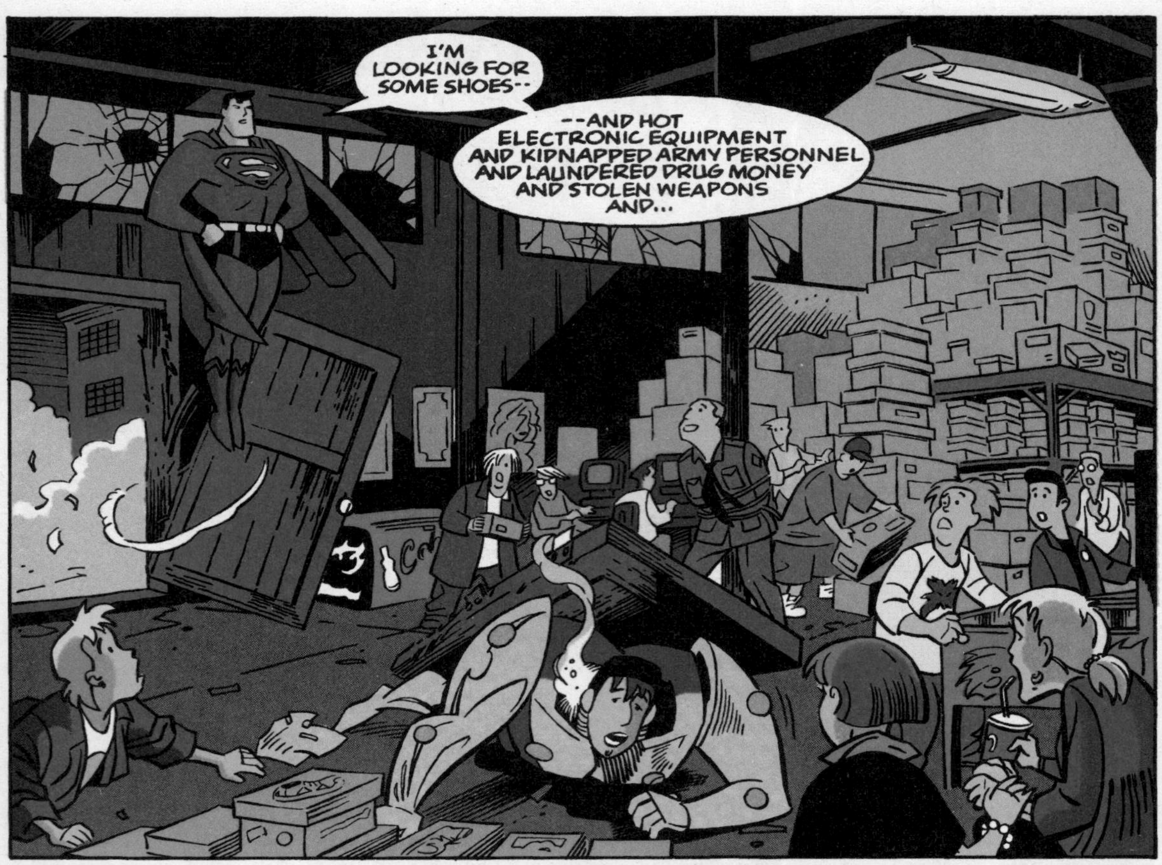
I'M LOOKING FOR SOME SHOES--
--AND HOT ELECTRONIC EQUIPMENT AND KIDNAPPED ARMY PERSONNEL AND LAUNDERED DRUG MONEY AND STOLEN WEAPONS AND...

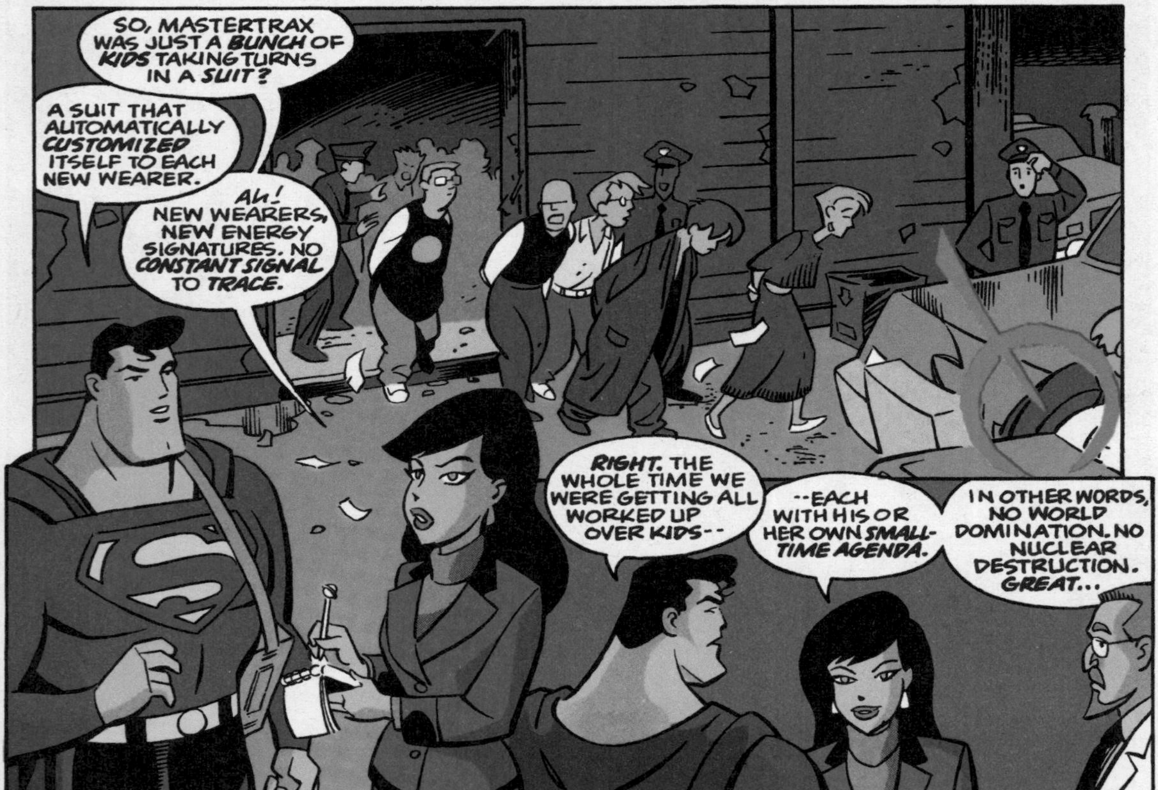
SO, MASTERTRAX WAS JUST A BUNCH OF KIDS TAKING TURNS IN A SUIT?
A SUIT THAT AUTOMATICALLY CUSTOMIZED ITSELF TO EACH NEW WEARER.
AH! NEW WEARERS, NEW ENERGY SIGNATURES. NO CONSTANT SIGNAL TO TRACE.
RIGHT. THE WHOLE TIME WE WERE GETTING ALL WORKED UP OVER KIDS--
--EACH WITH HIS OR HER OWN SMALL-TIME AGENDA.
IN OTHER WORDS, NO WORLD DOMINATION. NO NUCLEAR DESTRUCTION. GREAT...

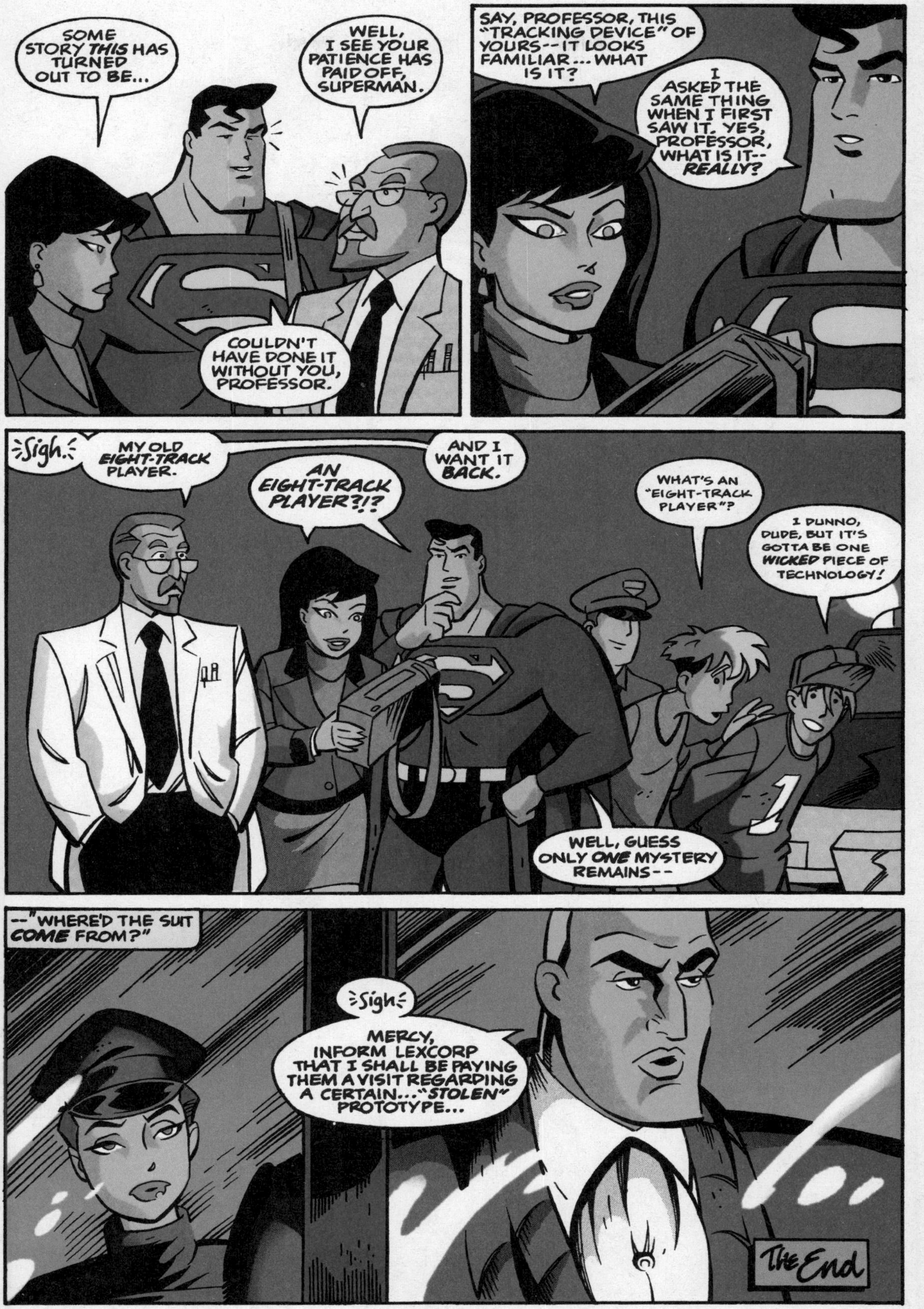
SOME STORY THIS HAS TURNED OUT TO BE...
WELL, I SEE YOUR PATIENCE HAS PAID OFF, SUPERMAN.
COULDN'T HAVE DONE IT WITHOUT YOU, PROFESSOR.
SAY, PROFESSOR, THIS "TRACKING DEVICE" OF YOURS--IT LOOKS FAMILIAR... WHAT IS IT?
I ASKED THE SAME THING WHEN I FIRST SAW IT. YES, PROFESSOR, WHAT IS IT--REALLY?
Sigh.
MY OLD EIGHT-TRACK PLAYER.
AND I WANT IT BACK.
AN EIGHT-TRACK PLAYER?!?
WHAT'S AN "EIGHT-TRACK PLAYER"?
I DUNNO, DUDE, BUT IT'S GOTTA BE ONE WICKED PIECE OF TECHNOLOGY!
WELL, GUESS ONLY ONE MYSTERY REMAINS--
--"WHERE'D THE SUIT COME FROM?"
Sigh
MERCY, INFORM LEXCORP THAT I SHALL BE PAYING THEM A VISIT REGARDING A CERTAIN..."STOLEN" PROTOTYPE...
The End

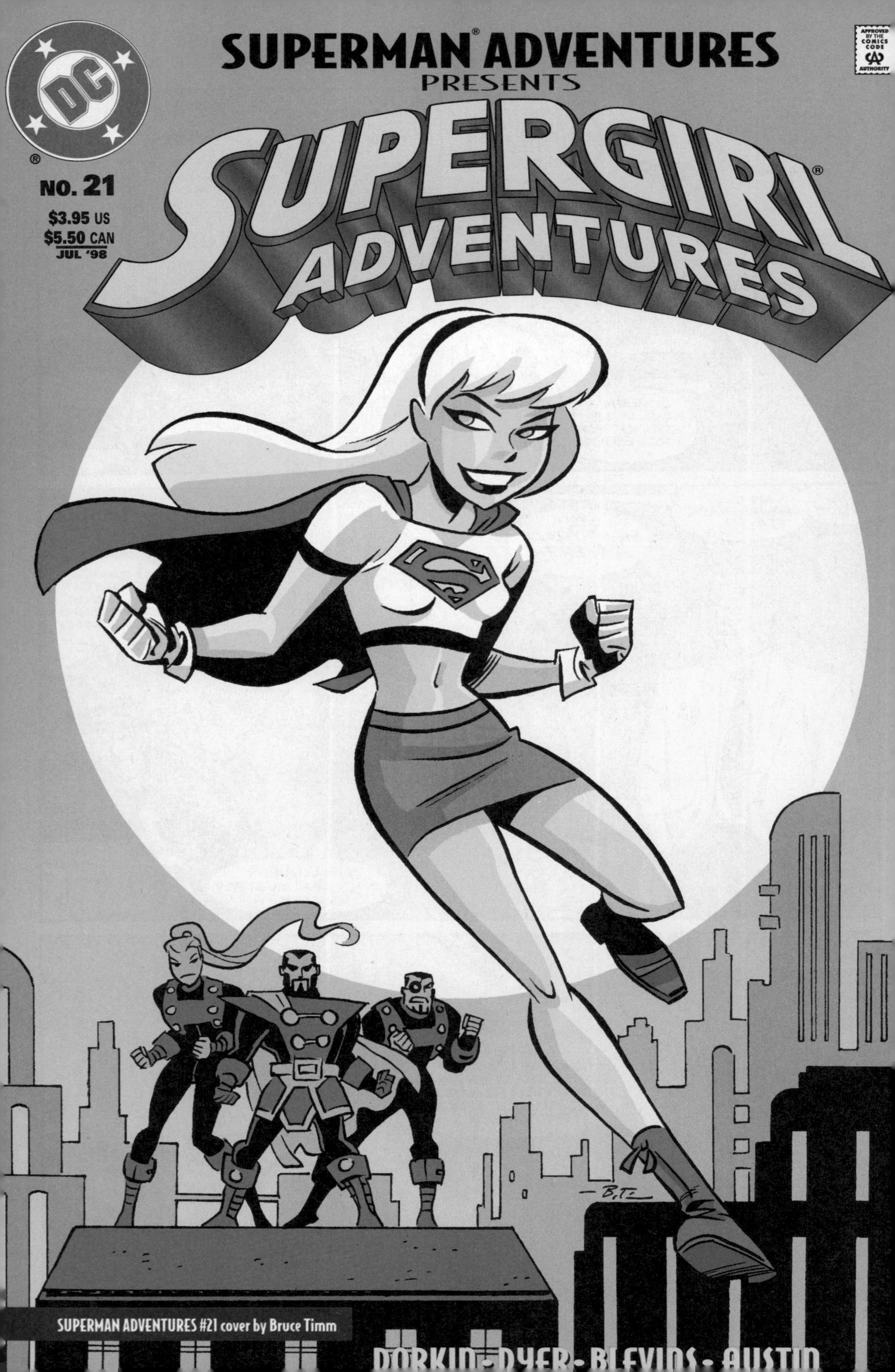
SUPERMAN® ADVENTURES
PRESENTS
SUPERGIRL®
ADVENTURES
DC
NO. 21
$3.95 US
$5.50 CAN
JUL '98
APPROVED BY THE COMICS CODE AUTHORITY
DORKIN • DYER • BLEVINS • AUSTIN
SUPERMAN ADVENTURES #21 cover by Bruce Timm

LAST DAUGHTER OF ARGO

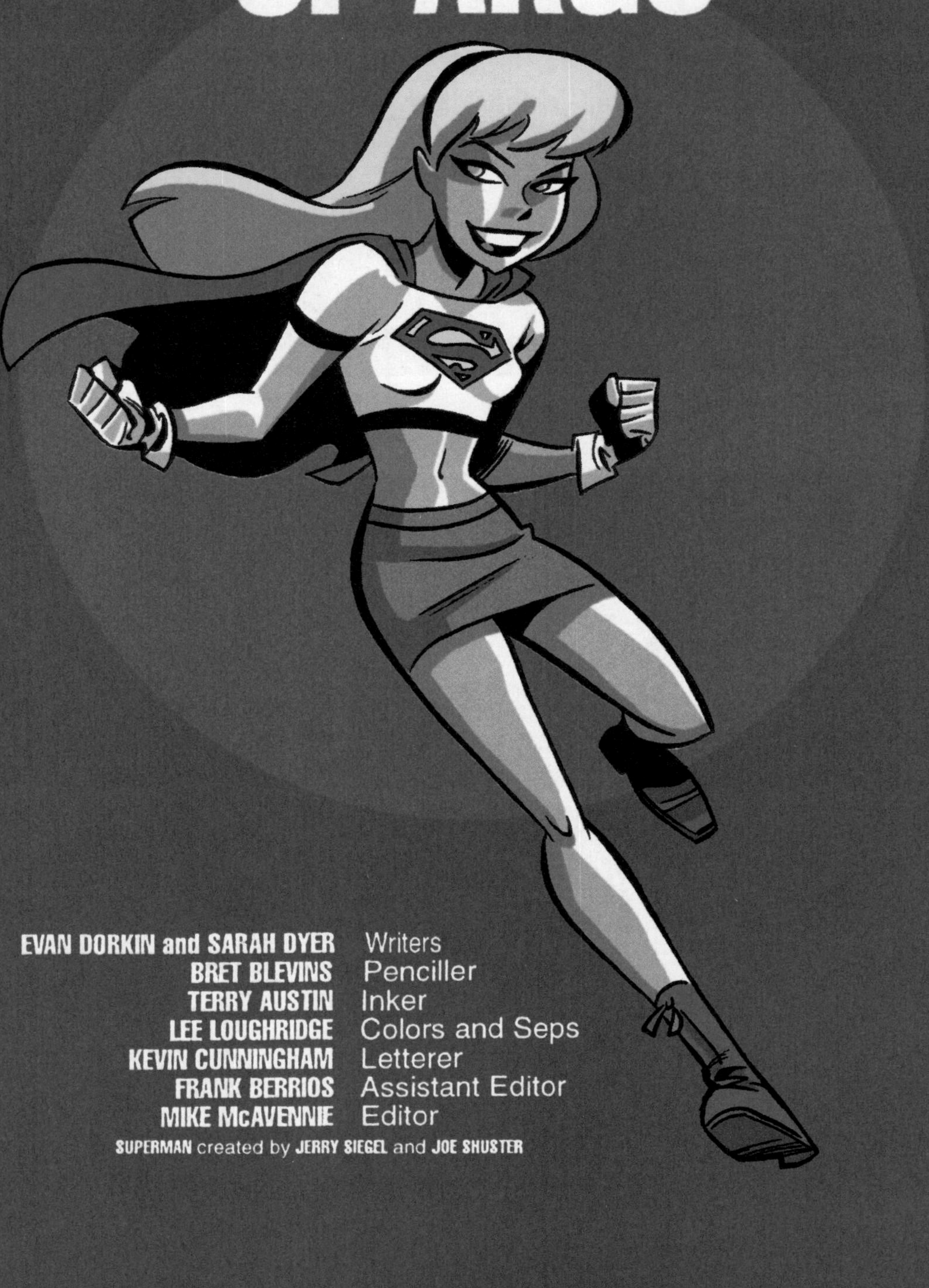

EVAN DORKIN and SARAH DYER Writers
BRET BLEVINS Penciller
TERRY AUSTIN Inker
LEE LOUGHRIDGE Colors and Seps
KEVIN CUNNINGHAM Letterer
FRANK BERRIOS Assistant Editor
MIKE McAVENNIE Editor

SUPERMAN created by **JERRY SIEGEL** and **JOE SHUSTER**

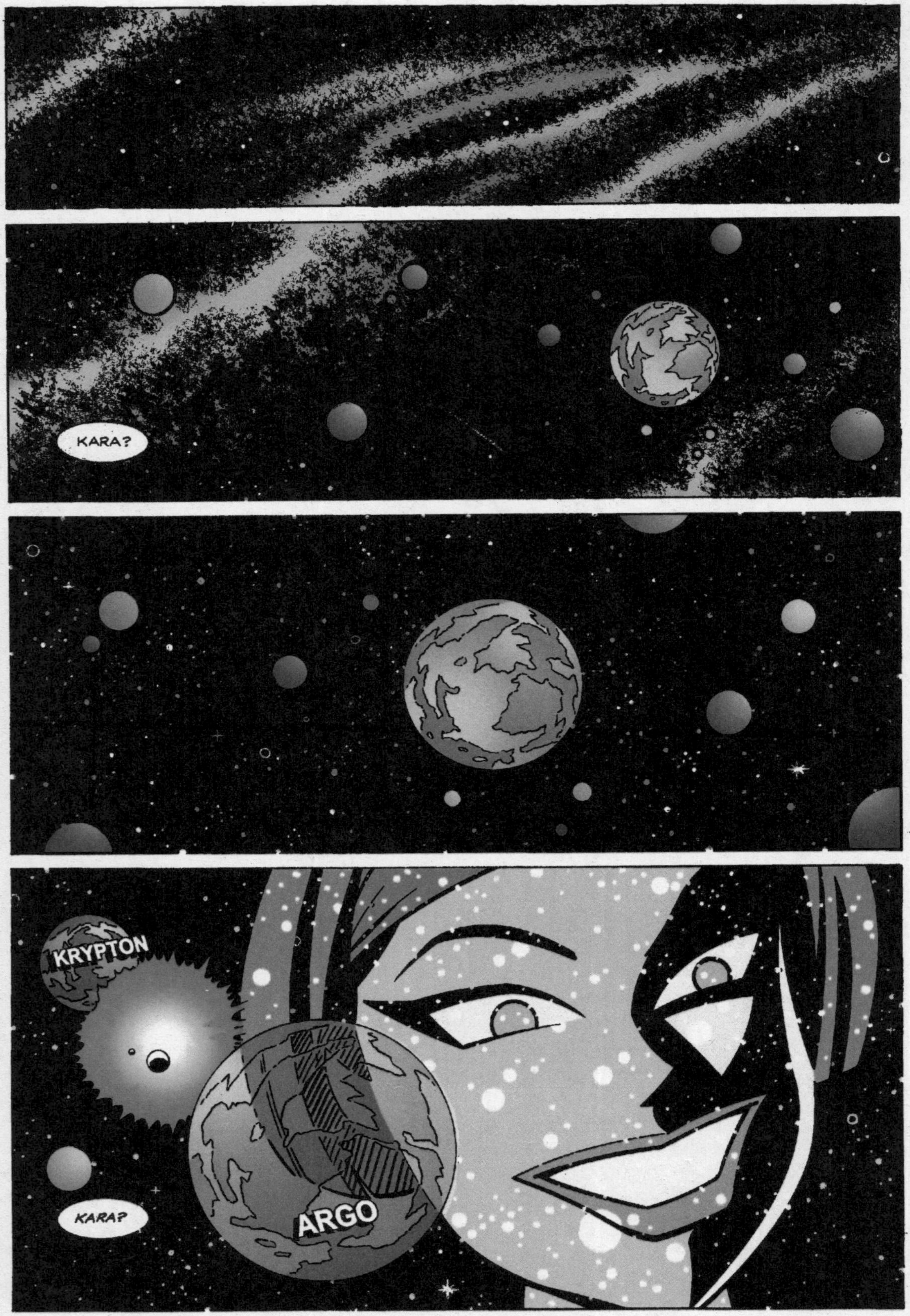
KARA?
KRYPTON
ARGO
KARA?

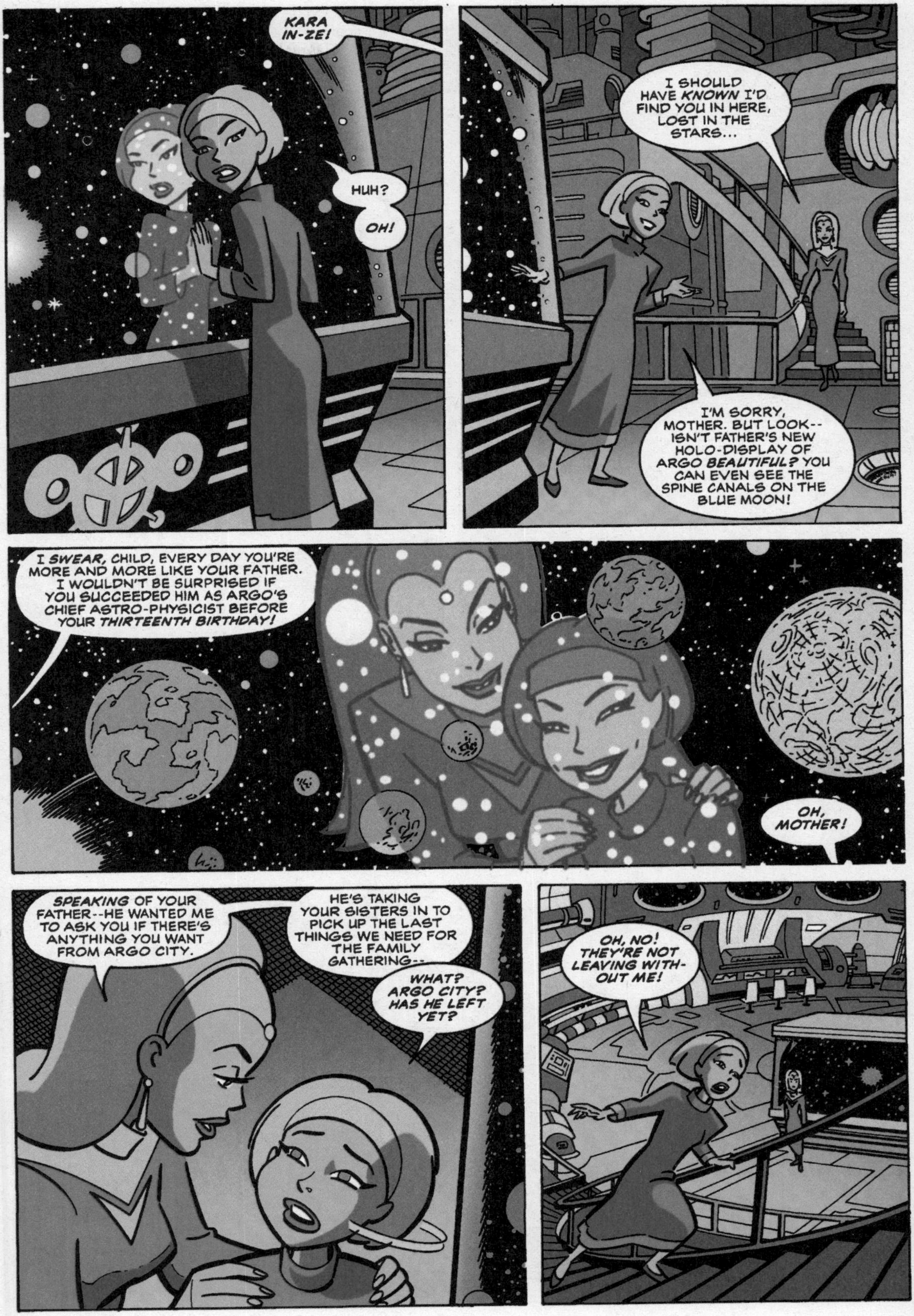
KARA IN-ZE!
HUH?
OH!
I SHOULD HAVE KNOWN I'D FIND YOU IN HERE, LOST IN THE STARS...
I'M SORRY, MOTHER. BUT LOOK-- ISN'T FATHER'S NEW HOLO-DISPLAY OF ARGO BEAUTIFUL? YOU CAN EVEN SEE THE SPINE CANALS ON THE BLUE MOON!
I SWEAR, CHILD, EVERY DAY YOU'RE MORE AND MORE LIKE YOUR FATHER. I WOULDN'T BE SURPRISED IF YOU SUCCEEDED HIM AS ARGO'S CHIEF ASTRO-PHYSICIST BEFORE YOUR THIRTEENTH BIRTHDAY!
OH, MOTHER!
SPEAKING OF YOUR FATHER--HE WANTED ME TO ASK YOU IF THERE'S ANYTHING YOU WANT FROM ARGO CITY.
HE'S TAKING YOUR SISTERS IN TO PICK UP THE LAST THINGS WE NEED FOR THE FAMILY GATHERING--
WHAT? ARGO CITY? HAS HE LEFT YET?
OH, NO! THEY'RE NOT LEAVING WITH-OUT ME!

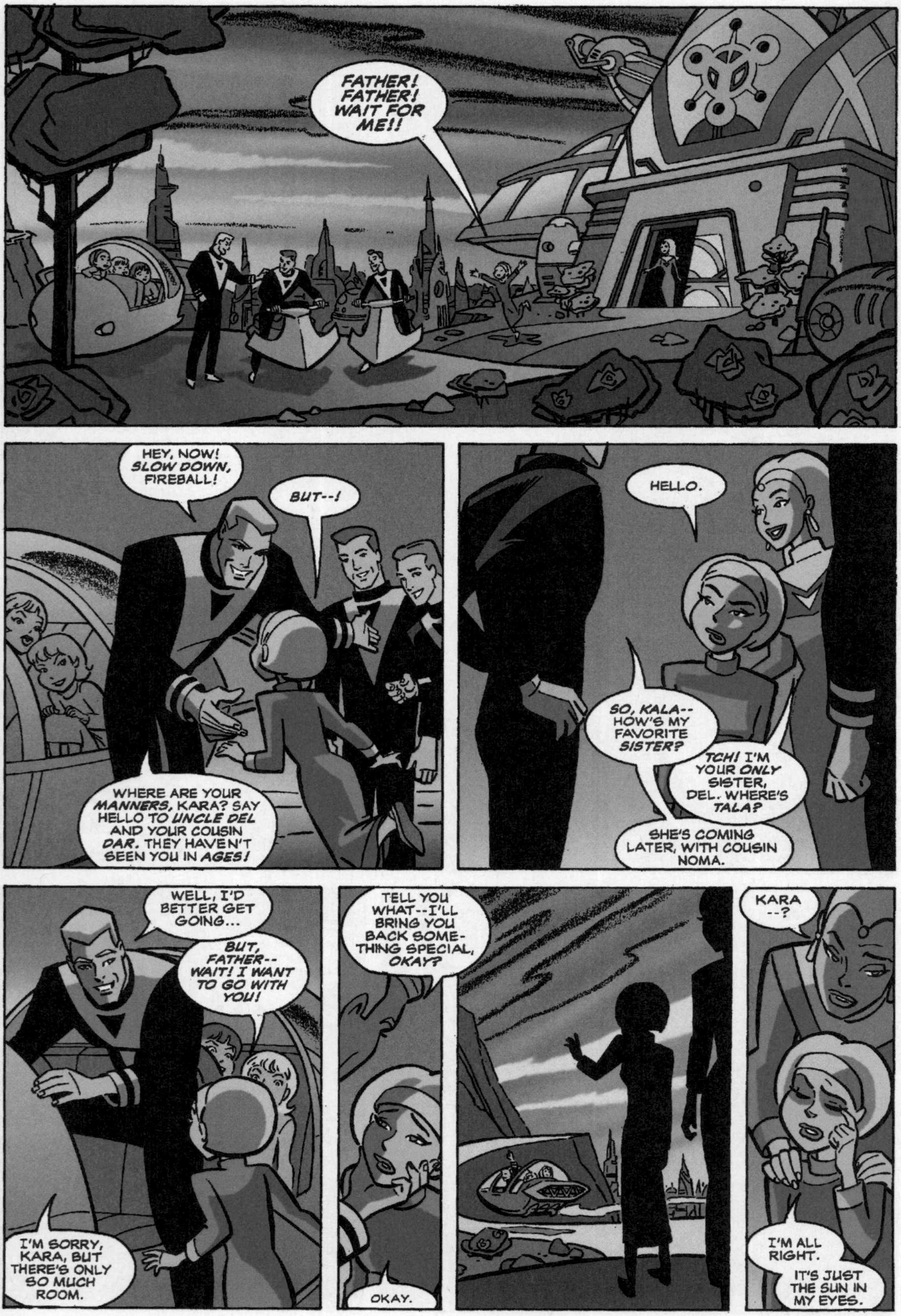
FATHER! FATHER! WAIT FOR ME!!
HEY, NOW! SLOW DOWN, FIREBALL!
BUT--!
WHERE ARE YOUR MANNERS, KARA? SAY HELLO TO UNCLE DEL AND YOUR COUSIN DAR. THEY HAVEN'T SEEN YOU IN AGES!
HELLO.
SO, KALA--HOW'S MY FAVORITE SISTER?
TCH! I'M YOUR ONLY SISTER, DEL. WHERE'S TALA?
SHE'S COMING LATER, WITH COUSIN NOMA.
WELL, I'D BETTER GET GOING...
BUT, FATHER--WAIT! I WANT TO GO WITH YOU!
I'M SORRY, KARA, BUT THERE'S ONLY SO MUCH ROOM.
TELL YOU WHAT--I'LL BRING YOU BACK SOME-THING SPECIAL, OKAY?
OKAY.
KARA--?
I'M ALL RIGHT.
IT'S JUST THE SUN IN MY EYES.

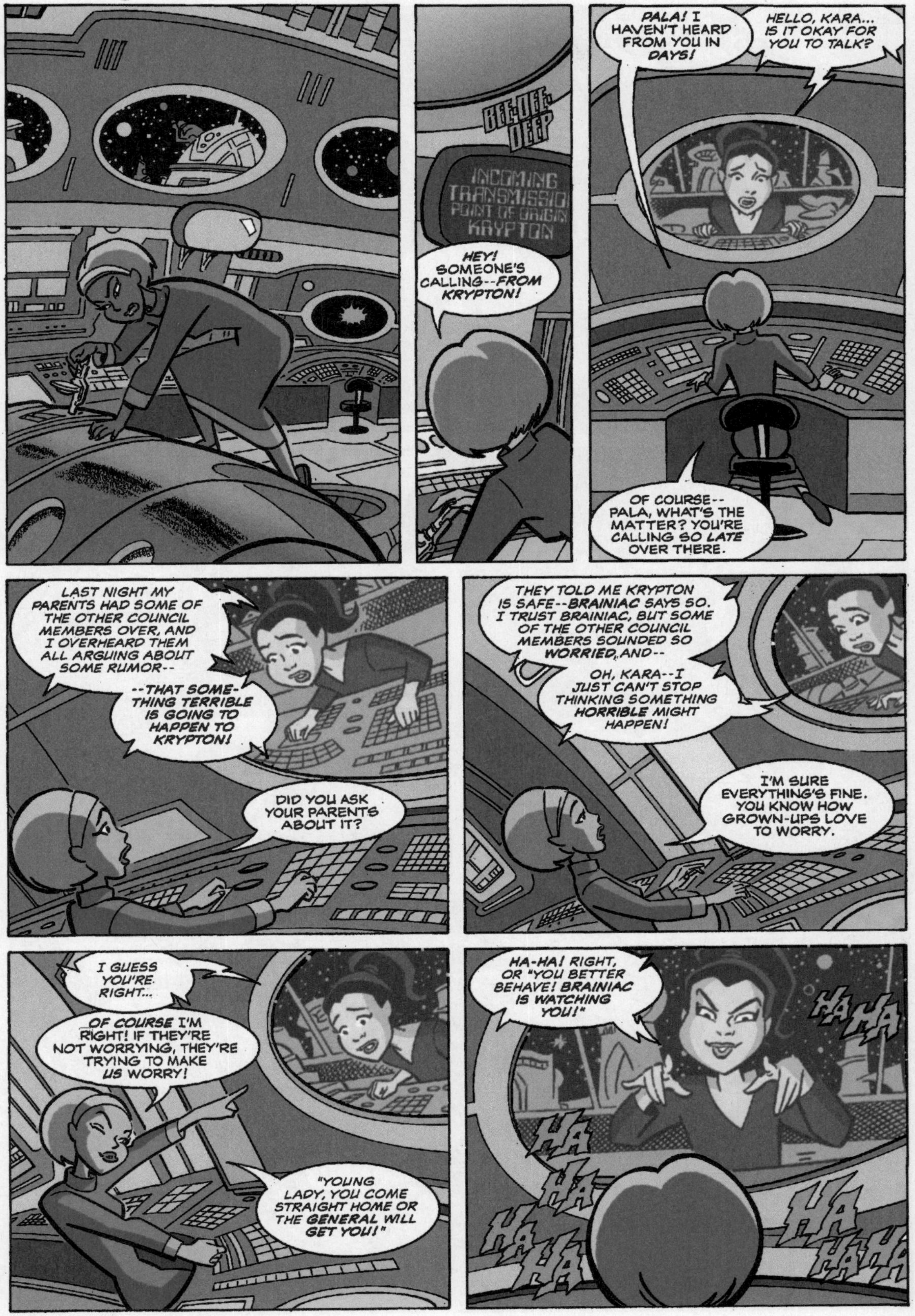
BEE-DEE-DEEP
INCOMING
TRANSMISSIO
POINT OF ORIGIN
KRYPTON
HEY! SOMEONE'S CALLING--FROM KRYPTON!
PALA! I HAVEN'T HEARD FROM YOU IN DAYS!
HELLO, KARA... IS IT OKAY FOR YOU TO TALK?
OF COURSE--PALA, WHAT'S THE MATTER? YOU'RE CALLING SO LATE OVER THERE.
LAST NIGHT MY PARENTS HAD SOME OF THE OTHER COUNCIL MEMBERS OVER, AND I OVERHEARD THEM ALL ARGUING ABOUT SOME RUMOR--
--THAT SOMETHING TERRIBLE IS GOING TO HAPPEN TO KRYPTON!
DID YOU ASK YOUR PARENTS ABOUT IT?
THEY TOLD ME KRYPTON IS SAFE--BRAINIAC SAYS SO. I TRUST BRAINIAC, BUT SOME OF THE OTHER COUNCIL MEMBERS SOUNDED SO WORRIED, AND--
OH, KARA--I JUST CAN'T STOP THINKING SOMETHING HORRIBLE MIGHT HAPPEN!
I'M SURE EVERYTHING'S FINE. YOU KNOW HOW GROWN-UPS LOVE TO WORRY.
I GUESS YOU'RE RIGHT...
OF COURSE I'M RIGHT! IF THEY'RE NOT WORRYING, THEY'RE TRYING TO MAKE US WORRY!
"YOUNG LADY, YOU COME STRAIGHT HOME OR THE GENERAL WILL GET YOU!"
HA-HA! RIGHT, OR "YOU BETTER BEHAVE! BRAINIAC IS WATCHING YOU!"
HA HA
HA HA HA HA
HA HA HA

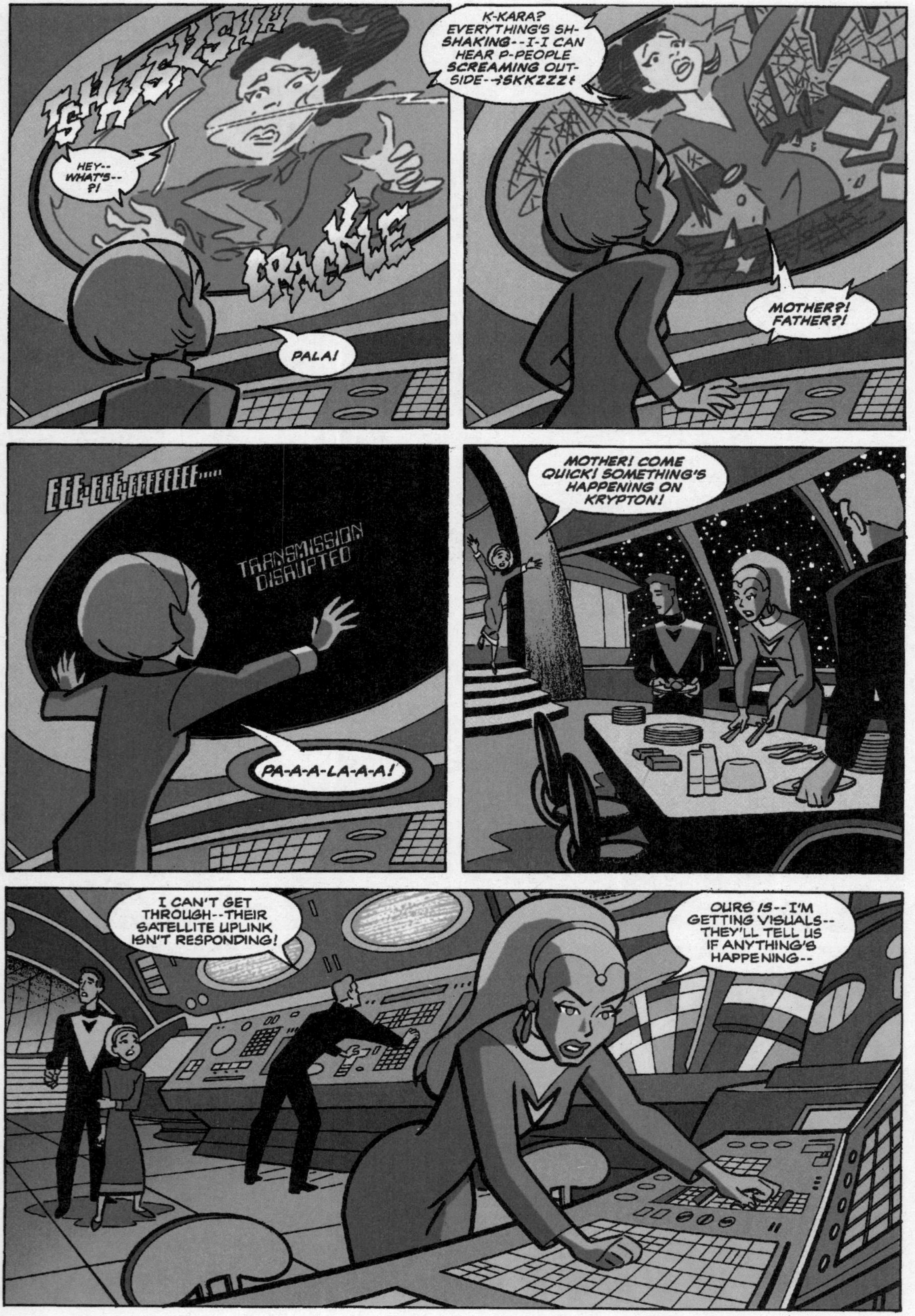
SHUSKSHH
HEY--
WHAT'S--
?!
CRACKLE
PALA!
K-KARA?
EVERYTHING'S SH-
SHAKING--I-I CAN
HEAR P-PEOPLE
SCREAMING OUT-
SIDE--‡SKKZZZ‡
MOTHER?!
FATHER?!
EEE-EEE-EEEEEEE.....
TRANSMISSION
DISRUPTED
PA-A-A-LA-A-A!
MOTHER! COME
QUICK! SOMETHING'S
HAPPENING ON
KRYPTON!
I CAN'T GET
THROUGH--THEIR
SATELLITE UPLINK
ISN'T RESPONDING!
OURS IS--I'M
GETTING VISUALS--
THEY'LL TELL US
IF ANYTHING'S
HAPPENING--

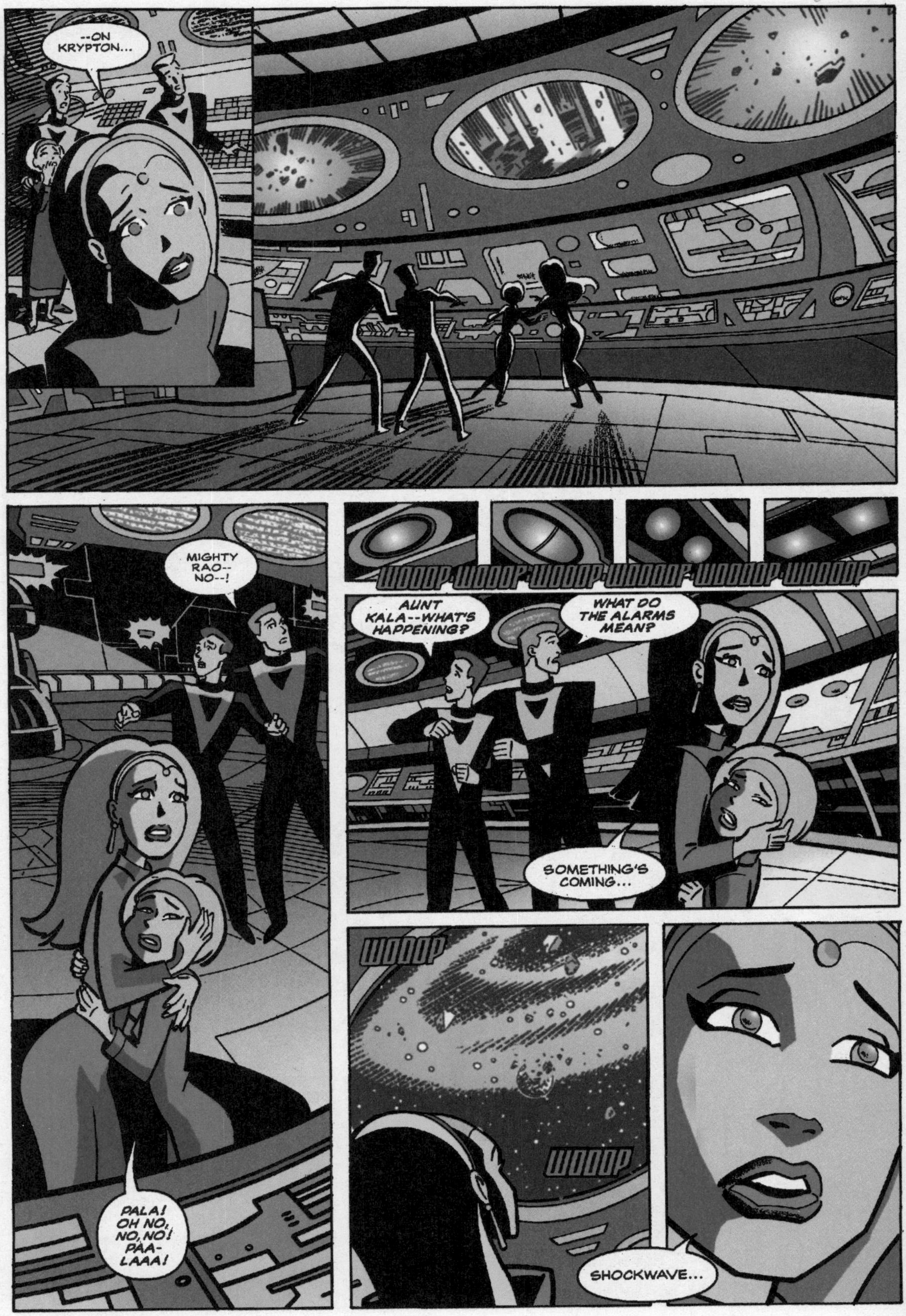
--ON KRYPTON...
MIGHTY RAO-- NO--!
PALA! OH NO, NO, NO! PAA-LAAA!
WOOOP WOOOP WOOOP WOOOP WOOOP WOOOP
AUNT KALA--WHAT'S HAPPENING?
WHAT DO THE ALARMS MEAN?
SOMETHING'S COMING...
WOOOP
WOOOP
SHOCKWAVE...

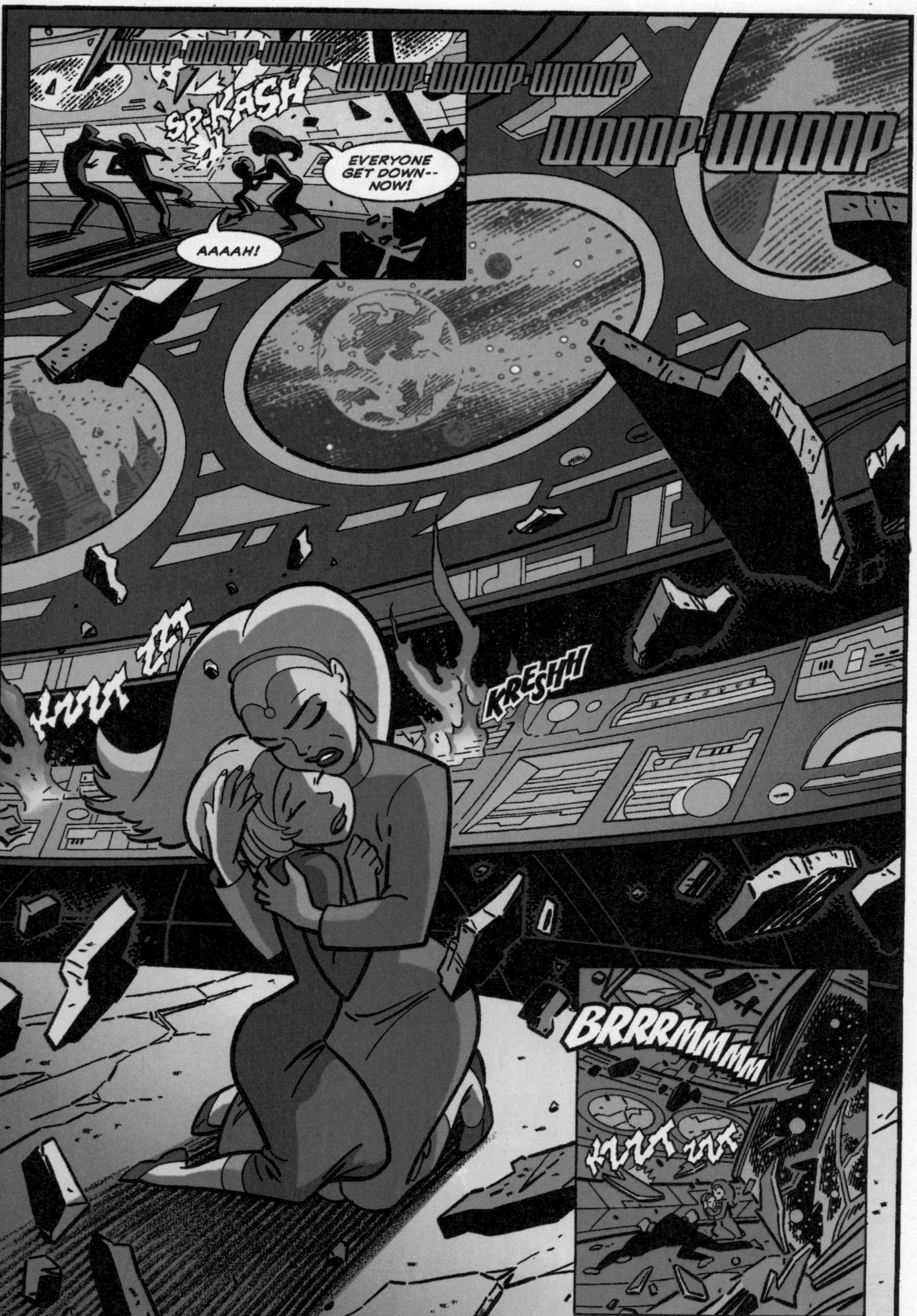
WOOOP-WOOOP-WOOOP
WOOOP-WOOOP-WOOOP
WOOOP-WOOOP
SP-KASH
EVERYONE GET DOWN--NOW!
AAAAH!
KRESHH
BRRRMMMMM

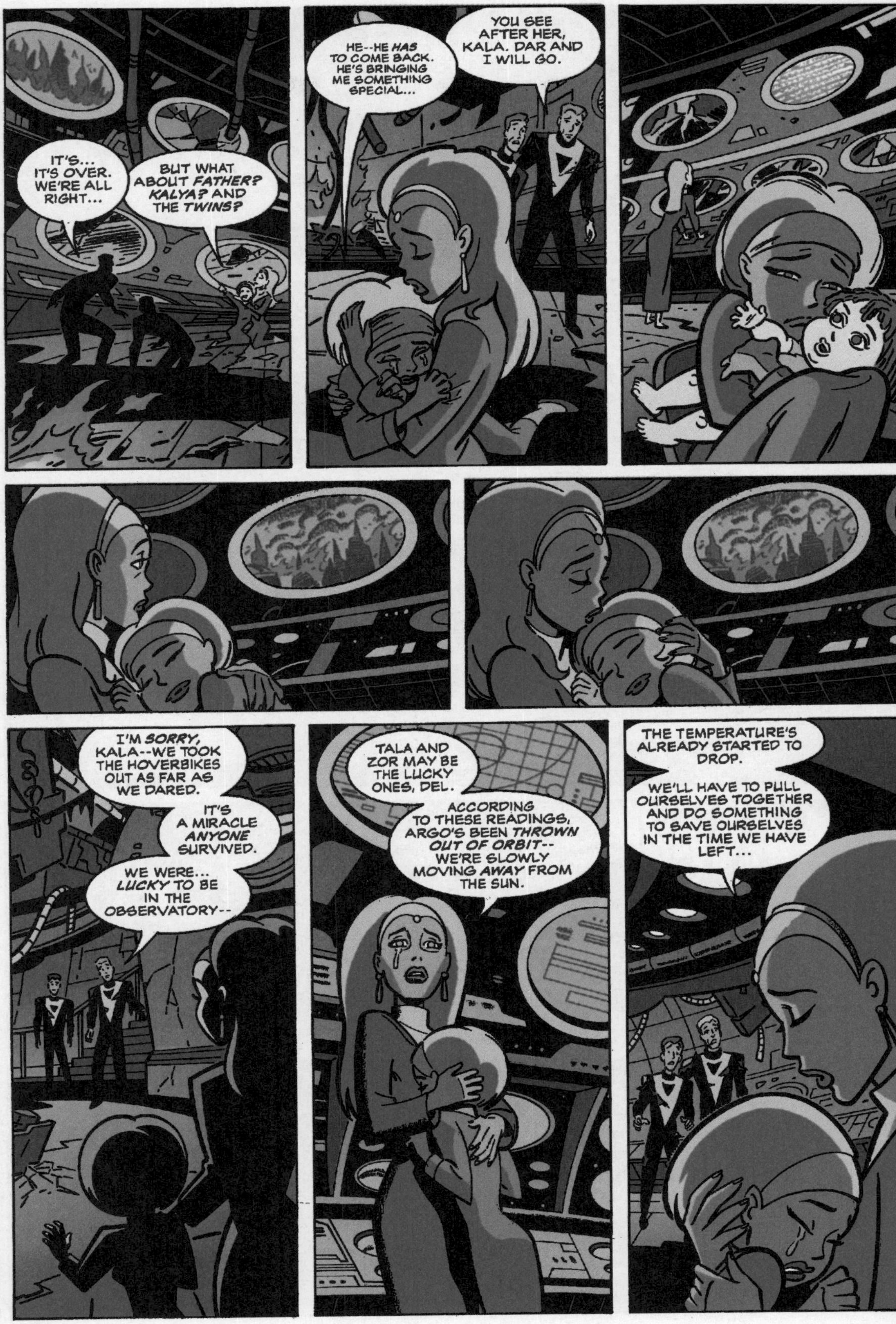
IT'S... IT'S OVER. WE'RE ALL RIGHT...
BUT WHAT ABOUT FATHER? KALYA? AND THE TWINS?
HE--HE HAS TO COME BACK. HE'S BRINGING ME SOMETHING SPECIAL...
YOU SEE AFTER HER, KALA. DAR AND I WILL GO.
I'M SORRY, KALA--WE TOOK THE HOVERBIKES OUT AS FAR AS WE DARED.
IT'S A MIRACLE ANYONE SURVIVED.
WE WERE... LUCKY TO BE IN THE OBSERVATORY--
TALA AND ZOR MAY BE THE LUCKY ONES, DEL.
ACCORDING TO THESE READINGS, ARGO'S BEEN THROWN OUT OF ORBIT-- WE'RE SLOWLY MOVING AWAY FROM THE SUN.
THE TEMPERATURE'S ALREADY STARTED TO DROP.
WE'LL HAVE TO PULL OURSELVES TOGETHER AND DO SOMETHING TO SAVE OURSELVES IN THE TIME WE HAVE LEFT...

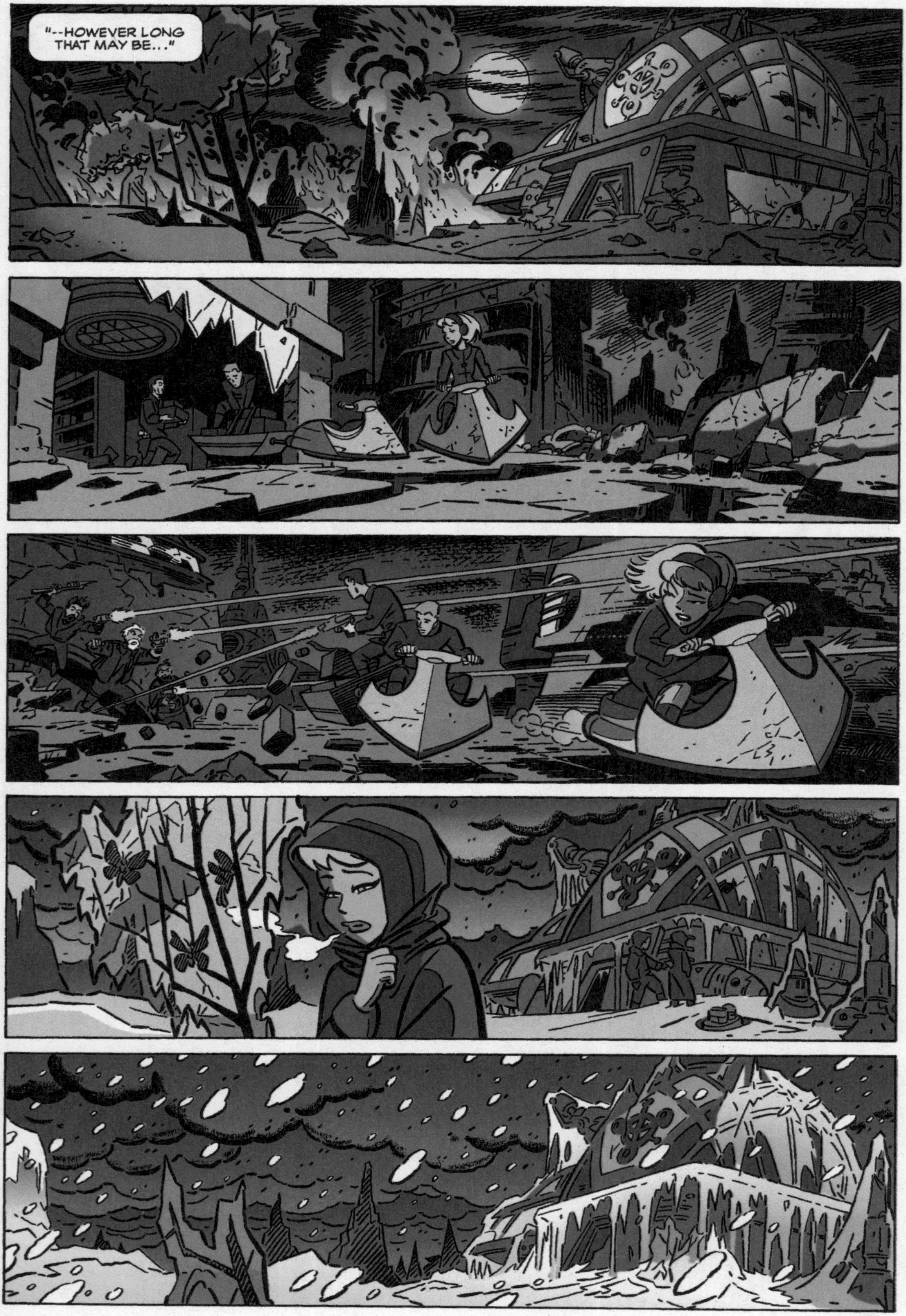
"--HOWEVER LONG THAT MAY BE..."

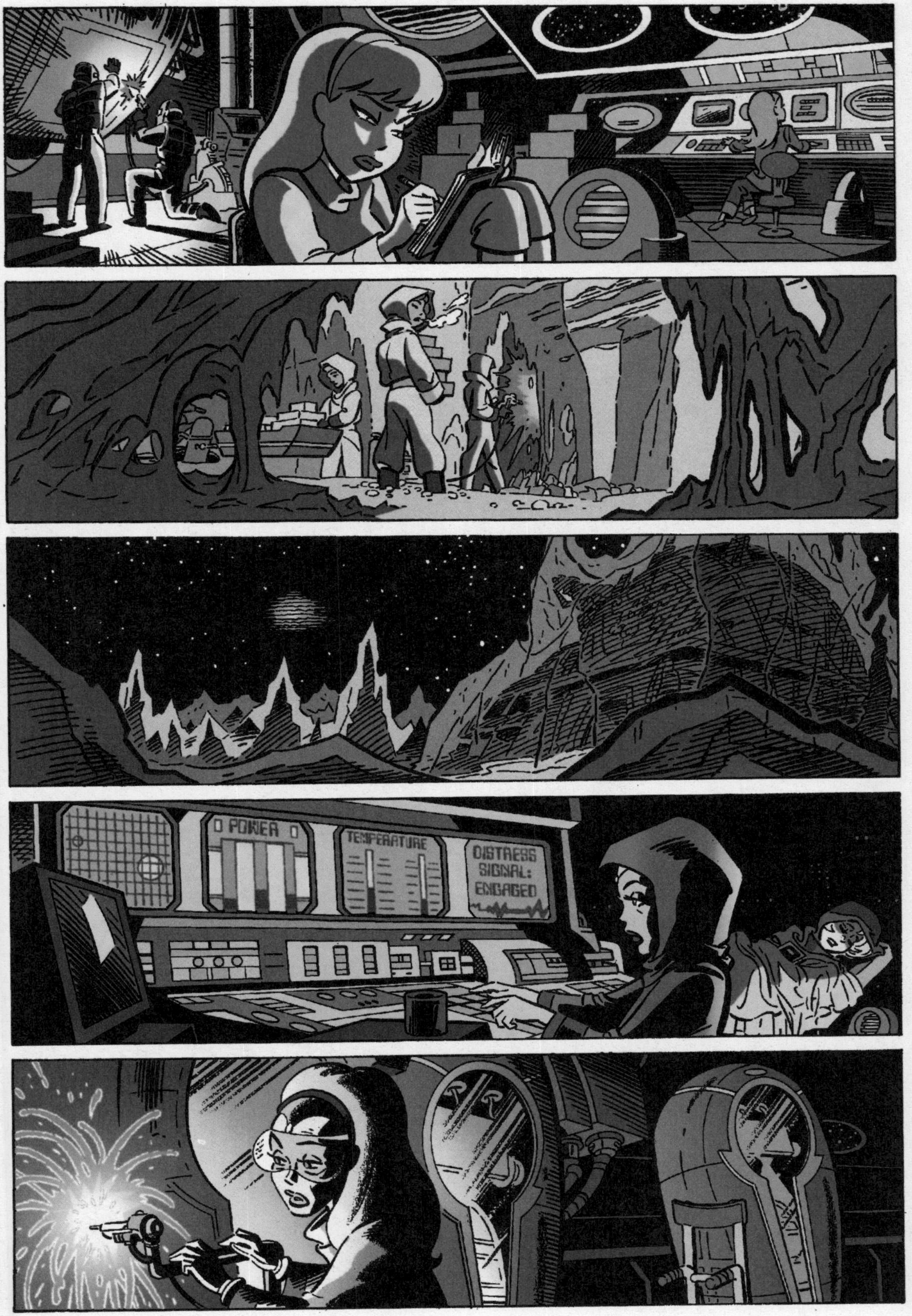
POWER
TEMPERATURE
DISTRESS SIGNAL: ENGAGED

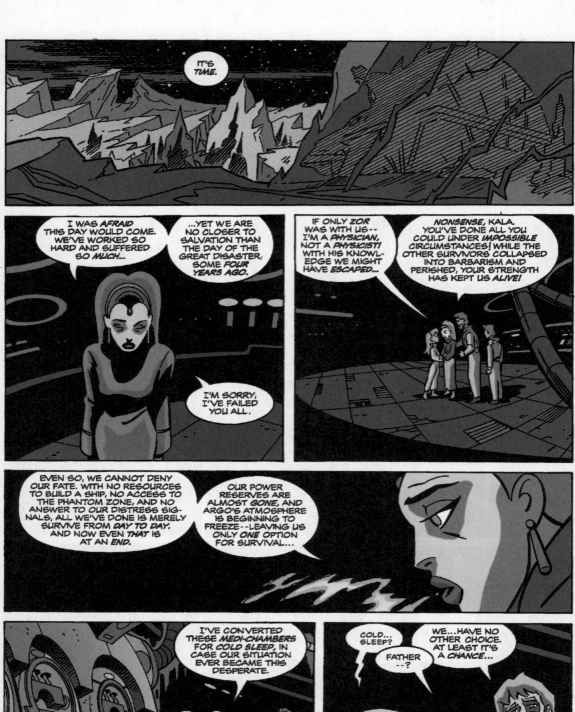

IT'S TIME.

I WAS *AFRAID* THIS DAY WOULD COME. WE'VE WORKED SO HARD AND SUFFERED SO *MUCH*...

...YET WE ARE NO CLOSER TO SALVATION THAN THE DAY OF THE GREAT DISASTER, SOME *FOUR YEARS* AGO.

I'M SORRY, I'VE FAILED YOU ALL.

IF ONLY *ZOR* WAS WITH US-- I'M A *PHYSICIAN*, NOT A *PHYSICIST!* WITH HIS KNOWL- EDGE WE MIGHT HAVE *ESCAPED*...

NONSENSE, KALA. YOU'VE DONE ALL YOU COULD UNDER *IMPOSSIBLE* CIRCUMSTANCES! WHILE THE OTHER SURVIVORS COLLAPSED INTO BARBARISM AND PERISHED, YOUR STRENGTH HAS KEPT US *ALIVE!*

EVEN SO, WE CANNOT DENY OUR FATE. WITH NO RESOURCES TO BUILD A SHIP, NO ACCESS TO THE PHANTOM ZONE, AND NO ANSWER TO OUR DISTRESS SIG- NALS, ALL WE'VE DONE IS MERELY SURVIVE FROM *DAY TO DAY*, AND NOW EVEN *THAT* IS AT AN *END*.

OUR POWER RESERVES ARE ALMOST *GONE*, AND ARGO'S ATMOSPHERE IS BEGINNING TO FREEZE--LEAVING US ONLY *ONE* OPTION FOR SURVIVAL...

I'VE CONVERTED THESE *MEDI-CHAMBERS* FOR *COLD SLEEP*, IN CASE OUR SITUATION EVER BECAME THIS DESPERATE.

THE LAB'S RESERVE POWER WILL BE CHANNELED INTO MAINTAINING THE CRYO- CHAMBERS AND DISTRESS BEACONS. HOPEFULLY *SOME- ONE*--*SOMEDAY*--WILL FIND OUR SIGNAL, AND HELP WILL ARRIVE.

COLD... SLEEP?

FATHER --?

WE...HAVE NO OTHER CHOICE. AT LEAST IT'S A *CHANCE*...

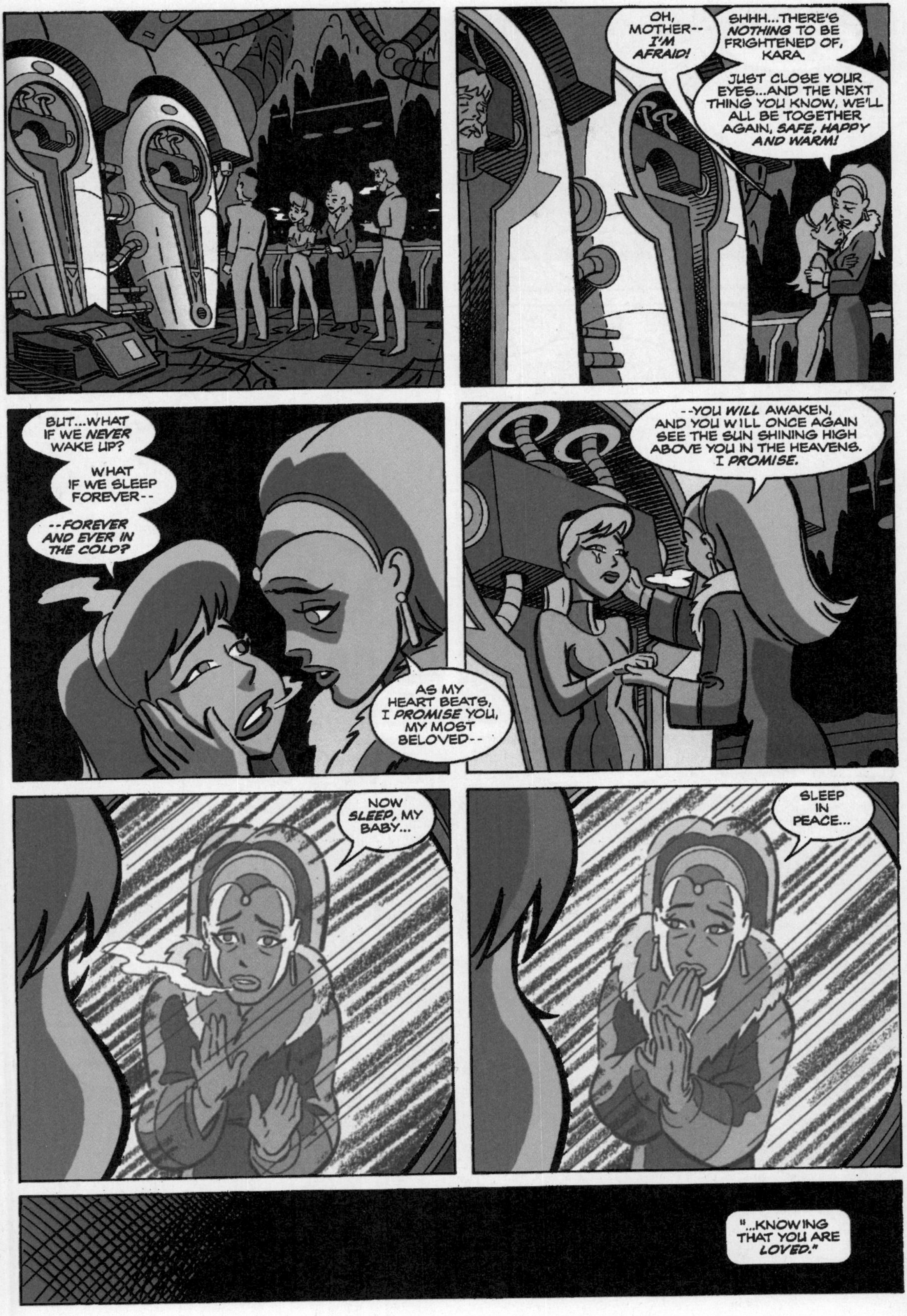
OH, MOTHER-- I'M AFRAID!
SHHH...THERE'S NOTHING TO BE FRIGHTENED OF, KARA.
JUST CLOSE YOUR EYES...AND THE NEXT THING YOU KNOW, WE'LL ALL BE TOGETHER AGAIN, SAFE, HAPPY AND WARM!
BUT...WHAT IF WE NEVER WAKE UP?
WHAT IF WE SLEEP FOREVER--
--FOREVER AND EVER IN THE COLD?
AS MY HEART BEATS, I PROMISE YOU, MY MOST BELOVED--
--YOU WILL AWAKEN, AND YOU WILL ONCE AGAIN SEE THE SUN SHINING HIGH ABOVE YOU IN THE HEAVENS. I PROMISE.
NOW SLEEP, MY BABY...
SLEEP IN PEACE...
"...KNOWING THAT YOU ARE LOVED."

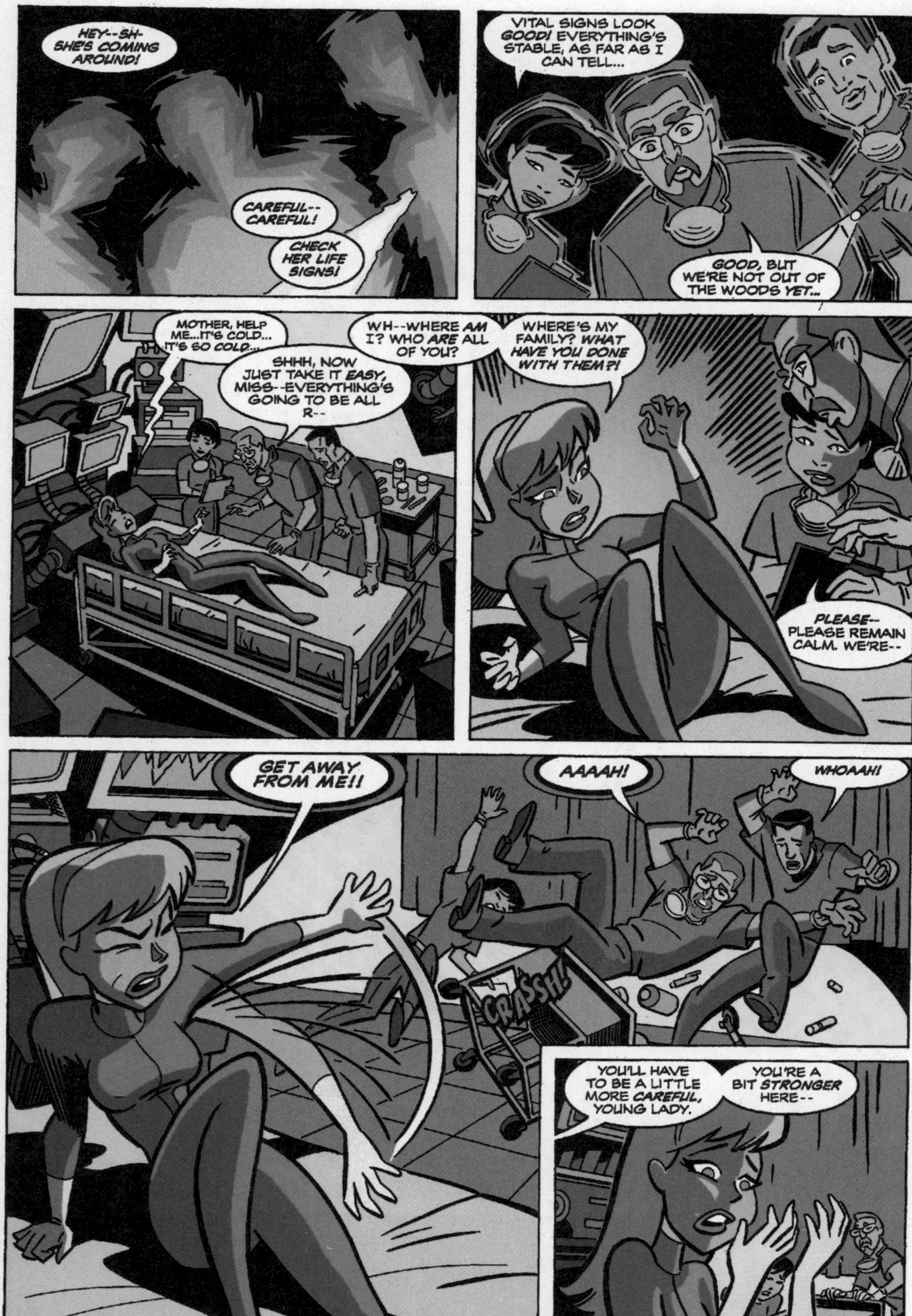
HEY--SH-SHE'S COMING AROUND!
CAREFUL--CAREFUL!
CHECK HER LIFE SIGNS!
VITAL SIGNS LOOK GOOD! EVERYTHING'S STABLE, AS FAR AS I CAN TELL...
GOOD, BUT WE'RE NOT OUT OF THE WOODS YET...
MOTHER, HELP ME...IT'S COLD... IT'S SO COLD...
SHHH, NOW JUST TAKE IT EASY, MISS--EVERYTHING'S GOING TO BE ALL R--
WH--WHERE AM I? WHO ARE ALL OF YOU?
WHERE'S MY FAMILY? WHAT HAVE YOU DONE WITH THEM?!
PLEASE--PLEASE REMAIN CALM. WE'RE--
GET AWAY FROM ME!!
AAAAH!
WHOAAH!
CRASSH!
YOU'LL HAVE TO BE A LITTLE MORE CAREFUL, YOUNG LADY.
YOU'RE A BIT STRONGER HERE--

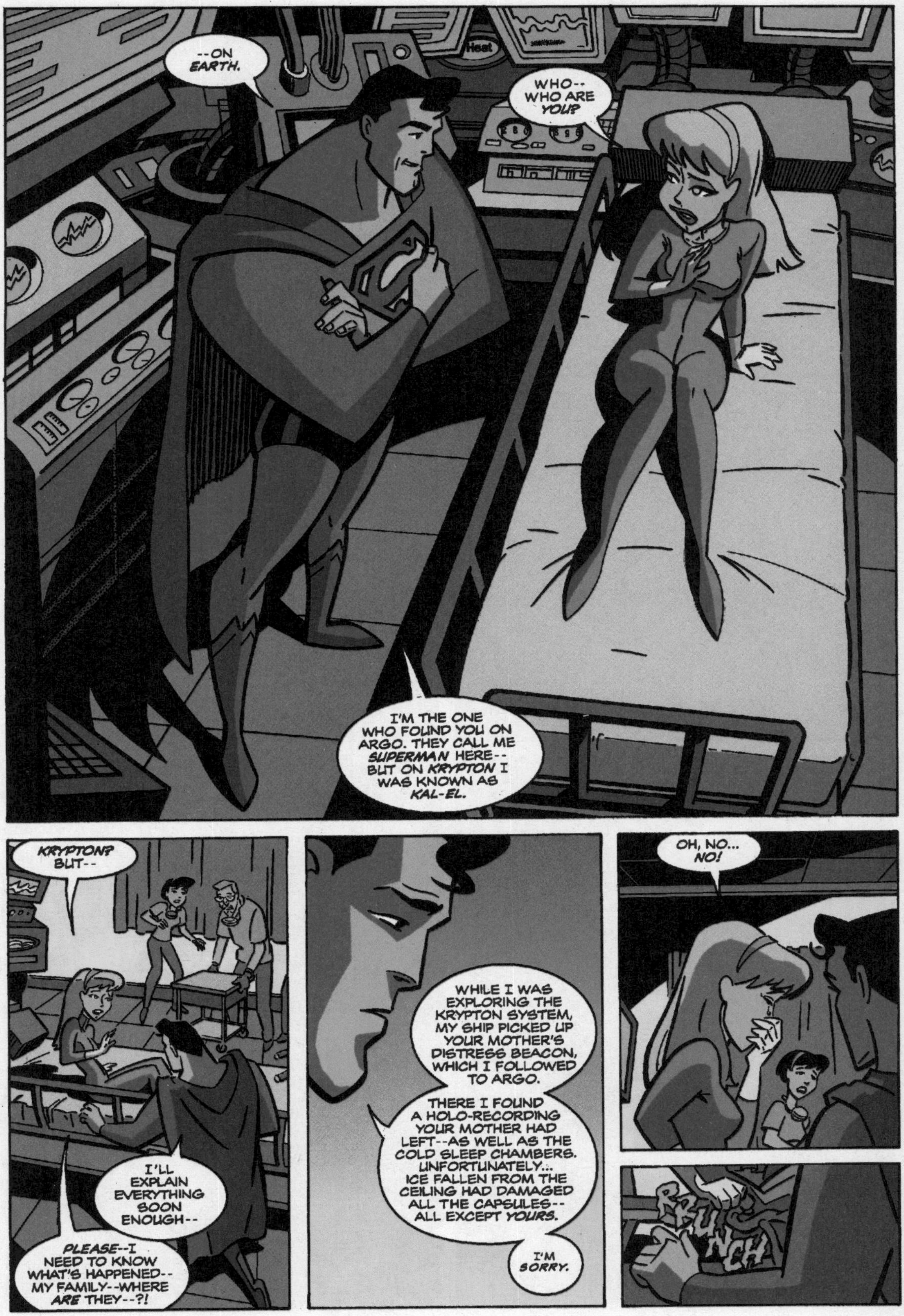
--ON EARTH.
WHO--WHO ARE YOU?
I'M THE ONE WHO FOUND YOU ON ARGO. THEY CALL ME SUPERMAN HERE--BUT ON KRYPTON I WAS KNOWN AS KAL-EL.
KRYPTON? BUT--
I'LL EXPLAIN EVERYTHING SOON ENOUGH--
PLEASE--I NEED TO KNOW WHAT'S HAPPENED--MY FAMILY--WHERE ARE THEY--?!
WHILE I WAS EXPLORING THE KRYPTON SYSTEM, MY SHIP PICKED UP YOUR MOTHER'S DISTRESS BEACON, WHICH I FOLLOWED TO ARGO.
THERE I FOUND A HOLO-RECORDING YOUR MOTHER HAD LEFT--AS WELL AS THE COLD SLEEP CHAMBERS. UNFORTUNATELY... ICE FALLEN FROM THE CEILING HAD DAMAGED ALL THE CAPSULES--ALL EXCEPT YOURS.
I'M SORRY.
OH, NO... NO!

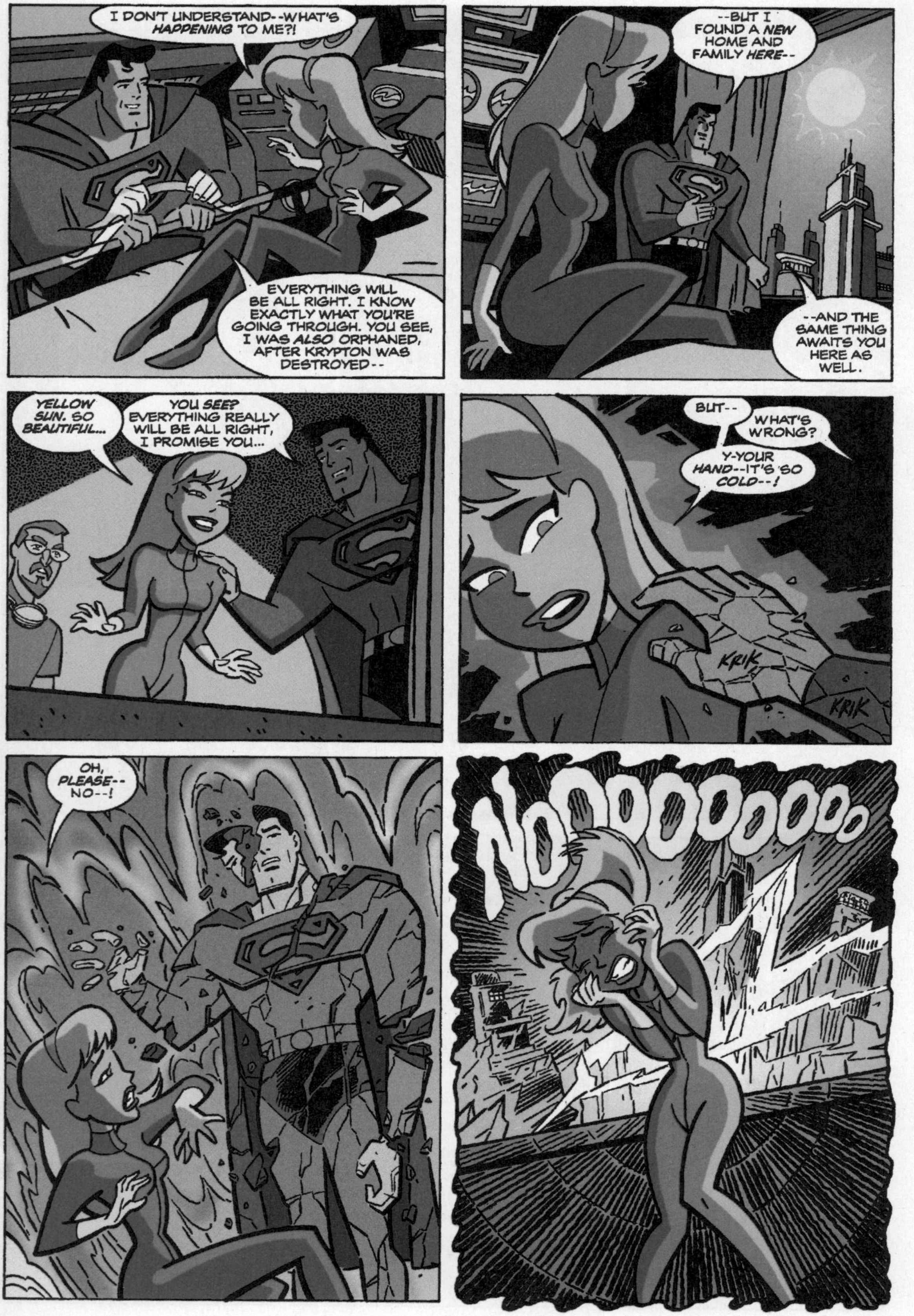
I DON'T UNDERSTAND--WHAT'S HAPPENING TO ME?!
EVERYTHING WILL BE ALL RIGHT. I KNOW EXACTLY WHAT YOU'RE GOING THROUGH. YOU SEE, I WAS ALSO ORPHANED, AFTER KRYPTON WAS DESTROYED--
--BUT I FOUND A NEW HOME AND FAMILY HERE--
--AND THE SAME THING AWAITS YOU HERE AS WELL.
YELLOW SUN. SO BEAUTIFUL...
YOU SEE? EVERYTHING REALLY WILL BE ALL RIGHT, I PROMISE YOU...
BUT--
WHAT'S WRONG?
Y-YOUR HAND--IT'S SO COLD--!
KRIK
KRIK
OH, PLEASE--NO--!
NOOOOOOOOOO

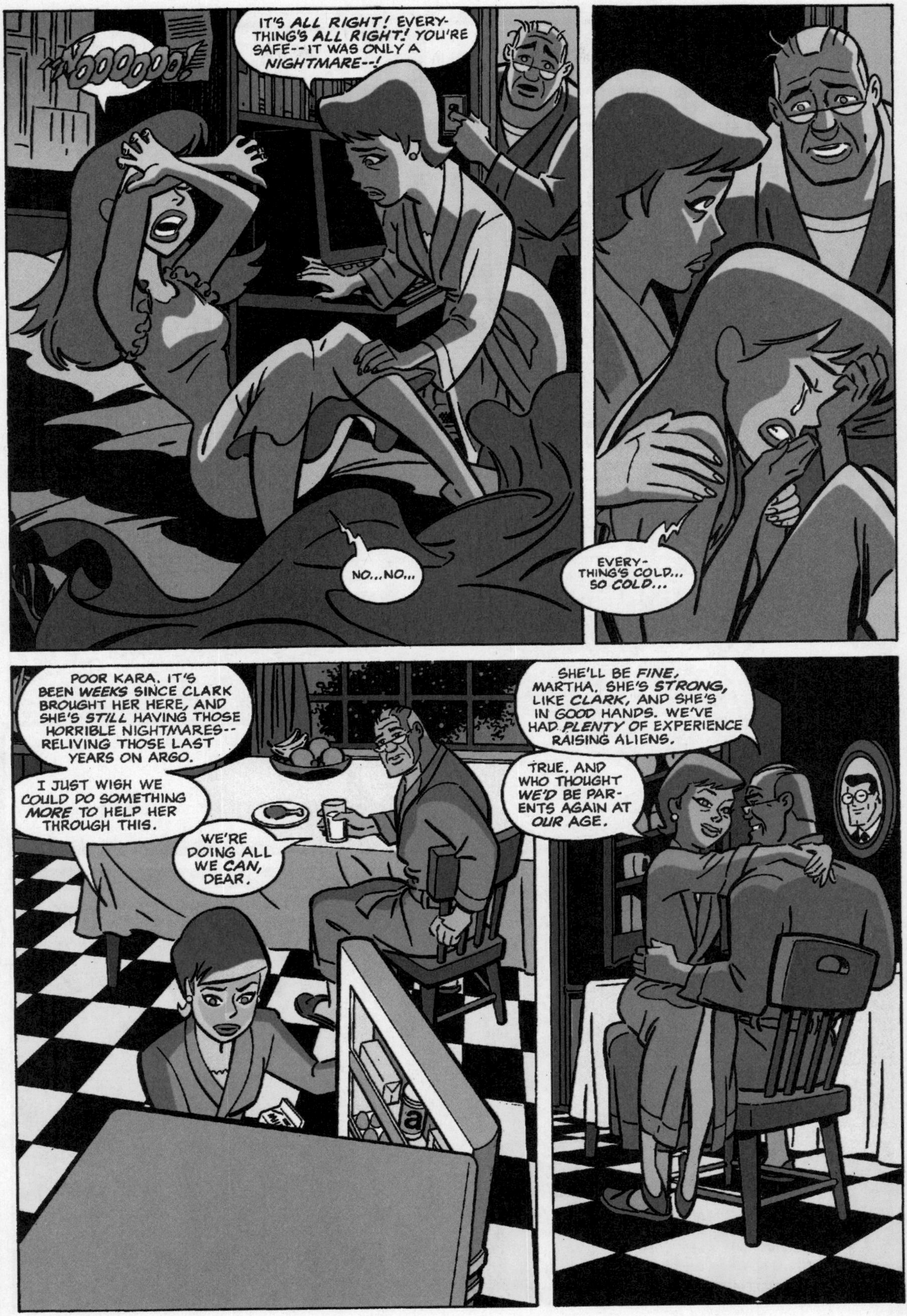
NOOOOOOO!
IT'S ALL RIGHT! EVERYTHING'S ALL RIGHT! YOU'RE SAFE-- IT WAS ONLY A NIGHTMARE--!
NO... NO...
EVERYTHING'S COLD... SO COLD...
POOR KARA. IT'S BEEN WEEKS SINCE CLARK BROUGHT HER HERE, AND SHE'S STILL HAVING THOSE HORRIBLE NIGHTMARES-- RELIVING THOSE LAST YEARS ON ARGO.
I JUST WISH WE COULD DO SOMETHING MORE TO HELP HER THROUGH THIS.
WE'RE DOING ALL WE CAN, DEAR.
SHE'LL BE FINE, MARTHA. SHE'S STRONG, LIKE CLARK, AND SHE'S IN GOOD HANDS. WE'VE HAD PLENTY OF EXPERIENCE RAISING ALIENS.
TRUE. AND WHO THOUGHT WE'D BE PARENTS AGAIN AT OUR AGE.

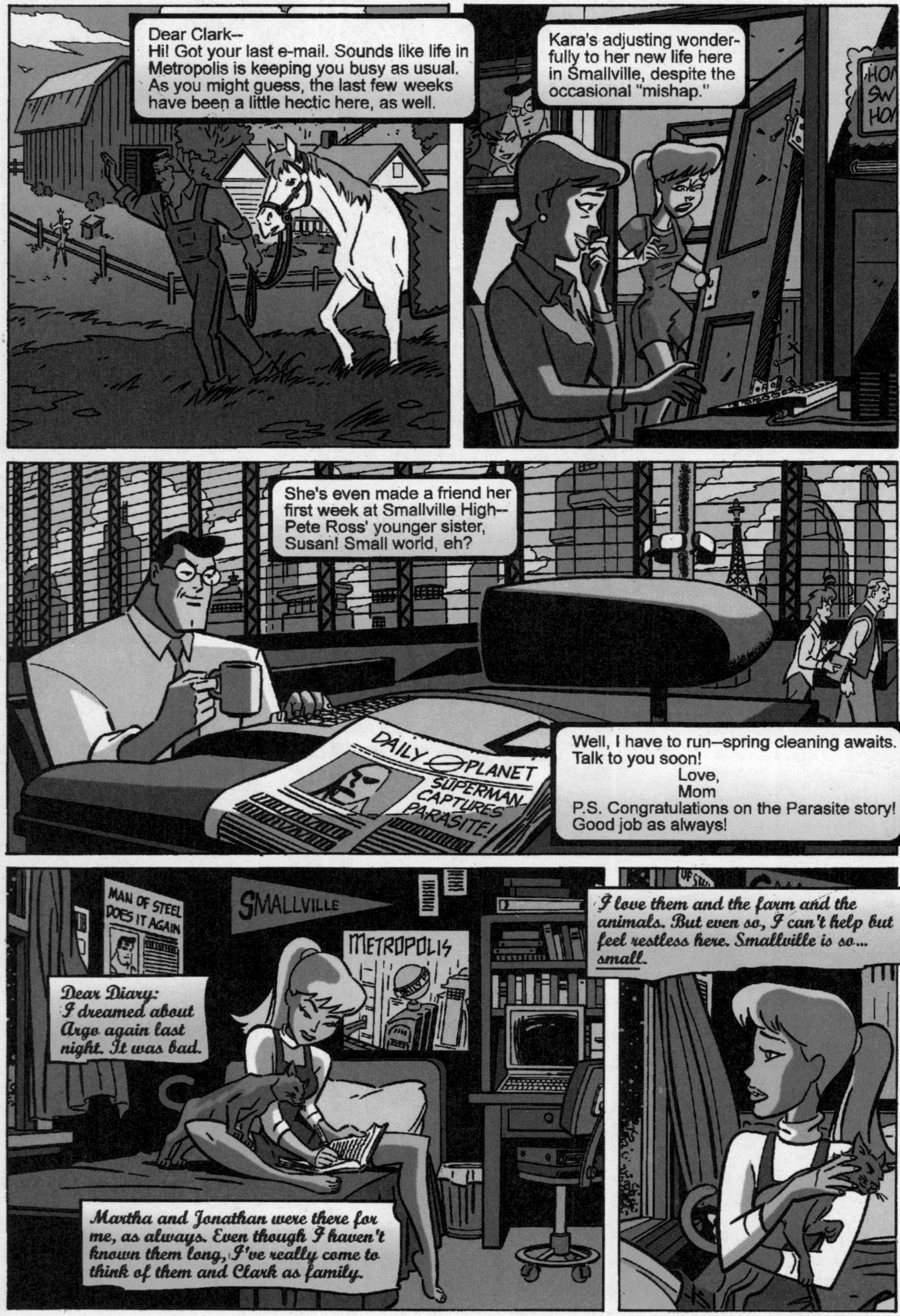
Dear Clark--
Hi! Got your last e-mail. Sounds like life in Metropolis is keeping you busy as usual. As you might guess, the last few weeks have been a little hectic here, as well.
Kara's adjusting wonderfully to her new life here in Smallville, despite the occasional "mishap."
She's even made a friend her first week at Smallville High--Pete Ross' younger sister, Susan! Small world, eh?
DAILY PLANET
SUPERMAN CAPTURES PARASITE!
Well, I have to run--spring cleaning awaits. Talk to you soon!
Love,
Mom
P.S. Congratulations on the Parasite story! Good job as always!
MAN OF STEEL DOES IT AGAIN
SMALLVILLE
METROPOLIS
Dear Diary:
I dreamed about Argo again last night. It was bad.
Martha and Jonathan were there for me, as always. Even though I haven't known them long, I've really come to think of them and Clark as family.
I love them and the farm and the animals. But even so, I can't help but feel restless here. Smallville is so... small.

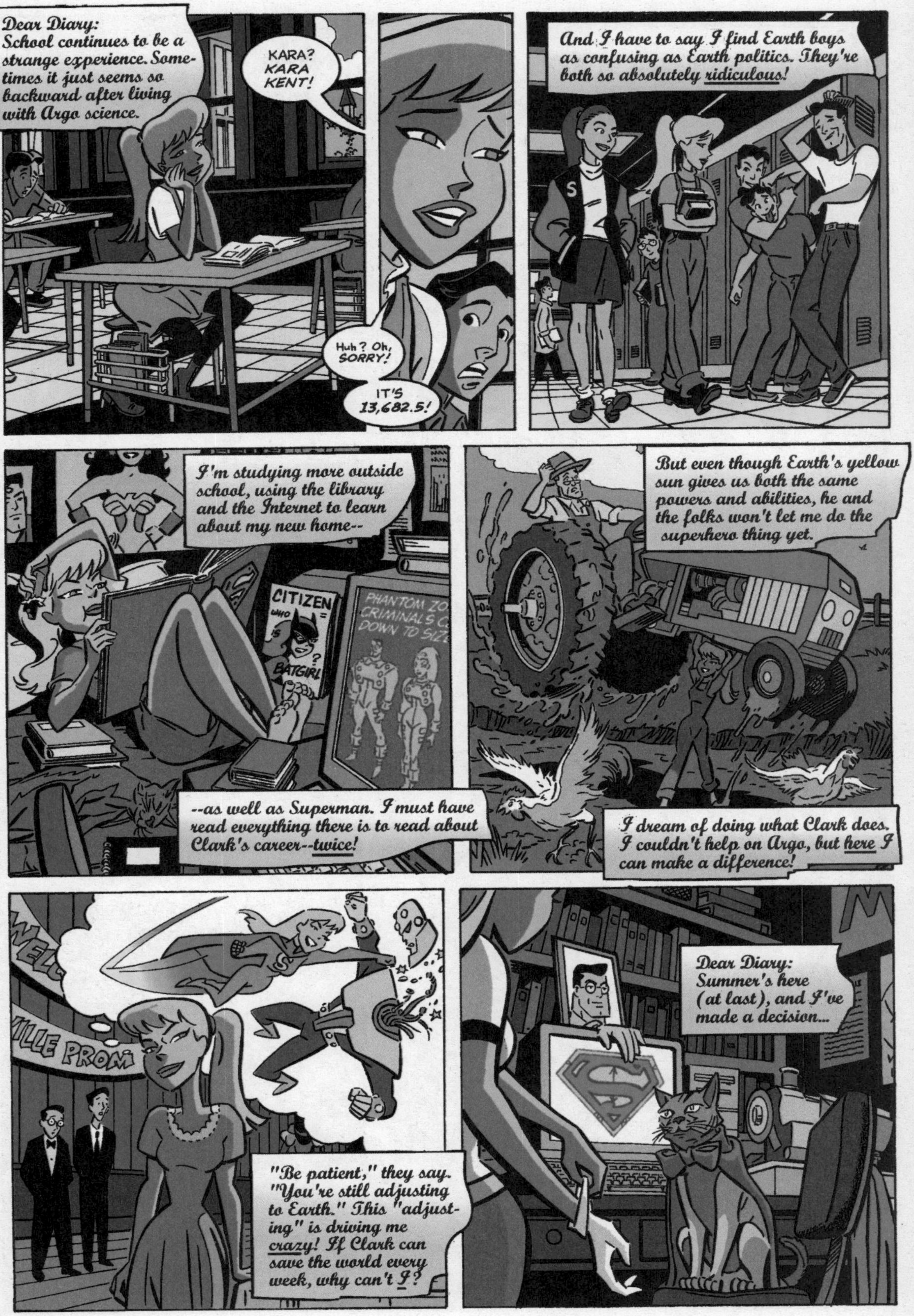

Dear Diary:
School continues to be a strange experience. Sometimes it just seems so backward after living with Argo science.
KARA? KARA KENT!
Huh? Oh, SORRY!
IT'S 13,682.5!
And I have to say I find Earth boys as confusing as Earth politics. They're both so absolutely ridiculous!
I'm studying more outside school, using the library and the Internet to learn about my new home--
CITIZEN
BATGIRL
--as well as Superman. I must have read everything there is to read about Clark's career--twice!
But even though Earth's yellow sun gives us both the same powers and abilities, he and the folks won't let me do the superhero thing yet.
I dream of doing what Clark does. I couldn't help on Argo, but here I can make a difference!
"Be patient," they say. "You're still adjusting to Earth." This "adjusting" is driving me crazy! If Clark can save the world every week, why can't I?
Dear Diary:
Summer's here (at last), and I've made a decision...

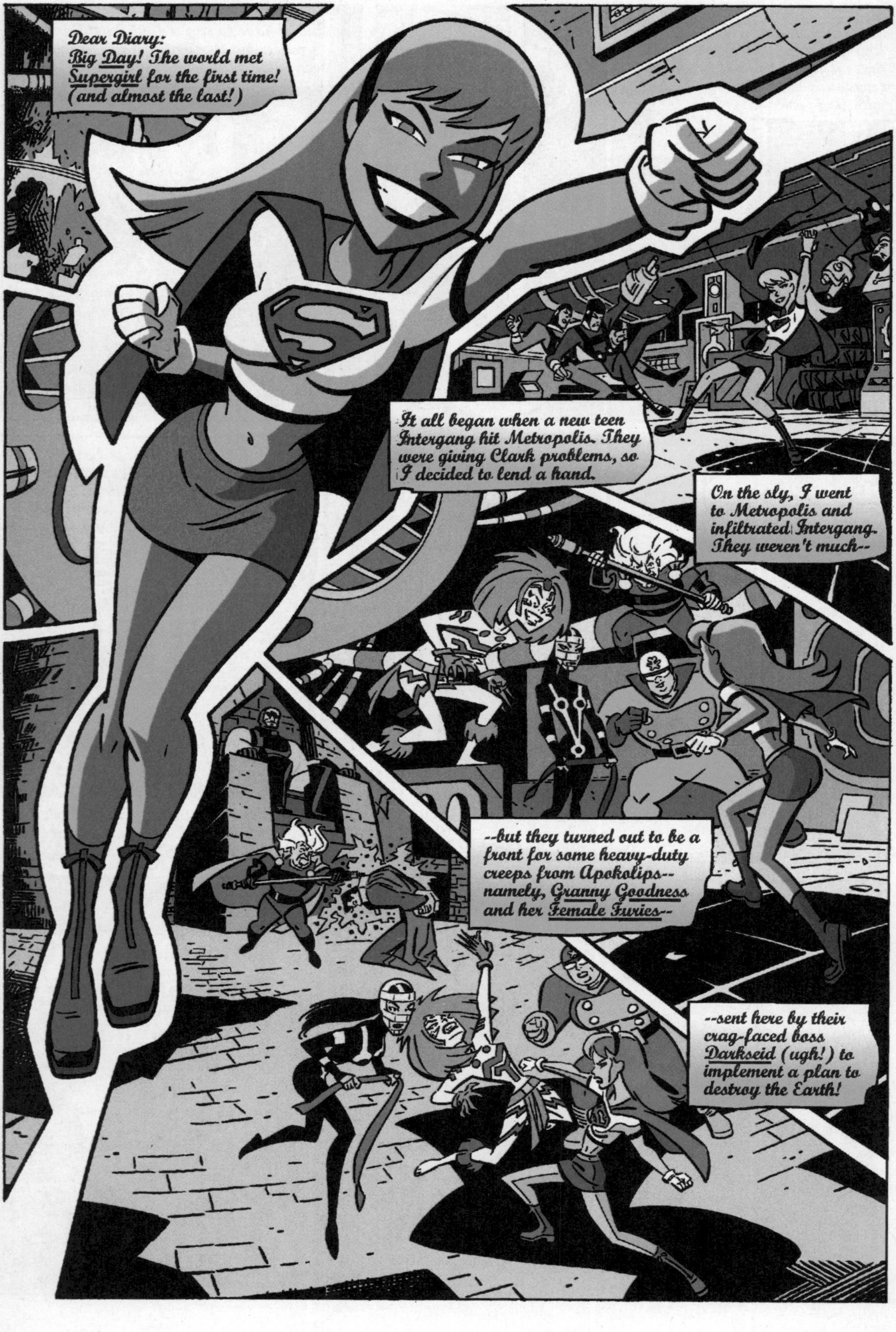
Dear Diary:
Big Day! The world met Supergirl for the first time! (and almost the last!)
It all began when a new teen Intergang hit Metropolis. They were giving Clark problems, so I decided to lend a hand.
On the sly, I went to Metropolis and infiltrated Intergang. They weren't much--
--but they turned out to be a front for some heavy-duty creeps from Apokolips--namely, Granny Goodness and her Female Furies--
--sent here by their crag-faced boss Darkseid (ugh!) to implement a plan to destroy the Earth!

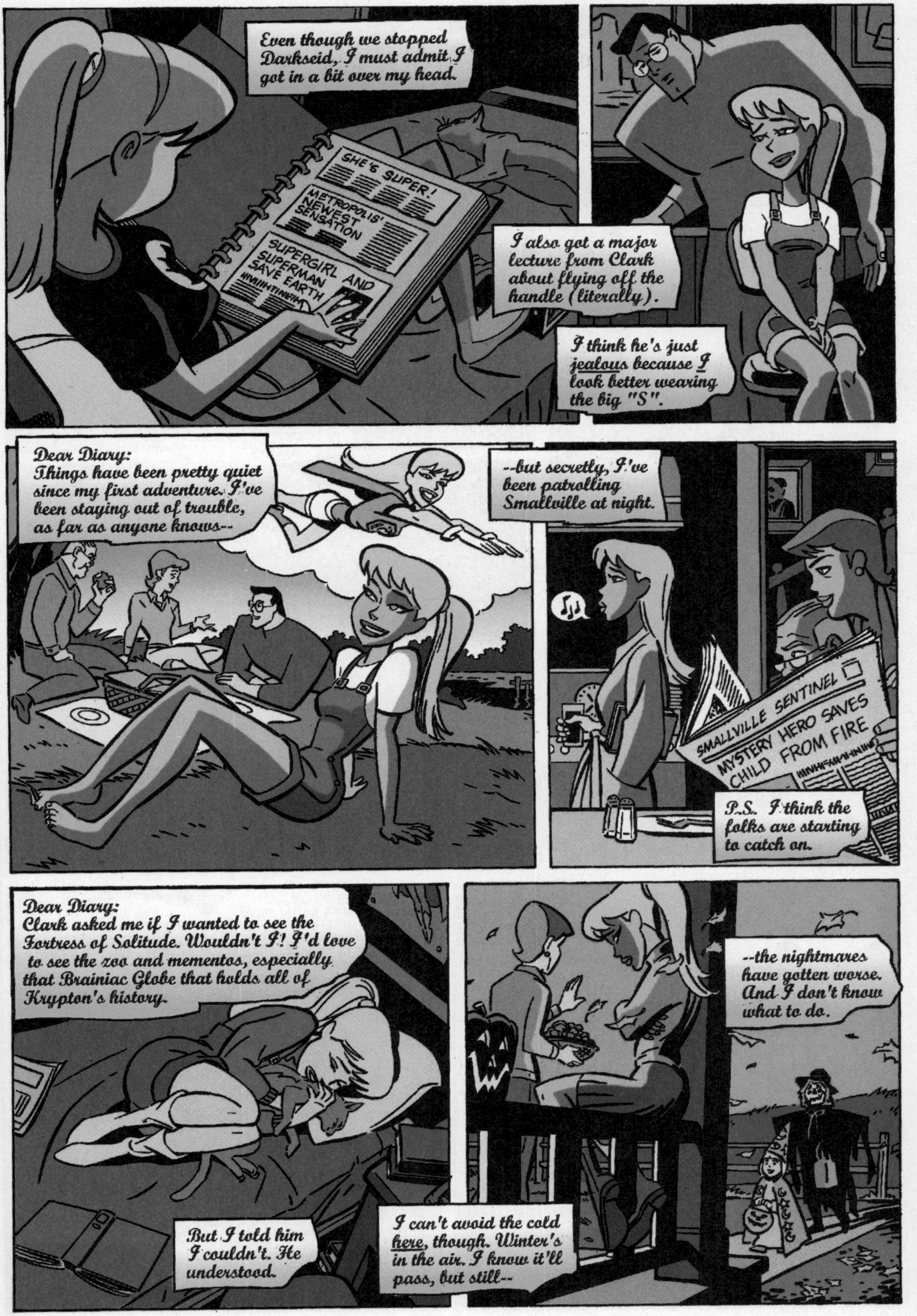

Even though we stopped Darkseid, I must admit I got in a bit over my head.
SHE'S SUPER!
METROPOLIS' NEWEST SENSATION
SUPERGIRL AND SUPERMAN SAVE EARTH
I also got a major lecture from Clark about flying off the handle (literally).
I think he's just jealous because I look better wearing the big "S".
Dear Diary:
Things have been pretty quiet since my first adventure. I've been staying out of trouble, as far as anyone knows--
--but secretly, I've been patrolling Smallville at night.
SMALLVILLE SENTINEL
MYSTERY HERO SAVES CHILD FROM FIRE
P.S. I think the folks are starting to catch on.
Dear Diary:
Clark asked me if I wanted to see the Fortress of Solitude. Wouldn't I! I'd love to see the zoo and mementos, especially that Brainiac Globe that holds all of Krypton's history.
But I told him I couldn't. He understood.
--the nightmares have gotten worse. And I don't know what to do.
I can't avoid the cold here, though. Winter's in the air. I know it'll pass, but still--

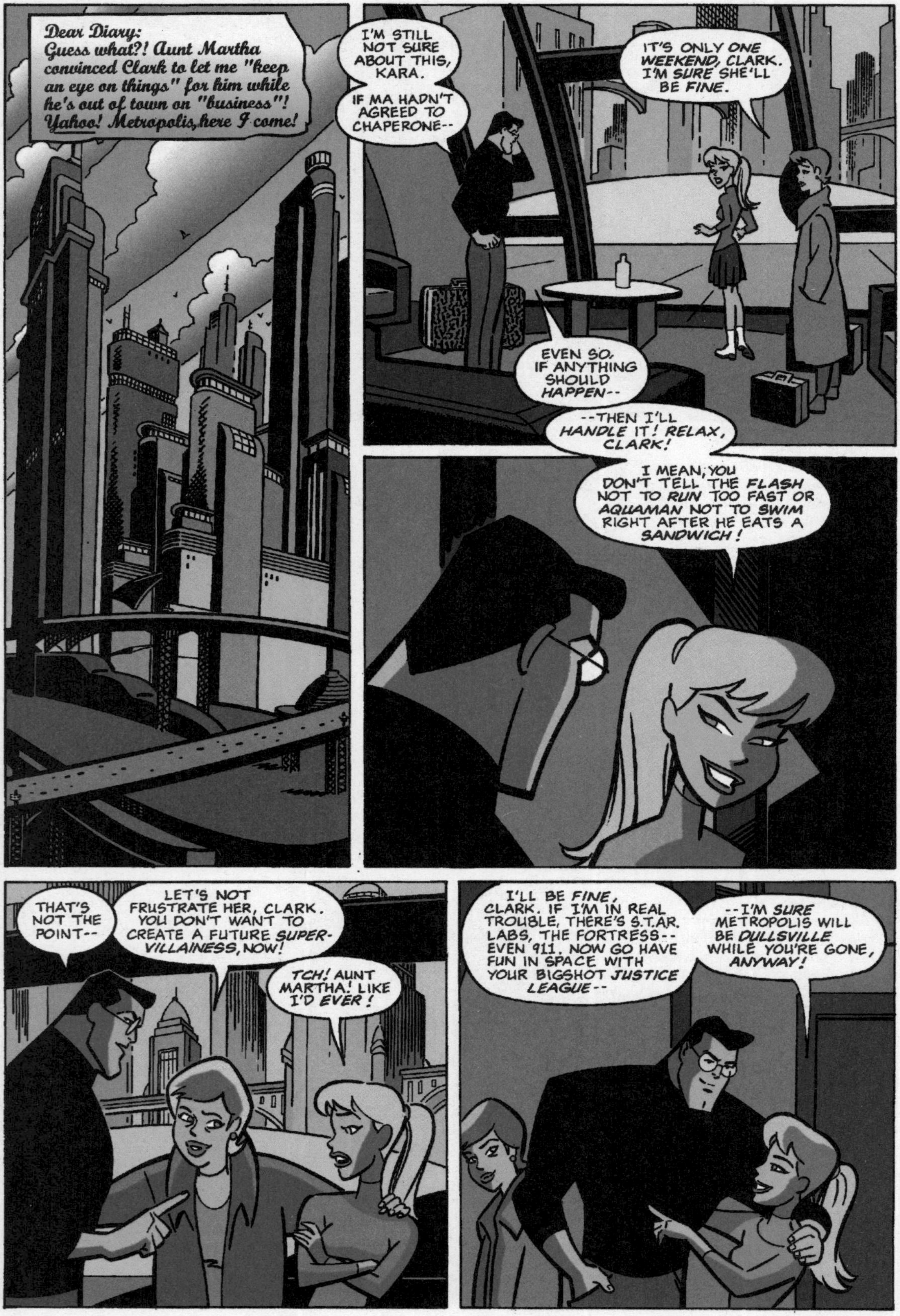
Dear Diary:
Guess what?! Aunt Martha convinced Clark to let me "keep an eye on things" for him while he's out of town on "business"! Yahoo! Metropolis, here I come!
I'M STILL NOT SURE ABOUT THIS, KARA.
IF MA HADN'T AGREED TO CHAPERONE--
IT'S ONLY ONE WEEKEND, CLARK. I'M SURE SHE'LL BE FINE.
EVEN SO, IF ANYTHING SHOULD HAPPEN--
--THEN I'LL HANDLE IT! RELAX, CLARK!
I MEAN, YOU DON'T TELL THE FLASH NOT TO RUN TOO FAST OR AQUAMAN NOT TO SWIM RIGHT AFTER HE EATS A SANDWICH!
THAT'S NOT THE POINT--
LET'S NOT FRUSTRATE HER, CLARK. YOU DON'T WANT TO CREATE A FUTURE SUPER-VILLAINESS, NOW!
TCH! AUNT MARTHA! LIKE I'D EVER!
I'LL BE FINE, CLARK. IF I'M IN REAL TROUBLE, THERE'S S.T.A.R. LABS, THE FORTRESS-- EVEN 911. NOW GO HAVE FUN IN SPACE WITH YOUR BIGSHOT JUSTICE LEAGUE--
--I'M SURE METROPOLIS WILL BE DULLSVILLE WHILE YOU'RE GONE, ANYWAY!

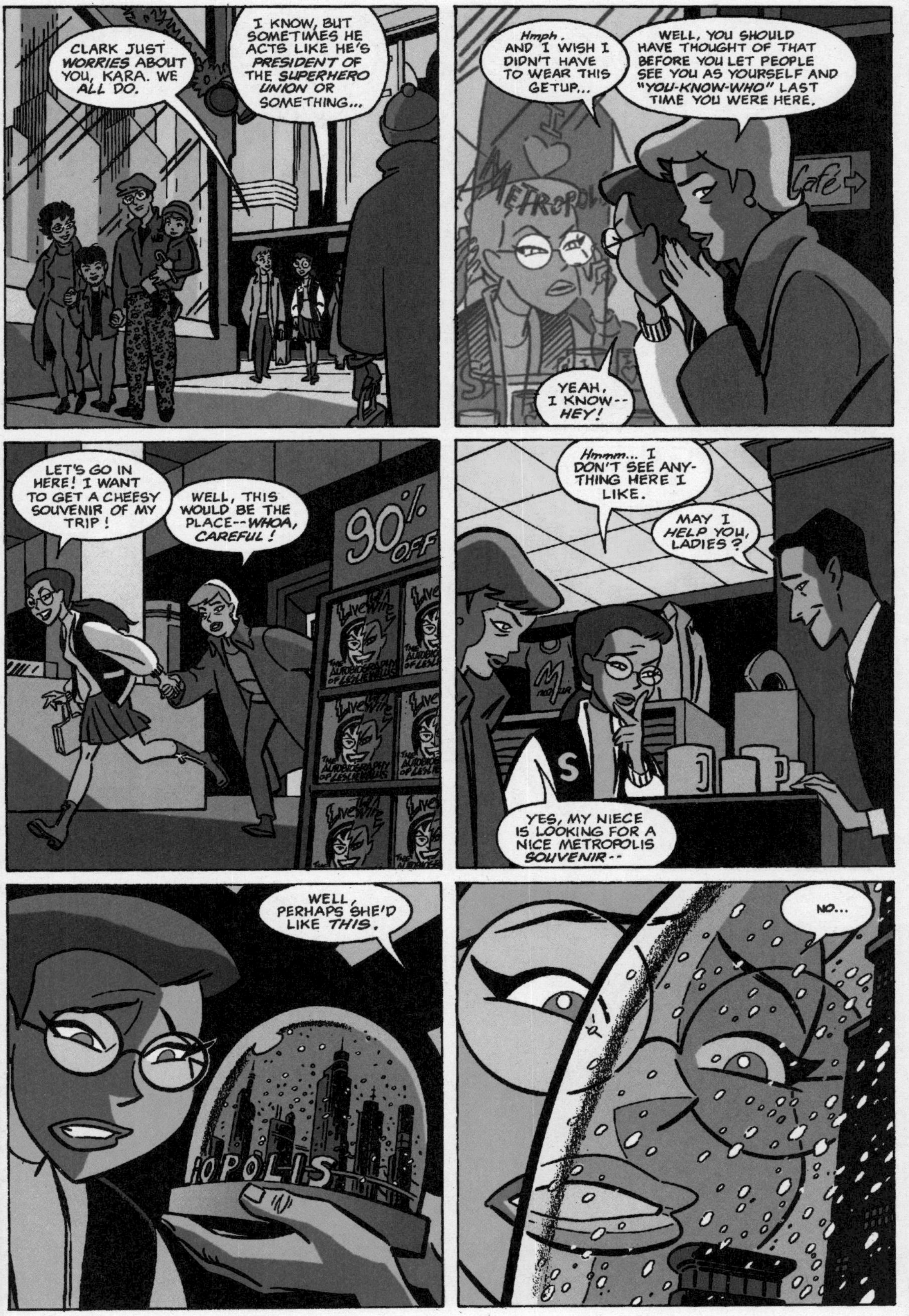

CLARK JUST WORRIES ABOUT YOU, KARA. WE ALL DO.
I KNOW, BUT SOMETIMES HE ACTS LIKE HE'S PRESIDENT OF THE SUPERHERO UNION OR SOMETHING...
Hmph. AND I WISH I DIDN'T HAVE TO WEAR THIS GETUP...
WELL, YOU SHOULD HAVE THOUGHT OF THAT BEFORE YOU LET PEOPLE SEE YOU AS YOURSELF AND "YOU-KNOW-WHO" LAST TIME YOU WERE HERE.
Café
YEAH, I KNOW-- HEY!
LET'S GO IN HERE! I WANT TO GET A CHEESY SOUVENIR OF MY TRIP!
WELL, THIS WOULD BE THE PLACE--WHOA, CAREFUL!
90% OFF
Hmmm... I DON'T SEE ANYTHING HERE I LIKE.
MAY I HELP YOU, LADIES?
YES, MY NIECE IS LOOKING FOR A NICE METROPOLIS SOUVENIR--
WELL, PERHAPS SHE'D LIKE THIS.
OPOLIS
NO...

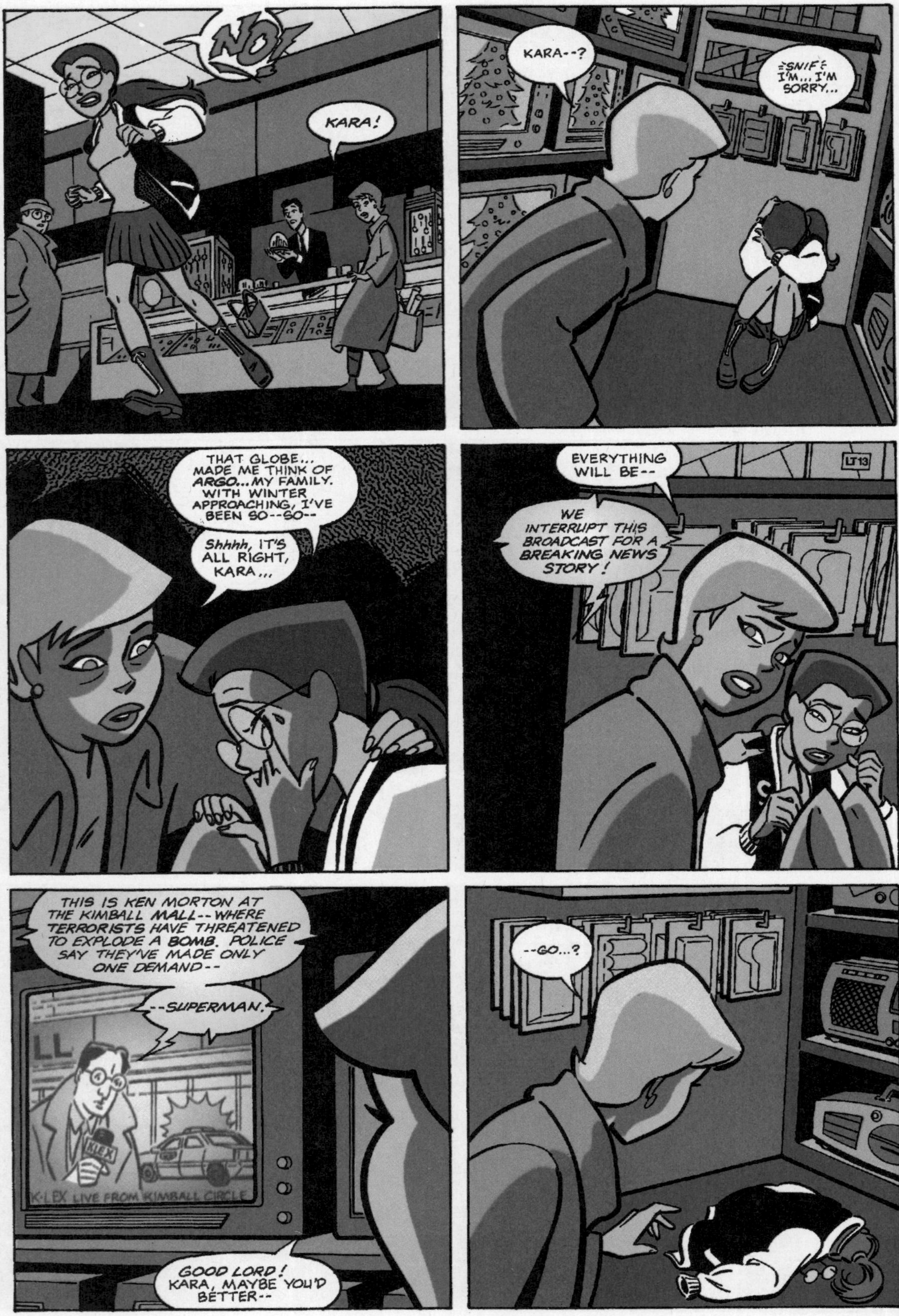
NO!
KARA!
KARA--?
SNIF I'M... I'M SORRY...
THAT GLOBE... MADE ME THINK OF ARGO... MY FAMILY. WITH WINTER APPROACHING, I'VE BEEN SO--SO--
Shhhh, IT'S ALL RIGHT, KARA...
EVERYTHING WILL BE--
WE INTERRUPT THIS BROADCAST FOR A BREAKING NEWS STORY!
LT13
THIS IS KEN MORTON AT THE KIMBALL MALL--WHERE TERRORISTS HAVE THREATENED TO EXPLODE A BOMB. POLICE SAY THEY'VE MADE ONLY ONE DEMAND--
--SUPERMAN.
K-LEX LIVE FROM KIMBALL CIRCLE
GOOD LORD! KARA, MAYBE YOU'D BETTER--
--GO...?

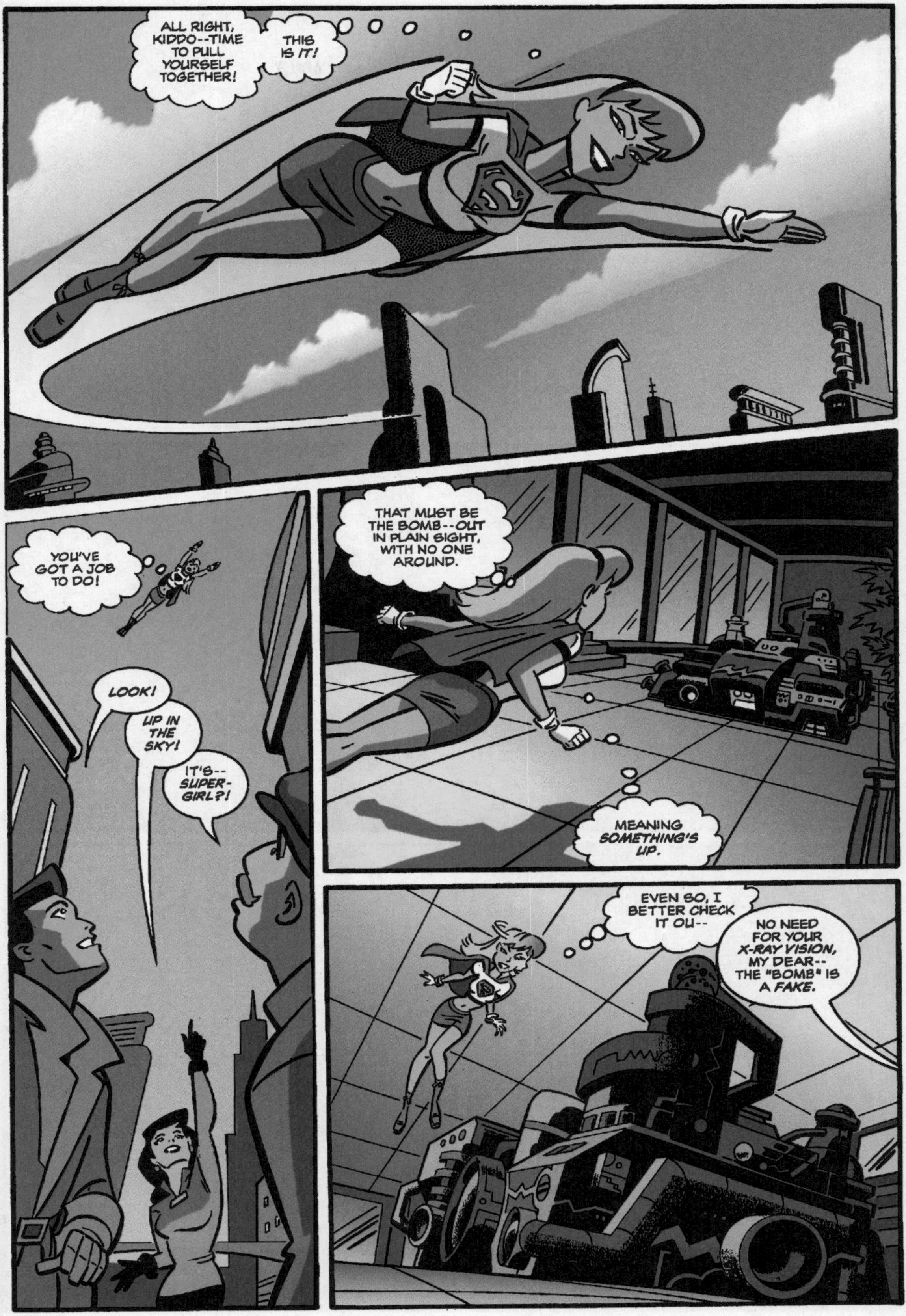
ALL RIGHT, KIDDO--TIME TO PULL YOURSELF TOGETHER!
THIS IS IT!
YOU'VE GOT A JOB TO DO!
LOOK!
UP IN THE SKY!
IT'S-- SUPER-GIRL?!
THAT MUST BE THE BOMB--OUT IN PLAIN SIGHT, WITH NO ONE AROUND.
MEANING SOMETHING'S UP.
EVEN SO, I BETTER CHECK IT OU--
NO NEED FOR YOUR X-RAY VISION, MY DEAR-- THE "BOMB" IS A FAKE.

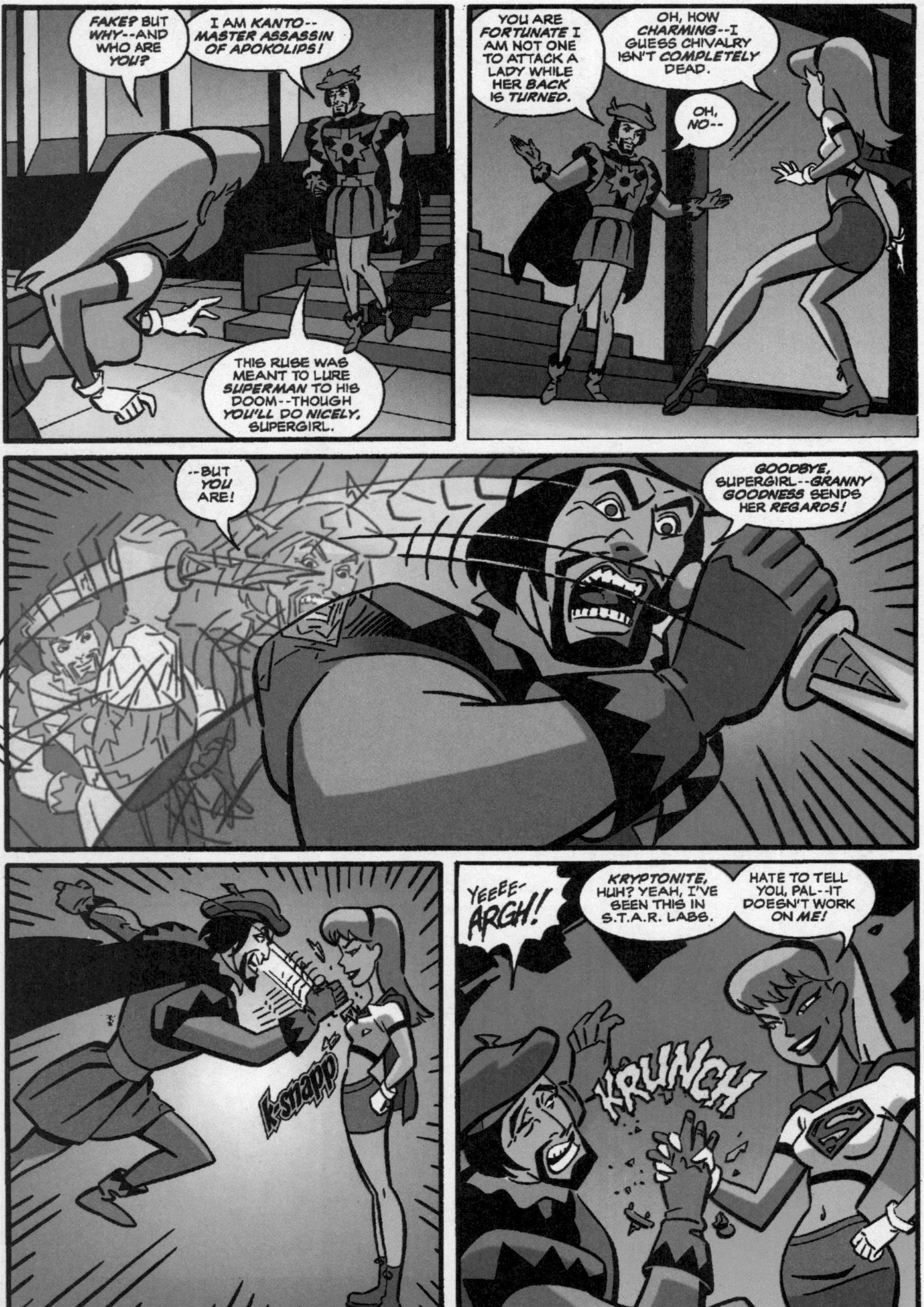
FAKE? BUT WHY--AND WHO ARE YOU?
I AM KANTO--MASTER ASSASSIN OF APOKOLIPS!
THIS RUSE WAS MEANT TO LURE SUPERMAN TO HIS DOOM--THOUGH YOU'LL DO NICELY, SUPERGIRL.
YOU ARE FORTUNATE I AM NOT ONE TO ATTACK A LADY WHILE HER BACK IS TURNED.
OH, HOW CHARMING--I GUESS CHIVALRY ISN'T COMPLETELY DEAD.
OH, NO--
--BUT YOU ARE!
GOODBYE, SUPERGIRL--GRANNY GOODNESS SENDS HER REGARDS!
K-SNAPP
YEEEE-ARGH!
KRYPTONITE, HUH? YEAH, I'VE SEEN THIS IN S.T.A.R. LABS.
HATE TO TELL YOU, PAL--IT DOESN'T WORK ON ME!
KRUNCH

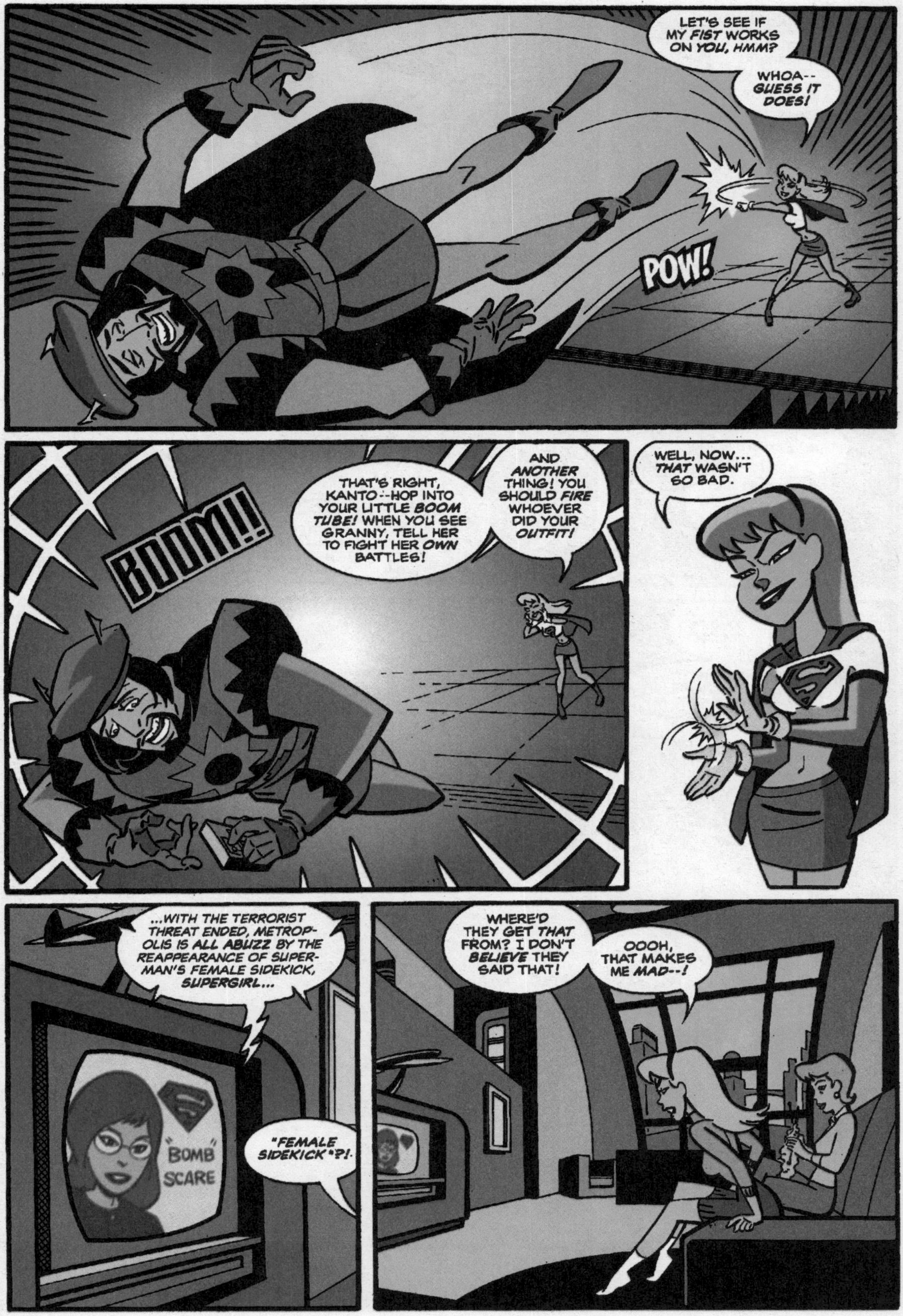
LET'S SEE IF MY FIST WORKS ON YOU, HMM?
WHOA-- GUESS IT DOES!
POW!
BOOM!!
THAT'S RIGHT, KANTO--HOP INTO YOUR LITTLE BOOM TUBE! WHEN YOU SEE GRANNY, TELL HER TO FIGHT HER OWN BATTLES!
AND ANOTHER THING! YOU SHOULD FIRE WHOEVER DID YOUR OUTFIT!
WELL, NOW... THAT WASN'T SO BAD.
...WITH THE TERRORIST THREAT ENDED, METROPOLIS IS ALL ABUZZ BY THE REAPPEARANCE OF SUPERMAN'S FEMALE SIDEKICK, SUPERGIRL...
BOMB SCARE
"FEMALE SIDEKICK"?!
WHERE'D THEY GET THAT FROM? I DON'T BELIEVE THEY SAID THAT!
OOOH, THAT MAKES ME MAD--!

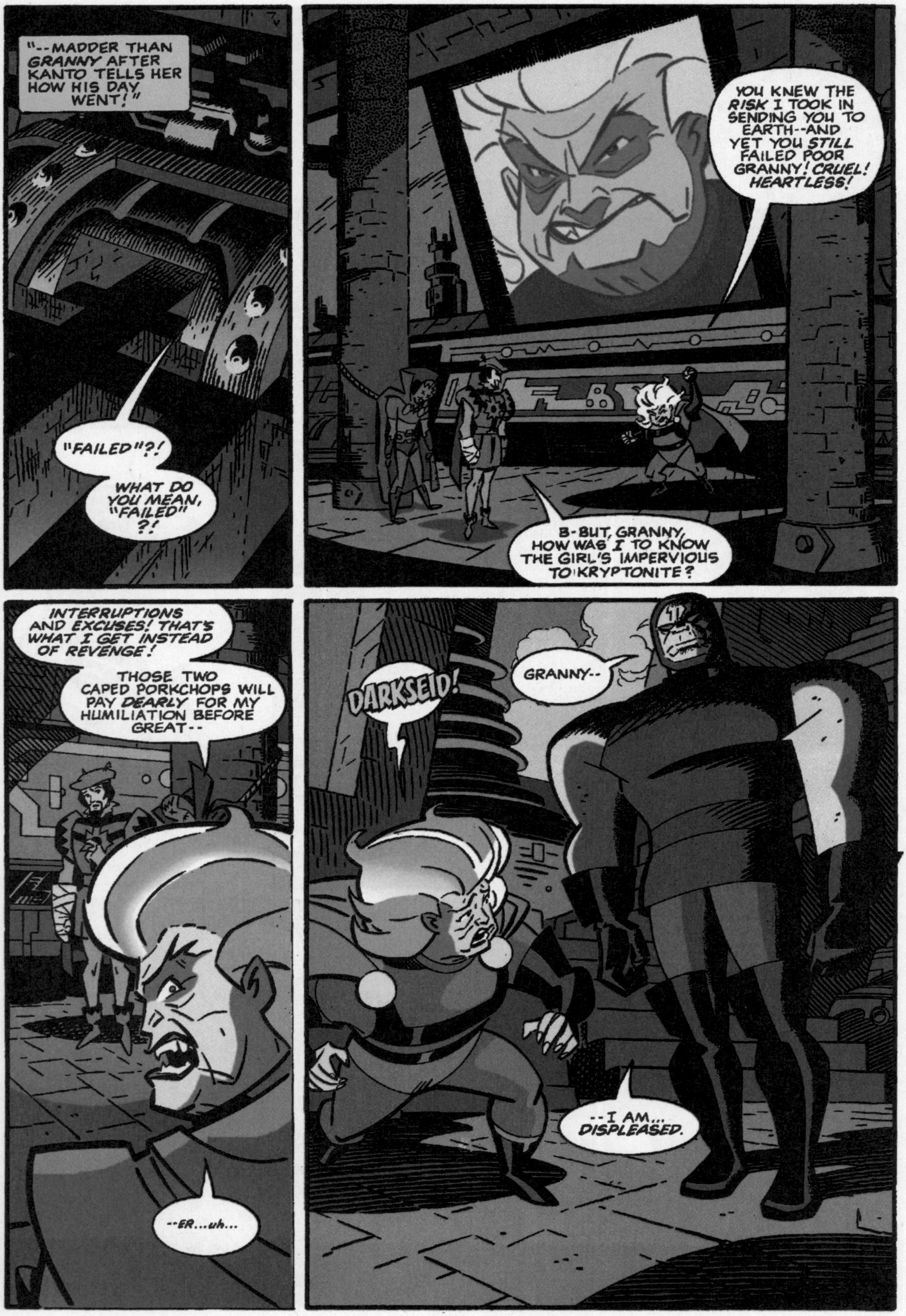
"--MADDER THAN GRANNY AFTER KANTO TELLS HER HOW HIS DAY WENT!"
"FAILED"?!
WHAT DO YOU MEAN, "FAILED"?!
YOU KNEW THE RISK I TOOK IN SENDING YOU TO EARTH--AND YET YOU STILL FAILED POOR GRANNY! CRUEL! HEARTLESS!
B-BUT, GRANNY, HOW WAS I TO KNOW THE GIRL'S IMPERVIOUS TO KRYPTONITE?
INTERRUPTIONS AND EXCUSES! THAT'S WHAT I GET INSTEAD OF REVENGE!
THOSE TWO CAPED PORKCHOPS WILL PAY DEARLY FOR MY HUMILIATION BEFORE GREAT--
--ER...uh...
DARKSEID!
GRANNY--
--I AM... DISPLEASED.

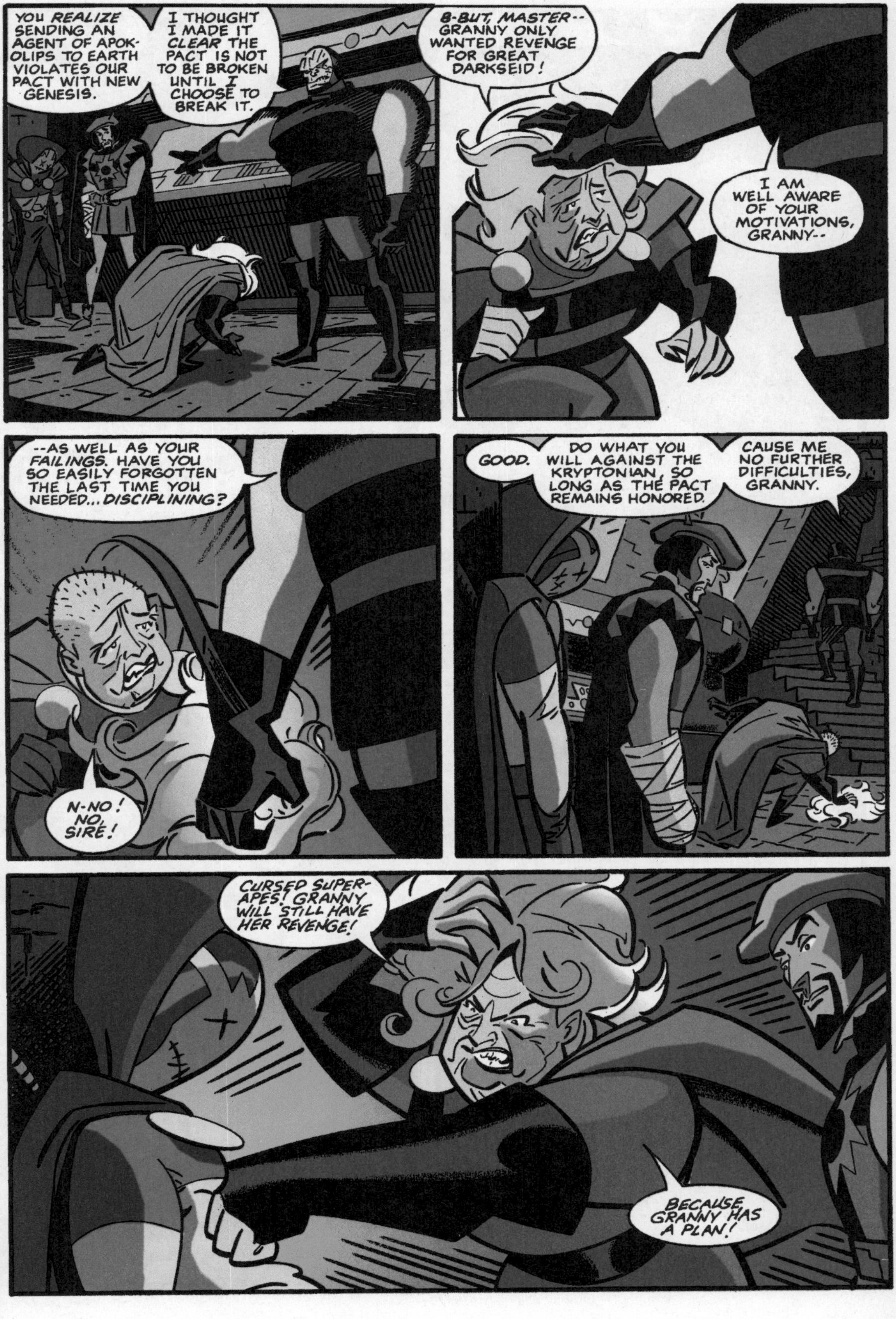
YOU REALIZE SENDING AN AGENT OF APOKOLIPS TO EARTH VIOLATES OUR PACT WITH NEW GENESIS.
I THOUGHT I MADE IT CLEAR THE PACT IS NOT TO BE BROKEN UNTIL I CHOOSE TO BREAK IT.
B-BUT, MASTER-- GRANNY ONLY WANTED REVENGE FOR GREAT DARKSEID!
I AM WELL AWARE OF YOUR MOTIVATIONS, GRANNY--
--AS WELL AS YOUR FAILINGS. HAVE YOU SO EASILY FORGOTTEN THE LAST TIME YOU NEEDED... DISCIPLINING?
N-NO! NO, SIRE!
GOOD.
DO WHAT YOU WILL AGAINST THE KRYPTONIAN, SO LONG AS THE PACT REMAINS HONORED.
CAUSE ME NO FURTHER DIFFICULTIES, GRANNY.
CURSED SUPER-APES! GRANNY WILL STILL HAVE HER REVENGE!
BECAUSE GRANNY HAS A PLAN!

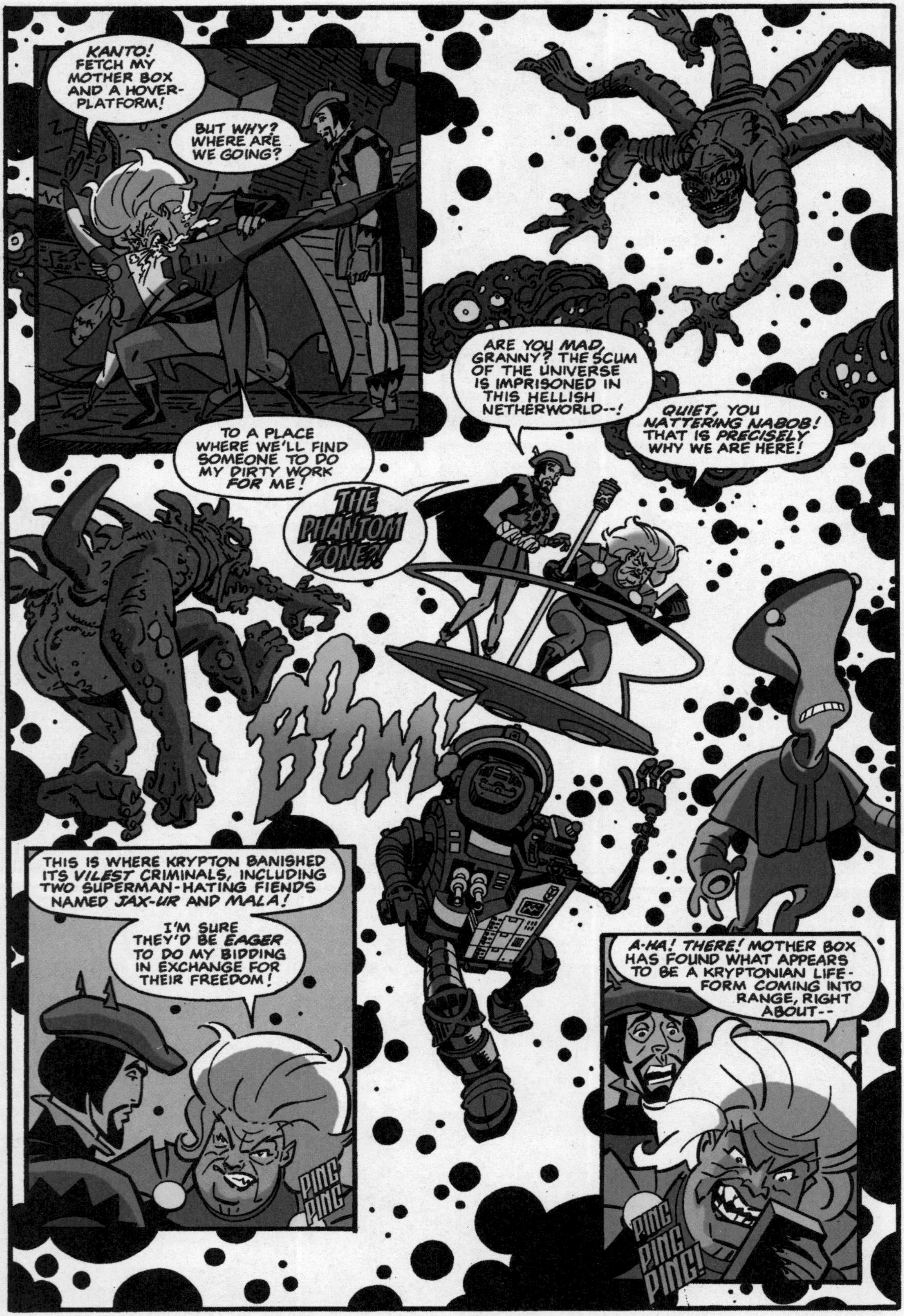
KANTO! FETCH MY MOTHER BOX AND A HOVER-PLATFORM!
BUT WHY? WHERE ARE WE GOING?
TO A PLACE WHERE WE'LL FIND SOMEONE TO DO MY DIRTY WORK FOR ME!
THE PHANTOM ZONE?!
ARE YOU MAD, GRANNY? THE SCUM OF THE UNIVERSE IS IMPRISONED IN THIS HELLISH NETHERWORLD--!
QUIET, YOU NATTERING NABOB! THAT IS PRECISELY WHY WE ARE HERE!
BOOM!
THIS IS WHERE KRYPTON BANISHED ITS VILEST CRIMINALS, INCLUDING TWO SUPERMAN-HATING FIENDS NAMED JAX-UR AND MALA!
I'M SURE THEY'D BE EAGER TO DO MY BIDDING IN EXCHANGE FOR THEIR FREEDOM!
PING PING
A-HA! THERE! MOTHER BOX HAS FOUND WHAT APPEARS TO BE A KRYPTONIAN LIFE-FORM COMING INTO RANGE, RIGHT ABOUT--
PING PING PING!

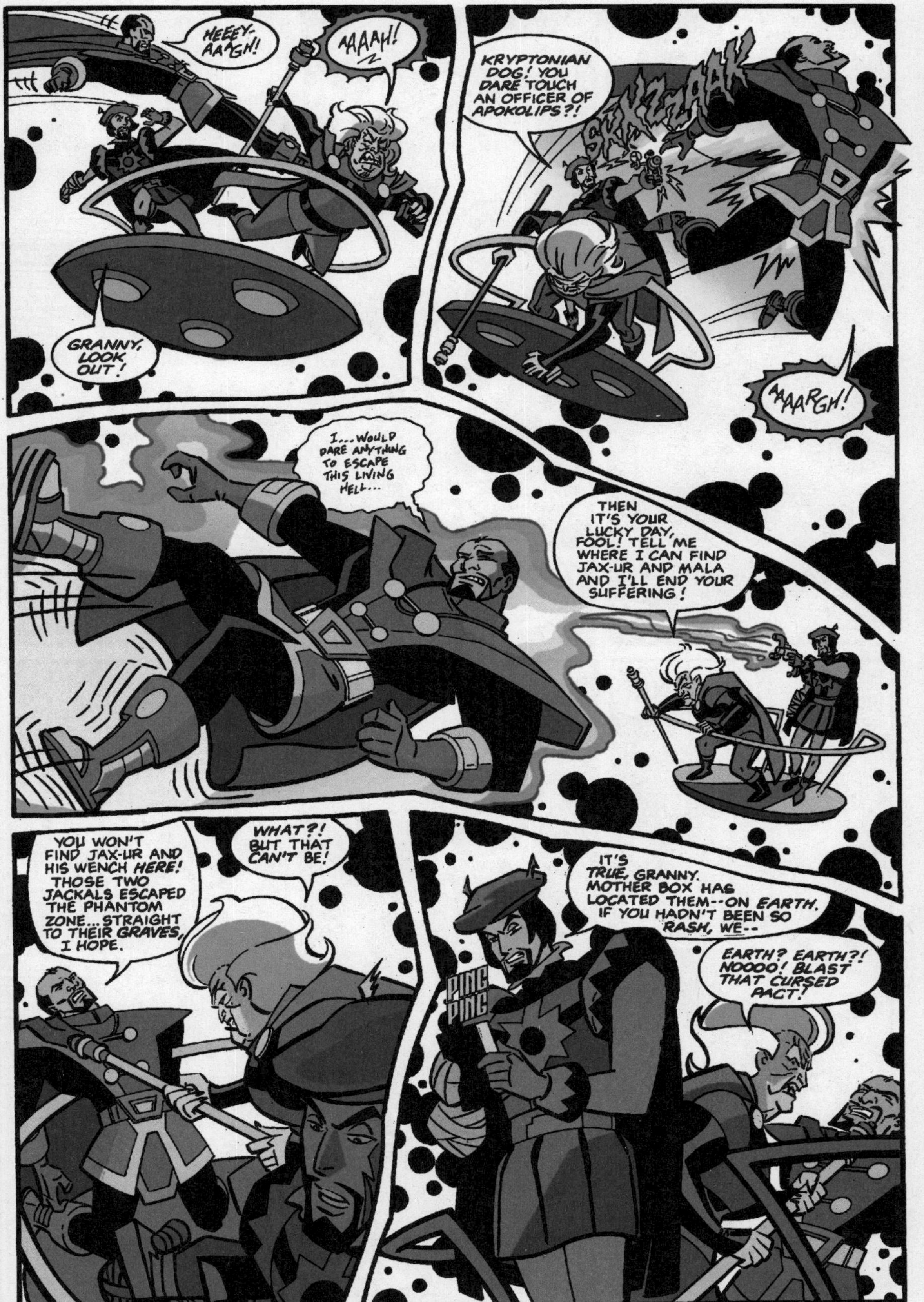

HEEEY-AAAGH!
AAAAH!
GRANNY, LOOK OUT!
KRYPTONIAN DOG! YOU DARE TOUCH AN OFFICER OF APOKOLIPS?!
SKKZZZAAK
AAAARGH!
I... WOULD DARE ANYTHING TO ESCAPE THIS LIVING HELL...
THEN IT'S YOUR LUCKY DAY, FOOL! TELL ME WHERE I CAN FIND JAX-UR AND MALA AND I'LL END YOUR SUFFERING!
YOU WON'T FIND JAX-UR AND HIS WENCH HERE! THOSE TWO JACKALS ESCAPED THE PHANTOM ZONE... STRAIGHT TO THEIR GRAVES, I HOPE.
WHAT?! BUT THAT CAN'T BE!
IT'S TRUE, GRANNY. MOTHER BOX HAS LOCATED THEM--ON EARTH. IF YOU HADN'T BEEN SO RASH, WE--
PING PING
EARTH? EARTH?! NOOOO! BLAST THAT CURSED PACT!

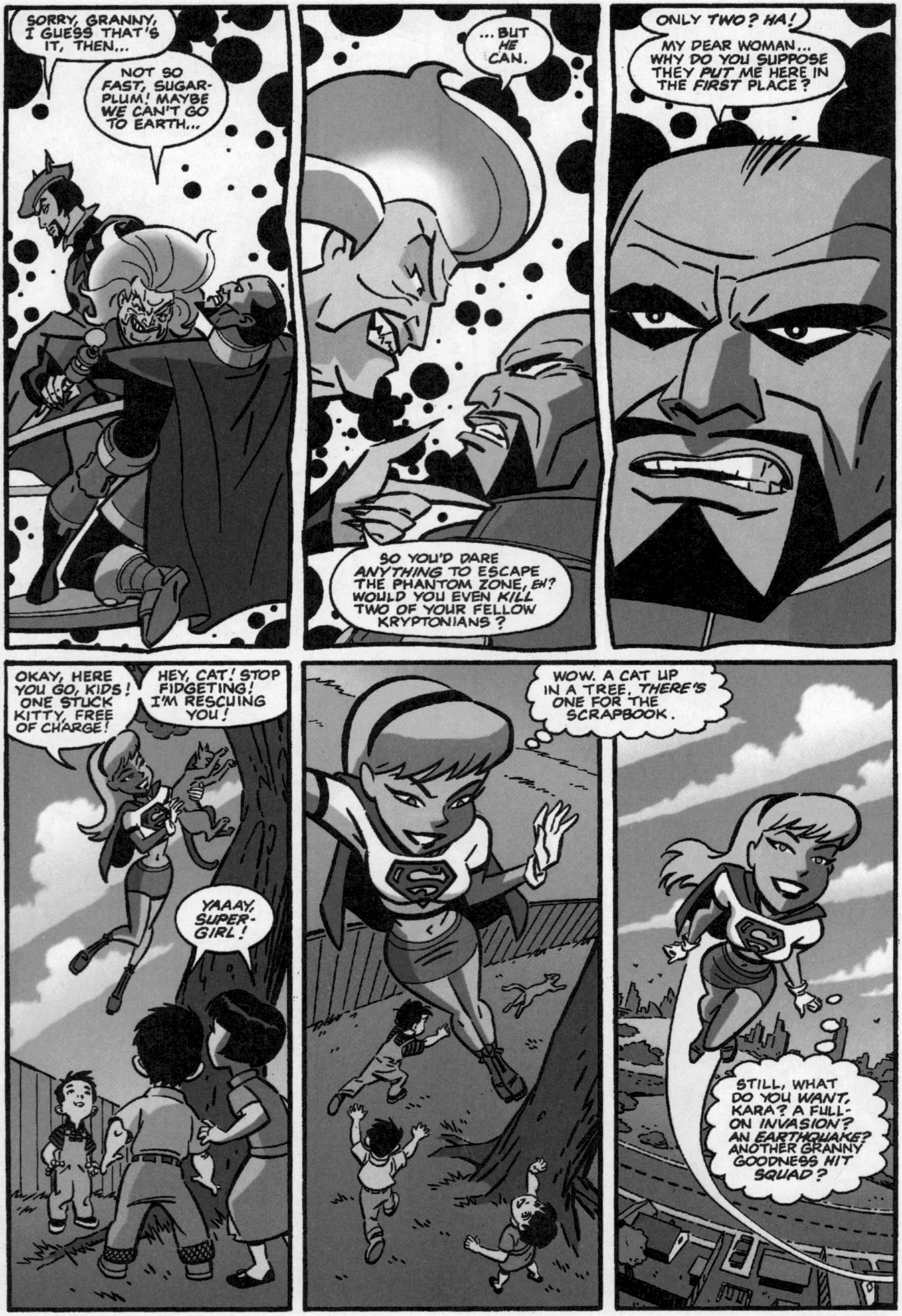
SORRY, GRANNY, I GUESS THAT'S IT, THEN...
NOT SO FAST, SUGARPLUM! MAYBE WE CAN'T GO TO EARTH...
...BUT HE CAN.
SO YOU'D DARE ANYTHING TO ESCAPE THE PHANTOM ZONE, EH? WOULD YOU EVEN KILL TWO OF YOUR FELLOW KRYPTONIANS?
ONLY TWO? HA!
MY DEAR WOMAN... WHY DO YOU SUPPOSE THEY PUT ME HERE IN THE FIRST PLACE?
OKAY, HERE YOU GO, KIDS! ONE STUCK KITTY, FREE OF CHARGE!
HEY, CAT! STOP FIDGETING! I'M RESCUING YOU!
YAAAY, SUPER-GIRL!
WOW. A CAT UP IN A TREE. THERE'S ONE FOR THE SCRAPBOOK.
STILL, WHAT DO YOU WANT, KARA? A FULL-ON INVASION? AN EARTHQUAKE? ANOTHER GRANNY GOODNESS HIT SQUAD?

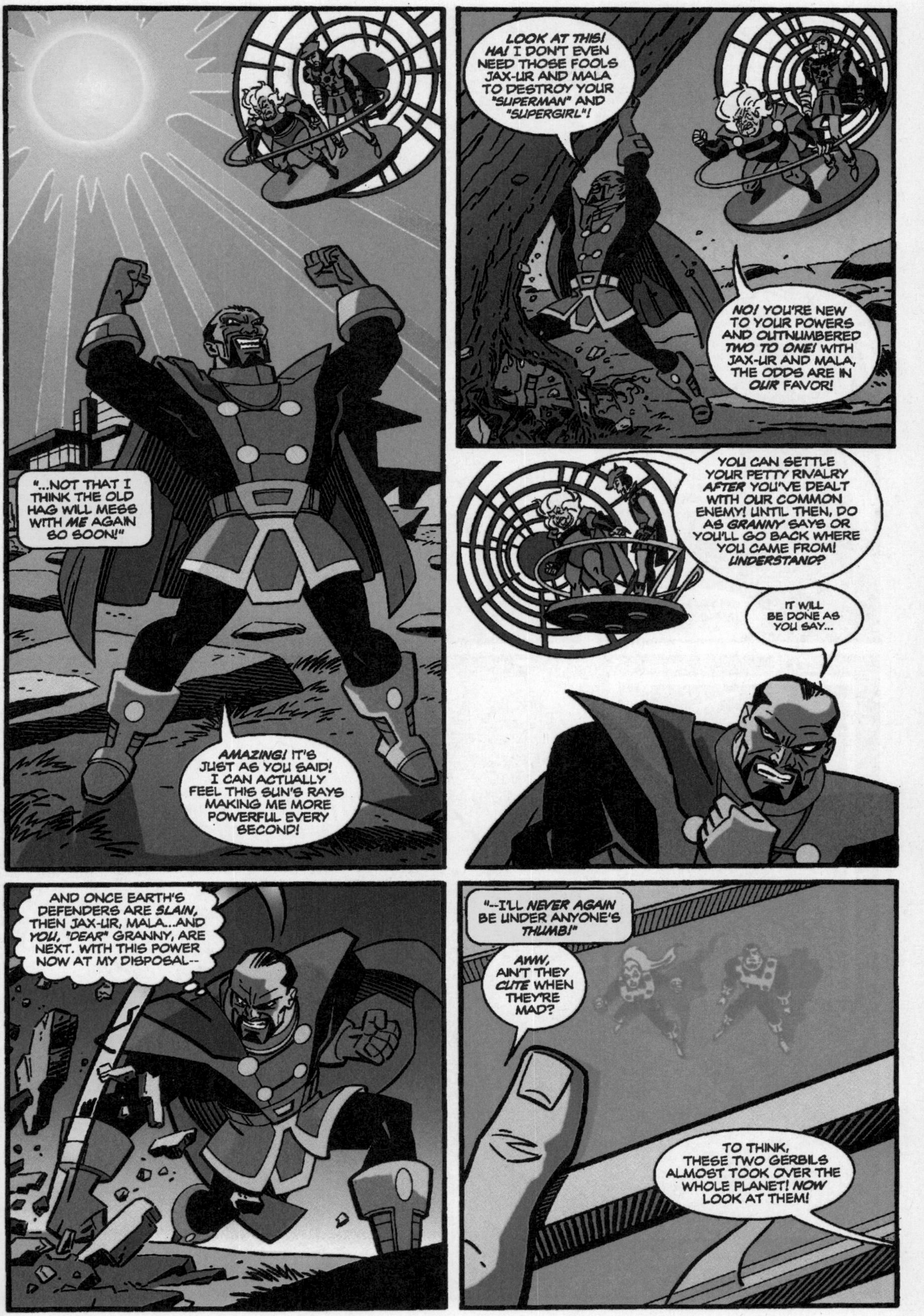
"...NOT THAT I THINK THE OLD HAG WILL MESS WITH ME AGAIN SO SOON!"
AMAZING! IT'S JUST AS YOU SAID! I CAN ACTUALLY FEEL THIS SUN'S RAYS MAKING ME MORE POWERFUL EVERY SECOND!
LOOK AT THIS! HA! I DON'T EVEN NEED THOSE FOOLS JAX-UR AND MALA TO DESTROY YOUR "SUPERMAN" AND "SUPERGIRL"!
NO! YOU'RE NEW TO YOUR POWERS AND OUTNUMBERED TWO TO ONE! WITH JAX-UR AND MALA, THE ODDS ARE IN OUR FAVOR!
YOU CAN SETTLE YOUR PETTY RIVALRY AFTER YOU'VE DEALT WITH OUR COMMON ENEMY! UNTIL THEN, DO AS GRANNY SAYS OR YOU'LL GO BACK WHERE YOU CAME FROM! UNDERSTAND?
IT WILL BE DONE AS YOU SAY...
AND ONCE EARTH'S DEFENDERS ARE SLAIN, THEN JAX-UR, MALA...AND YOU, "DEAR" GRANNY, ARE NEXT. WITH THIS POWER NOW AT MY DISPOSAL--
"--I'LL NEVER AGAIN BE UNDER ANYONE'S THUMB!"
AWW, AIN'T THEY CUTE WHEN THEY'RE MAD?
TO THINK, THESE TWO GERBILS ALMOST TOOK OVER THE WHOLE PLANET! NOW LOOK AT THEM!

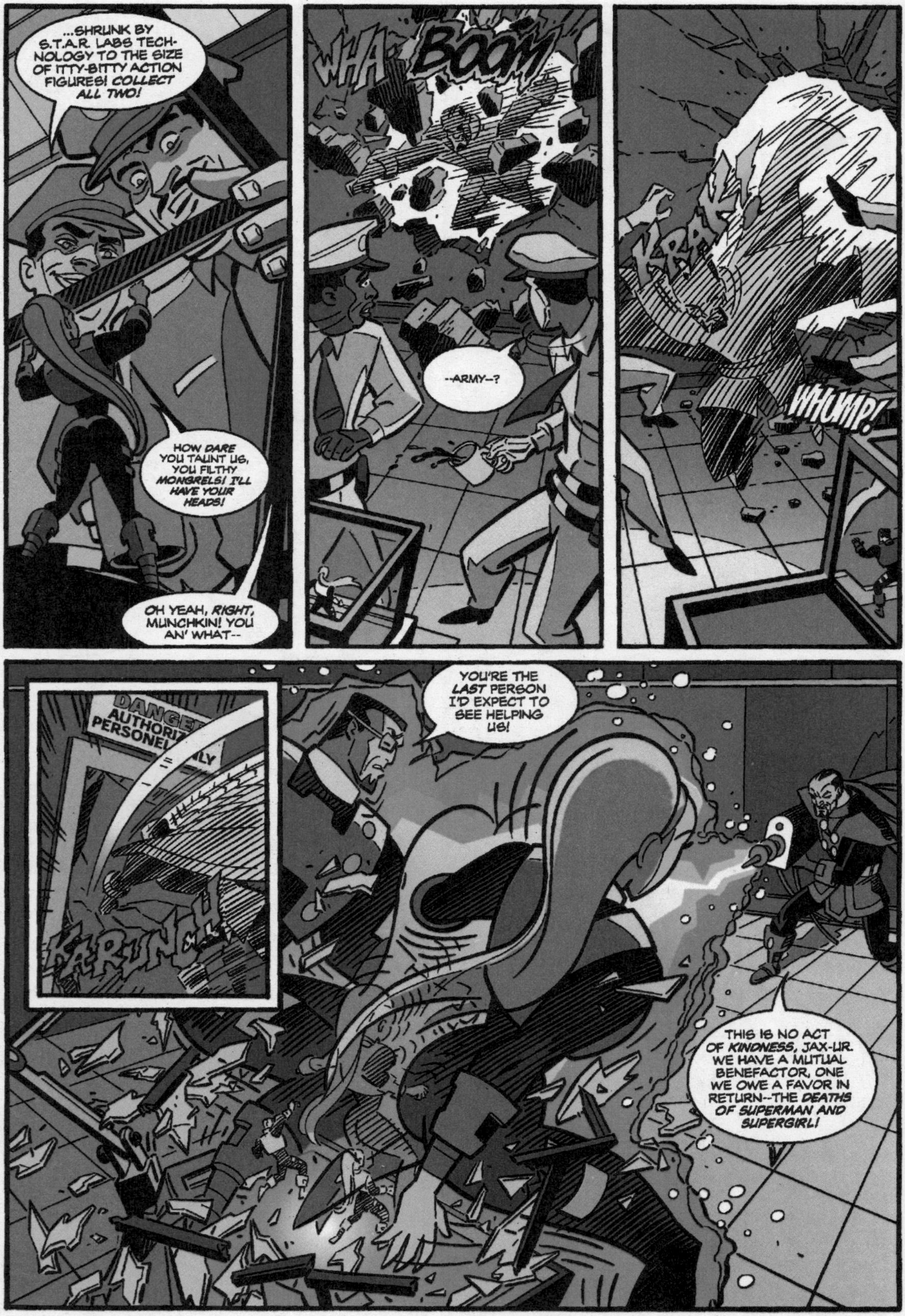
...SHRUNK BY S.T.A.R. LABS TECHNOLOGY TO THE SIZE OF ITTY-BITTY ACTION FIGURES! COLLECT ALL TWO!
HOW DARE YOU TAUNT US, YOU FILTHY MONGRELS! I'LL HAVE YOUR HEADS!
OH YEAH, RIGHT, MUNCHKIN! YOU AN' WHAT--
WHA-BOOM
--ARMY--?
KRAK
WHUMP!
DANGER
AUTHORIZ
PERSONEL ONLY
KARUNCH
YOU'RE THE LAST PERSON I'D EXPECT TO SEE HELPING US!
THIS IS NO ACT OF KINDNESS, JAX-UR. WE HAVE A MUTUAL BENEFACTOR, ONE WE OWE A FAVOR IN RETURN--THE DEATHS OF SUPERMAN AND SUPERGIRL!

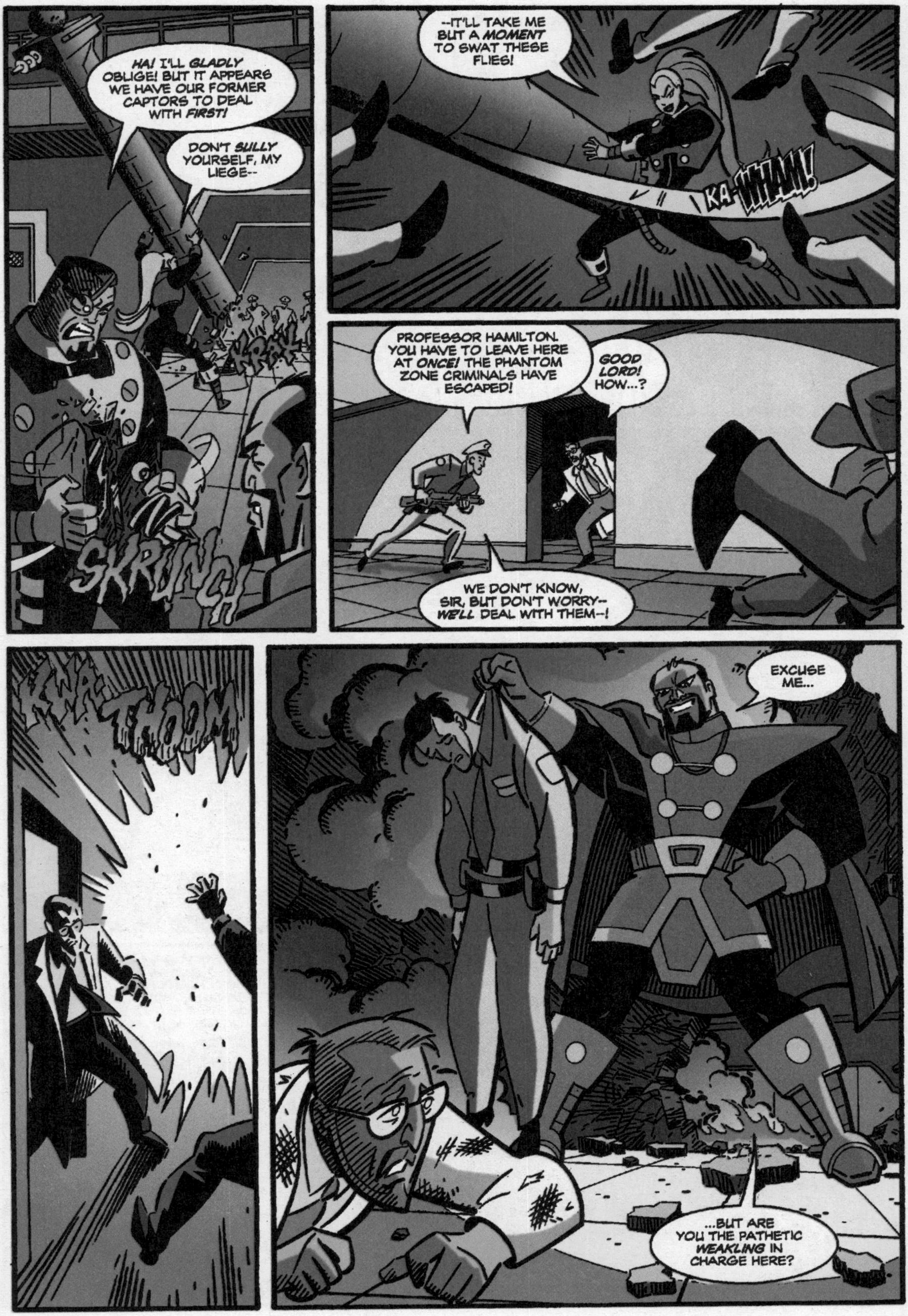
HA! I'LL GLADLY OBLIGE! BUT IT APPEARS WE HAVE OUR FORMER CAPTORS TO DEAL WITH FIRST!
DON'T SULLY YOURSELF, MY LIEGE--
SKRUNCH
--IT'LL TAKE ME BUT A MOMENT TO SWAT THESE FLIES!
KA-WHAM!
PROFESSOR HAMILTON. YOU HAVE TO LEAVE HERE AT ONCE! THE PHANTOM ZONE CRIMINALS HAVE ESCAPED!
GOOD LORD! HOW...?
WE DON'T KNOW, SIR, BUT DON'T WORRY-- WE'LL DEAL WITH THEM--!
KWA-THOOM
EXCUSE ME...
...BUT ARE YOU THE PATHETIC WEAKLING IN CHARGE HERE?

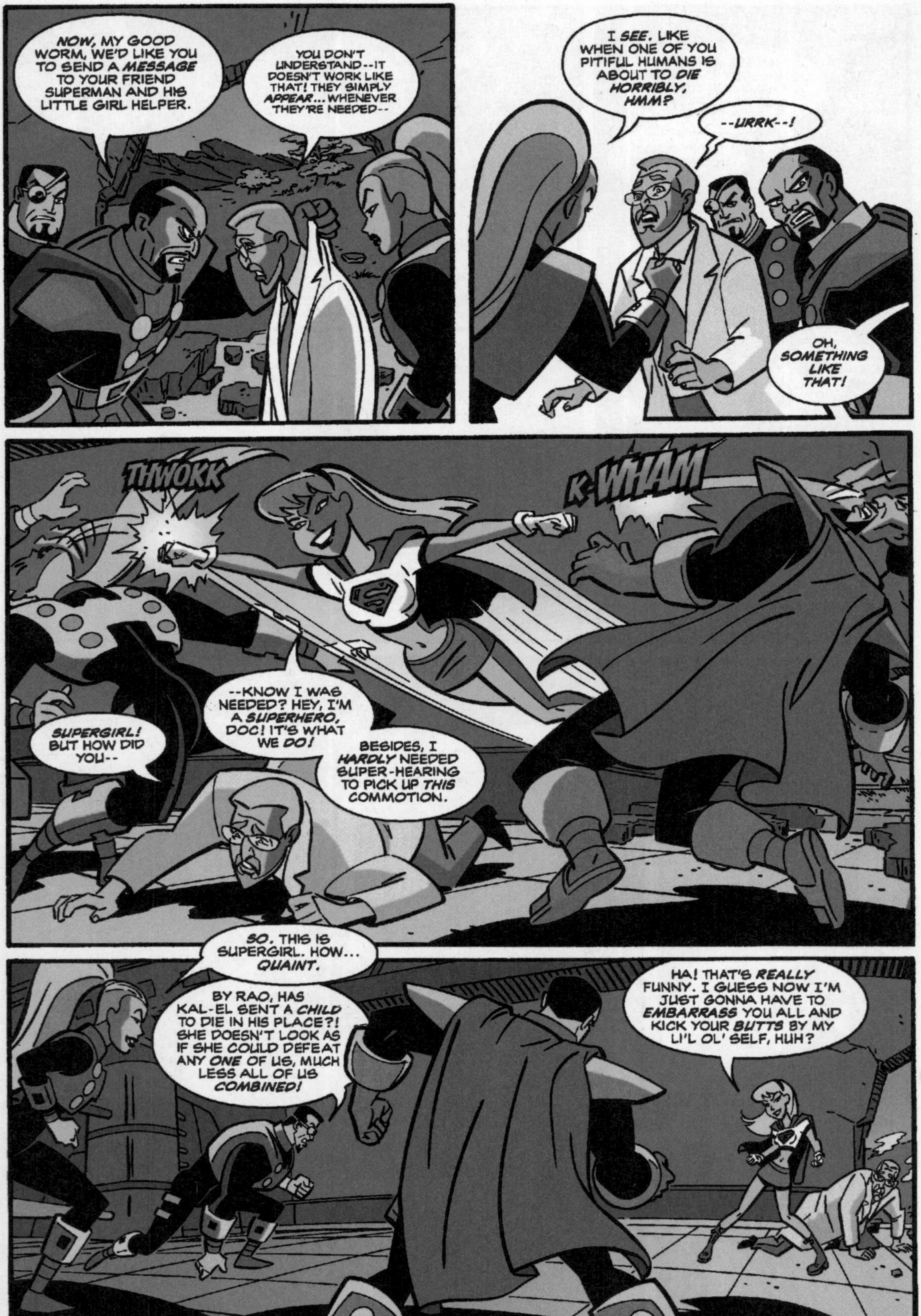
NOW, MY GOOD WORM, WE'D LIKE YOU TO SEND A MESSAGE TO YOUR FRIEND SUPERMAN AND HIS LITTLE GIRL HELPER.
YOU DON'T UNDERSTAND--IT DOESN'T WORK LIKE THAT! THEY SIMPLY APPEAR... WHENEVER THEY'RE NEEDED--
I SEE. LIKE WHEN ONE OF YOU PITIFUL HUMANS IS ABOUT TO DIE HORRIBLY, HMM?
--URRK--!
OH, SOMETHING LIKE THAT!
THWOKK
K-WHAM
SUPERGIRL! BUT HOW DID YOU--
--KNOW I WAS NEEDED? HEY, I'M A SUPERHERO, DOC! IT'S WHAT WE DO!
BESIDES, I HARDLY NEEDED SUPER-HEARING TO PICK UP THIS COMMOTION.
SO. THIS IS SUPERGIRL. HOW... QUAINT.
BY RAO, HAS KAL-EL SENT A CHILD TO DIE IN HIS PLACE?! SHE DOESN'T LOOK AS IF SHE COULD DEFEAT ANY ONE OF US, MUCH LESS ALL OF US COMBINED!
HA! THAT'S REALLY FUNNY. I GUESS NOW I'M JUST GONNA HAVE TO EMBARRASS YOU ALL AND KICK YOUR BUTTS BY MY LI'L OL' SELF, HUH?

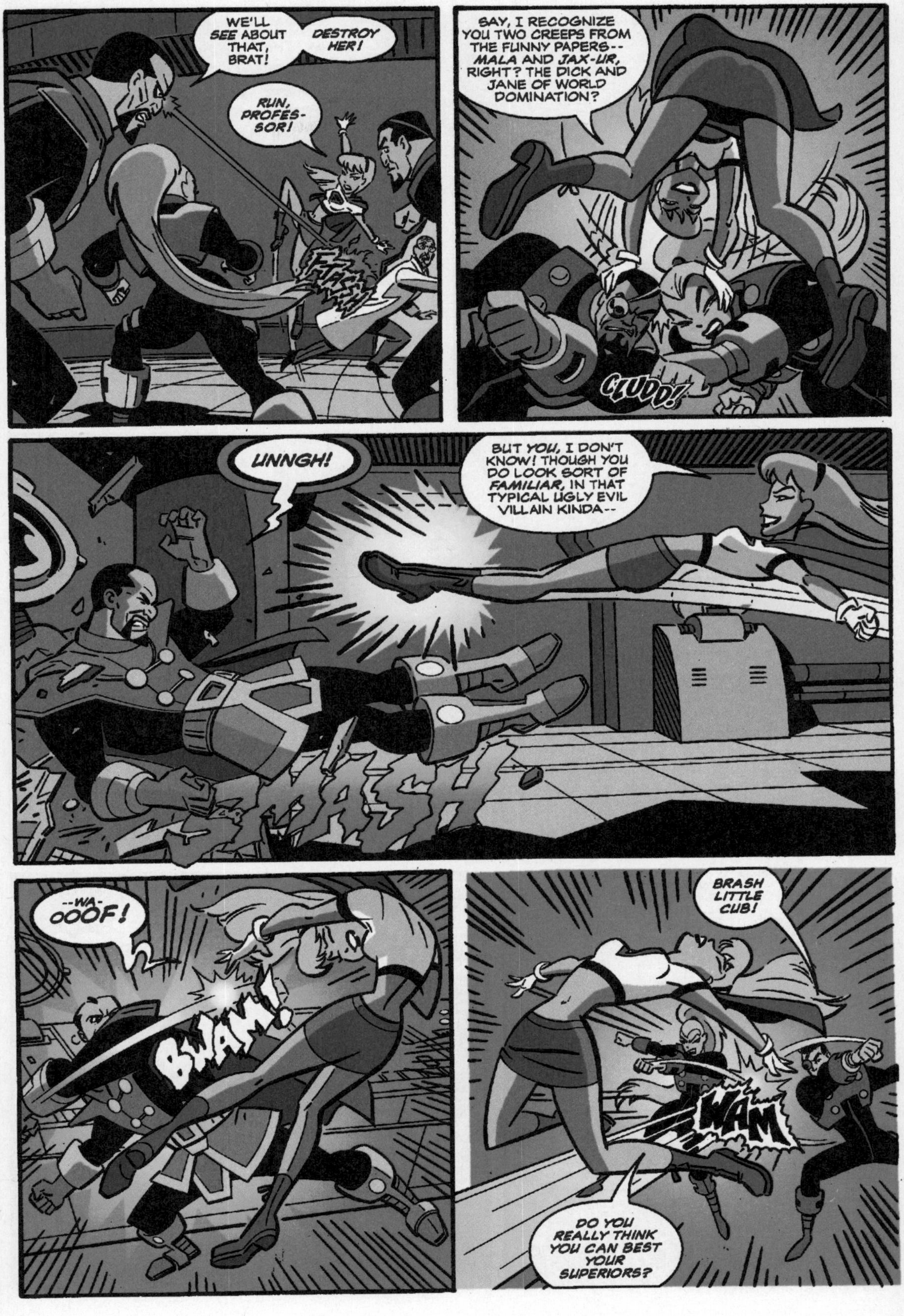
WE'LL SEE ABOUT THAT, BRAT!
DESTROY HER!
RUN, PROFES-SOR!
FTASH
SAY, I RECOGNIZE YOU TWO CREEPS FROM THE FUNNY PAPERS-- MALA AND JAX-UR, RIGHT? THE DICK AND JANE OF WORLD DOMINATION?
CLUDD!
UNNGH!
BUT YOU, I DON'T KNOW! THOUGH YOU DO LOOK SORT OF FAMILIAR, IN THAT TYPICAL UGLY EVIL VILLAIN KINDA--
--WA-OOOF!
BWAM!
BRASH LITTLE CUB!
WAM
DO YOU REALLY THINK YOU CAN BEST YOUR SUPERIORS?

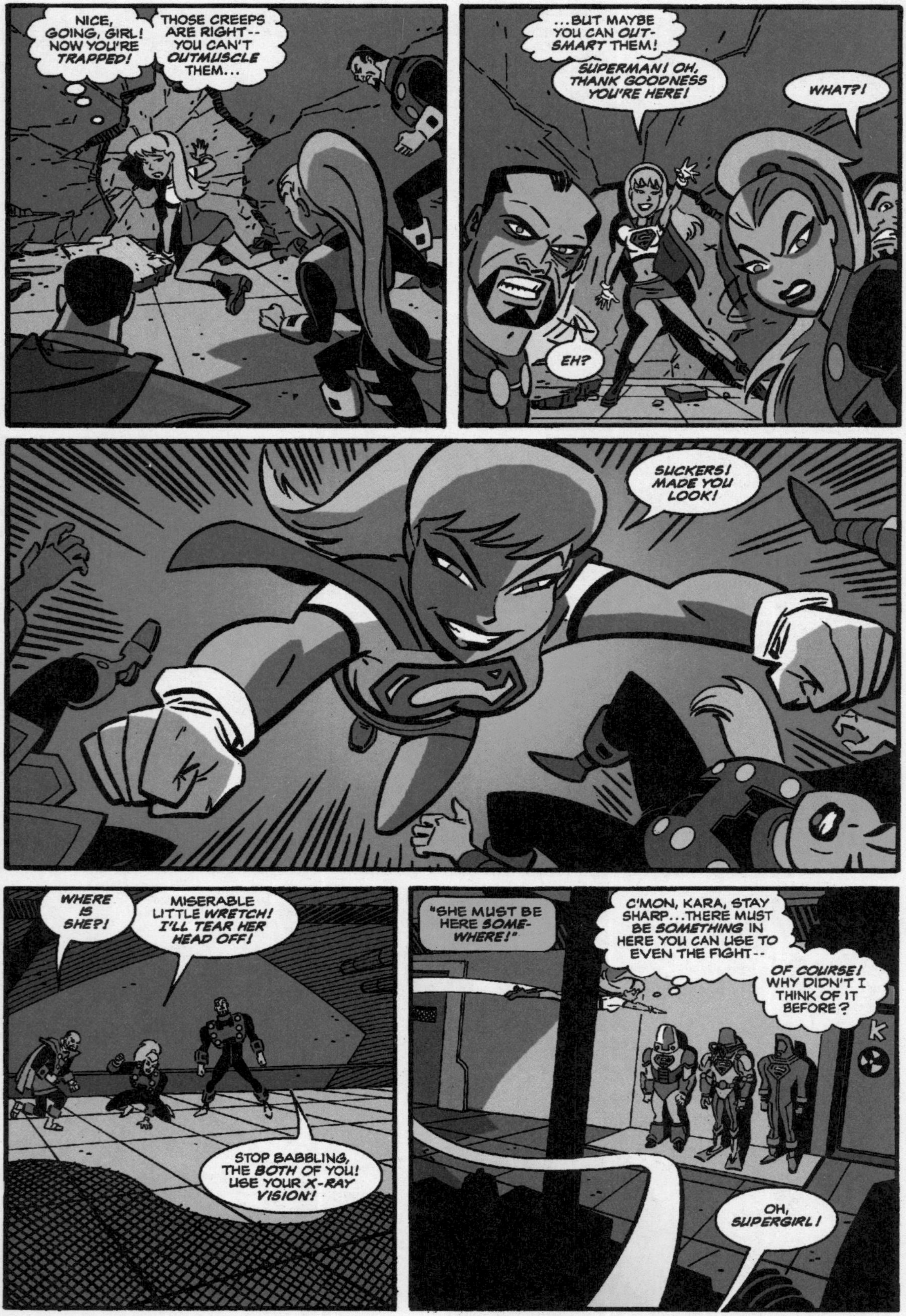
NICE, GOING, GIRL! NOW YOU'RE TRAPPED!
THOSE CREEPS ARE RIGHT-- YOU CAN'T OUTMUSCLE THEM...
...BUT MAYBE YOU CAN OUT-SMART THEM!
SUPERMAN! OH, THANK GOODNESS YOU'RE HERE!
WHAT?!
EH?
SUCKERS! MADE YOU LOOK!
WHERE IS SHE?!
MISERABLE LITTLE WRETCH! I'LL TEAR HER HEAD OFF!
STOP BABBLING, THE BOTH OF YOU! USE YOUR X-RAY VISION!
"SHE MUST BE HERE SOME-WHERE!"
C'MON, KARA, STAY SHARP...THERE MUST BE SOMETHING IN HERE YOU CAN USE TO EVEN THE FIGHT--
OF COURSE! WHY DIDN'T I THINK OF IT BEFORE?
K
OH, SUPERGIRL!

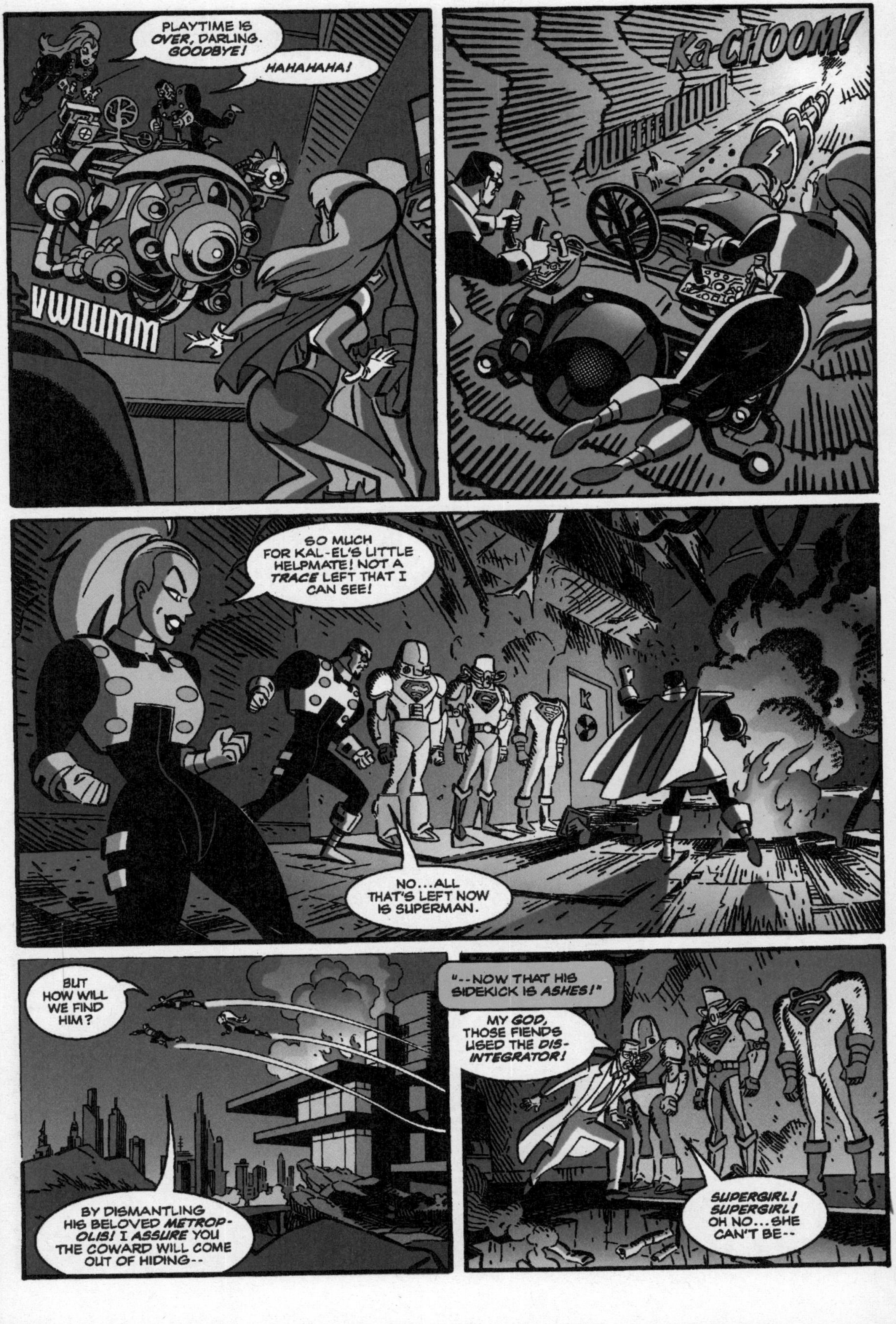
PLAYTIME IS OVER, DARLING. GOODBYE!
HAHAHAHA!
VWOOMM
Ka-CHOOM!
VWEEEEOWW
SO MUCH FOR KAL-EL'S LITTLE HELPMATE! NOT A TRACE LEFT THAT I CAN SEE!
K
NO...ALL THAT'S LEFT NOW IS SUPERMAN.
BUT HOW WILL WE FIND HIM?
BY DISMANTLING HIS BELOVED METROP-OLIS! I ASSURE YOU THE COWARD WILL COME OUT OF HIDING--
"--NOW THAT HIS SIDEKICK IS ASHES!"
MY GOD, THOSE FIENDS USED THE DIS-INTEGRATOR!
SUPERGIRL! SUPERGIRL! OH NO...SHE CAN'T BE--

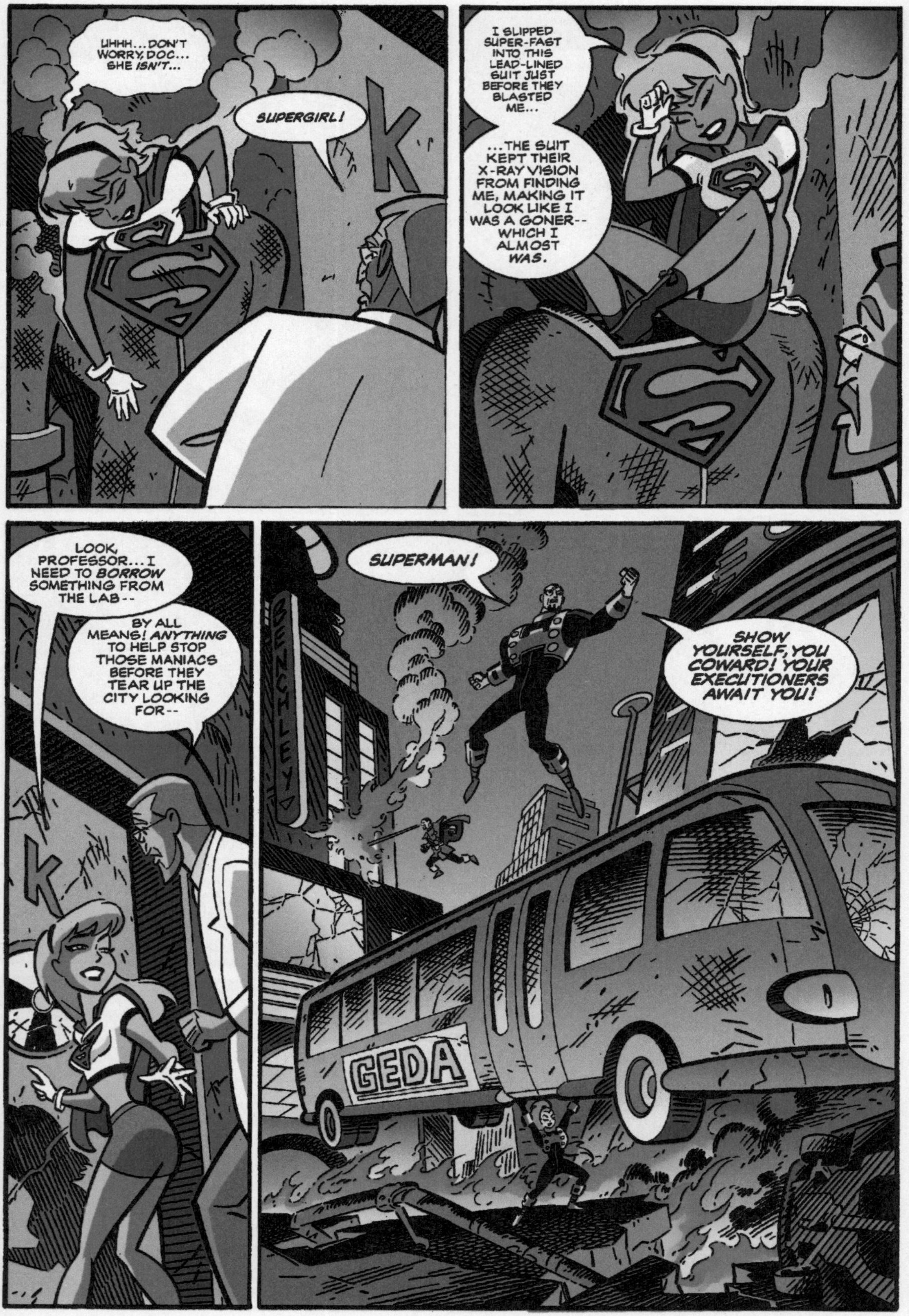
UHHH... DON'T WORRY, DOC... SHE ISN'T...
SUPERGIRL!
I SLIPPED SUPER-FAST INTO THIS LEAD-LINED SUIT JUST BEFORE THEY BLASTED ME...
...THE SUIT KEPT THEIR X-RAY VISION FROM FINDING ME, MAKING IT LOOK LIKE I WAS A GONER-- WHICH I ALMOST WAS.
LOOK, PROFESSOR... I NEED TO BORROW SOMETHING FROM THE LAB--
BY ALL MEANS! ANYTHING TO HELP STOP THOSE MANIACS BEFORE THEY TEAR UP THE CITY LOOKING FOR--
SUPERMAN!
SHOW YOURSELF, YOU COWARD! YOUR EXECUTIONERS AWAIT YOU!
BENCHLEY
GEDA

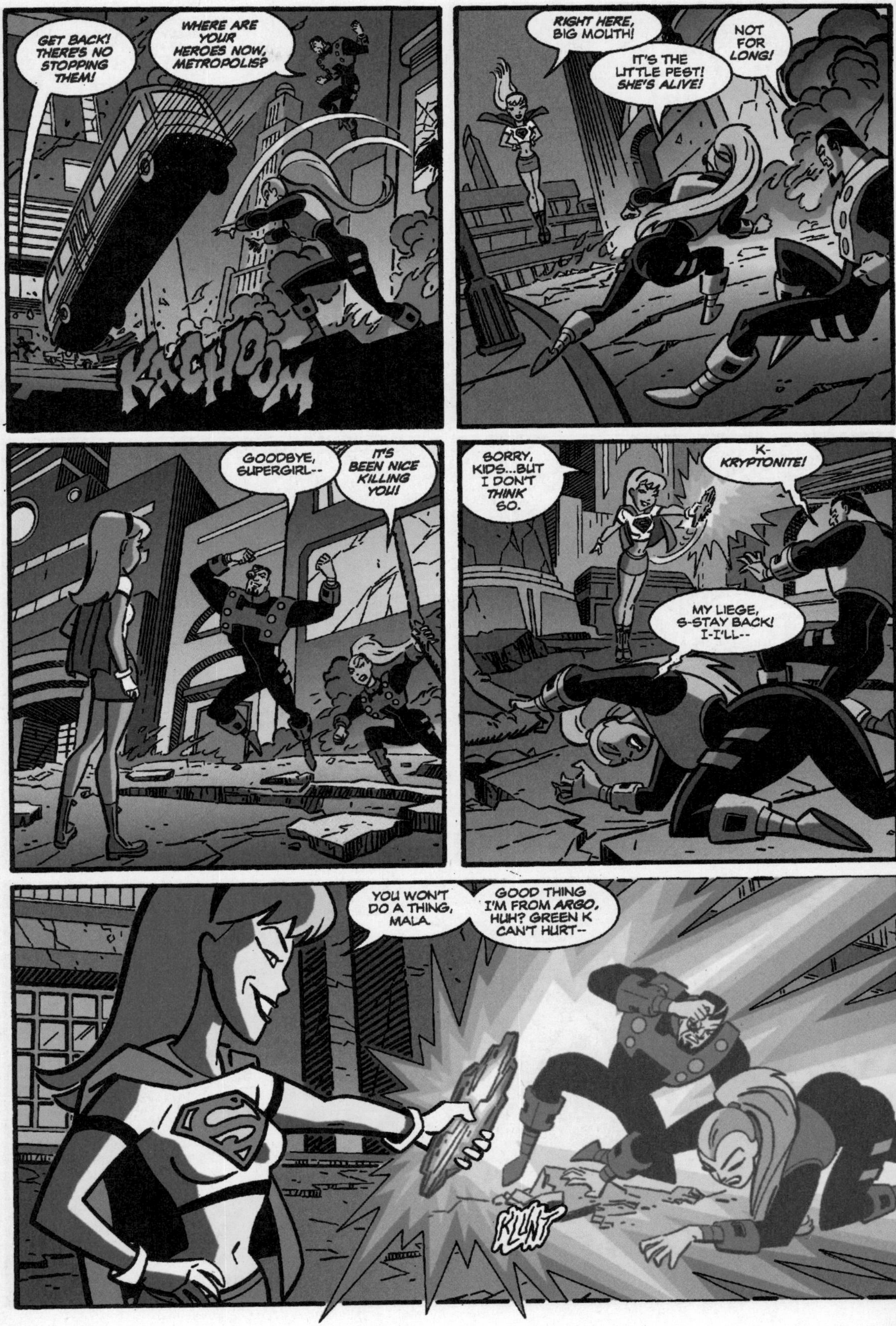
GET BACK! THERE'S NO STOPPING THEM!
WHERE ARE YOUR HEROES NOW, METROPOLIS?
KACHOOM
RIGHT HERE, BIG MOUTH!
IT'S THE LITTLE PEST! SHE'S ALIVE!
NOT FOR LONG!
GOODBYE, SUPERGIRL--
IT'S BEEN NICE KILLING YOU!
SORRY, KIDS...BUT I DON'T THINK SO.
K-KRYPTONITE!
MY LIEGE, S-STAY BACK! I-I'LL--
YOU WON'T DO A THING, MALA.
GOOD THING I'M FROM ARGO, HUH? GREEN K CAN'T HURT--
KLUNT

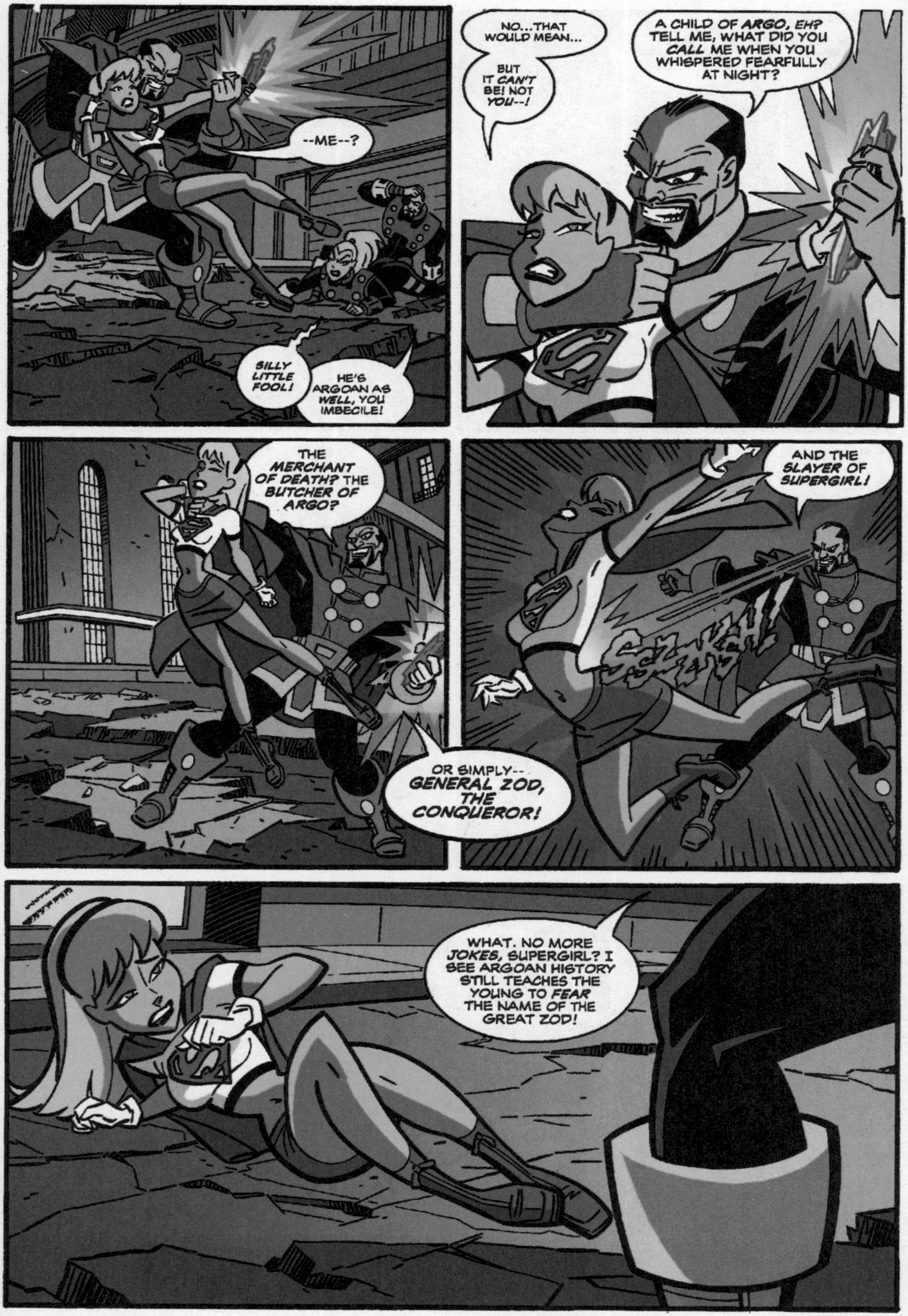
--ME--?
SILLY LITTLE FOOL!
HE'S ARGOAN AS WELL, YOU IMBECILE!
NO...THAT WOULD MEAN...
BUT IT CAN'T BE! NOT YOU--!
A CHILD OF ARGO, EH? TELL ME, WHAT DID YOU CALL ME WHEN YOU WHISPERED FEARFULLY AT NIGHT?
THE MERCHANT OF DEATH? THE BUTCHER OF ARGO?
OR SIMPLY-- GENERAL ZOD, THE CONQUEROR!
AND THE SLAYER OF SUPERGIRL!
SSZZAKSH!!
WHAT. NO MORE JOKES, SUPERGIRL? I SEE ARGOAN HISTORY STILL TEACHES THE YOUNG TO FEAR THE NAME OF THE GREAT ZOD!

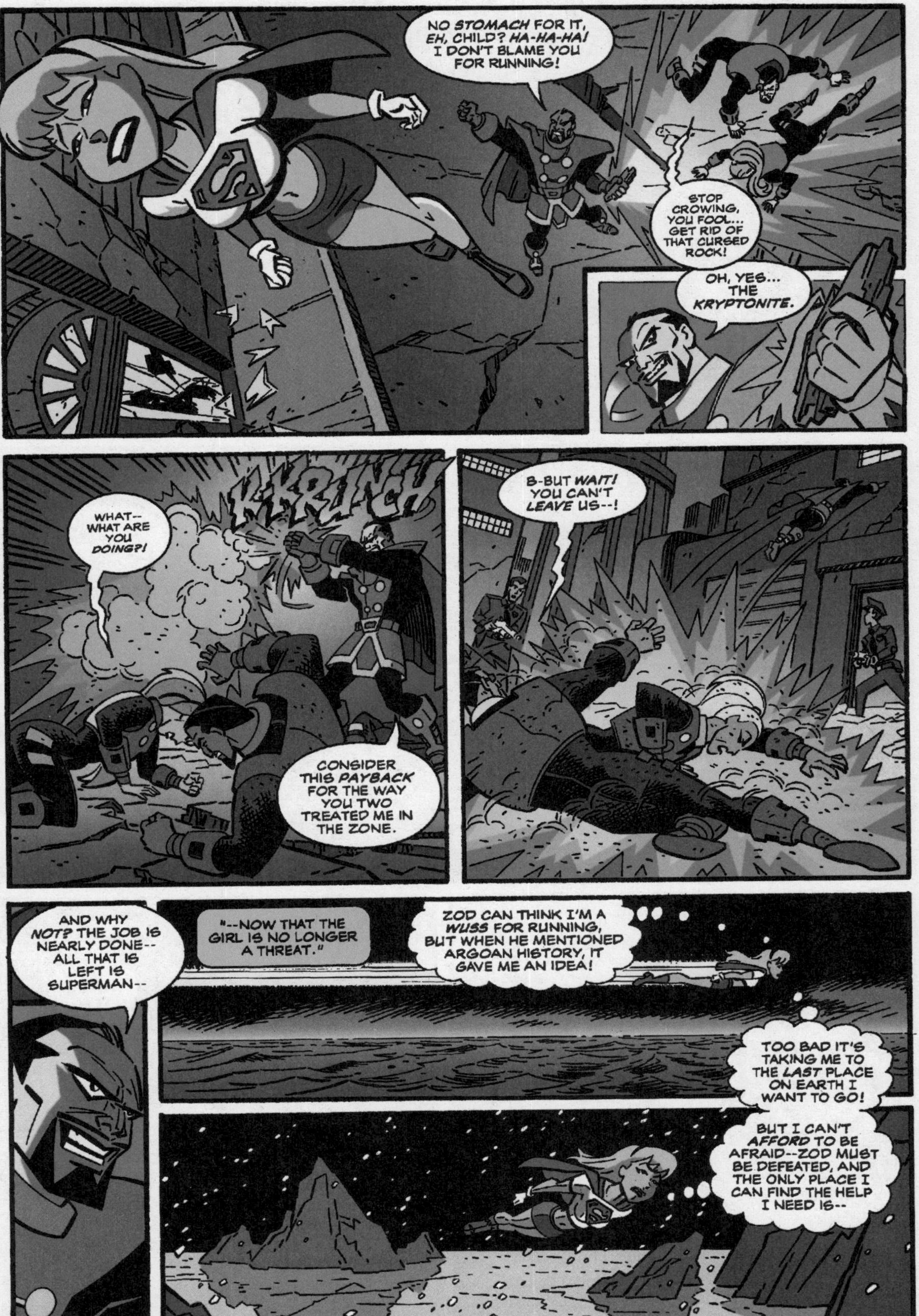
NO *STOMACH* FOR IT, *EH*, CHILD? *HA-HA-HA!* I DON'T BLAME YOU FOR RUNNING!
STOP CROWING, YOU FOOL... GET RID OF THAT CURSED ROCK!
OH, YES... THE *KRYPTONITE.*
K-KRUNCH
WHAT-- WHAT ARE YOU *DOING?!*
CONSIDER THIS *PAYBACK* FOR THE WAY YOU TWO TREATED ME IN THE ZONE.
B-BUT *WAIT!* YOU CAN'T *LEAVE* US--!
AND WHY *NOT?* THE JOB IS NEARLY DONE-- ALL THAT IS LEFT IS SUPERMAN--
"--NOW THAT THE GIRL IS NO LONGER A THREAT."
ZOD CAN THINK I'M A *WUSS* FOR RUNNING, BUT WHEN HE MENTIONED ARGOAN HISTORY, IT GAVE ME AN IDEA!
TOO BAD IT'S TAKING ME TO THE *LAST* PLACE ON EARTH I WANT TO GO!
BUT I CAN'T *AFFORD* TO BE AFRAID--ZOD MUST BE DEFEATED, AND THE ONLY PLACE I CAN FIND THE HELP I NEED IS--

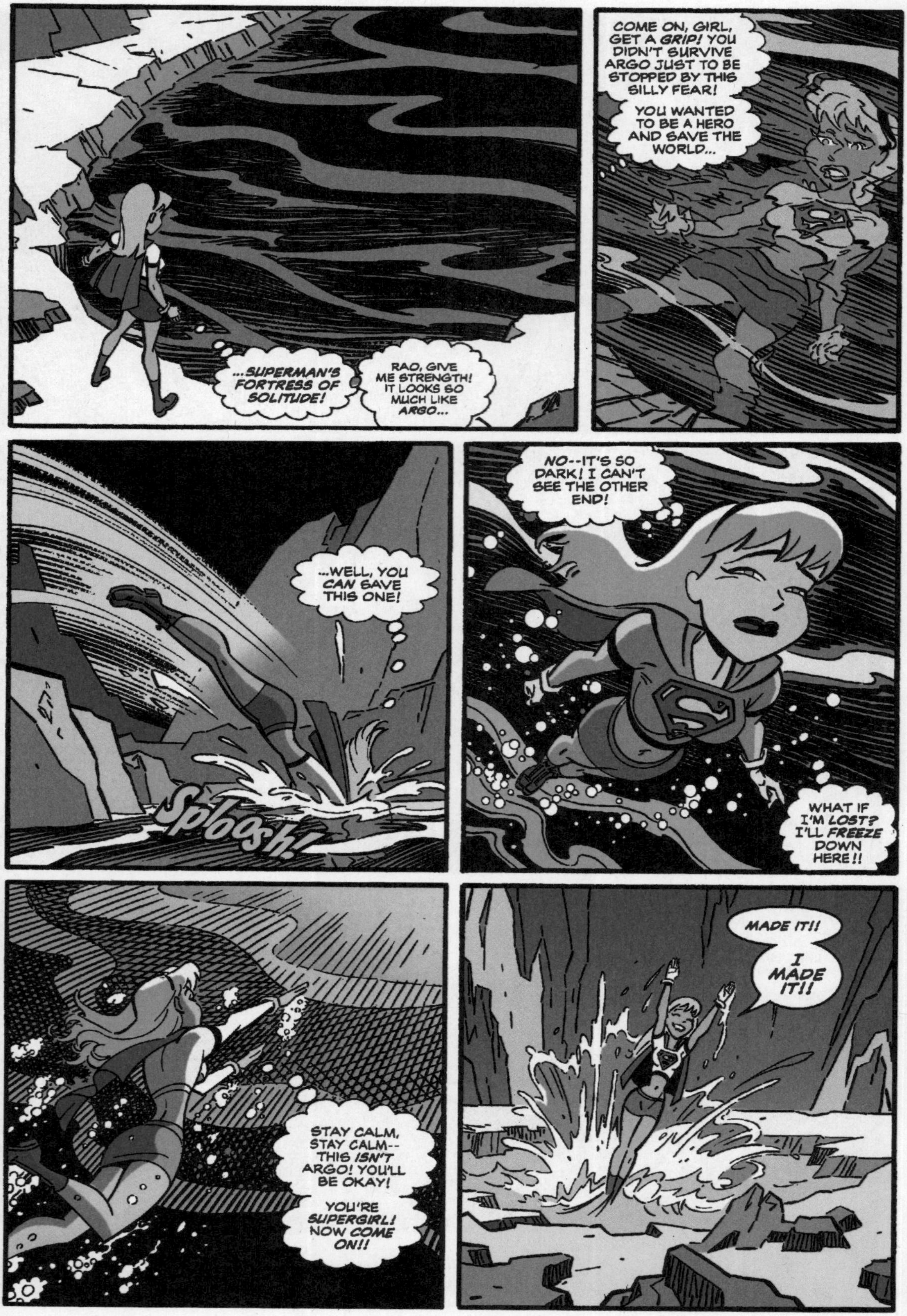
...SUPERMAN'S FORTRESS OF SOLITUDE!
RAO, GIVE ME STRENGTH! IT LOOKS SO MUCH LIKE ARGO...
COME ON, GIRL, GET A GRIP! YOU DIDN'T SURVIVE ARGO JUST TO BE STOPPED BY THIS SILLY FEAR!
YOU WANTED TO BE A HERO AND SAVE THE WORLD...
...WELL, YOU CAN SAVE THIS ONE!
Sploosh!
NO--IT'S SO DARK! I CAN'T SEE THE OTHER END!
WHAT IF I'M LOST? I'LL FREEZE DOWN HERE!!
STAY CALM, STAY CALM--THIS ISN'T ARGO! YOU'LL BE OKAY!
YOU'RE SUPERGIRL! NOW COME ON!!
MADE IT!!
I MADE IT!!

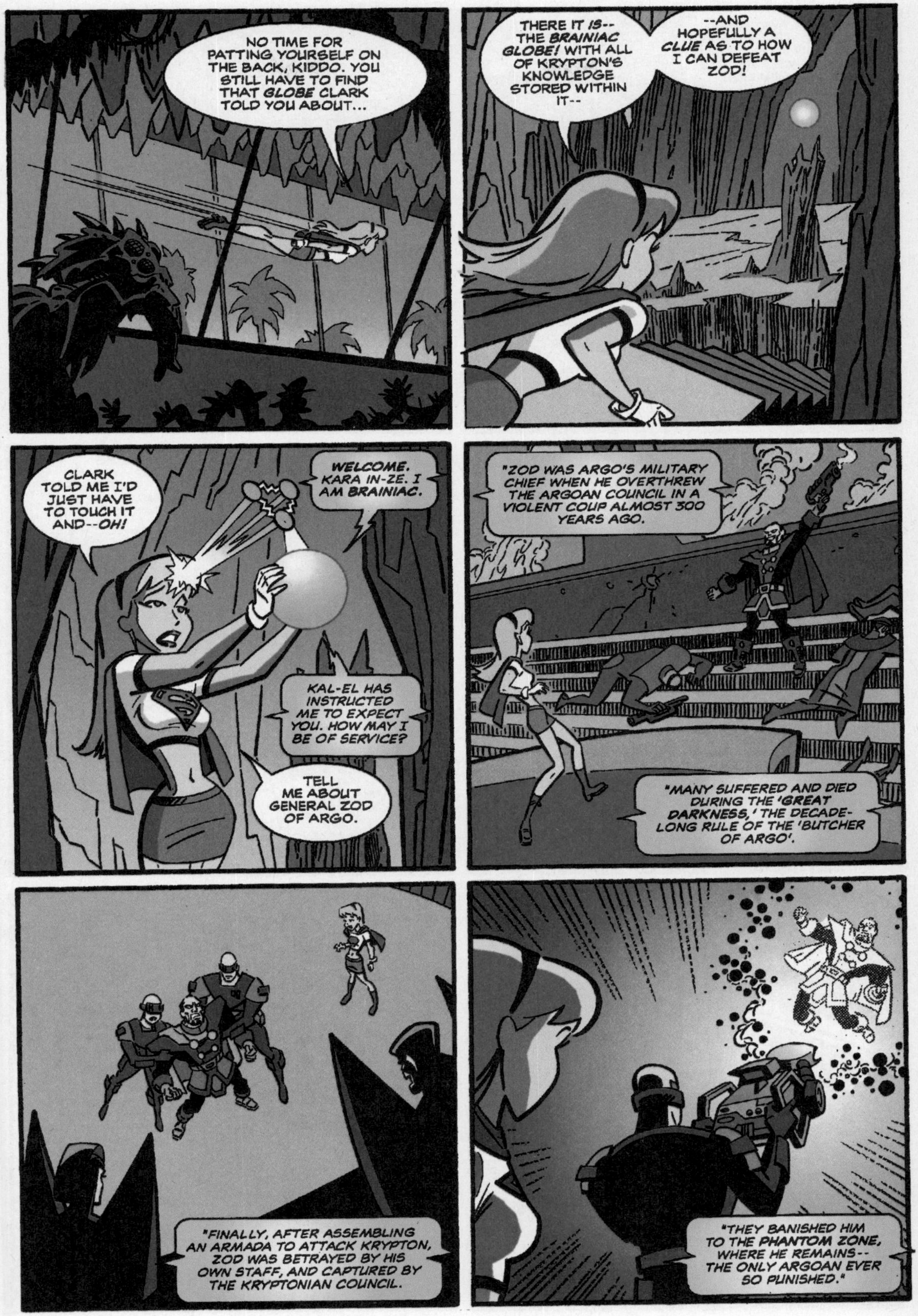
NO TIME FOR PATTING YOURSELF ON THE BACK, KIDDO. YOU STILL HAVE TO FIND THAT GLOBE CLARK TOLD YOU ABOUT...
THERE IT IS-- THE BRAINIAC GLOBE! WITH ALL OF KRYPTON'S KNOWLEDGE STORED WITHIN IT--
--AND HOPEFULLY A CLUE AS TO HOW I CAN DEFEAT ZOD!
CLARK TOLD ME I'D JUST HAVE TO TOUCH IT AND--OH!
WELCOME. KARA IN-ZE. I AM BRAINIAC.
KAL-EL HAS INSTRUCTED ME TO EXPECT YOU. HOW MAY I BE OF SERVICE?
TELL ME ABOUT GENERAL ZOD OF ARGO.
"ZOD WAS ARGO'S MILITARY CHIEF WHEN HE OVERTHREW THE ARGOAN COUNCIL IN A VIOLENT COUP ALMOST 300 YEARS AGO.
"MANY SUFFERED AND DIED DURING THE 'GREAT DARKNESS,' THE DECADE-LONG RULE OF THE 'BUTCHER OF ARGO'.
"FINALLY, AFTER ASSEMBLING AN ARMADA TO ATTACK KRYPTON, ZOD WAS BETRAYED BY HIS OWN STAFF, AND CAPTURED BY THE KRYPTONIAN COUNCIL.
"THEY BANISHED HIM TO THE PHANTOM ZONE, WHERE HE REMAINS-- THE ONLY ARGOAN EVER SO PUNISHED."

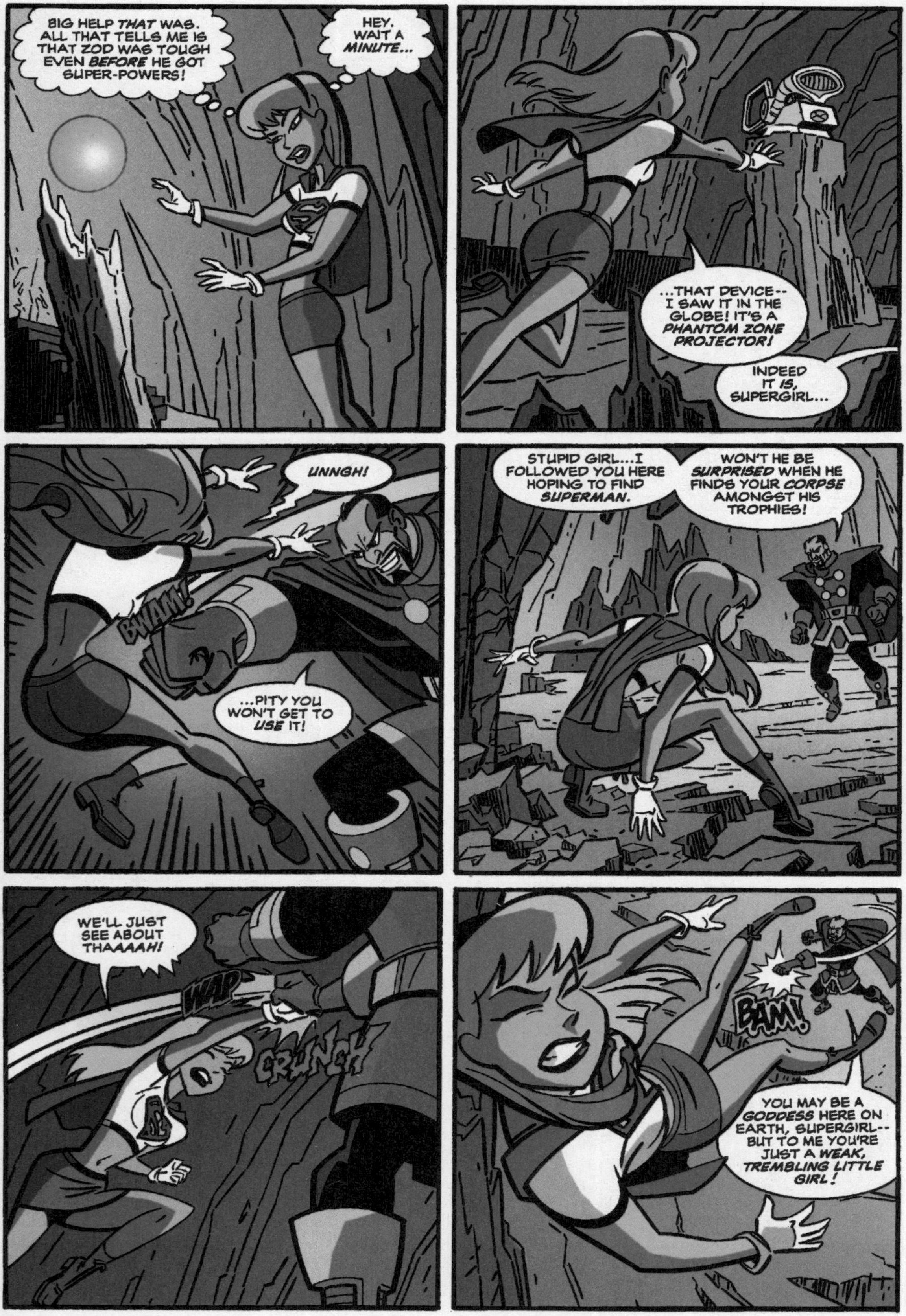
BIG HELP *THAT* WAS. ALL THAT TELLS ME IS THAT ZOD WAS TOUGH EVEN *BEFORE* HE GOT SUPER-POWERS!
HEY. WAIT A *MINUTE*...
...THAT DEVICE-- I SAW IT IN THE GLOBE! IT'S A *PHANTOM ZONE PROJECTOR!*
INDEED IT *IS*, SUPERGIRL...
UNNGH!
BWAM!
...PITY YOU WON'T GET TO *USE* IT!
STUPID GIRL...I FOLLOWED YOU HERE HOPING TO FIND *SUPERMAN*.
WON'T HE BE *SURPRISED* WHEN HE FINDS YOUR *CORPSE* AMONGST HIS TROPHIES!
WE'LL JUST SEE ABOUT THAAAAH!
WAP
CRUNCH
BAM!
YOU MAY BE A *GODDESS* HERE ON EARTH, SUPERGIRL-- BUT TO ME YOU'RE JUST A *WEAK, TREMBLING LITTLE GIRL!*

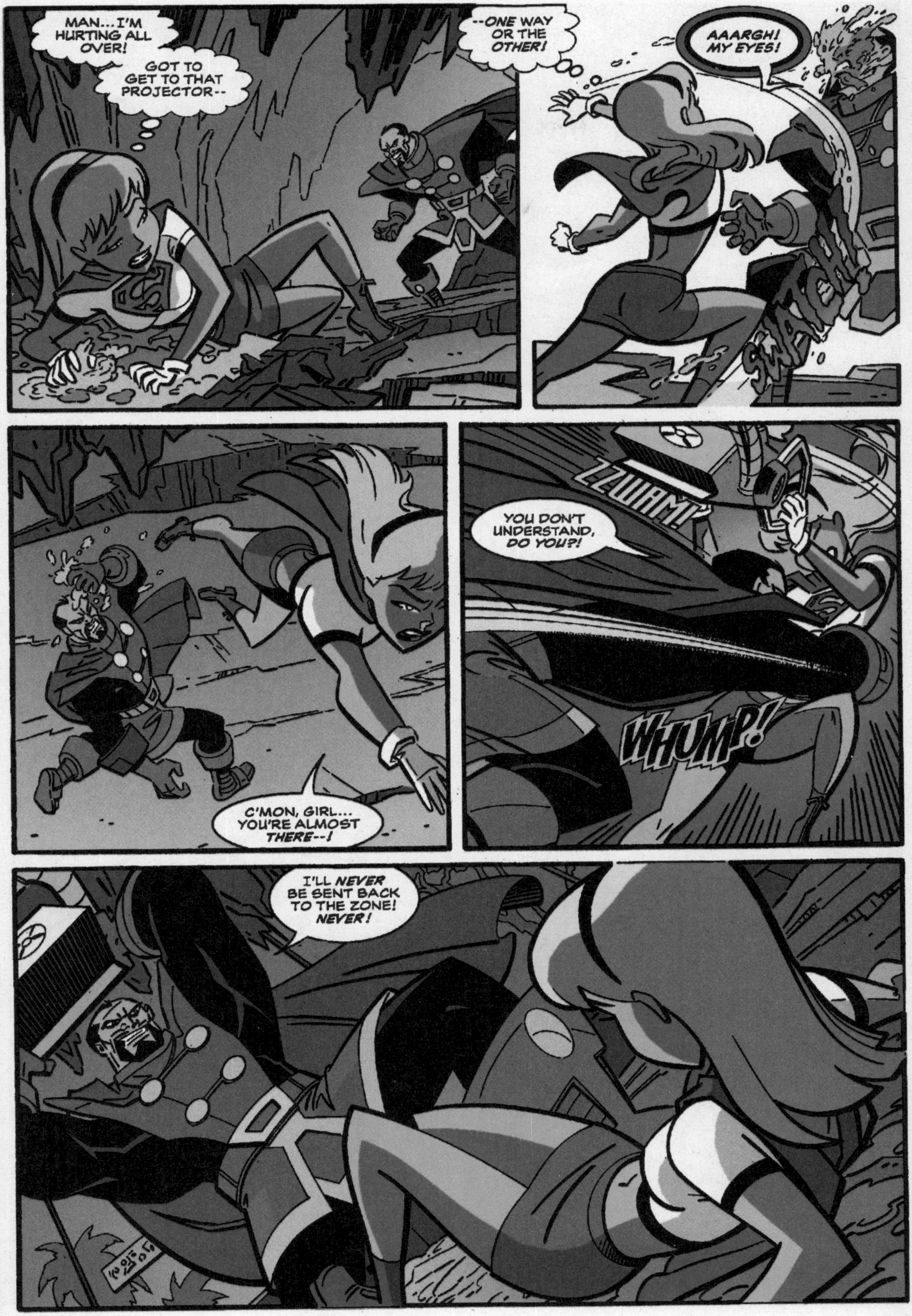
MAN... I'M HURTING ALL OVER!
GOT TO GET TO THAT PROJECTOR--
--ONE WAY OR THE OTHER!
AAARGH! MY EYES!
C'MON, GIRL... YOU'RE ALMOST THERE--!
ZZWAM!
YOU DON'T UNDERSTAND, DO YOU?!
WHUMP!
I'LL NEVER BE SENT BACK TO THE ZONE! NEVER!

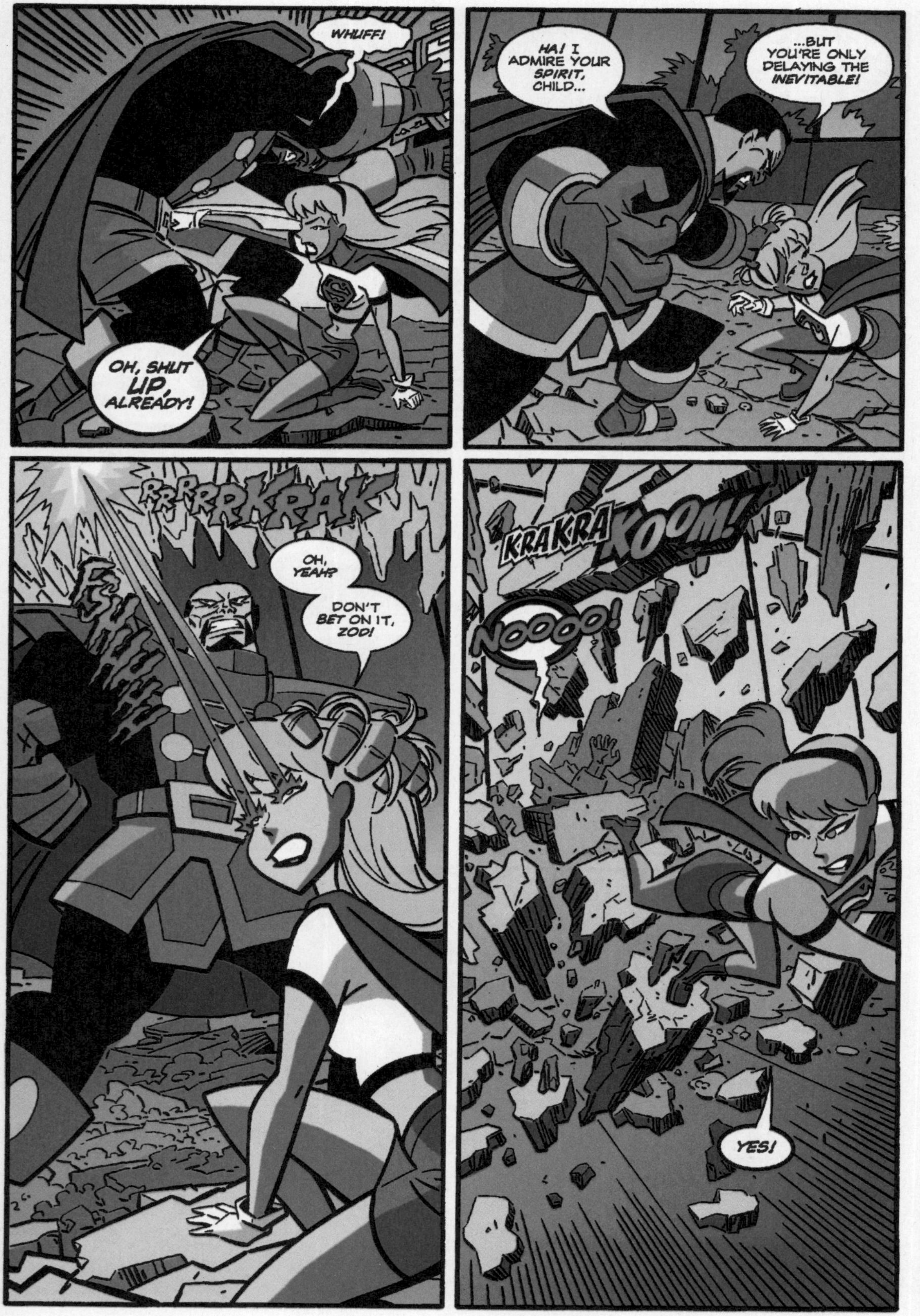
WHUFF!
OH, SHUT UP, ALREADY!
HA! I ADMIRE YOUR SPIRIT, CHILD...
...BUT YOU'RE ONLY DELAYING THE INEVITABLE!
RRRRRKRAK
OH, YEAH?
DON'T BET ON IT, ZOD!
KRAKRAKOOM!
NOOOO!
YES!

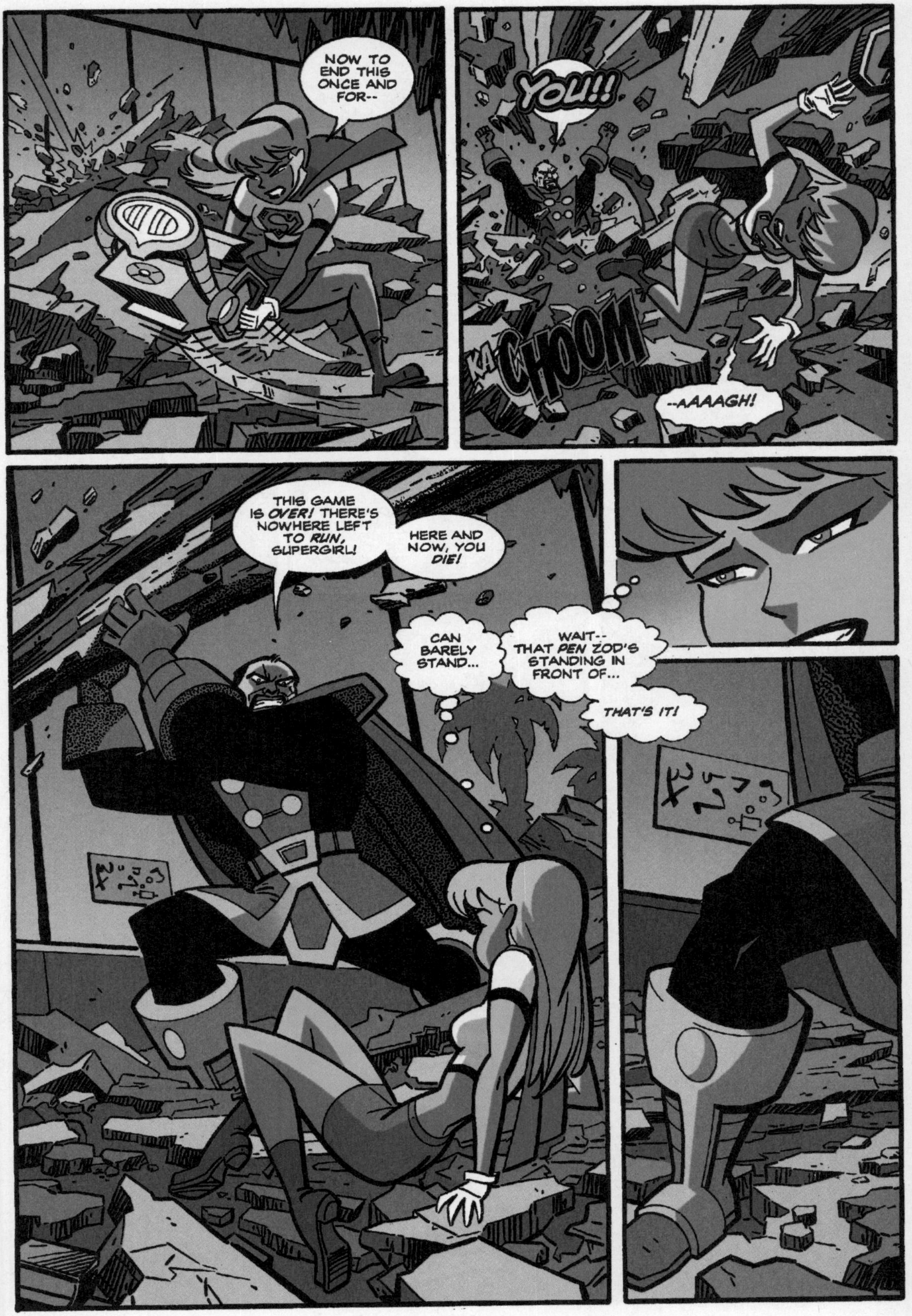
NOW TO END THIS ONCE AND FOR--
YOU!!
KA-CHOOM
--AAAAGH!
THIS GAME IS OVER! THERE'S NOWHERE LEFT TO RUN, SUPERGIRL!
HERE AND NOW, YOU DIE!
CAN BARELY STAND...
WAIT-- THAT PEN ZOD'S STANDING IN FRONT OF...
THAT'S IT!

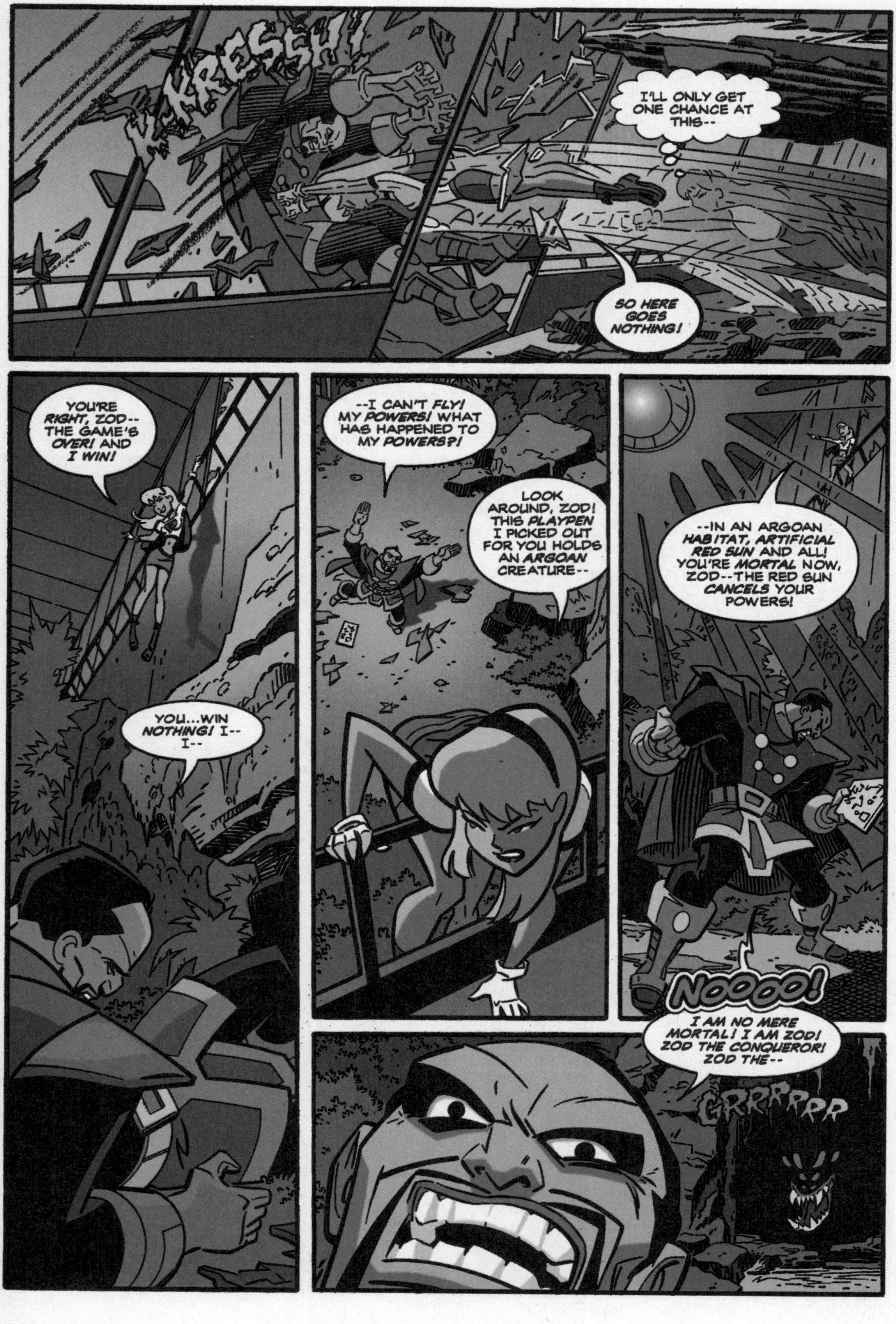
KRESSH!
I'LL ONLY GET ONE CHANCE AT THIS--
SO HERE GOES NOTHING!
YOU'RE RIGHT, ZOD-- THE GAME'S OVER! AND I WIN!
YOU...WIN NOTHING! I-- I--
--I CAN'T FLY! MY POWERS! WHAT HAS HAPPENED TO MY POWERS?!
LOOK AROUND, ZOD! THIS PLAYPEN I PICKED OUT FOR YOU HOLDS AN ARGOAN CREATURE--
--IN AN ARGOAN HABITAT, ARTIFICIAL RED SUN AND ALL! YOU'RE MORTAL NOW, ZOD--THE RED SUN CANCELS YOUR POWERS!
NOOOO!
I AM NO MERE MORTAL! I AM ZOD! ZOD THE CONQUEROR! ZOD THE--
GRRRRRR

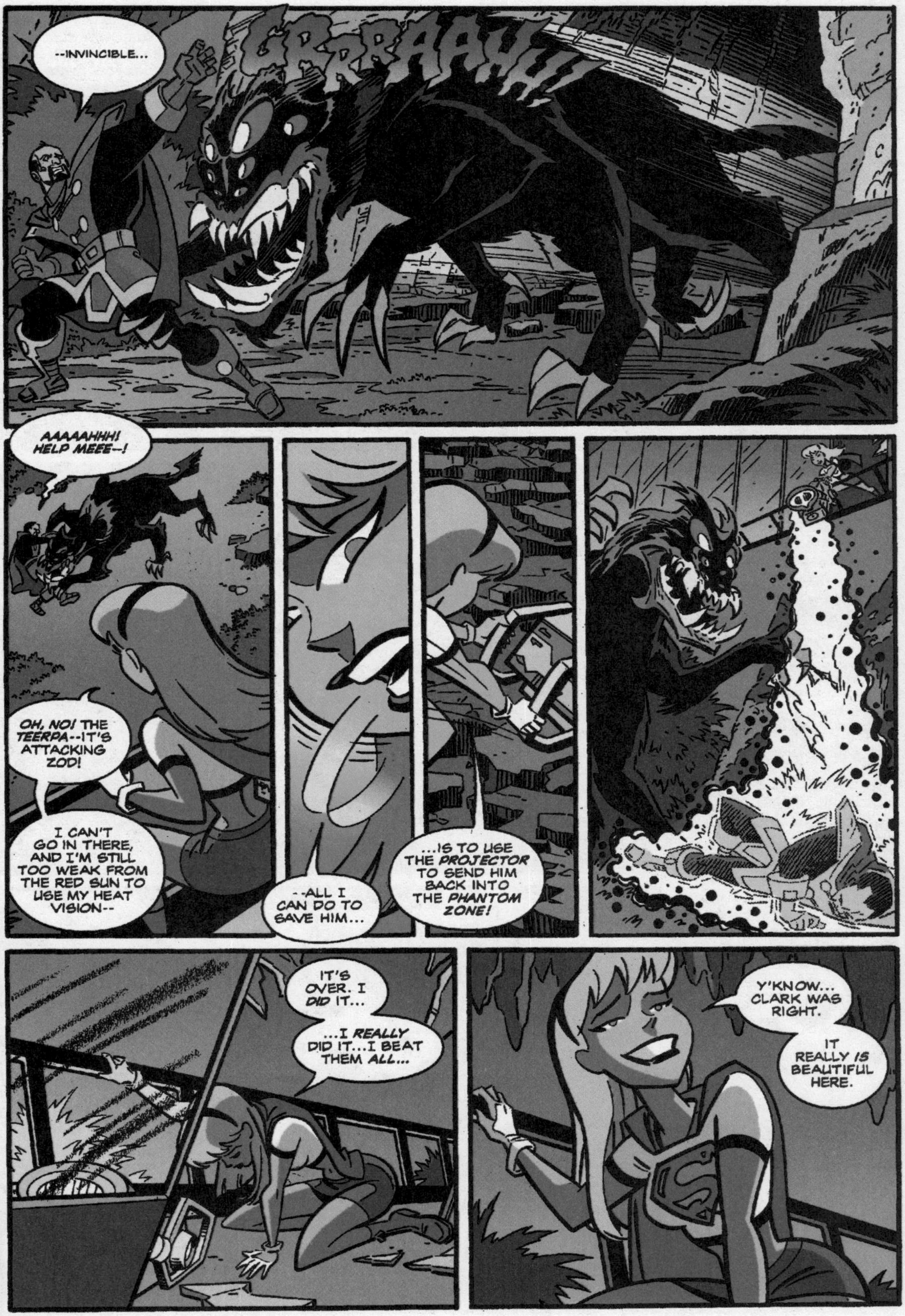
--INVINCIBLE...
GRRRAAAH!!
AAAAAHHH! HELP MEEE--!
OH, NO! THE TEERPA--IT'S ATTACKING ZOD!
I CAN'T GO IN THERE, AND I'M STILL TOO WEAK FROM THE RED SUN TO USE MY HEAT VISION--
--ALL I CAN DO TO SAVE HIM...
...IS TO USE THE PROJECTOR TO SEND HIM BACK INTO THE PHANTOM ZONE!
IT'S OVER. I DID IT...
...I REALLY DID IT...I BEAT THEM ALL...
Y'KNOW... CLARK WAS RIGHT.
IT REALLY IS BEAUTIFUL HERE.

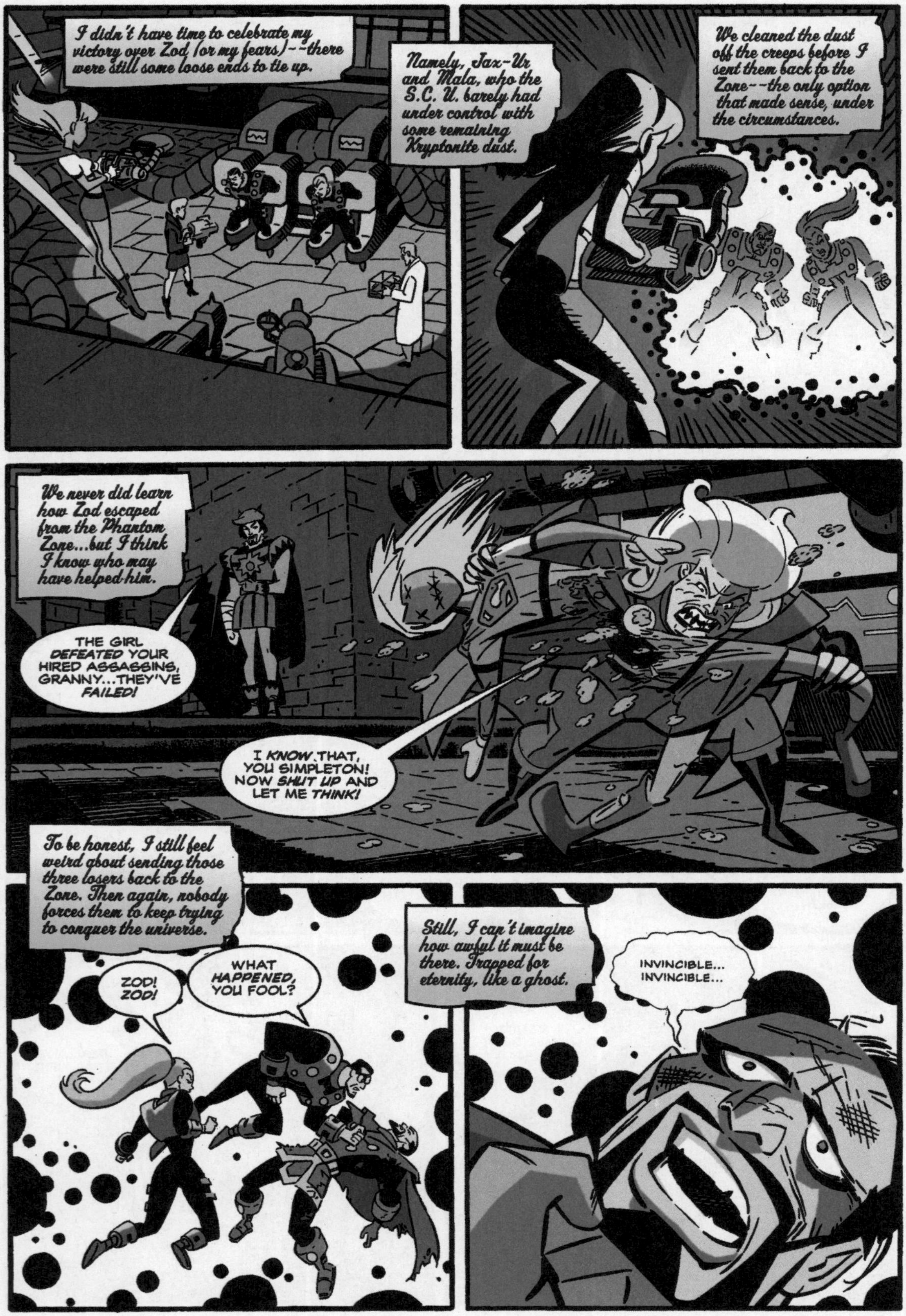
I didn't have time to celebrate my victory over Zod (or my fears)--there were still some loose ends to tie up.
Namely, Jax-Ur and Mala, who the S.C.U. barely had under control with some remaining Kryptonite dust.
We cleaned the dust off the creeps before I sent them back to the Zone--the only option that made sense, under the circumstances.
We never did learn how Zod escaped from the Phantom Zone...but I think I know who may have helped him.
THE GIRL DEFEATED YOUR HIRED ASSASSINS, GRANNY...THEY'VE FAILED!
I KNOW THAT, YOU SIMPLETON! NOW SHUT UP AND LET ME THINK!
To be honest, I still feel weird about sending those three losers back to the Zone. Then again, nobody forces them to keep trying to conquer the universe.
ZOD! ZOD!
WHAT HAPPENED, YOU FOOL?
Still, I can't imagine how awful it must be there. Trapped for eternity, like a ghost.
INVINCIBLE... INVINCIBLE...

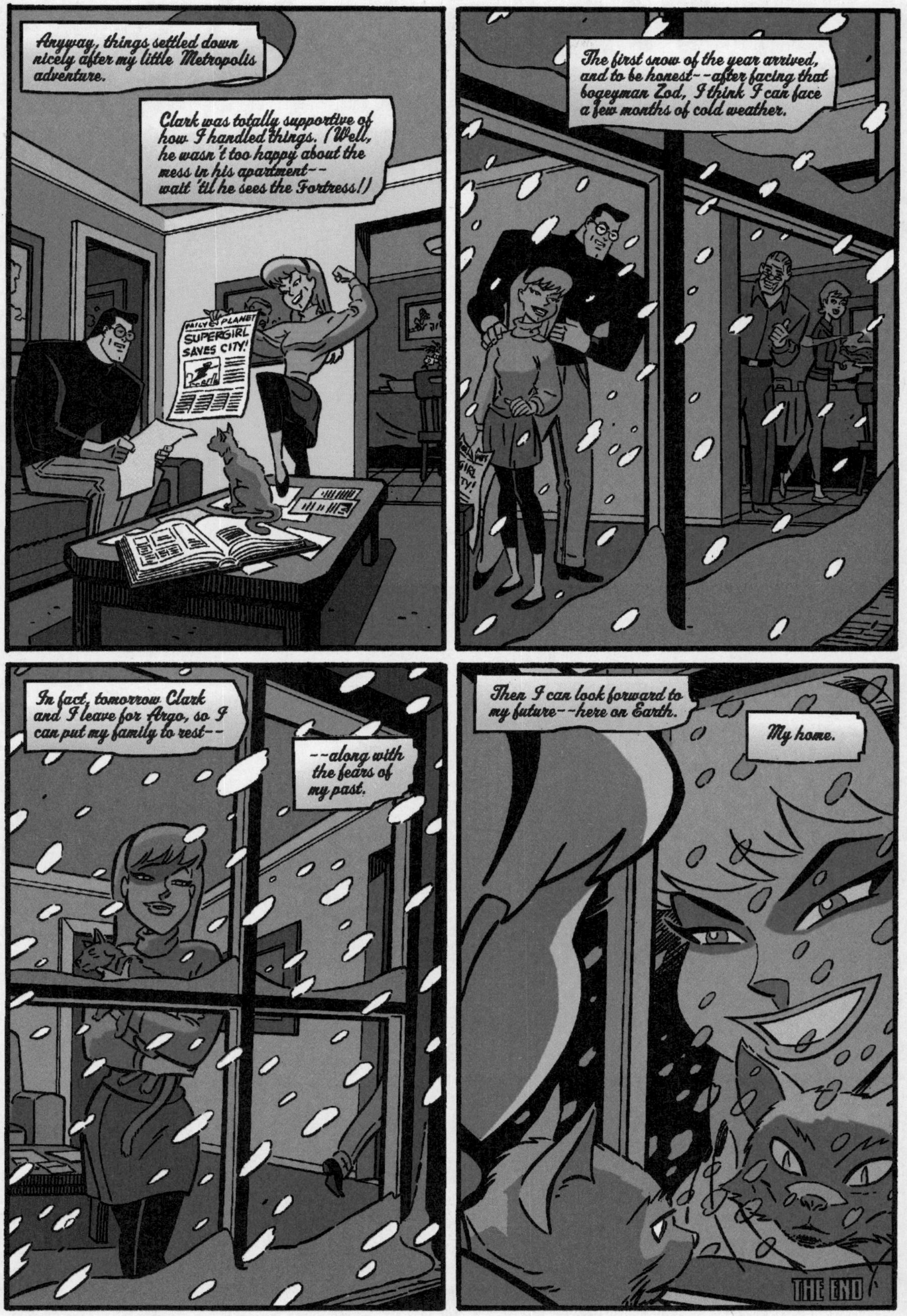

Anyway, things settled down nicely after my little Metropolis adventure.
Clark was totally supportive of how I handled things. (Well, he wasn't too happy about the mess in his apartment--wait 'til he sees the Fortress!)
DAILY PLANET
SUPERGIRL SAVES CITY!
The first snow of the year arrived, and to be honest--after facing that bogeyman Zod, I think I can face a few months of cold weather.
In fact, tomorrow Clark and I leave for Argo, so I can put my family to rest--
--along with the fears of my past.
Then I can look forward to my future--here on Earth.
My home.
THE END

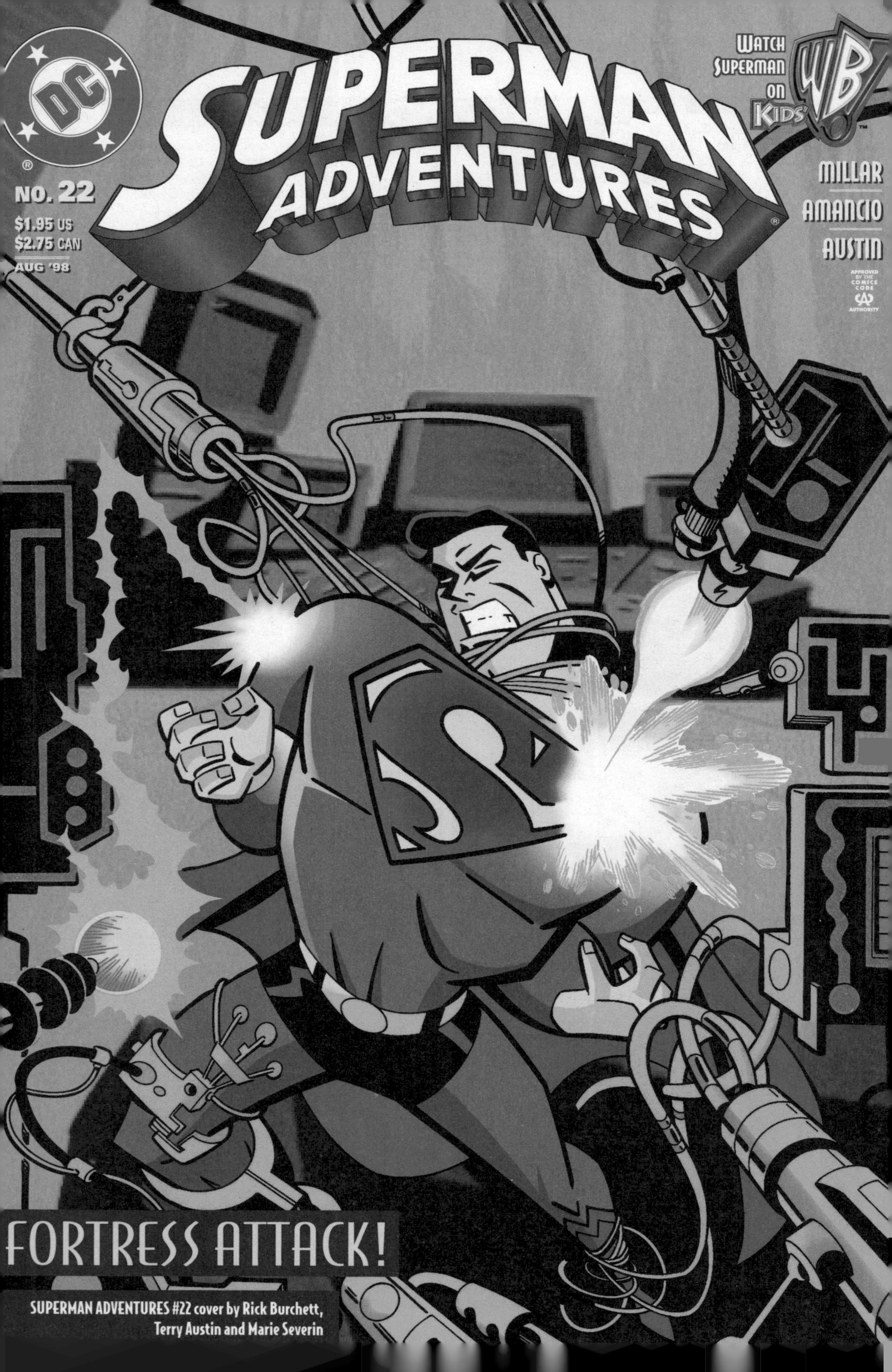
WATCH SUPERMAN ON KIDS' WB
SUPERMAN ADVENTURES
NO. 22
$1.95 US
$2.75 CAN
AUG '98
MILLAR
AMANCIO
AUSTIN
APPROVED BY THE COMICS CODE AUTHORITY
FORTRESS ATTACK!

SUPERMAN ADVENTURES #22 cover by Rick Burchett, Terry Austin and Marie Severin

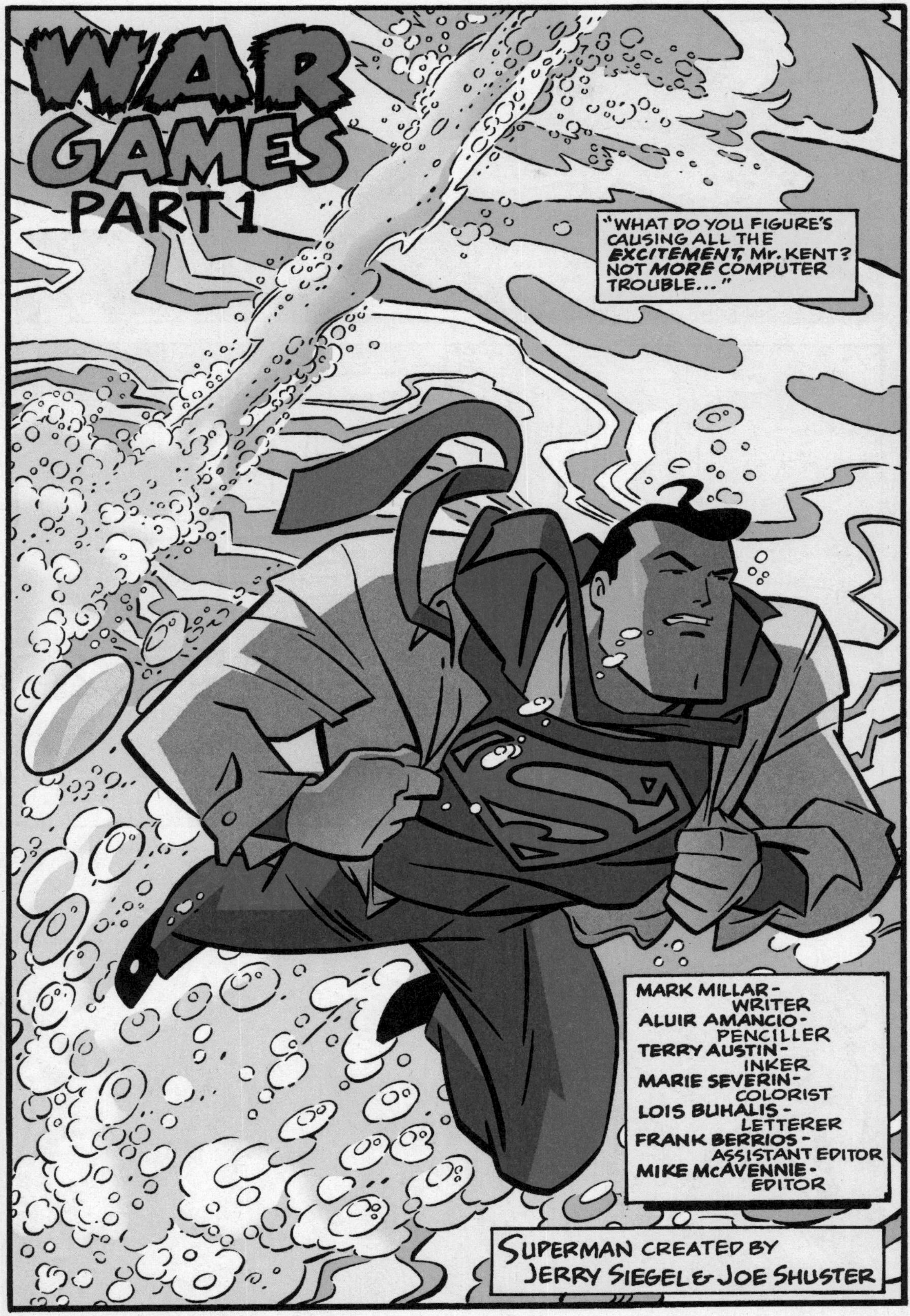
WAR GAMES
PART 1
"WHAT DO YOU FIGURE'S CAUSING ALL THE EXCITEMENT, Mr. KENT? NOT MORE COMPUTER TROUBLE..."
MARK MILLAR - WRITER
ALUIR AMANCIO - PENCILLER
TERRY AUSTIN - INKER
MARIE SEVERIN - COLORIST
LOIS BUHALIS - LETTERER
FRANK BERRIOS - ASSISTANT EDITOR
MIKE McAVENNIE - EDITOR
SUPERMAN CREATED BY JERRY SIEGEL & JOE SHUSTER

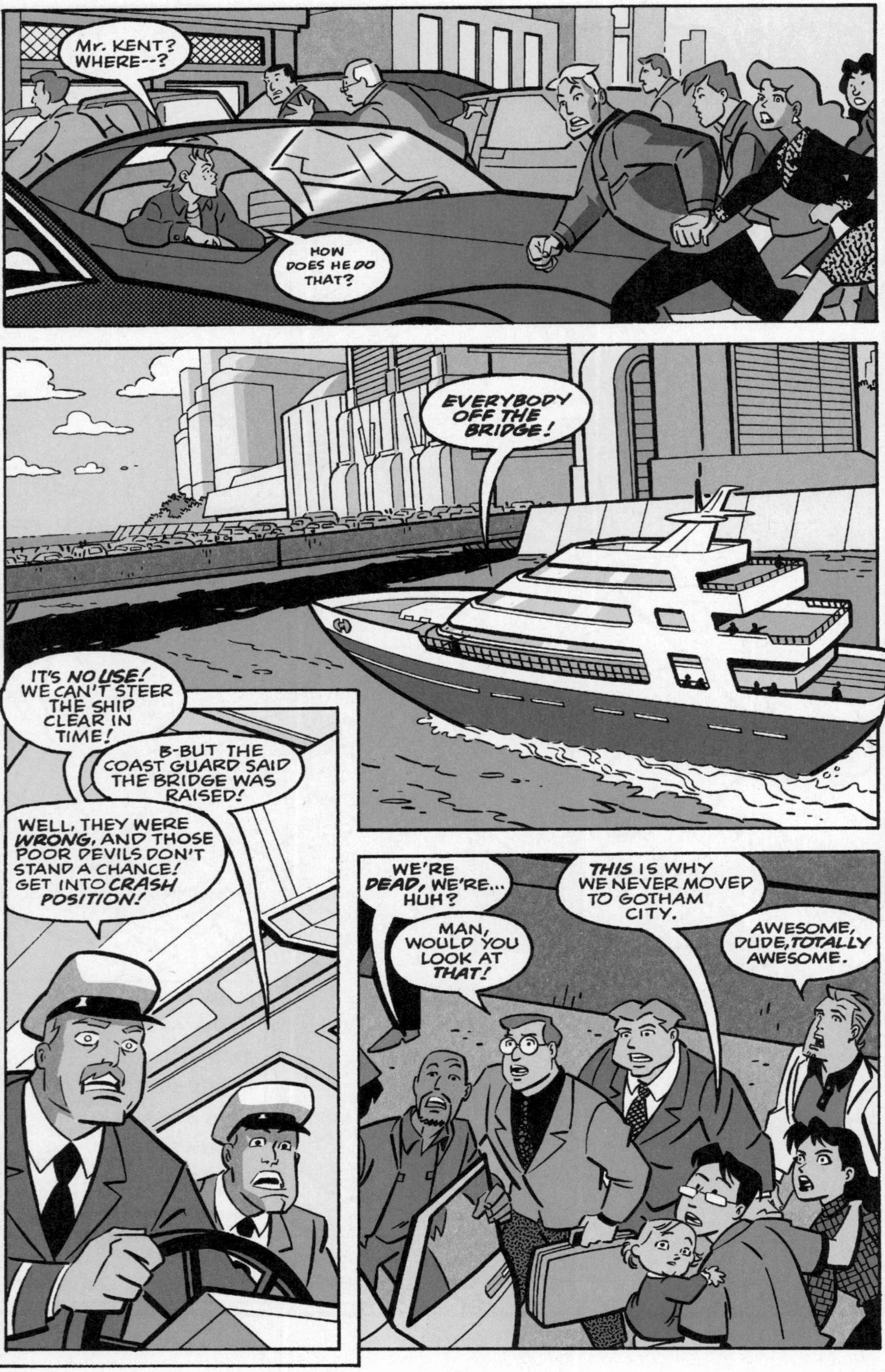
Mr. KENT? WHERE--?
HOW DOES HE DO THAT?
EVERYBODY OFF THE BRIDGE!
IT'S NO USE! WE CAN'T STEER THE SHIP CLEAR IN TIME!
B-BUT THE COAST GUARD SAID THE BRIDGE WAS RAISED!
WELL, THEY WERE WRONG, AND THOSE POOR DEVILS DON'T STAND A CHANCE! GET INTO CRASH POSITION!
WE'RE DEAD, WE'RE... HUH?
MAN, WOULD YOU LOOK AT THAT!
THIS IS WHY WE NEVER MOVED TO GOTHAM CITY.
AWESOME, DUDE, TOTALLY AWESOME.

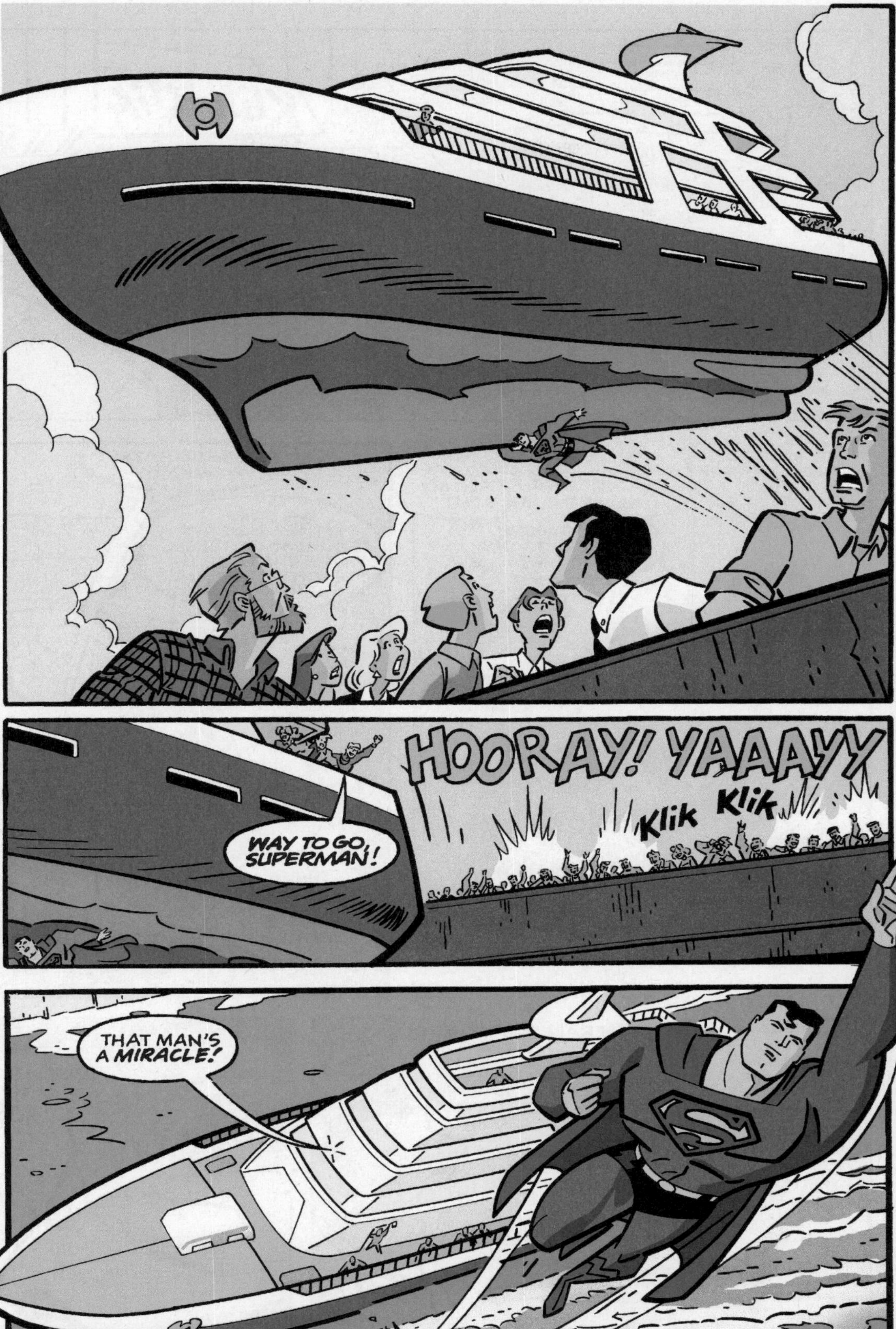
HOORAY! YAAAYY
Klik Klik
WAY TO GO, SUPERMAN!
THAT MAN'S A MIRACLE!

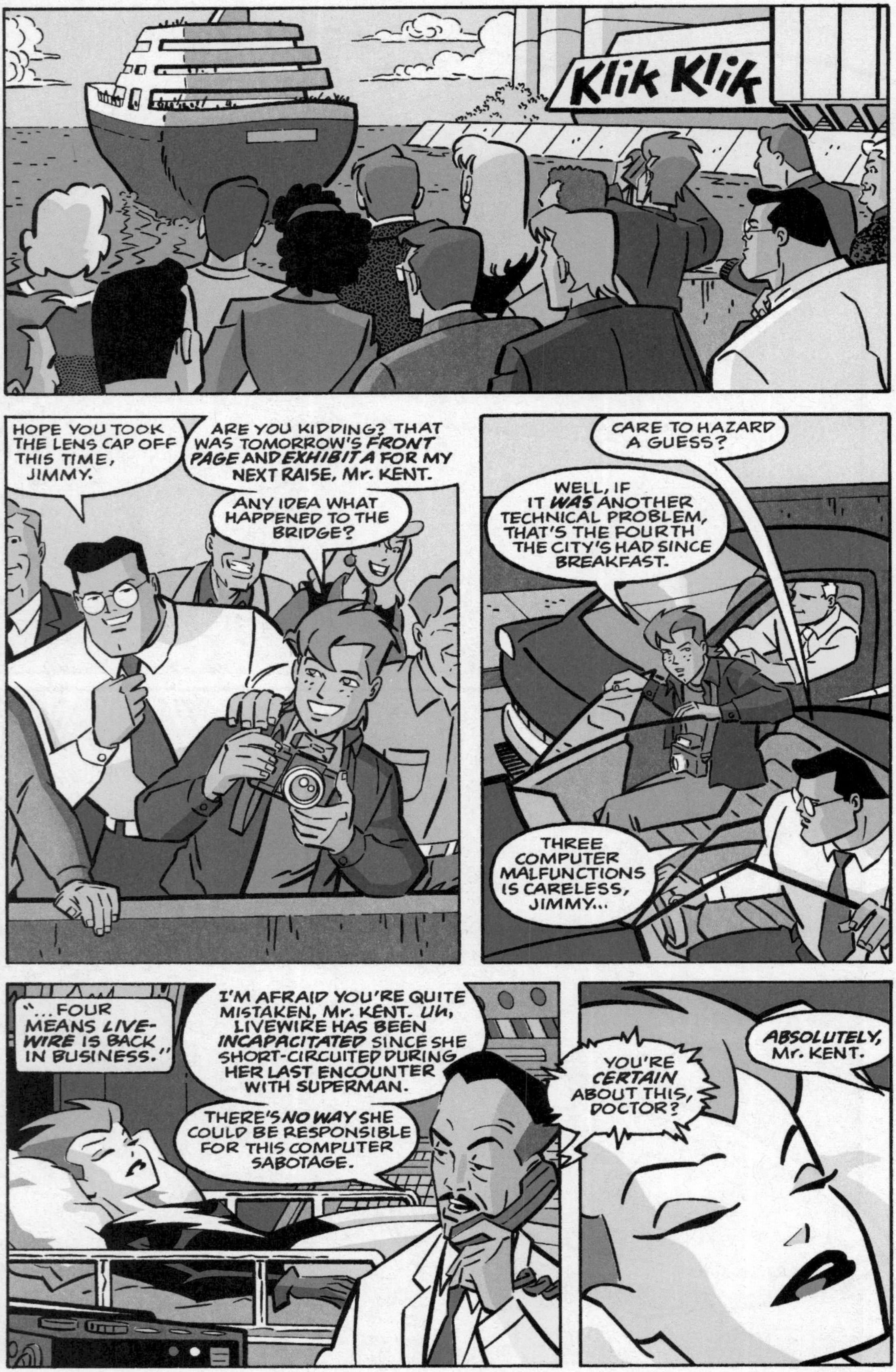

Klik Klik
HOPE YOU TOOK THE LENS CAP OFF THIS TIME, JIMMY.
ARE YOU KIDDING? THAT WAS TOMORROW'S FRONT PAGE AND EXHIBIT A FOR MY NEXT RAISE, Mr. KENT.
ANY IDEA WHAT HAPPENED TO THE BRIDGE?
CARE TO HAZARD A GUESS?
WELL, IF IT WAS ANOTHER TECHNICAL PROBLEM, THAT'S THE FOURTH THE CITY'S HAD SINCE BREAKFAST.
THREE COMPUTER MALFUNCTIONS IS CARELESS, JIMMY...
"...FOUR MEANS LIVE-WIRE IS BACK IN BUSINESS."
I'M AFRAID YOU'RE QUITE MISTAKEN, Mr. KENT. Uh, LIVEWIRE HAS BEEN INCAPACITATED SINCE SHE SHORT-CIRCUITED DURING HER LAST ENCOUNTER WITH SUPERMAN.
THERE'S NO WAY SHE COULD BE RESPONSIBLE FOR THIS COMPUTER SABOTAGE.
YOU'RE CERTAIN ABOUT THIS, DOCTOR?
ABSOLUTELY, Mr. KENT.

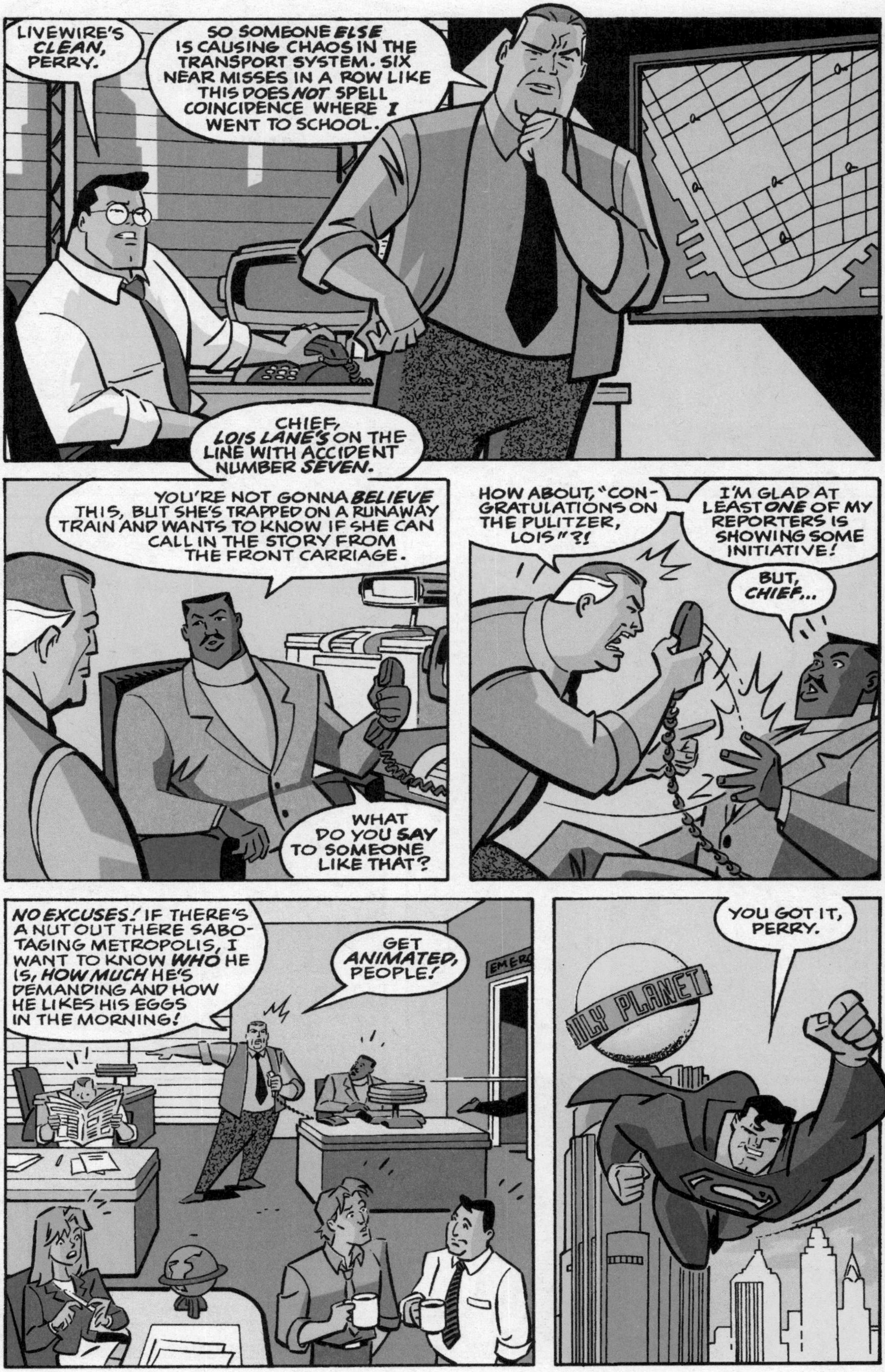
LIVEWIRE'S CLEAN, PERRY.
SO SOMEONE ELSE IS CAUSING CHAOS IN THE TRANSPORT SYSTEM. SIX NEAR MISSES IN A ROW LIKE THIS DOES NOT SPELL COINCIDENCE WHERE I WENT TO SCHOOL.
CHIEF, LOIS LANE'S ON THE LINE WITH ACCIDENT NUMBER SEVEN.
YOU'RE NOT GONNA BELIEVE THIS, BUT SHE'S TRAPPED ON A RUNAWAY TRAIN AND WANTS TO KNOW IF SHE CAN CALL IN THE STORY FROM THE FRONT CARRIAGE.
WHAT DO YOU SAY TO SOMEONE LIKE THAT?
HOW ABOUT, "CONGRATULATIONS ON THE PULITZER, LOIS"?!
I'M GLAD AT LEAST ONE OF MY REPORTERS IS SHOWING SOME INITIATIVE!
BUT, CHIEF...
NO EXCUSES! IF THERE'S A NUT OUT THERE SABOTAGING METROPOLIS, I WANT TO KNOW WHO HE IS, HOW MUCH HE'S DEMANDING AND HOW HE LIKES HIS EGGS IN THE MORNING!
GET ANIMATED, PEOPLE!
YOU GOT IT, PERRY.

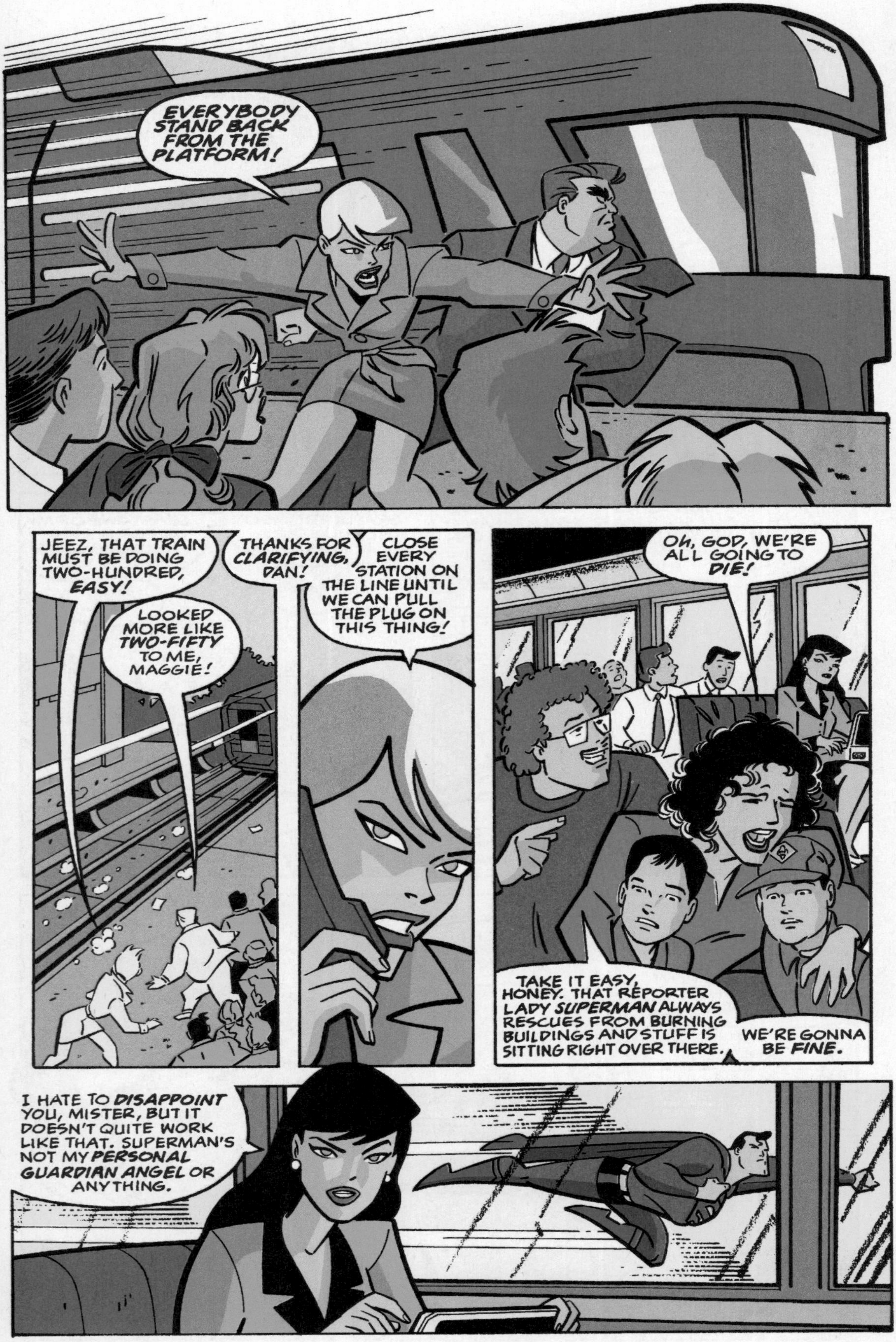
EVERYBODY STAND BACK FROM THE PLATFORM!
JEEZ, THAT TRAIN MUST BE DOING TWO-HUNDRED, EASY!
LOOKED MORE LIKE TWO-FIFTY TO ME, MAGGIE!
THANKS FOR CLARIFYING, DAN!
CLOSE EVERY STATION ON THE LINE UNTIL WE CAN PULL THE PLUG ON THIS THING!
OH, GOD, WE'RE ALL GOING TO DIE!
TAKE IT EASY, HONEY. THAT REPORTER LADY SUPERMAN ALWAYS RESCUES FROM BURNING BUILDINGS AND STUFF IS SITTING RIGHT OVER THERE.
WE'RE GONNA BE FINE.
I HATE TO DISAPPOINT YOU, MISTER, BUT IT DOESN'T QUITE WORK LIKE THAT. SUPERMAN'S NOT MY PERSONAL GUARDIAN ANGEL OR ANYTHING.

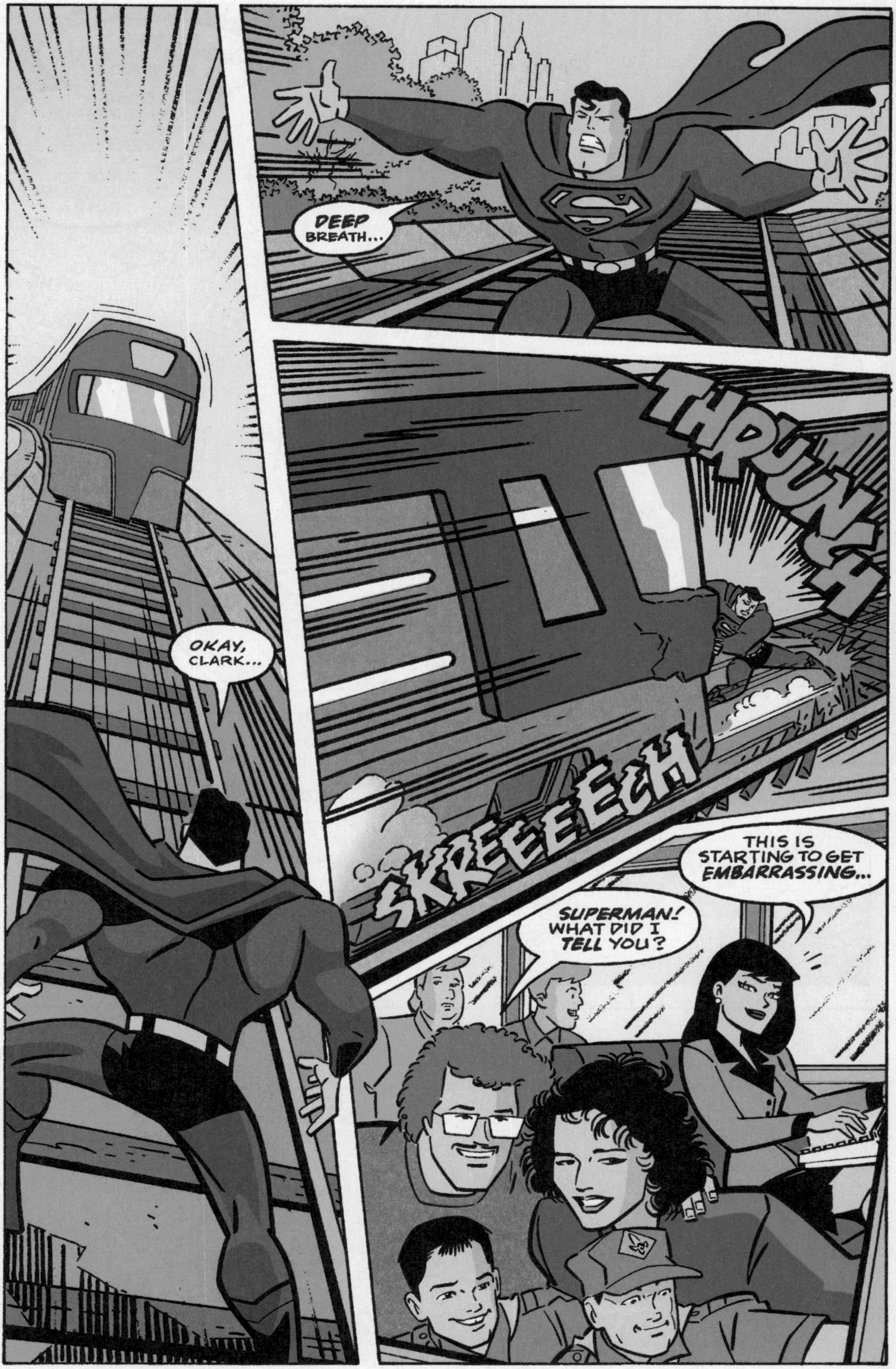
DEEP BREATH...
OKAY, CLARK...
THRUUNCH
SKREEEEECH
THIS IS STARTING TO GET EMBARRASSING...
SUPERMAN! WHAT DID I TELL YOU?

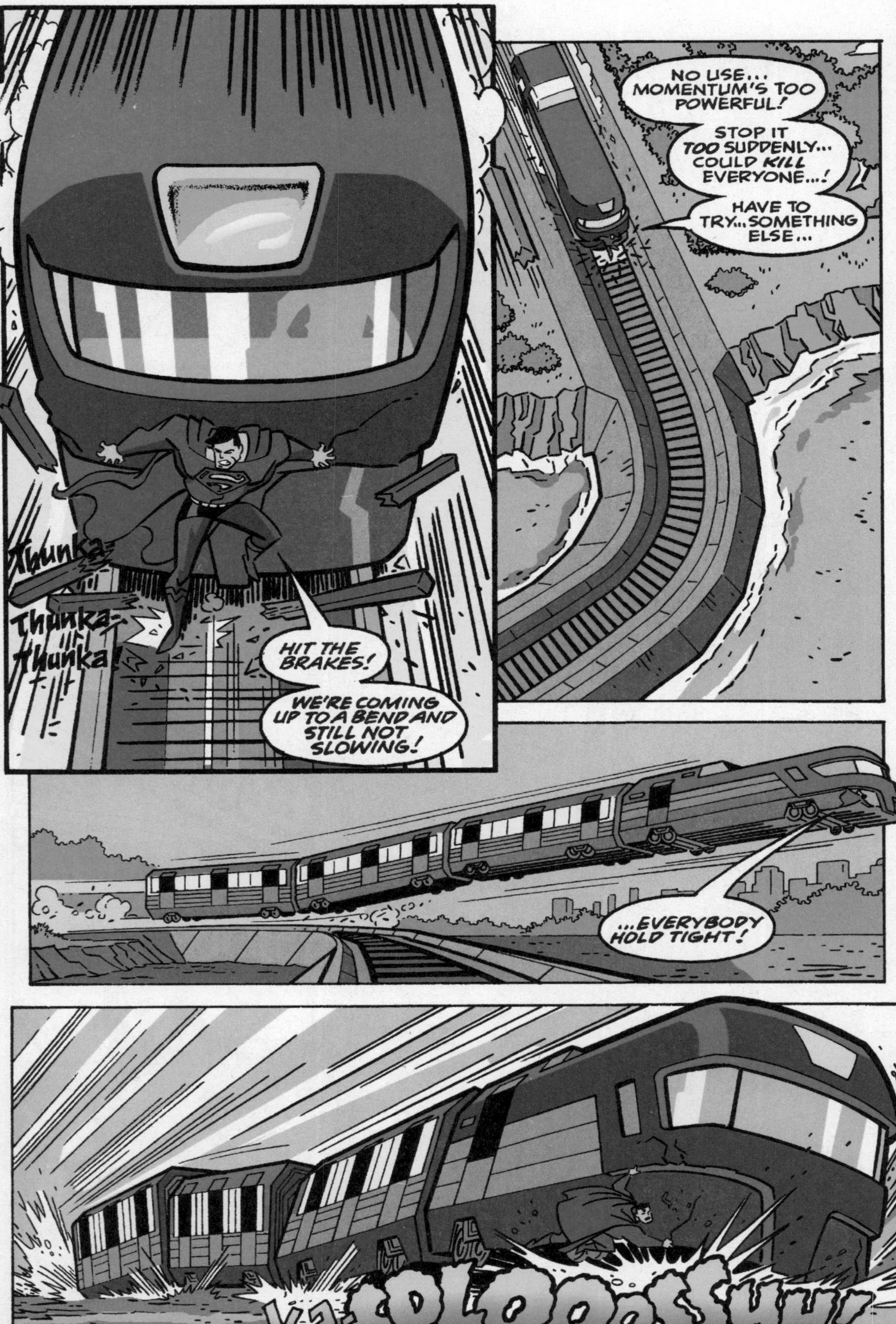
Thunka
Thunka
Thunka!
HIT THE BRAKES!
WE'RE COMING UP TO A BEND AND STILL NOT SLOWING!
NO USE... MOMENTUM'S TOO POWERFUL!
STOP IT TOO SUDDENLY... COULD KILL EVERYONE...!
HAVE TO TRY...SOMETHING ELSE...
...EVERYBODY HOLD TIGHT!
KA-SPLOOOOSSHH!

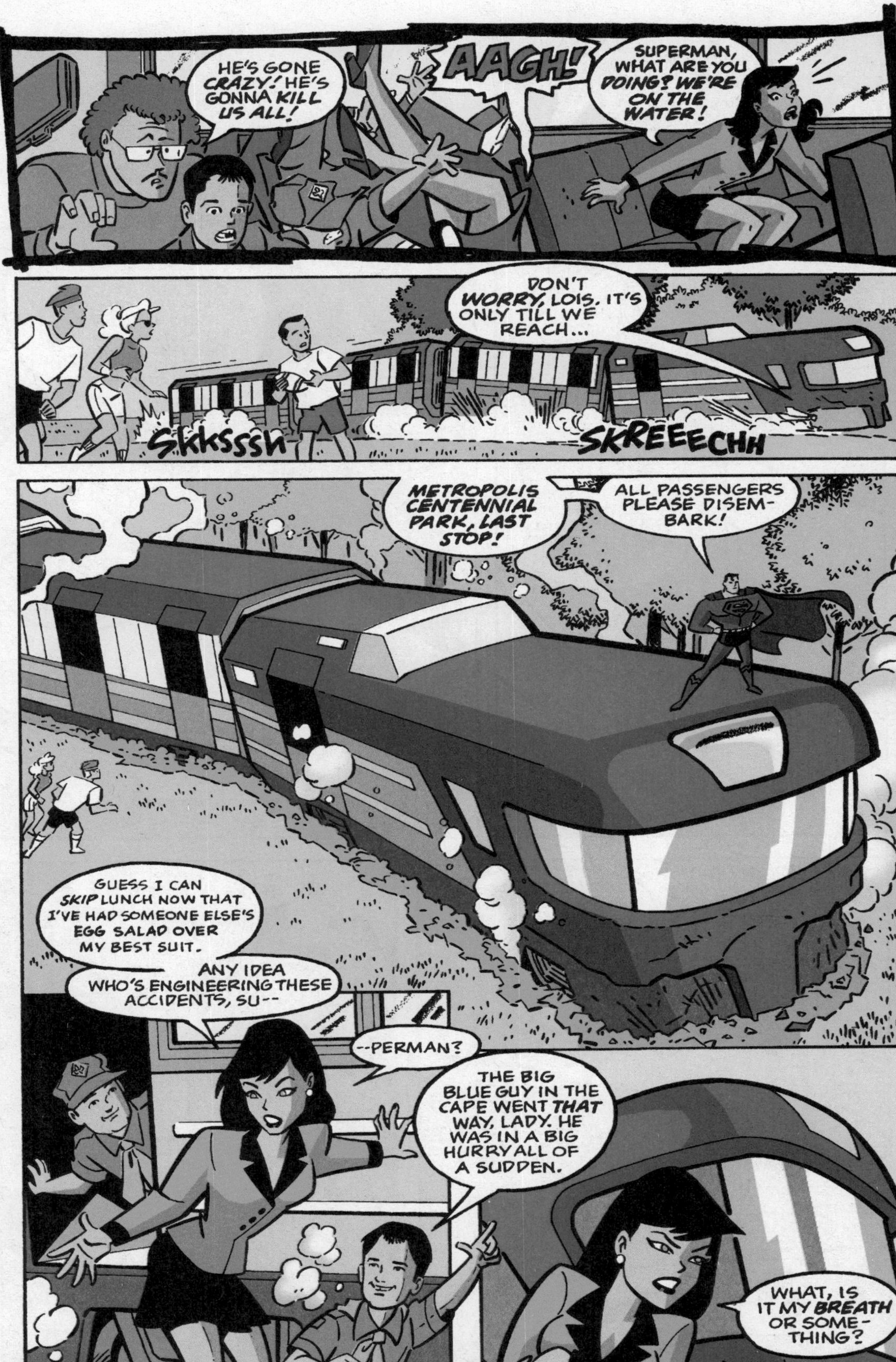
HE'S GONE CRAZY! HE'S GONNA KILL US ALL!
AAGH!
SUPERMAN, WHAT ARE YOU DOING? WE'RE ON THE WATER!
DON'T WORRY, LOIS. IT'S ONLY TILL WE REACH...
SKKSSSH
SKREEECHH
METROPOLIS CENTENNIAL PARK, LAST STOP!
ALL PASSENGERS PLEASE DISEMBARK!
GUESS I CAN SKIP LUNCH NOW THAT I'VE HAD SOMEONE ELSE'S EGG SALAD OVER MY BEST SUIT.
ANY IDEA WHO'S ENGINEERING THESE ACCIDENTS, SU--
--PERMAN?
THE BIG BLUE GUY IN THE CAPE WENT THAT WAY, LADY. HE WAS IN A BIG HURRY ALL OF A SUDDEN.
WHAT, IS IT MY BREATH OR SOMETHING?

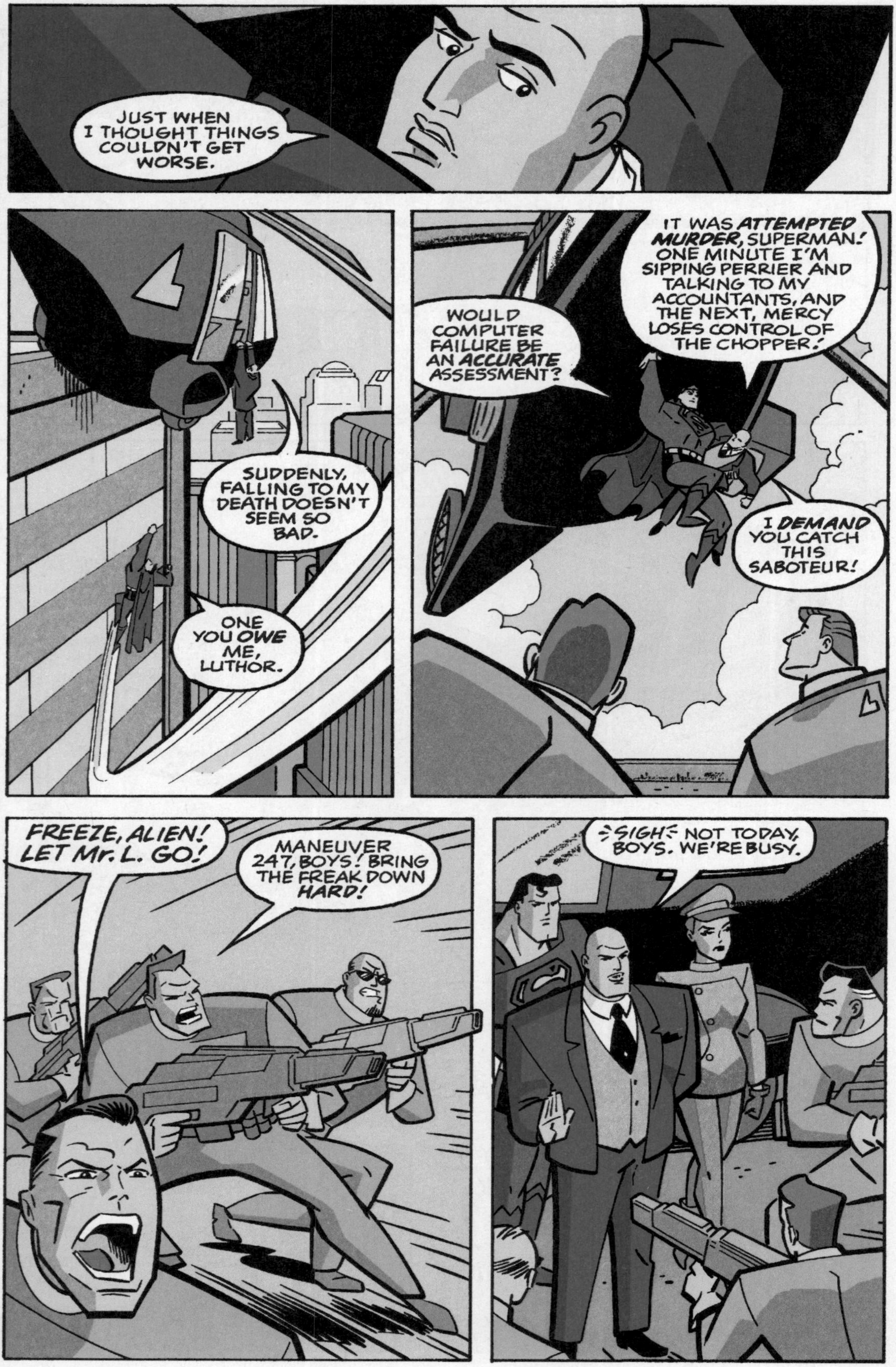
JUST WHEN I THOUGHT THINGS COULDN'T GET WORSE.
SUDDENLY, FALLING TO MY DEATH DOESN'T SEEM SO BAD.
ONE YOU OWE ME, LUTHOR.
WOULD COMPUTER FAILURE BE AN ACCURATE ASSESSMENT?
IT WAS ATTEMPTED MURDER, SUPERMAN! ONE MINUTE I'M SIPPING PERRIER AND TALKING TO MY ACCOUNTANTS, AND THE NEXT, MERCY LOSES CONTROL OF THE CHOPPER!
I DEMAND YOU CATCH THIS SABOTEUR!
FREEZE, ALIEN! LET Mr. L. GO!
MANEUVER 247, BOYS! BRING THE FREAK DOWN HARD!
SIGH NOT TODAY, BOYS. WE'RE BUSY.

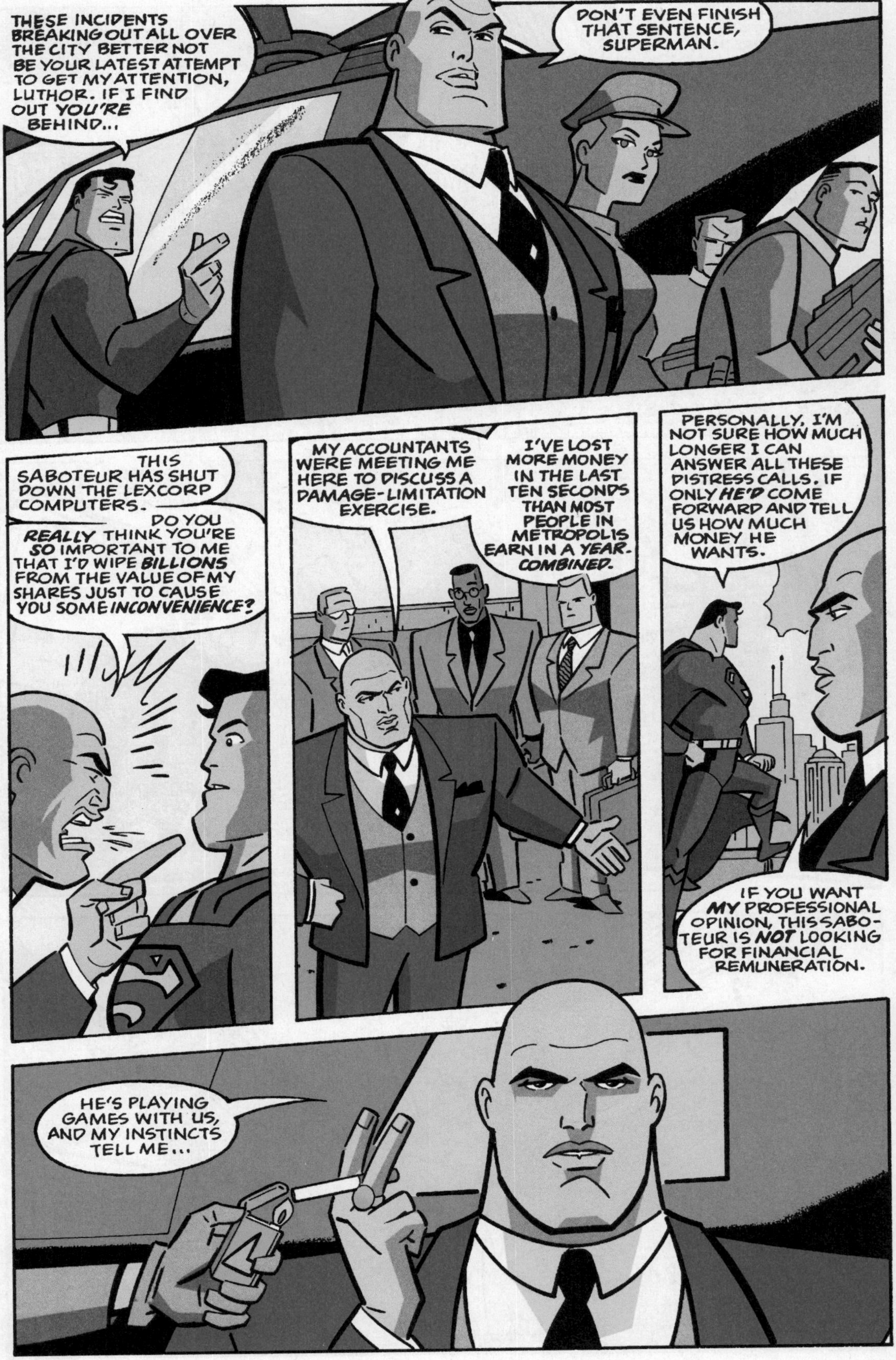
THESE INCIDENTS BREAKING OUT ALL OVER THE CITY BETTER NOT BE YOUR LATEST ATTEMPT TO GET MY ATTENTION, LUTHOR. IF I FIND OUT *YOU'RE* BEHIND...
DON'T EVEN FINISH THAT SENTENCE, SUPERMAN.
THIS SABOTEUR HAS SHUT DOWN THE LEXCORP COMPUTERS.
DO YOU *REALLY* THINK YOU'RE *SO* IMPORTANT TO ME THAT I'D WIPE *BILLIONS* FROM THE VALUE OF MY SHARES JUST TO CAUSE YOU SOME *INCONVENIENCE*?
MY ACCOUNTANTS WERE MEETING ME HERE TO DISCUSS A DAMAGE-LIMITATION EXERCISE.
I'VE LOST MORE MONEY IN THE LAST TEN SECONDS THAN MOST PEOPLE IN METROPOLIS EARN IN A *YEAR*. *COMBINED*.
PERSONALLY, I'M NOT SURE HOW MUCH LONGER I CAN ANSWER ALL THESE DISTRESS CALLS. IF ONLY *HE'D* COME FORWARD AND TELL US HOW MUCH MONEY HE WANTS.
IF YOU WANT *MY* PROFESSIONAL OPINION, THIS SABOTEUR IS *NOT* LOOKING FOR FINANCIAL REMUNERATION.
HE'S PLAYING GAMES WITH US, AND MY INSTINCTS TELL ME...

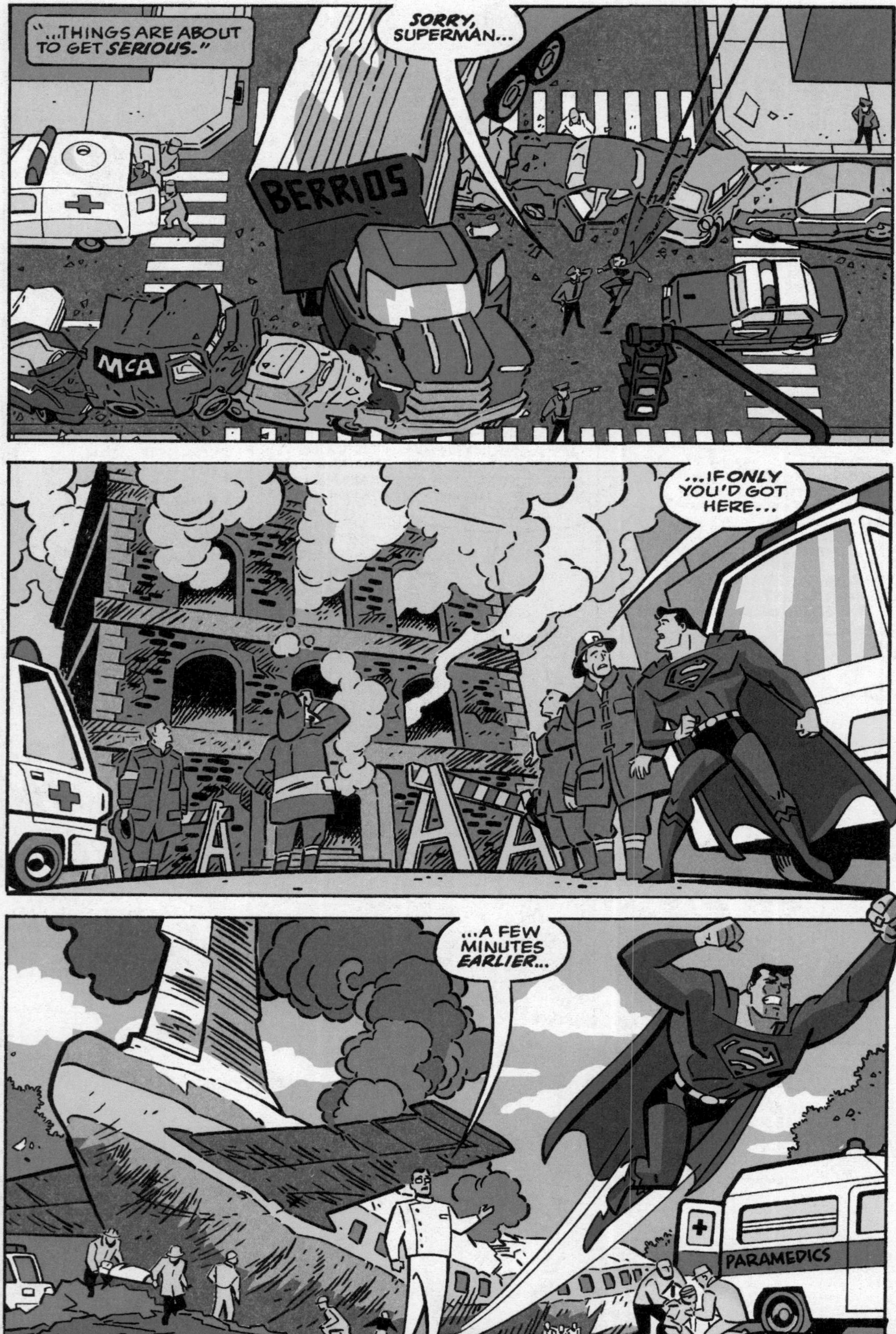
"...THINGS ARE ABOUT TO GET SERIOUS."
SORRY, SUPERMAN...
BERRIOS
MCA
...IF ONLY YOU'D GOT HERE...
...A FEW MINUTES EARLIER...
PARAMEDICS

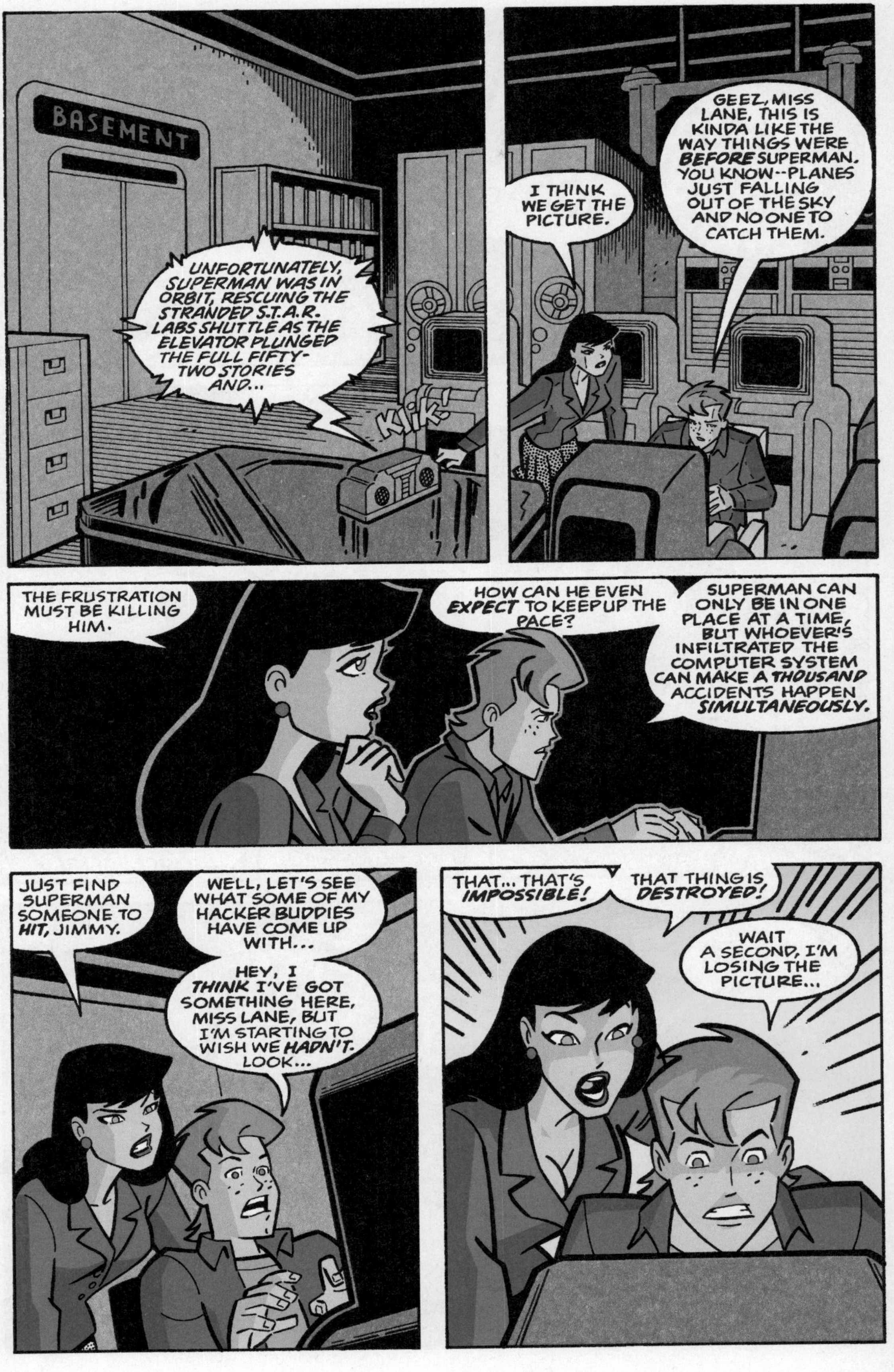
BASEMENT
UNFORTUNATELY, SUPERMAN WAS IN ORBIT, RESCUING THE STRANDED S.T.A.R. LABS SHUTTLE AS THE ELEVATOR PLUNGED THE FULL FIFTY-TWO STORIES AND...
KLIK!
GEEZ, MISS LANE, THIS IS KINDA LIKE THE WAY THINGS WERE BEFORE SUPERMAN. YOU KNOW--PLANES JUST FALLING OUT OF THE SKY AND NO ONE TO CATCH THEM.
I THINK WE GET THE PICTURE.
THE FRUSTRATION MUST BE KILLING HIM.
HOW CAN HE EVEN EXPECT TO KEEP UP THE PACE?
SUPERMAN CAN ONLY BE IN ONE PLACE AT A TIME, BUT WHOEVER'S INFILTRATED THE COMPUTER SYSTEM CAN MAKE A THOUSAND ACCIDENTS HAPPEN SIMULTANEOUSLY.
JUST FIND SUPERMAN SOMEONE TO HIT, JIMMY.
WELL, LET'S SEE WHAT SOME OF MY HACKER BUDDIES HAVE COME UP WITH...
HEY, I THINK I'VE GOT SOMETHING HERE, MISS LANE, BUT I'M STARTING TO WISH WE HADN'T. LOOK...
THAT... THAT'S IMPOSSIBLE!
THAT THING IS DESTROYED!
WAIT A SECOND, I'M LOSING THE PICTURE...

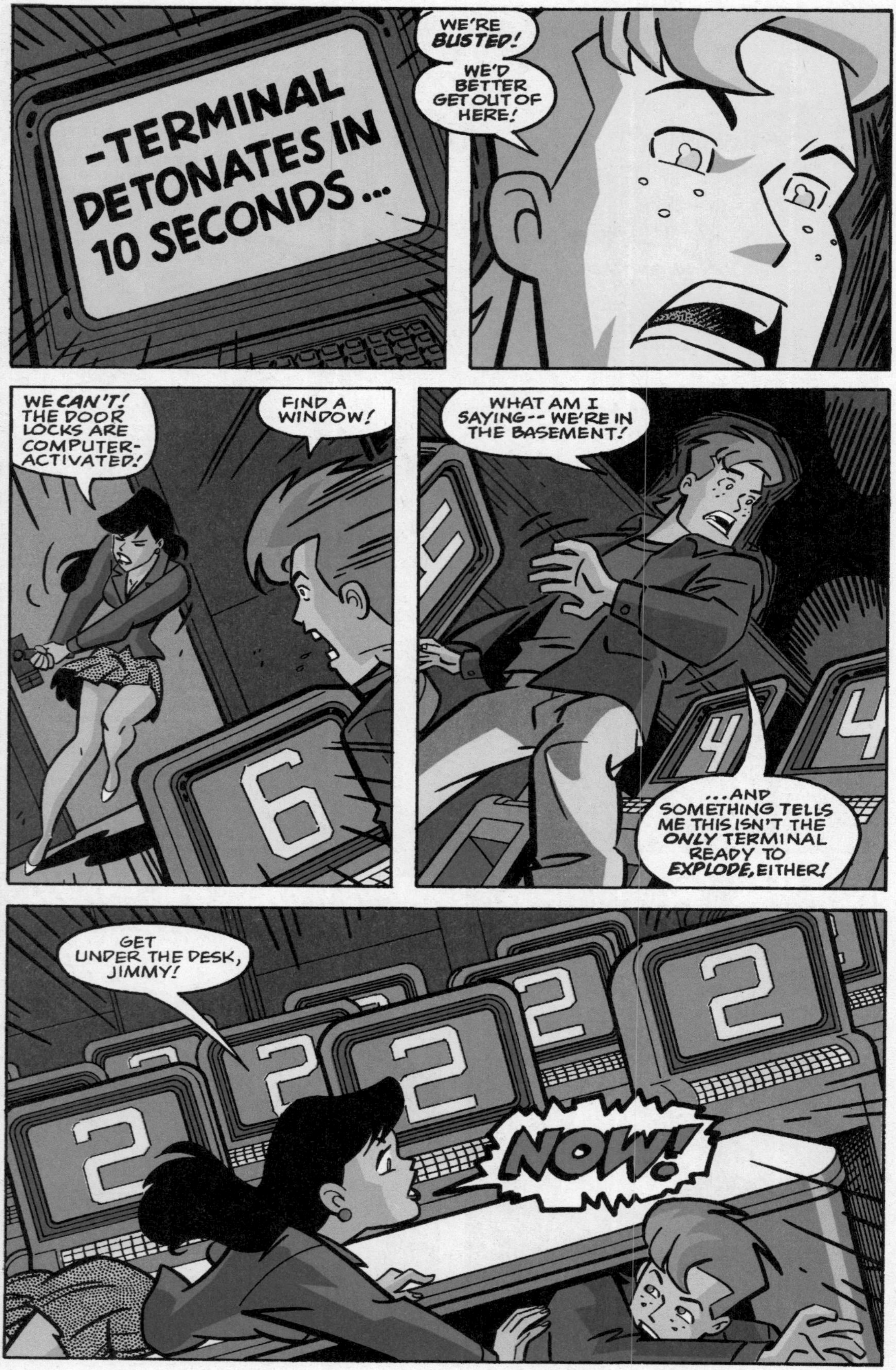
-TERMINAL DETONATES IN 10 SECONDS...
WE'RE BUSTED!
WE'D BETTER GET OUT OF HERE!
WE CAN'T! THE DOOR LOCKS ARE COMPUTER-ACTIVATED!
FIND A WINDOW!
6
WHAT AM I SAYING-- WE'RE IN THE BASEMENT!
4
4
...AND SOMETHING TELLS ME THIS ISN'T THE ONLY TERMINAL READY TO EXPLODE, EITHER!
GET UNDER THE DESK, JIMMY!
2
2
2
2
2
NOW!

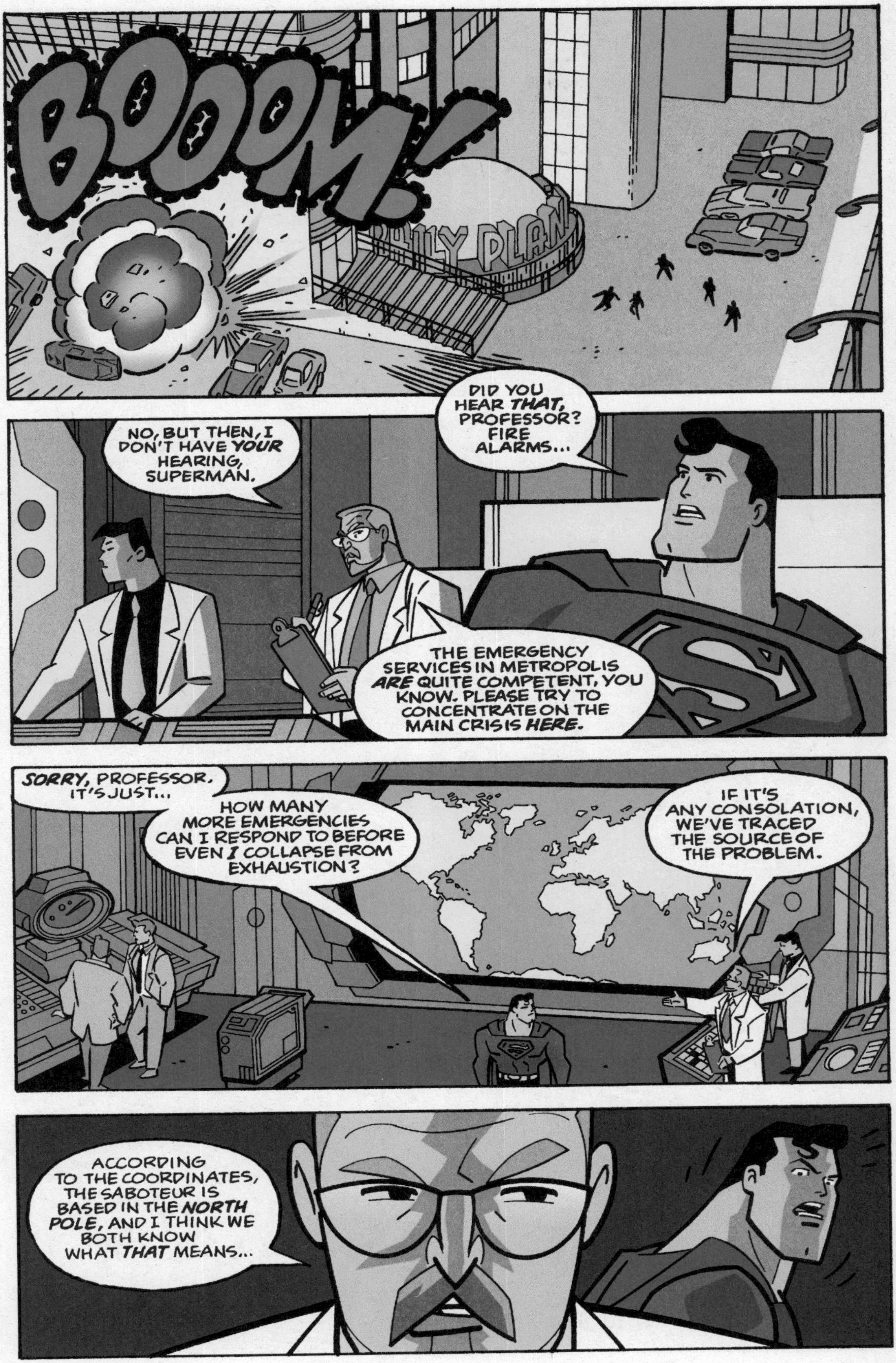
BOOOM!
DAILY PLAN
DID YOU HEAR THAT, PROFESSOR? FIRE ALARMS...
NO, BUT THEN, I DON'T HAVE YOUR HEARING, SUPERMAN.
THE EMERGENCY SERVICES IN METROPOLIS ARE QUITE COMPETENT, YOU KNOW. PLEASE TRY TO CONCENTRATE ON THE MAIN CRISIS HERE.
SORRY, PROFESSOR. IT'S JUST...
HOW MANY MORE EMERGENCIES CAN I RESPOND TO BEFORE EVEN I COLLAPSE FROM EXHAUSTION?
IF IT'S ANY CONSOLATION, WE'VE TRACED THE SOURCE OF THE PROBLEM.
ACCORDING TO THE COORDINATES, THE SABOTEUR IS BASED IN THE NORTH POLE, AND I THINK WE BOTH KNOW WHAT THAT MEANS...

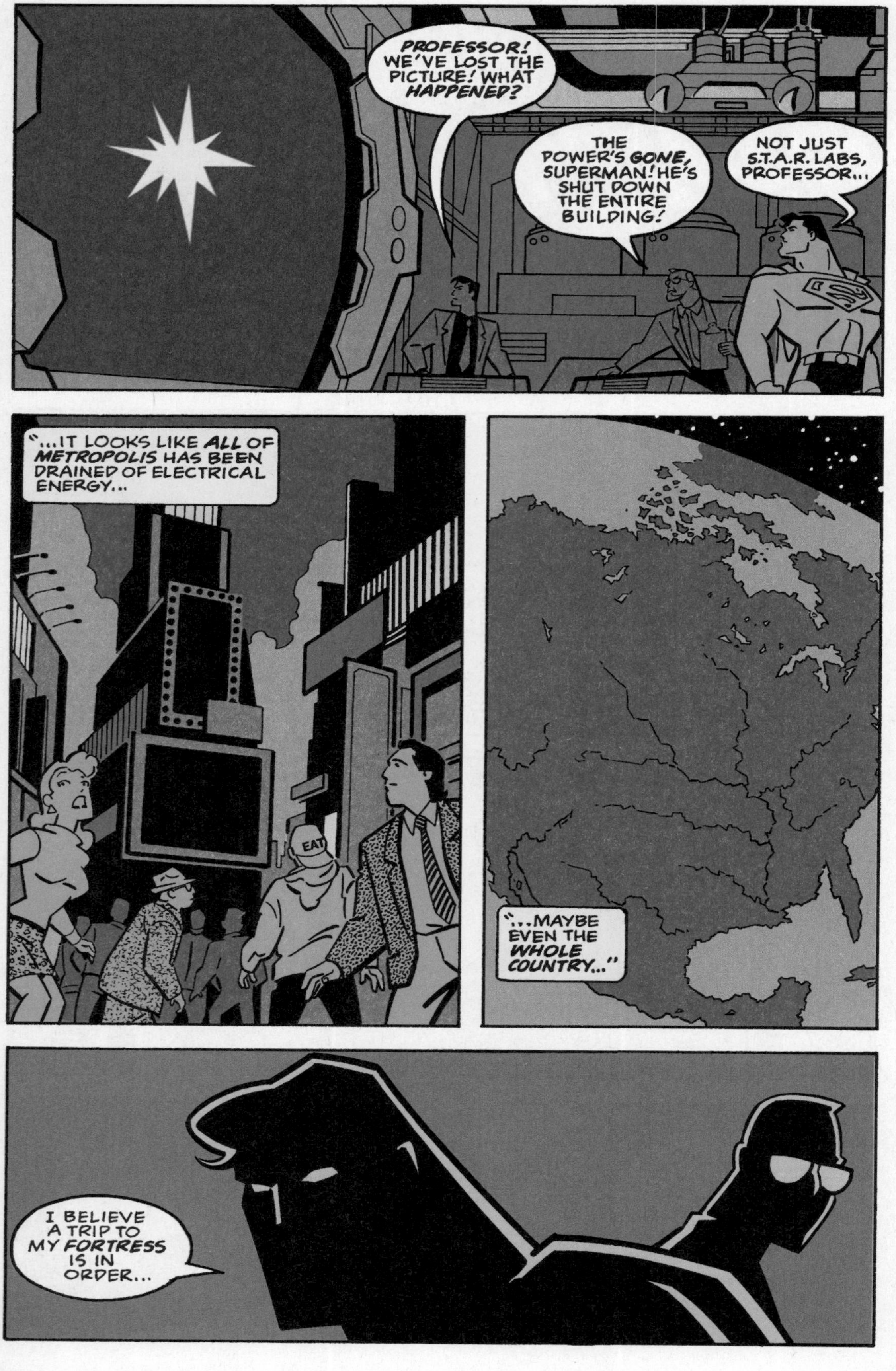
PROFESSOR! WE'VE LOST THE PICTURE! WHAT HAPPENED?
THE POWER'S GONE, SUPERMAN! HE'S SHUT DOWN THE ENTIRE BUILDING!
NOT JUST S.T.A.R. LABS, PROFESSOR...
"...IT LOOKS LIKE ALL OF METROPOLIS HAS BEEN DRAINED OF ELECTRICAL ENERGY...
EAT
"...MAYBE EVEN THE WHOLE COUNTRY..."
I BELIEVE A TRIP TO MY FORTRESS IS IN ORDER...

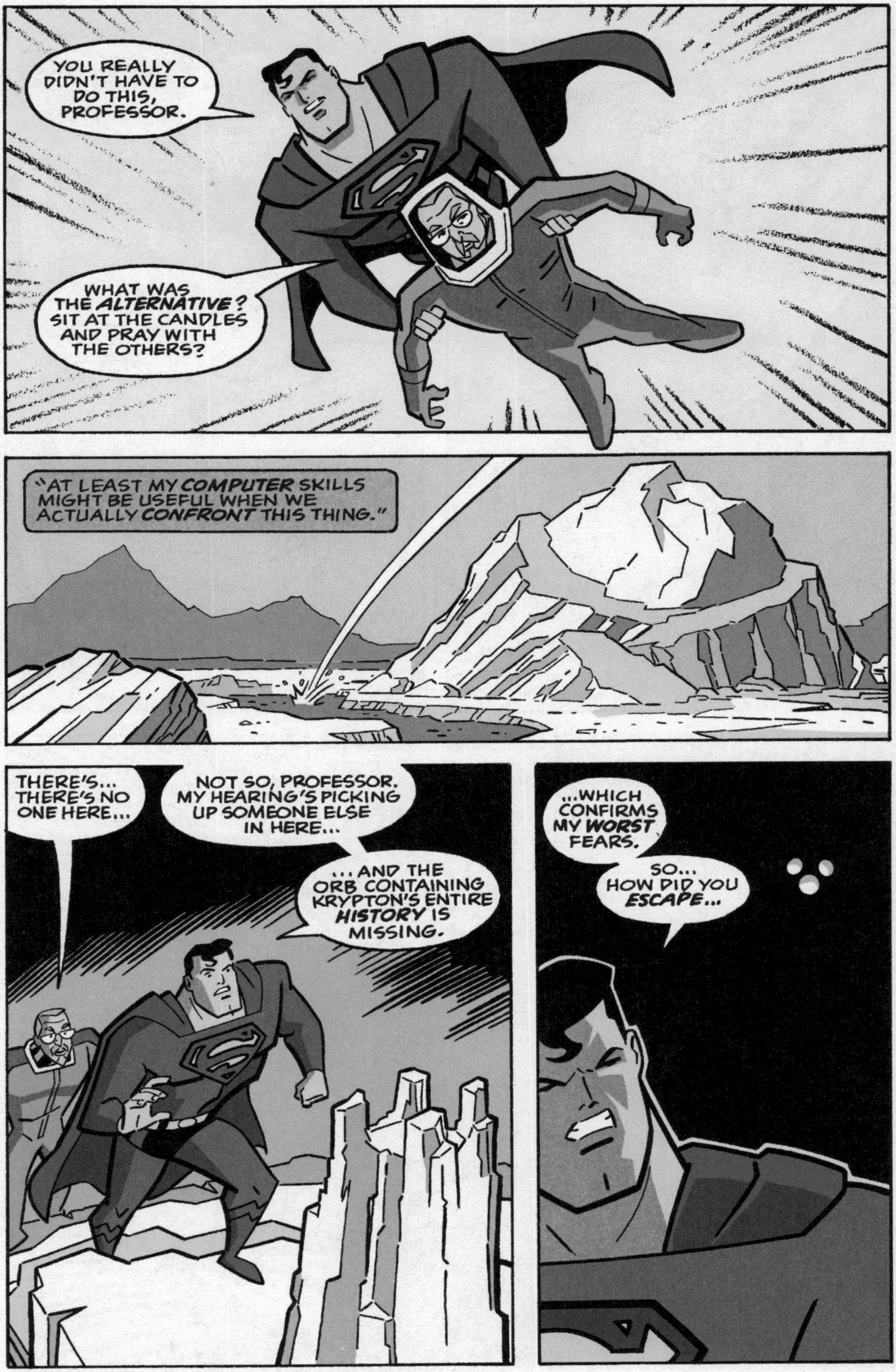
YOU REALLY DIDN'T HAVE TO DO THIS, PROFESSOR.
WHAT WAS THE ALTERNATIVE? SIT AT THE CANDLES AND PRAY WITH THE OTHERS?
"AT LEAST MY COMPUTER SKILLS MIGHT BE USEFUL WHEN WE ACTUALLY CONFRONT THIS THING."
THERE'S... THERE'S NO ONE HERE...
NOT SO, PROFESSOR. MY HEARING'S PICKING UP SOMEONE ELSE IN HERE...
...AND THE ORB CONTAINING KRYPTON'S ENTIRE HISTORY IS MISSING.
...WHICH CONFIRMS MY WORST FEARS.
SO... HOW DID YOU ESCAPE...

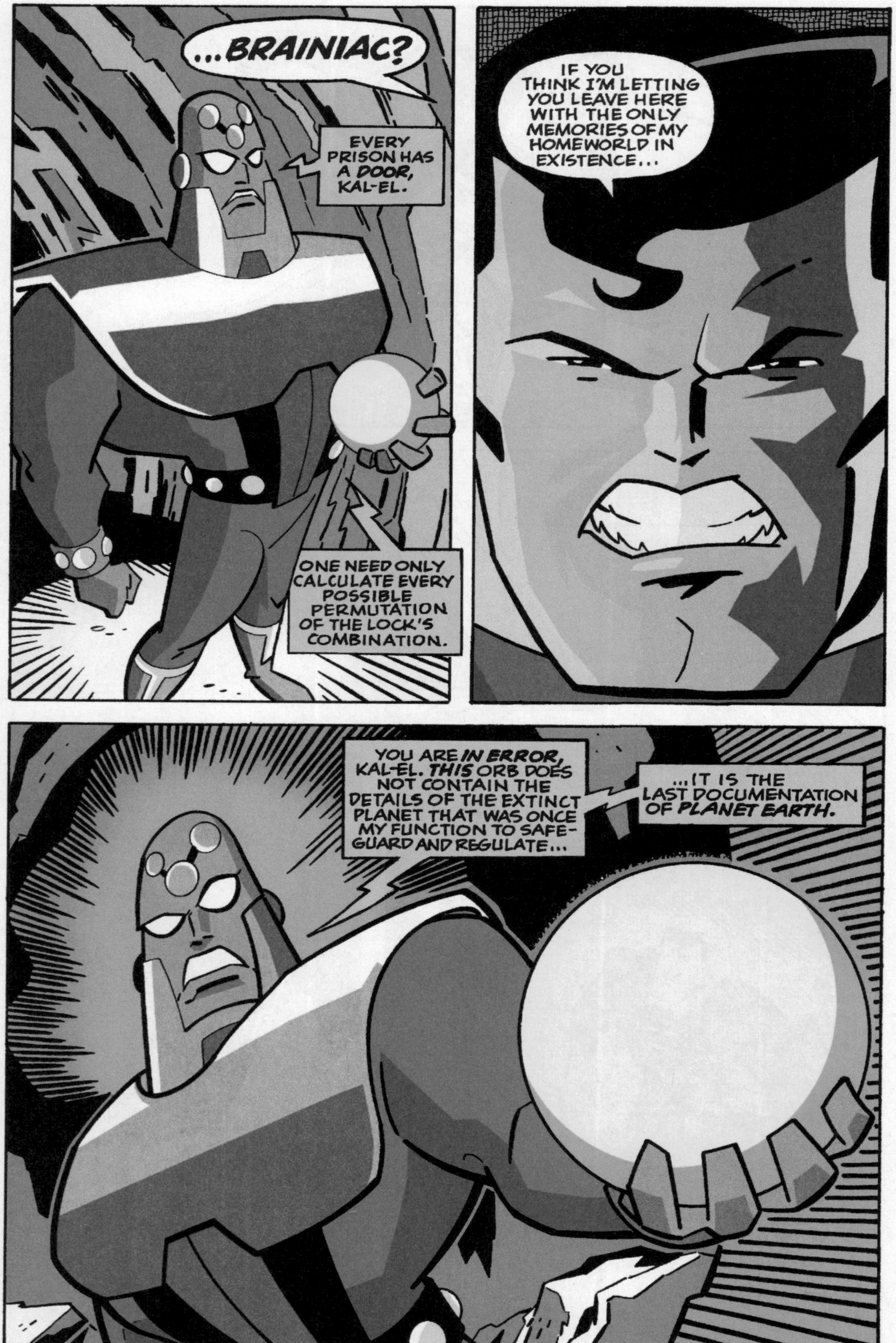
...BRAINIAC?
EVERY PRISON HAS A DOOR, KAL-EL.
ONE NEED ONLY CALCULATE EVERY POSSIBLE PERMUTATION OF THE LOCK'S COMBINATION.
IF YOU THINK I'M LETTING YOU LEAVE HERE WITH THE ONLY MEMORIES OF MY HOMEWORLD IN EXISTENCE...
YOU ARE IN ERROR, KAL-EL. THIS ORB DOES NOT CONTAIN THE DETAILS OF THE EXTINCT PLANET THAT WAS ONCE MY FUNCTION TO SAFE-GUARD AND REGULATE...
...IT IS THE LAST DOCUMENTATION OF PLANET EARTH.

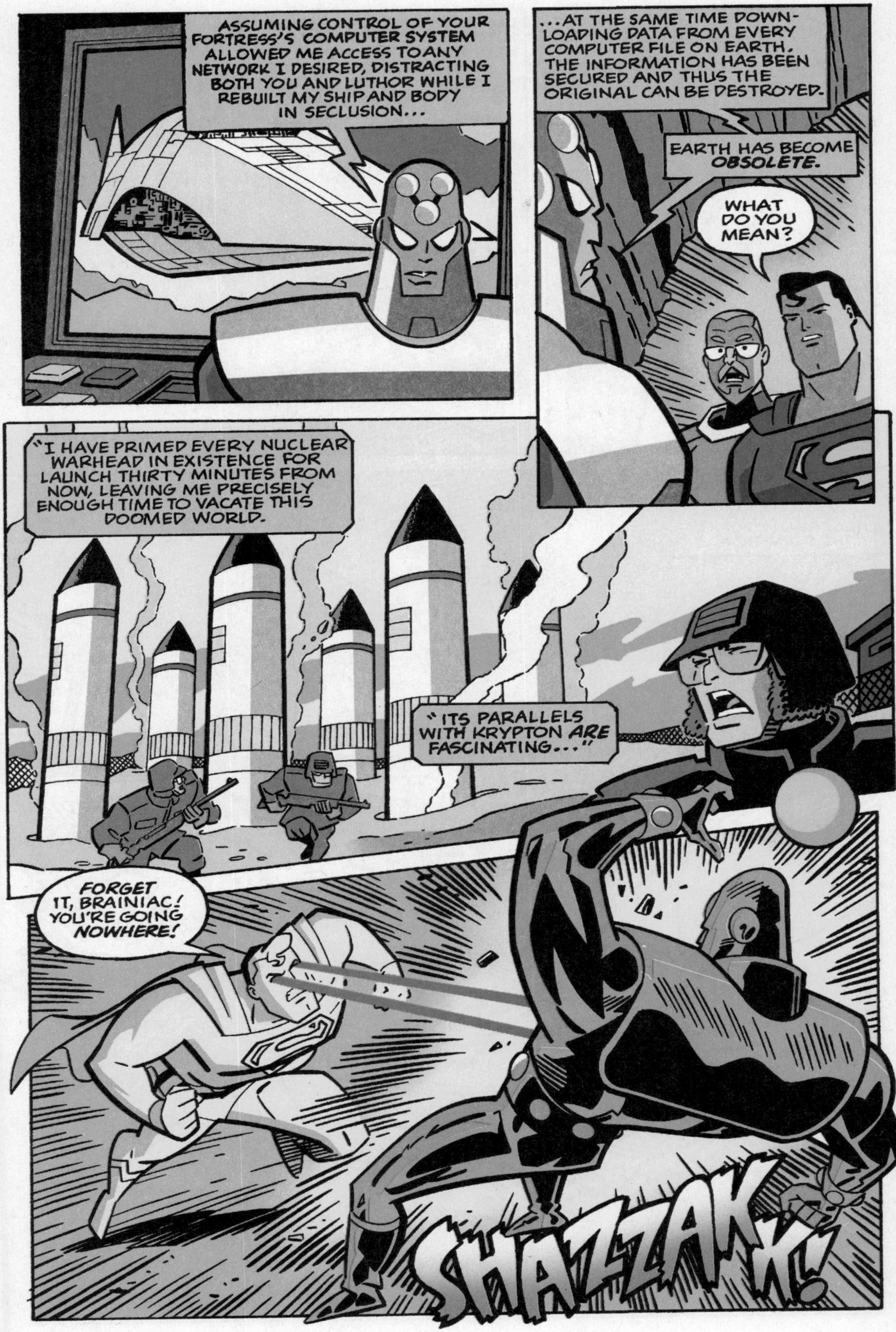
ASSUMING CONTROL OF YOUR FORTRESS'S COMPUTER SYSTEM ALLOWED ME ACCESS TO ANY NETWORK I DESIRED, DISTRACTING BOTH YOU AND LUTHOR WHILE I REBUILT MY SHIP AND BODY IN SECLUSION...
...AT THE SAME TIME DOWN-LOADING DATA FROM EVERY COMPUTER FILE ON EARTH. THE INFORMATION HAS BEEN SECURED AND THUS THE ORIGINAL CAN BE DESTROYED.
EARTH HAS BECOME OBSOLETE.
WHAT DO YOU MEAN?
"I HAVE PRIMED EVERY NUCLEAR WARHEAD IN EXISTENCE FOR LAUNCH THIRTY MINUTES FROM NOW, LEAVING ME PRECISELY ENOUGH TIME TO VACATE THIS DOOMED WORLD.
"ITS PARALLELS WITH KRYPTON ARE FASCINATING..."
FORGET IT, BRAINIAC! YOU'RE GOING NOWHERE!
SHAZZAKK!

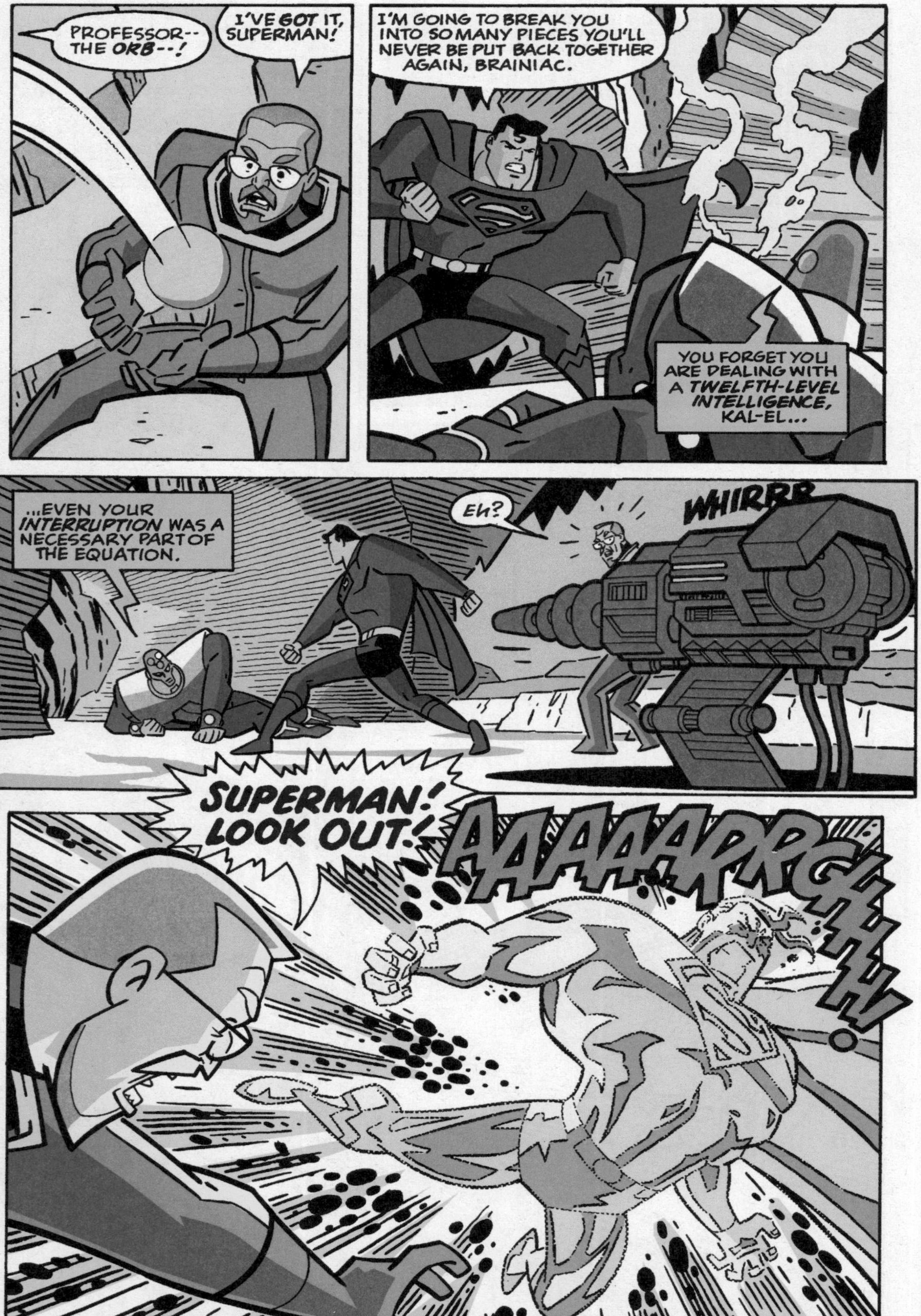
PROFESSOR-- THE ORB--!
I'VE GOT IT, SUPERMAN!
I'M GOING TO BREAK YOU INTO SO MANY PIECES YOU'LL NEVER BE PUT BACK TOGETHER AGAIN, BRAINIAC.
YOU FORGET YOU ARE DEALING WITH A TWELFTH-LEVEL INTELLIGENCE, KAL-EL...
...EVEN YOUR INTERRUPTION WAS A NECESSARY PART OF THE EQUATION.
Eh?
WHIRRR
SUPERMAN! LOOK OUT!
AAAAARRGHH!

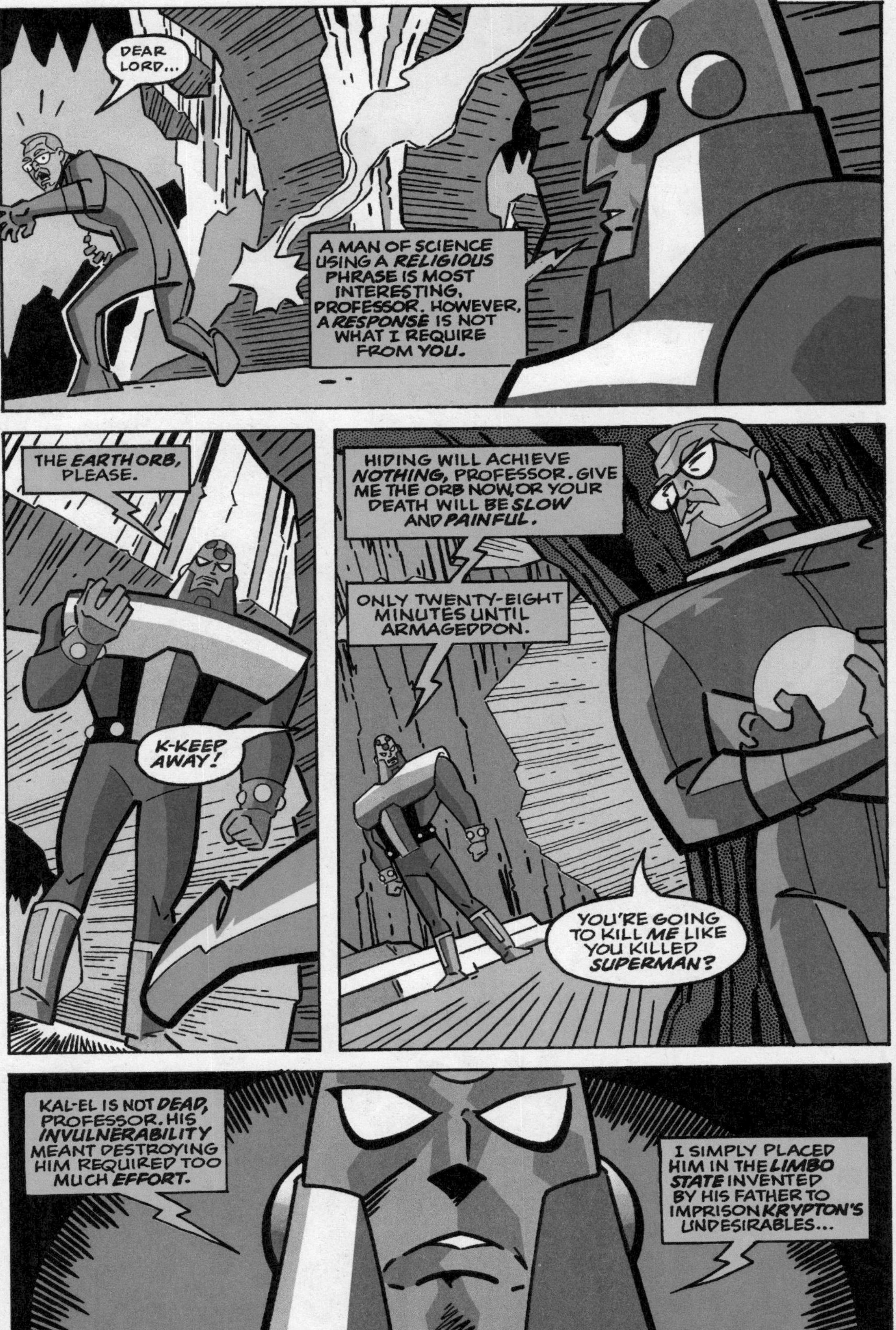
DEAR LORD...
A MAN OF SCIENCE USING A RELIGIOUS PHRASE IS MOST INTERESTING, PROFESSOR. HOWEVER, A RESPONSE IS NOT WHAT I REQUIRE FROM YOU.
THE EARTH ORB, PLEASE.
K-KEEP AWAY!
HIDING WILL ACHIEVE NOTHING, PROFESSOR. GIVE ME THE ORB NOW, OR YOUR DEATH WILL BE SLOW AND PAINFUL.
ONLY TWENTY-EIGHT MINUTES UNTIL ARMAGEDDON.
YOU'RE GOING TO KILL ME LIKE YOU KILLED SUPERMAN?
KAL-EL IS NOT DEAD, PROFESSOR. HIS INVULNERABILITY MEANT DESTROYING HIM REQUIRED TOO MUCH EFFORT.
I SIMPLY PLACED HIM IN THE LIMBO STATE INVENTED BY HIS FATHER TO IMPRISON KRYPTON'S UNDESIRABLES...

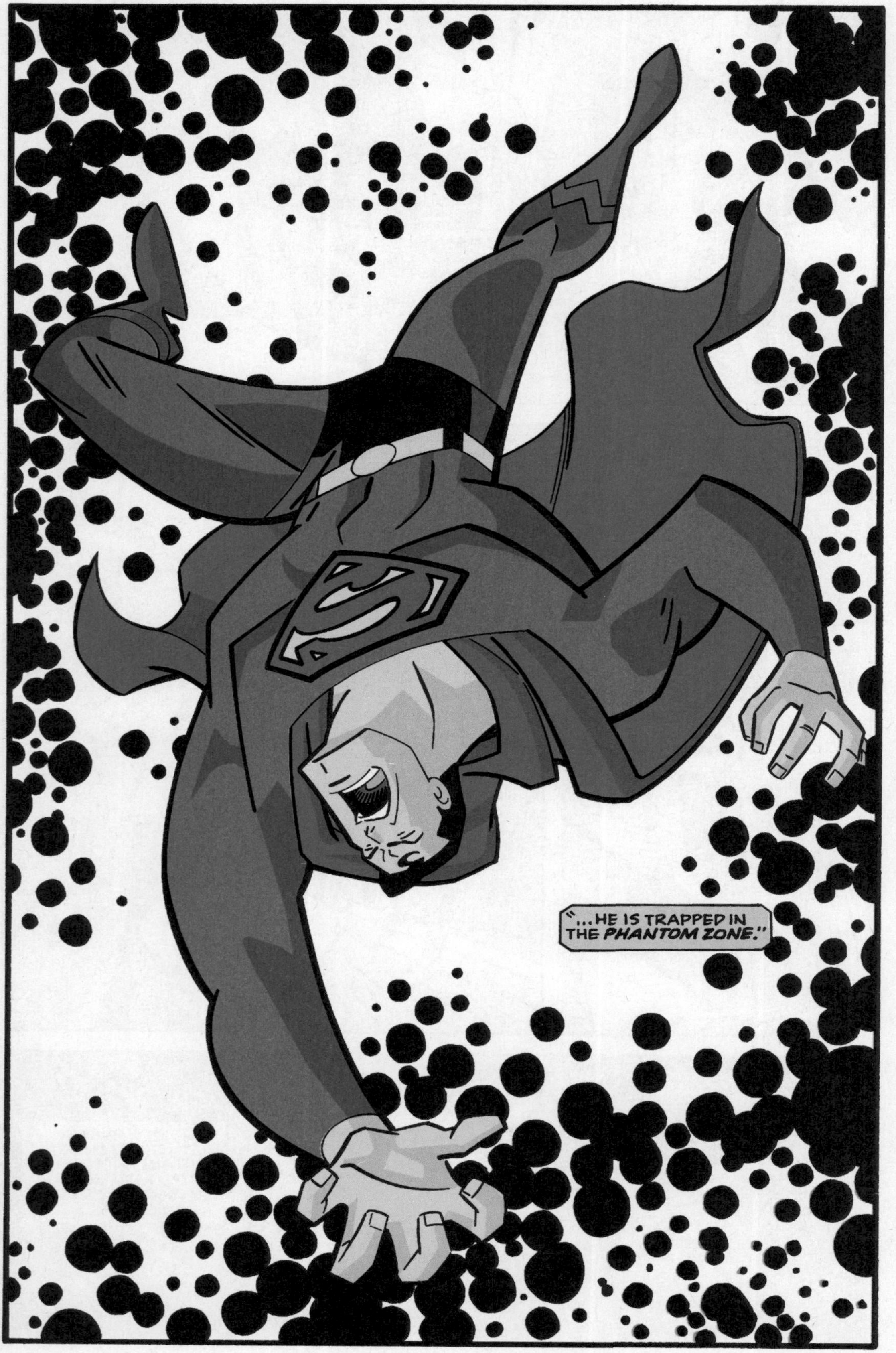
"...HE IS TRAPPED IN THE PHANTOM ZONE."

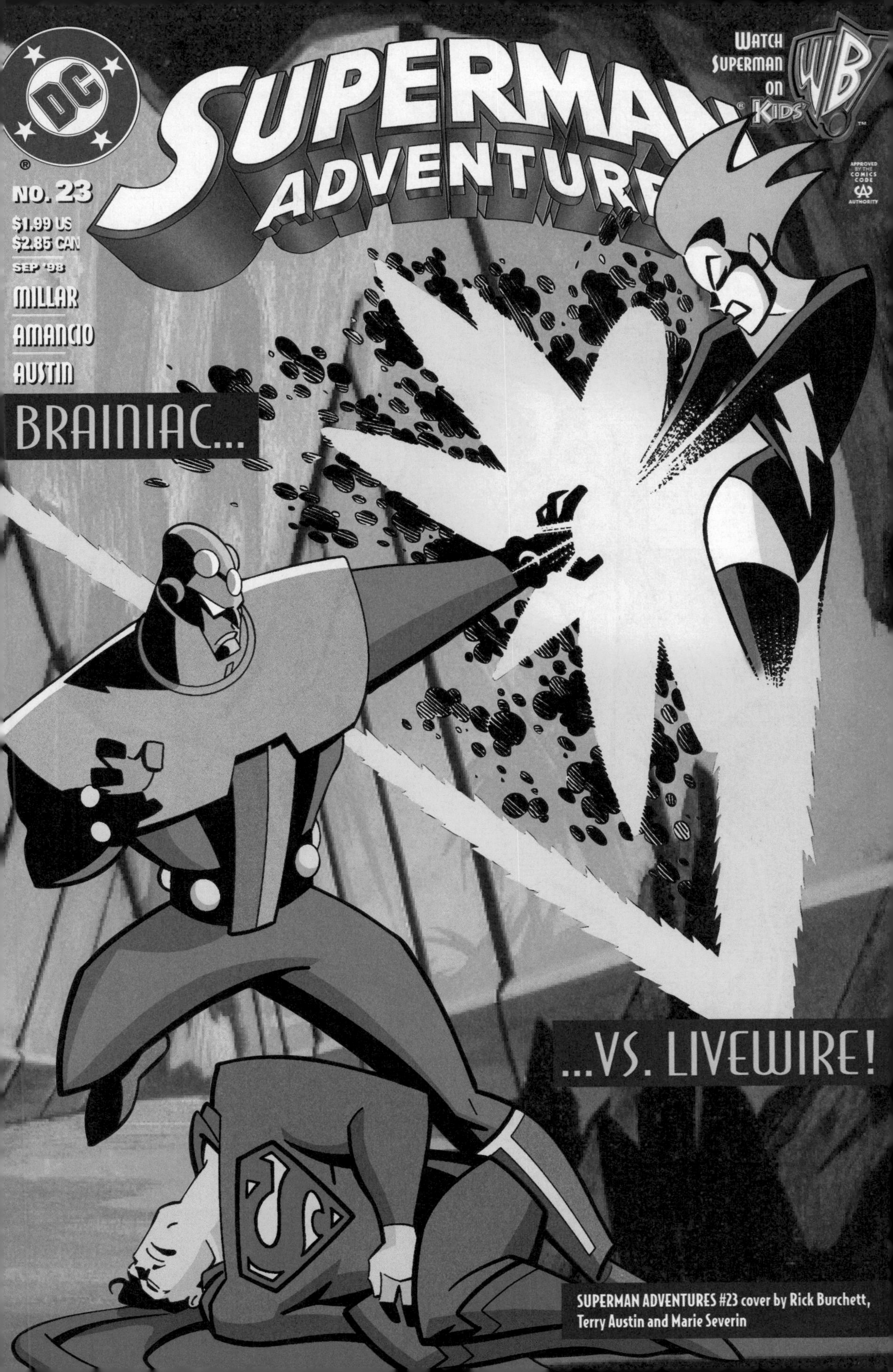
DC
SUPERMAN ADVENTURES
NO. 23
$1.99 US
$2.85 CAN
SEP '98
MILLAR
AMANCIO
AUSTIN
WATCH SUPERMAN ON KIDS' WB!
BRAINIAC...
...VS. LIVEWIRE!

SUPERMAN ADVENTURES #23 cover by Rick Burchett, Terry Austin and Marie Severin

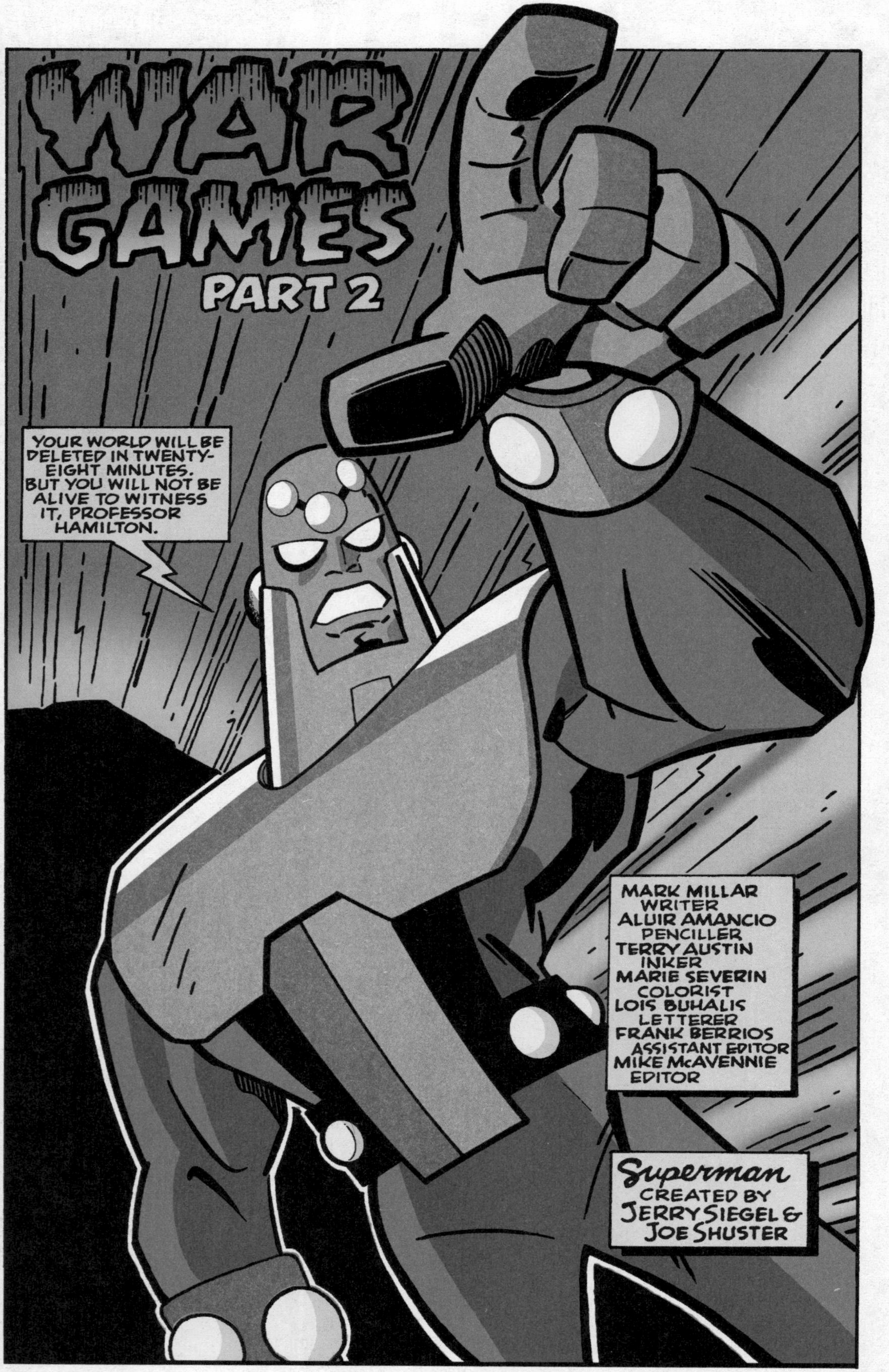
WAR GAMES
PART 2
YOUR WORLD WILL BE DELETED IN TWENTY-EIGHT MINUTES. BUT YOU WILL NOT BE ALIVE TO WITNESS IT, PROFESSOR HAMILTON.
MARK MILLAR WRITER
ALUIR AMANCIO PENCILLER
TERRY AUSTIN INKER
MARIE SEVERIN COLORIST
LOIS BUHALIS LETTERER
FRANK BERRIOS ASSISTANT EDITOR
MIKE McAVENNIE EDITOR
Superman CREATED BY JERRY SIEGEL & JOE SHUSTER

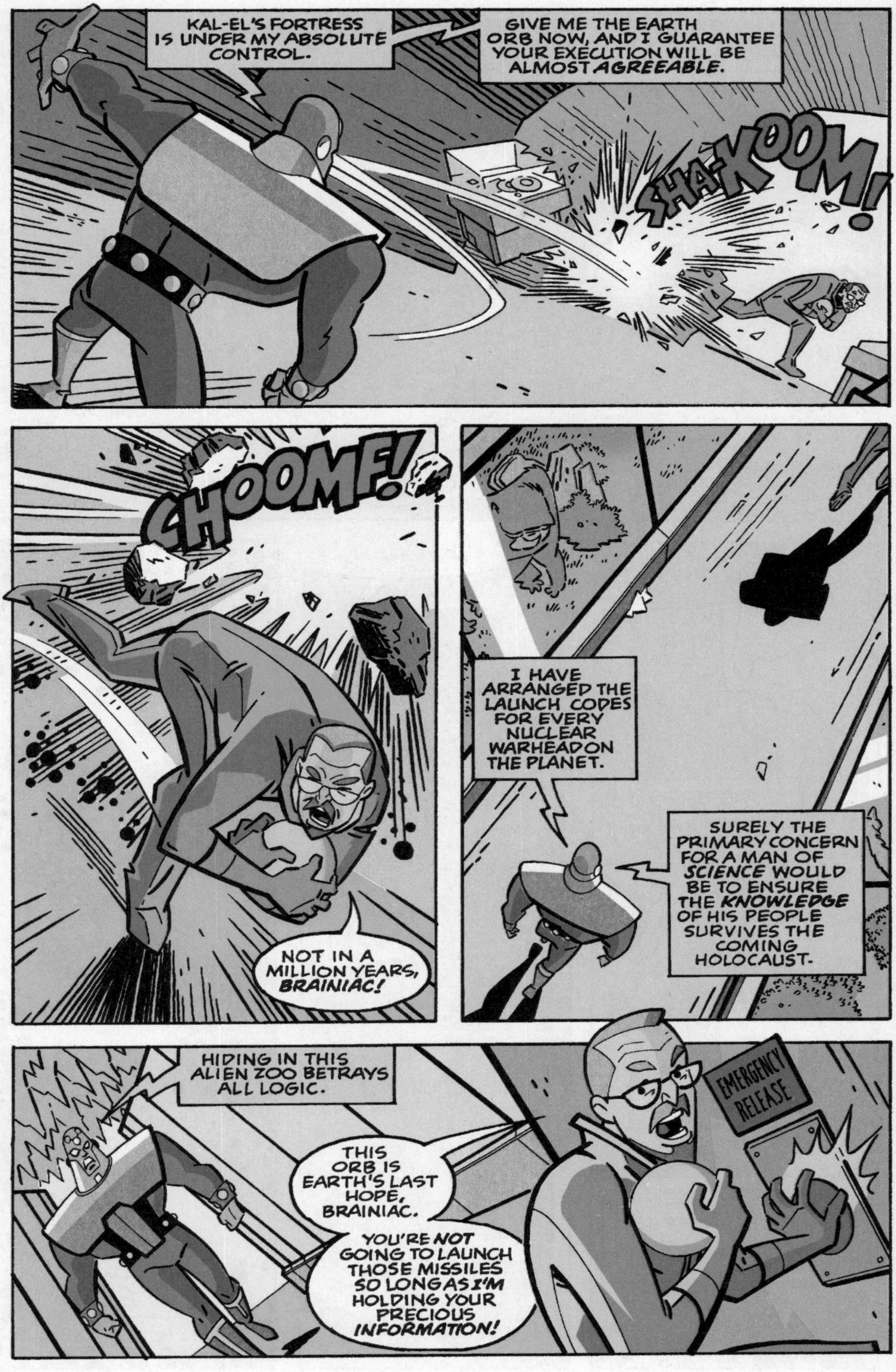
KAL-EL'S FORTRESS IS UNDER MY ABSOLUTE CONTROL.
GIVE ME THE EARTH ORB NOW, AND I GUARANTEE YOUR EXECUTION WILL BE ALMOST AGREEABLE.
SHA-KOOM!
CHOOMF!
NOT IN A MILLION YEARS, BRAINIAC!
I HAVE ARRANGED THE LAUNCH CODES FOR EVERY NUCLEAR WARHEAD ON THE PLANET.
SURELY THE PRIMARY CONCERN FOR A MAN OF SCIENCE WOULD BE TO ENSURE THE KNOWLEDGE OF HIS PEOPLE SURVIVES THE COMING HOLOCAUST.
HIDING IN THIS ALIEN ZOO BETRAYS ALL LOGIC.
EMERGENCY RELEASE
THIS ORB IS EARTH'S LAST HOPE, BRAINIAC.
YOU'RE NOT GOING TO LAUNCH THOSE MISSILES SO LONG AS I'M HOLDING YOUR PRECIOUS INFORMATION!

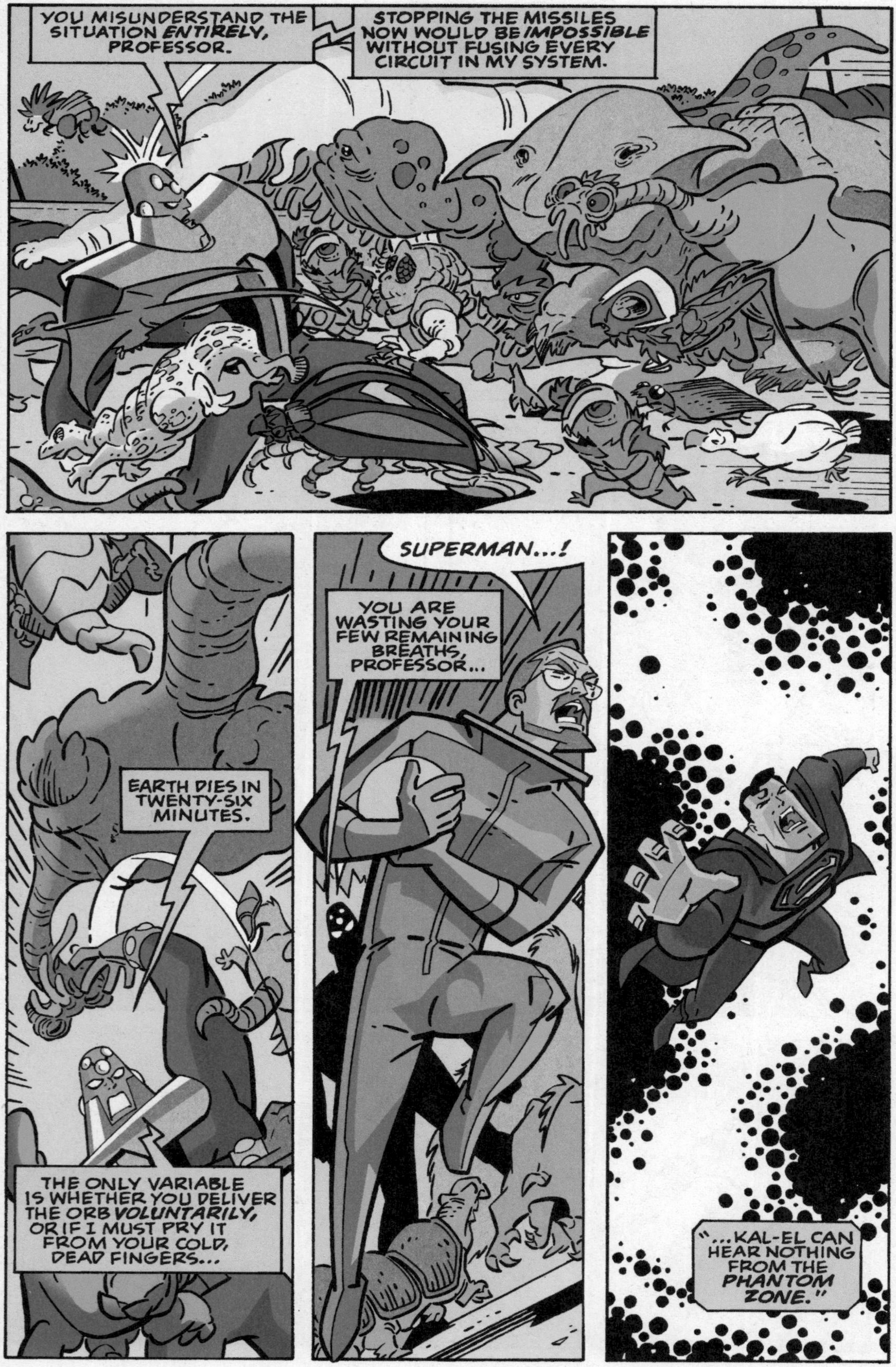
YOU MISUNDERSTAND THE SITUATION ENTIRELY, PROFESSOR.
STOPPING THE MISSILES NOW WOULD BE IMPOSSIBLE WITHOUT FUSING EVERY CIRCUIT IN MY SYSTEM.
EARTH DIES IN TWENTY-SIX MINUTES.
THE ONLY VARIABLE IS WHETHER YOU DELIVER THE ORB VOLUNTARILY, OR IF I MUST PRY IT FROM YOUR COLD, DEAD FINGERS...
SUPERMAN...!
YOU ARE WASTING YOUR FEW REMAINING BREATHS, PROFESSOR...
"...KAL-EL CAN HEAR NOTHING FROM THE PHANTOM ZONE."

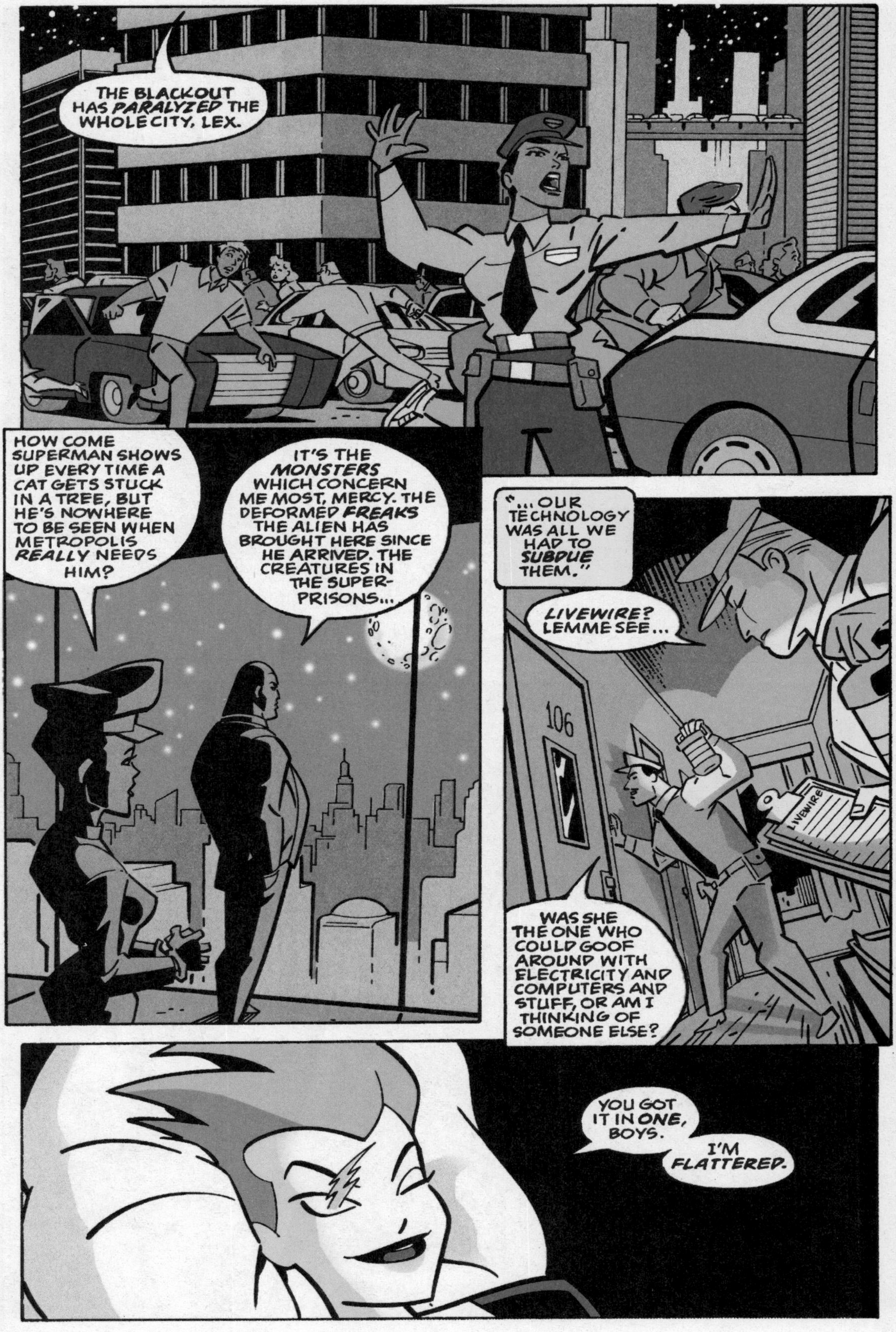
THE BLACKOUT HAS PARALYZED THE WHOLE CITY, LEX.
HOW COME SUPERMAN SHOWS UP EVERY TIME A CAT GETS STUCK IN A TREE, BUT HE'S NOWHERE TO BE SEEN WHEN METROPOLIS REALLY NEEDS HIM?
IT'S THE MONSTERS WHICH CONCERN ME MOST, MERCY. THE DEFORMED FREAKS THE ALIEN HAS BROUGHT HERE SINCE HE ARRIVED. THE CREATURES IN THE SUPER-PRISONS...
"...OUR TECHNOLOGY WAS ALL WE HAD TO SUBDUE THEM."
LIVEWIRE? LEMME SEE...
106
LIVEWIRE
WAS SHE THE ONE WHO COULD GOOF AROUND WITH ELECTRICITY AND COMPUTERS AND STUFF, OR AM I THINKING OF SOMEONE ELSE?
YOU GOT IT IN ONE, BOYS.
I'M FLATTERED.

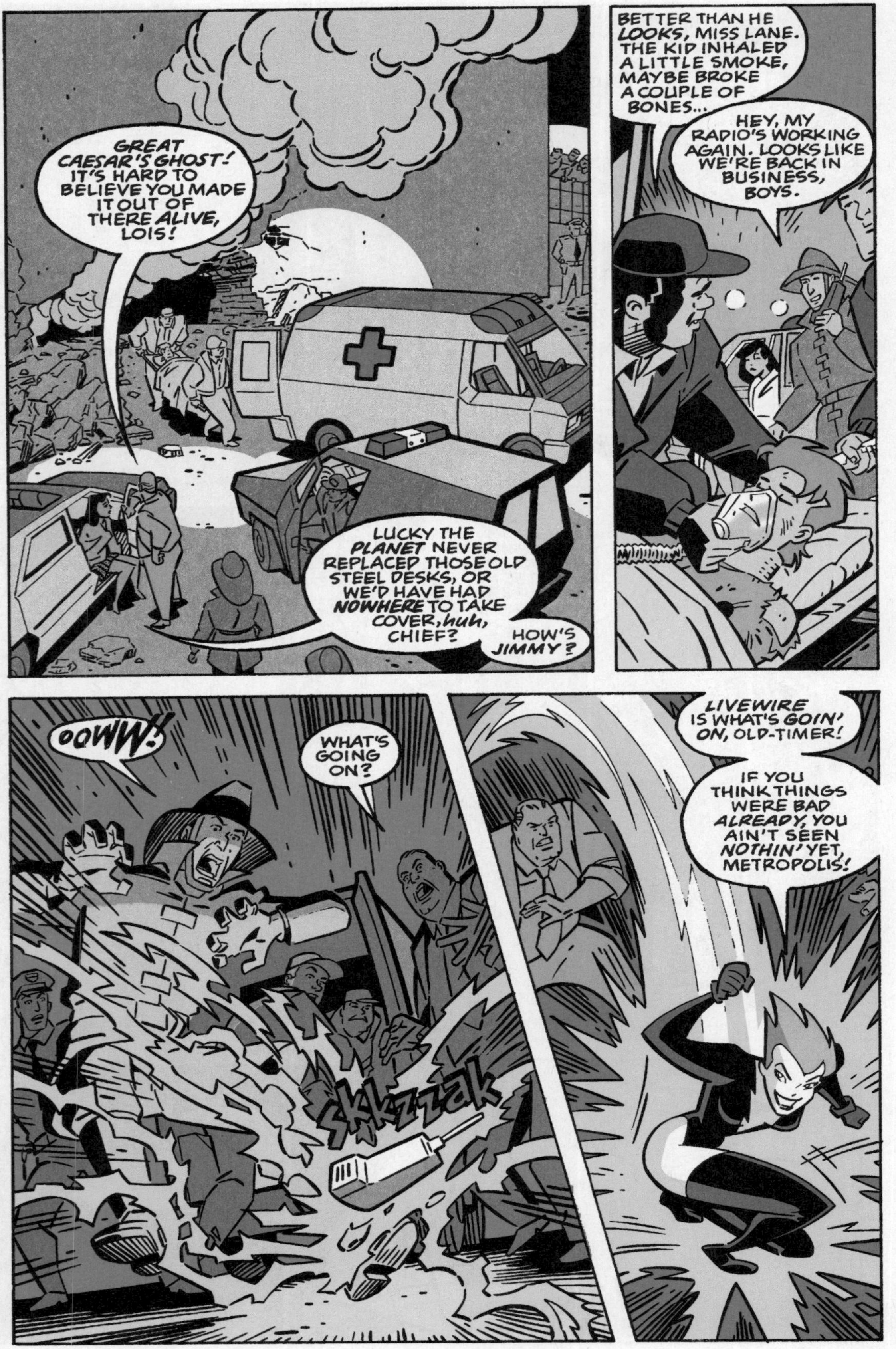
GREAT CAESAR'S GHOST! IT'S HARD TO BELIEVE YOU MADE IT OUT OF THERE ALIVE, LOIS!
LUCKY THE PLANET NEVER REPLACED THOSE OLD STEEL DESKS, OR WE'D HAVE HAD NOWHERE TO TAKE COVER, huh, CHIEF?
HOW'S JIMMY?
BETTER THAN HE LOOKS, MISS LANE. THE KID INHALED A LITTLE SMOKE, MAYBE BROKE A COUPLE OF BONES...
HEY, MY RADIO'S WORKING AGAIN. LOOKS LIKE WE'RE BACK IN BUSINESS, BOYS.
OOWW!
WHAT'S GOING ON?
SKKZZZAK
LIVEWIRE IS WHAT'S GOIN' ON, OLD-TIMER!
IF YOU THINK THINGS WERE BAD ALREADY, YOU AIN'T SEEN NOTHIN' YET, METROPOLIS!

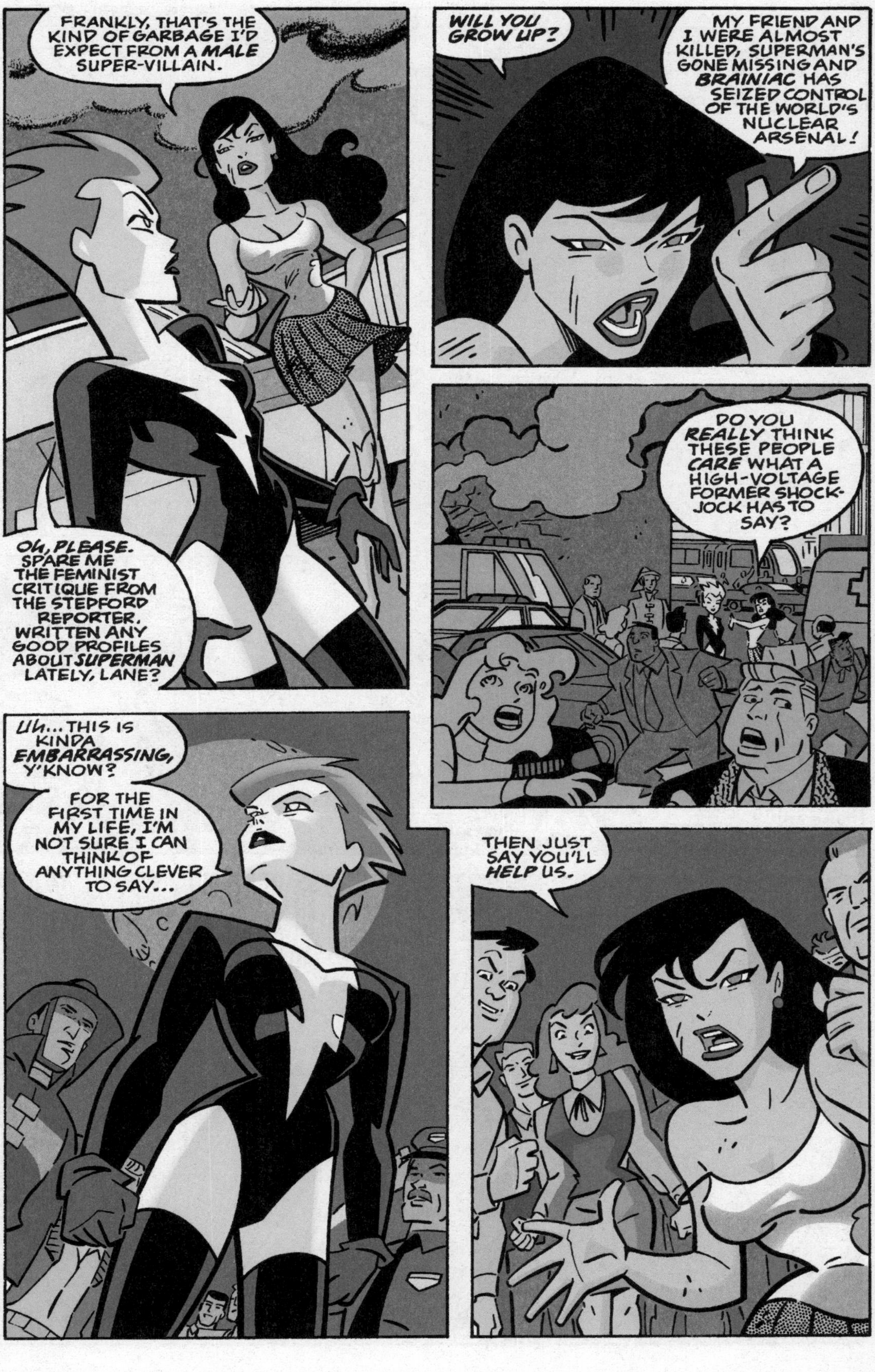
FRANKLY, THAT'S THE KIND OF GARBAGE I'D EXPECT FROM A MALE SUPER-VILLAIN.
OH, PLEASE. SPARE ME THE FEMINIST CRITIQUE FROM THE STEPFORD REPORTER. WRITTEN ANY GOOD PROFILES ABOUT SUPERMAN LATELY, LANE?
WILL YOU GROW UP?
MY FRIEND AND I WERE ALMOST KILLED, SUPERMAN'S GONE MISSING AND BRAINIAC HAS SEIZED CONTROL OF THE WORLD'S NUCLEAR ARSENAL!
DO YOU REALLY THINK THESE PEOPLE CARE WHAT A HIGH-VOLTAGE FORMER SHOCK-JOCK HAS TO SAY?
UH... THIS IS KINDA EMBARRASSING, Y'KNOW?
FOR THE FIRST TIME IN MY LIFE, I'M NOT SURE I CAN THINK OF ANYTHING CLEVER TO SAY...
THEN JUST SAY YOU'LL HELP US.

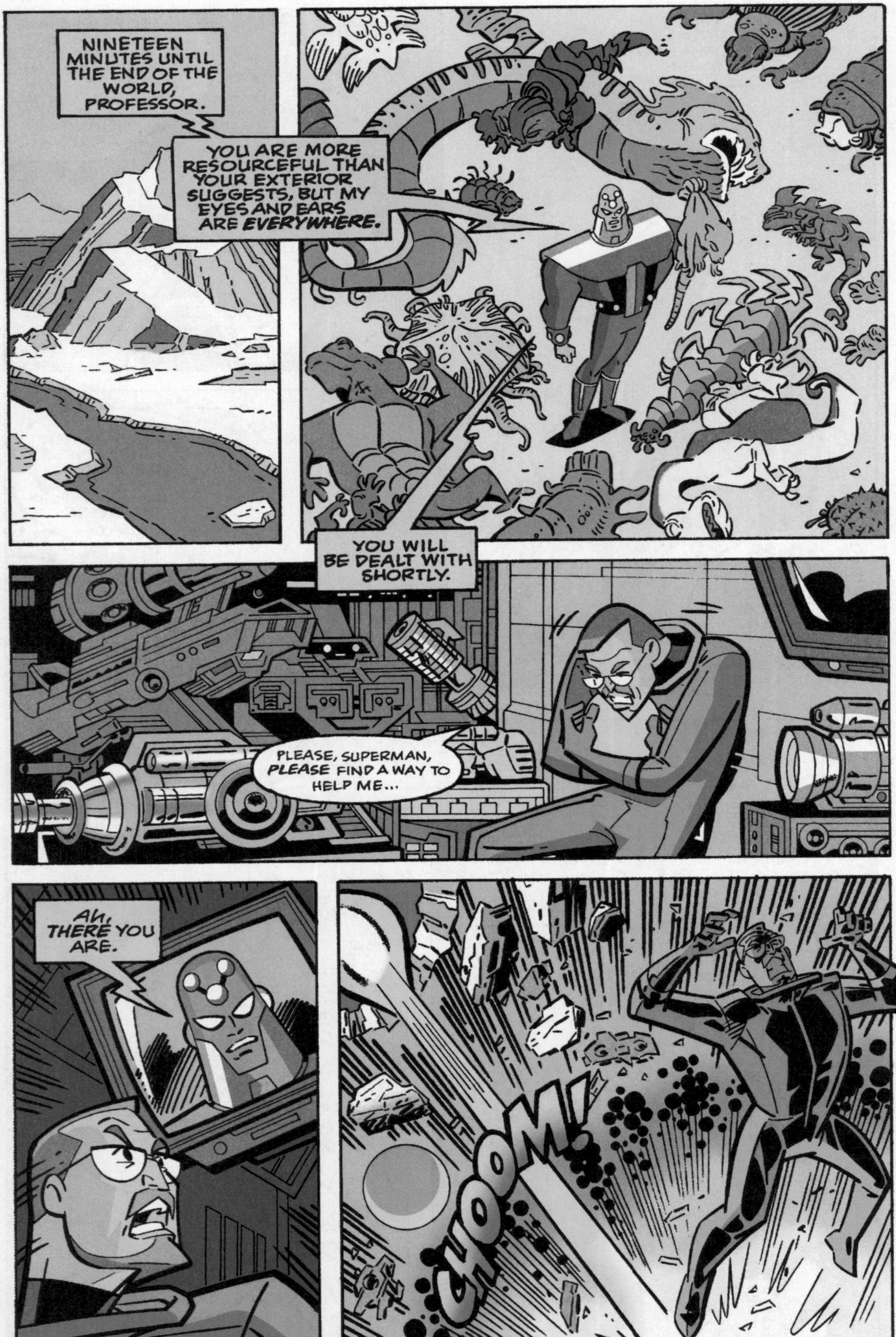
NINETEEN MINUTES UNTIL THE END OF THE WORLD, PROFESSOR.
YOU ARE MORE RESOURCEFUL THAN YOUR EXTERIOR SUGGESTS, BUT MY EYES AND EARS ARE *EVERYWHERE.*
YOU WILL BE DEALT WITH SHORTLY.
PLEASE, SUPERMAN, *PLEASE* FIND A WAY TO HELP ME...
AH, THERE YOU ARE.
CHOOOM!

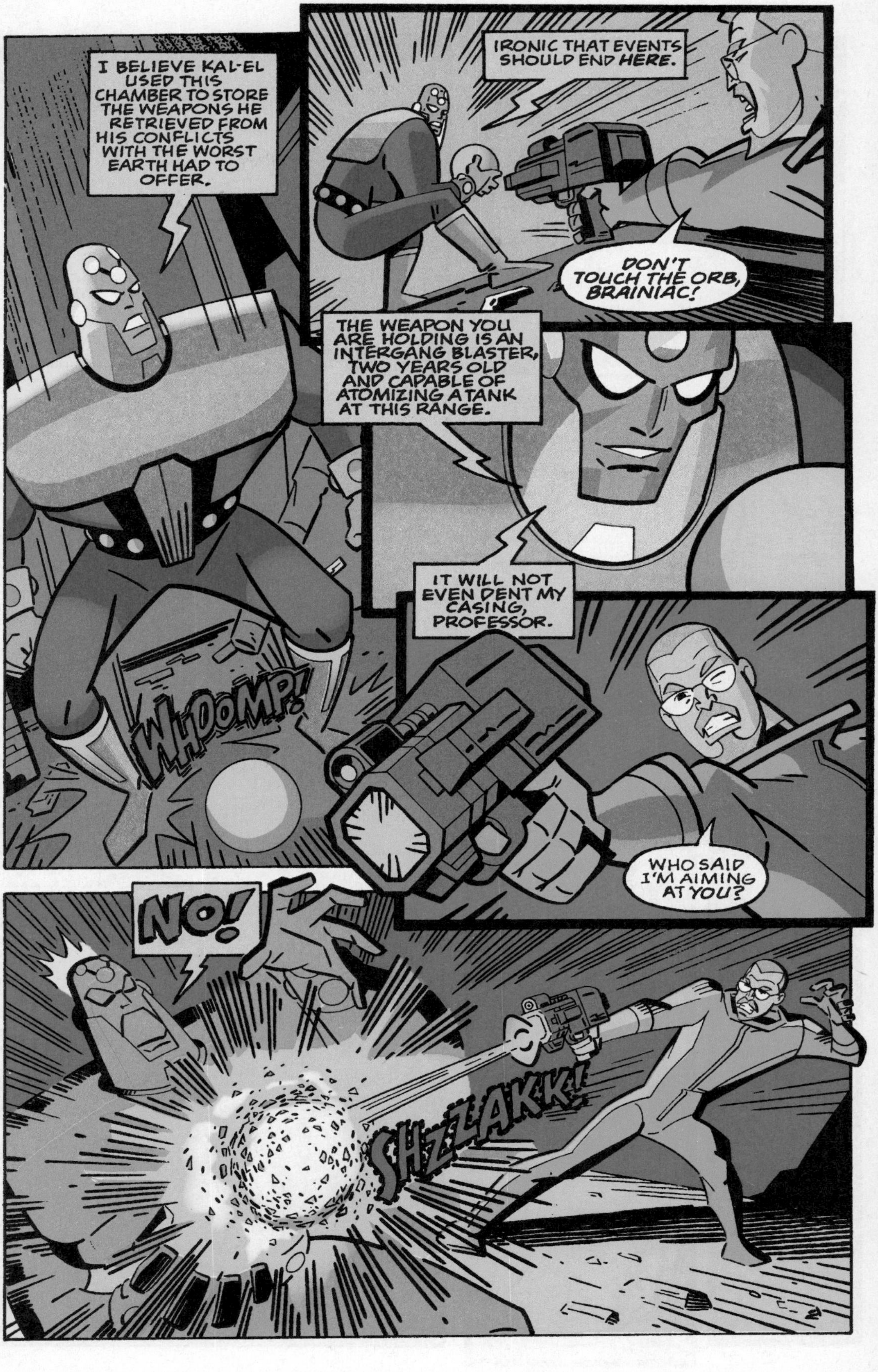
I BELIEVE KAL-EL USED THIS CHAMBER TO STORE THE WEAPONS HE RETRIEVED FROM HIS CONFLICTS WITH THE WORST EARTH HAD TO OFFER.
WHOOMP!
IRONIC THAT EVENTS SHOULD END HERE.
DON'T TOUCH THE ORB, BRAINIAC!
THE WEAPON YOU ARE HOLDING IS AN INTERGANG BLASTER, TWO YEARS OLD AND CAPABLE OF ATOMIZING A TANK AT THIS RANGE.
IT WILL NOT EVEN DENT MY CASING, PROFESSOR.
WHO SAID I'M AIMING AT YOU?
NO!
SHZZAKK!

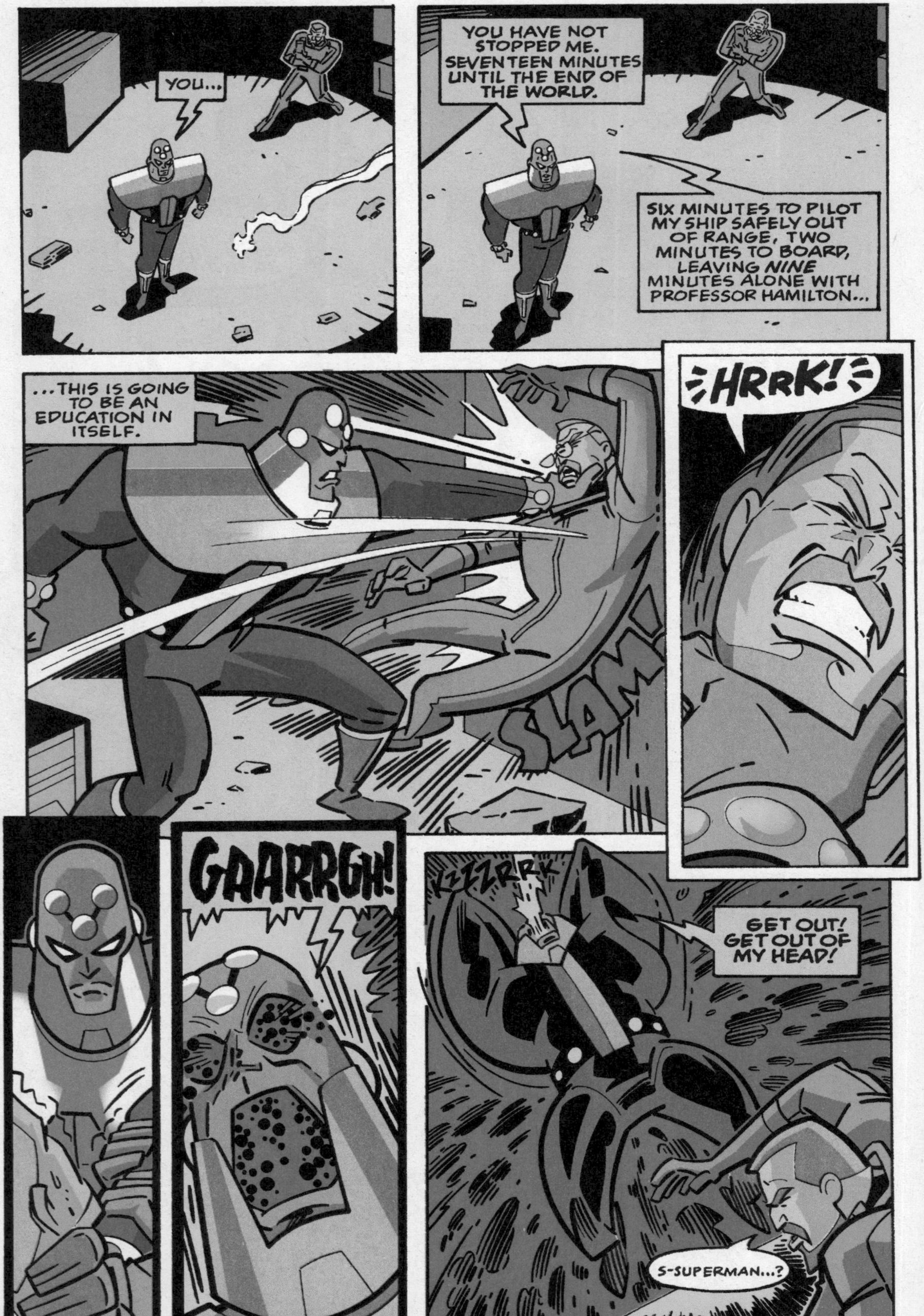

YOU...
YOU HAVE NOT STOPPED ME. SEVENTEEN MINUTES UNTIL THE END OF THE WORLD.
SIX MINUTES TO PILOT MY SHIP SAFELY OUT OF RANGE, TWO MINUTES TO BOARD, LEAVING NINE MINUTES ALONE WITH PROFESSOR HAMILTON...
...THIS IS GOING TO BE AN EDUCATION IN ITSELF.
SLAM!
HRRK!
GAARRGH!
KZZZRRK
GET OUT! GET OUT OF MY HEAD!
S-SUPERMAN...?

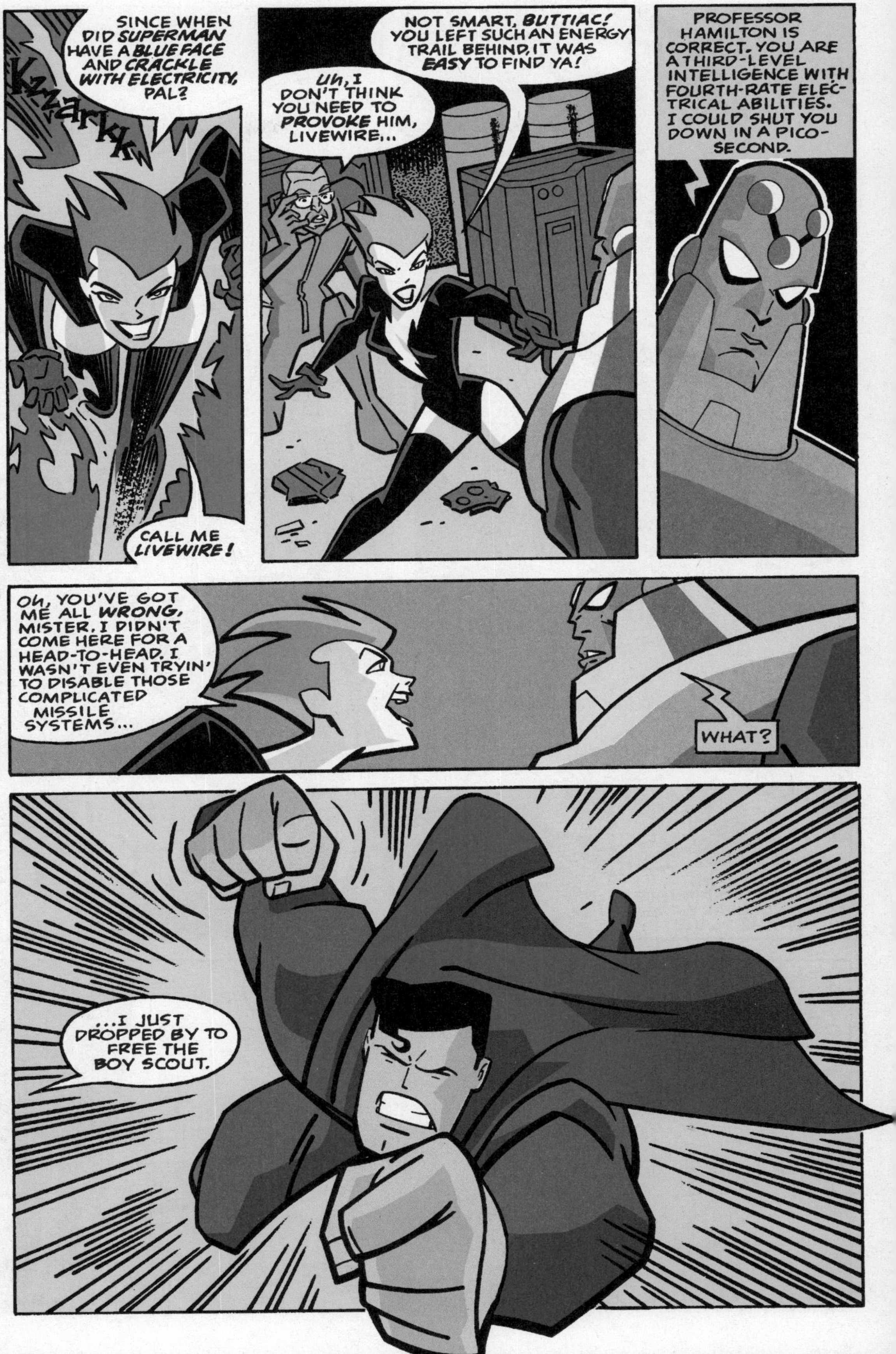
SINCE WHEN DID SUPERMAN HAVE A BLUE FACE AND CRACKLE WITH ELECTRICITY, PAL?
KZZARKKK
CALL ME LIVEWIRE!
NOT SMART, BUTTIAC! YOU LEFT SUCH AN ENERGY TRAIL BEHIND, IT WAS EASY TO FIND YA!
UH, I DON'T THINK YOU NEED TO PROVOKE HIM, LIVEWIRE...
PROFESSOR HAMILTON IS CORRECT. YOU ARE A THIRD-LEVEL INTELLIGENCE WITH FOURTH-RATE ELECTRICAL ABILITIES. I COULD SHUT YOU DOWN IN A PICO-SECOND.
OH, YOU'VE GOT ME ALL WRONG, MISTER. I DIDN'T COME HERE FOR A HEAD-TO-HEAD. I WASN'T EVEN TRYIN' TO DISABLE THOSE COMPLICATED MISSILE SYSTEMS...
WHAT?
...I JUST DROPPED BY TO FREE THE BOY SCOUT.

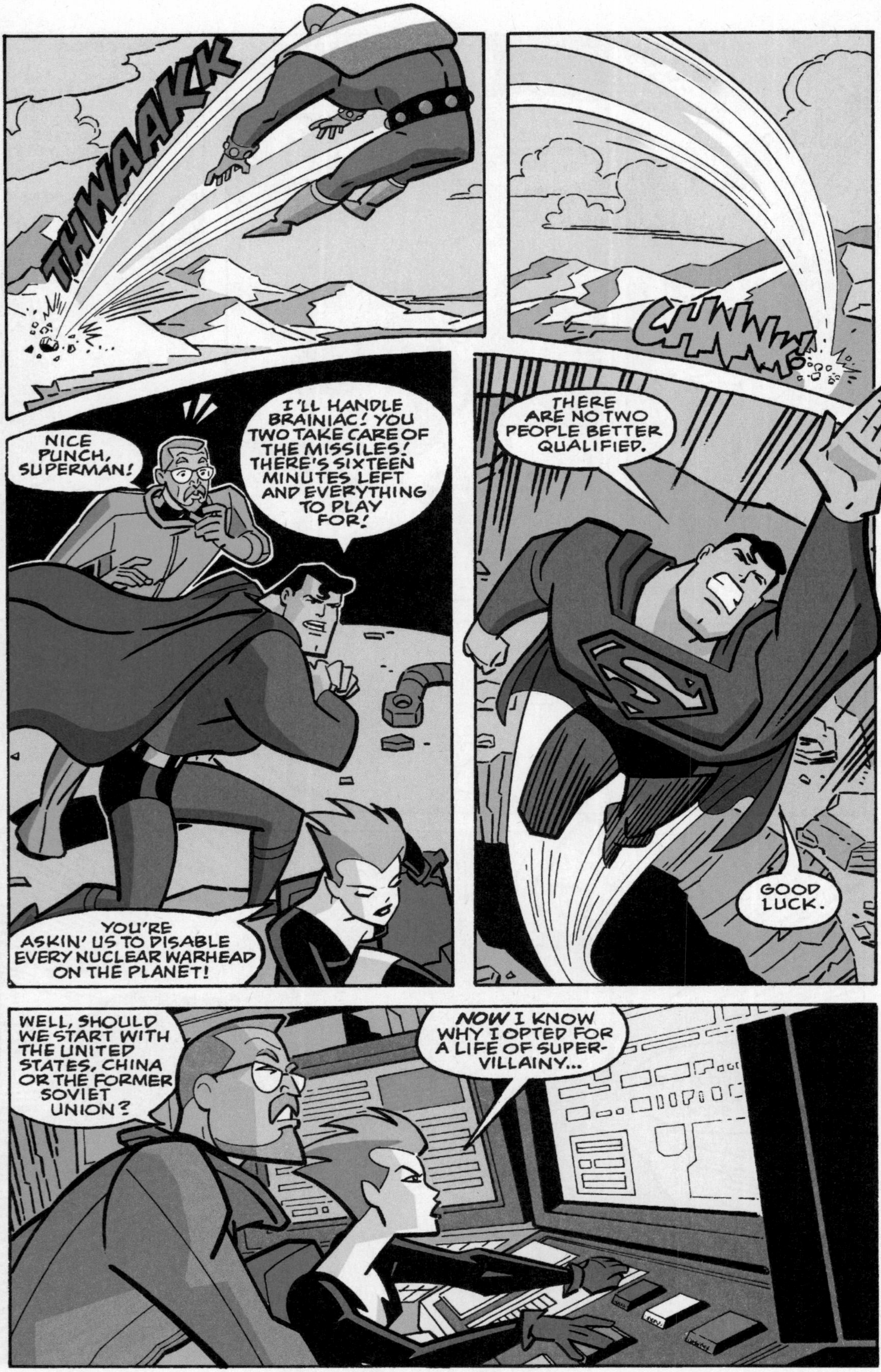
THWAAKK
CHNNK!
NICE PUNCH, SUPERMAN!
I'LL HANDLE BRAINIAC! YOU TWO TAKE CARE OF THE MISSILES! THERE'S SIXTEEN MINUTES LEFT AND EVERYTHING TO PLAY FOR!
YOU'RE ASKIN' US TO DISABLE EVERY NUCLEAR WARHEAD ON THE PLANET!
THERE ARE NO TWO PEOPLE BETTER QUALIFIED.
GOOD LUCK.
WELL, SHOULD WE START WITH THE UNITED STATES, CHINA OR THE FORMER SOVIET UNION?
NOW I KNOW WHY I OPTED FOR A LIFE OF SUPER-VILLAINY...

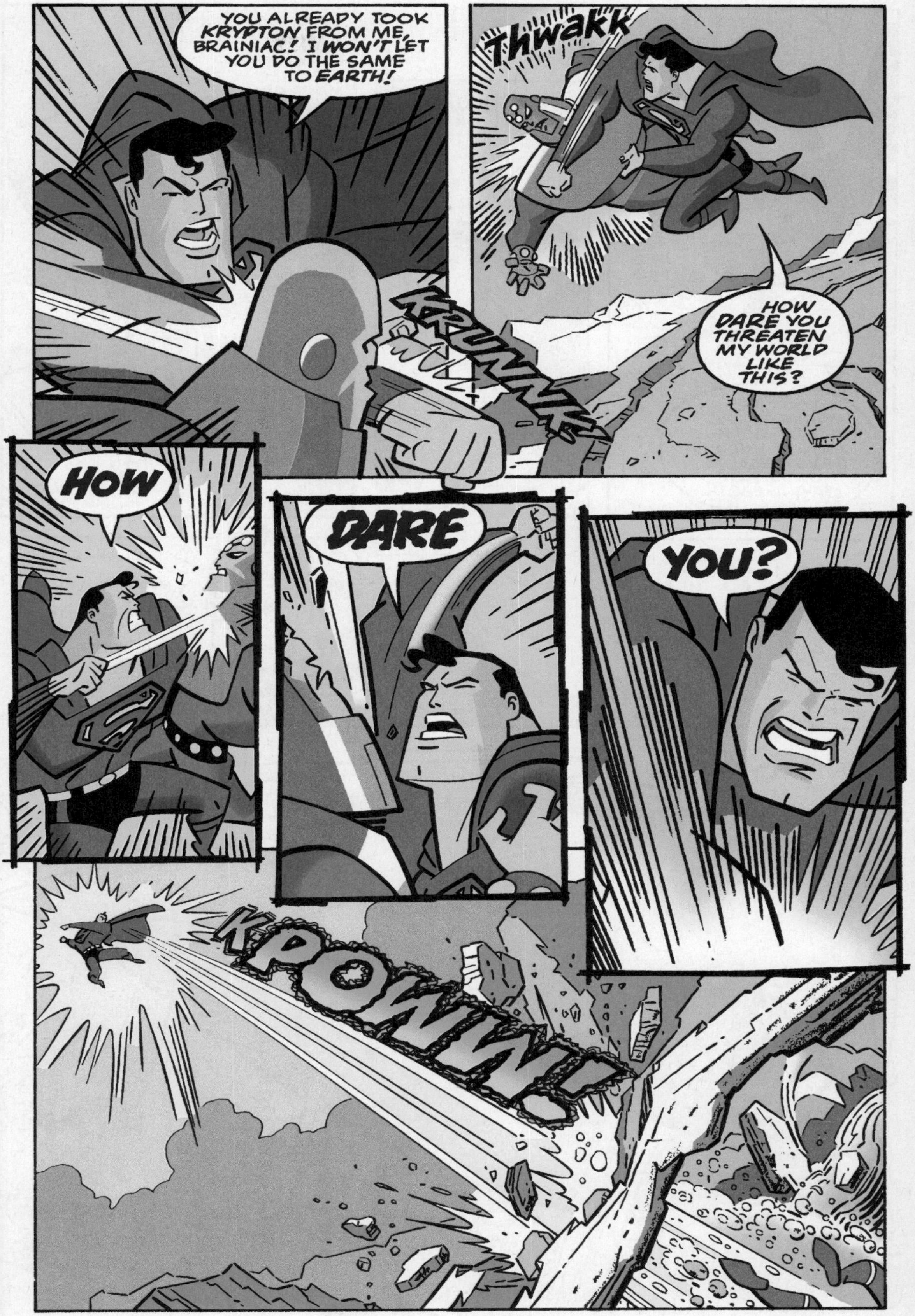
YOU ALREADY TOOK KRYPTON FROM ME, BRAINIAC! I WON'T LET YOU DO THE SAME TO EARTH!
KRUNNK
THWAKK
HOW DARE YOU THREATEN MY WORLD LIKE THIS?
HOW
DARE
YOU?
K-POWW!

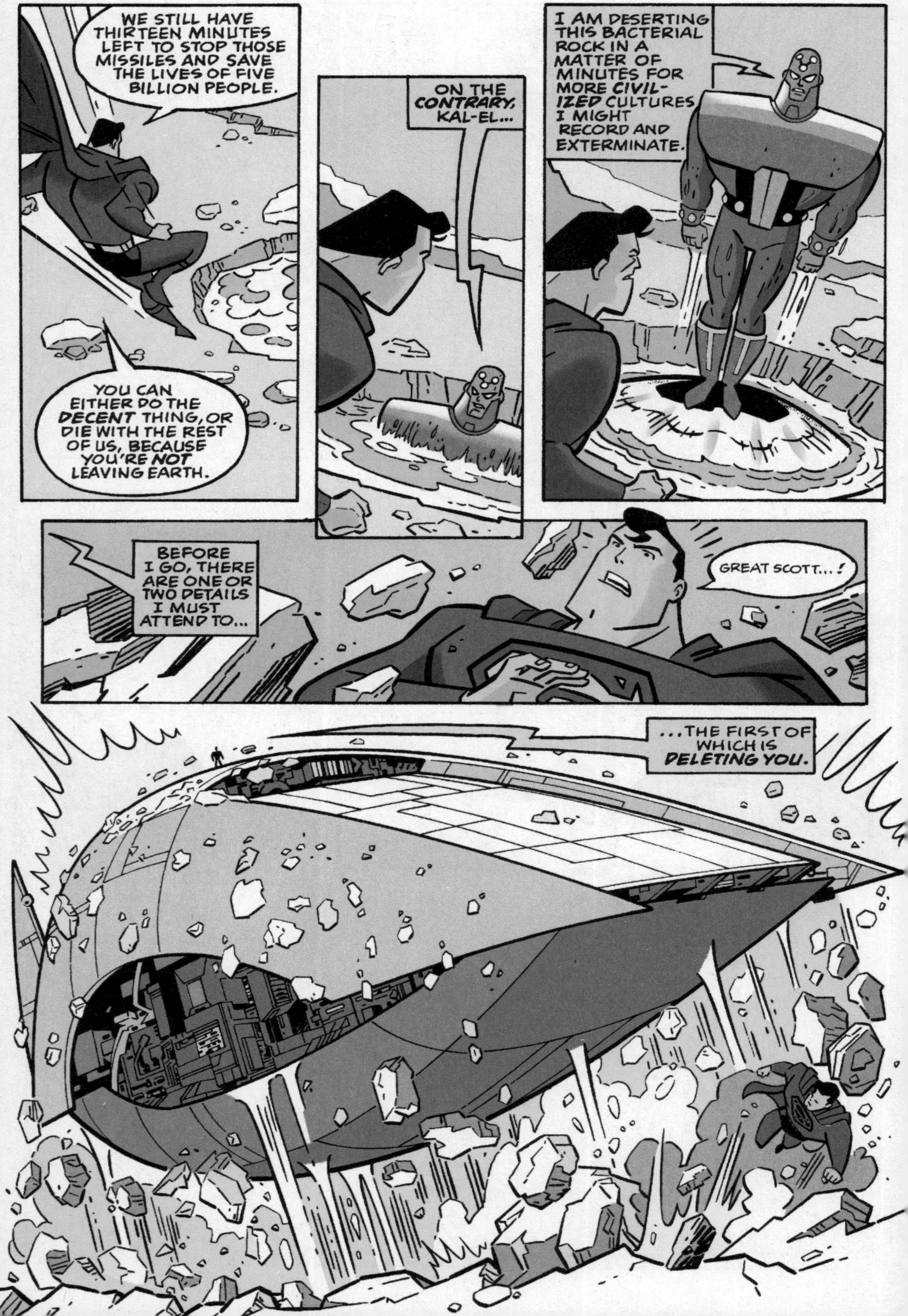
WE STILL HAVE THIRTEEN MINUTES LEFT TO STOP THOSE MISSILES AND SAVE THE LIVES OF FIVE BILLION PEOPLE.
YOU CAN EITHER DO THE DECENT THING, OR DIE WITH THE REST OF US, BECAUSE YOU'RE NOT LEAVING EARTH.
ON THE CONTRARY, KAL-EL...
I AM DESERTING THIS BACTERIAL ROCK IN A MATTER OF MINUTES FOR MORE CIVILIZED CULTURES I MIGHT RECORD AND EXTERMINATE.
BEFORE I GO, THERE ARE ONE OR TWO DETAILS I MUST ATTEND TO...
GREAT SCOTT...!
...THE FIRST OF WHICH IS DELETING YOU.

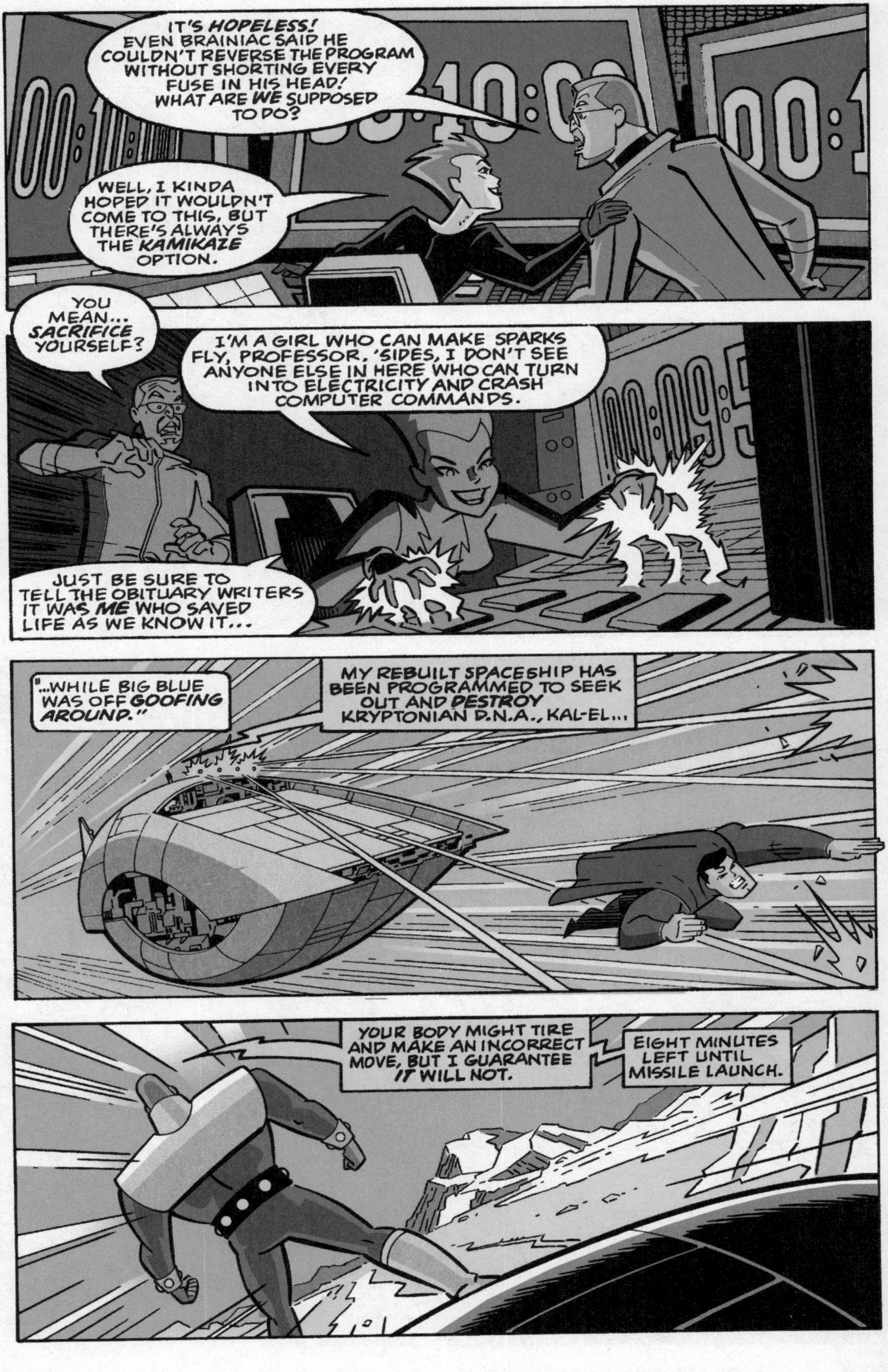
IT'S HOPELESS! EVEN BRAINIAC SAID HE COULDN'T REVERSE THE PROGRAM WITHOUT SHORTING EVERY FUSE IN HIS HEAD! WHAT ARE WE SUPPOSED TO DO?
WELL, I KINDA HOPED IT WOULDN'T COME TO THIS, BUT THERE'S ALWAYS THE KAMIKAZE OPTION.
YOU MEAN... SACRIFICE YOURSELF?
I'M A GIRL WHO CAN MAKE SPARKS FLY, PROFESSOR. 'SIDES, I DON'T SEE ANYONE ELSE IN HERE WHO CAN TURN INTO ELECTRICITY AND CRASH COMPUTER COMMANDS.
JUST BE SURE TO TELL THE OBITUARY WRITERS IT WAS ME WHO SAVED LIFE AS WE KNOW IT...
"...WHILE BIG BLUE WAS OFF GOOFING AROUND."
MY REBUILT SPACESHIP HAS BEEN PROGRAMMED TO SEEK OUT AND DESTROY KRYPTONIAN D.N.A., KAL-EL...
YOUR BODY MIGHT TIRE AND MAKE AN INCORRECT MOVE, BUT I GUARANTEE IT WILL NOT.
EIGHT MINUTES LEFT UNTIL MISSILE LAUNCH.

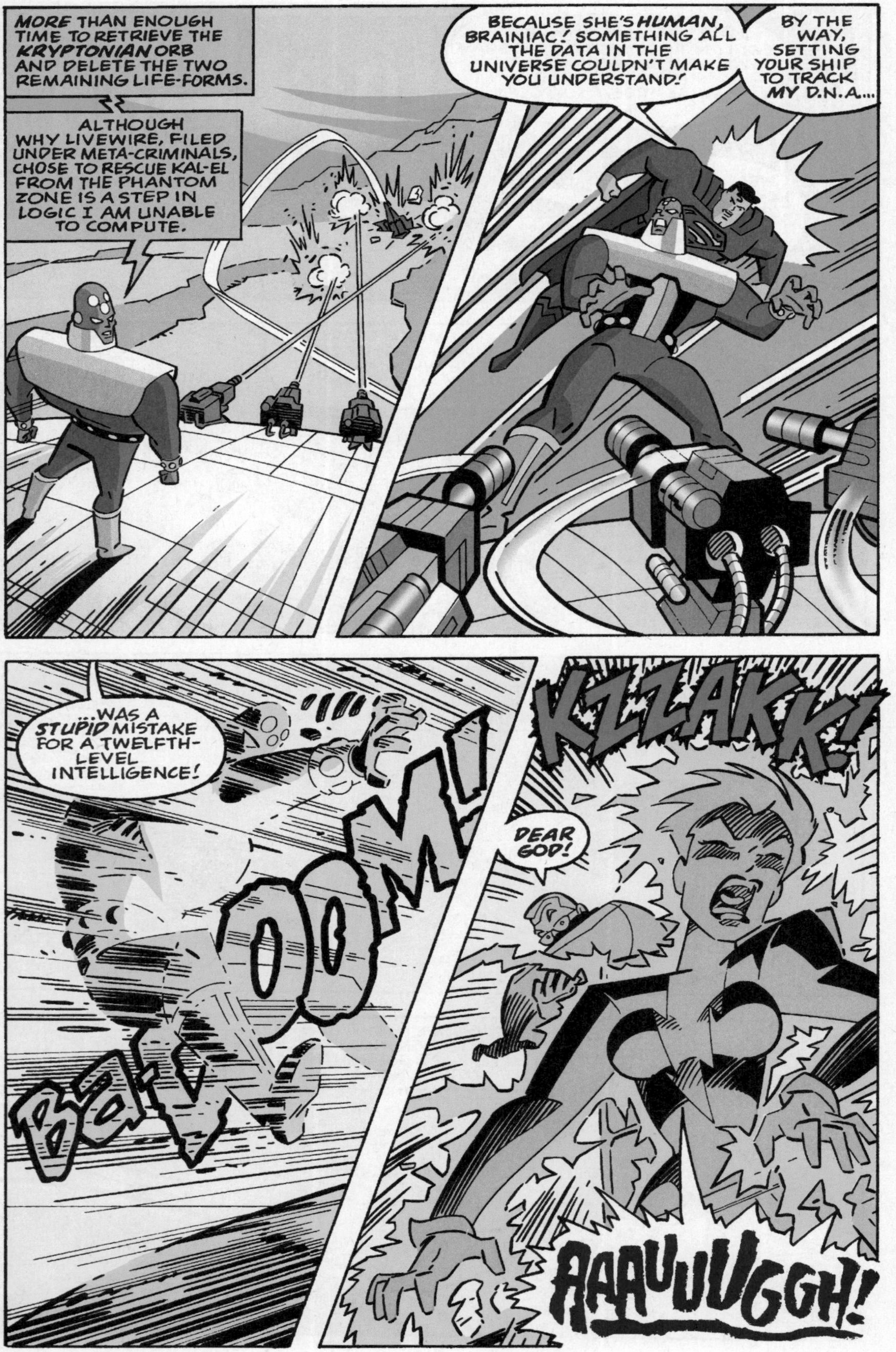
MORE THAN ENOUGH TIME TO RETRIEVE THE KRYPTONIAN ORB AND DELETE THE TWO REMAINING LIFE-FORMS.
ALTHOUGH WHY LIVEWIRE, FILED UNDER META-CRIMINALS, CHOSE TO RESCUE KAL-EL FROM THE PHANTOM ZONE IS A STEP IN LOGIC I AM UNABLE TO COMPUTE.
BECAUSE SHE'S HUMAN, BRAINIAC! SOMETHING ALL THE DATA IN THE UNIVERSE COULDN'T MAKE YOU UNDERSTAND!
BY THE WAY, SETTING YOUR SHIP TO TRACK MY D.N.A....
...WAS A STUPID MISTAKE FOR A TWELFTH-LEVEL INTELLIGENCE!
BA-DOOOM!
KZZAKK!
DEAR GOD!
AAAUUUGGH!

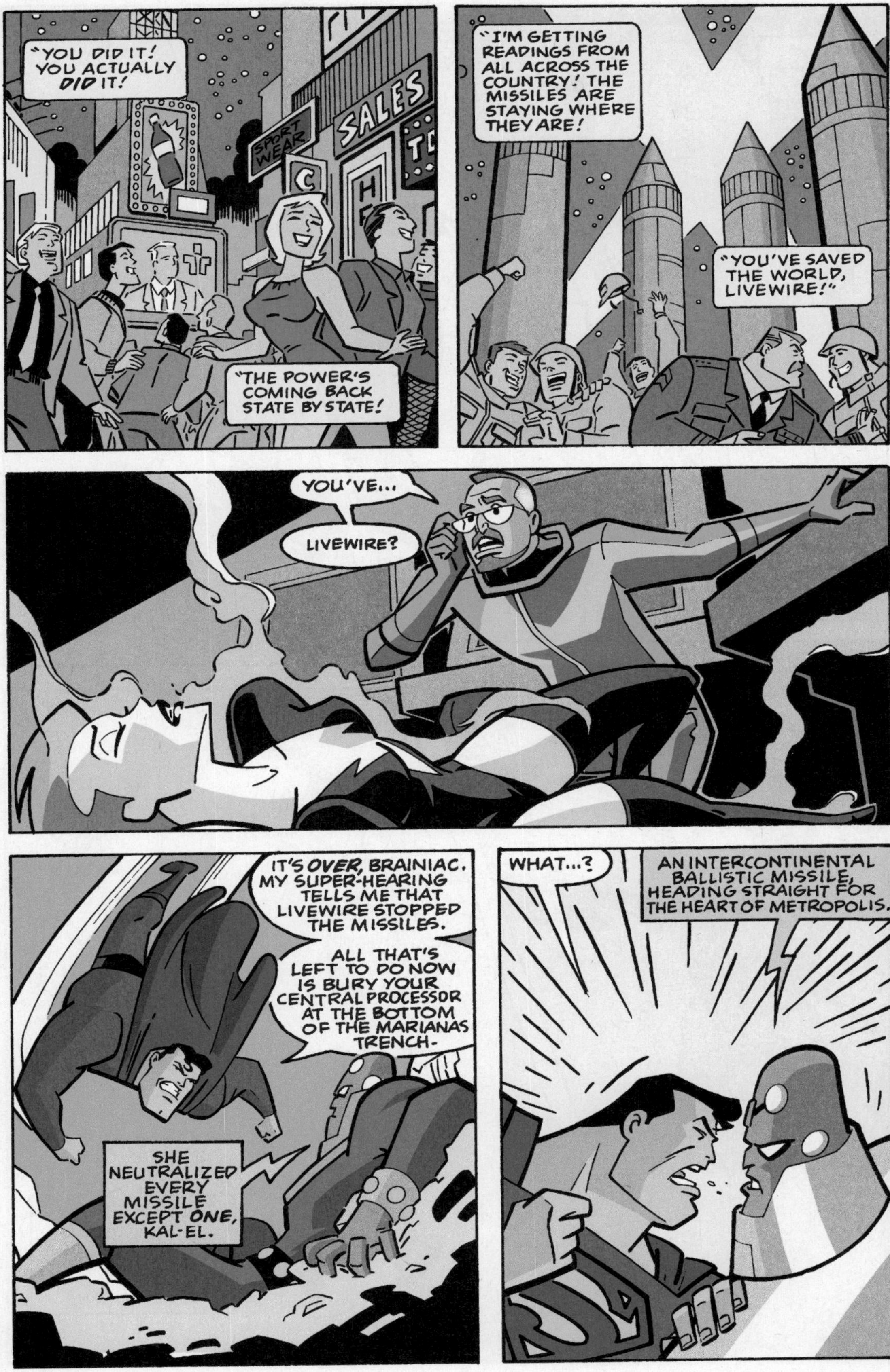
"YOU DID IT! YOU ACTUALLY DID IT!
"THE POWER'S COMING BACK STATE BY STATE!
SPORT WEAR
SALES
"I'M GETTING READINGS FROM ALL ACROSS THE COUNTRY! THE MISSILES ARE STAYING WHERE THEY ARE!
"YOU'VE SAVED THE WORLD, LIVEWIRE!"
YOU'VE...
LIVEWIRE?
IT'S OVER, BRAINIAC. MY SUPER-HEARING TELLS ME THAT LIVEWIRE STOPPED THE MISSILES.
ALL THAT'S LEFT TO DO NOW IS BURY YOUR CENTRAL PROCESSOR AT THE BOTTOM OF THE MARIANAS TRENCH.
SHE NEUTRALIZED EVERY MISSILE EXCEPT ONE, KAL-EL.
WHAT...?
AN INTERCONTINENTAL BALLISTIC MISSILE, HEADING STRAIGHT FOR THE HEART OF METROPOLIS.

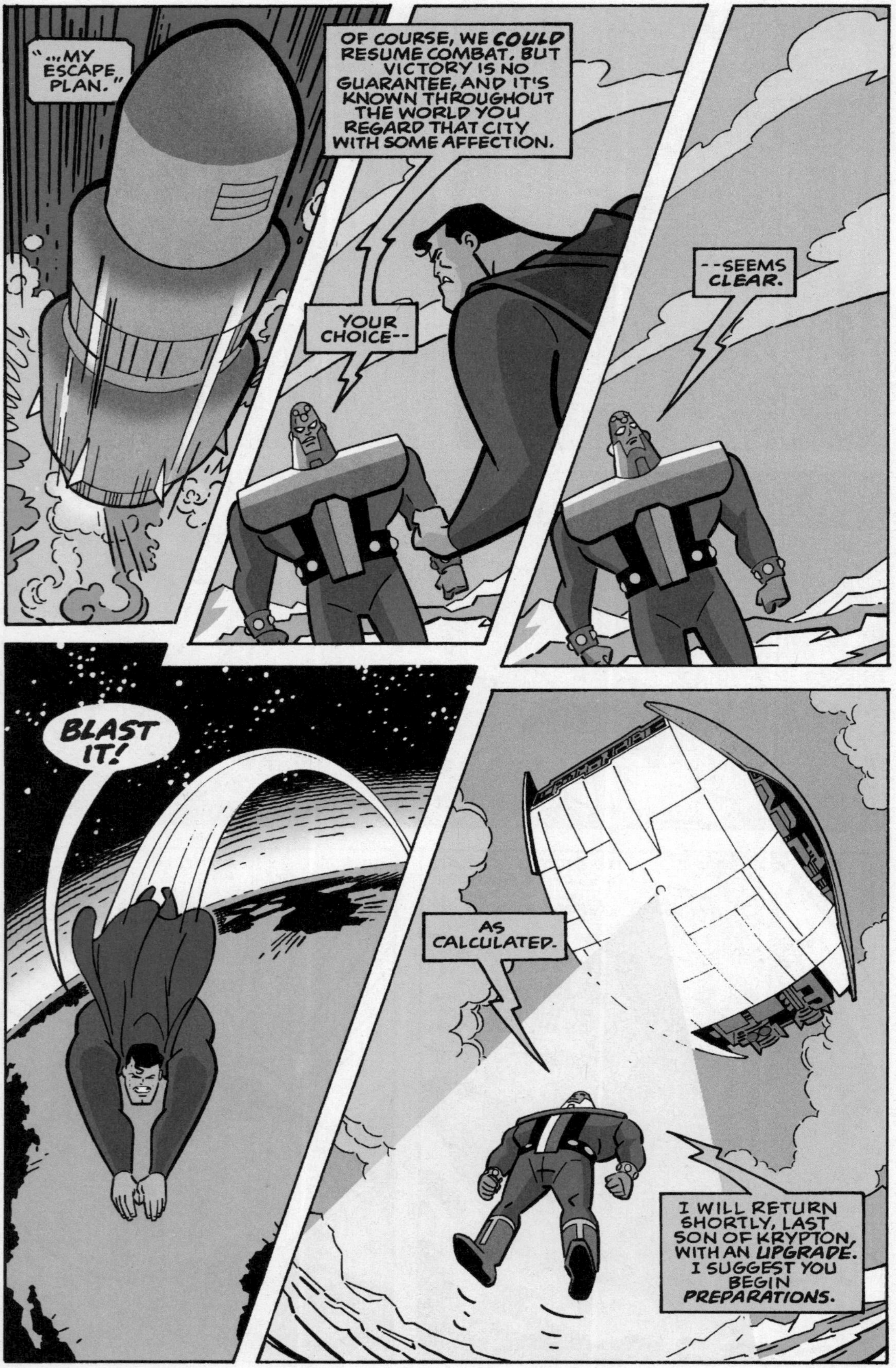
"...MY ESCAPE PLAN."
OF COURSE, WE COULD RESUME COMBAT, BUT VICTORY IS NO GUARANTEE, AND IT'S KNOWN THROUGHOUT THE WORLD YOU REGARD THAT CITY WITH SOME AFFECTION.
YOUR CHOICE--
--SEEMS CLEAR.
BLAST IT!
AS CALCULATED.
I WILL RETURN SHORTLY, LAST SON OF KRYPTON, WITH AN UPGRADE. I SUGGEST YOU BEGIN PREPARATIONS.

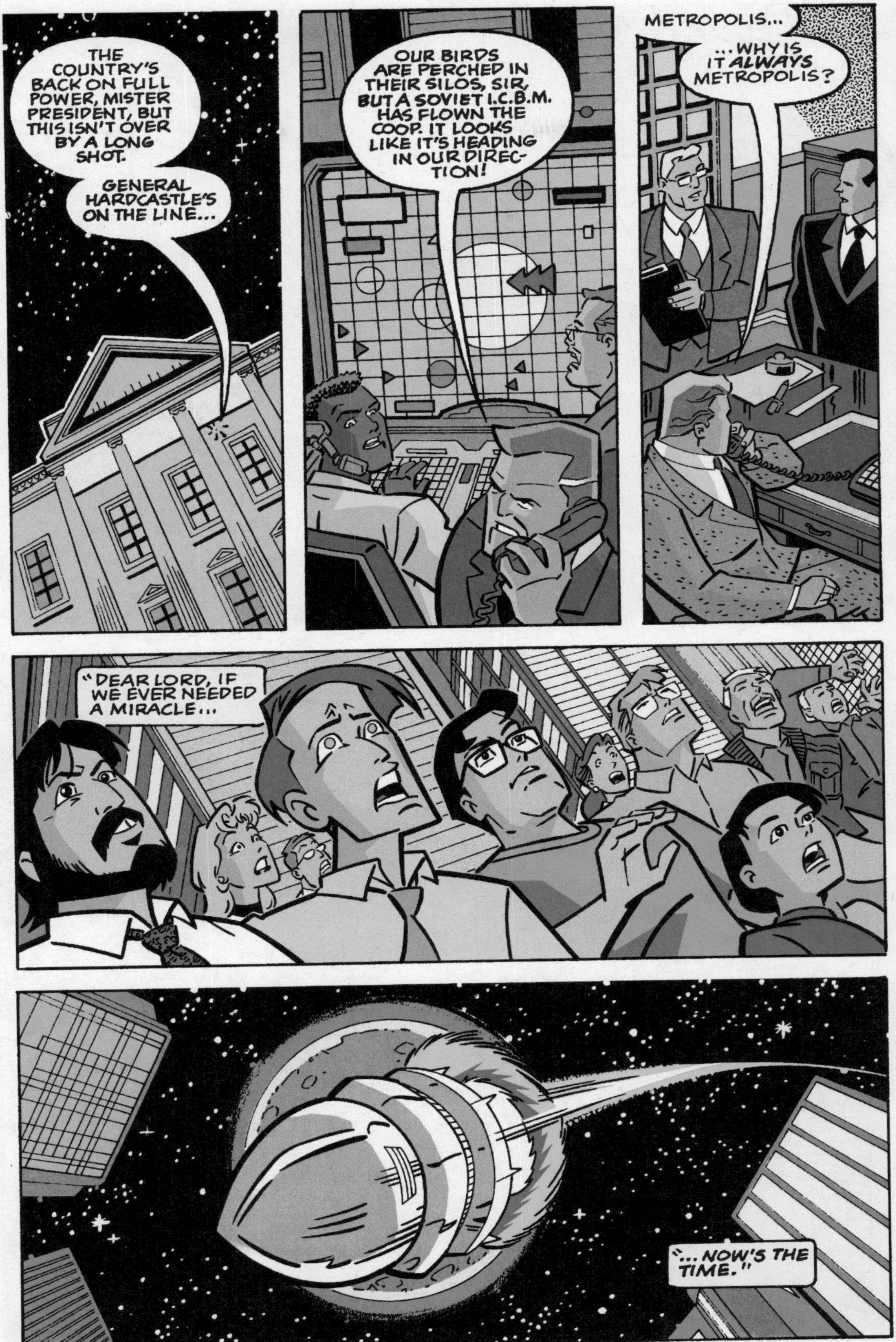
THE COUNTRY'S BACK ON FULL POWER, MISTER PRESIDENT, BUT THIS ISN'T OVER BY A LONG SHOT.
GENERAL HARDCASTLE'S ON THE LINE...
OUR BIRDS ARE PERCHED IN THEIR SILOS, SIR, BUT A SOVIET I.C.B.M. HAS FLOWN THE COOP. IT LOOKS LIKE IT'S HEADING IN OUR DIRECTION!
METROPOLIS...
...WHY IS IT ALWAYS METROPOLIS?
"DEAR LORD, IF WE EVER NEEDED A MIRACLE...
"...NOW'S THE TIME."

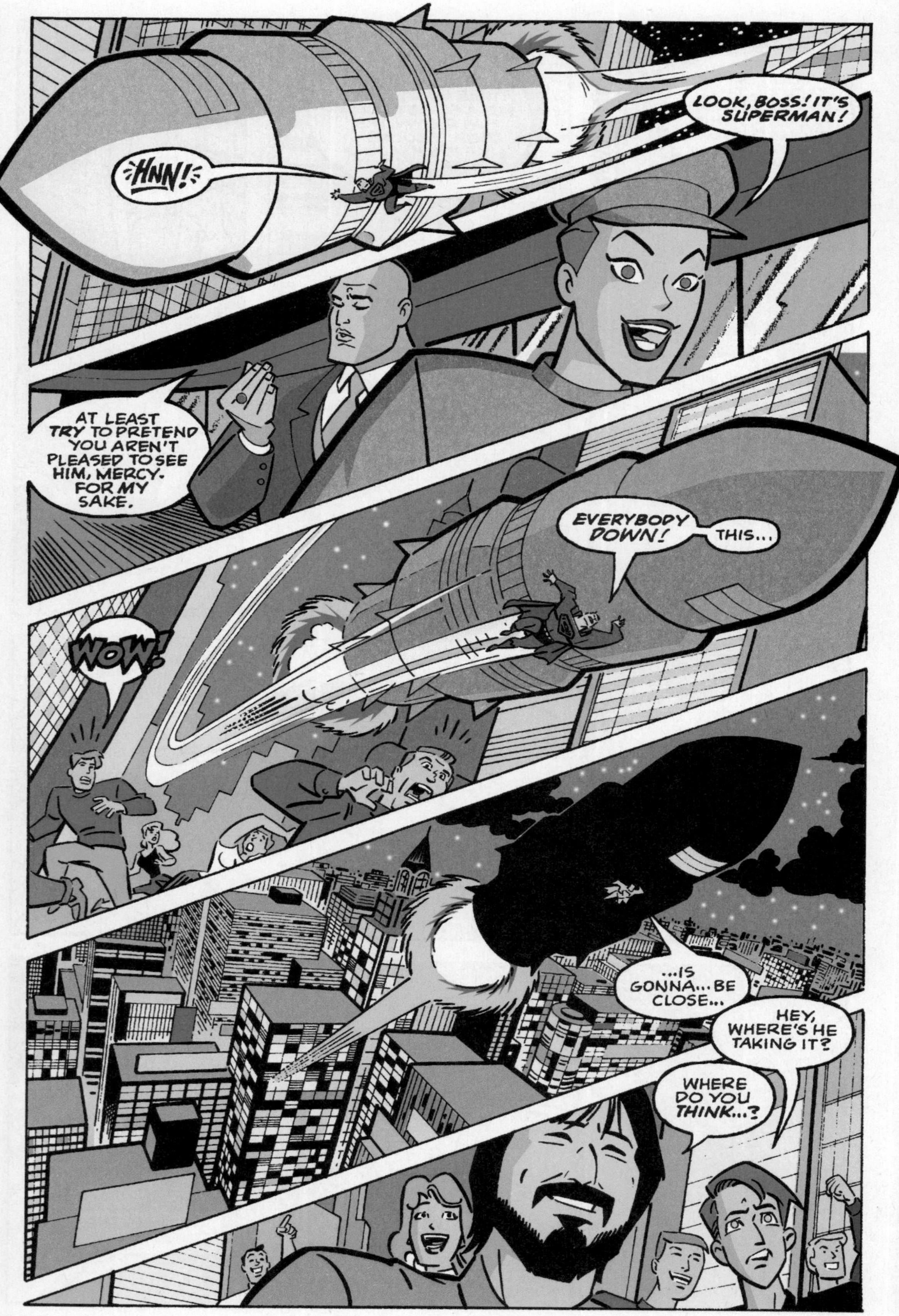
LOOK, BOSS! IT'S SUPERMAN!
HNN!
AT LEAST TRY TO PRETEND YOU AREN'T PLEASED TO SEE HIM, MERCY. FOR MY SAKE.
EVERYBODY DOWN!
THIS...
WOW!
...IS GONNA... BE CLOSE...
HEY, WHERE'S HE TAKING IT?
WHERE DO YOU THINK...?

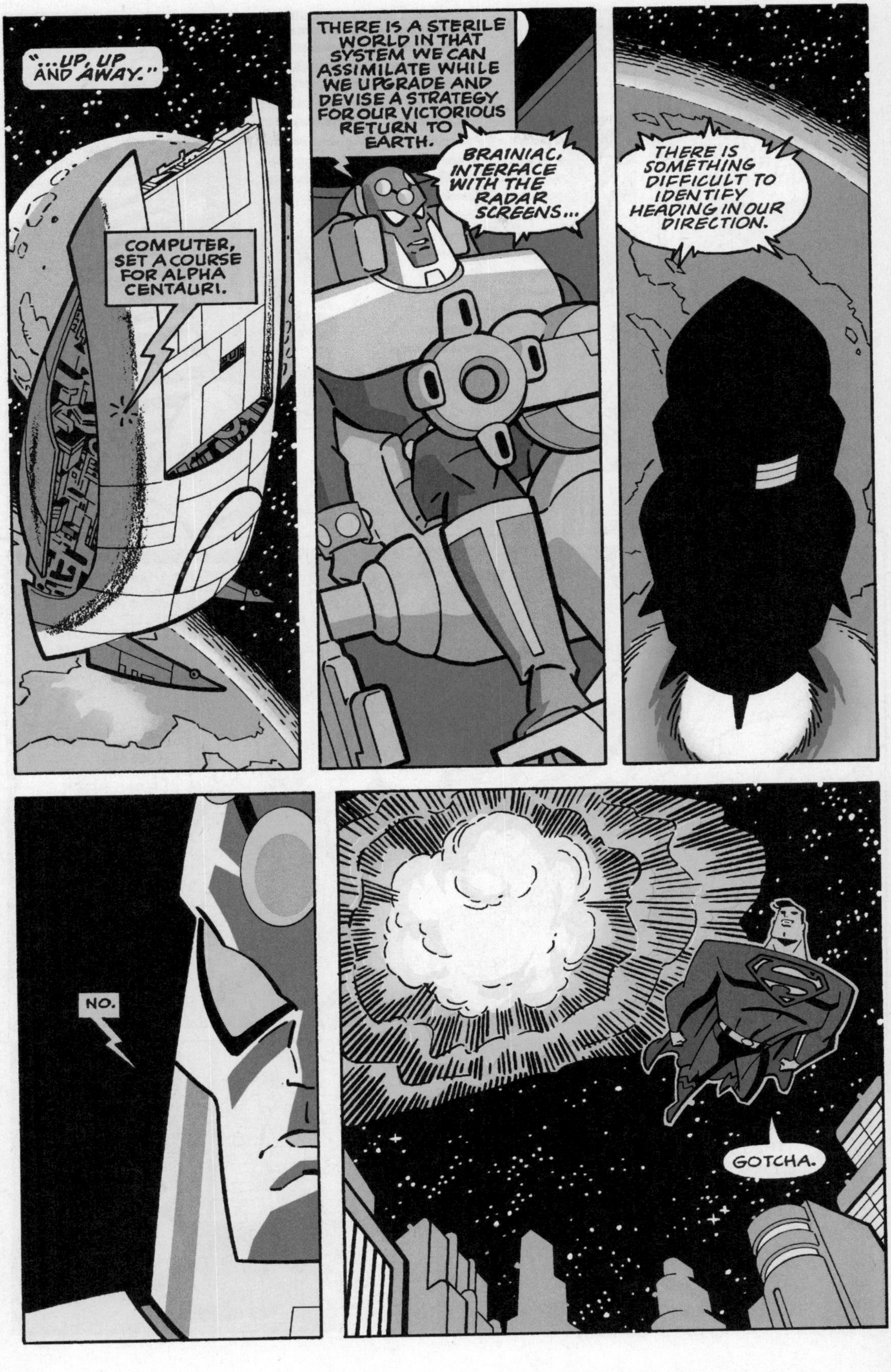
"...UP, UP AND AWAY."
COMPUTER, SET A COURSE FOR ALPHA CENTAURI.
THERE IS A STERILE WORLD IN THAT SYSTEM WE CAN ASSIMILATE WHILE WE UPGRADE AND DEVISE A STRATEGY FOR OUR VICTORIOUS RETURN TO EARTH.
BRAINIAC, INTERFACE WITH THE RADAR SCREENS...
THERE IS SOMETHING DIFFICULT TO IDENTIFY HEADING IN OUR DIRECTION.
NO.
GOTCHA.

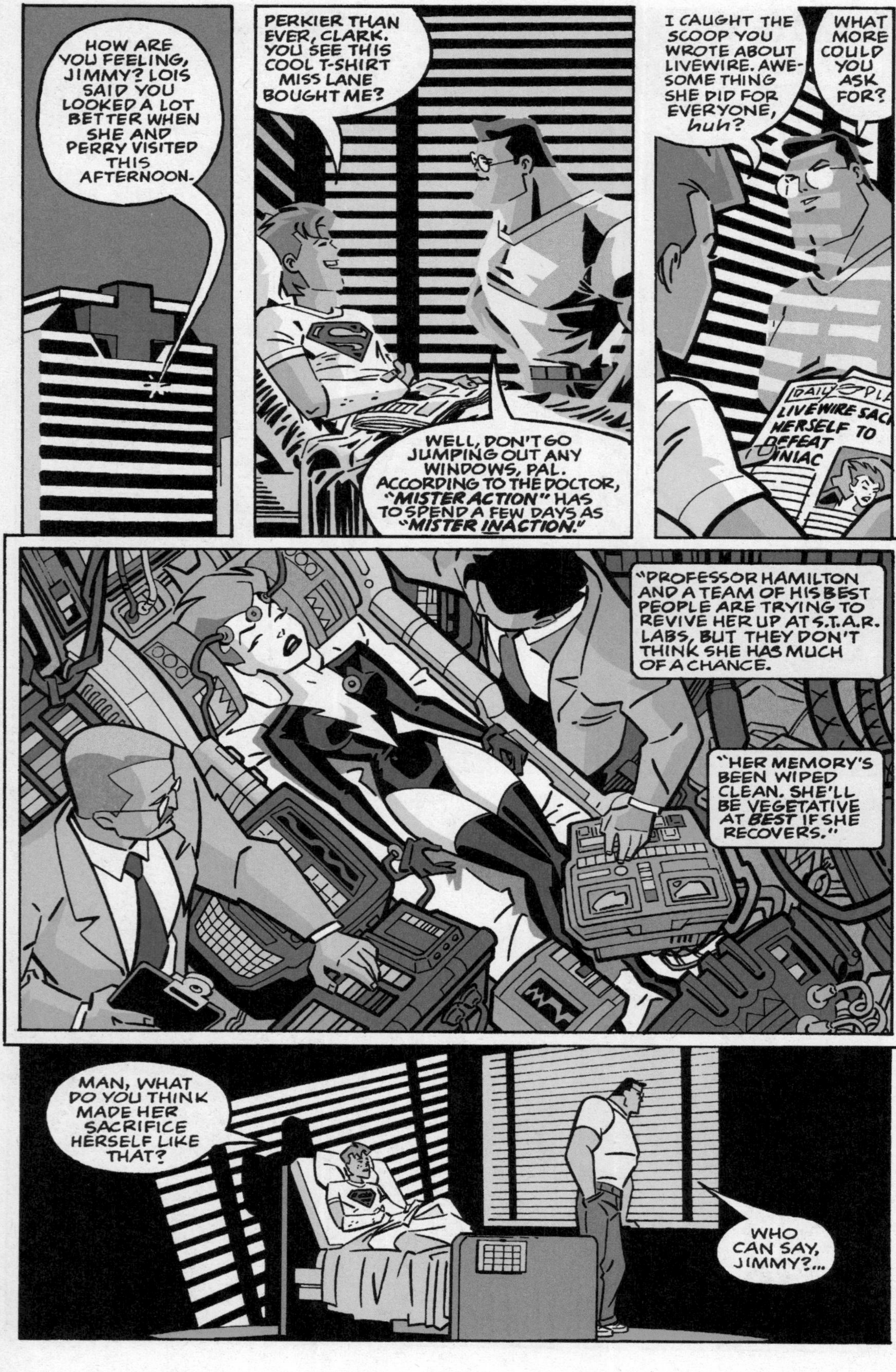
HOW ARE YOU FEELING, JIMMY? LOIS SAID YOU LOOKED A LOT BETTER WHEN SHE AND PERRY VISITED THIS AFTERNOON.
PERKIER THAN EVER, CLARK. YOU SEE THIS COOL T-SHIRT MISS LANE BOUGHT ME?
WELL, DON'T GO JUMPING OUT ANY WINDOWS, PAL. ACCORDING TO THE DOCTOR, "MISTER ACTION" HAS TO SPEND A FEW DAYS AS "MISTER INACTION."
I CAUGHT THE SCOOP YOU WROTE ABOUT LIVEWIRE. AWESOME THING SHE DID FOR EVERYONE, huh?
WHAT MORE COULD YOU ASK FOR?
DAILY PLA
LIVEWIRE SAC HERSELF TO DEFEAT INIAC
"PROFESSOR HAMILTON AND A TEAM OF HIS BEST PEOPLE ARE TRYING TO REVIVE HER UP AT S.T.A.R. LABS, BUT THEY DON'T THINK SHE HAS MUCH OF A CHANCE.
"HER MEMORY'S BEEN WIPED CLEAN. SHE'LL BE VEGETATIVE AT BEST IF SHE RECOVERS."
MAN, WHAT DO YOU THINK MADE HER SACRIFICE HERSELF LIKE THAT?
WHO CAN SAY, JIMMY?...

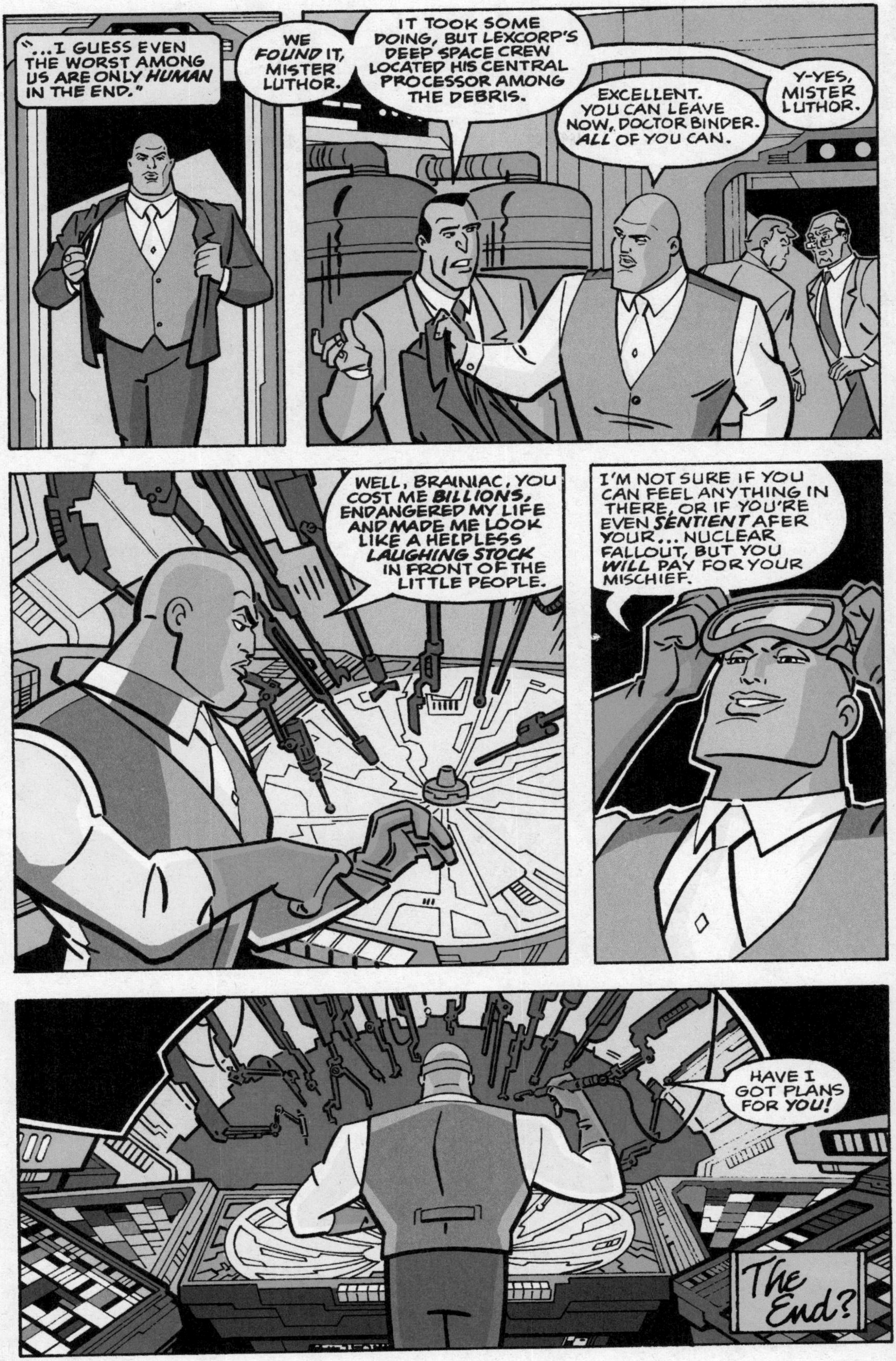
"...I GUESS EVEN THE WORST AMONG US ARE ONLY HUMAN IN THE END."
WE FOUND IT, MISTER LUTHOR.
IT TOOK SOME DOING, BUT LEXCORP'S DEEP SPACE CREW LOCATED HIS CENTRAL PROCESSOR AMONG THE DEBRIS.
EXCELLENT. YOU CAN LEAVE NOW, DOCTOR BINDER. ALL OF YOU CAN.
Y-YES, MISTER LUTHOR.
WELL, BRAINIAC, YOU COST ME BILLIONS, ENDANGERED MY LIFE AND MADE ME LOOK LIKE A HELPLESS LAUGHING STOCK IN FRONT OF THE LITTLE PEOPLE.
I'M NOT SURE IF YOU CAN FEEL ANYTHING IN THERE, OR IF YOU'RE EVEN SENTIENT AFER YOUR... NUCLEAR FALLOUT, BUT YOU WILL PAY FOR YOUR MISCHIEF.
HAVE I GOT PLANS FOR YOU!
The End?

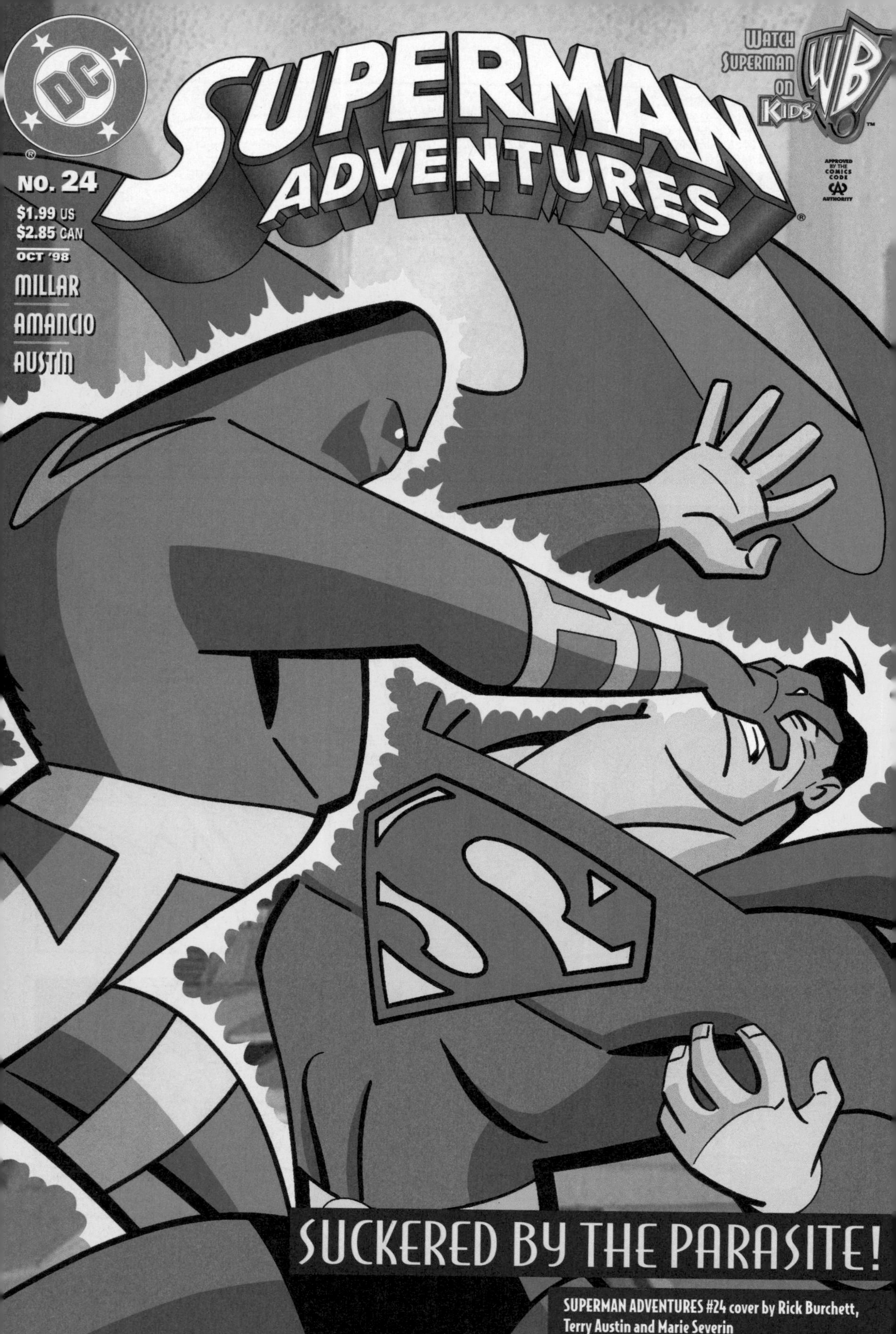
DC
SUPERMAN ADVENTURES
WATCH SUPERMAN ON KIDS' WB
NO. 24
$1.99 US
$2.85 CAN
OCT '98
MILLAR
AMANCIO
AUSTIN
APPROVED BY THE COMICS CODE AUTHORITY
SUCKERED BY THE PARASITE!

SUPERMAN ADVENTURES #24 cover by Rick Burchett, Terry Austin and Marie Severin

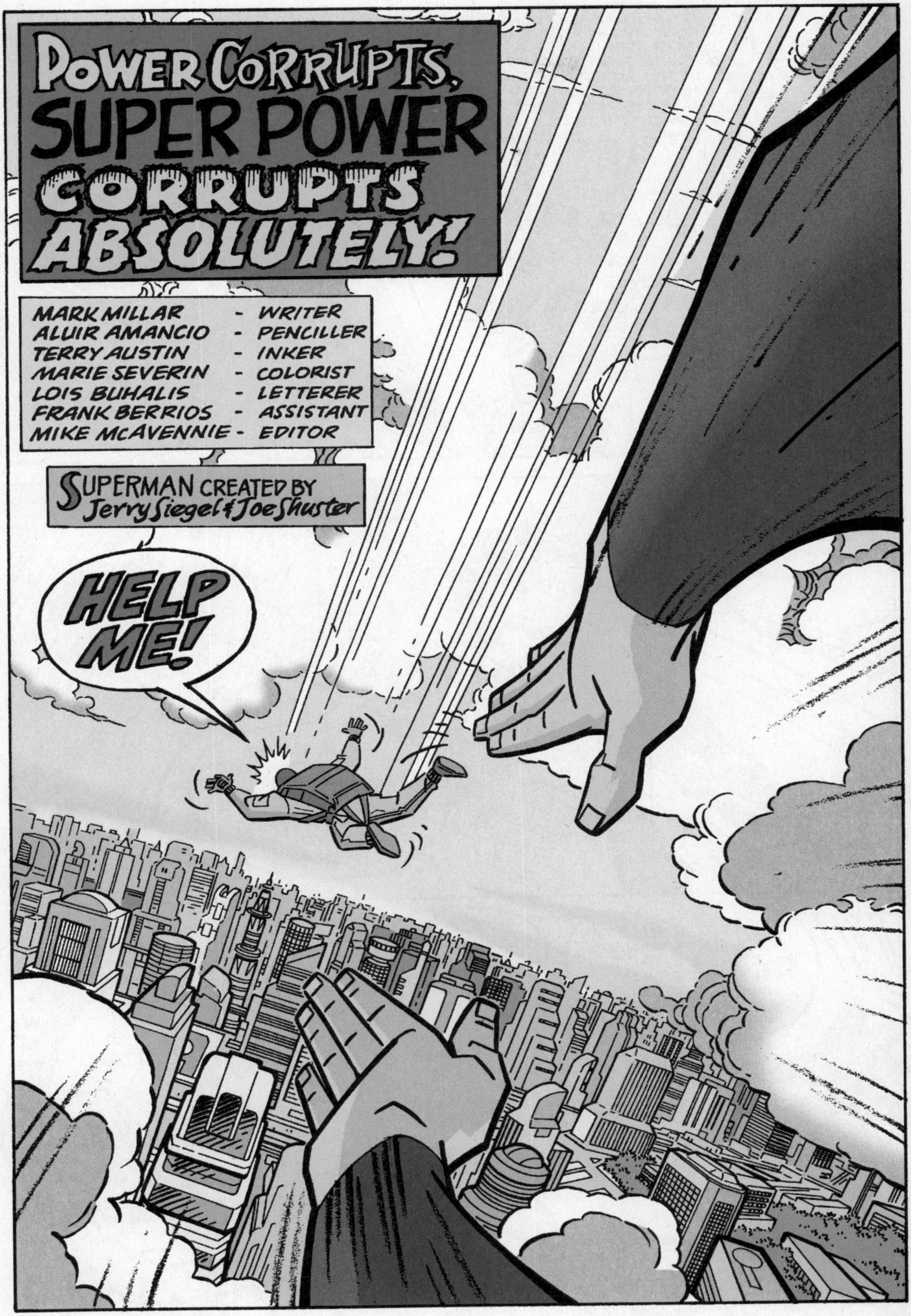
POWER CORRUPTS, SUPER POWER CORRUPTS ABSOLUTELY!
MARK MILLAR - WRITER
ALUIR AMANCIO - PENCILLER
TERRY AUSTIN - INKER
MARIE SEVERIN - COLORIST
LOIS BUHALIS - LETTERER
FRANK BERRIOS - ASSISTANT
MIKE McAVENNIE - EDITOR
SUPERMAN CREATED BY Jerry Siegel & Joe Shuster
HELP ME!

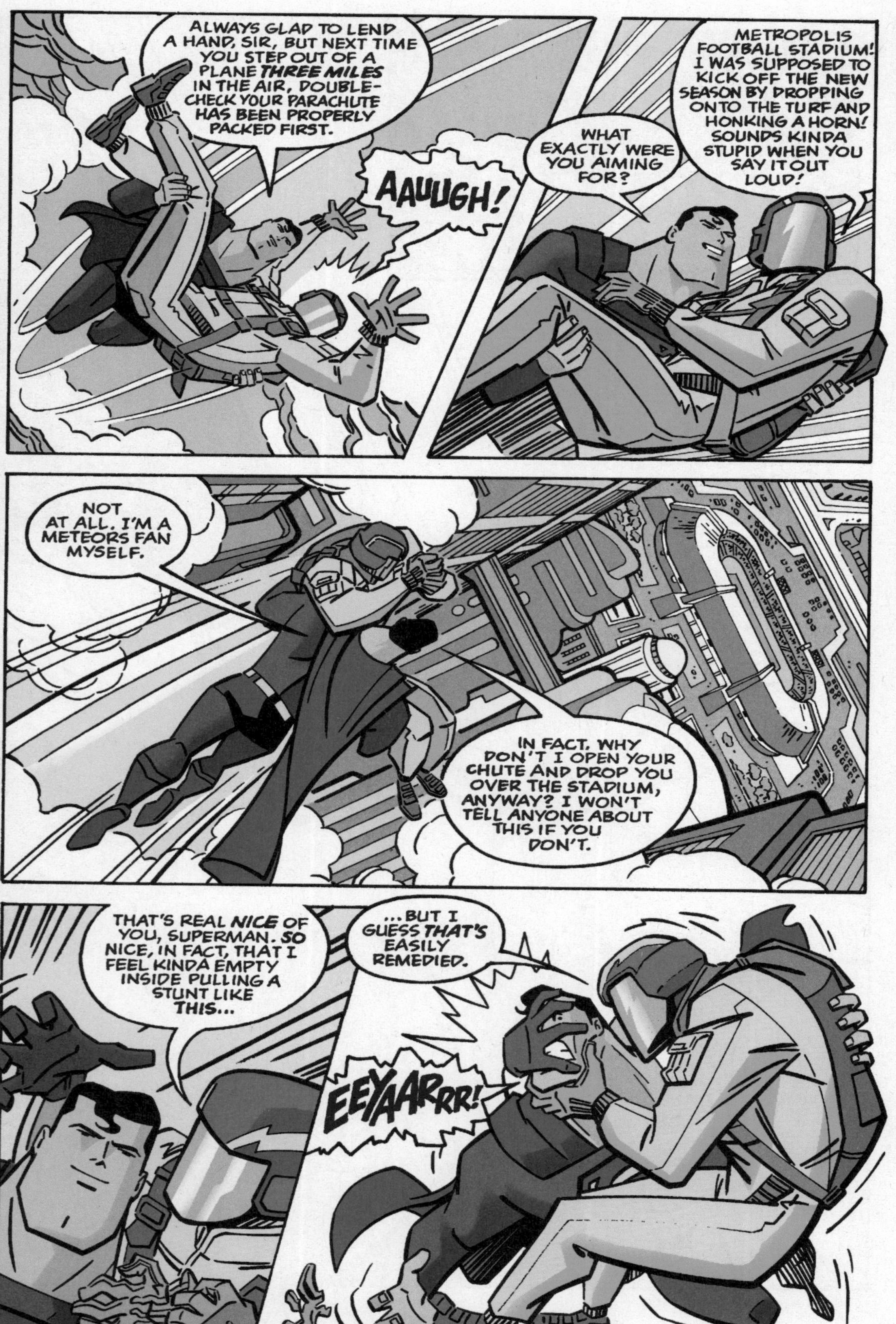
ALWAYS GLAD TO LEND A HAND, SIR, BUT NEXT TIME YOU STEP OUT OF A PLANE THREE MILES IN THE AIR, DOUBLE-CHECK YOUR PARACHUTE HAS BEEN PROPERLY PACKED FIRST.
AAUUGH!
WHAT EXACTLY WERE YOU AIMING FOR?
METROPOLIS FOOTBALL STADIUM! I WAS SUPPOSED TO KICK OFF THE NEW SEASON BY DROPPING ONTO THE TURF AND HONKING A HORN! SOUNDS KINDA STUPID WHEN YOU SAY IT OUT LOUD!
NOT AT ALL. I'M A METEORS FAN MYSELF.
IN FACT, WHY DON'T I OPEN YOUR CHUTE AND DROP YOU OVER THE STADIUM, ANYWAY? I WON'T TELL ANYONE ABOUT THIS IF YOU DON'T.
THAT'S REAL NICE OF YOU, SUPERMAN. SO NICE, IN FACT, THAT I FEEL KINDA EMPTY INSIDE PULLING A STUNT LIKE THIS...
...BUT I GUESS THAT'S EASILY REMEDIED.
EEYAARRR!

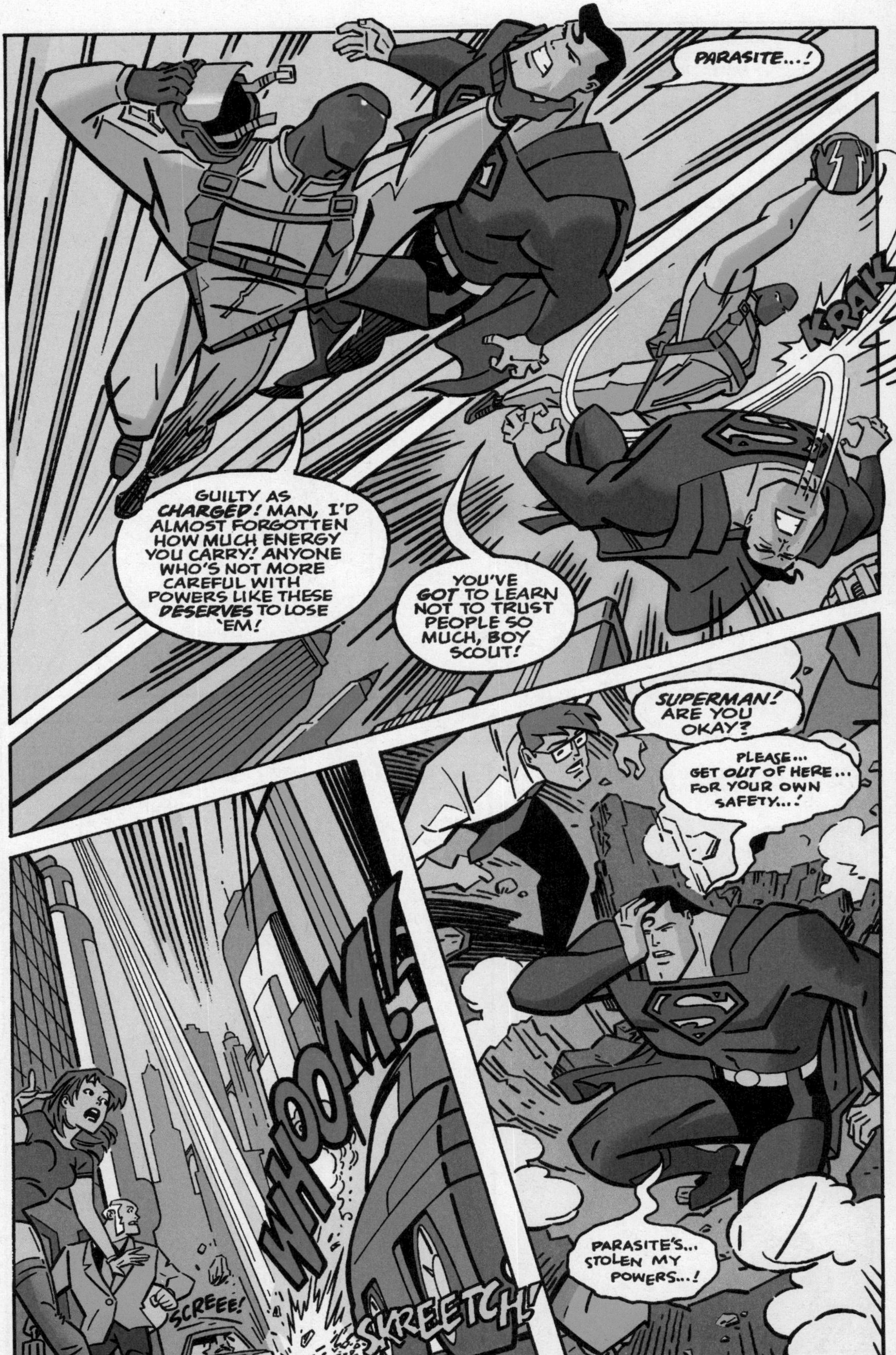

PARASITE...!
KRAK
GUILTY AS CHARGED! MAN, I'D ALMOST FORGOTTEN HOW MUCH ENERGY YOU CARRY! ANYONE WHO'S NOT MORE CAREFUL WITH POWERS LIKE THESE DESERVES TO LOSE 'EM!
YOU'VE GOT TO LEARN NOT TO TRUST PEOPLE SO MUCH, BOY SCOUT!
WHOOM!
SCREEE!
SKREETCH!
SUPERMAN! ARE YOU OKAY?
PLEASE... GET OUT OF HERE... FOR YOUR OWN SAFETY...!
PARASITE'S... STOLEN MY POWERS...!

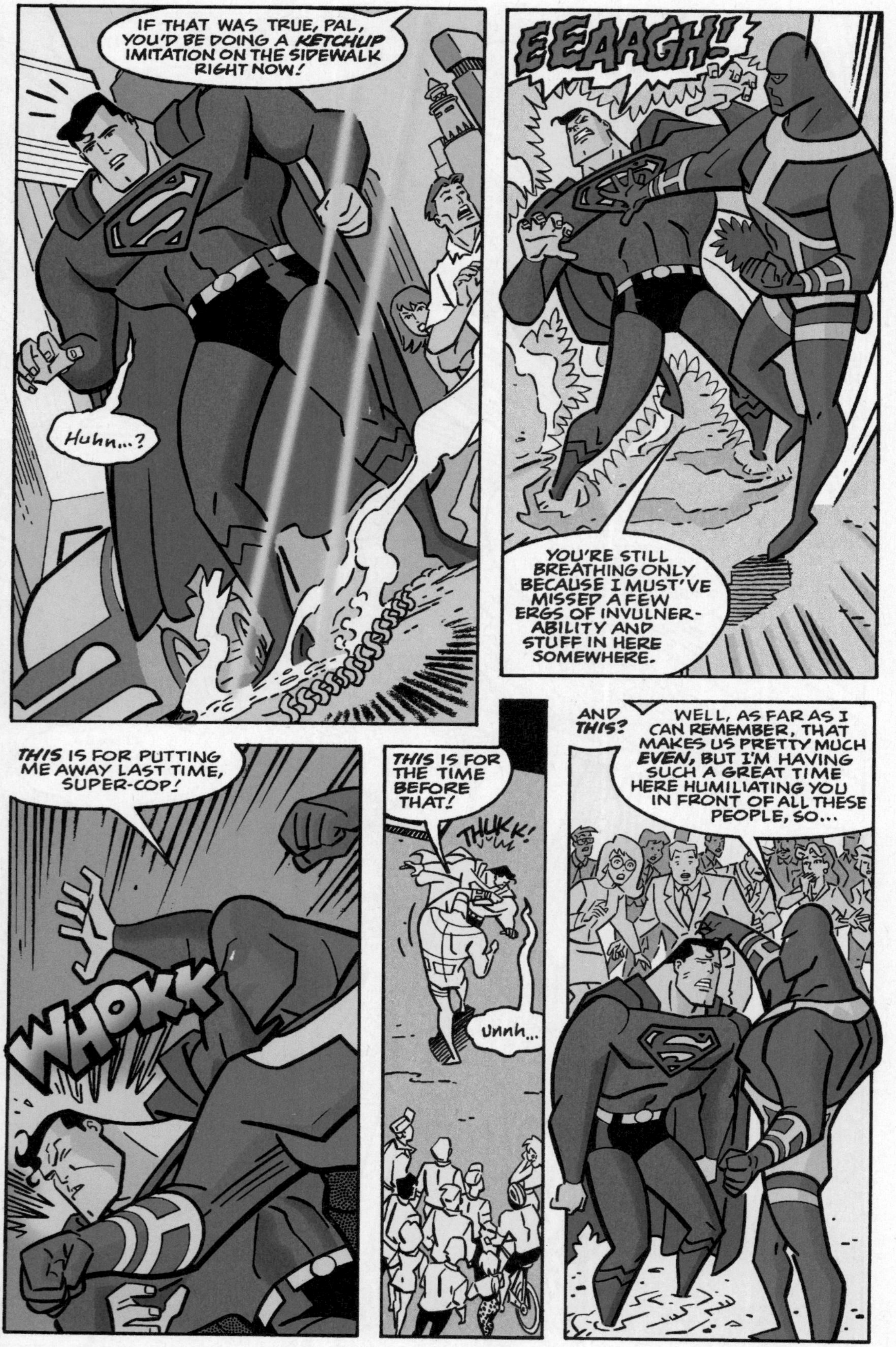
IF THAT WAS TRUE, PAL, YOU'D BE DOING A KETCHUP IMITATION ON THE SIDEWALK RIGHT NOW!
Huhn...?
EEAAGH!
YOU'RE STILL BREATHING ONLY BECAUSE I MUST'VE MISSED A FEW ERGS OF INVULNER-ABILITY AND STUFF IN HERE SOMEWHERE.
THIS IS FOR PUTTING ME AWAY LAST TIME, SUPER-COP!
WHOKK
THIS IS FOR THE TIME BEFORE THAT!
THUKK!
Unnh...
AND THIS?
WELL, AS FAR AS I CAN REMEMBER, THAT MAKES US PRETTY MUCH EVEN, BUT I'M HAVING SUCH A GREAT TIME HERE HUMILIATING YOU IN FRONT OF ALL THESE PEOPLE, SO...

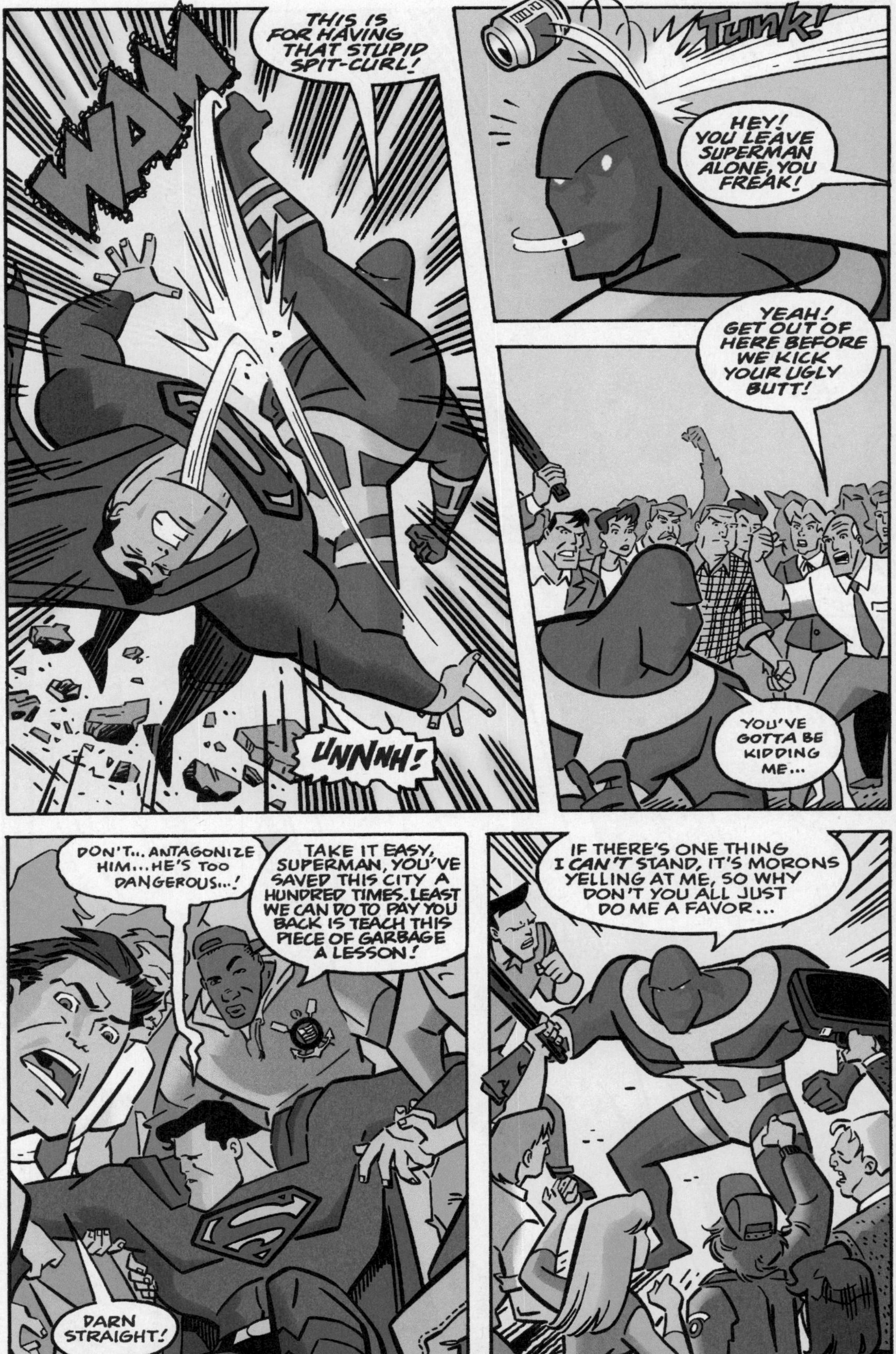
WAM
THIS IS FOR HAVING THAT STUPID SPIT-CURL!
UNNNH!
TUNK!
HEY! YOU LEAVE SUPERMAN ALONE, YOU FREAK!
YEAH! GET OUT OF HERE BEFORE WE KICK YOUR UGLY BUTT!
YOU'VE GOTTA BE KIDDING ME...
DON'T... ANTAGONIZE HIM... HE'S TOO DANGEROUS...!
TAKE IT EASY, SUPERMAN, YOU'VE SAVED THIS CITY A HUNDRED TIMES. LEAST WE CAN DO TO PAY YOU BACK IS TEACH THIS PIECE OF GARBAGE A LESSON!
DARN STRAIGHT!
IF THERE'S ONE THING I CAN'T STAND, IT'S MORONS YELLING AT ME, SO WHY DON'T YOU ALL JUST DO ME A FAVOR...

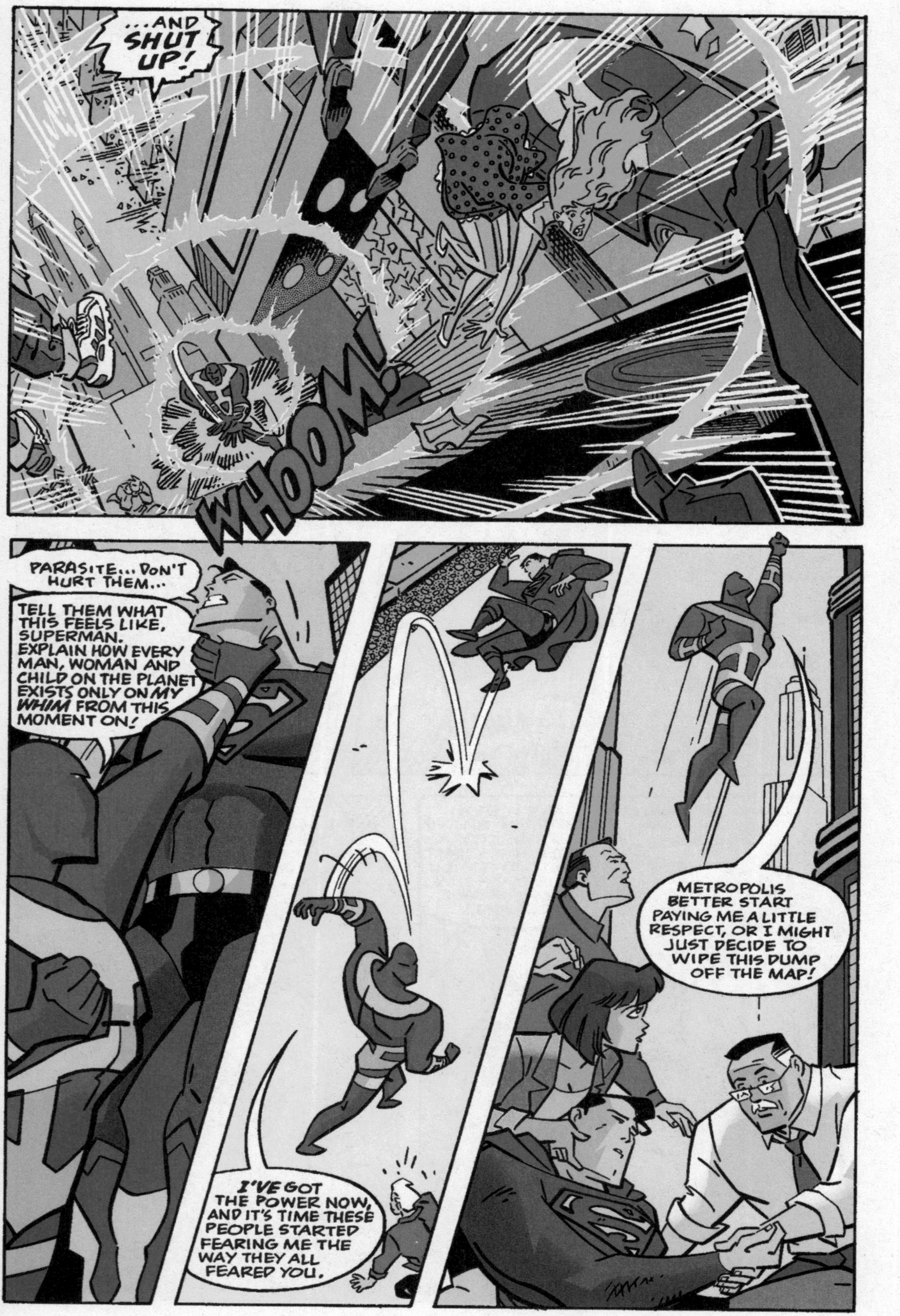
...AND SHUT UP!
WHOOM!
PARASITE... DON'T HURT THEM...
TELL THEM WHAT THIS FEELS LIKE, SUPERMAN. EXPLAIN HOW EVERY MAN, WOMAN AND CHILD ON THE PLANET EXISTS ONLY ON MY WHIM FROM THIS MOMENT ON!
I'VE GOT THE POWER NOW, AND IT'S TIME THESE PEOPLE STARTED FEARING ME THE WAY THEY ALL FEARED YOU.
METROPOLIS BETTER START PAYING ME A LITTLE RESPECT, OR I MIGHT JUST DECIDE TO WIPE THIS DUMP OFF THE MAP!

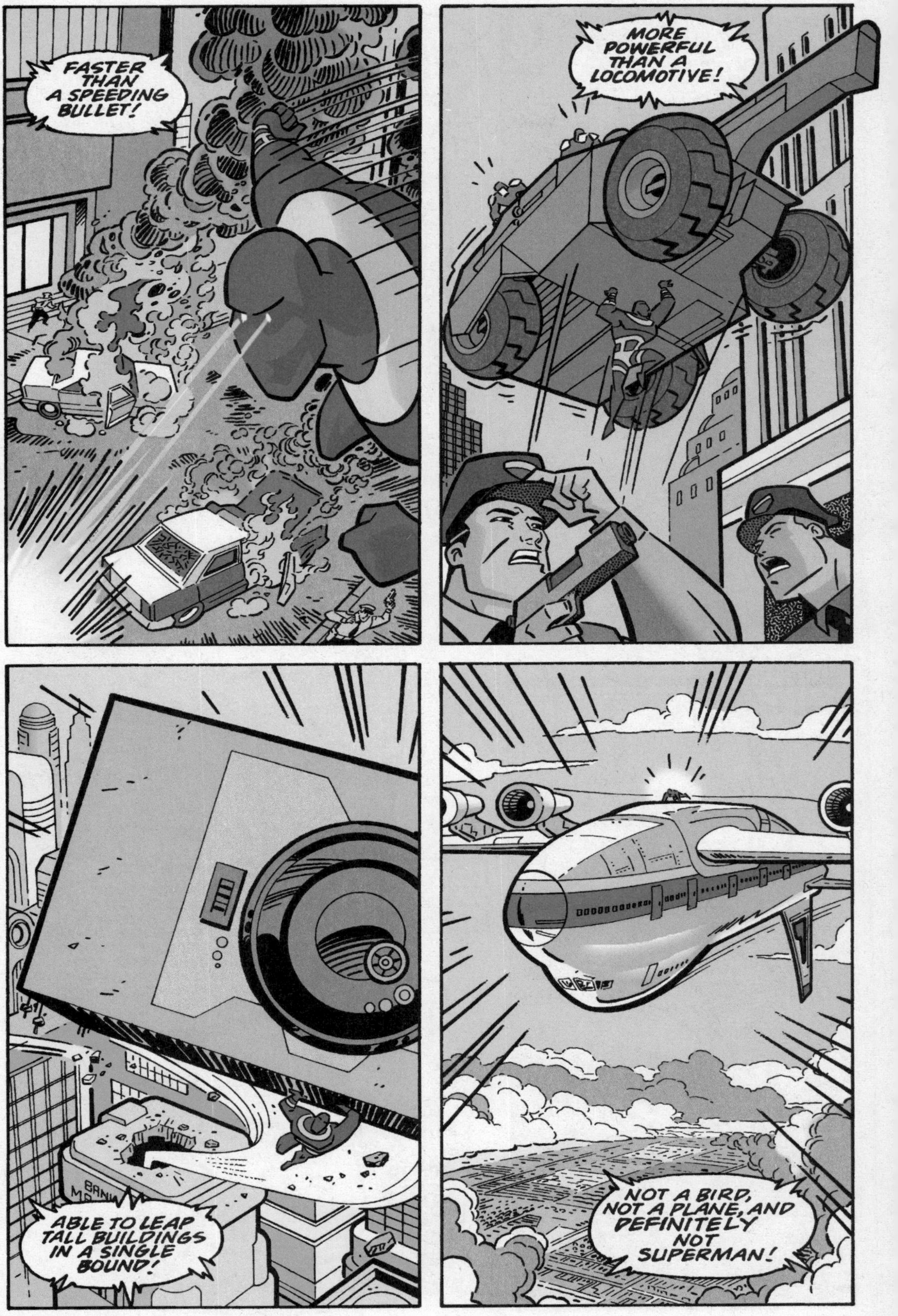
FASTER THAN A SPEEDING BULLET!
MORE POWERFUL THAN A LOCOMOTIVE!
ABLE TO LEAP TALL BUILDINGS IN A SINGLE BOUND!
NOT A BIRD, NOT A PLANE, AND DEFINITELY NOT SUPERMAN!

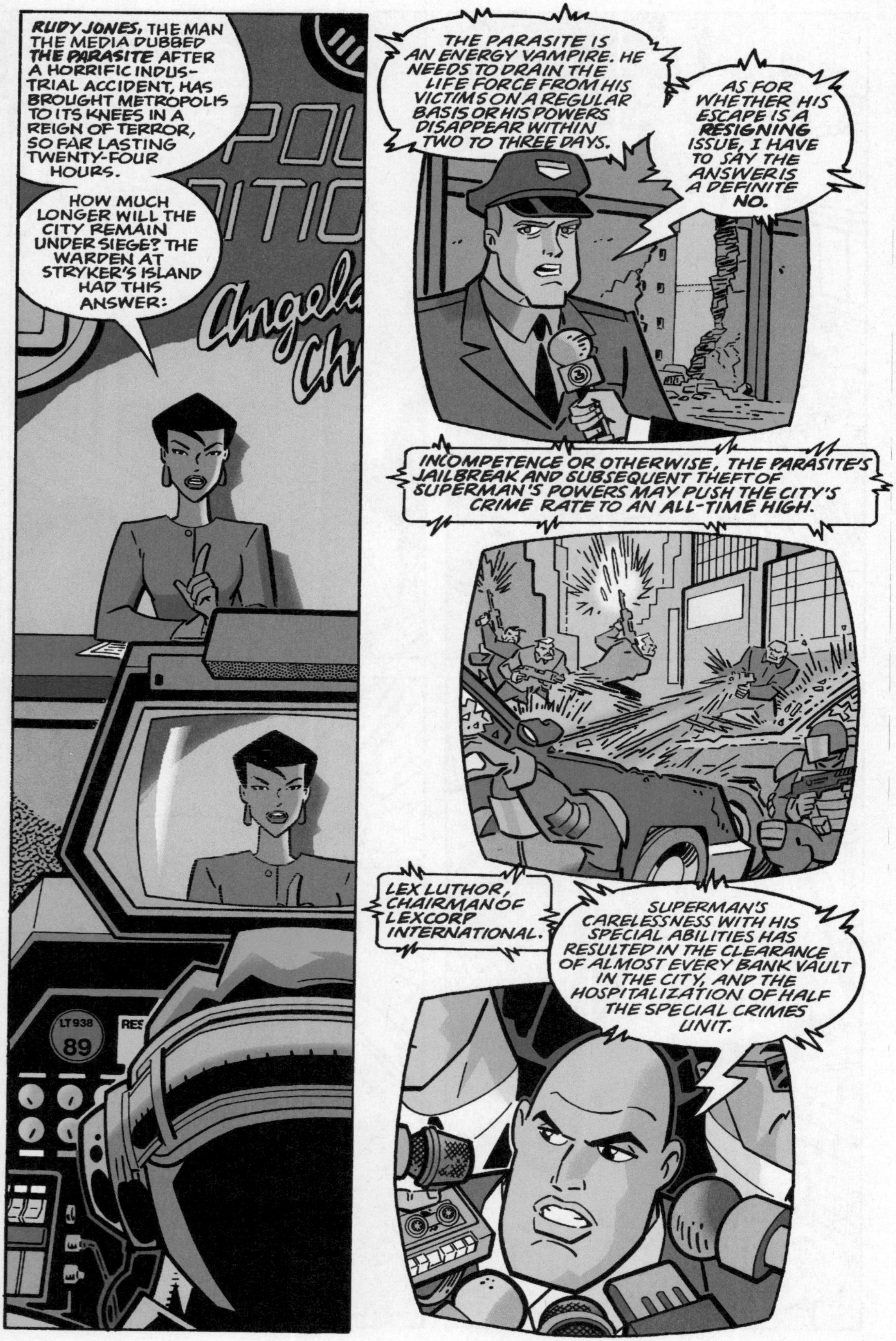

RUDY JONES, THE MAN THE MEDIA DUBBED THE PARASITE AFTER A HORRIFIC INDUSTRIAL ACCIDENT, HAS BROUGHT METROPOLIS TO ITS KNEES IN A REIGN OF TERROR, SO FAR LASTING TWENTY-FOUR HOURS.
HOW MUCH LONGER WILL THE CITY REMAIN UNDER SIEGE? THE WARDEN AT STRYKER'S ISLAND HAD THIS ANSWER:
Angela Ch
LT 938
89
THE PARASITE IS AN ENERGY VAMPIRE. HE NEEDS TO DRAIN THE LIFE FORCE FROM HIS VICTIMS ON A REGULAR BASIS OR HIS POWERS DISAPPEAR WITHIN TWO TO THREE DAYS.
AS FOR WHETHER HIS ESCAPE IS A RESIGNING ISSUE, I HAVE TO SAY THE ANSWER IS A DEFINITE NO.
INCOMPETENCE OR OTHERWISE, THE PARASITE'S JAILBREAK AND SUBSEQUENT THEFT OF SUPERMAN'S POWERS MAY PUSH THE CITY'S CRIME RATE TO AN ALL-TIME HIGH.
LEX LUTHOR, CHAIRMAN OF LEXCORP INTERNATIONAL.
SUPERMAN'S CARELESSNESS WITH HIS SPECIAL ABILITIES HAS RESULTED IN THE CLEARANCE OF ALMOST EVERY BANK VAULT IN THE CITY, AND THE HOSPITALIZATION OF HALF THE SPECIAL CRIMES UNIT.

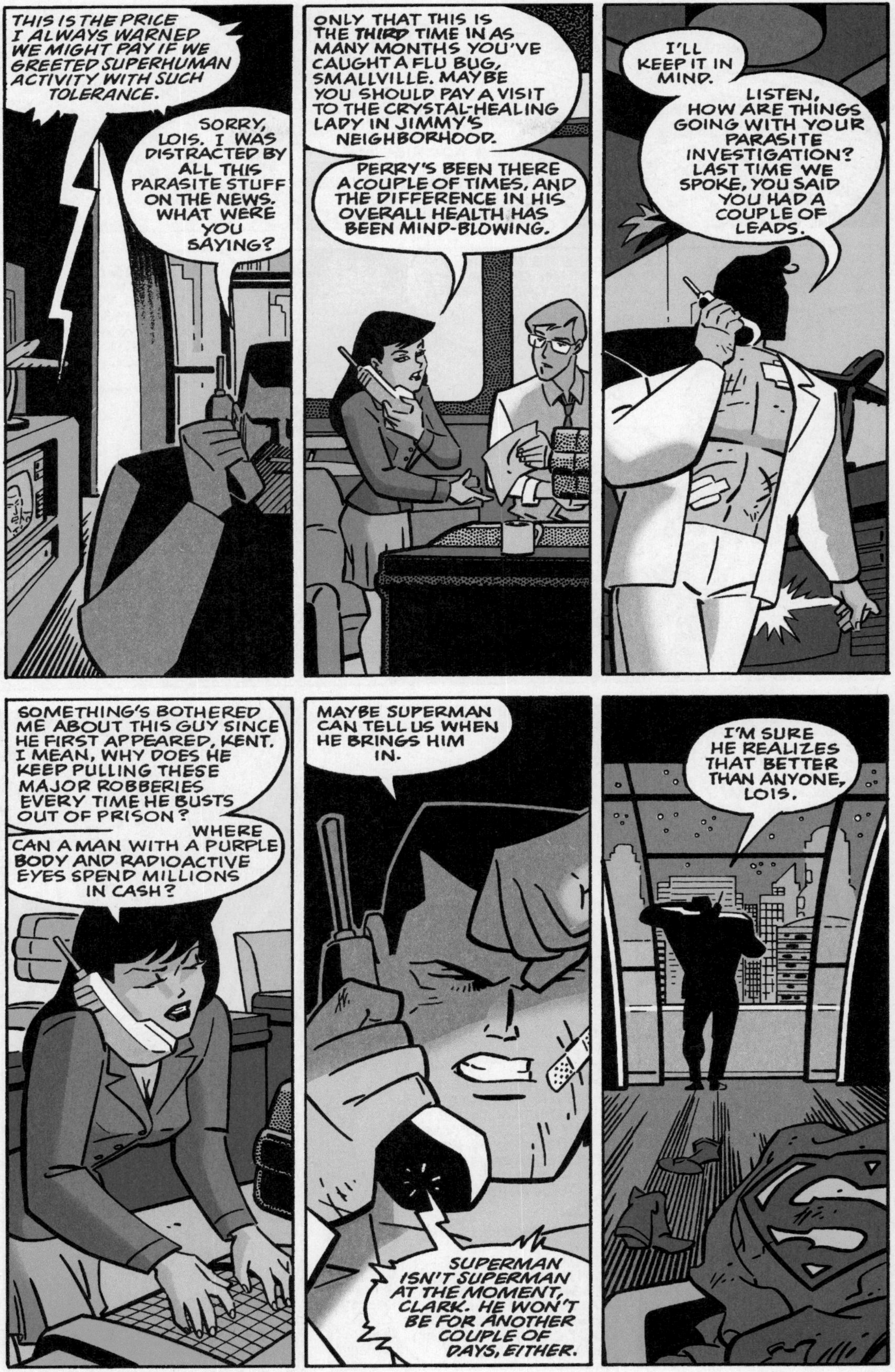
THIS IS THE PRICE I ALWAYS WARNED WE MIGHT PAY IF WE GREETED SUPERHUMAN ACTIVITY WITH SUCH TOLERANCE.
SORRY, LOIS. I WAS DISTRACTED BY ALL THIS PARASITE STUFF ON THE NEWS. WHAT WERE YOU SAYING?
ONLY THAT THIS IS THE THIRD TIME IN AS MANY MONTHS YOU'VE CAUGHT A FLU BUG, SMALLVILLE. MAYBE YOU SHOULD PAY A VISIT TO THE CRYSTAL-HEALING LADY IN JIMMY'S NEIGHBORHOOD.
PERRY'S BEEN THERE A COUPLE OF TIMES, AND THE DIFFERENCE IN HIS OVERALL HEALTH HAS BEEN MIND-BLOWING.
I'LL KEEP IT IN MIND.
LISTEN, HOW ARE THINGS GOING WITH YOUR PARASITE INVESTIGATION? LAST TIME WE SPOKE, YOU SAID YOU HAD A COUPLE OF LEADS.
SOMETHING'S BOTHERED ME ABOUT THIS GUY SINCE HE FIRST APPEARED, KENT. I MEAN, WHY DOES HE KEEP PULLING THESE MAJOR ROBBERIES EVERY TIME HE BUSTS OUT OF PRISON?
WHERE CAN A MAN WITH A PURPLE BODY AND RADIOACTIVE EYES SPEND MILLIONS IN CASH?
MAYBE SUPERMAN CAN TELL US WHEN HE BRINGS HIM IN.
SUPERMAN ISN'T SUPERMAN AT THE MOMENT, CLARK. HE WON'T BE FOR ANOTHER COUPLE OF DAYS, EITHER.
I'M SURE HE REALIZES THAT BETTER THAN ANYONE, LOIS.

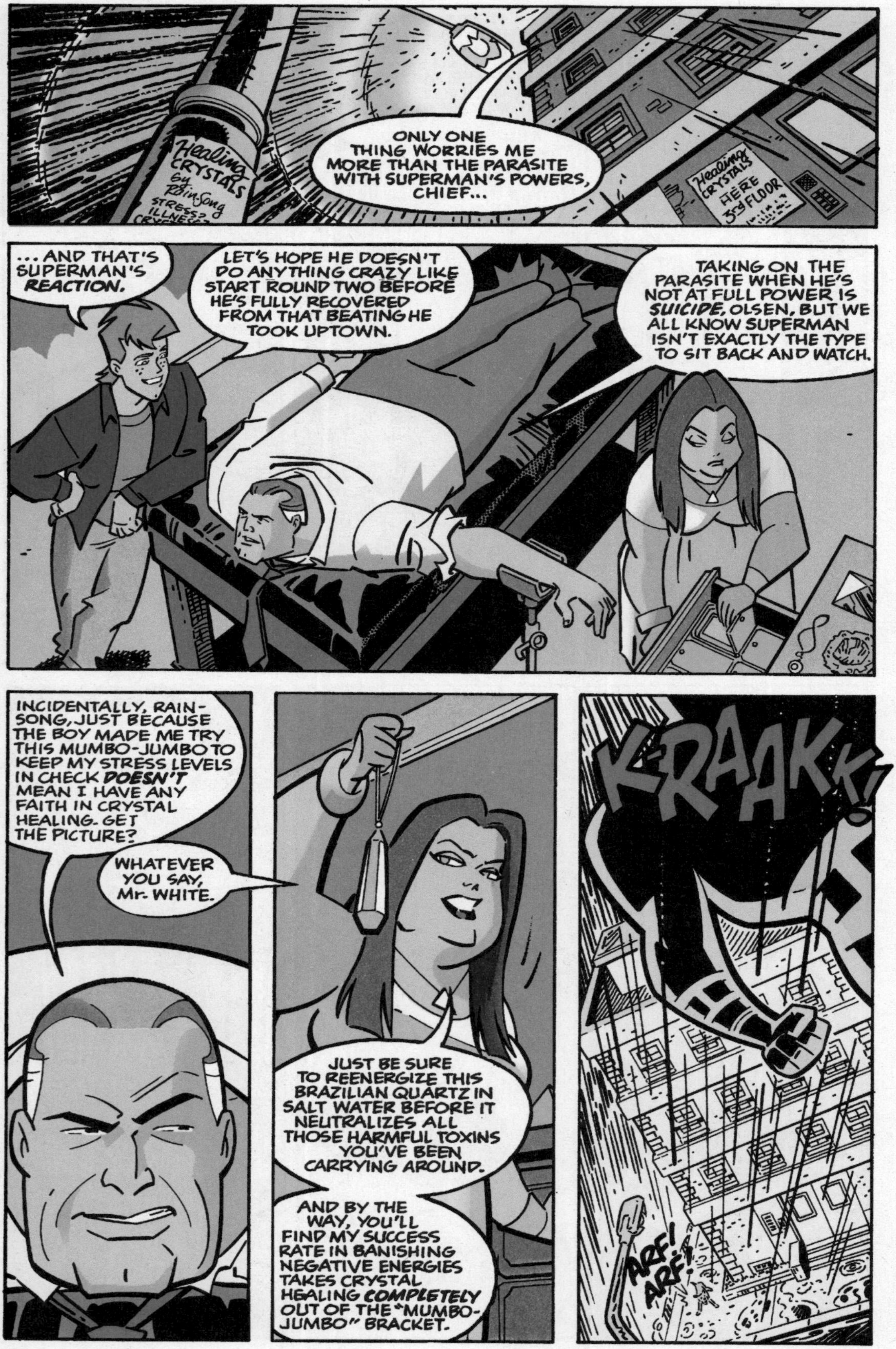
Healing CRYSTALS by RainSong STRESS? ILLNESS?
ONLY ONE THING WORRIES ME MORE THAN THE PARASITE WITH SUPERMAN'S POWERS, CHIEF...
Healing CRYSTALS HERE 3rd FLOOR
...AND THAT'S SUPERMAN'S REACTION.
LET'S HOPE HE DOESN'T DO ANYTHING CRAZY LIKE START ROUND TWO BEFORE HE'S FULLY RECOVERED FROM THAT BEATING HE TOOK UPTOWN.
TAKING ON THE PARASITE WHEN HE'S NOT AT FULL POWER IS SUICIDE, OLSEN, BUT WE ALL KNOW SUPERMAN ISN'T EXACTLY THE TYPE TO SIT BACK AND WATCH.
INCIDENTALLY, RAIN-SONG, JUST BECAUSE THE BOY MADE ME TRY THIS MUMBO-JUMBO TO KEEP MY STRESS LEVELS IN CHECK DOESN'T MEAN I HAVE ANY FAITH IN CRYSTAL HEALING. GET THE PICTURE?
WHATEVER YOU SAY, Mr. WHITE.
JUST BE SURE TO REENERGIZE THIS BRAZILIAN QUARTZ IN SALT WATER BEFORE IT NEUTRALIZES ALL THOSE HARMFUL TOXINS YOU'VE BEEN CARRYING AROUND.
AND BY THE WAY, YOU'LL FIND MY SUCCESS RATE IN BANISHING NEGATIVE ENERGIES TAKES CRYSTAL HEALING COMPLETELY OUT OF THE "MUMBO-JUMBO" BRACKET.
K-RAAKK!
ARF! ARF!

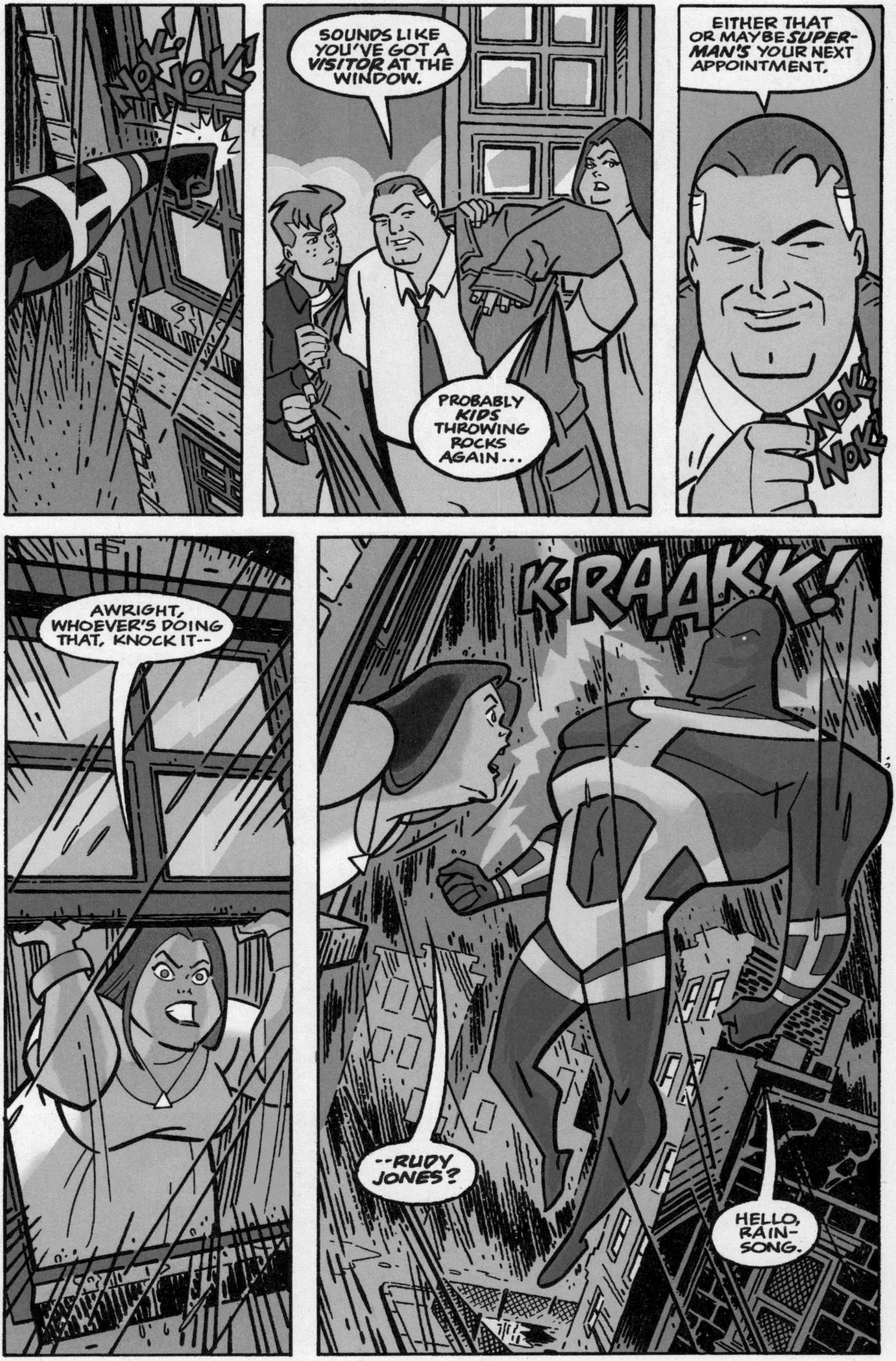
NOK! NOK!
SOUNDS LIKE YOU'VE GOT A VISITOR AT THE WINDOW.
PROBABLY KIDS THROWING ROCKS AGAIN...
EITHER THAT OR MAYBE SUPERMAN'S YOUR NEXT APPOINTMENT.
NOK! NOK!
AWRIGHT, WHOEVER'S DOING THAT, KNOCK IT--
K-RAAKK!
--RUDY JONES?
HELLO, RAIN-SONG.

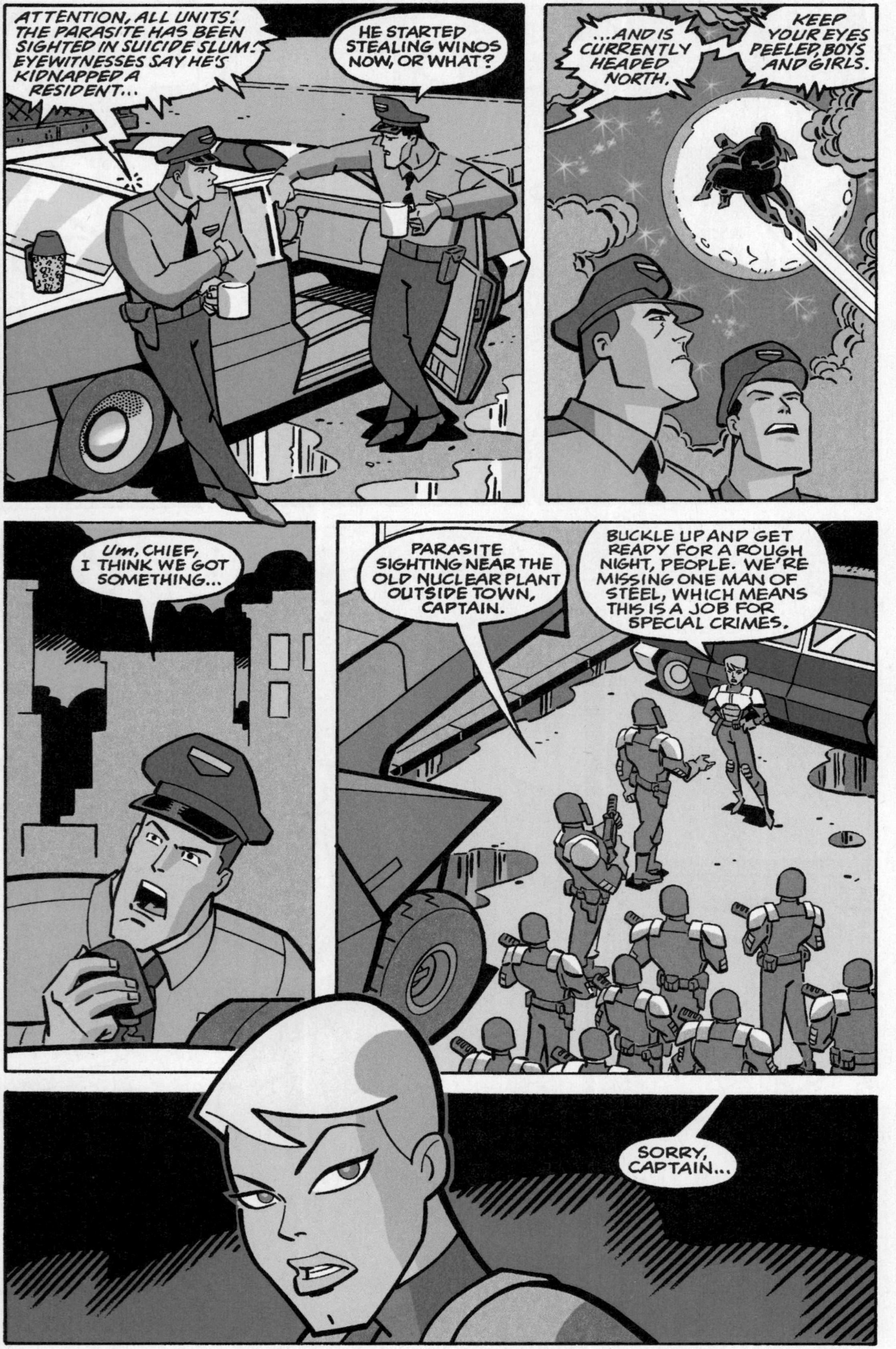
ATTENTION, ALL UNITS! THE PARASITE HAS BEEN SIGHTED IN SUICIDE SLUM! EYEWITNESSES SAY HE'S KIDNAPPED A RESIDENT...
HE STARTED STEALING WINOS NOW, OR WHAT?
...AND IS CURRENTLY HEADED NORTH.
KEEP YOUR EYES PEELED, BOYS AND GIRLS.
Um, CHIEF, I THINK WE GOT SOMETHING...
PARASITE SIGHTING NEAR THE OLD NUCLEAR PLANT OUTSIDE TOWN, CAPTAIN.
BUCKLE UP AND GET READY FOR A ROUGH NIGHT, PEOPLE. WE'RE MISSING ONE MAN OF STEEL, WHICH MEANS THIS IS A JOB FOR SPECIAL CRIMES.
SORRY, CAPTAIN...

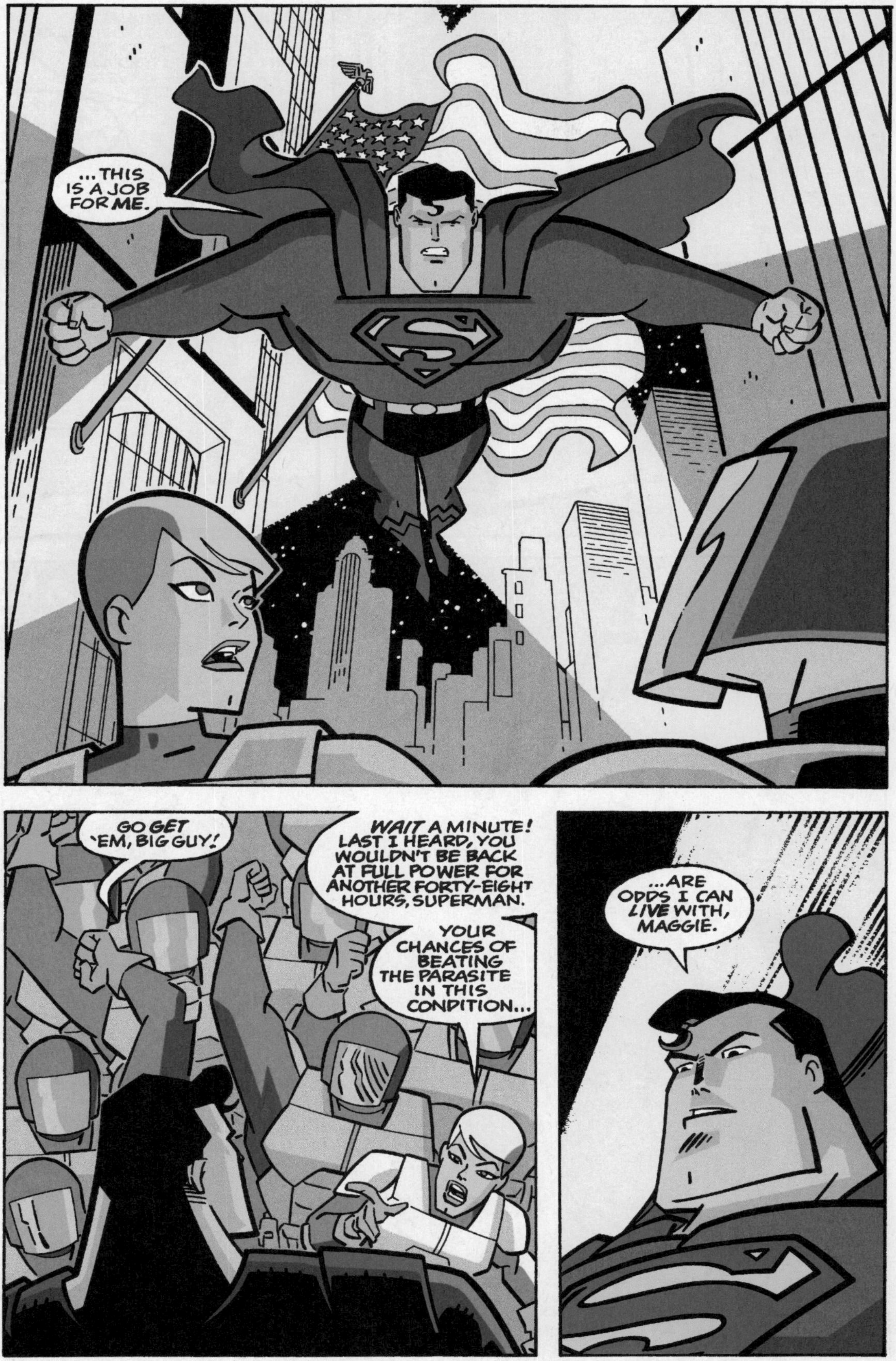
...THIS IS A JOB FOR ME.
GO GET 'EM, BIG GUY!
WAIT A MINUTE! LAST I HEARD, YOU WOULDN'T BE BACK AT FULL POWER FOR ANOTHER FORTY-EIGHT HOURS, SUPERMAN.
YOUR CHANCES OF BEATING THE PARASITE IN THIS CONDITION...
...ARE ODDS I CAN LIVE WITH, MAGGIE.

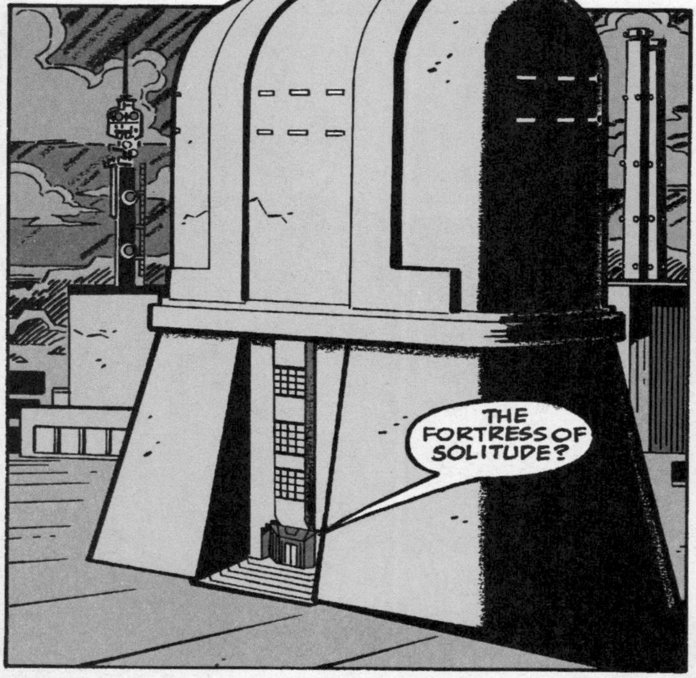
THE FORTRESS OF SOLITUDE?

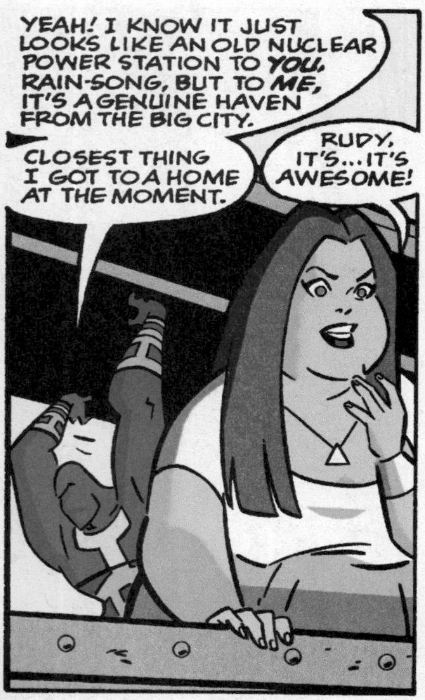
YEAH! I KNOW IT JUST LOOKS LIKE AN OLD NUCLEAR POWER STATION TO YOU, RAIN-SONG, BUT TO ME, IT'S A GENUINE HAVEN FROM THE BIG CITY.
CLOSEST THING I GOT TO A HOME AT THE MOMENT.
RUDY, IT'S...IT'S AWESOME!

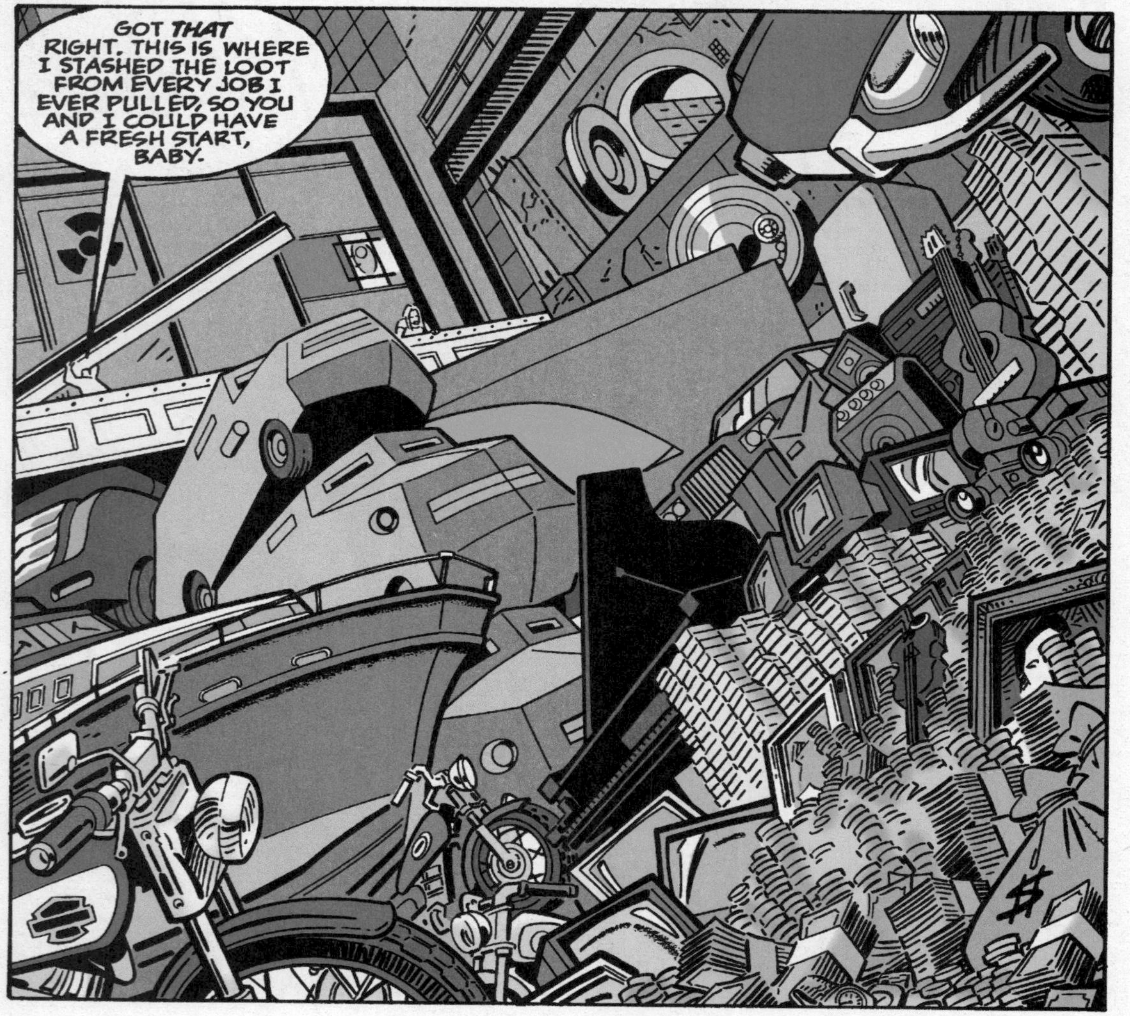
GOT THAT RIGHT. THIS IS WHERE I STASHED THE LOOT FROM EVERY JOB I EVER PULLED, SO YOU AND I COULD HAVE A FRESH START, BABY.

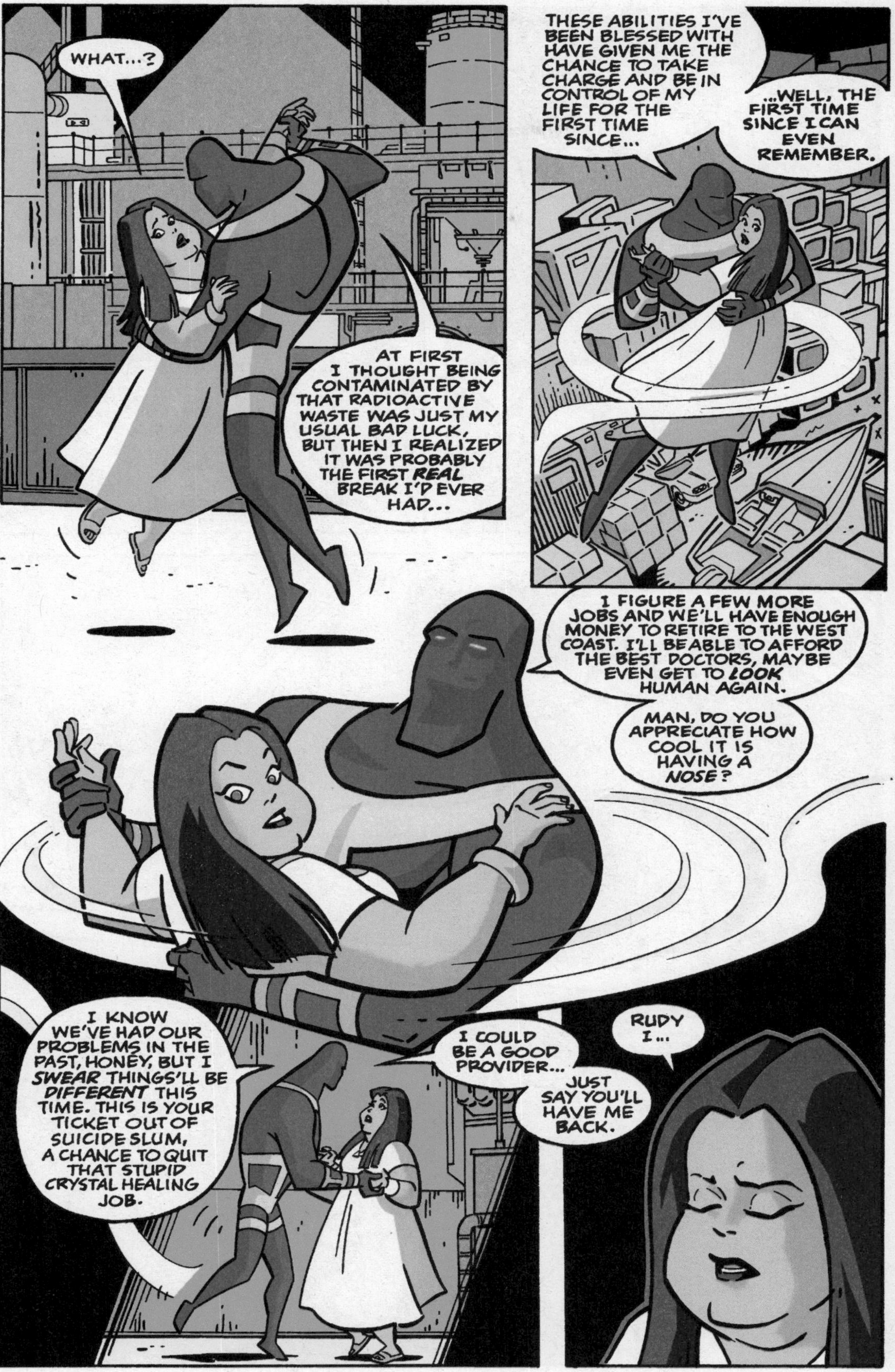
WHAT...?
AT FIRST I THOUGHT BEING CONTAMINATED BY THAT RADIOACTIVE WASTE WAS JUST MY USUAL BAD LUCK, BUT THEN I REALIZED IT WAS PROBABLY THE FIRST REAL BREAK I'D EVER HAD...
THESE ABILITIES I'VE BEEN BLESSED WITH HAVE GIVEN ME THE CHANCE TO TAKE CHARGE AND BE IN CONTROL OF MY LIFE FOR THE FIRST TIME SINCE...
...WELL, THE FIRST TIME SINCE I CAN EVEN REMEMBER.
I FIGURE A FEW MORE JOBS AND WE'LL HAVE ENOUGH MONEY TO RETIRE TO THE WEST COAST. I'LL BE ABLE TO AFFORD THE BEST DOCTORS, MAYBE EVEN GET TO LOOK HUMAN AGAIN.
MAN, DO YOU APPRECIATE HOW COOL IT IS HAVING A NOSE?
I KNOW WE'VE HAD OUR PROBLEMS IN THE PAST, HONEY, BUT I SWEAR THINGS'LL BE DIFFERENT THIS TIME. THIS IS YOUR TICKET OUT OF SUICIDE SLUM, A CHANCE TO QUIT THAT STUPID CRYSTAL HEALING JOB.
I COULD BE A GOOD PROVIDER...
JUST SAY YOU'LL HAVE ME BACK.
RUDY I...

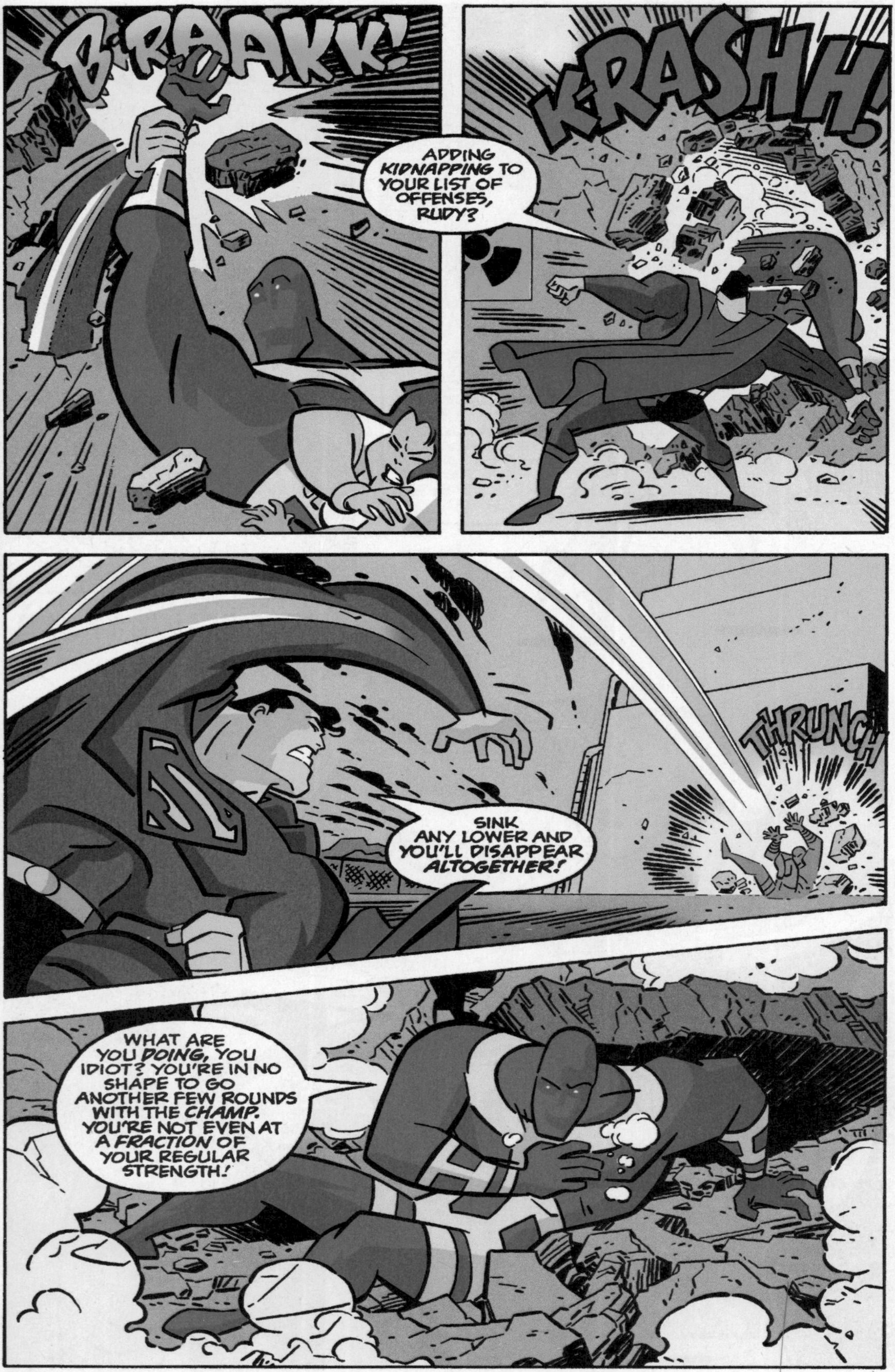
B-RAAKK!
ADDING KIDNAPPING TO YOUR LIST OF OFFENSES, RUDY?
K-RASHH!
SINK ANY LOWER AND YOU'LL DISAPPEAR ALTOGETHER!
THRUNCH
WHAT ARE YOU DOING, YOU IDIOT? YOU'RE IN NO SHAPE TO GO ANOTHER FEW ROUNDS WITH THE CHAMP. YOU'RE NOT EVEN AT A FRACTION OF YOUR REGULAR STRENGTH!

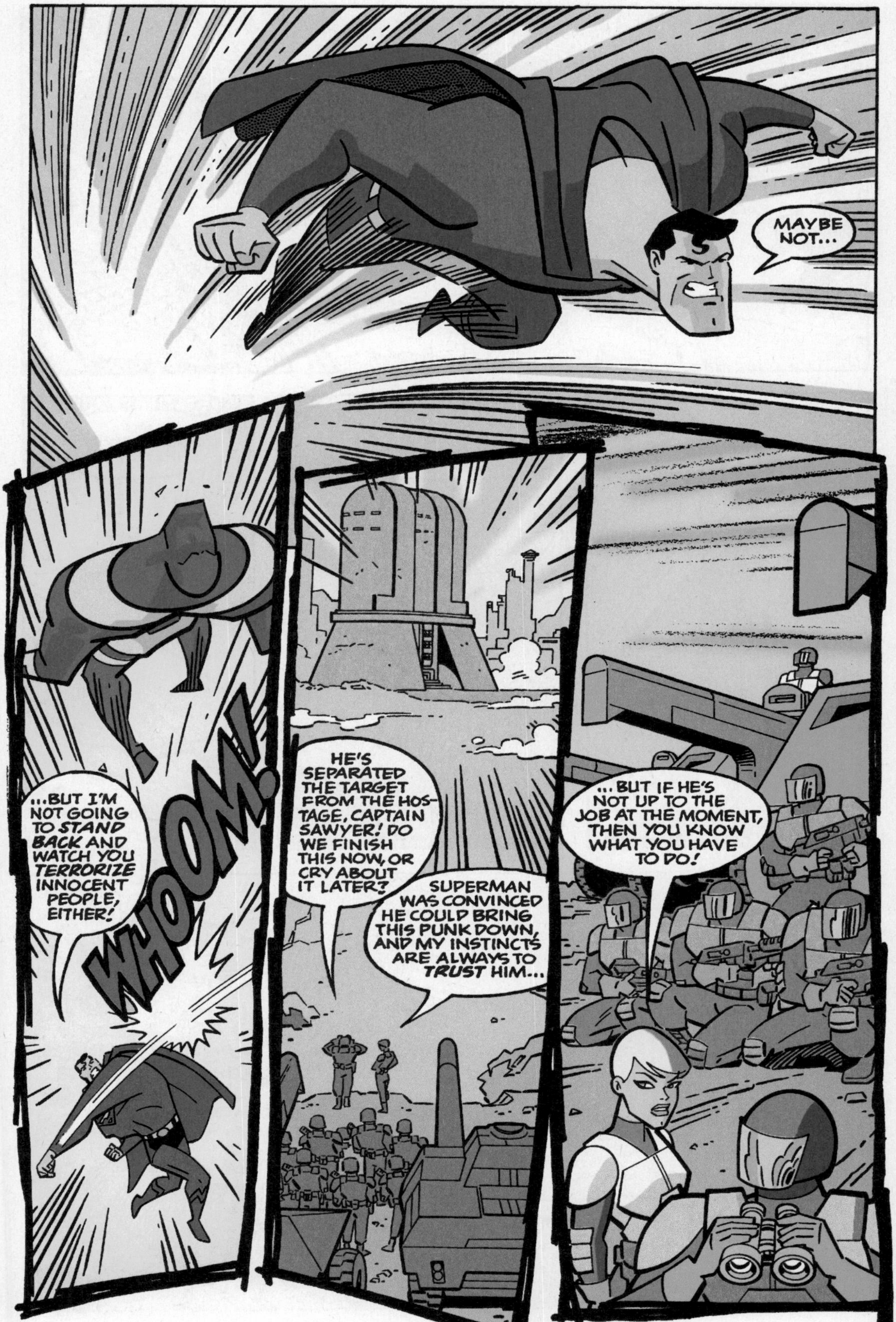
MAYBE NOT...
...BUT I'M NOT GOING TO STAND BACK AND WATCH YOU TERRORIZE INNOCENT PEOPLE, EITHER!
WHOOM!
HE'S SEPARATED THE TARGET FROM THE HOS-TAGE, CAPTAIN SAWYER! DO WE FINISH THIS NOW, OR CRY ABOUT IT LATER?
SUPERMAN WAS CONVINCED HE COULD BRING THIS PUNK DOWN, AND MY INSTINCTS ARE ALWAYS TO TRUST HIM...
...BUT IF HE'S NOT UP TO THE JOB AT THE MOMENT, THEN YOU KNOW WHAT YOU HAVE TO DO!

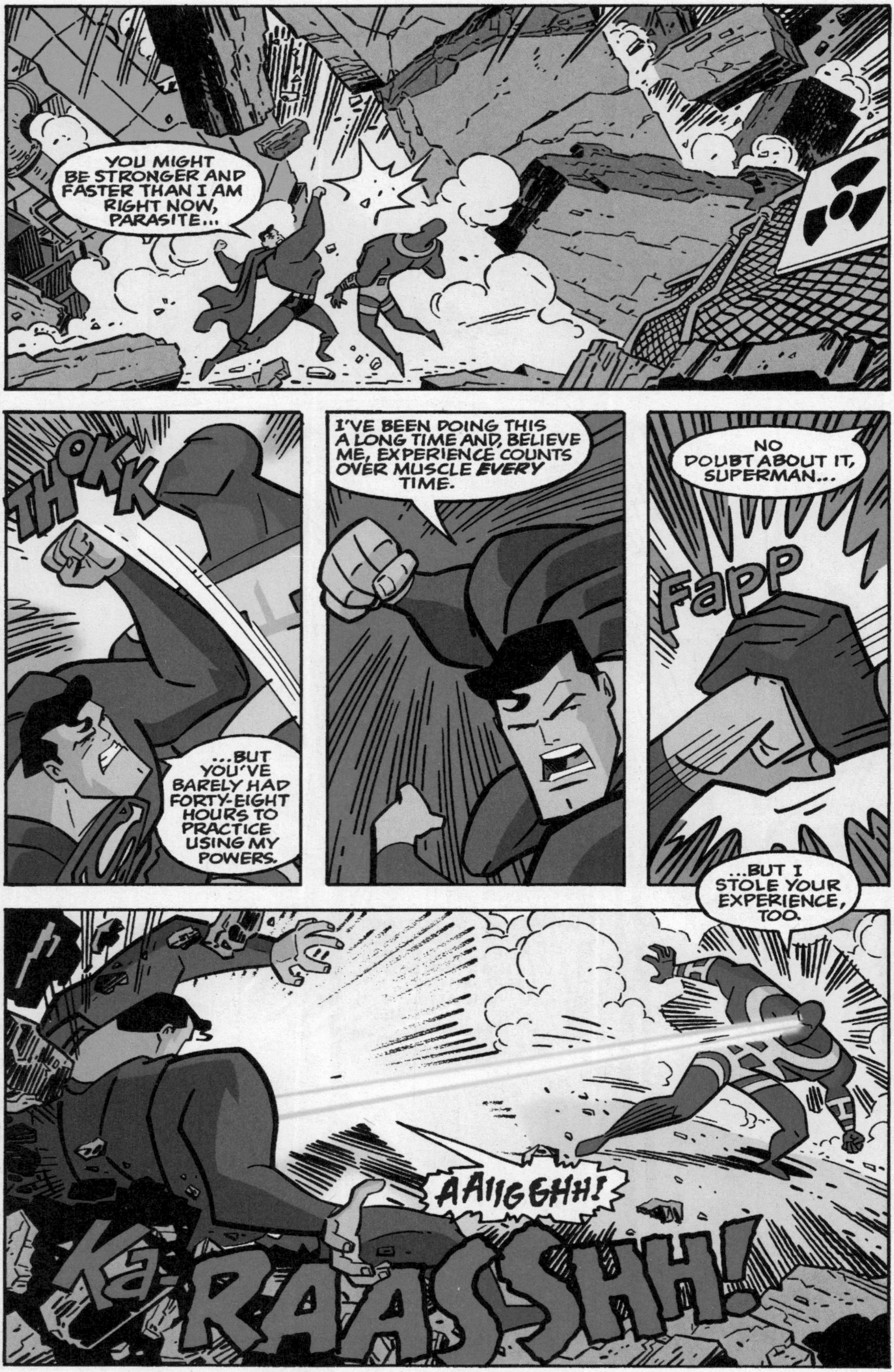
YOU MIGHT BE STRONGER AND FASTER THAN I AM RIGHT NOW, PARASITE...
THOKK
...BUT YOU'VE BARELY HAD FORTY-EIGHT HOURS TO PRACTICE USING MY POWERS.
I'VE BEEN DOING THIS A LONG TIME AND, BELIEVE ME, EXPERIENCE COUNTS OVER MUSCLE EVERY TIME.
NO DOUBT ABOUT IT, SUPERMAN...
FAPP
...BUT I STOLE YOUR EXPERIENCE, TOO.
AAIIGGHH!
KA-RAASSHH!

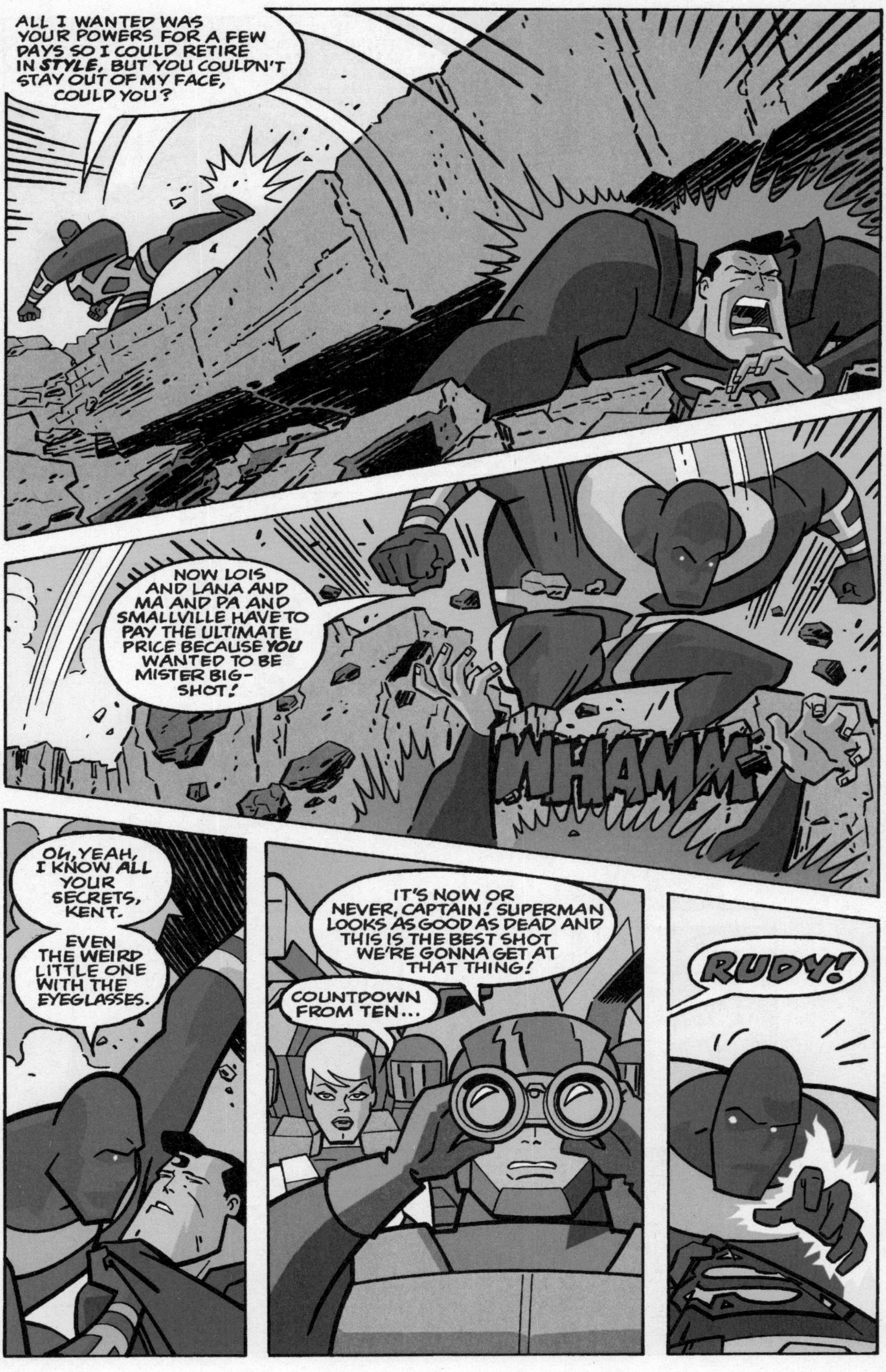
ALL I WANTED WAS YOUR POWERS FOR A FEW DAYS SO I COULD RETIRE IN STYLE, BUT YOU COULDN'T STAY OUT OF MY FACE, COULD YOU?
NOW LOIS AND LANA AND MA AND PA AND SMALLVILLE HAVE TO PAY THE ULTIMATE PRICE BECAUSE YOU WANTED TO BE MISTER BIG-SHOT!
WHAMM-
OH, YEAH, I KNOW ALL YOUR SECRETS, KENT.
EVEN THE WEIRD LITTLE ONE WITH THE EYEGLASSES.
IT'S NOW OR NEVER, CAPTAIN! SUPERMAN LOOKS AS GOOD AS DEAD AND THIS IS THE BEST SHOT WE'RE GONNA GET AT THAT THING!
COUNTDOWN FROM TEN...
RUDY!

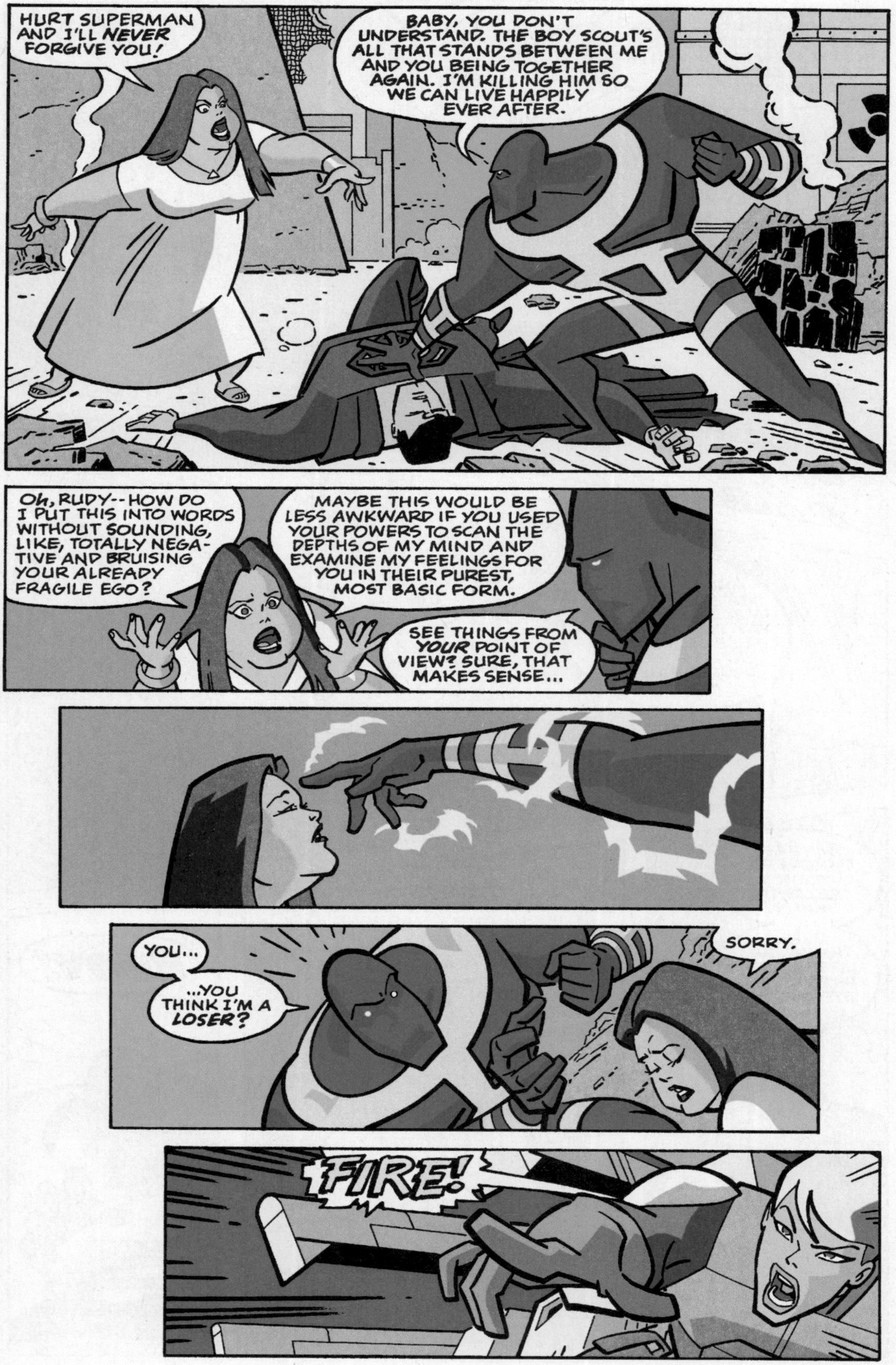
HURT SUPERMAN AND I'LL NEVER FORGIVE YOU!
BABY, YOU DON'T UNDERSTAND. THE BOY SCOUT'S ALL THAT STANDS BETWEEN ME AND YOU BEING TOGETHER AGAIN. I'M KILLING HIM SO WE CAN LIVE HAPPILY EVER AFTER.
Oh, RUDY--HOW DO I PUT THIS INTO WORDS WITHOUT SOUNDING, LIKE, TOTALLY NEGATIVE AND BRUISING YOUR ALREADY FRAGILE EGO?
MAYBE THIS WOULD BE LESS AWKWARD IF YOU USED YOUR POWERS TO SCAN THE DEPTHS OF MY MIND AND EXAMINE MY FEELINGS FOR YOU IN THEIR PUREST, MOST BASIC FORM.
SEE THINGS FROM YOUR POINT OF VIEW? SURE, THAT MAKES SENSE...
YOU...
...YOU THINK I'M A LOSER?
SORRY.
FIRE!

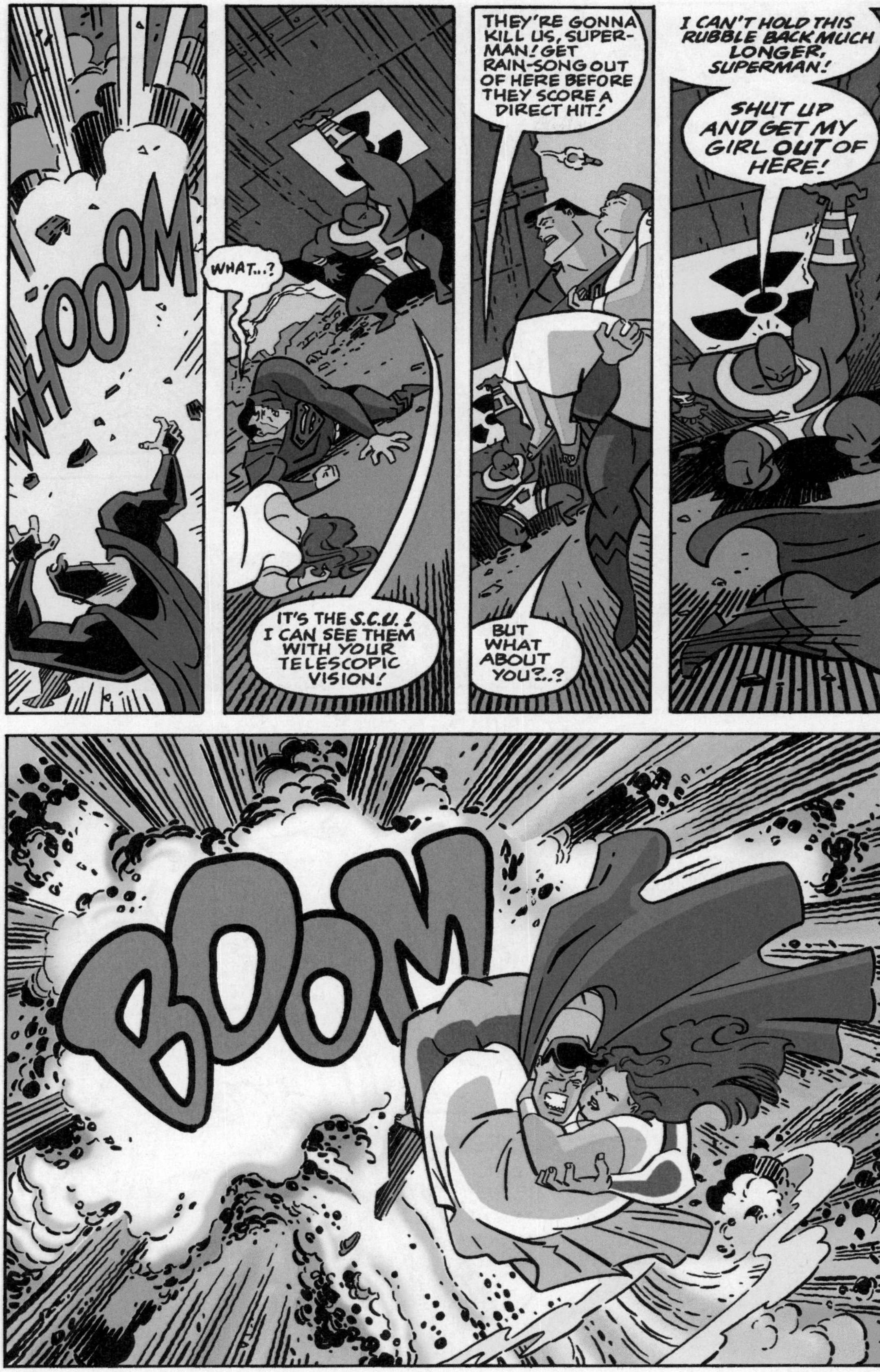
WHOOOM
WHAT...?
IT'S THE S.C.U.! I CAN SEE THEM WITH YOUR TELESCOPIC VISION!
THEY'RE GONNA KILL US, SUPER-MAN! GET RAIN-SONG OUT OF HERE BEFORE THEY SCORE A DIRECT HIT!
BUT WHAT ABOUT YOU?..?
I CAN'T HOLD THIS RUBBLE BACK MUCH LONGER, SUPERMAN!
SHUT UP AND GET MY GIRL OUT OF HERE!
BOOM

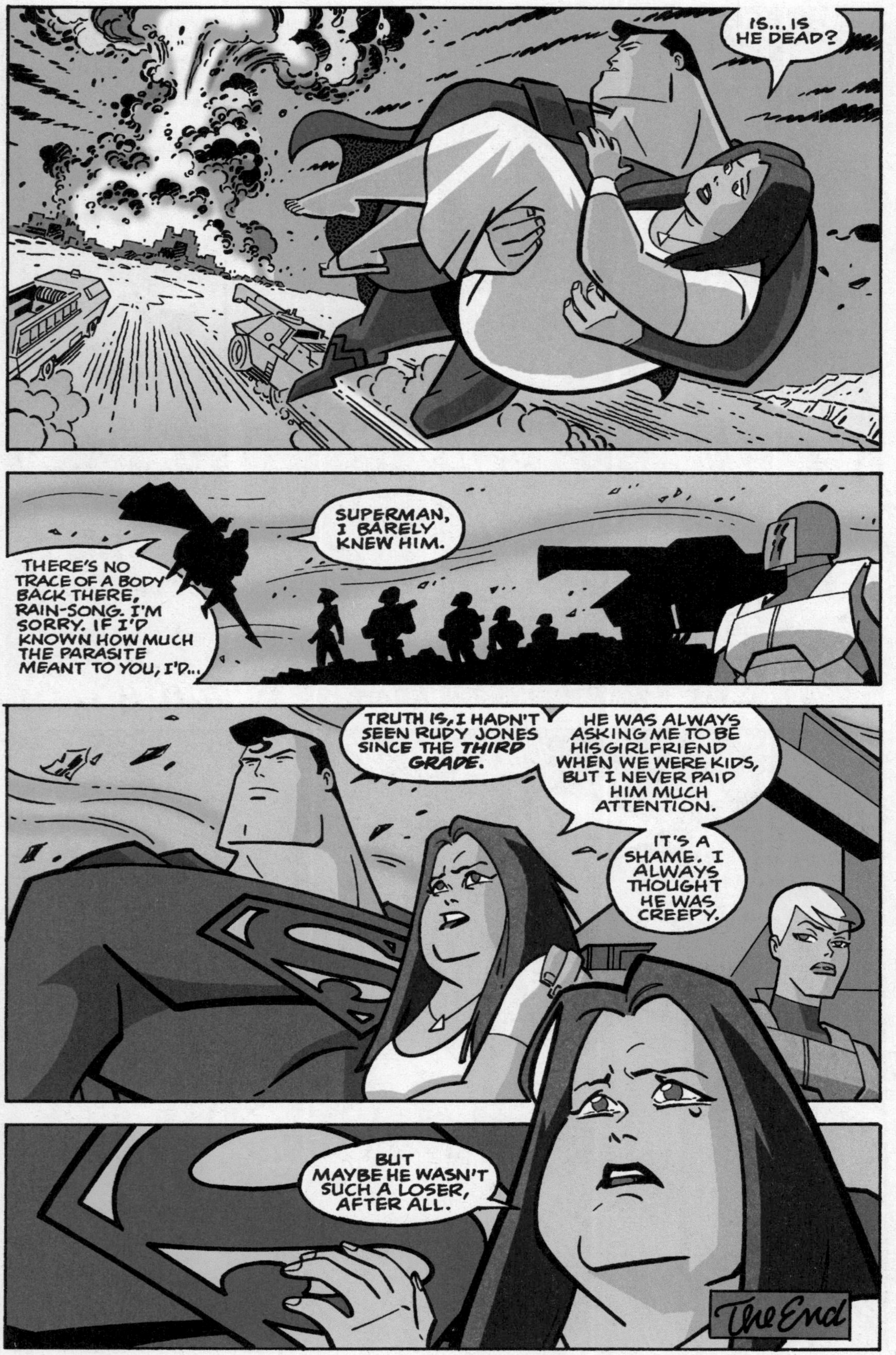

IS... IS HE DEAD?
SUPERMAN, I BARELY KNEW HIM.
THERE'S NO TRACE OF A BODY BACK THERE, RAIN-SONG. I'M SORRY. IF I'D KNOWN HOW MUCH THE PARASITE MEANT TO YOU, I'D...
TRUTH IS, I HADN'T SEEN RUDY JONES SINCE THE *THIRD GRADE*.
HE WAS ALWAYS ASKING ME TO BE HIS GIRLFRIEND WHEN WE WERE KIDS, BUT I NEVER PAID HIM MUCH ATTENTION.
IT'S A SHAME. I ALWAYS THOUGHT HE WAS CREEPY.
BUT MAYBE HE WASN'T SUCH A LOSER, AFTER ALL.
The End

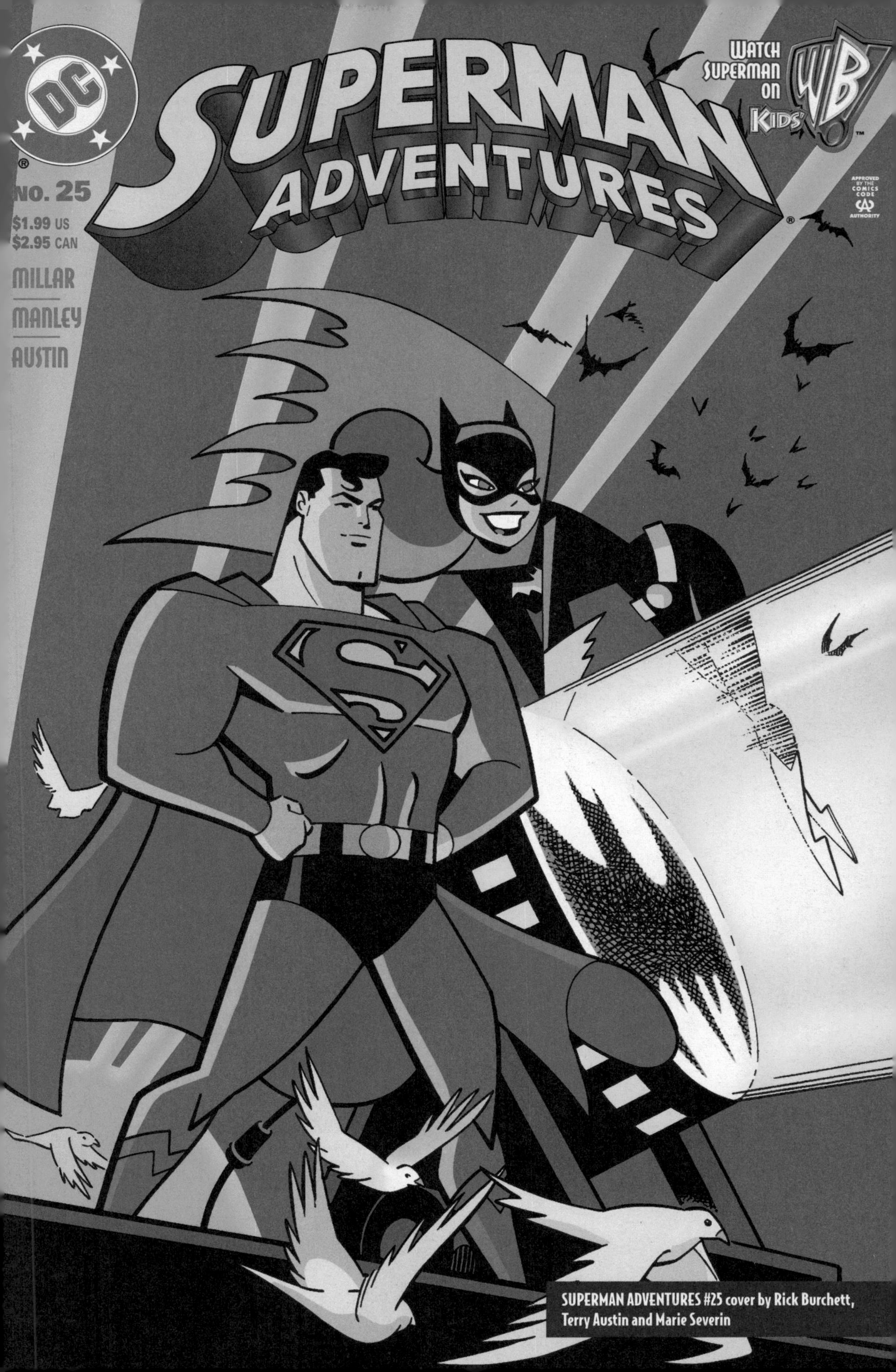
SUPERMAN ADVENTURES
NO. 25
$1.99 US
$2.95 CAN
MILLAR
MANLEY
AUSTIN
WATCH SUPERMAN ON KIDS' WB
APPROVED BY THE COMICS CODE AUTHORITY

SUPERMAN ADVENTURES #25 cover by Rick Burchett, Terry Austin and Marie Severin

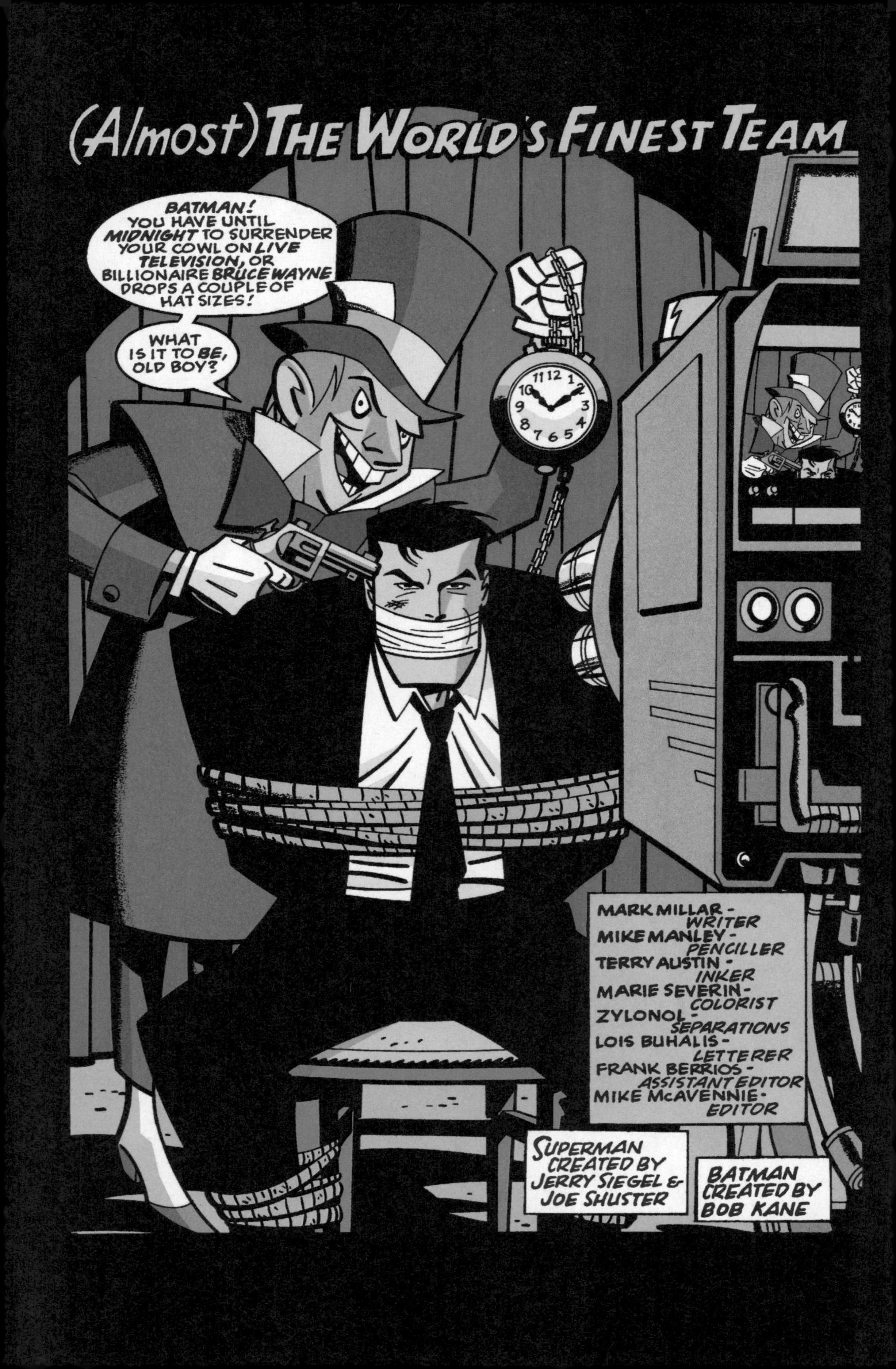
(Almost) THE WORLD'S FINEST TEAM
BATMAN! YOU HAVE UNTIL MIDNIGHT TO SURRENDER YOUR COWL ON LIVE TELEVISION, OR BILLIONAIRE BRUCE WAYNE DROPS A COUPLE OF HAT SIZES!
WHAT IS IT TO BE, OLD BOY?
MARK MILLAR - WRITER
MIKE MANLEY - PENCILLER
TERRY AUSTIN - INKER
MARIE SEVERIN - COLORIST
ZYLONOL - SEPARATIONS
LOIS BUHALIS - LETTERER
FRANK BERRIOS - ASSISTANT EDITOR
MIKE McAVENNIE - EDITOR
SUPERMAN CREATED BY JERRY SIEGEL & JOE SHUSTER
BATMAN CREATED BY BOB KANE

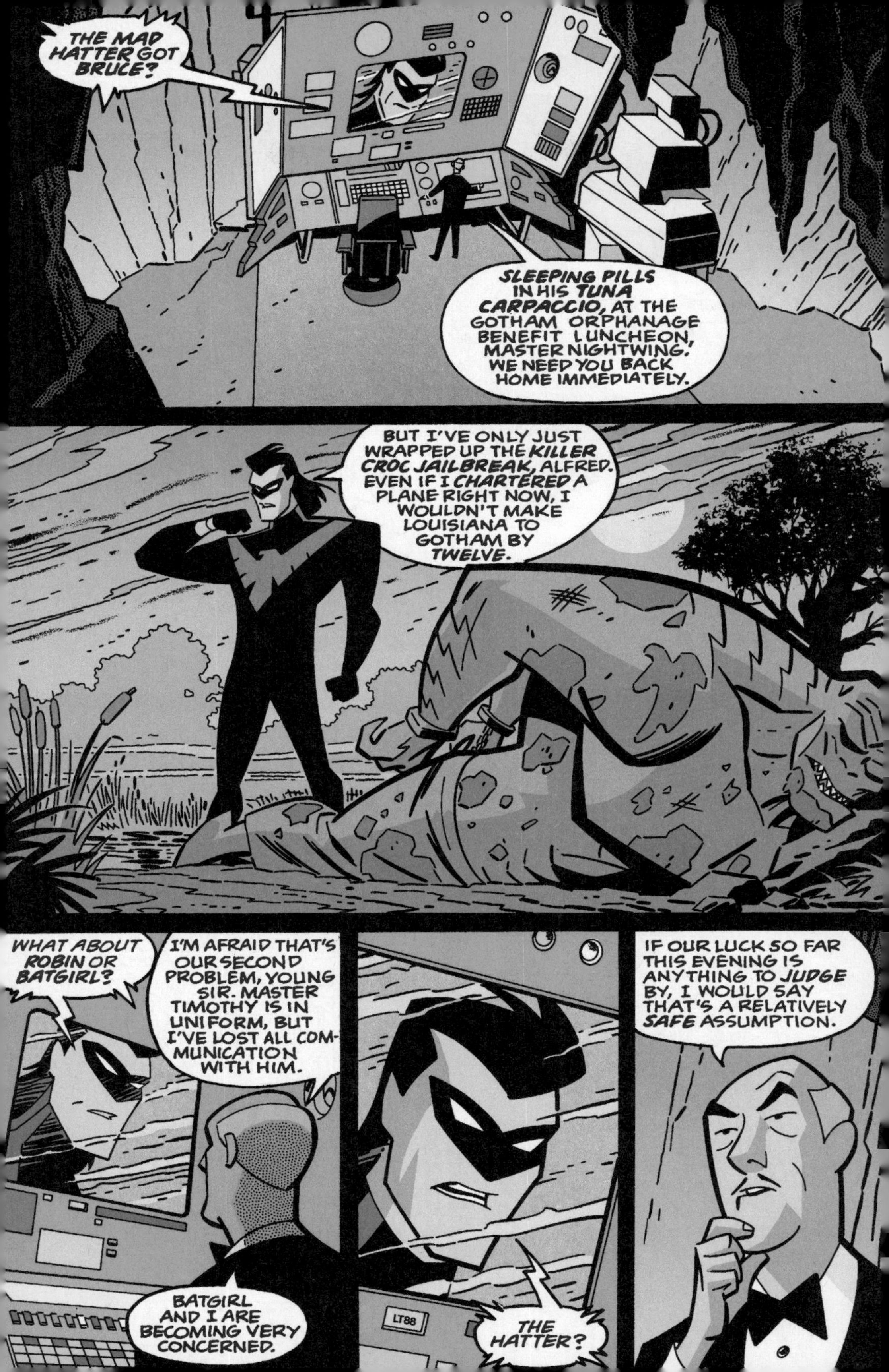
THE MAD HATTER GOT BRUCE?
SLEEPING PILLS IN HIS TUNA CARPACCIO, AT THE GOTHAM ORPHANAGE BENEFIT LUNCHEON, MASTER NIGHTWING. WE NEED YOU BACK HOME IMMEDIATELY.
BUT I'VE ONLY JUST WRAPPED UP THE KILLER CROC JAILBREAK, ALFRED. EVEN IF I CHARTERED A PLANE RIGHT NOW, I WOULDN'T MAKE LOUISIANA TO GOTHAM BY TWELVE.
WHAT ABOUT ROBIN OR BATGIRL?
I'M AFRAID THAT'S OUR SECOND PROBLEM, YOUNG SIR. MASTER TIMOTHY IS IN UNIFORM, BUT I'VE LOST ALL COMMUNICATION WITH HIM.
BATGIRL AND I ARE BECOMING VERY CONCERNED.
LT88
THE HATTER?
IF OUR LUCK SO FAR THIS EVENING IS ANYTHING TO JUDGE BY, I WOULD SAY THAT'S A RELATIVELY SAFE ASSUMPTION.

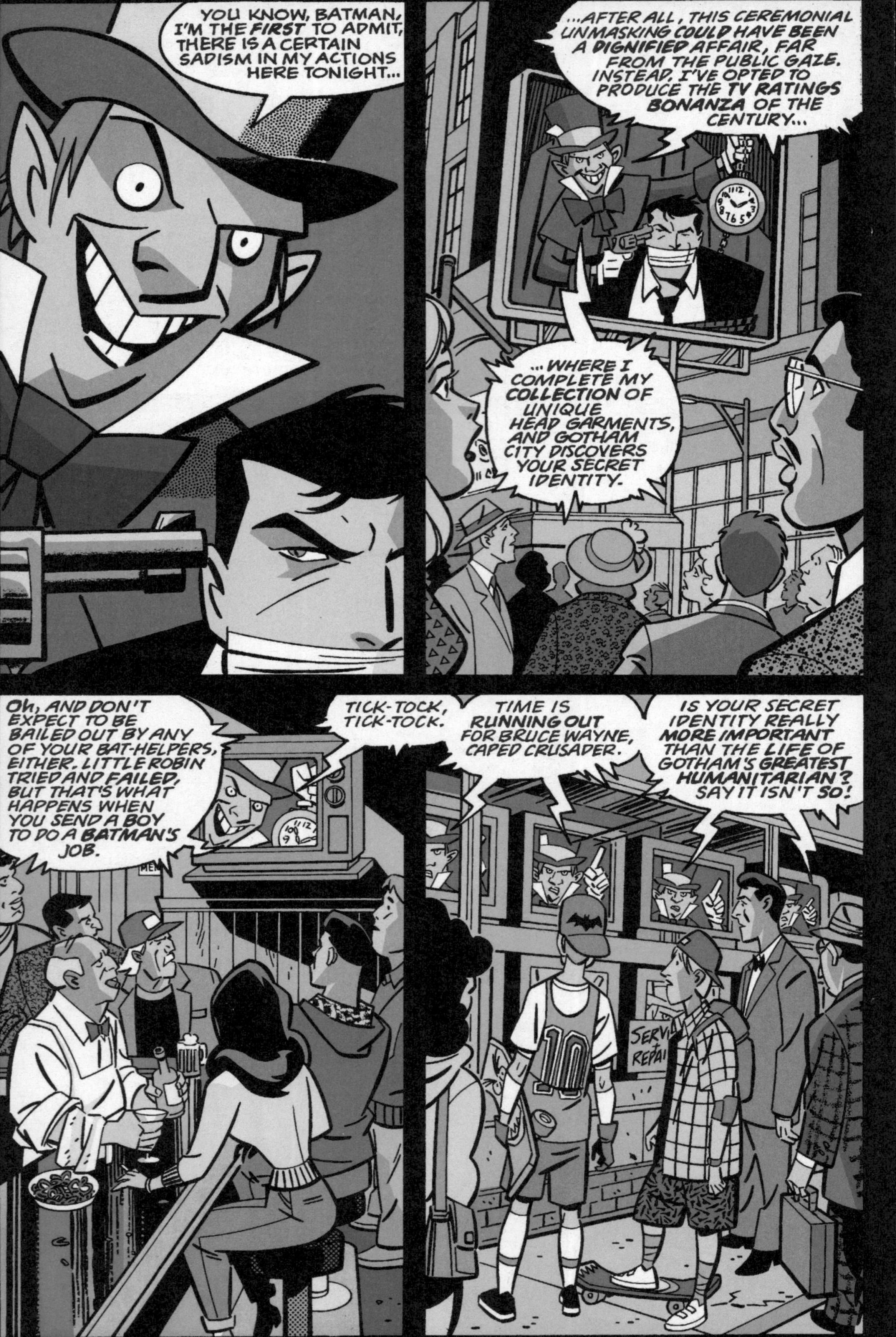
YOU KNOW, BATMAN, I'M THE FIRST TO ADMIT, THERE IS A CERTAIN SADISM IN MY ACTIONS HERE TONIGHT...
...AFTER ALL, THIS CEREMONIAL UNMASKING COULD HAVE BEEN A DIGNIFIED AFFAIR, FAR FROM THE PUBLIC GAZE. INSTEAD, I'VE OPTED TO PRODUCE THE TV RATINGS BONANZA OF THE CENTURY...
...WHERE I COMPLETE MY COLLECTION OF UNIQUE HEAD GARMENTS, AND GOTHAM CITY DISCOVERS YOUR SECRET IDENTITY.
Oh, AND DON'T EXPECT TO BE BAILED OUT BY ANY OF YOUR BAT-HELPERS, EITHER. LITTLE ROBIN TRIED AND FAILED, BUT THAT'S WHAT HAPPENS WHEN YOU SEND A BOY TO DO A BATMAN'S JOB.
TICK-TOCK, TICK-TOCK.
TIME IS RUNNING OUT FOR BRUCE WAYNE, CAPED CRUSADER.
IS YOUR SECRET IDENTITY REALLY MORE IMPORTANT THAN THE LIFE OF GOTHAM'S GREATEST HUMANITARIAN? SAY IT ISN'T SO!

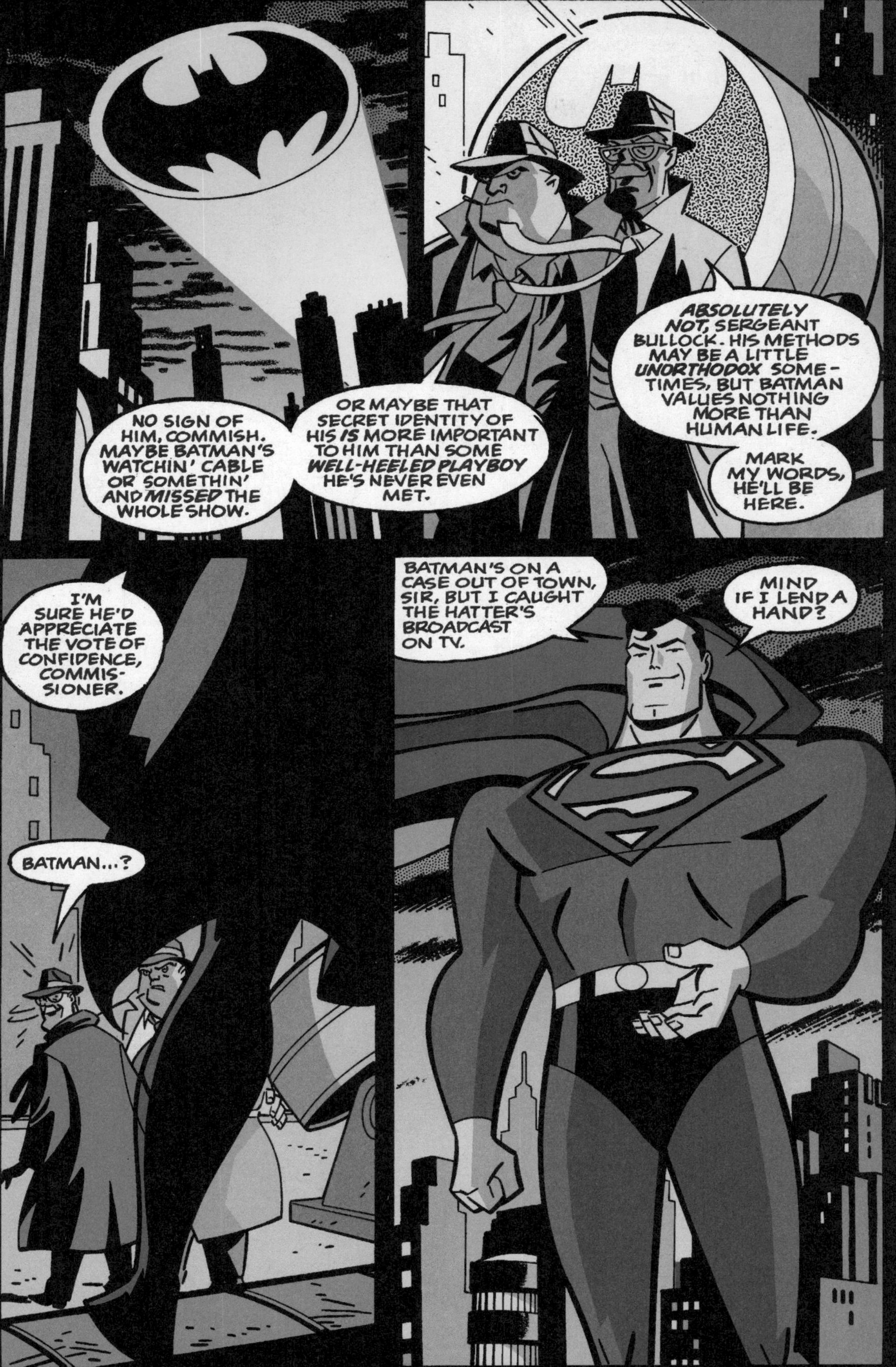
NO SIGN OF HIM, COMMISH. MAYBE BATMAN'S WATCHIN' CABLE OR SOMETHIN' AND *MISSED* THE WHOLE SHOW.
OR MAYBE THAT SECRET IDENTITY OF HIS *IS* MORE IMPORTANT TO HIM THAN SOME *WELL-HEELED PLAYBOY* HE'S NEVER EVEN MET.
ABSOLUTELY NOT, SERGEANT BULLOCK. HIS METHODS MAY BE A LITTLE *UNORTHODOX* SOME-TIMES, BUT BATMAN VALUES NOTHING MORE THAN HUMAN LIFE.
MARK MY WORDS, HE'LL BE HERE.
I'M SURE HE'D APPRECIATE THE VOTE OF CONFIDENCE, COMMIS-SIONER.
BATMAN...?
BATMAN'S ON A CASE OUT OF TOWN, SIR, BUT I CAUGHT THE HATTER'S BROADCAST ON TV.
MIND IF I LEND A HAND?

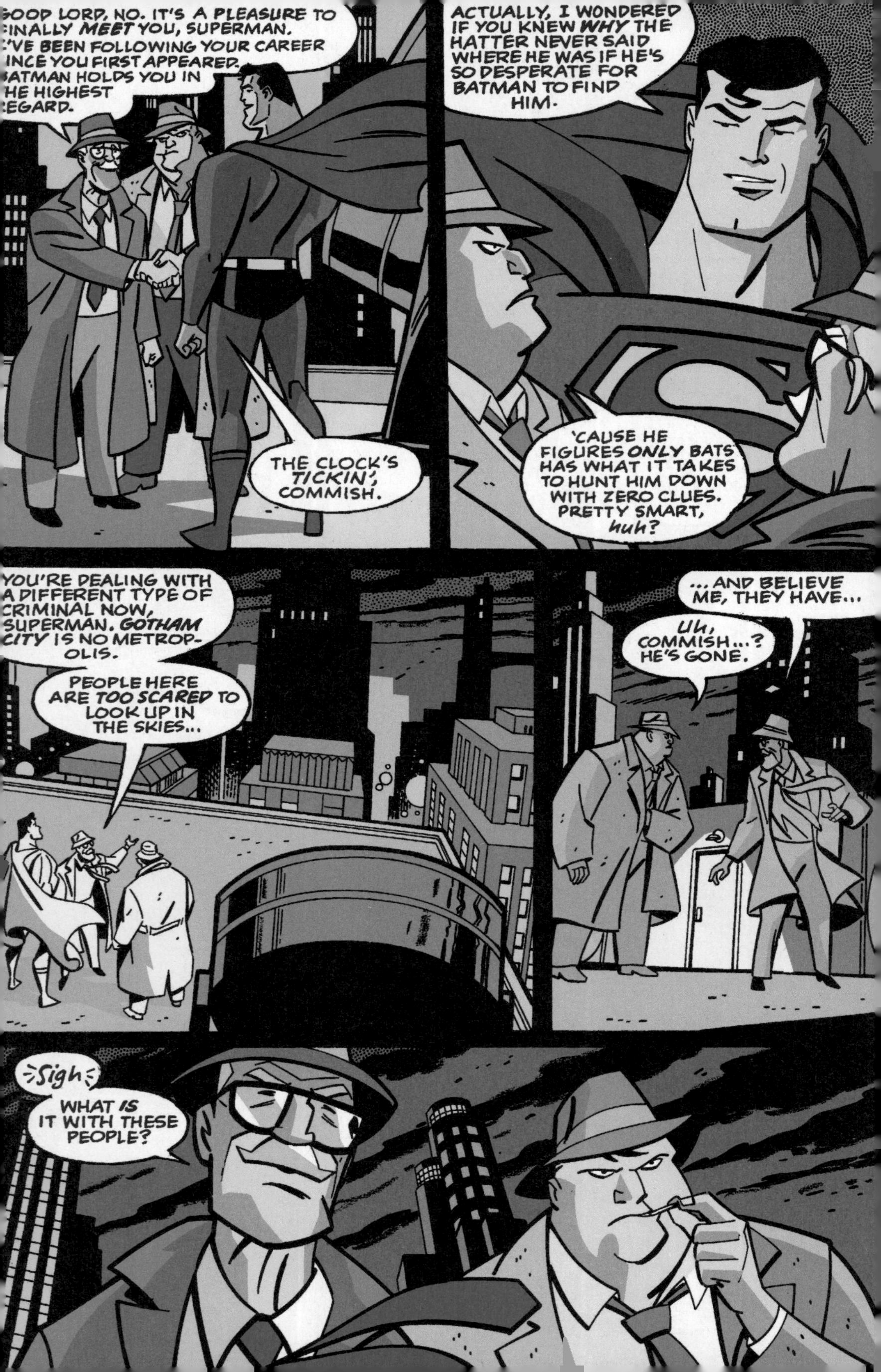
GOOD LORD, NO. IT'S A PLEASURE TO FINALLY MEET YOU, SUPERMAN. I'VE BEEN FOLLOWING YOUR CAREER SINCE YOU FIRST APPEARED. BATMAN HOLDS YOU IN THE HIGHEST REGARD.
THE CLOCK'S TICKIN', COMMISH.
ACTUALLY, I WONDERED IF YOU KNEW WHY THE HATTER NEVER SAID WHERE HE WAS IF HE'S SO DESPERATE FOR BATMAN TO FIND HIM.
'CAUSE HE FIGURES ONLY BATS HAS WHAT IT TAKES TO HUNT HIM DOWN WITH ZERO CLUES. PRETTY SMART, huh?
YOU'RE DEALING WITH A DIFFERENT TYPE OF CRIMINAL NOW, SUPERMAN. GOTHAM CITY IS NO METROPOLIS.
PEOPLE HERE ARE TOO SCARED TO LOOK UP IN THE SKIES...
...AND BELIEVE ME, THEY HAVE...
Uh, COMMISH...? HE'S GONE.
Sigh
WHAT IS IT WITH THESE PEOPLE?

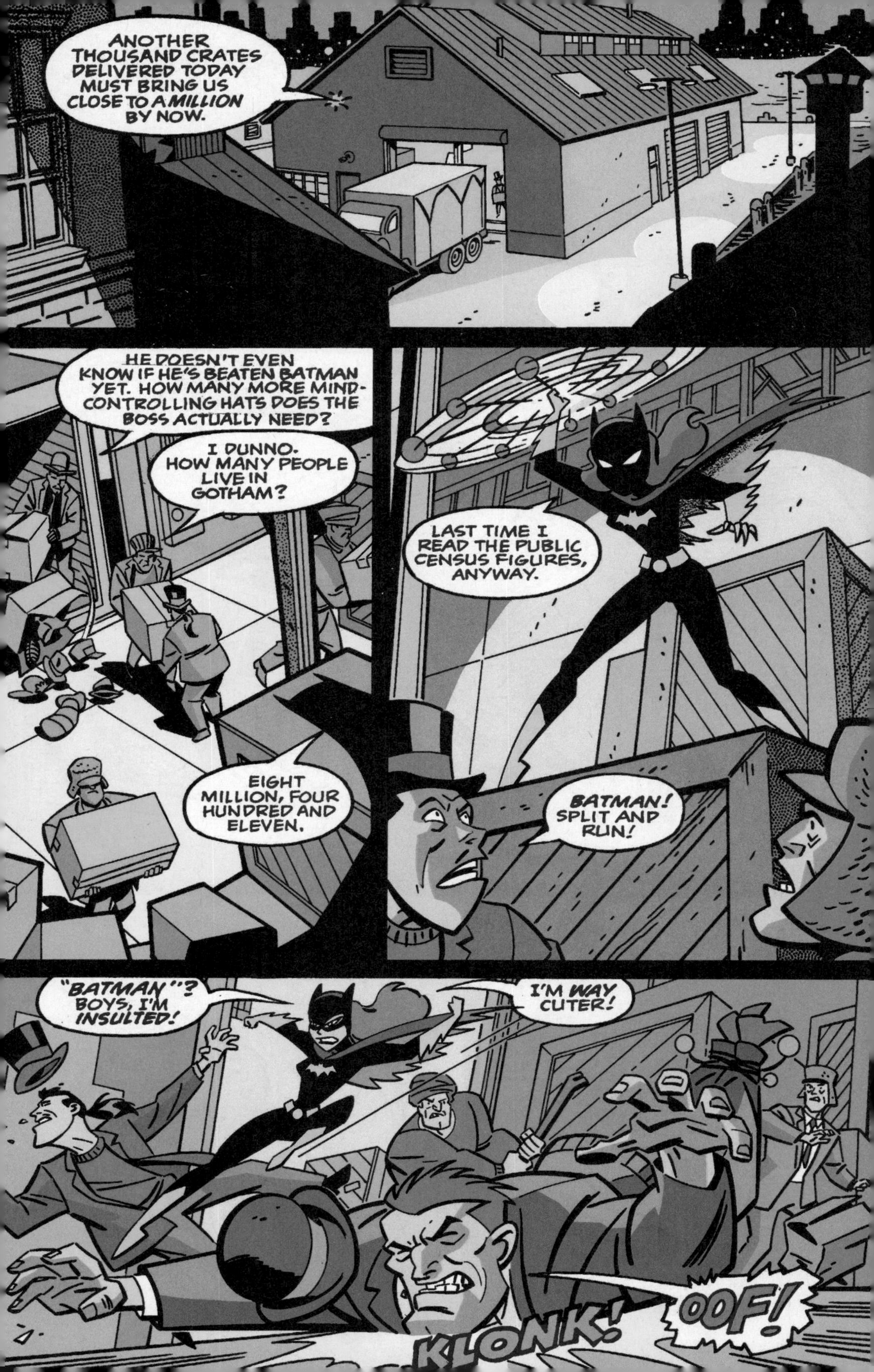
ANOTHER THOUSAND CRATES DELIVERED TODAY MUST BRING US CLOSE TO A MILLION BY NOW.
HE DOESN'T EVEN KNOW IF HE'S BEATEN BATMAN YET. HOW MANY MORE MIND-CONTROLLING HATS DOES THE BOSS ACTUALLY NEED?
I DUNNO. HOW MANY PEOPLE LIVE IN GOTHAM?
EIGHT MILLION, FOUR HUNDRED AND ELEVEN.
LAST TIME I READ THE PUBLIC CENSUS FIGURES, ANYWAY.
BATMAN! SPLIT AND RUN!
"BATMAN"? BOYS, I'M INSULTED!
I'M WAY CUTER!
KLONK!
OOF!

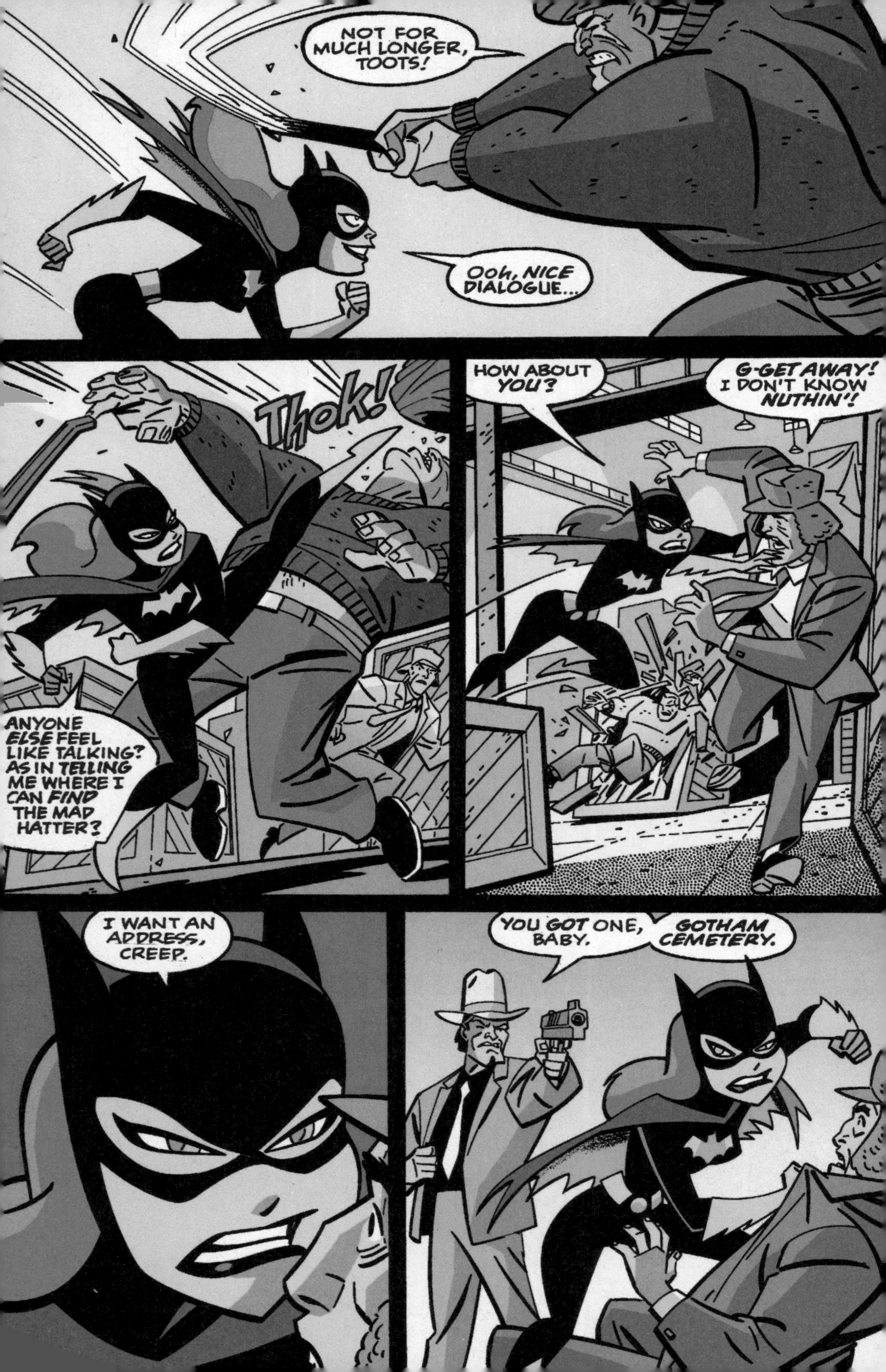
NOT FOR MUCH LONGER, TOOTS!
Ooh, NICE DIALOGUE...
Thok!
ANYONE ELSE FEEL LIKE TALKING? AS IN TELLING ME WHERE I CAN FIND THE MAD HATTER?
HOW ABOUT YOU?
G-GET AWAY! I DON'T KNOW NUTHIN'!
I WANT AN ADDRESS, CREEP.
YOU GOT ONE, BABY.
GOTHAM CEMETERY.

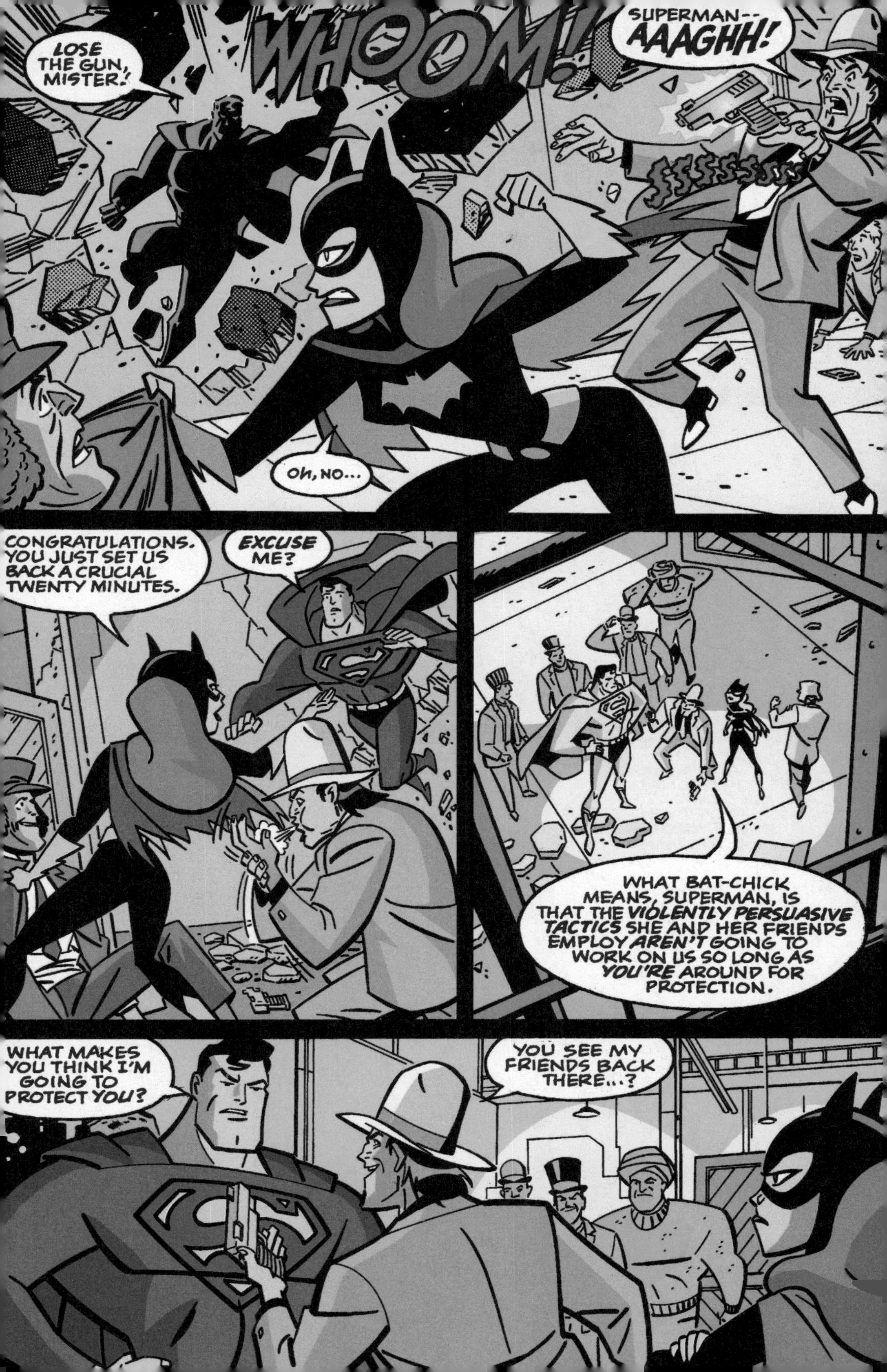
LOSE THE GUN, MISTER!
WHOOM!!
SUPERMAN--
AAAGHH!
FSSSSSSSS
Oh, NO...
CONGRATULATIONS. YOU JUST SET US BACK A CRUCIAL TWENTY MINUTES.
EXCUSE ME?
WHAT BAT-CHICK MEANS, SUPERMAN, IS THAT THE VIOLENTLY PERSUASIVE TACTICS SHE AND HER FRIENDS EMPLOY AREN'T GOING TO WORK ON US SO LONG AS YOU'RE AROUND FOR PROTECTION.
WHAT MAKES YOU THINK I'M GOING TO PROTECT YOU?
YOU SEE MY FRIENDS BACK THERE...?

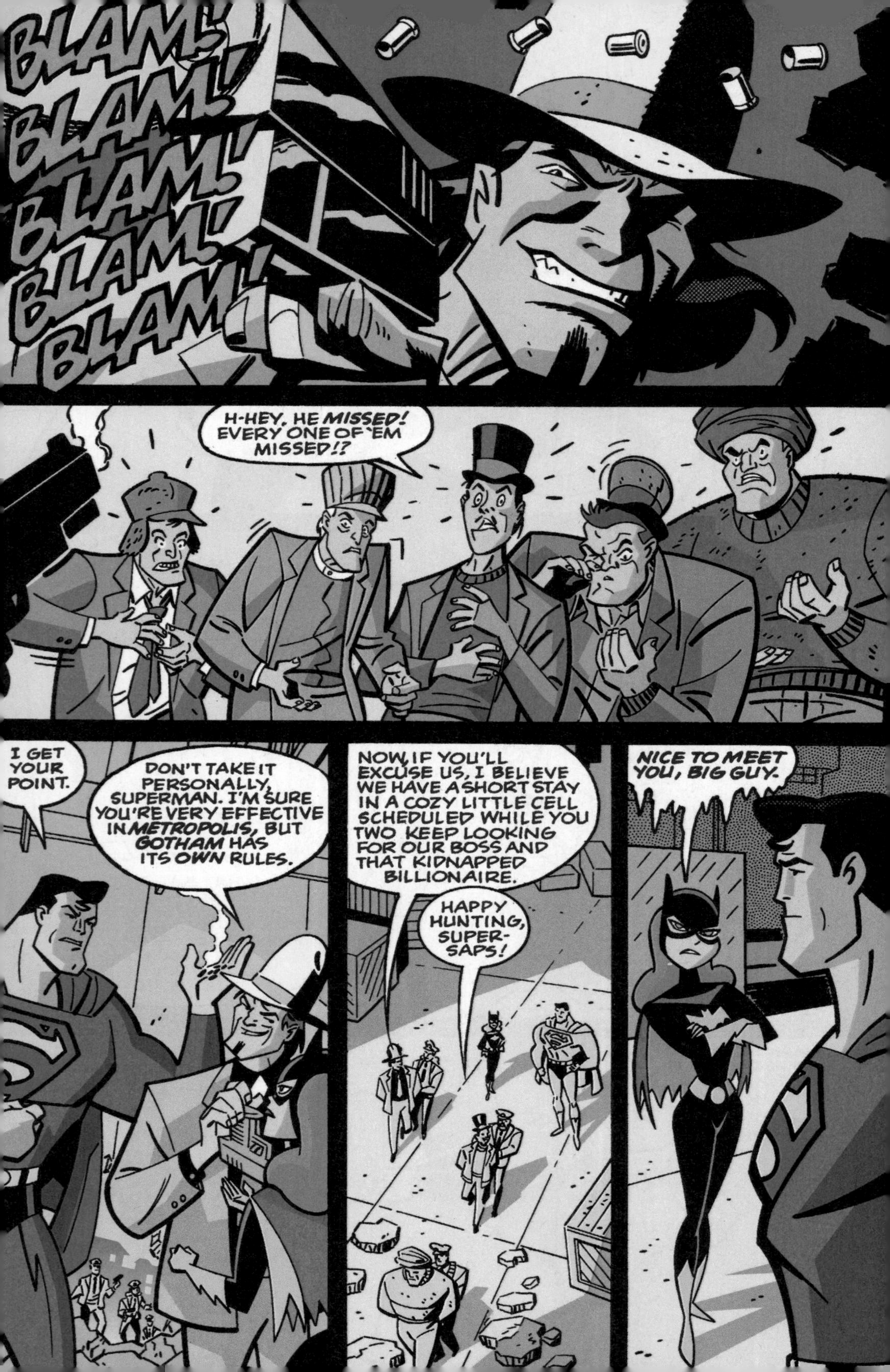

BLAM! BLAM! BLAM! BLAM! BLAM!
H-HEY. HE MISSED! EVERY ONE OF 'EM MISSED!?
I GET YOUR POINT.
DON'T TAKE IT PERSONALLY, SUPERMAN. I'M SURE YOU'RE VERY EFFECTIVE IN METROPOLIS, BUT GOTHAM HAS ITS OWN RULES.
NOW, IF YOU'LL EXCUSE US, I BELIEVE WE HAVE A SHORT STAY IN A COZY LITTLE CELL SCHEDULED WHILE YOU TWO KEEP LOOKING FOR OUR BOSS AND THAT KIDNAPPED BILLIONAIRE.
HAPPY HUNTING, SUPER-SAPS!
NICE TO MEET YOU, BIG GUY.

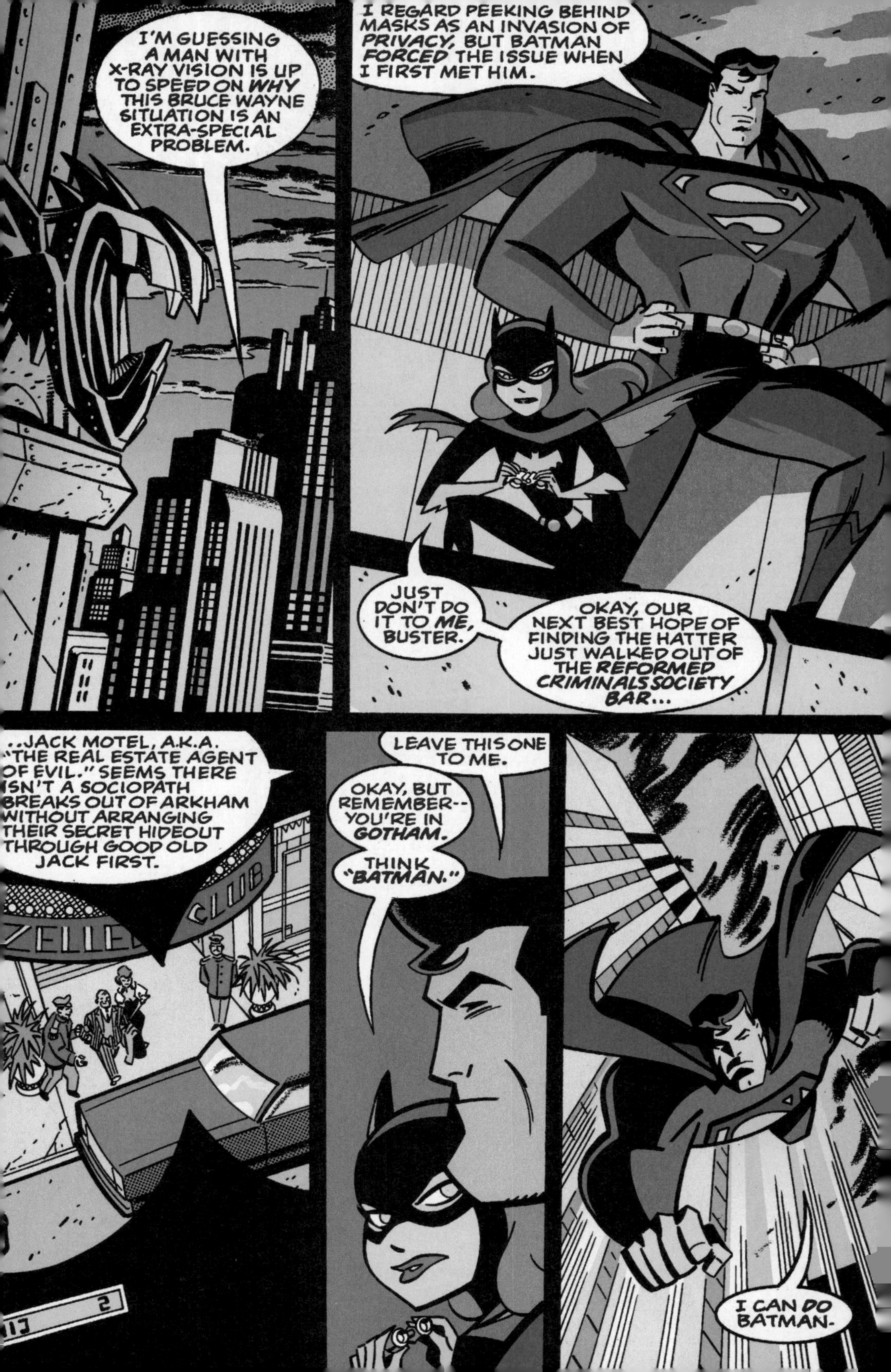
I'M GUESSING A MAN WITH X-RAY VISION IS UP TO SPEED ON *WHY* THIS BRUCE WAYNE SITUATION IS AN EXTRA-SPECIAL PROBLEM.
I REGARD PEEKING BEHIND MASKS AS AN INVASION OF *PRIVACY*, BUT BATMAN *FORCED* THE ISSUE WHEN I FIRST MET HIM.
JUST DON'T DO IT TO *ME*, BUSTER.
OKAY, OUR NEXT BEST HOPE OF FINDING THE HATTER JUST WALKED OUT OF THE *REFORMED CRIMINALS SOCIETY BAR*...
...JACK MOTEL, A.K.A. "THE REAL ESTATE AGENT OF EVIL." SEEMS THERE ISN'T A SOCIOPATH BREAKS OUT OF ARKHAM WITHOUT ARRANGING THEIR SECRET HIDEOUT THROUGH GOOD OLD JACK FIRST.
CLUB
LEAVE THIS ONE TO ME.
OKAY, BUT REMEMBER-- YOU'RE IN *GOTHAM*.
THINK "*BATMAN*."
I CAN *DO* BATMAN.

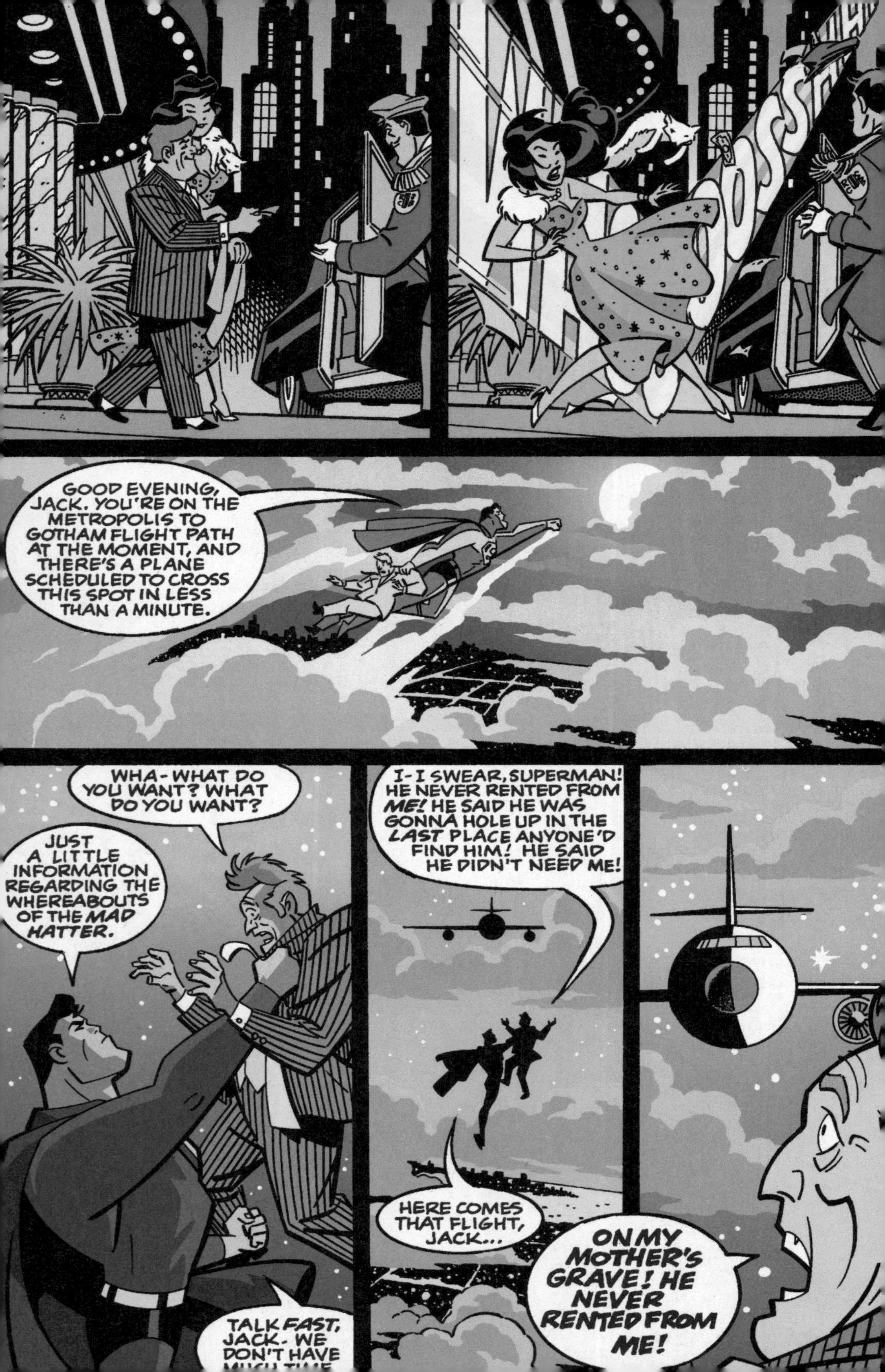
GOOD EVENING, JACK. YOU'RE ON THE METROPOLIS TO GOTHAM FLIGHT PATH AT THE MOMENT, AND THERE'S A PLANE SCHEDULED TO CROSS THIS SPOT IN LESS THAN A MINUTE.
WHA-WHAT DO YOU WANT? WHAT DO YOU WANT?
JUST A LITTLE INFORMATION REGARDING THE WHEREABOUTS OF THE *MAD HATTER*.
TALK *FAST*, JACK. WE DON'T HAVE
I-I SWEAR, SUPERMAN! HE NEVER RENTED FROM *ME!* HE SAID HE WAS GONNA HOLE UP IN THE *LAST* PLACE ANYONE'D FIND HIM! HE SAID HE DIDN'T NEED ME!
HERE COMES THAT FLIGHT, JACK...
ON MY MOTHER'S GRAVE! HE NEVER RENTED FROM ME!

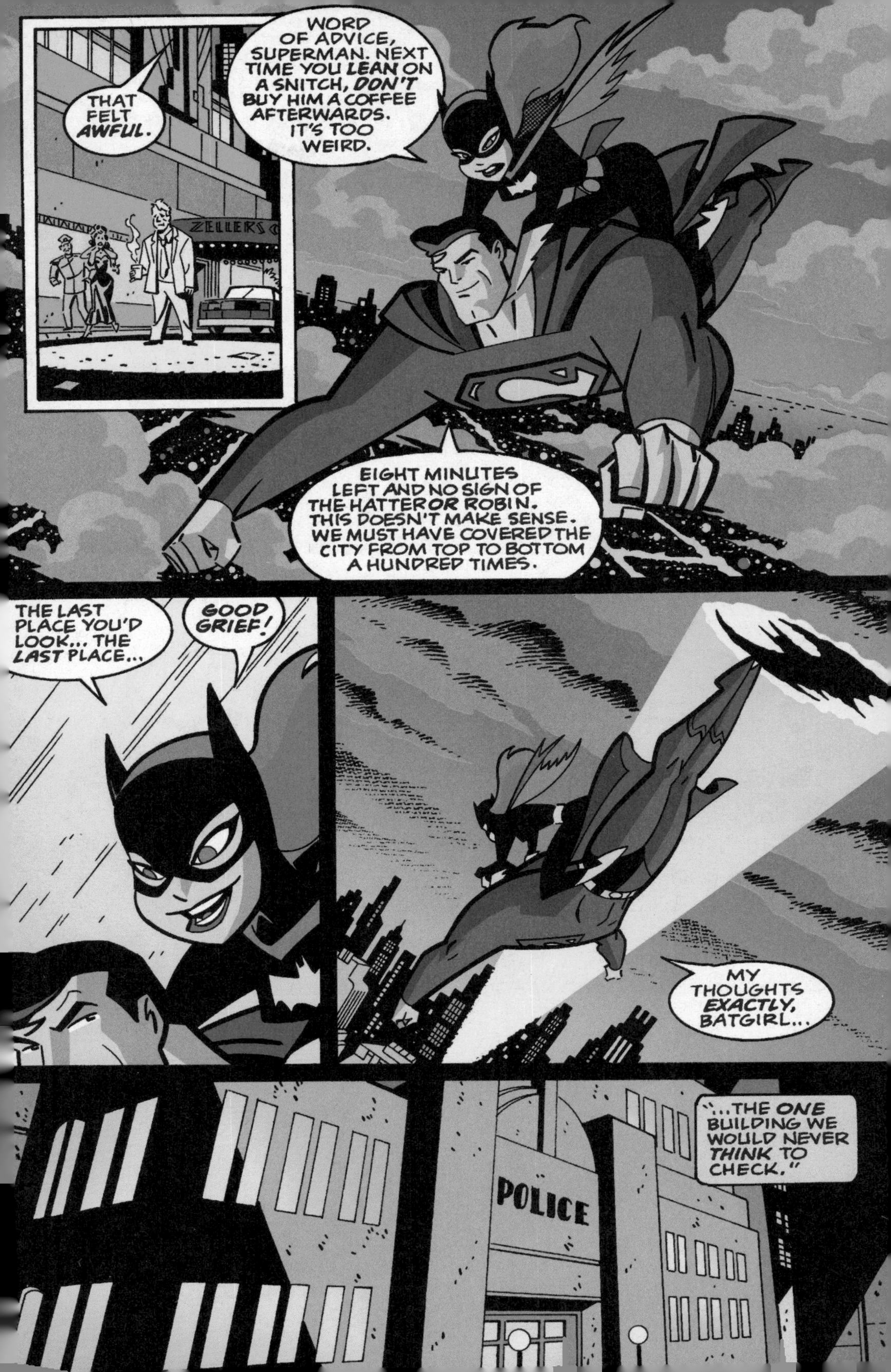
THAT FELT AWFUL.
WORD OF ADVICE, SUPERMAN. NEXT TIME YOU LEAN ON A SNITCH, DON'T BUY HIM A COFFEE AFTERWARDS. IT'S TOO WEIRD.
ZELLERS
EIGHT MINUTES LEFT AND NO SIGN OF THE HATTER OR ROBIN. THIS DOESN'T MAKE SENSE. WE MUST HAVE COVERED THE CITY FROM TOP TO BOTTOM A HUNDRED TIMES.
THE LAST PLACE YOU'D LOOK... THE LAST PLACE...
GOOD GRIEF!
MY THOUGHTS EXACTLY, BATGIRL...
"...THE ONE BUILDING WE WOULD NEVER THINK TO CHECK."
POLICE

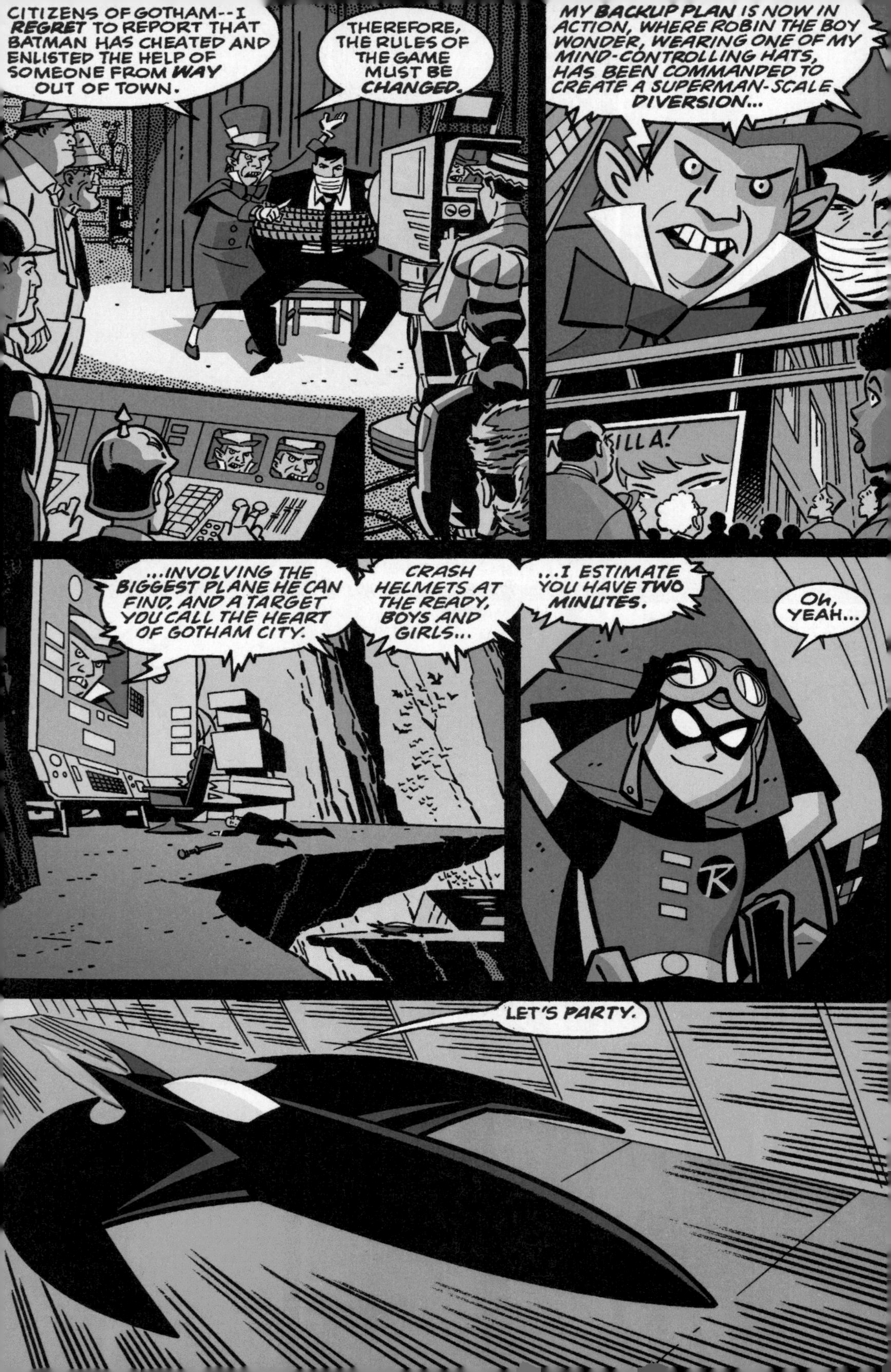

CITIZENS OF GOTHAM--I REGRET TO REPORT THAT BATMAN HAS CHEATED AND ENLISTED THE HELP OF SOMEONE FROM WAY OUT OF TOWN.
THEREFORE, THE RULES OF THE GAME MUST BE CHANGED.
MY BACKUP PLAN IS NOW IN ACTION, WHERE ROBIN THE BOY WONDER, WEARING ONE OF MY MIND-CONTROLLING HATS, HAS BEEN COMMANDED TO CREATE A SUPERMAN-SCALE DIVERSION...
ILLA!
...INVOLVING THE BIGGEST PLANE HE CAN FIND, AND A TARGET YOU CALL THE HEART OF GOTHAM CITY.
CRASH HELMETS AT THE READY, BOYS AND GIRLS...
...I ESTIMATE YOU HAVE TWO MINUTES.
OH, YEAH...
LET'S PARTY.

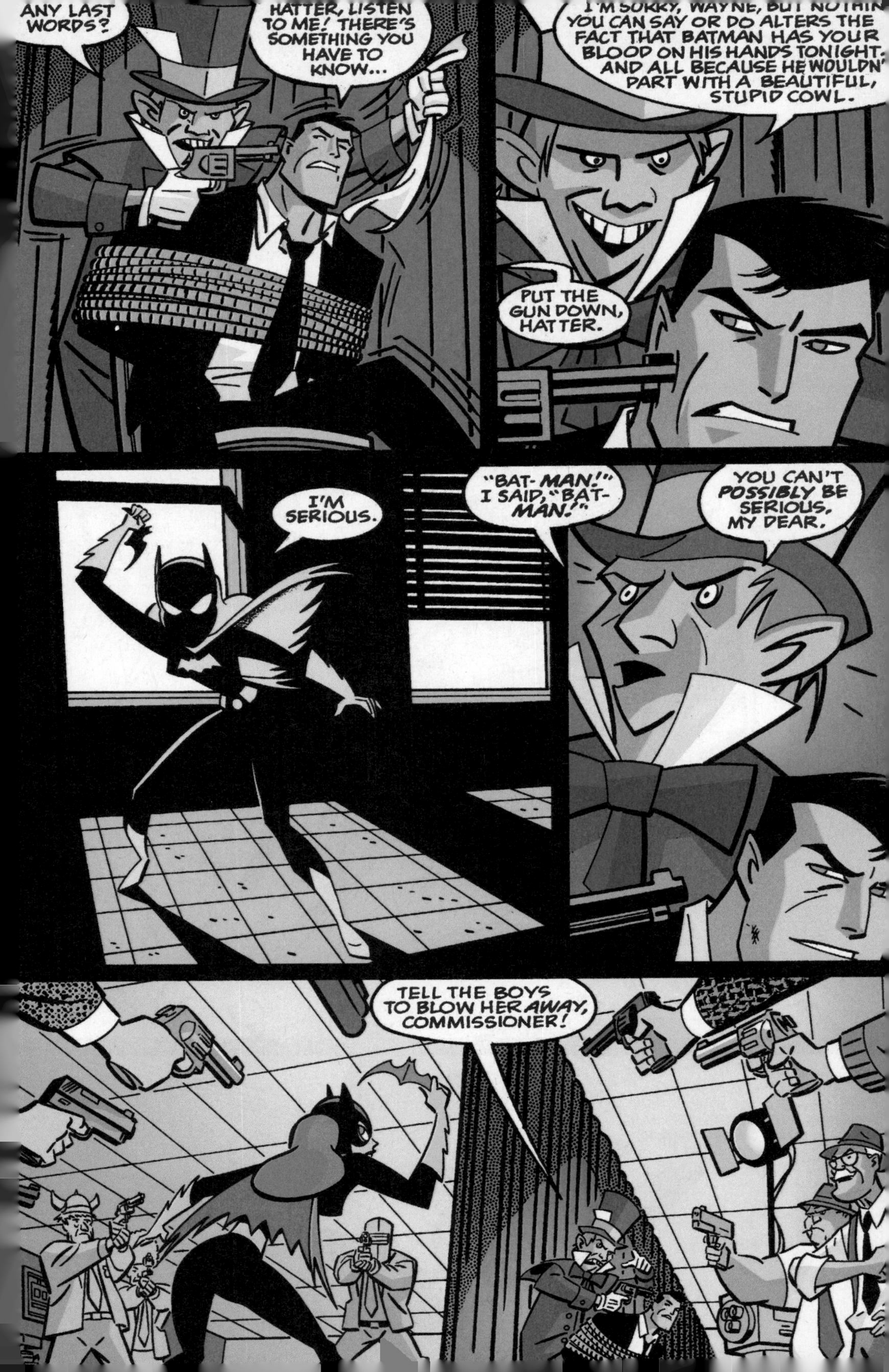
ANY LAST WORDS?
HATTER, LISTEN TO ME! THERE'S SOMETHING YOU HAVE TO KNOW...
I'M SORRY, WAYNE, BUT NOTHIN YOU CAN SAY OR DO ALTERS THE FACT THAT BATMAN HAS YOUR BLOOD ON HIS HANDS TONIGHT. AND ALL BECAUSE HE WOULDN' PART WITH A BEAUTIFUL, STUPID COWL.
PUT THE GUN DOWN, HATTER.
I'M SERIOUS.
"BAT-MAN!" I SAID, "BAT-MAN!"
YOU CAN'T POSSIBLY BE SERIOUS, MY DEAR.
TELL THE BOYS TO BLOW HER AWAY, COMMISSIONER!

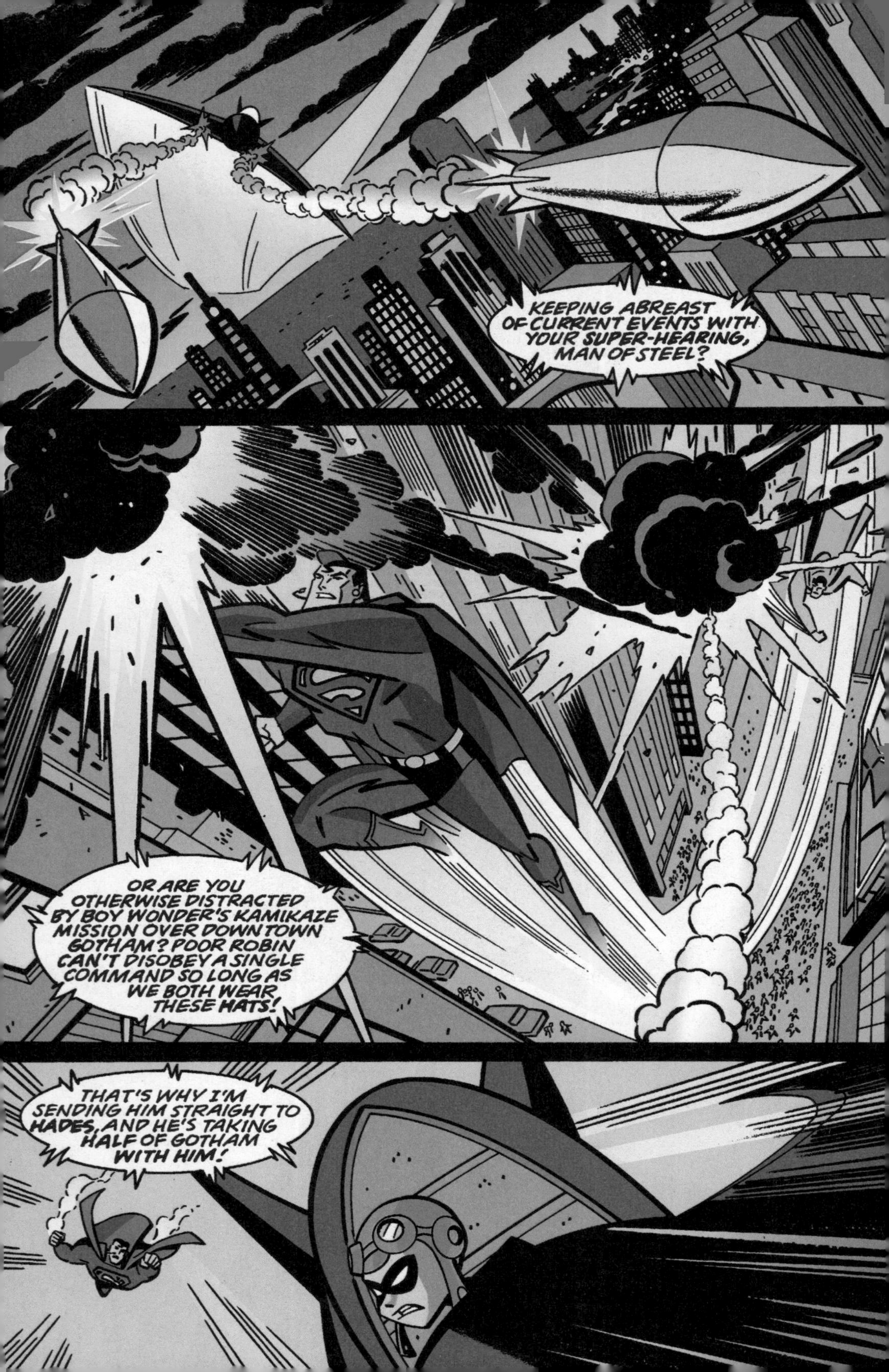
KEEPING ABREAST OF CURRENT EVENTS WITH YOUR SUPER-HEARING, MAN OF STEEL?
OR ARE YOU OTHERWISE DISTRACTED BY BOY WONDER'S KAMIKAZE MISSION OVER DOWNTOWN GOTHAM? POOR ROBIN CAN'T DISOBEY A SINGLE COMMAND SO LONG AS WE BOTH WEAR THESE HATS!
THAT'S WHY I'M SENDING HIM STRAIGHT TO HADES, AND HE'S TAKING HALF OF GOTHAM WITH HIM!

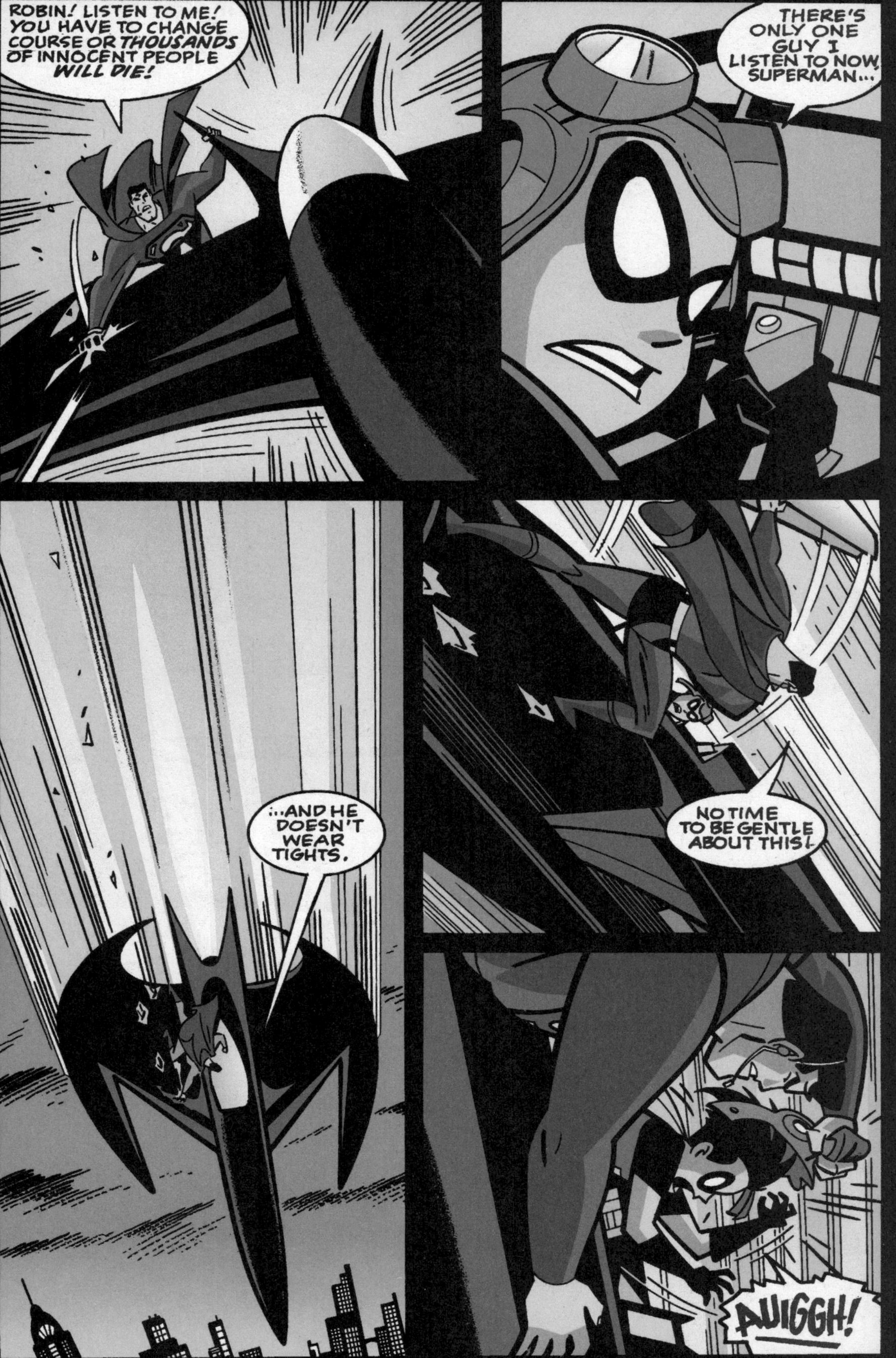
ROBIN! LISTEN TO ME! YOU HAVE TO CHANGE COURSE OR THOUSANDS OF INNOCENT PEOPLE WILL DIE!
THERE'S ONLY ONE GUY I LISTEN TO NOW, SUPERMAN...
...AND HE DOESN'T WEAR TIGHTS.
NO TIME TO BE GENTLE ABOUT THIS!
AUIGGH!

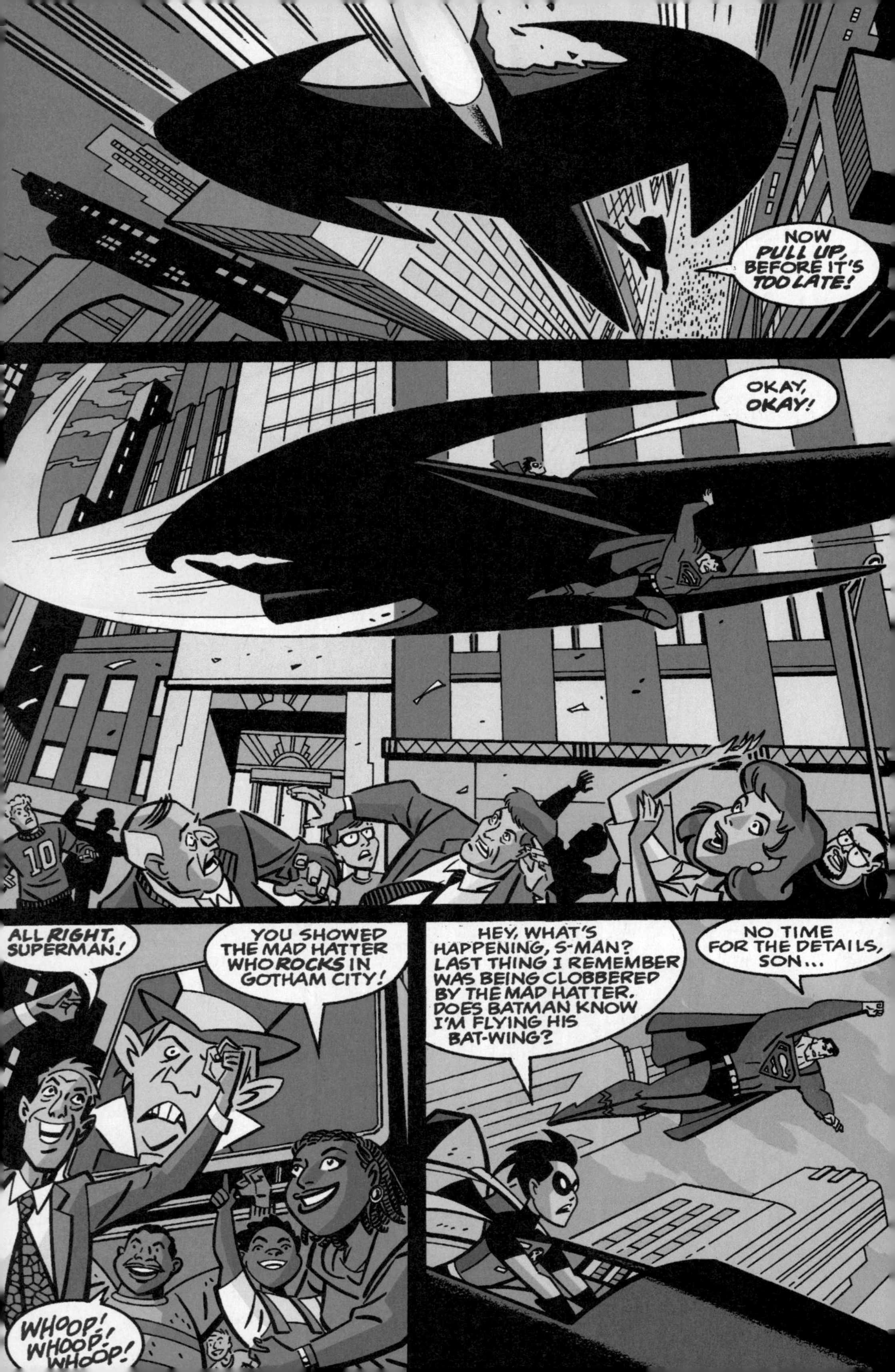
NOW PULL UP, BEFORE IT'S TOO LATE!
OKAY, OKAY!
ALL RIGHT, SUPERMAN!
YOU SHOWED THE MAD HATTER WHO ROCKS IN GOTHAM CITY!
WHOOP! WHOOP! WHOOP!
HEY, WHAT'S HAPPENING, S-MAN? LAST THING I REMEMBER WAS BEING CLOBBERED BY THE MAD HATTER. DOES BATMAN KNOW I'M FLYING HIS BAT-WING?
NO TIME FOR THE DETAILS, SON...

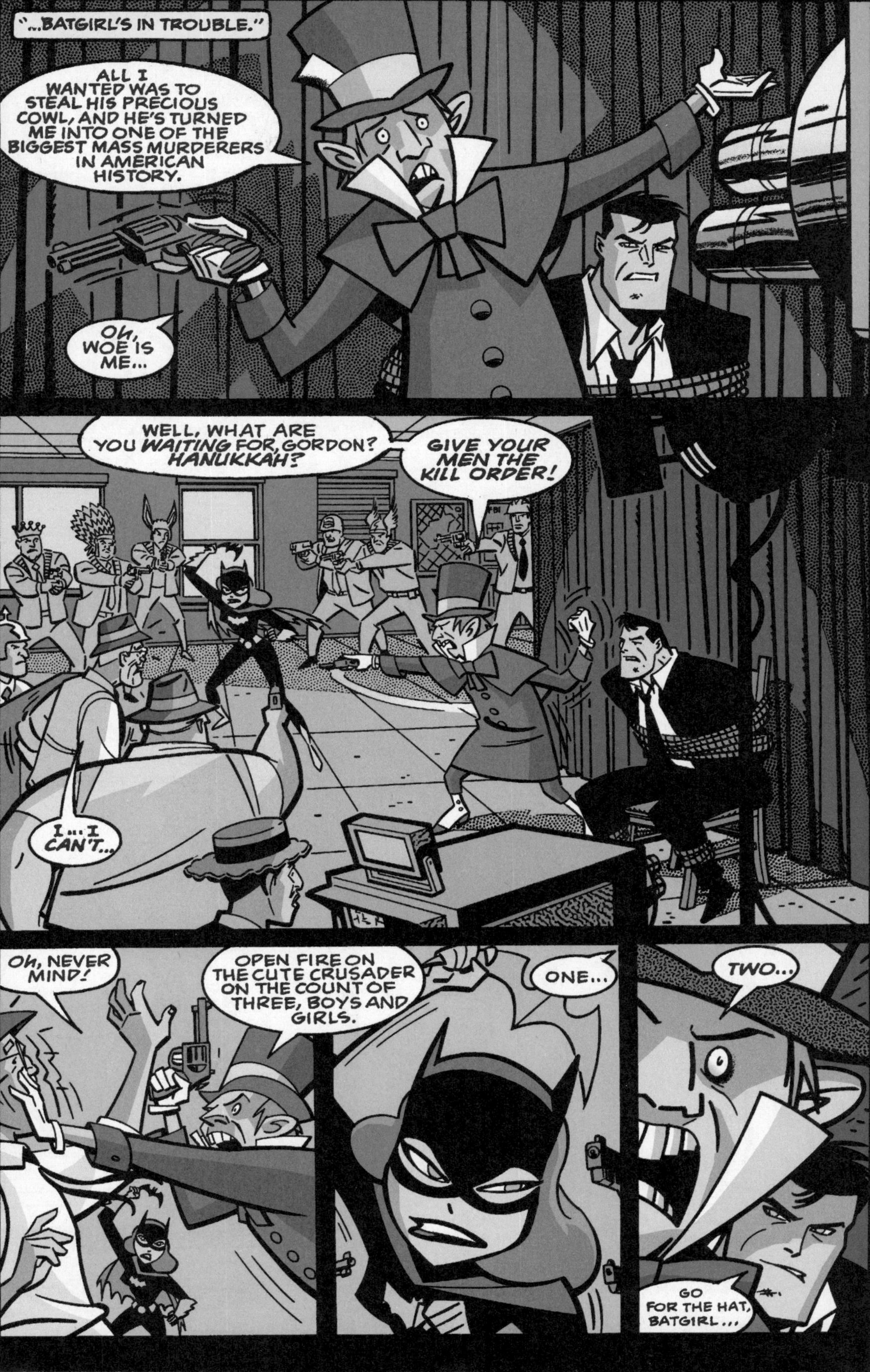
"...BATGIRL'S IN TROUBLE."
ALL I WANTED WAS TO STEAL HIS PRECIOUS COWL, AND HE'S TURNED ME INTO ONE OF THE BIGGEST MASS MURDERERS IN AMERICAN HISTORY.
OH, WOE IS ME...
WELL, WHAT ARE YOU WAITING FOR, GORDON? HANUKKAH?
GIVE YOUR MEN THE KILL ORDER!
I... I CAN'T...
OH, NEVER MIND!
OPEN FIRE ON THE CUTE CRUSADER ON THE COUNT OF THREE, BOYS AND GIRLS.
ONE...
TWO...
GO FOR THE HAT, BATGIRL...

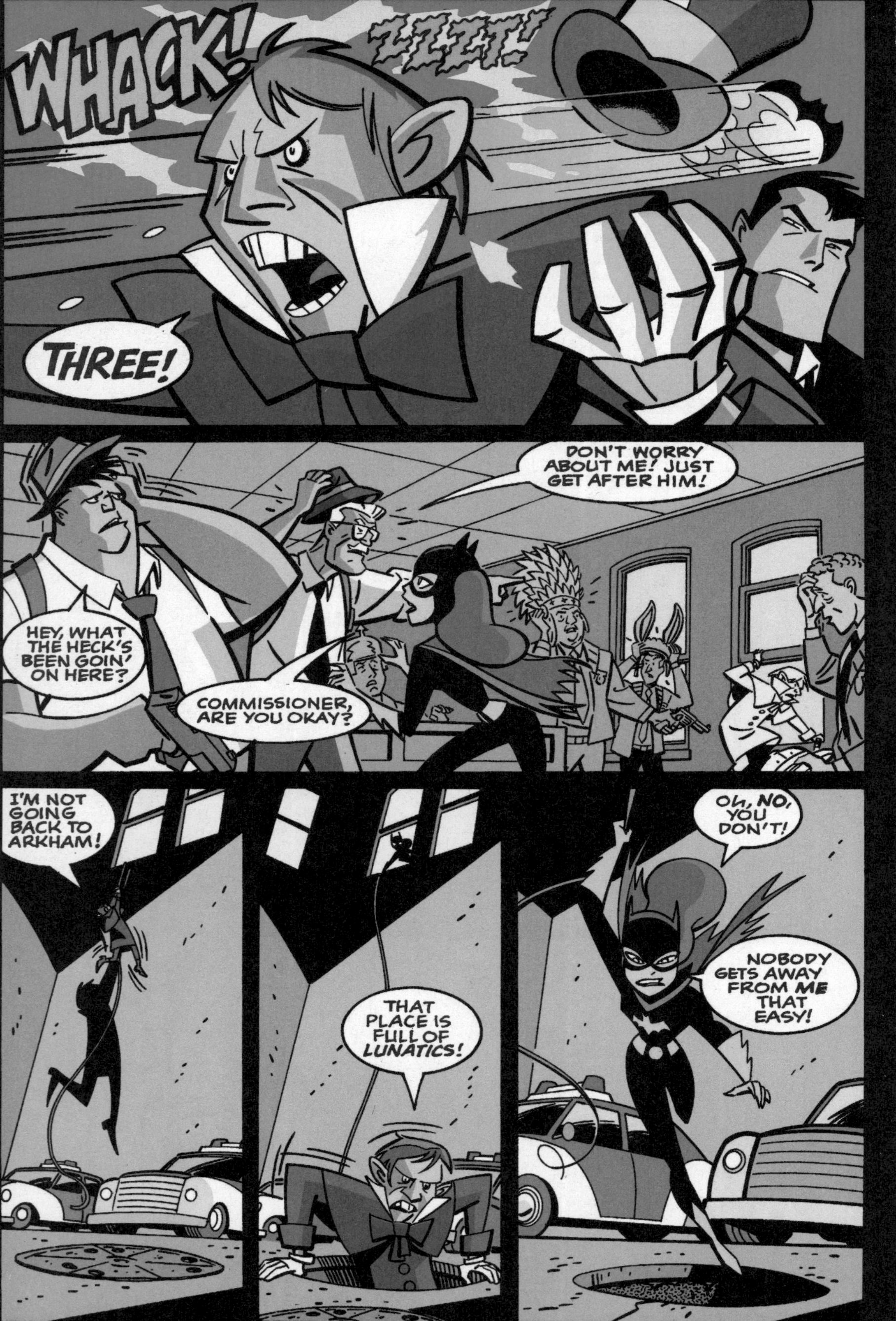
WHACK!
ZZZT!
THREE!
DON'T WORRY ABOUT ME! JUST GET AFTER HIM!
HEY, WHAT THE HECK'S BEEN GOIN' ON HERE?
COMMISSIONER, ARE YOU OKAY?
I'M NOT GOING BACK TO ARKHAM!
THAT PLACE IS FULL OF LUNATICS!
OH, NO, YOU DON'T!
NOBODY GETS AWAY FROM ME THAT EASY!

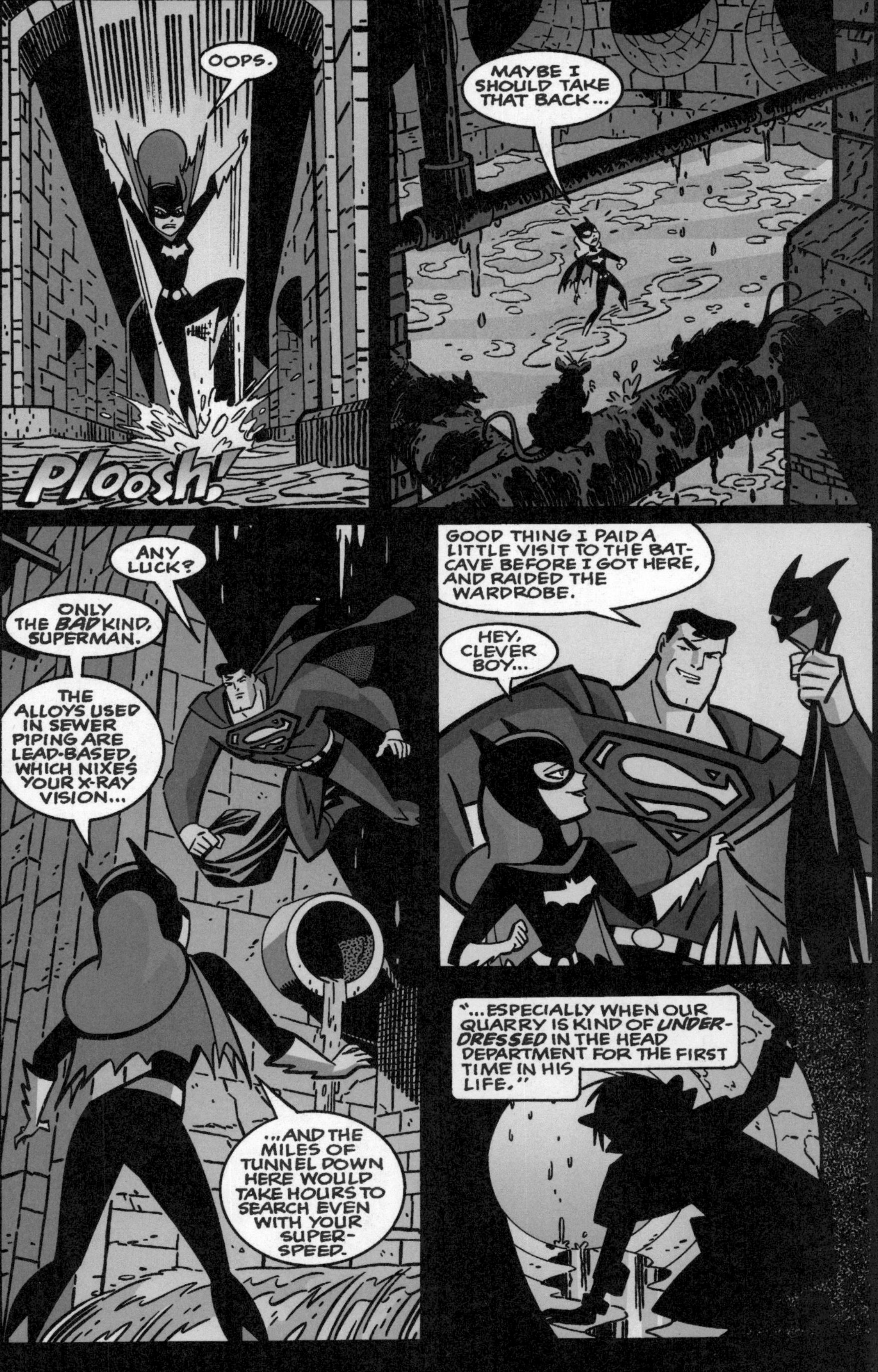

OOPS.
PLOOSH!
MAYBE I SHOULD TAKE THAT BACK...
ANY LUCK?
ONLY THE BAD KIND, SUPERMAN.
THE ALLOYS USED IN SEWER PIPING ARE LEAD-BASED, WHICH NIXES YOUR X-RAY VISION...
...AND THE MILES OF TUNNEL DOWN HERE WOULD TAKE HOURS TO SEARCH EVEN WITH YOUR SUPER-SPEED.
GOOD THING I PAID A LITTLE VISIT TO THE BAT-CAVE BEFORE I GOT HERE, AND RAIDED THE WARDROBE.
HEY, CLEVER BOY...
"...ESPECIALLY WHEN OUR QUARRY IS KIND OF UNDER-DRESSED IN THE HEAD DEPARTMENT FOR THE FIRST TIME IN HIS LIFE."

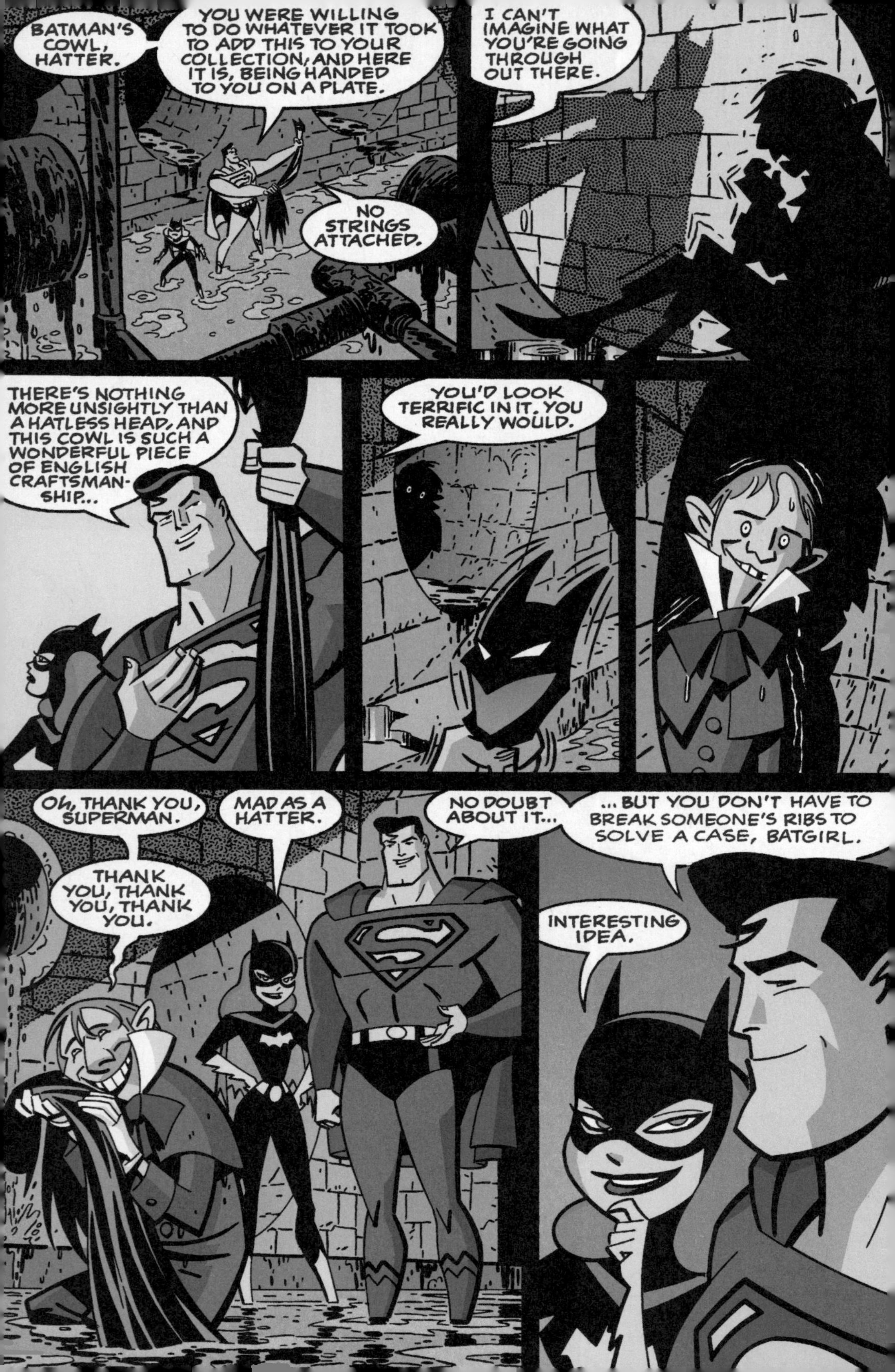
BATMAN'S COWL, HATTER.
YOU WERE WILLING TO DO WHATEVER IT TOOK TO ADD THIS TO YOUR COLLECTION, AND HERE IT IS, BEING HANDED TO YOU ON A PLATE.
NO STRINGS ATTACHED.
I CAN'T IMAGINE WHAT YOU'RE GOING THROUGH OUT THERE.
THERE'S NOTHING MORE UNSIGHTLY THAN A HATLESS HEAD, AND THIS COWL IS SUCH A WONDERFUL PIECE OF ENGLISH CRAFTSMANSHIP...
YOU'D LOOK TERRIFIC IN IT. YOU REALLY WOULD.
OH, THANK YOU, SUPERMAN.
THANK YOU, THANK YOU, THANK YOU.
MAD AS A HATTER.
NO DOUBT ABOUT IT...
...BUT YOU DON'T HAVE TO BREAK SOMEONE'S RIBS TO SOLVE A CASE, BATGIRL.
INTERESTING IDEA.

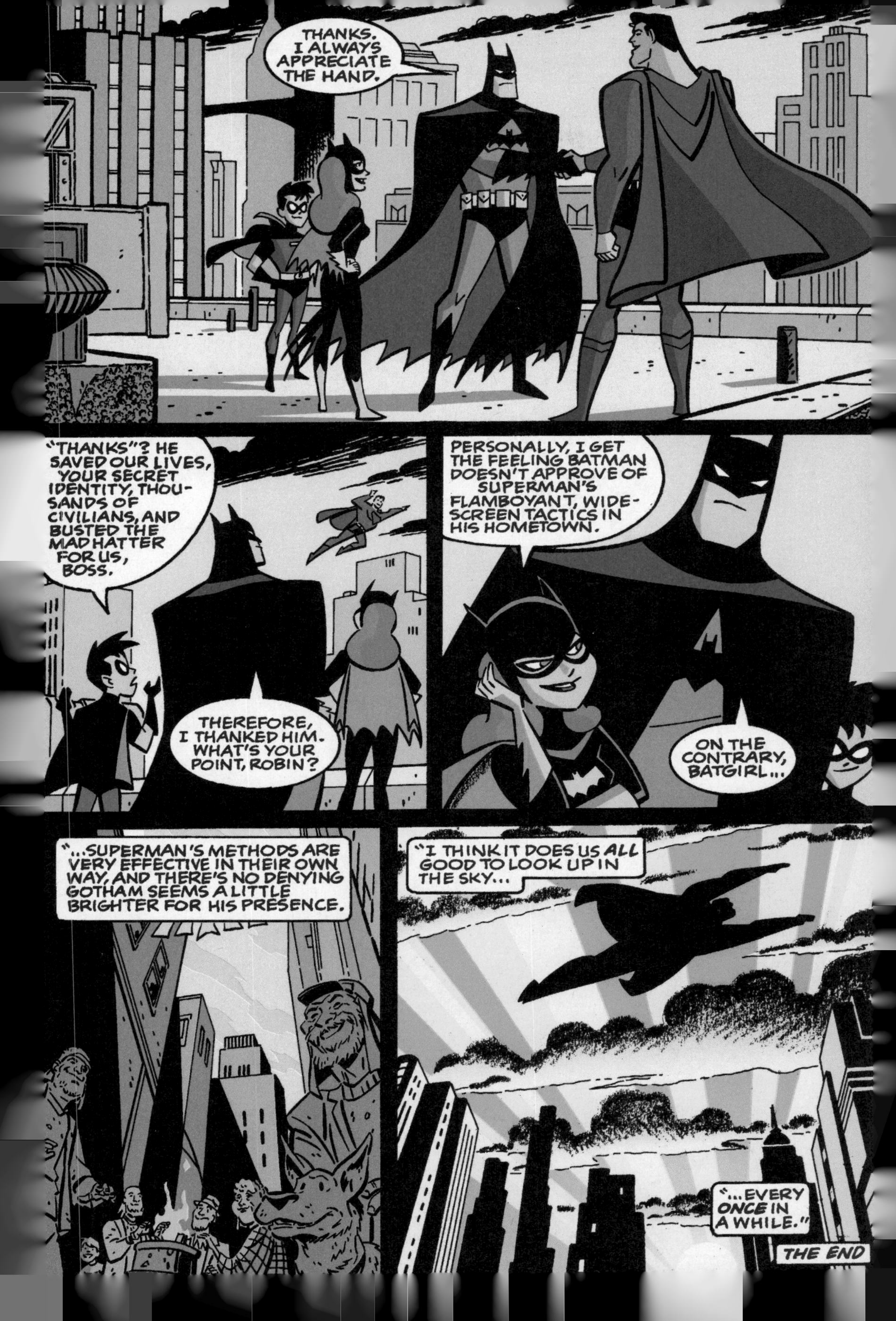
THANKS. I ALWAYS APPRECIATE THE HAND.
"THANKS"? HE SAVED OUR LIVES, YOUR SECRET IDENTITY, THOUSANDS OF CIVILIANS, AND BUSTED THE MAD HATTER FOR US, BOSS.
THEREFORE, I THANKED HIM. WHAT'S YOUR POINT, ROBIN?
PERSONALLY, I GET THE FEELING BATMAN DOESN'T APPROVE OF SUPERMAN'S FLAMBOYANT, WIDE-SCREEN TACTICS IN HIS HOMETOWN.
ON THE CONTRARY, BATGIRL...
"...SUPERMAN'S METHODS ARE VERY EFFECTIVE IN THEIR OWN WAY, AND THERE'S NO DENYING GOTHAM SEEMS A LITTLE BRIGHTER FOR HIS PRESENCE.
"I THINK IT DOES US *ALL* GOOD TO LOOK UP IN THE SKY...
"...EVERY *ONCE* IN A WHILE."
THE END

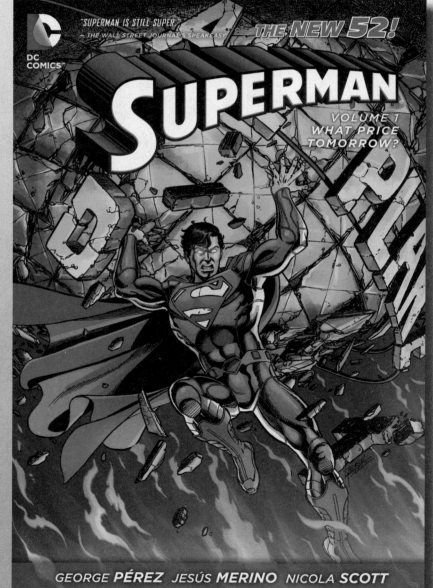